D0934885

PARK SYNAGOGUE
CLEVELAND, OHIO
PRESENTED BY
IN MEMORY OF
KRAVITZ MEMORIAL LIBRARY

TRENDS AND ISSUES IN JEWISH SOCIAL WELFARE IN THE UNITED STATES, 1899-1958

COMPILED BY

The National Conference of Jewish Communal Service

EDITED BY

ROBERT MORRIS

Professor of Social Planning at the Florence Heller Graduate School for Advanced Studies in Social Welfare, Brandeis University

AND BY

MICHAEL FREUND

Formerly Research Director of the Council of Jewish Federations and Welfare Funds

TRENDS AND ISSUES IN JEWISH SOCIAL WELFARE IN THE UNITED STATES, 1899-1952

The history of American Jewish social welfare, seen through the proceedings and reports of The National Conference of Jewish Communal Service

THE JEWISH PUBLICATION SOCIETY OF AMERICA

5726-1966 PHILADELPHIA

FIRST EDITION

LIBRARY OF CONGRESS
CATALOG CARD NUMBER 66-17827
MANUFACTURED IN THE UNITED STATES OF AMERICA
Designed By Sidney Feinberg

66-98

CONTRIBUTORS WHO HELPED MAKE THIS PUBLICATION POSSIBLE

JEWISH FEDERATION, *Chicago*

JEWISH COMMUNITY FEDERATION, *Cleveland*

BEN D. ZEVIN FUND, *Cleveland*

UNITED JEWISH CHARITIES, *Detroit*

DINAH CONNELL FUND, *Los Angeles*

AMERICAN JEWISH JOINT DISTRIBUTION COMMITTEE, *New York City*

Mrs. Richard J. Bernhard, *New York City*
Milton J. Bluestein, *New York City*

FEDERATION OF JEWISH PHILANTHROPIES, *New York City*
JEWISH CHILD CARE ASSOCIATION, *New York City*

SAMUEL LEMBERG FOUNDATION, *New York City*
PETER J. SCHWEITZER FOUNDATION, *New York City*
Eli Wishnick, *New York City*
Robert I. Wishnick, *New York City*
Ira M. Younker, *New York City*
HERMAN M. PEKARSKY MEMORIAL FUND, *Newark*
Alfred Goldsmith, *Philadelphia*
JEWISH SOCIAL SERVICE FEDERATION, *San Antonio*

Foreword

In the course of the past two thousand years, Jewish concepts of charity and social welfare have evolved out of the deepest religious commitments of the Jewish people and under whatsoever conditions they lived. For much of the time, charity and philanthropy were a natural expression of group mutual aid. Communities were small, slow to change, and organized mainly around the teachings of the Torah and the synagogue. In the United States, the early rooting of Jewish life followed essentially the same pattern; but by 1898 a new direction could be discerned. The generally benign American scene encouraged experimental action in minority groups, while the demands of life in an industrial and urban society subjected traditional ways of behaving to irresistible pressures. By 1898, the newly evolving expressions of communal responsibility were sufficiently strong to organize the first Conference of Jewish Charities.

During the sixty years that followed, the Conference[1] acted as a window through which one could see the operation of the forces which shaped and reshaped the character of Jewish charity in America; and the Conference itself also influenced the evolution of

[1] The Conference changed its name as events required, becoming the Conference of Jewish Social Service in 1919; the Conference of Jewish Social Welfare in 1937; the Conference of Jewish Communal Service in 1952. In the latter period the Conference brought together in one association the independent organizations of Jewish center workers, Jewish educators, community relations workers, and social workers.

a unique form of Jewish communal life. The new community came to have a form and structure capable of encompassing many special views about religious and sectarian matters, as well as of relating itself to the surrounding culture of the American city. The newly emergent community was, for perhaps the first time in Jewish life, organized to a significant extent around secular organizations and philanthropies. Religious life always remained primary, vital, and basic, but *Tsedakah* took new forms. This volume is an effort to recapture the evolution of this vigorous form of Jewish charity, which helped Jewish communities confront the upheavals of the twentieth century, and which also contributed much to the evolution of social-welfare concepts in American society generally.

The papers included in this volume were culled by the editors from a sixty-year written record. Others might well have chosen other documents; but in the judgment of the editors, the selected papers fairly represent the main course of evolution, at least as reported in the Conference *Proceedings*. Much of course was not covered, and the Conference is not the definitive source of data about American or Jewish history in the United States. Within the limits of its scope and purpose, however, the Conference remains the major source of information about Jewish philanthropy. Until comprehensive research can add other strands of information, these papers contribute substantially to an understanding of an exciting history. At the same time, they may preserve for the veterans, as well as for the new generations of social workers and their supporting Jewish communities, the views and beliefs of many great figures in social welfare whose work, kept alive in the oral tradition of their peers, may now be preserved in more permanent fashion.

Those who wish to untangle other strands of this history not covered by this selection will find the cumulative index of the Conference *Proceedings* an invaluable and intriguing guide; while the standard histories of the times, by Bogen, Lurie, Karpf, Baron, Frisch, Elbogen, and Stein, remain necessary reading.

In a very special sense the publication of this review is a testimonial to the life and work of Michael Freund, who did not live to enjoy its completion. To him is due the major credit, for it was out of his painstaking study of the Conference papers, and his rich knowledge of American Jewish affairs that the basic outlines of this history were sketched.

Thanks are due to many who shared in this work: to Miss Miriam R. Ephraim, during whose terms as President of the Conference the idea for this documentary history took form, and who by her inspiring leadership and patient, persevering guidance in her role as Chairman of the Conference History Committee was largely responsible for the completion of the project. Thanks are also due to Preston David, Philip Soskis and Judah Shapiro for continuous support, encouragement, and criticism; and to the members of the Conference Publication Committee.

Alfred Kutzik reviewed the manuscript in the light of recent historical studies and is responsible for valuable footnote additions to many documents. His work was especially valuable in correcting common misconceptions about the character and form of Jewish organization during the early and middle nineteenth century.

Jacob Sloan also reviewed the manuscript for omissions and gaps and strengthened the final work by his careful editorial work.

The Jewish Publication Society and its editorial staff contributed immeasurably to the completion of this history. Dr. Grayzel supported the idea from the start and offered editorial advice. Special thanks are due to Mrs. Evelyn Weiman, whose editorial help was always perceptive, sensitive to the subject, and painstaking in its attention to detail.

ROBERT MORRIS

November, 1965

SPECIAL ACKNOWLEDGMENTS

In the Foreword to this volume, Professor Robert Morris places the material in historical perspective, and acknowledges the contribution of a number of persons who helped in the development of the publication.

The Conference would be in error if it did not pay similar tribute to the outstanding accomplishment of Dr. Morris himself. The final selection of papers, the detail of editing, and the writing of the "connective issue," were executed at the high level of competence that uniformly distinguishes the work of this nationally known scholar.

At another level, special acknowledgments are due as well to a number of contributors to the financing of the project. These are listed elsewhere in this volume. Without their generous help and the cooperation of the publisher, the Jewish Publication Society, the publication would not have become a reality.

The final work on the history and the actual publication plans were completed under the administration of Conference President Maurice Bernstein (1965-66). To him the Conference is especially grateful for having cleared away the myriad of details and problems which confront a project of this character under the auspices of a voluntary association.

He brought to final fruition the publication of a history to which his predecessor presidents contributed both in the making and in the writing. They are listed separately in this volume.

Of course, no list of acknowledgments is complete and the Conference History does not break with this tradition. For the many who helped and who remain anonymous, their labor, we hope, found its own reward.

—WILLIAM AVRUNIN
President (1966-67)
National Conference of Jewish Communal Service

Contents

Foreword vii

Special Acknowledgments xi

Introduction xxiii

PART ONE

THE YEARS OF IMMIGRANT ADJUSTMENT
1899-1919

Survey of the Years 1899-1919 3

I Mass Immigration and Immigrant Aid—Long Range Adjustment Programs 13

1. Jewish Mass Immigration to the United States 15
SAMUEL JOSEPH

2. The Baron de Hirsch Fund 23
EUGENE S. BENJAMIN

3. Removal Work—Further Efforts 34
DAVID M. BRESSLER

4. The Galveston Movement — 39
DAVID M. BRESSLER

5. Agricultural and Vocational Education — 43
H. L. SABSOVICH

II Services for Individuals and Families — 49

1. Causes of Poverty and the Remedial Work of Organized Charity — 52
MORRIS GOLDSTEIN

2. The Russian Jew Looks at Organized Charity — 57
HAROLD SILVER

3. Adequacy of Relief — 60
SOLOMON LOWENSTEIN

4. The National Desertion Bureau — 66
CHARLES ZUNSER

5. Report of Committee on Transportation — 76

6. Tuberculosis as Affecting Jewish Charity Organizations — 78
LEE K. FRANKEL

III Child Care and Protection — 89

1. Report of the Committee on Dependent Children — 90
LEE K. FRANKEL

2. The Problem of Boarding and Placing Out Jewish Dependent Children — 103
LUDWIG B. BERNSTEIN

3. Prevention of Delinquency — 110
JULIAN W. MACK

IV Social Adjustment—Approaches and Methods 113

1. Preventive Work On the East Side 115
DAVID BLAUSTEIN

2. East Side Preventive Work 118
A. H. FROMENSON

3. Advanced Settlement Work 124
JACOB BILLIKOPF

4. The Public School as the Neighborhood Center 129
JENNIE F. PURVIN

V Responsibilities of Wartime Jewish Agencies 135

1. The Jewish Soldiers 136
EDITORIAL, *Jewish Charities*

2. Reconstruction 137
BORIS D. BOGEN

3. The Ten-Million-Dollar Campaign 141
JACOB BILLIKOPF

VI Toward Inter-Group Cooperation and Community Organization 143

1. Federation or Consolidation of Jewish Charities 144
MORRIS LOEB

2. Cooperation Between All Groups in A Community 148
MORRIS D. WALDMAN

PART TWO

THE AMERICAN JEWISH COMMUNITY MATURES 1920-1929

Survey of the Years 1920-1929 159

I Problems and Needs at the Opening of the Decade 167

1. Preliminary Report of the Committee of Nine 168
LOUIS M. CAHN

2. New Issues in Federation 173
MORRIS D. WALDMAN

II Relation of Jewish Services to the General Social-Work Program 177

1. Visible Effects of the Present Immigration Policy in the Work of Jewish Family Agencies 179
HYMAN KAPLAN

2. Changing Ideals in Jewish Social Work 188
FRANCES TAUSSIG

3. Character of Relationships of Jewish Agencies with Public or Non-Sectarian Agencies in the Field of Family Welfare 194
HARRY L. LURIE

III What Makes Jewish Social Work "Jewish?" 207

1. What Makes Jewish Social Work "Jewish?" Historical Aspects 209
ABRAHAM CRONBACH

2. Communal Aspects 214
JOHN SLAWSON

3. Facing Reality 218

4. The Place of Jewish Education in Jewish Social Service 220
ALEXANDER M. DUSHKIN

HARRY L. GLUCKSMAN

5. Tendencies in the Jewish Center Movement 225

IV New Problems in Jewish Communal Life 231

1. Jewish Communal Organization in America 234
SOLOMON LOWENSTEIN

2. Our Contemporary Ancestors 239
DOROTHY S. KAHN

3. Certain Present Tendencies in the Federation Movement in American Jewish Philanthropy 244
MAURICE B. HEXTER

4. What Have Been the Effects in Jewish Social Agencies of Membership in Community Chests and Councils of Social Agencies? 247
RAYMOND CLAPP

Discussion 251
MORRIS D. WALDMAN

5. Jewish Community Chests 254
SAMUEL C. KOHS

V National Organizations and Their Effect on Community Programs. Toward a Federation of Federations 259

1. Budgeting National Organizations 260
A COMMITTEE REPORT

2. The Question of Financing Non-Local Jewish Philanthropies 267
SAMUEL A. GOLDSMITH

3. The National Appeals Information Service Moves Forward 272
WILLIAM J. SHRODER

PART THREE

ECONOMIC AND POLITICAL CHALLENGES 1930-1945

Survey of the Years 1930-1945 279

I Economic Crisis: The Rise of Public Relief and Social Security 287

1. What Do We Owe to Peter Stuyvesant? 288
I. M. RUBINOW

2. The Cleveland Conference of Federation Executives—A Statement of Principles 298

3. A Call to the President and Congress of the United States from the National Conference of Jewish Social Service 303

4. The Present Status of Jewish Social Work: The Need for Critical Examination. A Symposium 305
HARRY L. LURIE, SOLOMON LOWENSTEIN, FRANCES TAUSSIG

5. Wanted—A Return to Basic Values 311
MAURICE J. KARPF

6. The Relation of Public and Private Social Work 316
HARRY GREENSTEIN

II Economic Welfare: Jobs, Professions and Discrimination 327

1. The Economic and Industrial Status of American Jewry 329
I. M. Rubinow

2. Planning for Economic Welfare 343
Ben M. Selekman

3. Organization and Administration of Vocational Services under Jewish Auspices. An Outline Statement to the Institute on Social Work Programs of Federations 351

III Anti-Semitism Renewed: Widening Approaches to Jewish Community Relations 357

1. Problems Facing the Jews Throughout the World and Their Implications for American Jewry 359
Morris D. Waldman

2. The Jew and Social and Economic Conditions in the United States—Report of a Committee of Practitioners 363

3. Developments in Jewish Civic and Protective Activity in the United States 370
Harry L. Lurie

4. Methods of Dealing With Problems Affecting Jewish and General Relationships 376
I. M. Rubinow

IV Organization for Refugee Service 385

1. Changes in Jewish Social Work Structure Under the Impact of Refugee Problems 387
Solomon Lowenstein

2. Local Organization for Refugee Service 392
Samuel A. Goldsmith

Discussion 404
SAMUEL S. KOHS

3. Backgrounds of Some Refugees As Factors in Their Orientation 407
CHARLES H. JORDAN

V Broadening the Jewish Community Base 413

1. Developments in Jewish Community Organization 415
HARRY L. LURIE

2. The Community Council Idea 425
ISAAC FRANCK

3. Jewish Social Services in a Nation at War 437
LOUIS KRAFT

4. The Impact of War Upon Jewish Social Service 447
PHILIP BERNSTEIN

PART FOUR

YEARS OF CONSOLIDATION
1946-1958

Survey of the Years 1946-1958 463

I The Jewish Health and Welfare Services—Purposes and Goals 467

1. Current Purposes and Goals of Jewish Family Agencies 469
MARCEL KOVARSKY

2. Changes in Child Care and Their Implications 476
MARTHA K. SELIG

3. Trends in the Care of the Aged 494
MORRIS ZELDITCH

4. The Function of a Jewish Vocational Agency 507
SIDNEY LEWINE

5. Local Community Planning Towards an Integrated Health Program 516
ROBERT MORRIS

II Communal and Educational Developments 523

1. Current National Trends Affecting Jewish Communities 527
GEORGE W. RABINOFF

2. The Place of the Jewish Community Center in Jewish Life 534
SANFORD SOLENDER

3. Trends and Recent Developments in the Field of Jewish Education 559
LOUIS L. RUFFMAN

4. New Developments in Jewish Community Organization 574
HERMAN M. PEKARSKY

PART FIVE

RETROSPECT AND PROSPECT

1899-1958 591

1. A Backward Look 595
MORRIS D. WALDMAN

2. The Next Twenty-Five Years in Jewish Communal Service 602
MAURICE B. HEXTER

APPENDIX 619

1. Program of the First Meeting of the Conference, June 11-13, 1900 620

2. The Raison D'Etre of the Conference 622
MAX SENIOR

3. Constitution of the National Conference of Jewish Charities—1900 624

4. Excerpts from Constitution and By-Laws of the Conference of Jewish Communal Service—1953 625

5. Conference Publications 626

6. Years and Meeting Places of Biennial and Annual Conferences, 1900-1958 628

7. Past Presidents of the Conference 631

8. Past Secretaries of the Conference 632

Biographical Notes 633

INTRODUCTION: THE MEANING OF THE CONFERENCE FOR THE AMERICAN JEWISH COMMUNITY *

BY MIRIAM R. EPHRAIM

IN an era of "atomic clocks" that permit time measurements to accuracies of better than one part in a million, how does one begin to measure the impact of the National Conference of Jewish Communal Service on the American Jewish community?

It has occurred to me that, for our purposes, one could establish three broad eras or epochs which highlight the contributions of the Conference to the evolving Jewish communal services in America during the past sixty years. I do not imply that these three eras had their clear-cut beginnings and endings within specific time periods. Elements of these different eras continue to have their ebb and flow in the stream of development of the Conference. They stand out, however, at particular times, as major aspects of growth and change in the Conference and in the Jewish communal services which have significance for us as we look toward the future.

The post-Civil War period to 1880 was marked by social and economic expansion in America. American Jewry at this time was largely Western European, urban, and middle or upper class. For these Jews, it was, in the main, a period of adjustment and adaptation, giving rise to many institutions and organizations, such as the forerunners of the YMHA's and Jewish community centers of today, Reform Judaism, Jewish hospitals, and Jewish philanthropic

* Adapted from the Presidential Address to the Annual Meeting of the National Conference of Jewish Communal Service, Chicago, Illinois, May 19, 1958.

and cultural voluntary organizations. The proliferation of voluntary-service agencies gave rise in the 1870's to the charity organization movement in the community at large.

Then came the pogroms and persecution in Russia and Poland which led to the mass migrations to America. It is said that within twelve years after the first Russian refugee had been received, the numbers that entered equalled the total Jewish population in the United States before their arrival. In the course of a single generation, one out of every three Jews living in Russia, Austria-Hungary of pre-war days, and Roumania left the land of his birth.

The great needs and problems arising out of these conditions led to the first national meeting for the purpose of conferring on problems of charity. A major concern at this meeting in St. Louis in 1885, under the chairmanship of Marcus Bernheimer, was to divert the new immigrant from the large cities and have the smaller communities assume some of the burdens imposed by the immigration. For several years thereafter, representatives of the leading societies were called together to meet some current crisis. They agreed on the action to be taken, and adjourned.

In 1899, Cincinnati issued a call to other cities for a meeting. Delegates came from a score of societies to what I. S. Isaacs, writing in the publication *Jewish Charity,* called "A two days' meeting that was harmonious and enjoyable. . . ." Mr. Isaacs further stated: "The requisite number of adherents having been obtained, the National Conference of Jewish Charities was formed."

Thus was our Conference born and the first of the three aspects of its contribution to the development of the Jewish communal services in America was set in motion. I think of this period as highlighting the *what* in Jewish social work. The founding fathers were dedicated laymen, intuitively responding to need, endeavoring to coordinate where services existed and to cooperate in the establishment of new services where needed, such as the creation of the Industrial Removal Office in 1901.

In 1902, Max Senior, president of the Conference, said that

mass migration had made volunteer administration of charity increasingly unworkable, and by the same token was changing the concept of charity from the prevalent practice of giving aid for relief of economic distress to one of providing many and varied services, such as help in adjusting to a new environment, removal of immigrants from New York to other parts of the country, legal aid, vocational guidance, and the like. In 1909, a study of Jewish philanthropy revealed that 1,191 agencies were helping about 40,000 people and spending ten million dollars annually; there were only seventy-three paid workers. The study referred to the prevailing low salaries and low status of the workers.

As another illustration of the contribution of the Conference in its early years to the creation of new agencies, may I remind you that in 1916 the National Conference of Jewish Charities established a field bureau "to disseminate information about the organization and administration of Jewish social-service activities." The Field Bureau also conducted surveys, the most notable example being the Chicago Survey of Jewish Charities, which, I believe, was the first thorough survey of the entire social-work program of a large city. Simultaneously, the New York City Bureau of Philanthropic Research, which had been organized by the *kehillah* and the Local Council of Communal Institutes, was helping in the study of local social agencies. The work of this Bureau was merged in 1919 with the Conference Field Bureau. The Bureau of Jewish Statistics and Research, which had been established in 1914 by the American Jewish Committee, formed the Bureau of Jewish Social Research "to serve American Jewry in the study and promotion of Jewish social and communal activity." This was one of the predecessor organizations of the Council of Jewish Federations and Welfare Funds.

During these years there was a continual increase in paid personnel. It is significant that in 1918 the Conference passed a resolution calling for the establishment of a Standing Committee on Standards and Qualifications for Jewish Social Workers, with power to prepare a registration form, for use to January 1, 1920.

After this date only those who came up to the standards set by that time would be registered as Jewish social workers. The plan did not go through, chiefly because of the interruption of the service of the secretary of the Conference who was called to overseas duty, but also because of "the resistance of some workers." In the earliest days of the Conference, the United Hebrew Charities conducted training programs in cooperation with the New York School of Philanthropy, and other courses were offered for the volunteers doing social work. Michael Freund, in his important history of the Training Bureau for Jewish Communal Service, describes the great variety of early undertakings to train employed personnel. From 1918 to 1924 the Conference was actively involved in the development of plans for a School for Social Work, which resulted in the opening of the Graduate School in July 1925, with Dr. Maurice Karpf as director.

These activities, the changing nature and nomenclature of the Conference, and its annual Conference programs reflect the second major aspect of the contribution of the Conference to the enrichment of Jewish communal services. We had moved from the concern with the *what* to an ever increasing emphasis on the *how*—the improvement of methods of work, standards of operation and training, and a concern for better working conditions, security for the worker and improvement of his status. The general field of social work was working in these directions; not only were we moving along with our colleagues, but in no small measure we were contributing leadership in these directions within the National Conference of Social Work, the American Association of Social Workers, and other groups. The refinement of skills and the development of the profession contributed to the enrichment of service and to our status as professional workers.

The third broad area of importance in evaluating the contribution of the Conference to Jewish communal service in America perhaps represents the major challenge: it is what I designate as the *why* phase of our being. There have been years in which our annual meetings reflected doubts and conflicts about the basic philosophies of organized Jewish community life in America and their implications for practice and for the fixing of program priorities. This also has been true in relation to individual aspects of social work philosophy and their application to the development of Jewish community services in America.

While this shows a continuous thread in the development of the Conference, it was perhaps in the 1930's that we had our most severe "growing pains"; it was our period of *sturm und drang,* connected with the period of economic depression and widespread unemployment. The rise of Nazism and Fascism convulsed the world and renewed the crisis and despair of world Jewry, as in the days before the establishment of our Conference.

The great depression affected workers and clients alike; governmental social-welfare programs were introduced on a large scale to meet the needs of the people, and the WPA projects brought blessings as well as problems, not the least of which was the impact on hard-won standards and professional development. It was a time of general ferment and the growth of radical movements. Heavy caseloads and increasing calls for service enlarged the numbers of rank-and-file workers and gave impetus to the development of trade unionism in social work. The distance between lay and professional leadership was widened. Resistance was built up to the leadership role in the Conference of executives and administrators. Influenced by the teachings of Mary Richmond, there was a movement away from the so-called applied psychology approach in dealing with people and their problems and toward a greater concern for social action as a way of affecting the environment for the prevention of problems. It is in this period that the family agencies began to shift to the public agencies such clients as required long-term financial assistance, while the private agencies began placing greater emphasis on counselling services. Relationships with governmental and non-sectarian community agencies stimulated thinking through the problem of "who are we and what are we," so that the local agencies and Conference programs became involved in ideological conflicts of fundamental significance. The 1936 annual meeting of the Conference gave major consideration to the following topics: anti-Semitism, aspects of American Jewish youth problems, group work and case work, and Jewish content in Jewish social work.

While it is true that much of the violent emotion involved in discussions around the *why* of social work have diminished, and much progress has been made in the acceptance of the reality of an American Jewish community, nevertheless many unresolved issues confront us in all aspects of Jewish communal service. These concern how best to serve our constituencies in regard to their Jewishness and the role and responsibility of the Jewish social worker in building a creative Jewish community life.

A very positive contribution has been made by the National Conference of Jewish Communal Service in bringing together the various functional fields that serve the Jewish people of America. To the degree to which this association under Conference auspices can become increasingly meaningful in the sharing of common concerns, it will stimulate significant gains for the total Jewish community. Not the least of the contributions emanating from the Conference, of course, is the qualified personnel who over the years have given leadership in the Jewish and general community and in the professional associations.

The Journal of Jewish Communal Service should be mentioned as an outstanding contribution to the development of Jewish communal service and to the total field of social work in America.

We may now be ready, somewhat like the scientists in the international geophysical year, for a series of explorations, innovations, and earnest studies of the forces in the Jewish and general worlds which have an impact upon us as members of the human race, as Jews, and as professional workers who can help to make this a better world to live in. Certainly there is much unfinished business in the areas of relationships with the general community on many fronts, and—a task of major proportions—in strengthening the quality of Jewish communal living in America. These are times in which we, along with all humanity, are involved in problems of survival and world peace, and there are many opportunities for us to share with colleagues in other associations, and with our fellow-citizens, in the great tasks that lie ahead.

The Rockefeller Brothers Fund Report on the American Economy is an important document well worth study. To quote its closing statement:

> This report has dealt largely with the material and physical well-being of our citizens. But these gains will have only partial meaning unless they are accompanied by the fullest possible realization by the individual of his spiritual, intellectual, and cultural capacities. Our democratic faith is a faith in the whole human being. We are concerned for the individual's life and health, his security and comfort; but even more we must be concerned for his highest aspirations.

Our Jewish cultural heritage regards man as created in the image of God, capable and worthy of the good life. As members of the National Conference of Jewish Communal Service, in our various ways, individually and collectively, it is in our hands to help our fellow-men achieve the good life and the full life.

TRENDS AND ISSUES IN JEWISH SOCIAL WELFARE IN THE UNITED STATES, 1899-1958

PART ONE
THE YEARS OF IMMIGRANT ADJUSTMENT

An American Jewish Community Emerges
1899-1919

SURVEY OF THE YEARS 1899–1919

THE American Jewish community and its social-welfare institutions have evolved out of a continuous interplay between the conditions of American society, Jewish group needs, and Jewish historical imperatives. The emergence of the Jewish community in its American and secular, rather than its religious, aspect has been due in large part to the social-welfare activities undertaken by Jews individually and in groups. At no time was this more evident than in the first two decades of the twentieth century. This creative period was one in which an urban Jewish community life in the United States came clearly into being, to replace the family, *Landsmanschaft* and synagogal forms of Jewish life of the nineteenth century.

The first two decades of the twentieth century saw the emergence of a strong, industrialized and unified United States, but also of the American social conscience in its contemporary form. The continent was now occupied; the foundations of a great industrial and urban society had already replaced agricultural and pioneer origins; and the major cleavages of civil war were closed. But the exciting economic and industrial growth of the nineteenth century also exacted a terrible human price in industrial injury and death, in social dislocation as immigrants and farmers moved to the cities, in sweated labor and child labor, and in cyclical unemployment. In the period 1899 to 1919, some dedicated Americans fought for social legislation and new philanthropic instruments with which to close the gap between the American promise and the rigors of rapid industrialization. The impetus for social innovation was expressed through social legislation: mother's pensions, workmen's compensation, tenement laws, the U. S. Children's Bureau, and public health services; and through voluntary social agencies: councils of social agencies and community chests, foster homes for children, the case-work method, settlement houses.

American Jews entered this period with community institutions capable of responding to new demands and also flexible enough to grow and change. Jewish immigrants in the early nineteenth century brought with them their families and synagogues, which constituted their first resources for group survival in a new world. As early as the 1820's, however, American communities combined one or more synagogues with non-synagogal charities and this became widespread by mid-century. In the earliest days of the republic, Jewish communities were secular as well as religious in function, although congregational in form.[1] By 1854, the charitable soci-

[1] See Jacob R. Marcus, *Early American Jewry,* vol. II, chapter 18 (Philadelphia, 1953); and Hyman B. Grinstein, *The Rise of the Jewish Community of New York, 1654-1860* (Philadelphia, 1947).

eties and agencies of Philadelphia had become so numerous that a Hebrew Charitable Fund had to be organized; this pattern was repeated in Chicago by 1859 with the formation of a United Helfsmans Relief Association. By 1845, Chicago had its Jewish Hospital, and by 1855 Philadelphia had its childrens' orphan asylum. The capacity to organize and create such agencies fitted well into a rapidly expanding American society. Although the originating communities lacked a wide communal discipline or an ideology sufficient to see them through the industrial and social upheavals of the approaching twentieth century, the early welfare structure provided a suitable foundation for the required expansion.

The late nineteenth and early twentieth centuries catapulted American Jews and their institutions into the turmoil of the changing social structure. In 1880 there were an estimated 250,000 Jews in the United States. Between 1880 and 1900 more than 500,000 additional Jews emigrated to the United States, followed by another 1,250,000 between 1900 and 1914.[2] Families were separated and traditional family stability and security was threatened and often destroyed; parents and children were alienated from each other by a new language, new mores, and new moralities; sweated and child labor was common; economic insecurity was the rule rather than the exception. Jewish life began to experience desertions, alcoholism, tuberculosis, juvenile delinquency—all the stigmata of rapid industrialization and urbanization.

The period brought into high focus the question of the Jewish group's responsibility for itself, its character, its survival. In these two decades not only did the American Jewish community take its shape, but the direction was set for evolution during the succeeding fifty years of American Jewish social work. Most of the concepts and institutions which now characterize the Jewish community and its social-welfare institutions were projected and tested during this period.

The building of a Jewish community thus coincided with a pe-

[2] See estimates in Solomon Grayzel, *The History of the Jews* (Philadelphia, 1947); and Glazer, Nathan, *American Judaism* (Chicago, 1957).

riod in American history which was especially rich in social inventiveness and social ferment. For the whole of American society was also adjusting itself to the demands of late nineteenth and early twentieth century industrialization and urbanization.

Through the records of the National Conference of Jewish Charities can be seen the main outlines of the history suggested above: (1) the emergence of a viable American Jewish community (2) the founding of contemporary Jewish social work. They reflect the experiences of individuals and groups, and the exchange of views which did much to sift the acceptable and workable material from the undesirable or unmanageable. The Conference papers are a curious blend of homely and practical details and broad-gauge planning; of critical self-analysis and uncritical prejudice; of cultural narrowness and wise adjustment.

The plans of the Baron de Hirsch Fund and the Industrial Removal Office led inevitably to a roughly outlined policy, a long-range program of national and communal responsibility for immigration to replace the earlier individual and emergency efforts. As a result, local efforts were based upon analyses of European needs, on planned arrangements for immigrant reception, on systematic financial aid, on resettlement and industrial or agricultural retraining, and on inter-city cooperation. These efforts were initiated by a few wealthy families and represented an attempt to plan with complete logic, although in the end, they affected only a small proportion of the flood of new immigrants soon to swamp the already settled Jewish population. True, some of the motives were less than purely altruistic; the new immigrants often aroused such dislike among some Americans that the newcomers' removal to distant places seemed to be merely a step toward good community relations. Nonetheless, such plans to assist them in their resettlement were not only broad in scope, but forced a major reconstruction of Jewish social institutions. Various synagogal and small relief societies tried to meet the first flood of needs but were wholly unequipped to do so. The late nineteenth century American experience with charity organization societies encouraged the unification of Jewish relief societies into community welfare societies.

At the same time, the relative compactness of Jewish community life made possible certain innovations for serving native and immigrant alike. It was not sufficient to unify relief work in order to save money and to make the work more efficient. Between 1902 and 1910 attention was regularly called to the social causes of individual and family distress, which could no longer be attributed to individual defects or weaknesses alone. Prevention was considered as important as the relief of suffering. Family rehabilitation and conservation of family strengths were fixed as primary goals. Adequate relief was insisted upon on the grounds that inadequate relief served only to pauperize. As early as 1904, adequate relief was urged to enable mothers to stay at home rather than work and risk the break-up of their families. These concepts, with their contemporary familiarity, characterize the approach of most Jewish welfare organizations in 1960, but in 1900 they were strange and unfamiliar.

The general relief societies of the last century were inadequate to meet the multiplicity of problems encountered in the new American cities. In response, individuals and groups experimented with many new types of service and new forms of organization. By 1902 some form of personal service was proposed, apart from relief, on the grounds that urban life presented many economically independent families with problems for which they needed help, which they would not take from a relief or charity organization. The special problems of juvenile delinquency, tuberculosis, transiency, family desertion, and Americanization—all called for new and often specialized treatment, which was beyond the capacity of the simple welfare societies of the 1800's.

Most of these problems were dealt with by means of local experimentation and creativity. But here and there, problems were clearly national in scope, and the earliest form of national voluntary planning by Jewish philanthropy began to appear. Transiency, the 1900 term for the population mobility of the 1960's, and family desertions were early recognized in Conference discussion as being national social problems. Standards and procedures were set through Conference committees in order to guide communities to help transients constructively when they asked for relief away from their home communities. But, while accepting the general American pattern, Jewish groups insisted on elaborating their own version of residence laws and seldom relied upon governmental organizations, as did other welfare agencies of the day.

Similarly, the prevailing concepts about enforcement of marital responsibility were adopted regarding family desertions, but a distinctive Jewish institution, the National Desertion Bureau, was created to supplement legal enforcement with voluntary efforts, thus retaining the freedom to relax legal controls if individual cases seemed to warrant it.

In the area of child welfare, the Jewish communities at first reflected the common premises of the surrounding communities. Early child welfare efforts were concentrated in large congregate institutions, and this was considered essential in 1902. By 1906 the conflict between foster family and institutional care was in full swing among Jewish spokesmen. Although a few far-sighted leaders were ahead of their times, their attempt was limited by lack of knowledge about the varieties of children's needs.

However, not all developments were concentrated on distinctive Jewish solutions within the generally accepted American philosophies of the time. In 1900 some Jewish writers analyzed the consequences of tuberculosis in essentially social terms, and called for general community rather than sectarian solutions. Others pointed out that transiency was only one manifestation of a general social problem characteristic of urban society, and that its solution required governmental attention, since its requirements far exceeded the resources of private charity. These early voices were far ahead of their time, since scientific knowledge and analysis required several decades to take effective hold of people's minds; large sanatoria were erected in Denver and upper New York state to serve sick persons from all parts of the country long after the scientific justification for such institutions was established.

The pressures of the period led to the creation of quite new social institutions, having little connection with nineteenth-century forms of Jewish life. One of the most distinctive was the Jewish settlement, one of the forerunners of the modern Jewish community center, whose origin was in part in the settlement-house movement of the late nineteenth century in England and the United States. From the beginning, the Jewish settlement agency confronted its supporters with a dilemma as to its purpose: Was its function to Americanize Jews (and what did this entail?) or to preserve their Jewishness? At first, the belief in Americanization seemed dominant, and the main purpose of the settlements was to teach English and help the Jews of the big city ghettos learn American ways as fast as possible. By the outbreak of the war in 1914, these institutions, along with their wartime associates in the Jewish Welfare Board, were conscious of the dualism of their mission: to find a place for the immigrants in the general American scene, and also to create a distinctively Jewish place in it.

Between 1899 and 1914, there emerged another characteristic of American and Jewish social welfare—social action by individuals to improve government programs for social needs. Many early Jewish social workers achieved general recognition; men like Lee Frankel, I. M. Rubinow, Boris Bogen and Julian Mack shared the efforts of other American social workers to advance effective social security systems, state mothers' pension laws, workmen's compensation laws, juvenile courts, and a federal Children's Bureau. While these general activities do not appear prominently in the early *Proceedings* of the Conference, the men and women who took part in them do appear as active Conference participants, discussing matters of specific Jewish interest. This led to a cross-fertilization between leaders active in both Jewish and general social welfare affairs, to the enrichment of both. The political atmosphere of the times—the New Freedom of Wilson and the Bull Moose Party of Theodore Roosevelt—was congenial to such social-welfare leadership. Leading social workers contributed directly to the platforms on social legislation which were adopted by major political parties, marking a high point in social and political effectiveness for social work in America.

The course of events confronted community workers with a great need for information. A number of fact-finding and technical facilities were therefore organized which became the foundation for later organizations, such as the Bureau of Social Research and the Council of Jewish Federations. In 1914, the American Jewish Committee formed a Bureau of Jewish Social Research "to serve American Jewry in the study and promotion of Jewish social and communal activity."

The Conference took an active lead in this development; in 1916 it established a Field Bureau "to disseminate information about the organization and administration of Jewish social-service activities," whch conducted pioneering studies of all Jewish social services in Chicago. At about the same time, the *kehillah*[3] of New York City organized its Bureau of Philanthropic Research, which was merged with the Conference Bureau in 1919.

These early research or fact-finding bodies were characterized by a breadth of scope which could encompass nearly all phases of community life, and, although the Conference focused its activities on social welfare events, it interpreted the term welfare liberally.

By the end of World War I the foundations for American Jewish communities and American Jewish social work were well set. Scores of thousands of new Jewish residents had not only been received but settled. True, the newcomers did not lose their identity in relation to earlier Jewish settlers any more than the first Jews had in relation to their Christian neighbors. Some Jews were still organizing community and welfare services according to the country of origin or the religious choice of the sponsors. But the aims, purposes, and organizational forms in most cities were now community-wide, as well as synagogue or *Landsmanschaft* based. Relief societies were becoming social-welfare agencies, with codes

[3] The organized Jewish community.

and standards. Through the medium of National Conferences, views were exchanged on a national platform, and new experiments were tested in a national laboratory of opinion. Jews were committed to making their own contribution to the national effort in wartime, rather than becoming submerged in the activities of other sectarian and secular welfare programs. The problems of post-war reconstruction in Europe could be faced by an American Jewry fortified by two decades of experience in national, American, and Jewish efforts to supplement local and individual philanthropy.

I Mass Immigration and Immigrant Aid—Long Range Adjustment Programs

In 1900 it was estimated that there were 1,058,000 Jews living in the United States, and in that year alone over 40,000 Jewish immigrants entered the country. At the peak of the post-World War II migration, when there was an American Jewish population of about 5,000,000, the annual inflow of known Jewish migrants did not exceed 40,000. Planning for this influx was characterized by a remarkable self-confidence and hopefulness, although social institutions were primitive, funds were not yet raised, and personnel was untrained and inexperienced.

Thc rapidity with which Jewish efforts matured is dramatic. A paper read in 1902 expressed attitudes of the day towards new immigrants: "They are lazy, don't want to work, they hide behind their religious habits of the old country, and should be made to work or walk on, regardless of the conditions of work or pay." By 1904, the Bressler paper indicates a more perceptive attitude, and there is a plea to view the immigrant in light of his personal history and needs, rather than in light of "our ideas of what is best for him." In 1900, the immigrant was expected to take any job at any pay; but other workers complained bitterly about this undercutting of wage levels and the whole process fed anti-foreign and anti-immigrant passions of the day. By 1904, it was recognized that the immigrant had a right to his own standards of life and also a right to a place in the American society of which he was becoming a part.

The pattern of modern immigrant resettlement is foreshadowed in the centrally worked out plans of the Industrial Removal Office. Accurate data about population flow is sought for, and investigators go to the country of origin in Europe; reception at boatside is organized; training is provided; an attempt is made to organize a network of field services to keep local efforts in step with the in-pouring demands at the eastern ports of entry; plans are made centrally and from a national position, although carrying them out depends upon local organization, understanding, and support. In some respects the planning in 1900 was more broad and ambitious than that of 1950. Note the attempt to create whole new communities, such as Woodbine, N.J., with new agriculture and industry. The quick-learning pragmatic leaders of the time soon discovered the limitations of private philanthropy, no matter how ambitious its intentions. The welfare program soon shifted its emphasis to adjustment of new immigrants to the city, since the demands of the industrial period required that the majority of newcomers settle there. Even here, the early efforts at vocational training and re-training were colored by recognition that even these activities would be better carried out through public educational facilities in the future.

The Jewish organizational response to the large-city slums, that consequence of nineteenth-century industrialization, was in many ways distinctive from the efforts of other American social reformers of the period. While many individual Jewish citizens participated in the fight for social legislation to relieve the human tragedies of the city slums, Jewish organizational efforts first took the form of efforts to move poor Jews from the overcrowded ghettos to other parts of the country, and especially to rural areas. Only when these measures proved inadequate was attention directed to work in the slums, and a slower-paced movement within the city itself was adopted.

1. Jewish Mass Immigration to the United States*

BY SAMUEL JOSEPH

Jews have been in this country since its very beginnings.[1] Their presence in small numbers was noted in Colonial days. Those were mainly Spanish and Portuguese Jews. German Jews began to enter in the fifties of the past century, following the political disturbances in Germany of that time.[2] About a quarter of a million Jews were estimated to be living here around 1880.

The mass movement of Jews to the United States begins with the immigration of Russian Jews.[3] Their entry was dramatically staged by the pogroms in southern Russia in the spring of 1881, which in a few months sent hundreds of refugees to our ports in indescribable misery. Few realized at the time that they were beholding in the terror-stricken Russian-Jewish families at Castle Garden, then the immigrant-receiving station of New York, the advance-guard of a stream of Jewish immigrants that was even-

* From "Survey of Jewish Immigration to the United States," *Jewish Social Service Quarterly,* vol. XV, no. 2 (March 1939), pp. 299-304.

[1] For a more extensive treatment of Jewish immigration to the United States, see: Samuel Joseph, *Jewish Immigration to the United States from 1881 to 1910* (New York, Columbia University Press, 1914); Elias Tcherikower, *The Early Jewish Labor Movement in the United States,* tr. and rev. by Aaron Antonovsky (New York, Yiddish Scientific Institute—YIVO, 1961); Mark Wischnitzer, *To Dwell in Safety: The Story of Jewish Migration Since 1800* (Philadelphia, 1948); Maurice R. Davie, *Refugees in America* (New York 1947); Oscar and Mary Handlin, "A Century of Jewish Immigration to the United States," *American Jewish Year Book,* vol. 50, 1948-49.

[2] Recent scholarship has established that Ashkenazi Jews from England, Holland, Germany, and other European countries soon followed the Spanish and Portuguese Sephardim and by 1725 they constituted the majority of the Jewish population in New York and elsewhere. See Bernard D. Weinryb, "Jewish Immigration and Accommodation to America," *Publication of the American Jewish Historical Society* (*PAJHS*), vol. XLVI, no. 3-4 (March, 1957).

[3] The first mass Jewish immigration is now understood to have begun in 1836. See Nathan Glazer, *American Judaism* (Chicago, 1957), p. 23.

tually to land, within one short generation, over two million Jews upon our shores.

It was a fateful moment in modern Jewish history. At a memorable meeting of protest in London held on February 1, 1882, the call for which was signed by the greatest Englishmen of that day, including Charles Darwin, James Bryce, and Robert Browning, Cardinal Manning spoke these words:

> We have all watched for the last twelve months what is called the anti-Semitic movement in Germany. I look upon it with a two-fold feeling: In the first place I look upon it with abhorrence as tending to disintegrate the foundations of social life, and, secondly, with great fear lest it may tend to light up an animosity which has already taken fire in Russia and may spread elsewhere.

The formation of the famous Mansion House Committee followed. Along with the many other voluntary committees of Jews and Christians in Europe and the United States, it began the first great international effort to aid the victims of Russian autocracy.

In this crisis Jewish leadership fell to the directors of the Alliance Israelite Universelle,[4] the then representative international Jewish body, with branches in Europe and America. Charles Netter, veteran Alliance worker, writing from Brody, the Austrian frontier town where hundreds of Jewish families were huddled, and hundreds more arriving daily, swiftly summed up the situation in a sentence: "There is need for a permanent resettlement of millions of Russian Jews."

The inertia and immobility of the East European Jew had given way, and a steady stream of immigrants followed the first refugees. Ten years later, with the introduction of the May Laws and the widespread feeling that no hope remained for the Jews in Russia,

[4] The Alliance Israelite Universelle was organized in Paris, France, in 1860, "to work everywhere for the emancipation and moral progress of the Jews; to lend effectual support to those who suffer through being Jews; to encourage every publication intended to bring about this result." (Jacques Bigart, "The Alliance Israelite Universelle," *American Jewish Year Book*, vol. 2 [1900-1901], p. 46.)

an immense outpouring began. An American observer sent to Europe described the situation:

During the last four months, from April to August 1891, about 35,000 Jews have passed the borders in flight from Russia; of these some 25,000 Jews have means of their own; 10,000 are destitute. The German committees at the borders and the seaports have made a careful selection of those to be sent forward, and several thousands are to be returned to Russia.

The American Jewish leaders of that day had only the barest inkling of the tremendous difficulties with which the European committees were grappling. Nor, for that matter, had the European Jews any clearer understanding of the conditions in this country. In the eighties, and later again in the early nineties, the great question for millions of Russian Jews was: Whither to go? Possible outlets for emigration were earnestly canvassed by the Alliance Committees in Paris, Berlin, Vienna, and London. Attention was focused on the newer and comparatively undeveloped countries—South America, South Africa, Australia, Canada, and, above all, the United States—with their vast tracts of land and sparse populations. America offered the broadest possibilities in this time of need. Here were boundless territory, inexhaustible resources, an expanding commerce and industry, and not least, a welcoming hand. Here, too, the leaders of the Alliance had paved the way in the seventies by sending out small groups of Russian Jewish families, and entrusting them to the care of the Board of Delegates of American Israelites.[5] (Others had been attracted here by eco-

[5] Actually the "welcoming hand" of the Board of Delegates of American Israelites was extended rather grudgingly. The Board kept insisting through the 70's that "the dispatch of poor emigrants to America has long constituted a burden and an unjust tax upon our large cities" and "sought to check this abuse at a period when it threatened to be more than ordinarily vexatious." It favored, however, a scheme of emigration which "shall assist energetic and industrious youth to a new field, a new home in favored districts, of the Old or the New World, which shall exclude the listless and improvident, and leave the unhappy clan or chronic poor to the benevolence and resource of their place of residence." (Max J. Kohler, "The Board of Delegates of American Israelites, 1859-1878," *PAJHS,* no. 29, pp. 101-02, 114-16.) All told, no more than about 600 immigrants were

nomic opportunity, so that at the beginning of the eighties, there were in the United States some 40,000 Russian and Polish Jews.)

The late Dr. I. M. Rubinow, writing as a participant in a European conference for the relief of the German Jews,[6] mentioned the problems of temporary emergency and of more permanent economic adjustment, and emphasized other matters as well—legal problems of right of entry, right of transit, right of sojourn, and most important, the right to engage in remunerative employment. He added that the social attitudes of the native population must be taken into consideration. The danger of direct stimulation of anti-Jewish sentiments should not be disregarded, since sympathy for refugees might yield to the natural fear of economic competitors. He also feared that the strain upon local Jewish communities in Europe might result in producing a dangerous class of immigrants or transients, thus introducing an element of strife between Jewries of different countries.

All these complex questions arising out of a forced emigration were multiplied a thousandfold in the Russian Jewish emigration that ended only with the onset of the last war. One must visualize the restless, disorganized flow of the immigrant Jewish tide in the thirty years that followed the pogroms of southern Russia. Every month and nearly every day of these long years witnessed seaports, liners, immigrant stations seething with mainly destitute immigrants, often with their wives and children, looking forward eagerly to their new homeland, but entering it with the uncertainty, fear, and foreboding with which the unknown is faced. Within twelve years after the first Russian refugees had been received, the

---

assisted by the Board during the years 1870-73. A similar attitude toward large-scale immigration of East European Jews was taken in the 80's and the 90's by its successor, the Board of Delegates of the Union of American Hebrew Congregations. See: E. Tcherikower, *The Early Jewish Labor Movement in the United States,* pp. 108-109; also Zosa Szajkowski, "The Attitudes of American Jews to East European Jewish Immigration, 1881-1893," *PAJHS,* vol. 40, no. 3 (March 1951), 221-280.

[6] I. M. Rubinow, "What Happened in London," *B'nai B'rith Magazine* (December 1933), pp. 84-5.

numbers that had entered equalled the total Jewish population in the United States before their arrival. In two years, 1891 and 1892, over 10,000 Jews landed in the country. It was a tidal wave, incredible in its swiftness and extent. The Jews, with a relatively small population to draw from, as compared to the immigrants pouring in from the countries of Europe, nevertheless constituted one-tenth of the whole immigration to the United States in the twenty-five years before the war. In the course of a single generation, one out of every three Jews living in Russia, the Austria-Hungary of pre-war days, and Roumania had left his land. Within a comparatively short time, the Jewish emigrés here had practically all the components of a total society. All generations, all classes, and nearly every occupation typical of a normal social group were represented. It took many years for American Jews and Christians alike to realize that this was no ordinary, bird-of-passage movement of immigrants motivated largely or solely by economic considerations, as was the case with practically all the other groups entering this land. It had reached the magnitude of the migration of a people.

Some interesting characteristics of the Russian Jews may be here noted in connection with the problems of adjustment they had to face. The disproportionately large number of women and children, greater by far than that of any other immigrant group, burdened the Russian Jewish immigrants with a large number of dependents; this, together with their meager financial resources, made the task of getting an economic foothold in the country very difficult. On the other hand, the family rather than the individual became the unit for social living, making for a normal home life and associations, as well as, through the children, a rapid cultural assimilation.

The proportion of skilled workers was high. The largest group was composed of needle workers, including tailors, dressmakers and seamstresses and allied trades. The garment workers composed practically one half of the entire body of skilled laborers. Carpenters, joiners, cabinet makers, painters, glaziers, shoemakers, bakers, locksmiths, blacksmiths, clerks, and accountants were the principal occupations reported. These comprised four-fifths of the total reported skilled occupations. Twenty-two other skilled occupations were also reported.

The impression that every Jew could read and write was dispelled by the relatively high rate of illiteracy found. This was partly explained by the lack of educational facilities offered in the countries of Eastern Europe, and partly by the tendency among the Orthodox pre-revolution Russian Jews to neglect the education of females.

An early survey of the immigrant Jews in New York City in 1890 revealed surprising facts and checked alarmist concern about their adjustment both among Jews and the non-Jews in the city. It was shown that the typical Russian Jewish family had nearly five members—almost the same as that of the normal American population of the country. Over one-half of this group were children under fourteen. Economic conditions, it is true, were deplorable: low wages and overcrowded rooms, the latter chiefly because of the necessity of eking out a living through boarders and lodgers. English was spoken by less than one-third of the adults. Only one-third of the heads of families were naturalized. But the health of the newcomers compared favorably with that of other immigrant groups and even of the native population. Jacob Riis, reporting the results of this census,[7] drew the conclusion that "the evidence is after all, that, even here, with a tremendous inpour of a destitute, ignorant people, and with the employment of child labor on a large scale, the cause of progress was holding its own."

For a period of twenty years, from 1880 to about the beginning of this century, the adjustment and accommodation of these rapidly augmenting hordes, "this mass of illiterate, uncouth, mainly superstitious foreigners"—as a Jewish member of the New York community, later to become an eminent economist, described them in print—bristled with difficulties of all sorts. Poverty, overwork, congestion in slums, home overcrowding, anxiety

[7] Jacob A. Riis, *The Children of the Poor* (New York, 1892), pp. 49-55.

about the fate of their relatives abroad, proved a strain that severely taxed the immigrants and the social agencies, particularly of the port cities, and above all of New York City, where 70 per cent of the arrivals regularly remained. The early generous reception and friendly but impractical offers of aid from various states, notably the South, which lacked immigrants, gradually subsided, and the burden of their immediate care fell upon the various Jewish communities in the United States. Here New York naturally took the lead.

The problems were new. Little was known about the incorporation of immigrant groups into American ways of life. The settlement worker, the social worker, and the communal organizer were yet to arrive. Furthermore, prejudice was rife among the leaders of the Jewish communities, who knew little of the East European Jew, and who felt that this immigration would "inevitably accentuate and immensely increase the growing prejudice against Jews in America." The United Hebrew Charities (of New York), forerunner of the Jewish Social Service Association, nevertheless began its seemingly hopeless, endless tasks of aid.

Two conditions made the work easier. One was that the great majority of the Russian Jews vigorously proved their ability to enter into the economic and cultural life of the country. The story of their business success and educational success has been told and retold. Suffice it to say that they have been held up before all the other immigrant groups of the country as models of economic independence, of cultural activity, and for their contribution to the country almost from the beginning.

But aid was needed at various periods from organized charity. This was particularly true of the years preceding the beginning of this century, when the Russian Jews were gaining a foothold and their organizations and institutions were only taking form. By the time the pogroms of 1905-06 had electrified the world, Russian Jews through their *Landsmanschaften* and other agencies did heroic service in pouring out money for relief, and in sending and caring for relatives and friends.

From the standpoint of organized help, the greatest service was performed in 1891 by Baron de Hirsch, when he announced the founding of the ICA in Europe and the formation of the Baron de Hirsch Fund in America. What was virtually flight became transformed into an orderly, and to some degree, controlled immigration. In the United States, through the efforts of the trustees of the Baron de Hirsch Fund, the relief tasks of the beginning gradually gave way to permanent constructive work, largely along the lines laid down by Baron de Hirsch. The adjustment and assimilation of the immigrant Jewish population was attacked mainly from four angles. These were training in trades, agriculture, removal, and Americanization. The short-course trade school which the Fund organized was planned to teach young immigrants "American" trades and American mechanical processes and methods. It was hoped that the door would be opened for them by American firms, and that opportunities for advancement in their field through entry into business or the professions would be presented. In part the trade school solved the need of many who had had technical experience in the "old" country. To those who believed the widespread idea that Jews were fit only for business or peddling, it was a surprise to learn that many of them were possessed of a great deal of mechanical ability. On the other hand, the school led to a much wider appreciation of the importance of technical training by the immigrants themselves. Many of the 9,000 graduates opened small shops in plumbing, sign painting, machinist, electrical wiring, show-card writing, and other trades.

To turn the East European Jews into farmers proved a more difficult undertaking. The record of the many colonies founded by Russian Jews either with idealistic or practical aims is, on the whole, disheartening, yet constitutes a tribute to their courage. Inexperience, lack of capital, separation from fellow Jews and from a wholesome Jewish community life were obstacles too great to overcome. The Irish, themselves a rural folk, became wholly urbanized in this country. Individual farmers with fairly adequate resources succeeded better. Gradually, a farm movement began at the turn of the century, with the result that about 10,000 Jews are now largely dependent upon their farms for their living. Many of these have made their way without the aid of philanthropic associations like the Jewish Agricultural Society, a subsidiary of the ICA and in recent years of the Baron de Hirsch Fund. This organization has served as a remarkable experiment station, unique in many respects, for the aid of Jewish farmers and of farm settlements.

The concentration of immigrants in the port cities of Boston, Philadelphia, Baltimore, and particularly New York, with their widely advertised slums, was viewed with fear by American Jews; much of the agricultural and other activity of the Fund was devoted to an effort to distribute them throughout the country, particularly in the smaller communities of the West and the South. A more organized effort in this direction under the name of "Industrial Removal" later attempted to do this work on a large scale. Educational and so-called Americanization work was carried on in the large cities.

2. The Baron de Hirsch Fund*

BY EUGENE S. BENJAMIN

The Baron de Hirsch Fund was founded in 1891 by the Baron Maurice de Hirsch, who gave to a committee of nine gentlemen and their successors the sum of $2,400,000 in trust for the purposes mentioned in the deed. The original trustees were Myer S.

* National Conference of Jewish Charities, *Proceedings* (1906), pp. 156-70. Presented at the Fourth Biennial Meeting of the National Conference of Jewish Charities, Philadelphia, Pa., May 6-8, 1906. For a detailed account of the work of the Baron de Hirsch Fund up to 1935, see: Samuel Joseph, *History of the Baron de Hirsch Fund* (Philadelphia, 1935), XVII, 305 pp.

Isaacs, Jesse Seligman, Jacob H. Schiff, Oscar S. Straus, Henry Rice, James H. Hoffman, Julius Goldman, Mayer Sulzberger, and William B. Hackenburg.

The objects and purposes as expressed in the deed of trust were as follows:

1. Loans to emigrants from Russia or Roumania, agriculturists, settlers within the United States, upon real or chattel security.
2. Provision for the transportation of immigrants selected (after their arrival at any American port) with reference to their age, character, and capacity, to be placed where it is expected the conditions of the labor market or the residence of friends will tend to make them self-supporting.
3. Provision for training immigrants in a handicraft and contributing to their support while learning such handicraft, and for furnishing the necessary tools and implements and other assistance to enable them to earn a livelihood.
4. Provision for improved mechanical training for adults and youths—immigrants and their children—whereby persons of industry and capacity may acquire some remunerative employment, either by the payment of apprenticeship, or tuition fees, or the instruction of adults and minors in trade schools or otherwise, with contributions for temporary support.
5. Provision for instruction in the English language and in the duties and obligations of life and citizenship in the United States, and for technical and trade education, and the establishment and subvention of special schools, workshops, and other suitable agencies for promotion and maintenance of such instruction.
6. Provision for instruction in agricultural work and improved methods of farming and for aiding settlers with tools and implements, and the practical supervision of such instruction, conducted upon suitable tracts of land and in necessary buildings.
7. Cooperation with established agencies in various sections of the United States, whose duty it shall be in whole or in part to furnish aid or relief, and education to needy and deserving applicants coming within the classes designated herein.
8. Contributions towards the maintenance of individuals and families, while temporarily awaiting work, or when settled in the new homes in which they may be established.
9. Such other and further modes of relief and such other and further

contributions to education and in such departments of knowledge as the said trustees or their successors shall from time to time decide.

The Fund, thus established by the Baron de Hirsch, was subsequently very largely increased by a donation made by the Baroness de Hirsch in 1898, and still further by a bequest received under her will.

A portion of the principal was expended at once, under the provisions of the Deed of Trust, in the purchase of land and the erection of buildings at Woodbine, New Jersey; the balance of the principal of the Fund has been kept intact by the trustees, and now (1906) amounts to $3,800,000, and only the income thereof is used. This income, however, is by no means sufficient to defray the cost of the work undertaken by the trustees, and we are only able to continue our many activities through the generous financial assistance annually rendered us by the Jewish Colonization Association of Paris.

Having thus concisely stated the origin of the Fund and the sources of its income, I shall proceed to give you a brief summary of the different kinds of work undertaken or fostered by it. For the purpose of this address, I shall divide the work into five groups, viz.: general aid to the immigrant; removal work; educational work; Woodbine and other industrial activities; and agricultural work.

General Aid to the Immigrant

During the first two years of his stay in this country, we regard the immigrant in some respects as our ward, and as one who is entitled to our help. Upon his arrival at Ellis Island, an agent of the United Hebrew Charities, who is paid by us, meets the immigrant and gives him such information, advice, and other assistance as the circumstances of the case may require. If the immigrant is a woman arriving here unattended, an agent of the Council of Jewish Women, for whose services we likewise make the necessary financial provision, looks after her welfare and prevents her going astray; if she has no proper place to go to, until she gets a position or is otherwise satisfactorily placed, she is cared for at the downtown lodging house for immigrant girls conducted by the Clara de Hirsch Home, a lodging house maintained in part by our financial assistance.

If the new arrival, through illness or other misfortune, fails to succeed, he is furnished with the necessary tools or implements of his trade, employment is found for him, a trade taught him or temporary financial assistance given him.

In New York City this assistance is given through the agency of the United Hebrew Charities; and in Philadelphia and Baltimore through branch committees of the Fund. To all of these we supply the funds necessary to do this work. To a smaller extent funds are also supplied to Boston for similar work.

Removal Work

This work was initiated in 1891 with a view to relieving the pressure on the seaport cities at the time of the heavy immigration of Jews to the United States, and large numbers of the immigrants were settled in manufacturing towns in the East and West. This work became so extensive and its beneficient results so apparent that in 1900 it was decided to thoroughly systematize it and conduct it on a large and permanent scale. Accordingly, the Jewish Agricultural and Industrial Aid Society was organized, and to a branch of that society, known as the Removal Committee, this work has been entrusted.[1] Numerous agencies have been established and working arrangements made with local societies, or with committees of public-spirited citizens in most of the important centers of the United States, and about 6,000 persons are removed

[1] For a more detailed treatment of early removal work and the activities of the Jewish Agricultural and Industrial Aid Society and the Removal Office, see William Kahn, "Removal Work—Early Experience," National Conference of Jewish Charities, *Proceedings* (1902), pp. 83-91.

annually from New York City alone, and self-sustaining positions found elsewhere for all of them.

Educational Work

It is of vital importance that the adult immigrant should promptly obtain a knowledge of the English language, and in the interest of good government that he should become familiar with the customs of the country and the theory of our government; and in the case of the child, that he should be prepared as promptly as possible to take his proper grade in the public school, or if it is necessary for him to go to work, that he should quickly receive the minimum of education which is required by the State before he is excused from attending the public schools.

To accomplish these purposes the educational work of the society is conducted. In New York City the Educational Alliance, through funds furnished by us, maintains day classes for children and adults, where the pupils are kept for a period ranging from three months to a year and half. . . . In the same way, a night school is maintained, supplementing the public night schools; it is kept open from April to September, when the public night schools are closed. This night school is attended by adults ranging in age from seventeen to fifty.

In Brooklyn we aid the Hebrew Educational Society; in Philadelphia, the Hebrew Educational Society; in Pittsburgh, the Columbian Council; and in St. Louis, the Jewish Educational Society. All of these maintain classes similar to those conducted by the Educational Alliance in New York City.

A very important feature of our educational work is the Baron de Hirsch Trade School in New York City. This is a fully equipped and well-housed school for the teaching of trades. With a course of instruction of five and one-half months, it fits boys to qualify as helpers in certain mechanical trades. The trades taught are those of the carpenter, machinist, plumber, electrician, and house and sign painter. The capacity of the school is taxed to its utmost. In this school we try to get down to a practical basis, and to give such instruction as will prepare the boy to become a valuable helper to a journeyman workman. While we do not aim to teach a trade thoroughly, it is, nevertheless, a fact that a fair proportion of the graduates of the school quickly become journeymen workmen and earn journeymen wages. I might say that while this school was originally instituted only for boys of foreign birth, we have of late years allowed those born here to partake of its benefits; but it is true in this school, as in our agricultural school, that the foreign-born boy is more efficient, earnest, and successful.

Woodbine and Other Industrial Activities

One of the desires of the Baron de Hirsch was the establishment of an agricultural and industrial colony in this country where the newly arrived immigrant might settle. One of the first acts of the trustees of the Fund, in furtherance of this wish, was the purchase in the fall of 1891 of a tract of land of over 5,000 acres in southern New Jersey, where the town of Woodbine was established. On this tract a town site was laid out, and the surrounding country was set apart for farms.

The town has had many vicissitudes, but is today a self-governing and self-respecting community with about 2,000 inhabitants, a large proportion of whom rely for their subsistence on the several factories which have been built and established there through the agency of the Fund.

Most of the heads of families own their own houses, for the Fund has made it possible for a man to acquire title to his home by a monthly payment amounting, in most cases, to one-half of what he would pay for three rooms in a crowded tenement house in New York City.

In the year 1903, the town received its charter as an independent community; it is now governed by its own Mayor and Common

Council. Every municipal office is filled by a Jew, and the affairs of the town have always been well and economically administered.

When the colony was first started, we were obliged to subsidize all industries that we induced to locate there, in order to provide employment for the immigrants. Even with all the fostering care and large financial assistance which we gave it, the success of the colony was for many years in doubt; but we are able now to say that the industries of Woodbine are practically on a self-sustaining basis. The only aid which they receive from the Fund is the grant in a few cases of free rent, power, and light, which is no greater inducement than is held out by other small towns to manufacturing concerns.

When the town was established by the Baron de Hirsch Fund, it was intended that its inhabitants should be industrial workers and farmers. A large part of the tract of 5,000 acres owned by the Fund was divided into small farms, and a number of farmers were settled on them. While a small proportion of those farmers have been able to make a living and improve their condition, it is but fair to say that as a farming experiment Woodbine has not been a success, partly because of its distance from a profitable market, and partly because most of the men had no previous experience in the cultivation of land. It was found also that one of the causes that operated against the success of the farmer was the inducement that the factory held out to him of employment at weekly wages; it is a well recognized fact that a man cannot be a worker in a factory and a successful farmer at the same time.

We have lately undertaken to develop along new lines the farming possibilities of Woodbine. With the knowledge gained by years of experience, we have every hope of being able, within a few years, to cite Woodbine as a success from an agricultural as well as from an industrial standpoint.

In South Jersey, about twenty miles from Woodbine, but nearer to Philadelphia, are the other so-called South Jersey Colonies of Alliance—Rosenhayn, Carmel, Norma, and Brotmanville—which were established in the '80's and '90's by various philanthropic societies. Since 1900 the Jewish Agricultural and Industrial Aid Society has undertaken the duty of bettering the physical and moral condition of these early settlers. We have established several modern factories; maintained night schools and provided scholarships in high schools in neighboring towns for pupils of promise; cooperated in building a canning factory; provided a resident director of social and educational work, who has done and is doing much to elevate the general moral tone of the community; provided free lecture courses; built social halls; subsidized resident physicians; established libraries; and have in numerous instances made loans to the farmers of these communities. The farmers have, as a rule, been successful, but the factories have not always prospered.

I do not desire to be understood as advocating the establishment of other colonies on the plan of Woodbine. The amount of money, time and energy spent in bringing this industrial settlement to its present condition is out of all proportion to the number of our coreligionists who were benefited thereby. This same amount of money spent in removal work or in building up a farming class among the Jews would produce better, surer, and more far-reaching results.

At one time it was believed that we could remove large numbers of factory workers from the cities to rural communities, provided we could supply them with employment at the place to which they were sent, and several large and costly experiments were undertaken along these lines; but they have all proved failures. It was found that we could successfully remove city dwellers to points where there was an established industry offering them employment, as is evidenced by the work of the removal office; it was also found that we could establish industries in a place like Woodbine, where we already had a sufficient permanent population to supply the industry with workmen; but it was not found either feasible or practical to remove both the industry and the industrial worker, for reasons which it would take too long to discuss in this paper.

Agricultural Work

The founders of the Fund were most anxious to encourage the Jewish immigrant in the pursuit of agriculture. The trustees have devoted much of their time and attention to the carrying out of this aim, and have sought in every way to induce the immigrant to settle on land and to become a farmer. It was thought that this work could best be accomplished by first teaching the rudiments of agriculture to those who were not farmers, and second, by rendering financial assistance to those who were farmers but had not the means to establish themselves on farms. To teach agriculture we have established the agricultural school and Woodbine, and the so-called test farm at Kings Park, L.I.

The Woodbine agricultural school was established to teach agriculture to boys. It was founded in 1895 and seeks to give a boy an amount of technical education in the school and practical training on the school-farm sufficient to qualify him for filling a position as a helper on a farm—with the promise held out to him of assistance in the purchase of a farm of his own when he reaches the proper age and has demonstrated his ability to managc it.

The school has been to a large extent an experiment, and from time to time we have changed the curriculum as suggested by experience. The present requirements for admission are that the applicant should be about the age of eighteen, should be physically capacitated for the work of farming, and should have an elementary knowledge of English. The student is given one year of practical and technical education, and then secured a position on a farm; if he retains his position and sticks to the work and desires further instruction of a technical or practical character, he may take an advanced course the following winter. The school undertakes only to give the boy sufficient instruction and experience to enable him to work satisfactorily on a farm as a helper, and makes no attempt to compete with the many excellent agricultural schools in the country where the *science* of agriculture is taught.

The problem of the school is a difficult one. There is no difficulty in finding places for graduates as farm helpers, but our main trouble heretofore has been that boys would take advantage of the opportunities offered them by the school to secure a general training and education, and would ultimately forsake farming. Nevertheless, we have a large number of very creditable graduates who are pursuing agriculture as a livelihood.

An equally interesting experiment is the work of the Test Farm at Kings Park, L.I. A tract of 500 acres of good land was purchased there and equipped with modern buildings and farming implements, and houses were erected for twelve families. We locate at this test farm each year about twelve families. We provide the heads of the families with work as farm laborers, teaching them American methods of agriculture. We pay them daily wages, out of which they provide for the support of their families and pay rent for the houses which they occupy. We also allot to each one of them a small plot of ground for raising the garden truck needed for his family.

After a year, if they have shown a likelihood of success as farmers, we assist them in finding farms of their own and enable them to settle on them under favorable conditions.

The Fund has also, through the medium of the Jewish Agricultural and Industrial Aid Society, provided the means by which various agricultural experiments have been conducted throughout the United States, such as the Colony of Arpin, Wisconsin, conducted by the Milwaukee Agricultural Association.

All of the agricultural work which I have described is conducted under the auspices of the Jewish Agricultural and Industrial Aid Society. In 1900 we found that our agricultural, industrial and removal work had become so extended that it was necessary to found a separate society to take charge of these activities; hence the establishment of this Society, which is maintained partly by the funds donated by the Baron de Hirsch Fund, and partly by contributions from the Jewish Colonization Association of Paris.

A very large part of the funds of this Society is used in making loans to farmers. These loans are of such a nature that they could not possibly be obtained from any other source. They therefore encourage and aid men with limited means to become farmers.

This farm loan work has grown steadily each year. The records of the Society show that (as of 1906) there are 1,382 Jewish farmers of whom we have cognizance in one way or another, with a total farming population of 7,491 souls, cultivating 125,434 acres, with a real-estate value of $2,170,850, and with a personal property value of $545,799.

These figures by no means account for the total Jewish farming population of the United States and Canada, since from experience we have reason to believe that there are fully as many more of whom we have no records who are cultivating farms in the United States and Canada.

In addition to this, we make home-building loans to dwellers in small cities and villages who wish to acquire their own homes.

The foregoing completes the very general outline of the numerous activities in which the income of the Baron de Hirsch Fund is utilized. No adequate conception, however, can be given of the immense amount of detail and executive work found necessary to give this work proper supervision.

We maintain three separate organizations: one to do the work of the Fund proper, one to do the work of the Jewish Agricultural and Industrial Aid Society, and a third to do the work of the Removal Office.

For the fruits of all these undertakings we must perhaps look largely to the future, because the work is of such a kind that immediate results are not always discernible. Certainly those branches of the work which are concerned with the removal of the new immigrants to places outside of the large cities, with the education and Americanizing of those immigrants and their children who elect to stay in the large cities, with the teaching to a large number of boys of trades which have previously not been generally adopted by the Jews, and with the encouragement of the Jew to become a farmer, are all efforts which tend to the uplifting of the Jewish immigrant as a class, and which will produce good results not only now, but to a much greater extent in the years to come.

3. Removal Work—Further Efforts*

BY DAVID M. BRESSLER

The question: "What is the Removal Office?" is a question that is heard far more frequently in this city (New York) than in any other place in this country. Yet, the main scene of its activity is set in this seaport metropolis. To me, this ignorance of the movement among a large number of intelligent and even public-spirited Jews is simply an indication of the many diversified movements and social activities that engage the interest of New York Jews; the fact that there are so many local problems and philanthropic institutions, interest in which excludes even a knowledge of removal work, is the surest evidence that the Jewish population of New York is already large enough to present a national problem. Removal has been opposed and opposed stoutly, but only by such as make capital of the ghetto. Even those theorists intensely Jewish in feeling who believe that distribution means ultimate assimilation admit that the congestion of Jews in certain districts of New York contains elements of danger. There are others who look askance at the distribution of our people, because in their opinion it will kindle the flame of anti-Semitism in those cities and villages where the Jew is as yet unknown. Interesting as this phase of the question may be, I do not think that it deserves prominent consideration in the councils of this Conference. To say that they love us only at a distance would, it seems to me, be an unwarranted offense against the tolerance and fair-mindedness of our non-

* National Conference of Jewish Charities, *Proceedings* (1904), pp. 141-48. Presented at the Third Biennial Conference of Jewish Charities, New York City, May 24-27, 1904.

Jewish neighbors. There is need for removal; greater need than ever before. The immigration last year (1903) was 63,000 as against 54,000 of the year previous, and this year it will reach, if not exceed, 75,000.[1] And if this continues, even with the improved city transportation facilities to the suburbs, it must give us concern to think what the results may be.

It is erroneously believed even by many engaged in assisting removal work that our chief aim is to depopulate or decentralize the ghetto. Whether this be a consummation devoutly to be wished or not, a serious attempt to do this would be the height of quixotic extravagance. It would no more be possible to decentralize the large Jewish quarters of this city than it would be to obliterate anti-Semitism from off the face of the earth. . . . The Removal Office does not attempt any such Utopian scheme as this. It merely recognizes the evils of present overcrowding in New York and organizes the efforts of the Jewish community of America to divert the stream of Jewish immigration away from New York and into the interior. Judging superficially, one would quickly come to the conclusion that even this is a hopeless task. Last year about 43,000 immigrants remained in the city of New York, and only 5,525 were sent out by the Removal Office; that is to say, only one-eighth, approximately. The work of the Removal Office must, therefore, apparently make very little impression upon the conditions which it seeks to relieve. But a careful study of the immigration figures presents reasonable hope of ultimate success. In the years 1900, 1901, and 1902, 73 per cent had the city of New York as their ultimate destination: of those arriving in 1903, 69.5 per cent were destined for New York, which on the basis of immigration for that year shows that the number of persons removed directly and at their own expense to the interior towns was 3.5 per cent or 2,224 more than in 1902. Furthermore, the unfailing experience for the past twenty years has been that the establishment

[1] These appear to be New York City statistics. The actual figures nationally were 1902—57,688; 1903—76,203; 1904—106,236. See Wischnitzer, *op. cit.*, p. 289.

of a number of Jewish immigrants at a given place speedily results in attracting a considerable additional number to that same place; so it is reasonable to expect that the 12,000 persons who have been sent away in the past three years will succeed in attracting a considerable number of friends and relatives who would otherwise settle in New York City.

Removal is interesting from many points of view, both as a theory and as a practical philanthropic and sociological movement. We who are constantly driving the moving van, so to speak, must be alert to adjust and reconcile in every practical and legitimate manner the prejudice and timidity of the immigrant with exactly the same qualities that characterize in a different form the majority of the people of the interior. Our difficulties, therefore, are two-fold: first, to gain the confidence of the beneficiary, and secondly, to gain the confidence of the benefactor. That we have been able to do this, even in a limited degree, seems to me to be a sure sign that Israel is still one.

The communities in the interior have shown that they recognize the problem to be an important and pressing one; but without reflecting upon their willingness to assist in this solution, I make bold to say that they do not realize how important and how pressing it is. Above all they do not appreciate how difficult it is. They still regard their acceptance of new immigrants as a favor bestowed upon New York, when they should regard the problem of this large immigration as much theirs as that of New York. It is not their open denial or refutation of the truth of this argument so much as the thousand and one restrictions placed upon us by them that convinces me that many of them have not yet acquired the true point of view. One community will say, You may send us only newly arrived immigrants; another, You may send us only mechanics; another, only laborers; another, only such as speak English, and so on. Such orders would be helpful provided every Jew in New York were willing to leave the city. It must be remembered that comparatively few persons apply at the office, and of them only a part are possessed of handicrafts for which there is a general demand. It can, therefore, be seen readily that in order that the work may be promoted in the most effective manner, the Bureau must not be regarded as an employment agency, whose province it is to cater to the demands of employers. Of course, the Removal Office must always be kept informed of the actual industrial conditions in all parts of the country, in order that an intelligent distribution may be made; but the cooperating communities must be prepared to take people whether there is a crying demand for them or not. Particularly of late, many of our applicants have been men of no skilled trade and some of them are physically unable to do very laborious work. It must be remembered that a very large proportion of our immigrants were students, merchants, and small tradesmen abroad. For such men special efforts must be made, and our cooperating communities must be willing to accept them. What is to become of them? It is hard for them to accept employment in factories in New England and New Jersey, for the simple reason that most of the work done in such establishments can be done by female help; and even were these men prepared to enter into these factories, they would find it difficult to do so, because they more or less have family responsibilities and cannot work for the low wages that are offered. Then, too, it is questionable whether they would be taken, for the simple reason that in these mills quickness and dexterity are the qualities demanded, and such qualities can more readily be found among girls and young women than among men. The only way in which these helpless ones can be made self-supporting is for the communities to receive them and make special efforts in their behalf. That this can be done successfully I know from experience, provided the whole country gives us its hearty assistance. Unfortunately, we have up to this time depended largely upon one or two sections of the country; I have no hesitation in saying that if our efforts had not been limited to so few cities, the results would have been far more satisfactory. If every town in the country in which there is a community of Jews would be prepared to take on an average of say, one immigrant a week, or even two a month, these less endowed but equally deserving men would not be forced to leave our office in despair. It would then be possible for us to send a smaller number of people to those cities that have thus far borne the brunt of the burden, and they, in turn, would have better opportunities to place people whom they have been reluctant to receive.

In the early years of East European immigration, most of this class entered the needle trades. Today there is no other industry which they can take up so readily to any large extent. Not being able to find work in New York, they should be scattered throughout the whole country in as large numbers, but in as small groups, as possible, in order that they may be placed in the appropriate vacancies of the mercantile and industrial structure. This conviction has been forcing itself upon me the longer I deal with the problem, and I can find no solution to it, except in the generous cooperation of every small and large community.

When the world was startled by the shocking news of the Kishinev horrors [1903], an impetus apparently was given to the removal project. Unsolicited, a large number of communities gave us authority to send them Kishinev refugees. They were prompted by a sympathetic desire to assist these unfortunates, but their sympathy was confined to Kishinev refugees alone. However, since only a handful of these persons arrived in this country, most of whom were solicitously cared for by their friends and relatives in New York, the sympathy of these interior communities was wasted upon the desert air. We had no Kishinev survivors to send them, and we had not the right to send them men from other parts of East Europe. For want of an object upon which to bestow their pity, their true sentiment was wasted. Had Kishinevers applied to us, we could have sent hundreds every week, but as it was, we were forced to turn away large numbers of other applicants because of the narrow restrictions placed upon us. In other words, the sympathy of these communities was not expressed in terms broad enough to embrace the general principles underlying removal. As far as ultimate results are concerned, it is immaterial whether a Kishinev-er, Bialystock-er, Warsaw-er, Jassy-er or Cracow-er is removed from New York. Each person removed means relief, by one, of the deplorable overcrowding.

We dare not lull ourselves into the belief that this immigration problem is one for us Jews alone to solve. Immigration into this country has always found opposition from one source or another, even at a time when everybody agreed that the country's progress actually depended upon it. But the timid murmurs that were heard fifteen or twenty years ago have become fearless denunciations. The distant rumblings have become imminent thunderclaps. . . . Mark the bills introduced into Congress at the last session. Granted that the solution of the Jewish problem lies in Russia, or even granted that the solution lies in Zion. That solution is so remote that we in America cannot, with any pretense of fairness and charity, regard with indifference a serious attempt to close the doors to many of our unhappy co-religionists. And surely there is no more powerful weapon in the hands of advocates against immigration than the congestion in the seaport cities. . . .

4. The Galveston Movement*

BY DAVID M. BRESSLER

The removal movement was inaugurated and supported by the generosity of Mr. Jacob H. Schiff. Its purpose is to divert Jewish immigration from the Eastern seaboard towns to the territory west of the Mississippi River, with Galveston as the port of entry, and it

* From "The Removal Work Including Galveston," National Conference of Jewish Charities, *Proceedings* (1910), pp. 123-40. Presented at the Sixth Biennial Meeting of the National Conference of Jewish Charities, St. Louis, Mo., May 17-19, 1910.

is the first deliberate [organized] effort in America to divert the Jewish immigrant from the Atlantic port cities. It is an attempt to divert the current from those few places where it has come to a head, and where the height of the tide is creating problems of great import to American Jewry.

The East European immigration, with its source in Russia, Roumania, Galicia, and Hungary empties into the strip of territory which borders the Atlantic Coast; and except for the overflow into the large inland cities of Chicago, St. Louis, Cincinnati, and Cleveland, and the dribble into the Pacific port towns, it is at points contiguous to the Atlantic Coast that the largest volume remains. New York, Philadelphia, Baltimore, and Boston absorb the greater part of this new influx. So that while the center of population in the United States is moving westward and may soon tilt southwestward, what may be considered the Jewish center of population has not followed this normal shift.

Although the cost of transportation and the social attraction of large centers have contributed to retarding the immigrant drift westward, the uncertainty regarding the material advantages in the small town has also been a large factor in determining where the mass of immigrants will gravitate. If this holds good for the section east of the Mississippi, how much more unattractive, even repelling, must the hinterland appear, a veritable land of mystery both to the recent newcomer and the intending emigrant from Eastern Europe.

The port of Galveston invited entry; but the plunge into the hinterland, where Yiddish may be an unknown tongue, kosher food an unknown thing, and labor opportunities limited, was taken only by the most daring. Those who might have previously penetrated this Far Western section and have won material success could hardly prove lodestones; for daring as the Russian is in his philosophy, he is conservative in action. He could make his wants known in his own language in New York and other Eastern cities; and if his wants were dire, his friends and fellowcountrymen were ready to lend a helping hand. The West, on the other hand, loomed chill. No Yiddish news emanated from it that could influence the East Sider of New York or reach across the sea. The very names of these cities were almost as unknown in New York as in the Pale. As a result, the Russian immigrant regarded the hinterland with the same feeling that a child might regard a dark room.

The answer to this question was the creation of the Galveston movement, organized with the purpose of popularizing the West and Southwest as objective points for Jewish immigration. The opportunities in what is as yet an undeveloped field bear out the contention that the immigrant, in throwing in his destiny with the newer sections of the United States, will reap the benefits of a growing country where the struggle for a livelihood is not so intense, and where the environment is more favorable. . . .

Even were the Galveston movement to be regarded as an experiment (hardly borne out by its record of nearly 2,000 immigrants distributed through the Port facilities in spite of the industrial panic that followed on the heels of its formation), the conditions favoring its success are natural ones and not the result of an artificial stimulus.[1] In the first place there is the demand for labor in the West and Southwest arising from the industrial development of these sections. The entrance of Russian Jewish labor into these parts is not an invasion but a necessary addition to the industrial growth of a dozen states. It is a notable fact, for instance, that immigrants coming through the Bureau are finding work in railroad shops, and even more significant than this is the fact that in quite a number of instances cooperating agencies have been able to find employment for the newly arrived immigrants at their own trades on the very day of their arrival in the new city. . . .

It has been noticed that the effect of the movement has been to infuse something akin to the pioneer spirit into the immigrant. That some of the immigrants should feel the lure of the Eastern

[1] See *Jewish Charity,* vol. V, no. 1, (August 1914). Nearly 10,000 immigrants were reported as settled through Galveston by July 1914.

cities and should drift there at the first opportunity is hardly surprising. A secondary drift takes place from the town in which the immigrant has been placed to the next larger town within striking distance, and there the initial impulse appears to exhaust itself. But a noteworthy feature is the frequent drift towards the smaller communities within easy reach. . . .

Whereas the success of the movement might have been jeopardized two decades ago by a very high percentage of unskilled labor, today, as already stated before, the industrial development of Russia and its trend towards modernity in method and production is developing an artisan who, except for a language handicap, compares much more favorably with the American artisan than was the case a decade or two ago. . . .

Transportation facilities have also contributed largely to the growth and development of every new settlement. But the crucial factor in any movement which has for its object the emigration of large bodies of people from the crowded sections to the as yet sparsely settled but promising territories is not that the person desiring to go westward has the choice of three or four or even five transportation lines. From New York to California, Washington, Oregon, or even Colorado and Iowa, the cost of transportation is the greatest obstacle; it is almost prohibitive to those pioneers who have the brain and the brawn so necessary to the development of newer sections of our country. The railroad companies would do well to recognize the commercial value of a steady stream of immigration to the undeveloped sections through which their roads run. They might well foresee that an augmented western population will mean a larger productivity for that region, with a resultant increase in the freight and passenger business. A reduction in the rate of transportation would not only facilitate the work of the distributing of immigrants; it would also enable workingmen of moderate means—who by reason of their longer stay in this country have acquired the language and have absorbed the spirit of American institutions—to take advantage of the improved opportunities which the West affords them.

5. Agricultural and Vocational Education*

BY H. L. SABSOVICH

In presenting to this Conference the subject of agricultural education for Jews in the United States, it is impossible to treat it independently of the general status of farming and agricultural education as carried on in this country.

In view of the great difficulties Jewish farming has encountered in the past, and which it must contend with even now, and in view of the general standing of farming, the question has arisen in the minds of many: "Is it *advisable* to direct the energies of the Jews into a new channel of activity—agriculture?" We will not consider Jewish farming here as the result of a spontaneous movement toward farming, but as the result of certain philanthropic efforts to regulate this movement, and prevent, if possible, an unnecessary waste of means, energy and enthusiasm in a large number of our co-religionists, principally newcomers, in their efforts to better their material conditions. I will therefore consider here Jewish farming as one of the preventive measures which present themselves to Jewish philanthropy in the United States.

The question of the *advisability* of fostering and encouraging Jewish farming by giving Jewish boys an agricultural training is not an idle one.

1. In comparing the numbers engaged in various employments, the compilers of the twelfth census report found that out of 29,287,070 persons of ten years of age and over who were in 1900 engaged in gainful occupations, 10,438,219 or 35.6 per cent, were following agricultural pursuits, while 24.3 per cent were engaged in manufacturing and mechanical arts; $20,439,901,164 were invested in farming, and $9,831,486,500 in manufacturing and mechanical trades. Therefore, farming is still the most important

* National Conference of Jewish Charities, *Proceedings* (1906), pp. 203-11. Presented at the Fourth Biennial Session of the Conference, Philadelphia, Pa., May 6-8, 1906.

industry in the United States. It is true, however, that during the past twenty years, the number engaged in manufacturing has increased 86.2 per cent, while in agriculture, only 34.6 per cent. . . .

2. The present agricultural situation in this country *justifies* our philanthropic efforts towards opening to the Jews new fields of employment and new means of earning a healthful living through the pursuit of farming. For the *general Jewish welfare* we must certainly have a farming population, as we will stand better with our neighbors when we are able to point out that the agricultural industries are taken up by us as a life vocation. From an *economic standpoint,* farming, as a new Jewish trade, is not only advisable, but is an absolute necessity.

In all large cities, Jewish committees are maintaining trade, industrial, and technical schools, following the general tendency in this country to replace the older form of apprenticeship by regular long and short courses of technical and trade training in special schools. In 1900, there existed in the United States over 110 educational institutions where manufacturing and mechanical arts were taught.

In 1900, the average number of wage earners employed in the hand trades—such as building trades, blacksmithing, wheelwrighting, furniture and cabinet making—was 801,284, hardly 2.75 per cent of the total number of wage-earners. The metal workers in this country, including iron and steel, number about 1,000,000 —less than 3.5 per cent. Workers in wood and those in the textile industries, including the manufacture of clothing, do not compose more than 5 and 10 per cent of the total labor population, and yet the total product of each enumerated group of industries exceeds the home consumption. These industries are well provided with labor, and observation points toward a state of affairs which is making employment in these branches of industry unsteady.

On the other hand, the agriculture industry gave employment in the same year to over 10,000,000 persons, or over 36 per cent of the total number of wage earners. While it is true that the country has produced more farm products than it needs, American farming, to a certain extent, does not meet such fierce competition in the world's market as American manufacturing and mechanical trades. Again, the farm labor market is not satiated. By giving an agricultural training to our youth, we will direct them from occupations that are already overcrowded into new fields of activity where their labor is more sought for.

3. Can we utilize the existing agencies for agricultural education to train Jewish youth for farming pursuits, or do we need to maintain special Jewish agricultural schools? These questions are of vital importance, since the Jewish communities are overwhelmed by problems which already heavily tax their financial resources.

Jewish organized charity should not only avoid duplicating existing agencies for dispensing charity in order to prevent waste of means and energy, but should especially abstain from competing with State and municipal institutions. To my mind the principal function of Jewish organized charity is to step in, then and there, when and where the State or municipality fails or cannot act, and to cooperate with existing institutions. It would, therefore, be not only unwise but wasteful to maintain special Jewish agricultural schools whenever the State school meets the Jewish need for agricultural education.

Unfortunately, however, none of the present schools meet fully the Jewish needs, for the obvious reason that all the agricultural colleges and agricultural high schools were established to *further* American agriculture, while we have yet to *create* Jewish farming. It is true that in view of the several thousands of Jewish families now engaged in farming in this country, our immediate task is no longer to demonstrate whether or not the Jew can be a farmer. But as yet, on account of small numbers, we can hardly consider Jewish farming a well-established economic factor in the life of the American Jew and as past its experimental stage. This is the case to a still greater degree in Jewish agricultural education, since it is an entirely new activity (about ten years old) and requires more fostering. Thus Jewish agricultural education cannot be accomplished by means of the existing general agricultural school.

The contingent from which we are to draw our agricultural school pupils is different from the contingent at the command of the American schools. The latter is composed of children of American farmers, who learn the practical operations of farming on their fathers' farms during their childhood, and go to the colleges and schools to study improved methods of farming. As a matter of fact, all the farm schools are not in operation during the summer months, and they are principally theoretical schools, though in some of them the methods of imparting agricultural knowledge may be eminently practical. Under these circumstances, should the children of the Americanized Jews be willing to study agriculture, their lack of knowledge of elementary farming operations and farm life would prevent them from taking advantage of the existing agricultural colleges and high schools. This is still the case with the main contingent from which we have to recruit our pupils, the immigrant Jew. To the absence of practical farming training which the Americanized Jew lacks may be added the lack of knowledge of the English language on the part of the immigrants, and of the American ways of life.

4. In order then, to enable both the Americanized and the immigrant Jewish youth to take advantage of the educational facilities offered by the state colleges and secondary agricultural schools, preparatory Jewish agricultural schools should be established where they can learn the farm operations and farm life. . . .

The Jewish agricultural school must train farm helpers who may, after several years of work for others, become independent farmers. The task of such a school is to train the young men for the rank and file, and not for leadership. No Jewish community can afford to equip and maintain a school which will equal even the most poorly equipped State institution, and therefore we cannot train leaders. With less sacrifice, if leaders are needed, individual communities can educate them in the higher agricultural educational institutions, such as Cornell University in the East and the Michigan Agricultural College in the West.

The *curriculum* of a Jewish agricultural school, accordingly, must be arranged so as to train the largest possible number, and with a view to making the pupils practical farmers. The age of the student must be sufficiently high and the course should not be too extended, since we must not forget that the boys are of an earning age and that their earnings are needed for their families. . . .

II Services for Individuals and Families

POPULATION upheaval, industrial and urban life, political and social change, and economic deprivation take their toll of all peoples. The new Jewish immigrant population of 1900 was no exception. The immigrant experienced the bitterness of tenement life, the break-up of families due to the husband's death, desertion, or his absence due to a search for work, juvenile delinquency among Jewish youth, widespread immorality among young girls, and the spread of chronic illness, especially tuberculosis. Of these, delinquency, housing, and chronic illness have a familiar ring, for they are among the major social-welfare problems of the 1960's. An early effort by Goldstein in 1902 compared the incidence of social problems among Jews and other Americans. While lacking a firm statistical base, the comparison indicates the extent to which social disorganization had set in among Jewish families in the early years of their migration, despite the safeguards of strong family life and the protection of Old World social institutions.

The Jewish social-welfare effort to provide services for individuals and families in the early 1900's matured with remarkable speed. Lowenstein in 1904 recognized the need for large-scale social action to strike at the causes of dependency, as well as for continued regard for the individual and his relief. He foreshadows the later social-work concept of relief as a tool in personal treatment and rehabilitation, and insists that "relief be well-handled." Here, too, is the early Jewish social work insistence that relief be

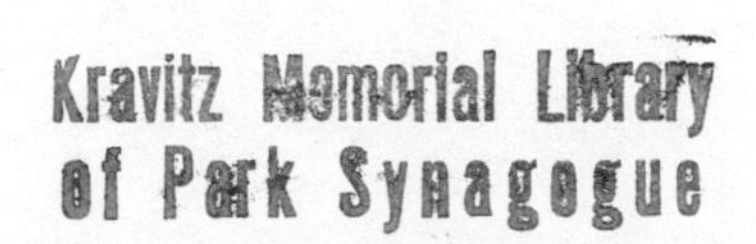

adequate for the individual's need, otherwise it only pauperizes the recipient.

Many social problems are already viewed comprehensively in the first two decades of the century. There is a modern ring to the insistence that a chronic disease like tuberculosis requires first treatment and arrest of the disease, then full and adequate care for the patient and adequate care for his dependent family, followed by full family rehabilitation when the patient can return home. The plans for handling widows and children foreshadow the goals of the Social Security Act of 1935—to keep families together rather than removing children for economic reasons. However, the emphasis upon "supervising the widows until children grow up" has an old-fashioned ring which may reflect the prevailing attitude toward women in the late nineteenth century. In the case of family desertions, more punitive attitudes are dominant, and Conference speakers insist that applicants be treated rigorously until their "investigator" is assured there is no collusion to get unjustified relief. This has the still-familiar sound of those who oppose the present-day program of Aid to Dependent Children. It was easy in 1900, and it is easy now, to argue that the social agency causes the problem which upsets society, forgetting that the problem came first and demanded society's attention, leading to the creation of social agencies to cope with it.

By 1910, the outlines of modern case-work service to families had already been drawn (see the text of the address by Jacob H. Hollander, professor of Economics at Johns Hopkins University and government financial advisor: "Rationalism in Jewish Philanthropy," Presidential Address, National Conference of Jewish Charities, *Proceedings* [1910] pp. 32 - 36). Personal problems began to be viewed as signs of social disorder and to be treated by a blend of scientific and common-sense methods, as opposed to emotionalism and fatalism. The key aspects of a community program were already seen as organization, federation (or coordination of effort), training for personnel, individual case study, personal service (as well as relief), and prevention.

The evolution of these guides was not easy, and the papers by Silver and Goldstein illustrate the two views of welfare and relief: one as seen by the giver (the older and predominantly German Jewish citizen), and the other by the receiver of relief (the predominantly East European immigrant). Aside from the echoes of cultural prejudice which appear, these papers are significant in that they mark the period in which modern Jewish social-work philosophy took its form, and stress the equal importance of compassion and personal understanding for the receiver of help, and an adequate administrative mechanism to achieve high social purposes.

The papers on desertion and transiency are significant for the depth of their early analysis of these social problems. They recognize that the causes of such problems lie not only in individual deficiency, but in the economic and social disorganization of the period and the mobility and anonymity of urban life. The early approaches as reflected in the Transportation Rules of the Conference and the National Desertion Bureau are based on social and legal analyses, not psychological ones. However, they are modified by substantial provision for individual treatment according to the needs of each situation. These approaches represent a major effort by private Jewish philanthropy to deal with a large national problem in national terms and by a systematic national approach. In the case of the National Desertion Bureau, a national agency is created. In the case of transiency, voluntary cooperation among scores of local agencies is furthered by a Conference Committee which is empowered to carry out a national policy through persuasion only.

1. Causes of Poverty and the Remedial Work of Organized Charity*

BY MORRIS GOLDSTEIN

What are the causes of poverty? This is a question that has in the last fifty years engaged the attention of students of social science in every civilized country. It is one of the most vexing questions, for the causes of poverty are to a great extent not possible to analyze. It requires much experience on the part of workers in charity to give even approximately the fundamental reasons why a certain family has come to destitution. Much time has been spent in classifying cases from records, but as the majority of social scientists are not personally acquainted with these cases, their classification is a very inadequate method of arriving at the truth. The question in the minds of those who undertake the investigation of the causes of poverty is this: Is poverty a misfortune or is it a fault? All endeavors to answer this question through scientific methods will not lead to a full and satisfactory answer. Careful and conscientious workers in charity have classified the alleged causes of poverty in two groups: first, causes indicating misconduct; second, causes indicating misfortune. In the first group are included intemperance, immorality, laziness, shiftlessness and inefficiency, crime and dishonesty, and a restless or unsatisfied disposition. Lack of normal support, matters of employment, matters of personal capacity, such as sickness or death in family and other misfortunes form the second group. The difficulty in such classification lies in the fact that there is hardly a case on record where destitution has resulted from a single cause, as one cause generally lies behind another. Intemperance is often the cause of lack of employment, of sickness, or accident. Lack of employment may lead to intemperance, immorality, or laziness. One of these causes

* National Conference of Jewish Charities, *Proceedings* (1902), pp. 78-85. Presented at the Second Biennial Meeting of the National Conference of Jewish Charities, Detroit, Michigan, May 26-28, 1902.

alone might not have been sufficient to produce poverty, had not others cooperated with it. . . . One has often to know the case quite well before he can determine the cause or combination of causes underlying the condition. Moreover, applicants for relief are always disposed to attribute their distress to circumstances beyond their control.

When we compare statistics gathered by charity organizations, we find that they vary very little in their classification. They tabulate the various causes of poverty as follows:

Lack of employment	23 per cent
Sickness and accident	20 per cent
Physical defect or old age	5 per cent
Death of wage earner	4 per cent
Desertion	3 per cent
Intemperance	20 per cent
Shiftlessness	15 per cent
Unknown, or no need of assistance	10 per cent

Those who tabulated these cases have discussed at great length the variations in the percentages as regards nationality, color and creed, but I failed to find any reference to any Jewish charitable organization. I have therefore examined and tabulated according to the same classification 200 successive applications from the records of the United Jewish Charities of Cincinnati. The result of their analysis is as follows:

Lack of employment	15 per cent
Sickness and accident	25 per cent
Physical defect or old age	10 per cent
Death of wage earner	5 per cent
Desertion	10 per cent
Shiftlessness	15 per cent
Unknown, or no need of assistance	20 per cent

In comparing these two tables, we find in ours a higher percentage of sickness and accident, of physical defect or old age, of desertion and of cases where there was found to be no need of assistance. We find a smaller percentage of lack of employment, shiftlessness, and intemperance. It is noticeable that in examining the 200 records mentioned, I could find no case of intemperance. I therefore examined the entire record of the past four years in search of cases of intemperance; the result was that in 1,900 applications I found four such cases, of which only one was termed habitual.

We find the same difficulties with regard to the treatment of the causes of poverty as we find in their analysis. The treatment which has been found to be the most advisable consists of friendly visiting and advice, provision of temporary help, referral to institutions, and locating employment where possible.

There are, however, causes of poverty which have not been tabulated, but which, in my estimation, are its real causes. We will easily find these causes when we examine the existing evils with which our charities have to contend. First, there are those able-bodied but, unfortunately, not able minded applicants who would rather peddle than work, and who, if they do accept regular work, are restricted in their activities and thus are undesirable employees. They are not unskilled and do not lack strength or ability, but their close religious observance, such as praying three times a day and refusing to work on the Sabbath and the holidays, seriously limits their employment potential. It is not my intention to criticize these habits, nor will the liberal-minded censure them for the expression of religion. But because times and conditions have changed, these people must also change their habits to fit the new conditions or they will meet with constantly increasing difficulties in maintaining themselves. . . . They are prevented from entering the industries of the times and the result is that the man who remains unemployed must resort to peddling. This seems to be the reason why every city in this land is infested with so many peddlers. . . . Our charities must discourage peddling by refusing assistance to an applicant for peddling outfits. Such refusals may and will force them to direct their energies in other channels. The city of Cincinnati had a vast number of peddlers, notably women, who supplemented their allowances from the charities by so-called peddling, which, however, was nothing less than an excuse for begging. These individuals became such an annoyance to our subscribers that something had to be done to diminish their numbers. The United Jewish Charities took the matter in hand, sent out warning circulars against chronic peddler-beggars, secured more honorable employment for the worthy, and increased the allowances of such as derived a necessary income from their peddling. The result is that we have at present less than 5 per cent of the number that we had four years ago.

We find another real cause of poverty in the early marriages among the poor and dependent classes. Those dependents are beneficiaries of our charities, their means of support being otherwise insufficient on account of the large number of dependent children in their families. We keep these cases on the lists for years in the hope that the growing children may in time become a help and support to the parents and younger sisters and brothers. But too often we meet with disappointment, for many of these growing children marry when hardly out of their teens and thus they neither become a help to their parents nor are they able to support their own families. . . . In view of the circumstances, organized charity must find remedial measures whereby this evil may be cured. The United Jewish Charities of Cincinnati has so far succeeded in checking child marriages among those who are in one way or another dependent upon the charities by threatening to withdraw assistance from a family in whose midst such a marriage is contemplated.

A large contributor to the real causes of poverty is also the testator. At the present time, when the solution of the problems of poor-relief is approaching the high mark of perfection, many of the legacies intended to benefit the poor have outlived their usefulness. It is claimed that the guiding spirit of many legacies is ostentation, vanity, superstition, or even revenge upon a disliked relative. We do not share this opinion; we believe that every charity legacy [in the past] was made with a good intention by the testator. But we do not believe that the judgment of a testator is infallible in thinking that he has made a provision that must prove adequate and wise for future generations. . . . We in Cincinnati are compelled to distribute large sums of money before each holiday among the poor in our charge for whom the charities fully provide. Charities which are dependent on legacies and occasional donations cannot do the work properly. The charity organization must have a fixed yearly income, like any other corporation based on the membership system. We do not need the endowments of past generations; neither do we need to provide for coming generations. These endowments are not all profit, for with them the dependent poor also are turned over to us. We should treat these poor not by doles, but by modern methods—by making them self-sustaining, so that there will be no dependent pauper class for the generation after us, and consequently there will be no need for legacies. The existing legacies, however, which are expended in mischievous doles, should be so administered that the communities have the power to modify the purposes of the endowments, thus making these bequests more useful.

There is one cause of poverty which is the most constant everywhere, at all times, and according to all investigators—that is sickness. Here the remedial work of the charities must consist in alleviating suffering, no matter what the cost may be. As regards the other causes of poverty, however, the charitable organizations should deal with the causes rather than with the results, and do preventive rather than relief work.

To make the remedial work effective in all classes, certain principles of true charity must be observed. We have to promote the cooperation of our charitable institutions for the furtherance of our common work. We have to discuss practical questions connected with our work, the reform of charitable administration generally, and methods of promotion of thrift and self-dependence. We have to bring into cooperation not only the various charitable agencies, but also the communities, so as to prevent the misapplication of relief and the evils of duplication. Few realize that the small success of such charitable work is probably due to a lack of education in charity on the part of those who engage in it. We must, therefore, learn and teach in order to train and educate ourselves and all those who are engaged in charitable work to do the work judiciously. If we are to act in the name of true charity, we must help thoroughly or refuse help rightly. We must not be too timid or too sentimental to refuse relief, if we think that gifts may have evil results. We must combine all existing charitable institutions and prevent new ones from coming into existence, for with the multiplication of relief societies, the craving for charity and the temptation to ask for relief grows. If such principles of true charity were observed, it would be found that much less monetary aid would be required. Monetary relief is not always charity; it often weakens the independence of the poor, and yet can never be a substitute for it. Only by their own endeavors can the poor maintain their independence. Let us aid them to do so, and we will less frequently ask the question: What are the causes of poverty?

2. The Russian Jew Looks at Organized Charity*

BY HAROLD SILVER

The influx of Russian immigrants into the United States after 1881 introduced a large alien element into the hitherto more or less homogeneous Jewish population. In charitable activities the new arrivals formed, as a group, the receiving class, while the older German settlers were, on the whole, the contributors and the directors of the agencies. Added to the other differentiating traits, this fact tended to draw a rather sharp line of separation between

* From "The Russian Jew Looks at Charity—A Study of the Attitudes of Russian Jewish Immigrants Toward Organized Jewish Charitable Agencies in the United States in 1890-1900," *Jewish Social Service Quarterly*, vol. IV, no. 2 (December 1927), pp. 129-44.

the two groups, which laid a basis for bitterness of feeling and much misunderstanding.

Attacks were made on the leaders and press of the German Jews for what was believed to be their opposition to further immigration, and their discrimination against and mistreatment of the Russian Jews in the agencies. There was particularly an objection to their attempts at "Americanization," which in those days meant a rather rapid substitution of the outward characteristics of "Americanism" in dress, language and habits for the cultural heritage of the immigrant. The more religiously inclined saw an even greater danger in this "Americanization"; for them it meant the dissolution of the bonds that held Israel together. The logical end result of "Americanization" they saw to be baptism.

Coming now to the criticism by the Yiddish press of the organized charity agencies, we find that it stemmed from two standpoints. The first was the East European's traditions with regard to charity and his past experiences with charitable activity. Charity was no new thing to the Russian Jew. His prayers reminded him of it several times a day. His communal institutions and closely knit communal life in general afforded him many opportunities for becoming familiar with it. His views on charity were well formulated by the Scriptures and the Talmud, and definitely molded by his concrete contacts with the numerous charitable *chevrahs* in his town. It was natural that he should apply to the charitable agencies in America the precepts of the sages, and measure them by the standards that were applicable in his native milieu.[1] The principle of investigation—quite superfluous in a primary group community—was alien to his philosophy and repugnant to his "Jewish heart." The record-and-account-keeping system of the American agency

[1] See "Jewish Charitable Activities in Russia," in the *Proceedings* of the National Conference of Jewish Charities (1908), pp. 31-48, for the historical backgrounds, structure, and functions of various activities, including Jewish community attitudes toward relief giving and receiving. The study was prepared by a Conference Committee consisting of H. L. Sabsovich, Elias Lewin-Epstein, Bernard G. Richards and David Blaustein. For a more recent and comprehensive study of East European charity, see Mark Zborowski and Elizabeth Herzog, *Life Is with People* (New York, 1952), pp. 191-213.

impressed him as a feelingless "charity machine," thoroughly un-Jewish in principle and action. He could not understand the horror of the businessman and director of any agency for indiscriminate, unplanned giving. Did not the Talmud say that small alms are better than one large donation? And did not a famous benevolent man order his servants to give even to *schnorrers* so that the *mitzvah* of giving charity might be fulfilled?

The second standpoint from which criticism of the agencies proceeded is one that would be acceptable to the modern social worker. It is the criterion of good and adequate work. The standard of judgment applied is, roughly speaking, the present-day standard, though the writer is aware of the unfairness of applying it to the agencies of that day.

The poor work of organized agencies proceeded from two sources: unfamiliarity with the psychology of the new type of client; and the inability of the agency and the community generally to care adequately for the needs that arose without warning and on such a large scale.

Organized labor objected to charity agencies on two counts: (1) the men at the helm of the agencies were hostile to labor, and (2) the agencies, particularly the Baron de Hirsch Fund and the (N. Y.) United Hebrew Charities, furnished strike-breakers and cheap labor to employers, thus undermining the union and lowering the wage standards.

While assailing the German Jews and criticizing their charity organizations, the Russian Jews were establishing their own institutions. Their most important charitable societies of this period in New York City were the Hachnosas Orchim and the Beth Israel Hospital, both established in the early nineties. A certain pride was taken in the fact that they were founded and were being maintained solely by downtown Jews. The proponents of these institutions made no secret of the fact that in addition to desiring a kosher ritual and to help the poor in their own spirit, they wanted to show the rich uptowners that the Russian Jews were not *schnorrers* or parasites.

Simultaneously with the resentments, objections and protests, and while "downtown" societies were springing up like mushrooms after rain, there were being sowed the seeds that later ripened into better understanding, cooperation, and the gradual elimination of the distinction between "German" and "Russian." This was made possible on the one hand by the realization by the Russians of their own shortcomings and their appreciation of the positive aspects of the ways of German charity; and, on the other hand, by the understanding by the Germans of the psychology of the Russian Jew and their assumption of a friendlier and more sympathetic attitude toward the more recent immigrants.

3. Adequacy of Relief*

BY SOLOMON LOWENSTEIN

For a long period, until within very recent years, it was the practice of those gathered together in conferences for the discussion of philanthropic questions to pay scant attention to material relief. Its baleful effects were fully exposed, the fear of pauperization through charity was constantly in the mind of the charitable worker, and substitutes of every sort were devised to make unnecessary the use of material assistance for any but emergency work. So overemphasized was this danger of the pauperizing of the applicant by means of indiscriminate money gifts that the result necessarily was the production of the idea of the harmfulness of material relief, and consequently, the abstinence from its use wherever possible. There can be little doubt that the general acceptance of these extreme views would rob the charitable agency of one of its most effective agents. We need not here proclaim the

* National Conference of Jewish Charities, *Proceedings* (1904), pp. 35-41. Presented at the Third Biennial Conference of Jewish Charities, New York City, May 24-27, 1904; see also "Free Loan Societies," by Morris Loeb, *Proceedings* of the Conference of Jewish Charities (1900), pp. 51-57.

merits of material assistance, nor define its defects. It is sufficient for our purpose that we recognize that it possesses both; that for the relief agent to be deprived of his power to use it would render him well nigh helpless; and that its use must be careful and cautious. We have learned that the danger of material relief consists not in its amount, nor in the frequency of its employment, but in its careless application. This has been the temper of all the more recent discussion on the subject. We cannot fail to conclude that for the alleviation of the individual cases of destitution which present themselves to the relief agent, the well-considered handling of material relief presents the first, the most natural, and the most potent agency.

The careful study of the causes of distress and poverty, and the endeavor to remove them, must, of course, constitute the ultimate endeavor of our relief organization; various agencies will contribute their forces to this removal, all of them valuable; but absolutely indispensable will be the power to supply the immediate need. Granting them the right and the necessity of the use of material relief, there follows as the corollary to this proposition that this relief should be adequate. It should need but little argument to prove that, if after careful deliberation in any particular case it has been decided to grant assistance, that assistance should be ample to supply the existing need. That he gives twice who gives quickly is a truism. After having taken due account of all the means of support existing within the family in our care, of all income possible from relatives, friends, societies, etc., this income should be supplemented in an amount ample to meet all legitimate needs. It should not be forgotten in any discussion of the possibility of pauperizing by means of material assistance, that the same result may as easily be brought about by too little as by too much relief. The consequent necessity of frequent, repeated appeals on the part of the applicant, his enforced demands at the doors of various agencies, very easily lead to a condition of willing dependence. Therefore, we may consider ourselves justified in assuming that on this point we may all agree that relief, to be effective, must be adequate, and that this may be considered the principle determining the amount and character of the assistance applied in any given case. Yet this consensus of opinion apparently leads to divergencies in application, if we may judge from the figures of relief expenditures submitted by societies in the larger Jewish communities.

We are not inclined to attach too great an importance to figures such as those gathered from reports which give no itemized accounts. Yet the contrasts are sufficiently striking to justify an inquiry into what should constitute an adequate handling of those typical classes of dependents present in all communities.

We need give but slight heed to those cases in which some temporary misfortune deranges the normal family life. Sudden illness or the loss of employment present situations which must be carefully attended in order to prevent undue dependence. But such causes of distress as are due to the temporary absence of wage-earning capacity present no great difficulties. Such assistance must make provision for any necessities which cannot be derived from the internal resources of the family. It would automatically cease with the restoration to health or employment of the family head.

If, however, we turn to those cases involving more complex questions—those in which the relief policy must be one adapted to a long-continued treatment—we are apt to meet with more difficulty in obtaining our definition of adequacy.

An examination of the causes of distress as exhibited by the annual reports of the various societies shows a decided parallel as to the causes producing the largest number of cases among us. These are: illness, lack of work, no male support, insufficient earnings. Practically all the cases of long duration on the books of our organizations are due to one of these four causes. We have spoken of cases of temporary illness and lack of employment above.

Of permanent cases due to illness, by far the most troublesome and therefore most important are the tubercular. In no other class of cases is adequate relief at once so imperative and so economical. The entire treatment of the disease demands extraordinary measures. First, the instruction of the patient in the proper means of caring for himself so as to improve his own condition and prevent his transmitting the disease to others; the establishment of the family in sanitary quarters as an additional protection; the furnishing of the extra nourishment required by the patient; and securing, while the disease is still in the curable stage, the requisite sanatorium treatment. It is in such cases that the economic value of an adequate treatment is best observed. In his last annual report, the president of the United Jewish Charities of Cincinnati calls attention to the fact that at the present time that Society is paying only one pension due to the presence of tuberculosis in the family, and that for almost two years no applications have been made for the admission of orphans from that city to the Cleveland institution.[1] In view of the fact that 52 per cent of the children in this orphanage owe their presence there to the death of one or both parents from consumption, the statement has added significance. These results were accomplished in Cincinnati by endeavoring to send every known case of tuberculosis to the Denver (National Jewish) Hospital as early as possible, to keep the patient in that institution until cured or sufficiently improved to warrant his discharge, and then to insist upon his remaining in that favorable climate. In order to do this, the family of the invalid was maintained at home until he was able to support it. Upon his discharge from the hospital, the man was established in such employment or business as promised him a livelihood, and the Denver authorities were guaranteed against expense on his account or that of his family. Such procedure naturally involves a large initial expenditure, but one easily counter-balanced by the saving in pensions, orphanage charges, and the restoration of the patient to economic independence. Such complete treatment is, of course, possible only where the number of cases is not excessive. In all cases, however, it ought to be possible to secure hospital treatment, to assist the family, and, upon recovery or improvement, to remove its mem-

[1] Reference to the Cleveland Jewish Orphan Asylum, organized in 1868 by the B'nai B'rith to serve the child-care needs of Districts 2, 6 and 7.

bers from overcrowded tenements to open, freer, healthier residences, supplying them with necessary additional nourishment and securing suitable employment. To do less than this is to fail in our plain obligation.

The next large cause of continued dependence is an absence of male support. These cases are mainly of two general classes: widows with small children below wage-earning age, and deserted women. The first impulse in dealing with widows with children, particularly in the smaller communities, has been to resort to an institution for the care of such of the children as could not support themselves or be maintained from the mother's earnings. It is outside our purpose to enter here upon a discussion as to the merits of institutional training. Suffice it to say that practically all are agreed that a good mother is far superior to the best institution, and it would appear the height of wisdom to grant sufficient subsidy in such cases to enable the family life to be preserved and its good influences to surround the growing children. Naturally, such grants will be subject to the most careful supervision, being graduated according to the increasing earning capacity of the older members of the family, and ceasing when these reach an amount permitting the withdrawal. We should not omit to mention the great influence that the proper agency may exert in the education of the children so as to equip them to assume their share of the family responsibility at an early period. One of the most distressing features of many of our cases is the failure of the young men and girls of our families to realize their duties in this respect; our constant endeavor in such pension cases should be, through our friendly visitors, to cultivate this attitude. Moreover, in our desire that the burden of support be shared as fully as possible by the family, we should not commit the error of forcing the mother to give so much of her time to labor that she will be unable to properly rear her children.

The deserted woman presents a much more difficult problem than the widow. We are not able to establish the relationship of desertion to charitable assistance. How much the despondent husband is induced to desert by his belief that his family will be cared for in his absence is a question that still awaits an answer. The possibility of collusion between the husband and wife is another factor; whether the husband will return sooner if his family is refused assistance is also open to doubt. That the evil is growing there can be no doubt. It is astonishing that of 10,924 cases handled by the United Hebrew Charities of New York in the last fiscal year, 1,052, or almost 10 per cent, were deserted women. Better methods to deal with such cases must be devised. Thus far our experience has taught us that we cannot allow the probably innocent wife and the certainly innocent children to suffer because of the desertion of the recreant husband. Therefore, after a diligent effort to trace the husband and a somewhat rigorous treatment of the family until the absence of collusion is determined, in the majority of cases the family receives the same assistance as does the widow.

The fourth large class of dependents consists of those making an effort at economic independence but whose earnings are insufficient to ensure self-support. Among this class are many whose weak physical condition should really place them among those whose need is due to illness. Others, again, because of age or earlier training incapacitating them from success at manual labor, find themselves forced into this class. If the dependent is possessed of any business ability, assistance in the form of a loan without interest, returnable in small payments, will often prove efficacious. The opportunities for the teaching of trades which require little skill and may be practiced in the home have not yet been as fully tried, but are also advisable methods in the treatment of this class of applicants. With an opportunity to learn a skill, some of these men ought to be able to increase their earning capacities by entry into the better-paid factory trades. The value of assistance in the family support during the weeks and even months of apprenticeship is too apparent to require exposition. We must, however, be careful to avoid the temptation to place our men in the easily acquired trades, which are overcrowded for this very reason, and which offer but little hope of a livelihood.

In conclusion, but one word of explanation. Throughout, we have laid stress upon the relief side of this question. I would not be understood as underrating the value of the various educational aids—particularly the trade schools—in the solution of the problems of dependence. With the better education and the equipping of our youth in practical matters, many of the questions which now perplex us should disappear in another generation; but in the present and in the preparation of this new generation, adequate assistance for the dependent must be our chief effort.

4. The National Desertion Bureau*

BY CHARLES ZUNSER

Thirteen years ago at a session of this Conference held in St. Louis, Morris D. Waldman read his epochal paper on family desertion. He outlined the extent of the problem and after giving a detailed and painstaking account of the causes of desertion, proposed that each of the constituent organizations of the Conference shall, during the forthcoming year, make an intensive study of its respective desertion problem . . . with a view to possible concerted action along certain lines, . . . proposals which were not to be acted upon until the following year at the Boston Conference. Even before that, the National Conference had interested itself in the problem. In the very comprehensive report of the committee on desertion presented to the National Conference of Jewish Charities

* From "The National Desertion Bureau. Its Functions, New Problems, and Relations with Local Agencies," National Conference of Jewish Social Service, *Proceedings* (1923), pp. 386-404. Presented at the Annual Meeting of the National Conference of Jewish Social Service, Washington, D.C., May 13-16, 1923.

in 1900 are given suggestions to prevent the evil of desertion. Briefly summed up, they are: 1. Elevation of the general moral outlook of our co-religionists. 2. The cooperation of the various Jewish charities in ferreting out the deserter, and in taking the proper steps towards his arrest and return to his residence for punishment. 3. Charitable societies should strive to influence legislation in different cities to make abandonment a criminal offense and to insure the return of fugitive husbands.

A study of actual cases made in Boston in 1901, and a similar study made by Mr. Waldman in 1902 in behalf of the United Hebrew Charities of New York, disclosed the fact that a large proportion of desertion was not due, as had been supposed, to unemployment or inability to earn a living, but to various forms of immorality, and that in addition to the usual reasons for desertion, there are specific causes that apply to cases of Jewish desertion. [In the wake of these studies] Dr. Lee K. Frankel, then manager of the United Hebrew Charities of New York, established a separate department in his organization to deal exclusively with these cases. Largely through his instrumentality, a law was passed in New York making the abandonment of minor children in destitute circumstances a felony. In a paper which Dr. Frankel wrote for the Fourth National Conference of Jewish Charities held in Philadelphia in 1906, he traced the methods then employed by the present reporter with a considerable measure of success. It was soon realized, however, that sporadic action here and there by various communities was not adequate to meet the need. This was, in a measure, the value of Mr. Waldman's paper in 1910.

In 1909, the extent of family desertion among Jews in the United States was indicated by the following figures: In Chicago, 204 or 11 per cent of the total number of agency applicants were deserted women; in New York, 1,046 or 10 per cent (the proportion of those applicants to whom relief was granted was 12.3 per cent of the total monies spent for relief. The following year it rose to 13.4 per cent). In Baltimore, it was 90, or 16 per cent. The belief grew stronger with each Conference that the principal method of checking desertion is the enactment and enforcement of proper laws, together with a strict prosecution of the deserter when feasible. In Boston in 1911 the foundations of what is now known as the National Desertion Bureau were laid, for the purpose of centralizing the treatment of family desertion by cities and assisting prosecution through the medium of publicity. An announcement was distributed among the constituent organizations of the Conference. It proposed "to ascertain the whereabouts of deserters and to induce them to reunite with and support their families, or failing this, to secure the conviction and imprisonment of such deserters." In the belief that the work heretofore done locally and sporadically could be successfully carried on in a comprehensive way throughout the country, the Bureau was established to act as a clearing house for all Jewish charitable organizations in the United States who desired to avail themselves of its assistance. The following general scheme was then outlined by Mr. Waldman, Mr. Fred M. Butzel, and the late Minnie F. Low, the committee assigned to the task:

1. Constituent societies of the Conference will send to the central Bureau a full statement regarding deserters whose families have applied for assistance. Where possible a photograph and a description of the deserter will accompany each report. 2. Upon receipt of this information, the Bureau will send copies of its report to the other constituent societies of the Conference, as well as to rabbis, lodges, benefit societies, or other organizations in various cities in the United States that may be interested. Should it be necessary, descriptions and photographs will be published in the Jewish press, copies of these newspapers being sent to the above-mentioned societies, organizations, and individuals who may receive these descriptions, which will be requested to have them exhibited publicly so that acquaintances and countrymen of the deserters may see them. 3. The societies will be requested to enlist the cooperation of local charities, which will be prepared to prosecute obstinate offenders when called upon by the Bureau.

As New York is the largest Jewish center and contains approximately half of the Jewish population of the United States, it was found expedient to establish the headquarters in that city. Mr.

Monroe M. Goldstein, an able and energetic young attorney, who had heretofore rendered effective services for the United Hebrew Charities of New York in similar work, was appointed secretary, and the Bureau began to function.

From its inception to the close of the year 1922, the Bureau has handled 12,413 cases. Of these, 4,221, or approximately one-third, were referred by interior communities (Brooklyn included); 6,085 originated in New York proper, and the balance in foreign countries. The work of locating family deserters, because it was socially important, warranted the formulating of a special and elaborate technique. The method pursued may be summed up briefly: 1. The establishment of a publicity technique by publishing photographs and stories of the deserters in cooperating Jewish newspapers in New York, Chicago, Montreal, and Toronto. Other newspapers, English and Yiddish, were utilized for the purpose of acquainting the general reading public, and particularly the Yiddish public, with the work of the Bureau in ferreting out deserters, and in general of popularizing the functions and efficiency of the Bureau as a deterrent. 2. The establishment of a network of several hundred cooperating social agencies, country-wide, even world-wide, which were urged to give immediate attention to the diligent investigation of desertion cases among the relatives, friends, *Landsleit* and fellow employees of deserters, as well as to tap all other available sources of information. 3. The establishment of a national body of correspondents and attorneys to deal with inquiries submitted by the Bureau and to represent applicants before the courts whenever necessary.

Having located the deserter, the next step was what to do with him. While every case presents unique factors and conditions, there are sufficient elements of similarity binding given cases into classes or groups, and it was possible in time to form a general policy with reference to such groups. Of primary importance, however, was the social viewpoint underlying the work of the Bureau, which sought to prevent family desertion by creating deterrents and preserving the family unity whenever possible. Therefore, it first attempted to reconcile husband and wife where possible and feasible. It sought to bring to justice vicious offenders: those who had previous criminal records; those whose desertions had extended over a prolonged period without satisfactory explanation and who were not in the least concerned that their wives and children had suffered through their meanness. Where such offenders showed pathological traces, either mental or physical, we enlisted the aid of social agencies that deal with such types. There was still a third or intermediate type of deserter: those who offered no scope for reconciliation and yet could not be classed as vicious offenders. With these we sought to effect an arrangement for separate support. It soon became apparent that the United Hebrew Charities of New York had experienced a net decrease in the number of desertion cases entered, as the following table will show.

Years	Number of deserted women to whom cash relief was granted	Proportion of total relief spent on deserted families
1910	487	13.4%
1911	431	11.5%
1912	313	9.0%
1913	298	9.2%
1914	234	8.6%
1915	267	8.1%
1916	195	7.9%
1917	185	7.7%
1918	137	7.3%
1919	193	8.4%
1920	216	11.0%
1921	189	10.2%
1922	192	9.3%

The very low figures for 1917, 1918, and 1919 are to be interpreted in the light of the fact that these were the years of the American participation in the World War. Not only was there practically no unemployment at that time, but many a prodigal husband and father, faced with the draft laws, suddenly reminded himself of his obligations to wife and children and incidentally of his right to claim exemption from military service. The rather startling increase of desertions in 1920, a year of extensive unemployment problems, post-war restlessness, and large numbers of demobilized soldiers who threw the labor market into disruption, can be attributed to post-bellum conditions. For the eleven years beginning with 1912, the average proportion of the total amount of relief expended by the United Hebrew Charities on deserted families is 8.98 per cent of the total. This constitutes a decrease of 4.42 per cent over 1910, the year before the establishment of the Bureau.

New Tendencies in Jewish Family Desertion

The causes of family desertion among Jews have been elaborately dealt with before by Mr. Waldman,[1] Mr. Liebman,[2] the Bureau's president, Mr. Goldstein,[3] as well as by others who have discussed the problem at various conferences. These may be briefly summarized under the following general captions: immorality of husband, of wife, or both; incompatibility of temper; shiftlessness; intemperance; economic conditions including industrial disturbances; financial depression; insufficient wages; illness; discrepancy in ages; interference of relatives; differences in nativity; forced marriages; and immigration of the husband ahead of his family. To these the experience of the Bureau cannot add any factor that could not be subsumed under any of the foregoing captions, except those which are a direct result of the war.

Our congressional lawmakers have been subjected to considera-

[1] *Reports,* National Conference of Jewish Charities, 1910, 1912.

[2] Walter H. Liebman, "Social Service in The Family Court." A paper read before the National Conference of Jewish Social Workers, Atlantic City, May, 1919. "Some General Aspects of Family Desertion," *Social Hygiene,* vol. VI, no. 2 (April 1920).

[3] Monroe M. Goldstein, "Report of the National Desertion Bureau 1912"; Report published in 1915; *Justice and the Poor and the Family Court.*

ble criticism because of the harshness of the present immigration laws. Perhaps it will come as a surprise to some of them to learn that this law has helped many a recreant husband and father to avoid fulfilling his obligation towards his wife and little ones across the ocean. The problem of the desertion by American husbands of immigrant women and children in foreign countries has become a difficult and embarrassing one. . . .

These cases, in the form in which they come up for treatment day by day at the Bureau, may be divided into two main classes: Class A, where the families are abroad; and Class B, where the families are either en route, have arrived at the port of entry, or have already been admitted. It should be stated at the outset that in all cases in Class A we have no legal means of compelling the deserter to either send for his family or to make provision for them, and can employ moral persuasion only. These cases [A] lend themselves to sub-division under the following general groupings:

1. Where the husbands remarry here in the belief or upon alleged information that the first wife in Europe died in war or pogrom, or in the pretended belief that the first wife died.

2. In cases where the families are still abroad, the work of the Bureau has been, after the husband has been located, to induce him to execute the necessary affidavits for visas and passports and to forward passage for the family; or failing this, to effect arrangements of separate support and maintenance in cases where husbands refuse reconciliation. In a large number of cases where the husbands refuse to send for their families, or where the families for some reason prefer to remain abroad, the Bureau has often been requested by referring agencies to procure lump sum settlements and ecclesiastical divorces or *gets*. The Bureau has at all times taken a strong stand against the indiscriminate issuance of *gets* by irresponsible rabbis in this country where the parties are both residents here, and the Bureau has taken an active part, in cooperation with other social agencies, in the curtailing of this practice. We nevertheless feel that in some cases where there is no likelihood or possibility of the families ever coming here, it is advisable

to assist in the rehabilitation of the family abroad by means of a lump settlement and a *get* arrangement which will enable the wife abroad to remarry.

3. In difficult cases, where the husband willfully refuses either to send for the family or to make provision for them, the Bureau will not hesitate to secure the deportation of alien husbands to their native countries as undesirable aliens. . . .

4. The Bureau has been called upon to defend suits for divorce instituted by deserters in this country against their wives, who are still abroad. This class of cases may be further sub-divided into: (a) cases in which the wife resides in a country with which the United States has diplomatic relations, and can therefore enter into a legal defense and appear before an American consular agent for acknowledgement of such legal documents as may have to be interposed. (b) Cases where the wife resides in a country with which we have no diplomatic relations (i.e., Russia), and may not, therefore, be able to successfully defend such suit, the husband thereupon obtaining a decree by default. (c) In this connection may also be mentioned those cases where the deserter had already obtained a decree by default, service by publication in newspapers (which the wife in Europe never sees), and where the statute of limitations of many states bars an action to set aside the decree.

5. The Bureau has also been called upon to handle cases in which the husband's whereabouts are unknown. If exhaustive investigations have failed, the usual publicity method employed by the Bureau to locate the deserters (publication of the photograph of the deserter in our gallery of missing husbands) cannot here be employed in the absence of the wife in view of our inability to safeguard the interests of newspapers, which may be sued for libel.

6. Cases wherein illegitimate children were born while the husband was in this country.

Class B. Within that group of cases where the families are either en route, held at port of entry, or have been permitted to land, the following sub-divisions may be listed:

1. In cooperation with the HIAS,[4] the Council of Jewish Women, and other organizations, the Bureau has been called upon to induce husbands to apply for the discharge of their families. This work often presents perplexing problems, and mention must be made at this time of the valuable assistance often rendered by relatives and *Landsmanshaften,* who place themselves at the disposal of the Bureau and render whatever services may be required of them.

2. While we are on the subject of non-support proceedings in family courts to compel the husbands to make provision for their immigrant families, it is interesting to note that some of the magistrates before whom these cases are brought fail utterly to visualize the problem of the wife and mother left in Europe before the war. Having gone through the ordeal of war and its aftermath with her children, after a great deal of privation and suffering the wife has succeeded in journeying here only to find her husband estranged from her, perhaps involved with another family. Court officials often look askance at the action of such women in applying to the court a day or two after their arrival in the United States. Social workers have a job enlightening the authorities. Emphasis must also be laid on the difficulties of Domestic Relations Court proceedings, due to our immigration laws. In most states, the complainant in a non-support proceeding is required to execute an affidavit to the effect that unless her husband is compelled by the court to make provision for her, she and her children are likely to become public charges. One can easily see how these affidavits may be interpreted in such a way as to make such families deportable under our immigration laws by the alien's own sworn statement. Recently, interviewers and workers of the Family Courts of New York have received instructions requiring them to ascertain the date of arrival, port of entry, and the name of the steamer of every complainant, and whether she is a deserted wife or an aged and indigent parent.

3. As an alternative to Domestic Relations Court proceedings,

[4] Hebrew Immigrant Aid Society.

resort may be had to the Supreme Courts, where actions may be instituted for separation and alimony. The drawbacks to such actions are manifold: Jurisdictional defects where the courts cannot acquire jurisdiction in a given case because the wife is still regarded as a non-resident, even though her husband may have established his legal domicile. Such proceedings are very cumbersome and costly and subject to great delays. There is also the ever-present danger that the husband is likely to abscond on being served with the necessary papers, unless an order of arrest accompanies the service of the motion papers for alimony, which is not always feasible.

4. Cases where validity of the marriage in Europe is contested by the husband. This often presents an insurmountable difficulty. Marriages celebrated under Mosaic laws in Tzarist Russia and Turkey are deemed sufficient, as Jews enjoyed religious autonomy in matters of marriage and divorce in those countries. But in Roumanian and Austrian marriages, such autonomy was not recognized by the laws of those countries, and although thousands of Jewish couples have had only a rabbinical marriage ceremony, the validity of such marriages has often been questioned. When this defense is raised by attorneys in behalf of the husbands of immigrant families, it often results in serious complications involving legitimacy of children, etc.

5. Cases wherein the husband and wife arrived together in the U. S. and were temporarily admitted, the bond having been furnished by relatives and family. The husband absconds soon thereafter, and the wife and children are deported. Through the Immigration Welfare Organization, efforts are made to obtain extensions from the Department of Labor while the husband is being looked for.

6. Cases in which the husband is located in an interior city, and families are sent there on admission. The question of the financial responsibility for the family in case of dependency, under the transportation rules adopted by the National Conference of Jewish Social Work, is raised by such interior cities. Because these fami-

lies arrived at the port of New York, some of the interior communities have taken the position that New York is financially responsible in the event of dependency.

Conclusion

In spite of the seriousness of this aspect of the problem, the Bureau believes that it can nevertheless be dealt with in an efficacious way. The conditions portrayed in the foregoing pages are merely the backwash of the great war. It is beyond our knowledge to foretell the duration of this period of adjustment, but we believe that in about ten years the more serious and dire aspects of the situation will be over with. A strong publicity campaign with the assistance of the Yiddish press should be begun forthwith to acquaint the Yiddish-speaking public of the seriousness of the problem, and to create favorable public opinion.

5. Report of Committee on Transportation*

Proposed Rules for the Regulation of Transportation

1. A transient shall mean any person (including his family) who shall have become a charge upon the charities of the city where he may be, within one year of the time of his arrival at that city, unless he shall have become dependent through unavoidable accident.

2. A telegraphic code now in preparation shall be used for the prompt and economical exchange of information regarding transportation between the constituent associations, and each association agrees and binds itself to reply to all inquiries submitted to it as soon as the necessary investigations can be made.

* National Conference of Jewish Charities, *Proceedings* (1900), pp. 19-22. Presented at First National Conference of Jewish Charities, Chicago, Ill., June 11-13, 1900.

3. No applicant for transportation shall be forwarded from one city to another, nor shall half-rate tickets, paid for by the applicant, be furnished without the advice and consent of the city of destination. But should the applicant be a transient within the meaning as above defined, he may be returned to the city from which he came within a year, provided the statement as to residence be confirmed by investigation in said city. Whenever transportation is furnished, even if paid for by the applicant, notice shall be sent to the city of destination.

4. Every initial city shall in all cases furnish transportation through to the city of destination. In the event of any violation of this rule, the receiving city shall at its option, after investigation, transport the applicant to his destination, or to the city from which he came, at the cost of the initial city.

5. Any woman wishing to seek or desiring to join her husband shall not be assisted with transportation under any circumstances without the consent of the city where it is claimed the husband resides.

6. Any violations, disputes, or misunderstandings between constituent associations under these rules shall be referred to the Committee on Transportation, which shall investigate the same, and whose decision shall be final and binding.

Substantially, these rules are the same as those framed and adopted at the Conference held at Cincinnati last year; though hastily drawn and considered then, the unanimity of their adoption was indicative that all had knowledge of the evils which it was proposed to remedy and felt the necessity for the formulation of some systematic and harmonious plan of action between the various communities.

In this progressive age, the administration of charity has become a science, and it behooves us to keep pace with the general advance. Poverty may not be abolished by the collection of statistics, nor the pangs of hunger allayed by filling up blank forms, but the worthy poor will be more readily assisted and the impostor more speedily detected where system and order govern.

It was in this spirit that these rules were framed, not merely from a desire to protect the various communities from fraud and imposition, but with the intention to most effectively aid those deserving assistance. It was felt that the time has come when we must put a stop to the too common practice of endeavoring to unload the poor of one city upon another community; of getting rid of a perpetual burden by placing it on someone else. The temptation is very strong to get rid of a disagreeable subject, possibly forever, by spending a few dollars in car-fare, or by suggesting to the persistent begger the advisability of trying some other sphere of action.[1]

6. Tuberculosis as Affecting Jewish Charity Organizations*

BY LEE K. FRANKEL

In a letter which the writer recently received from Mr. Alfred Muller, secretary of the National Jewish Hospital for Consumptives, was the following significant statement:

One of the matters that must be considered by the National Conference of Jewish Charities in Chicago, and one that will become serious if the rules of the Conference are to be enforced, is the question: "What to do with consumptives who reach Denver in a condition too sick to work and too well to go to the hospital, or who are unable to find occupation according to their requirements in Denver or Colo-

[1] The Committee on Transportation functioned for many years. Its revised rules were adopted by most Jewish agencies, and it served as advisor in many cases of inter-city dispute. See "Transportation Rules" as amended and adopted June 1925, and "Transients," by Boris D. Bogen in *Jewish Charities,* vol. II, no. 12 (July, 1912).

* National Conference of Jewish Charities, *Proceedings* (1900), pp. 87-98. Presented at First National Conference of Jewish Charities, Chicago, Ill., June 11-13, 1900.

rado"; also: "What should be done with convalescents after they leave the hospital?"

Following close upon the heels of this letter came another from Mr. Myer H. Levy, secretary of the Eureka Benevolent Society of San Francisco, from which I will take the liberty of quoting. After discussing the fact that it is necessary for the San Francisco society to divide their applicants into two classes, local and transients, he says:

Transients, however, are the bugbear. Unfortunately, our state has received a world-wide reputation as a sanitarium for consumptives, and there is hardly a week that passes that we do not receive from one to three applicants for assistance from strangers, who had been advised by some physician in the East to come here on account of the climate. After a week or month's residence, having exhausted their means, they apply to us for aid or transportation back to their homes, and out of self-protection we are forced to send them back where they belong. We cannot undertake to care for them. We have enough of what I have classed under the head of local cases, and no matter how much we sympathize with them, we have to stifle our sympathies and refuse them aid, except transportation back to their homes. The influx of consumptives here has become of such a serious nature that physicians and others interested are agitating the passage of a state quarantine law.

Statements such as these, coming as they do in any official manner from representative communities, at once take the question of the care of the tuberculous poor away from purely local lines, and make of it a national issue. I believe that many of you will agree with me that there is no question of equal importance before the Conference. Those of you who come into personal contact with charity administrations, particularly in the large cities, must have realized how difficult it is to find any permanent or thorough solution to the problem of the poor consumptive. It is therefore with a sense of pleasure, combined with one of relief, that I welcome the opportunity of presenting to the organization at its initial meeting the facts that have been especially brought to my attention in connection with the care of consumptives who apply at our charitable institutions, and for whom they must provide.

The question, "Is consumption on the increase among our co-religionists?" is at this time a very pertinent query. Is the disease sufficiently prevalent among the Jews to warrant such statements as have been made above? Is it no longer true that the Jew is less susceptible to tubercular disease than his Christian neighbor? It is now ten years since the United States Government published its pamphlet on the vital statistics of the Jews. In that publication a census of 10,000 Jewish families throughout the United States was taken, and revealed the somewhat startling fact that the ratio of deaths from consumption, between Jews and others, was one to three. It is questionable, however, how valuable these figures really are. The investigation comprised but 10,000 families, and, from information recently given to the writer, these families included but a few of that large bulk of Jewish population which has arrived here from Russia since 1881. Considering the conditions under which the latter live, and have lived since the enormous immigration to the United States began, it is doubtful if the splendid showing of the census would hold.

An attempt to gather statistics on the percentage of consumptives among Jews today has not met with much success. In fact, if anything has been demonstrated, it is the old adage that figures are unreliable. A few weeks ago, the writer sent a circular letter to the various Jewish charitable organizations, asking for information on the consumption question.

Replies were sent by the following cities: Helena, Mont.; Charleston, S.C.; Atlanta, Ga.; St. Paul, Minn.; Pittsburgh, Pa.; Cleveland, Ohio; Omaha, Neb.; Elmira, N.Y.; New Orleans, La.; Dallas, Tex.; Seattle, Wash.; Detroit, Mich.; Buffalo, N.Y.; New Haven, Conn.; Denver, Colo.; Baltimore, Md.; Washington, D.C.; Albany, N.Y.; Philadelphia, Pa.; Chicago, Ill.; Boston, Mass.; Hartford, Conn.; Montgomery, Ala.; Evansville, Ind.; Cincinnati, Ohio; Greenville, Miss.; Toledo, Ohio.

The replies which have been received are interesting and instructive, and are indicative of what might be done if a systematic plan of keeping records were to be introduced by each society. I have arranged the information sent to me, and believe it to be of sufficient value to incorporate in this paper.

Very few societies keep a careful record of their cases. A number of the smaller communities have no records. In New York, of the new applicants this year, over three per cent are consumptives. These, however, are cases where a physician's certificate gives indisputable evidence that the disease is present. The doubtful cases will double the percentage given, and there is every reason to believe that there are at present on the records of the United Hebrew Charities of New York at least one thousand families in which one or more members are afflicted with tuberculosis. In order to obtain some clue as to the comparative number of Jewish consumptives in New York City, the death records of the Board of Health were studied.

It is difficult to draw deductions from these figures owing to the inherent fault in their compilation, and to the comparatively few cases investigated. Such statistics should cover a period of years rather than of months. I think, however, that I am not going beyond the limits of reasonable conclusion in stating that such tuberculosis as exists is confined to the poorer element of the Jewish population, and that the foreigner who suffers from the disease has contracted it after his arrival in the United States. I think there can be little doubt from what has been said that tuberculosis is on the increase among our Jewish population. In New York, the increase in the number of consumptives who apply at the charities is distinctly apparent. In 1895, the ratio was but two per cent, whereas at present it is three per cent. Other cities likewise report an increase in the number of consumptive applicants. Figures to show that consumption is on the increase generally may be multiplied indefinitely. The causes of such increase are not difficult to find. They have their origin in those tides of emigration which have brought our oppressed and persecuted brethren to these shores; and in that peculiar clannishness of the Jew, which makes him seek the city rather than the town. Of the hundreds of thousands who have arrived in New York since 1885, 75 per cent have never passed beyond the city's limits. I believe the same is true of Philadelphia, Boston, and Baltimore. Those who were venturesome enough to pass beyond the portals of what was to them an unknown land, drifted to the large cities of the West and Southwest, and began their new life under conditions very similar to those of their eastern brethren.

And what were these conditions? In most cases, a state of appalling poverty brought with them from Europe and of long standing. A poverty so acute that it was necessary to seek relief on the day of arrival. A need so great that in the industrial competition it became necessary for father, mother, and children to enter the ranks of the industrial army, and to literally fight for their livelihood. In quarters unfit for human beings, where the landlord's greed necessitated such economies that the living room and the working room became one, these people slaved on, underfed, insufficiently clad, from early morning until late at night, in a stifling, suffocating atmosphere, daily bringing their systems into such a condition that it required but the entrance of the tuberculosis germ to complete the work.

You all know this picture. It is, I regret to state, not exaggerated. Indeed, I know of no pen that can do justice to the environment which produces such results, nor to the distress and suffering that is occasioned when consumption has once entered such a habitation.

The picture is dark, I admit. Looked at from certain positions, it appears still darker. When I think that the tide of emigration is not yet on the ebb, and that, from present indications, the 40,000 mark may be reached this year, I am tempted to wonder what will be the condition of affairs five and ten years from now. And then I see the brighter side of the picture. I realize that we live in an age of progress, in an age where the strides that have been made in the study of consumption are more than marvelous. It has been acknowledged by the most eminent specialists that we need not sit by idly and wait for our applicants to die, but that we may find the means, if we so wish, to help them to live. As has been aptly said, "The consumptive should be cared for until he is well, not until he is dead."

And here, to my mind, lies the crux of the entire question, so far as our charitable societies are concerned. How far will they be able to meet modern, scientific views on the care of the consumptive? To what extent will their policy and system of relief-giving permit them to follow in the wake of the most advanced medical research? Will it be possible for our Jewish societies and communities to realize that the tuberculosis question is not essentially a Jewish one, and that, in order to combat this dread disease most successfully, it will be necessary to join hands with other organizations which are striving for similar ends? Will it be possible for this Conference to educate its members so that they will in the future not act independently, but as a unit; so that each one will not follow his own line of thought but together they will accept as a plan of action what today is considered the only rational procedure for the treatment of the tuberculous poor?

I trust you will pardon me, if for a moment I grow technical and speak to you of the etiology of consumption. I do this merely to demonstrate to you that the causes which underlie tuberculosis are well known; that they are primarily due to a bacillus which finds nourishment in the human system only when it is below par, and that, when the system is restored to its normal state, the causes of infection are destroyed. In other words, the glorious discovery of recent medical research is the fact that consumption is not only preventable, but curable. Medical men are today almost united in declaring that if proper sanitary conditions could be secured, and the populace educated to its needs, the plague, if not entirely exterminated [can be greatly reduced].

What is, however, of even greater interest to us as charitable organizations is the well-founded belief among the medical fraternity that special climatic conditions for the treatment of tuberculosis are no longer necessary. Given fresh air in quantities, the proper nourishment, and medical care, as many cures are being effected at the seashore as in the mountains; as many sufferers grow well near the large cities as in the recesses of the forests. The sanitarium treatment, as it is called, is today looked upon as the best method for the care of the individual afflicted with tuberculosis. . . . The consumptive sanitarium is generally in a locality with pure air; it involves the erection of suitable buildings which should be especially adapted to the hygienic and dietetic treatment that may be necessary. It presupposes a rigid discipline, which educates the patient regarding his condition, and prevents him from infecting his neighbors and from reinfecting himself. It excludes the belief that climate is a specific, and leaving out of the question individuals whose idiosyncracies require special consideration, it contends that, if the above conditions can be obtained, one section of the country is as good as another for the treatment of tuberculosis.

It will readily be seen how the conception of a sanitarium near each community must radically affect and alter the work done by our relief societies, in that it gives the community the opportunity to care for their consumptive poor near home rather than at distant points. I trust that I shall not be misunderstood when I state that the tendency on the part of societies and individuals has been to shift the responsiblity to others in so far as consumptives are concerned. This is particularly true of physicians. It has not been at all uncommon in my experience for a physician to recommend a change of climate for his patient without any knowledge of the conditions which exist at such a place. Solly, in his *Handbook of Medical Climatology,* says: "If we consider how great a sacrifice of time, money, inclination and affection is involved when an invalid, under direction of a physician, leaves his home and journeys into another and perhaps a far country, we marvel at the small amount of thought and study that is bestowed by the majority of physicians upon the science of medical climatology, for without a fair knowledge and appreciation of this no rational selection of climate can be made." I am confident that when Solly wrote the above he had in mind the consumptive who was able to pay.

How much more strongly then does it apply to the poor consumptive who, without a dollar in his pocket, applies at our charity societies for transportation to Denver, Los Angeles, or other health resorts, in search of the *ignis fatuus* that has been revealed to him through the reprehensible action of his physician. I know of no more pitiful object than such a man refusing other relief that would ultimately do him more good, because the physician on whom he has pinned his faith has suggested Denver as the place where he might get well.

The day for such conduct is past. In the light of our new vision, our societies should move along the lines of organized, systematized charity, whose basic principle is the belief that no man can be given the assistance which he needs without an intelligent knowledge of his condition. It goes without saying that, in the case of the consumptive, the medical examination and report is the information most vital. Where it is possible this should be made by a specialist, since much depends upon diagnosing tuberculosis in its first stages and furnishing the necessary sanitarium treatment. Similarly it is a crime, unless hospital facilities are at hand, to remove from his home and his family the poor consumptive for whom there is no longer any hope. The report of the physician should indicate the treatment needed: whether the applicant should remain at home, whether sanitarium treatment in the neighborhood may be advisable, or whether owing to the applicant's idiosyncracies, a complete change of climate is desirable. In the first case, the society's opportunities for assistance through its visitors are endless. Aside from the monetary assistance which will be necessary, the intelligent visitor or nurse will undertake a campaign of education. He will teach his patient a knowledge of his condition, and instruct him not only how to care for himself but prevent him from infecting his family, by following the simple rules which have been laid down for the purpose, and which every relief society should distribute. As stated above, consumption is a preventable disease. It cannot be communicated except through the sputum. Even the dullest and most ignorant individual can be taught this fact and to observe simple rules of cleanliness. I take it to be the province of a Relief Society to do work of this kind.

Where sanitarium treatment is desirable, obstacles may be encountered in the lack of sufficient accommodations of this kind in the vicinity. Should this be absent, the opportunity will be afforded to you to provide it. The sanitarium treatment for consumptives is comparatively recent in the United States, and hence but few sanitaria are as yet to be found. Throughout continental Europe this treatment has been found to be so effective that sanitaria are to be found by the hundreds. The Bedford Sanitarium of the Montefiore Home in New York is an example of what private enterprise can do in this direction. Beginning with accommodations for 40 patients, the institution will soon be enlarged to accommodate 150. Should the occasion demand it, sanitaria similar to this should be instituted in all our large cities, so that each community may, to a great extent, work out its own salvation. As relief societies we may do even more than this by adding our voices to the many that are being raised, asking for state intervention in aiding the tuberculous poor. I am glad to report that not only the United Hebrew Charities, but other Jewish institutions in New York were heartily in favor of this movement and joined the other communal institutions in bringing about the passage of this bill. In Massachusetts, such a state sanitarium has been in existence several years and is doing splendid work. Among its inmates are sixteen Jewish consumptives, who were sent there by the Boston society. If there are no similar movements in the other cities, let the Jewish societies comprised in this Conference act as pioneers in furthering them.

To many of you, it may appear that all that has been so far said is but prefatory to the question which is of immediate importance, viz., the relation of this Conference to the National Jewish Hospital for Consumptives at Denver, Colorado. The city of Denver has today the unenviable reputation of possessing that peculiar climate which is one of the specifics for the improvement of tuberculosis. Although the medical world realizes that climate-therapy for pulmonary tuberculosis is not essential for the cure of the consumptive, Denver is still the place where he may find new life and health. The result is obvious. For years, Denver has been the Mecca of every unfortunate afflicted with pulmonary disease. So strongly was the belief implanted that if the consumptive could reach Denver he would be well, that many an unfortunate left home and friends frequently penniless, suffered untold tortures during the weary days and nights he was on the way, and at last reached his destination but to die.

Many other cases can be cited of those in whom the disease had only begun its ravages, but who, with slight means and with the hope of finding work, undertook a similar journey. To these, likewise, came disappointment. Unable to find work, their scanty funds exhausted, without friends and without acquaintances, lacking proper nourishment and badly housed, it was only a question of time until the disease laid them prostrate, even in that climate.

It was in the hope of aiding these unfortunates that the Denver Hospital was organized. As at present constituted, it has accommodations for sixty-eight patients, the costs of whose maintenance will approximatc $2,200. per annum. Since the opening of the Hospital, seventy-five patients have been admitted, of whom eighteen have been dismissed, sufficiently improved to follow their respective vocations and to take care of themselves. Eleven have died. There can be no doubt in the mind of any thinking man that this institution has the right to ask, and must receive, the support of the community at large in carrying on this praiseworthy undertaking. Personally, I have no doubt that the funds necessary to carry on its work properly, and even to increase its facilities, will be forthcoming. In a letter from the secretary on this subject, he suggests that the Conference should have representation in the corporation, which will take charge of the Hospital on January 1, 1901. He suggests, furthermore, that the Conference shall name one or two appointees, who shall be the representatives of the Conference on the General Board of the Hospital. I trust that this suggestion will receive the consideration it deserves, and that the action taken at this meeting will enable the Conference and the Hospital to work harmoniously together, and to be of service to each other. Paradoxical as it may seem, the societies comprising the National Conference can be of even greater service to the Hospital than in the ways enumerated above. I am strongly of the opinion that the work of our relief societies, with respect to the Hospital, should be preventive rather than curative; that their energies should be directed to relieving the Denver community of its burden, or at least to lessening it. With our present knowledge of the subject, all societies should follow the rule of not granting transportation to consumptives to Denver, or similar resorts, unless the testimony of a reputable physician absolutely demands it; and of not granting it even then, unless there is the positive assurance that the applicant will be self-supporting during his stay there, and that he will not become a charge upon the community. This is, however, but a portion of their work. Following the broader lines of activity which come within the province of a modern relief society, they should undertake the education of the community over whose poor they watch, and of the poor themselves, regarding the grave evils which arise from ill-considered and hasty transportation of the consumptive to distant points without the consent and advice of an experienced physician. They should endeavor to impress upon the physicians who come into contact with the consumptive poor the crime of fostering hopes in their patients which cannot be realized; they should make such propaganda in their respective communities as will lead to the establishment of sanitaria in their vicinities for the treatment of incipient cases, and of hospitals for the more advanced and hopeless ones. And, lastly, upon the broad basis of non-sectarian charity, they should unite with other institutions to secure for the poor consumptive the aid which he has the right to demand from the state. For the rich man, with the means to travel and the ability to humor any desire, the special health resort may be the means of recovery. For the poor man, the hope that the future has in store for him lies in the State Hospital and the State Sanitarium. . . .

III Child Care and Protection

THE Conference was the forum for advancing many ideas which were proved ahead of their time. The Frankel analysis of the controversy between institutional and foster care for children is thoughtful, and fully modern in its tone. It is significant that the continued dominance of congregate institutional care as early as 1900 seems due, not so much to conviction, as to lack of professional and administrative experience in locating and retaining suitable foster homes. It is startling to learn that even in 1902, the common public view about children's institutions was no longer supported by the facts—fewer than 10 per cent of Jewish children in institutions were even then full orphans.

The principles outlined in 1902 were not to be improved upon for several decades: cooperation with public child-care agencies; refusal to place small children in institutions; adequate relief to keep families together. There appears, perhaps for the first time, a plea to stress the reuniting of families, rather than controversy over the relative merits of institution and foster home, neither approach having given before 1902 much attention to the return of the child to his family.

The 1906 paper by Bernstein makes the case for institutional care. But even here there is advanced a plan which was not to receive general attention until the 1950's—special small-group homes for certain children, staffed by couples with special training and equipment. By 1911, the modern view had crystallized: A wide range of services for children is necessary; the choice of one among several possible courses is to be determined by the needs of the individual child; institutional care is only one of several possible choices. This 1911 approach varies from the present one mainly in the factors considered in making a choice.

Contrary to the common view that there were few delinquent Jewish youths, the Conference papers of 1904 and 1906 reveal a marked concern over the growing incidence of delinquency among youth in immigrant Jewish families. This concern led first to a demand for a special Jewish institution for such youths, so that Jews would not become a public burden. In 1906, Judge Mack outlined the position on institutions which has since been the accepted one for Jewish social work: a Jewish institution is justified only if it is state policy to use private institutions for the care of children committed to them. A preferable goal for Jewish citizens is the establishment of adequate public facilities open to all. Judge Mack's proposals for prevention reflect the period in their emphasis upon financial and social help to move families from poor environments, and vocational training to raise the goals and opportunities of youth. More modern is the proposal that recreation programs be designed for youth *and* their parents—an early case of family-oriented social work which has not yet been put into wide practice.

1. Report of the Committee on Dependent Children*

BY LEE K. FRANKEL, Chairman

Your Committee on Dependent Children has deemed it wise to devote its report to the present Conference to the consideration of

* National Conference of Jewish Charities, *Proceedings* (1902), pp. 107-21. Presented at the Second Conference of Jewish Charities, Detroit, Mich., May 26-29, 1902.

the question of caring for dependent Jewish children through other than institutional means. The Committee was led to this decision through the importance that has been attached in recent years, in particular by non-Jewish bodies, to the methods of caring for children through agencies, such as the boarding-out and the placing-out systems. In order that the report be representative and, if possible, authoritative, it was deemed inadvisable to make it voice the opinions of any or all of the Committee; rather, it should express the views of the Jewish community at large, and in particular should reflect the unprejudiced and impartial conclusions of those who are engaged in child-saving work. To this end, it was decided to make a study of the subject from a historical standpoint, and to obtain, where possible, information that might permit of subsequent deductions and generalizations.

As a basis of study [a series of] questions was submitted to the Jewish orphan asylums and children's institutions in the United States.[1]

From the replies that were received, the Committee has framed the following reports:

The institutional care of Jewish children dates back to the early part of the century. In 1822, the first Jewish Orphan Asylum in the United States was founded in the City of New York.[2] The example then set was followed by New Orleans and Philadelphia in 1855, by Cleveland in 1868, by San Francisco in 1871, by Baltimore in 1873, by Newark, N.J., in 1877, and by Brooklyn and HSGS [3] in New York in 1879. The last-named institution was unique in that

[1] The questionnaire is omitted because of limitations of space. The questions asked are indicated in the analysis of replies received.

[2] While a Society for the Education of Poor Children and the Relief of Indigent Persons of the Jewish Persuasion was organized in New York City in 1827 which, among its other functions, helped *support* orphans, the first Jewish agency providing orphans' *institutional* care in that city was the Hebrew Orphan Asylum established in 1859. The first American Jewish organization devoted to the support of orphans was the Society for the Relief of Orphans and Children of Indigent Parents founded in Charleston in 1802, and the first Jewish orphan asylum was established in Philadelphia in 1855.

[3] Hebrew Sheltering Guardian Society.

it admitted not only orphans and half-orphans, but likewise children who had become public charges through destitution or improper guardianship.

In 1881, the Rochester Asylum first opened its doors. Eight years later, in 1889, the IOBB [4] founded its second institution in Atlanta, Ga. Following the example of the other cities, Boston and Chicago built asylums for their orphaned children in 1890 and 1893, respectively. In 1895 the Hebrew Infant Asylum of New York attempted the novel experiment of caring for children under the age of five years. With a few exceptions, such as the Foster Home in Cincinnati, the recently organized Home for Hebrew Orphans in Philadelphia, and the Home for the Friendless in Chicago, the institutions enumerated comprise the entire organized effort that has been made by American Jewry towards solving the question of caring for its orphaned and destitute wards.

From the statistics which have been submitted, it appears that over 19,569 children have been inmates of the various Jewish asylums since their inception. During the past fiscal year, 3,572 children, 18 per cent of the total registration, were being cared for. It is noteworthy that of these 3,572 children, 2,172, or 60 per cent, were in institutions in New York and Brooklyn, and 500, or 14 per cent, in the Cleveland Orphan Asylum. Of the children at present in asylums, 309 are full orphans, 2,362 are half-orphans, and 630 are children with both parents living. These last figures do not include the institutions in Newark, N.J., and Atlanta, Ga., the statistics of which are not at hand. Of the 630 children with both parents living, 479 are with the Hebrew Sheltering Guardian Society of New York.

Practically all of the institutions admit full orphans, half-orphans, and, in exceptional cases, children with both parents living. In the main, the institutions do not admit children under three years of age. The prevailing age of admission is from three to five years, while children are discharged from fourteen to eighteen years.

[4] International Order of B'nai B'rith.

The average length of stay varies in the various institutions from two and one-half to ten years. None of the institutions has as yet attempted to care for its wards in small detached buildings, or what is known as the "Cottage Plan." Even the largest shelter their children under one roof. Practically all of the institutions make a determined effort to return children to their parents as soon as the latter are in a position to support them.

In the main, the children receive a public-school education, and in institutions like those in Chicago, and the HSGS of New York, San Francisco, New Orleans and Cleveland, manual training has been introduced. In Rochester the children are sent to the Mechanics' Institute; in Boston, manual training is taught in the public schools; in New York they attend the Hebrew Technical Institute. After children leave or are discharged from the asylums, the latter have endeavored, in nearly every instance, to keep some form of supervision over their graduates. In a number of institutions, alumni associations have been formed, and through these societies the subsequent careers of their former wards have been followed. It is not an exaggeration to say that no cause has been so potent in the strengthening of the belief in the value of institutional care of Jewish children as the splendid and even brilliant records of some of these orphans, and the uniformly successful results that have followed from this method of treatment.

There appears to be but little difference of opinion on the question of how graduates of these institutions, judged from their subsequent careers, compare with other children. The Rochester society notices no difference. In Philadelphia, Chicago, New York, San Francisco, New Orleans, Baltimore, Brooklyn, and Atlanta the children compare very favorably with other children. The authorities of the Cleveland Orphan Asylum and the Hebrew Infant Asylum do not hesitate to say that their children are superior to others from the same strata of society.

Of profound interest are the replies which have been received on the question of boarding out and placing out children. Rochester has found it almost impossible to board out children, except with their own mothers. In the few instances in which they have attempted to place out children in free homes, they have been unsuccessful. As a rule, the mother or some relative could give a home to those who were dismissed. Rochester is firmly opposed to institutions where hundreds of children are herded together, and believes that the child can be fully developed only in an institution the size of theirs. The Philadelphia society has attempted to board out children, at an average cost of $3.50 per week, and to place children in free homes, to have them indentured and adopted. The results were only partly successful. They are of the opinion that under proper conditions an institution is the equivalent of any other method of child care, and that the child's development is complete. They do not deem it feasible to place out Jewish children in Jewish homes. They consider the care received by the children in the institution superior to that which most poor people can bestow outside of the institution.

The Boston institution has not found any need for boarding out its children, probably owing to the small number of children at one time in the asylum. They have succeeded in having one child adopted in a well-to-do family. Speaking through its superintendent, the institution is opposed to placing children in private homes, although he states that hardly any of our large asylums are so managed that they develop a child in a natural way. Where an institution is well managed, it is felt that it is on a par with the home.

The Chicago institution does not deem it advisable to board out its children. They further state that it cannot be denied that no influence is so strong or beneficial to the child as the parental influence, and that it remains an open question whether a dependent child can have his or her full development in an institution such as theirs.

The Hebrew Sheltering Guardian Society of New York has not attempted to board out children. Attempts to place out or to indenture children, or to have them adopted, have been successful to a limited extent only. In their opinion, placing children in homes is feasible, provided that the latter are under constant supervision and that careful investigation is made of the homes and of the motives of those in whose charge the children are placed.

The New Orleans society has boarded out children at a cost of $200.00 per annum. No attempt has been made at placing out. The superintendent states that the full natural development of the child cannot be accomplished in an institution, although he doubts whether proper Jewish homes could be found either in the large cities or in smaller towns throughout the United States. In a paper which he read before the National Conference of Charities and Corrections in 1897 on "Jewish Child-Saving in the United States," there appeared the following statement:

Remove all children from the large cities, scatter them throughout the country, or raise them in agricultural or industrial colonies, make good farmers of them or teach them a trade by which they can make an honest living, and the problem of child-saving will be solved.[5]

Boarding out children has never been attempted by the Cleveland Asylum. Attempts to have full orphans adopted have rarely been successful. In their opinion, the institution under proper management is the ideal system; finding homes is not practicable. The fact that out of 1,700 children cared for by this institution there has been but five per cent of failures speaks volumes for the character of the training given here. The Hebrew Infant Asylum of New York has never been successful in having its children adopted, although they thoroughly believe that it would be to the best interest of the destitute and orphaned child if it could be adopted into a good Jewish home. Such a statement coming from an institution whose wards are under the age of five years of age has more than passing value. They are, however, absolutely opposed to boarding out small children, and maintain that the child receives better treatment in their institution than it would if placed out for pay or given to those families who make a business out of

[5] Presented by Michael Heymann, Supt., Jewish Orphans Home, New Orleans, La., at The National Conference of Charities and Corrections, Toronto. See *Proceedings,* 1897, pp. 108-110.

receiving children in board. The low death rate (six per cent) indicates how well children are cared for by this institution.

The Hebrew Orphan Asylum of New York in former years has made many efforts to place and to board out children in homes. At present the boys who attend the Hebrew Technical Institute and the New York City College are boarded out; generally speaking, the results have not been successful. The Newark, N.J. Asylum has boarded out children at a cost of $60.00 per annum. No attempt has been made to have them adopted or placed in free homes. Boarding out of children by the Baltimore Asylum has not been tried. Attempts to place children in free homes have been successful.[6] In their opinion, the institution is the equivalent of the private home, and frequently certain talents of the children are more carefully fostered in the former than in the latter.

The Brooklyn Orphan Asylum has boarded out children at a cost of from $8.00 to $10.00 per month. In their opinion, the full development of the child cannot be accomplished in the institution. Under favorable conditions and surroundings, private homes may prove satisfactory. The Hebrew Orphans' Home, in Atlanta, has indentured a few of its children with varying success. They have never attempted boarding out or placing out. They, too, believe that the full development of the child cannot be accomplished in an institution. The San Francisco Asylum boards out all children suffering from physical disability at a cost varying from $90.00 to $180.00 per annum. Placing out, adoption, and indenturing have not been tried.

The unsuccessful attempts on the part of the benevolent societies to board out children led to the establishment of the Orphan Asylum. It is their opinion that in a properly managed institution, development, both physical and mental, is accomplished more successfully than it is in the majority of the children in the poorer classes brought up in their own homes.

Your Committee has deemed it of interest as supplemental to the reports from institutions to obtain an expression of opinion

[6] Experience in later years proved this conclusion unduly optimistic. Abuse of child labor in many free homes led to almost universal reliance upon boarding homes compensated by placement agencies.

from the various Jewish benevolent and relief societies throughout the United States. To this end, a set of questions similar to those sent to Orphan Asylums was sent to each society. Three questions were added, viz.:

What disposition do you make of children with both parents living, if the latter are dependent on the community, or are improper guardians?

What do you do with abandoned children?

What do you do with children under two years of age?

Replies were received from twenty-six societies. Practically all societies make use of the institutions for the care of the half-orphan and full-orphan children who come under their charge; in many instances, where the institution is not available, the relief funds are freely used to subsidize the remaining parent or to place the child in a private family.

Without going further into detail, it may be stated that, judging from the replies which have been received, the majority of societies have at various times attempted to board out children, at a cost varying from $36.00 to $156.00 per annum, and with correspondingly varying degrees of success. Similarly, a number of societies have attempted to place out children in free homes and to have them adopted and indentured, with varying success.

It is to be regretted that in the replies which were sent, only a few societies gave any data regarding the number of children cared for in these various ways. As a result, no definite conclusions can be drawn, as no exact comparisons can be made, except from the general statements of the societies as to their success or non-success. The same fact is true with regard to the questions of the possibility of placing Jewish children in Jewish homes in cities and towns throughout the United States. A number of societies have never given any consideration to this question. Others have ignored it altogether. Out of twelve societies which sent answers, three are opposed to the plan of placing out, six believe in its practicability, while three are doubtful. The San Francisco society stands as an exponent of the opposition to such a movement, while the New Orleans society can be considered as a champion of this cause. In their reply, the first society states:

If our Jewish people were of the farming class and we could induce some of them to care for our dependent children, we would say it would be a good plan to place them out in that manner. But as we have none of that class, and as we would have to seek homes for them among the poor and ignorant members of the Jewish community, we say "no"; it would be bad for the children; they are a great deal better off brought up in an orphanage. Years ago, before our orphanage was established, our association was responsible for the care of all of the dependent children in this community, and we placed them in private families for pay. We could find no free homes for them, and our experience was disheartening—in fact, so bad that this was one of the reasons for the establishment of our Orphan Asylum. First of all, there was the distressing feature of the breaking-up of a family. The majority of our poor have large families; in the case of a family of from four to six children, two would be brought up with one person, two with another, etc., and in the course of time the children would become estranged from their families and would forget their brothers and sisters. Then, again, there was the extreme difficulty of having proper supervision over them to see that they were receiving proper education, that their character was being properly developed, and that they were not being made household drudges. Our efforts were so unsuccessful that, as we have said before, it led to our establishing the Orphan Asylum; the success that institution has had in properly bringing up our children will forever put a damper on the idea of placing out dependent children in private homes. We do not believe in it, and do not care to shirk out duty in that manner. The only trouble is that we have not enough Orphan Asylums. We know hundreds of children in this city that we would like to take away from their parents and place in the Orphan Asylum, where they would be brought up to make good men and good women, but, unfortunately for them, we cannot.

In the reply from the New Orleans Society, there occurs the following statement: "We are strongly of the opinion that dependent children should be placed in private families under the supervision of, let us call them, 'guardians.' We recognize that orphan asylums have to be resorted to; we have no other alternative now; we have, say, 150 families in the whole South who would take our children; but we confidently hope that the time will come when asylums are things of the past."

Conclusions

Your Committee does not deem it essential for the proper treatment of the subject to introduce any lengthy discussion of the relative merits of the institution and the private home in the care of the dependent child. Both systems have their ardent supporters and detractors, while the results that have been obtained from either could be used to demonstrate its superiority or inferiority to the other.

Like individuals, both institutions and private homes may run the gamut of virtues and vices, may be either models or awful examples—it will suffice to say that the home is a natural product, the institution an artificial one, and that all other things being equal, the former is to be preferred to the latter. From the standpoint of the Conference, the important question to consider is the feasibility and advisability of finding proper homes in which Jewish children can be cared for, and not whether the institution is superior to the home, or the reverse.

It cannot be gainsaid that the problem presents great difficulties. Of the 1,000,000 Jews in the United States, the large majority are residents in cities. Probably nearly 50 per cent reside in the city of New York, and no one knowing the conditions of overcrowding and congestion that exist there would advocate that any extensive effort be made to find homes in which children could be either adopted or boarded. Again, homes in the country among agriculturalists and farmers are equally impossible, owing to the exceedingly limited number of Jews who are engaged in such vocations. On the other hand, the question from the Jewish standpoint is very much simplified by the fact that of the 3,572 children presently in institutions, only 309—less than 10 per cent—are full orphans. It may be assumed that 50 per cent of these are over eight years of age, and even the strongest adherents of the placing-out system do not advocate placing out children over the age of eight years in private homes. In rare instances only are they able to adapt themselves to those intimate relationships which should exist between the foster parent and the foster child and which are so necessary in the true home. Working on the above assumption, it can be assumed that there are probably between 150 and 200 Jewish children at present in institutions throughout the United States who have no natural guardians or parental ties, and with whom it might be wise to make the experiment of having them boarded out or placed in free homes. In the face of evidence to the contrary, your Committee is of the opinion that such an experiment is worthy of a trial.

From the statistics that have been gathered, it is evident that no systematic effort has ever been made to find homes of the kind mentioned. The attempts in this direction on the part of the institution have been spasmodic and irregular. Cooperation with existing agencies, such as home-finding associations, children's-aid societies, placing-out bureaus, under state control and supervision, have rarely been tried. Systematic propaganda through the medium of newspapers, circulars, and bulletins is almost unknown. That it is possible to produce results through such media is evidenced by the fact that the State Charities Aid Society of New York has placed four Jewish children in Jewish homes, through advertisements in the secular press.

The Children's Aid Society of Brooklyn has suceeded in finding, without any difficulty, boarding homes for two of the children of the Brooklyn Hebrew Orphan Asylum. The success which has been obtained by the Federation of Jewish Charities of Boston in finding satisfactory Jewish homes in the state of Massachusetts by cooperating with state agencies augurs well for the possibility of finding even more homes of a similar kind. It is to be regretted that the work of the Orphans' Guardians' Society of Philadelphia has not been more fully developed, since the society has demonstrated to a limited extent that children can be placed in private homes under proper supervision and guardianship. The same is true of the Frank Fund in Chicago. It would assuredly be a sinister reflection on the well-earned reputation of the Jew as the champion of purity and integrity of the home to conclude, without thorough trial, that decent, desirable homes cannot be found throughout the length and breadth of the United States for a few hundred children.

Your Committee recommends the appointment of a committee empowered to thoroughly investigate the subject, with a view to the establishment of a National Jewish Home Bureau, which shall cooperate with the various Jewish institutions in finding homes for the orphans confided to their care.

The difficulties that surround the finding of homes for half-orphans are even more serious than with full orphans. The claims of the surviving parent to his or her children must always be considered. The institution must ever keep in sight the possibility of reuniting the family when the destitution which has occasioned the break-up has disappeared or been overcome. It is fortunate that the commitment of Jewish children to institutions is almost altogether due to destitution. Neglected or abandoned Jewish children are so few in number that they need not be considered in the discussion. Furthermore, the entire problem is very much simplified by this fact, since the institution has the possibility of reuniting the family or obviating its break-up by removing the destitution.

While your Committee has but few figures upon which to base an opinion, it is nevertheless of the impression that the placing out of many children could be prevented if the earnings of the surviving parent could be supplemented sufficiently to keep the family intact. This is particularly true in the cases where the surviving parent is the mother. It is immediately after her bereavement that the poor widow in her anguish and uncertainty turns to the institution as her only refuge; whereas if she could be properly cared for until the first sharp grief has passed away, she would gradually come to a realization of her responsibilities and be willing to assume them, if assured of the necessary support. There can be no doubt that the breaking-up of many a family could have been prevented if the mother had been subsidized and had been able to give her children the necessities of life. If greater cooperation could be effected between the institution and the benevolent societies, most admirable results would follow. A thorough boarding-out system should first of all consider the possibility of placing children with their own parents, the natural guardians, who have relinquished their proprietary rights through causes that can, in many cases, be readily overcome.

Whether Jewish children can be successfully boarded out with foster parents is still undetermined, notwithstanding the efforts that have been made in past years in this direction by a number of institutions. Your Committee is of the belief that speculation on this topic is idle, since the demonstration of its possibilities or impossibilities is a matter of experiment, and it therefore recommends referring the entire question to the Committee on Home Bureaus for investigation and report.

Regarding children in institutions who have both parents living, your Committee deems it inadvisable to attempt either placing out or boarding out. The efforts of Jewish institutions with such children have always been and should always be directed towards restoring the family to its normal condition at the first opportunity. If this can be enhanced by any system of subsidy or pension, it is worthy of encouragement.

Your Committee realizes that there still remain numbers of children who cannot be cared for by the above means, and for whom the institution is the best possible home. It is axiomatic to state that where the institution is required, the best possible results will be obtained from the cottage plan, through a system of small detached houses, rather than one large building in which all the children are housed. Such a plan is the closest approach to the home that can be attempted. None of the Jewish asylums has as yet attempted such a plan, primarily because Jewish institutions have been more like homes than institutions, and have fostered and perpetuated Jewish family ideals most worthily. This is the main reason why neither boarding out nor placing out has ever been systematically attempted by our Jewish asylums and orphanages.

2. The Problem of Boarding and Placing Out Jewish Dependent Children*

BY LUDWIG B. BERNSTEIN

Assuming that the normal parental home is the best child-caring method, it might be interesting to analyze some of the factors that help to make the parental home the very best and most natural method of taking care of children. So far as I can see, there are among other elements the following five, which we might call the essentials:

1. The affection and tender care given to the child even in the poorest home constitute the sunshine necessary for the natural growth of the child.

2. The frequent expressions of rapture, joy, and encouragement on the part of the parents over the slightest possible manifestation of progress in the child form a second important element, psychologically almost as strong and valuable as the first.

3. The child's contact in school with hundreds of other types of children of similar and different home surroundings; the numerous friendships, comradeships, and rivalries which a normal school life naturally engenders; and in general, the inter-relation of the two great social factors, the home and the public school, are powerful stimuli in the development of the child as a social being.

4. The consciousness on the part of the child that he occupies a distinct place in the family life, together with his observation of the relations of various members of the family with one another and with himself may be considered another important element in the social training of the child.

5. The varied acquaintance with practical problems of life and the knowledge of money values, which the child in the ordinary

* National Conference of Jewish Charities, *Proceedings* (1906) pp. 75-89. Presented at the Fourth Biennial Conference of Jewish Charities, Philadelphia, Pa., May 6-8, 1906.

home acquires as a matter of course; the daily relations of outside life to the home; and the numerous interests, proficiencies and accomplishments which the child in a parental home absorbs without conscious effort are valuable equipment for his future struggle in life.

Using the five essential characteristics of the normal parental home as a criterion by which to measure the relative merits of the various child-caring methods, we have to consider above all that plan which will make it possible to train the dependent child in his own parental home, namely:

1. *The Method of Pensioning Parent or Parents or the Family.* It is needless to argue that the preservation of family life is one of the fundamental concerns of organized society. The first great method of taking care of dependent children is therefore the same as that of taking care of non-dependent children: the natural home.

On theoretical grounds, a system of liberal pensions to prevent the breaking-up of families even temporarily is certainly the most natural, the most advisable, and I would say, the most advanced plan. Caution, of course, must be exercised that the child or the children in a family receiving pension should not be made to feel that they are dependent on or the recipients of charity. The supply to such children, for example, of wearing apparel bearing the distinctive mark of the "Charity Bureau quality" has a positively demoralizing effect. This method of pensioning presupposes first of all adequacy of pensioning; it furthermore takes into consideration supplementary supervision of children in case of sickness or physical incapacity on the part of one or both parents.

Semi-adequate or inadequate pension is an injustice to the children as well as to the parents. Its consequence may not be a normal, but an abnormal home; not a naturally poor home, encouraged by the hope of better days, but a miserable existence marked by unhappiness and by a lack of that individual care and attention which is the foremost characteristic of the normal home.

In the absence of funds adequate to pension a family on a self-respecting basis, it would seem to be much more advisable to relieve temporarily the parent or parents of the care of the children, and to give the struggling father or mother a chance to reach a self-supporting stage, with a view to returning the child to them as speedily as possible.

But whatever may be the just objections to an inadequate pension plan, let us remember that the natural parental home, adequately supported for the purpose of keeping it intact, holds the highest rank among the various methods of taking care of dependent children.

2. *Home of Adoption.* We now pass to the second child-caring program, which preserves practically all the characteristics of the natural parental home, i.e., the free home, or the home of adoption.

At this juncture the question arises as to whether, outside of the natural home, a child is better taken care of in a private home or in an institution. In the chaos of conflicting opinions on this subject, it is necessary to bear in mind the following:

The advocates of the institution plan concentrate their arguments on the contention that a well-managed institution gives the child a superior equipment for life. In support of such an argument they say that the institution offers to its wards, in addition to a sound scholastic and religious education, excellent facilities for social development, together with splendid opportunities for musical and manual training, military drill, athletics, etc. They furthermore claim in favor of the institution that its wards develop a very considerable degree of self-control, owing to the habits of regularity, obedience, and promptness which such children readily acquire in a short time.

On the other hand, the advocates of the home of adoption consider the home influence, the individualism of the child, and the realization of all the elements that enter into the development of the average child in the normal parental home as far more essential factors for the future adjustment of the child and his becoming a useful member of society than band music, military drill and manual training. They consider home life as even more important than the extraordinary advantages of acquiring habits of regularity, promptness, and obedience. Furthermore, they proffer the charge against the prevailing congregate institutions that in a number of instances their alumni, and especially those that spent a very long period in such institutions, have been found to be lacking in initiative, in self-reliance, and in those qualities that made for manhood and womanhood.

Confining ourselves to the problem of full orphans or totally abandoned children, or in other words, of children who are permanently deprived of a home, I may say that by far the weightier arguments are on the side of the home of adoption. Even the most enthusiastic adherent of the institution method will have to agree to the cardinal point, that it is a physical impossibility for the institution to offer that tender care and affection to each individual child that he is anxious to give [and which can be provided in the home]. The moment he admits the impossibility of doing so, he subscribes to the main contention advanced by the advocates of the free home.

Under what conditions is a home of adoption the best child-caring method? It is desirable, first, if the home is good and promising—promising as far as the future of the child is concerned. It is furthermore desirable if the foster parents have no children and are willing to assume the burden of bringing up a very young child. Thirdly, it is desirable only if an agreement is made by which the home can be made subject to frequent inspection before and, to some extent, after the adoption of the child.

On the other hand, the policy of placing children ranging between ten and fifteen years of age into distant homes of adoption, a policy by no means uncommon among non-Jewish child-placing agencies, must be emphatically condemned. In a number of instances it has resulted in ruined careers and in slavery.

Thus it will be seen that the home of adoption is the superior child-caring method only for full orphans and abandoned children up to ten years of age. It is not advisable for orphans of over ten years of age, or for half-orphans and temporarily destitute or dependent children. What is to become of the three classes of children just mentioned? Is it wiser to place them in a boarding home or in an institution?

3. *Boarding Home or Institution?* Using as a basis of judgment the five characteristics of the normal parental home, the enthusiast of the institutional method has again to yield to the superiority of the ideal boarding home, in which it is absolutely possible to obtain every essential characteristic of the natural home. But the difficulty of the whole question lies in this: Are the available boarding homes ideal, and with particular reference to the Jewish problem, are our Jewish boarding homes of such a nature as to make them a powerful rival of the best institutional care that has been devised for children who are temporarily dependent?

The city of Boston and the State of Massachusetts have permanently abandoned their children's homes by introducing a boarding-out system on a large scale. Homer Folks, in chapter XII of his book *The Care of Destitute, Neglected and Dependent Children,* in speaking of the present tendencies, remarks that it is doubtful whether any other states will emulate the example of Massachusetts and of Boston in doing away altogether with "temporary" institutions.

Edward T. Devine, in his excellent book *Principles of Relief,* coolly and impartially discusses the advantages and disadvantages of both methods without passing final judgment as to which is better.

In this connection, you must further consider the fact that the motive in applying for the care of a child in the case of the boarding mother is not quite as pure as that of the childless mother. Even in the good boarding homes, monetary consideration constitutes a more or less potent element, by which I do not mean to say that because of this element the home is necessarily bad. In my experience with Jewish boarding homes for children, I have found that the care and attention given by boarding mothers to a child are certainly out of all proportion to the small compensation given them. Moreover, I may definitely say that in a majority of cases the charitable instinct is at least as strong as the desire for compensation.

From the point of view of the child, it is a fact that certain children will never thrive and prosper in an institution: a certain class of children who are nervous by nature; children who are somewhat ungovernable, so-called mischievous children; some children who are semi-deficient mentally; and children who come from a physically weak ancestry, etc. Even the staunchest friends of the institution plan for temporarily dependent children will have to concede this point.

On the other hand, the enthusiasts of the boarding home, both Jewish and non-Jewish, will have to admit that there are certain children who need the trained skill of the pedagogue rather than the common-sense treatment that the average foster mother is capable of giving, and that the majority of the boarding mothers and fathers have to divide their cares between their own children and the children placed with them. The boarding-home friends will also have to admit reluctantly that the boarding home, as a rule, is not of the same high type as the free home.

Finally, they will have to admit that there are numerous children, the product of Jewish institutional training, who have indeed developed a high type of character and a rare degree of ability; that the Jewish institutions have a higher conception of their educational aims for their wards than some non-Jewish institutions; and that a fair majority of their alumni are certainly successful in life.

Summing up again the theoretical aspect of the question, it must be said that, if ideal boarding homes could be secured in large numbers, irrespective of cost and maintenance, I would consider this method as superior to that of the institution. But, on this point, theory and practical experience do not blend. There are homes, pseudo-homes, and miserable homes.

Until such time as it will be possible to secure a uniformly high standard of boarding homes, as high a type as that of the free home (and I do not say that this is impossible); until such time as the Jewish communities are willing to invest large sums of money to pay liberally for the highest possible class of boarding homes (and I hope that they will do so), the boarding homes will remain confined to the special class of temporarily dependent children referred to above, and the institution will remain the chief child-caring agency, especially if it frees itself of the just criticism and objections.

I refer here to the justified criticism that the congregate institution is carrying out on a similar scale the ancient Greek-Spartan tion is carrying out on a smaller scale the ancient Greek-Spartan ideal of the collective training of youth—an objection which the cottage-home institution has successfully met. The cottage home has also made adequate provision for practical training in economic values, and has made it possible to individualize children on a satisfactory basis.

4. *Scattered Cottage Plan* . . . I would like to mention one more child-caring method which, to my knowledge, has not yet been attempted in this country. It is a plan which combines all the intrinsic merits of the natural-home training without involving the difficulties encountered in finding first-class boarding homes for normally dependent children.

I refer to the plan of establishing scattered cottages with a trained woman, or possibly couples, to keep house in each cottage or flat for only five or six children. Such a mother, or matron, or cottage couple should be given a certain allowance for the economical management of their house or flat, and for the proper training to be given to the children. The supervision of all such cottages or flats could be made central.

I am satisfied that ultimately such a plan, which is theoretically closely akin to the ideal boarding home, might possibly yield better results than an elaborate cottage-home institution. . . .

3. Prevention of Delinquency*

BY JULIAN W. MACK

We must not, in our pride, hide the facts which are brought out daily in the juvenile and police courts. Delinquency is on the increase among our boys; no longer is the Jewish girl a synonym for virtue. This condition brings with it two problems—the care of the delinquent, and prevention of delinquency. . . .

Primarily, the care of these children is in the hands of the State, but frequently delinquent children are committed to private institutions. The facilities that the State afford too often fall short of the needs. The aim of the Juvenile Court—to train and to educate, not to punish and imprison—can be carried out only if the institutions are really schools and not prisons. In most cities it has become necessary, due to the lack of Jewish institutions and the inadequacy of the provisions made by the state, to send our children to institutions under non-Jewish control. New York, through its new Protectory, aims to check this practice. My own view is that a united public opinion should exercise pressure on the public authorities to provide full and complete facilities for all; but until that is done, it may be desirable to maintain a Jewish protectory.[1] Smaller communities in each state might band together and establish a farm school for delinquents, just as years ago the Cleveland Asylum was founded, and is now maintained by a number of cities.

The more important question, however, is not what we shall do to redeem the delinquent, but how shall we check delinquency. Primarily, we must study its causes; we must follow the conditions that produce the lapse. At times they are susceptible to medical

* From "Presidential Address," National Conference of Jewish Charities, *Proceedings* (1906), pp. 24-39; pp. 32-35 quoted.

[1] The creation of a protectory for Jewish delinquent children to prevent their commitment to orphan asylums or to non-Jewish institutions of reform was advocated by Edward Lauterbach at the 1904 Conference; see *Proceedings* (1904) pp. 62-68.

treatment; generally they are home conditions resulting from poverty and death and depriving the child of proper parental care; sometimes, but not very often among the Jews, parental depravity is responsible for the wrongs of the child; and too frequently, the environment of the neighborhood in which the child lives fully accounts for them. . . .

Though the stream of immigration may in time be partially diverted from our large cities, and with improved conditions in Europe be greatly checked, nevertheless we cannot hope radically to relieve the congestion of our so-called ghetto districts. As the prosperity of the people grows and their demands on life increase, there is a natural tendency to seek more comfortable quarters. But newcomers who cannot be persuaded to immigrate elsewhere are ever ready to take their places.

When the physical surroundings so react on the child as to produce delinquency or dependency, the Juvenile Courts can aid by conditioning his return to the home on the removal of the family to another section of the city. Private aid, too, [in the form of] paying higher rentals in better localities for families which give promise of their becoming self-supporting will doubtless accomplish much. But more must be done. We must bring in the good, if we want to drive out the bad.

The boy whose natural fondness for sport and athletics is encouraged in the gymnasium, the boys club, and the athletic field, is easily kept from the gambling dens that infest these regions and ultimately lead to theft and other delinquencies; the young girl who craves beautiful surroundings and who likes to dance is driven from a dingy overcrowded home into the gaudy palaces of vice and shame because of a lack of decent places of amusement.

Technical and trade schools are the most valuable agencies in training the young for successful industrial careers. Settlements at first attract the earnest children who are in small danger of going wrong; but when properly conducted so as to form a center of light and joy, with the workers living in the house and being an integral part of the neighborhood, the settlements can gradually draw in those who are not eager for book learning, but have the natural desire of every healthy young person for pleasure, and stimulate them to higher aims.

In some way, however, proper provision for decent recreation, for the game and the dance, the play and the song, must be made. And in satisfying the cravings of youth we should not neglect the needs of the parents. They, too, want a change from the oft-times dismal home. If they can have a share in their children's joys, perhaps there may be averted that separation in outlook and aspiration, with its loosening of the family ties and weakening of the parental authority, that is now responsible for many of the evils.

In furthering those great preventive movements that are endeavoring to make headway everywhere—the establishment of playgrounds and parks, the betterment of the public schools by the introduction of manual training, ungraded [class]rooms,[2] summer classes, free evening lectures and vacation school—we must join hands with our fellow-citizens.

We can gain much by a knowledge of their methods, particularly in preventive work, while they can perhaps learn from us in the management of institutions and in the federation of organizations.

[2] Special classrooms for slow-learning children, taught outside of the usual educational program of classes from 1 to 12.

IV Social Adjustment—Approaches and Methods

THE growing tide of immigration demanded much more than transportation and emergency or temporary relief measures. An early and major issue was very simply stated: How could America, and especially its then settled Jewish population, ever absorb so large a flood of newcomers, whose culture, traditions, habits, language were all so at variance with the established and accepted American way of doing things? Others were less concerned about the impact of American habits on the newcomer, but were troubled by the problem of the trauma he experienced in adjusting to an alien way of life in industrialized and urbanized America. Both anxieties found expression in many plans to ease the social adjustment of new immigrant families, the parents as well as the youth.

Jewish leadership, and especially the paid workers, early recognized the value of the very rich tapestry of native Jewish organizations which the new immigrants created for themselves in the major cities, and especially on the lower East Side of New York. The listing of neighborhood organizations by Blaustein reveals the native vitality and solidarity of the newcomers. In the opinion of philanthropic leaders of the time, however, most of the activities perpetuated the life from which the people had come; they did little either to ease the adjustment to America or to speed it up.

The Jewish settlement idea, one of the forerunners of the later community center, took early hold. From the start, its creators paid full tribute to borrowings from the general settlement-house movement already established in major cities. This movement's attention to basic problems of the poor in large cities, to social and economic betterment in the slums, to education for self-improvement, were all accepted and copied. However, the general settlements were not much used by the Jewish immigrant, who was suspicious of so foreign a way of behaving and unable to bridge the barriers of language, religion, and custom. The Jewish settlement seemed a logical answer, and early meetings discussed how a Jewish settlement, staffed and supported by Jews, would work wonders among new Jewish families. It was felt that the artificial barriers of culture and religion which generally separate the workers from the needy would thus be eliminated.

At the very least, the Jewish settlement was seen as a place for Jews of many backgrounds to meet without mutual distrust, to learn about each other, and to learn how best to get along in this new America.[1] For others, this new Jewish institution had a much more far-reaching purpose, that of carrying on the task of "Americanizing" the newly arrived youth. Robison, in his paper, takes the middle point of view, praising the work of the Y.M.H.A., with its stress upon American forms of education, sports and related activity, but adding that the aim here, too, is to help the newcomer answer affirmatively, "How can I be both a Jew and an American?"

These approaches are not the only ones. Some of the bitterness of the early struggle over immigrant adjustment can be discerned in Fromenson's harsh attack upon settlements. He blames them for the rise of juvenile delinquency in the urban slums, because they have abandoned the traditional Jewish rootedness and religion and culture which the Jews brought with them in favor of artificial "do-gooding."

The attempts of many groups to deal with these adjustment problems did more than lay the foundation for the modern network of Jewish community centers, with their cultural leisure-time facilities. The Billikopf paper offers a startling modern attempt to

[1] Cf. Moses J. Gries, "Settlement Work Among Jews," National Conference of Jewish Charities, *Proceedings* (1902), pp. 259-270 for the general case for adopting the settlement-house approach.

find a common bridge connecting the traditional forms of Jewish education (the *cheder* or Talmud Torah) with the new settlement-house approach. Each approach is viewed as partial and incomplete, although the great hold which traditional education has on Jewish families is recognized and praised. Nevertheless, an experiment is described whereby the Hebrew school, with its then Orthodox support, was housed in a general community center, with subsequent adjustment of programs by both school and center so that the children were able to benefit from both. This approach is hailed as serving Jew and American alike by overcoming the growing alienation of children from their parents, as the cultures of the two generations began to diverge. This promising effort proved to be only a trial balloon, however; fifty years later the separation of formal and informal Jewish education remains as great as ever.

Finally, Jennie Purvin raises an almost lone voice in 1914 for the use of the public schools as a social center for the poor and needy. Without touching upon the issues of group identity, she argues that voluntary settlements can pioneer, but can never meet the needs of more than a few; the public schools, on the other hand, are available to meet the adjustment and social needs of the great masses. Her paper is especially noteworthy for the reminder that, as early as 1914, the public schools of the core city had been virtually abandoned by the well-to-do families for private schools and left primarily to the use of the city's poor.

1. Preventive Work on the East Side*

BY DAVID BLAUSTEIN

Before speaking of the preventive work on the East Side, I wish to give you an idea of the character of the people of the neighborhood. . . .

* National Conference of Jewish Charities, *Proceedings* (1904), pp. 111-16. The essay is presented in re-written and abbreviated form.

I carried out a census of the lower East Side, which takes in about thirty-two streets, south of Houston Street and east of the Bowery. I tried to ascertain the number of families in each house, the nationality in each house, places of business . . . and the social, religious and educational institutions within this area. Not to tire you with figures, I will simply give you an idea of the character of this square mile. There are 5,107 tenement houses, with 64,268 families. Of these I found that 6,499 persons who work within the neighborhood have 84 different occupations. . . . There are, among 1,069 professional people, 361 teachers or proprietors of Hebrew schools.

In this section of the city there are as many as 306 synagogues. There are 22 churches and a Mission House, which are closed all the time. . . . The neighborhood contains 48 public schools and yet the schools are not large enough to accommodate the children, who can only attend half-time sessions.

As of May 1st, 1903, there were seventy-two entertainment places and literary and social clubs. Among the 306 synagogues, 276 are regular and only 30 are special. The highest seating capacity in any individual synagogue was 1,500, and the lowest 74. The total number of seats in these 306 synagogues is 71,024. It is primarily the men who attend services, and when seats are counted the juniors or young men under sixteen are almost never taken into consideration. The women comprise a very small percentage.

As to the character of these synagogues, only 25 were used for exclusively religious purposes; the rest were used for a variety of purposes during the week: 37 are used as dance halls; 77 serve as shops and factories; 36 are located in the rear of saloons; and 19 are meeting halls and private residences.

It may interest you to learn something about the *cheders*. The *cheders* discussed here do not include the religious schools of the Alliance. There are 307 *cheders*, where 8,616 boys and 361 girls receive instruction. Thus it is apparent that the religious instruction of girls is not considered nearly as essential as that of the boys. The ages of the majority of the pupils extend from eight to fifteen. The teachers work from eight in the morning until nine at night. There are all-day sessions as well as part-time sessions for children who are not yet of school age. The average income of a teacher per month is $80, yet the total amount paid out in this neighborhood for instruction amounts to $10,000 a month; $120,000 a year is paid out in this neighborhood for *cheders*. The *cheders* of this neighborhood are not supported by outsiders, but by the people of the lower East Side.

There are four theaters in this neighborhood, one of which is open Friday, Saturday, and Sunday. On week days, the theaters are used for benefit performances of the societies of the neighborhood. Any society may hire the theater, and there are people who do not attend theater except for such a benefit affair. Counting the four afternoons in the week in the four theaters, sixteen performances a week are possible, given by benevolent and charitable societies, lodges, unions, synagogues, and sometimes private individuals, if they need to raise money. In this way, an average of $1,800 a week is raised from entertainment. Since the theaters are open at least forty weeks a year, perhaps I have underestimated: it may be that $1,000,000 a year is raised by the people of this neighborhood to ameliorate conditions.

After having given you the background of this neighborhood, I wish to say something about what is being done in a more or less organized way by the settlements of the neighborhood and by the Educational Alliance, which particularly helps the Jews of the neighborhood. There are quite a number of settlements here on the lower East side; foremost among them are the University Settlement, the Corning Clark Memorial Building, the Music Settlement and so on. They do not administer charity; they are engaged in preventive work; and this is done in various ways. . . . The settlements are instrumental in starting all kinds of movements for the improvement of the neighborhood; the social centers, the playgrounds and the small parks are the work of the settlements.

The homes of the people are such that it is impossible for them to enjoy a social life at home. They cannot entertain strangers and they cannot meet socially. The settlement is a cheerful and bright place, where they can come together for social purposes. . . .

The children of the neighborhood are very progressive, and this often results in tragic conflicts between parent and child. After six months in this country the parents and the children often no longer understand one another. The parents speak Yiddish, and the children master the English language. The family circle practically ceases to exist. The children look forward too much, and the parents look backward too much; the parents become more conservative, and the children more progressive in their ideas, an inevitable result of the process of evolution. For this reason, the Educational Alliance has religious classes for boys as well as girls. In our two branches we have as many as 3,200 registered students; the girls come three times a week and the boys five times a week. Yet the parents are not satisfied; they want even more religious education for the children. We also conduct certain services and classes for the older people and the younger children, where conservative ideas are taught. We endeavor to reconcile the heart of the parent to the child. . . .

Have we had any results? It is hard to tell. Preventive work cannot be compared to charitable aid, where we can tell how much money is distributed. A settlement house is not like a hospital, where you can point to a patient recovered. We simply sow the seeds.

2. East Side Preventive Work*

BY A. H. FROMENSON

The fault with the preventive work on the East Side is that, for the most part, it is based upon theories and not upon realities. It

* National Conference of Jewish Charities, *Proceedings* (1904), pp. 116-24.

has not found its inspiration in the real needs of the immigrant, but was planned by people who made up their minds in advance that certain things were good things, and therefore should be offered to the people. In other words, instead of responding to a demand, the work has been rather in the nature of furnishing a supply and hoping for a demand.

The consequence of this illogical and unnatural method is a lack of proportionate response to the tremendous energy and the princely fortunes expended in abortive attempts to uplift and regenerate the denizens of the East Side. . . . The various institutions, the settlements and the Educational Alliance may offer bewildering arrays of statistics to prove "results," but such "results," as understood in the realm of social service, prove little or nothing. True, these institutions have their clientele. A certain number of people visit them a certain number of times a year, a month, or a week. Some more, some less. A certain very inconsiderable minority of the great mass of human beings take advantage of the opportunities offered by the Settlements and the Educational Alliance. When all is said and done, however, when every claim made for them by their most enthusiastic admirers and workers is conceded, the fact remains that as far as the overwhelming majority of the East Side residents are concerned, it is as if these institutions did not exist at all. Worse even than that, they are regarded by a very large number with absolute antipathy and by another very large number with mistrust.

Another and perhaps more serious fault of the settlements and kindred institutions is that having come into existence, they proceed at once to antagonize the people, instead of trying to win their sympathies and cooperation. Instead of shaping the work of these institutions in accordance with the real needs and desires of the people, the effort has been to shape the minds of the people in accordance with the theories of those who instituted the work.

The best evidence for this is found in the fact that these institutions have contributed practically next to nothing to the solution of the graver problems. It is true that they have, in some measure, helped to open up park space, and to protect the integrity of the present beneficient tenement-house laws, and in a few other ways aided to secure relief from some of the depressing conditions due to the East Side's congestion. But it is in preventive work of the higher kind, in spreading morality and checking the growth of criminality, that they have failed.

Recent occurrences on the East Side prove this. It is here that these uplifting, regenerating, and preventive institutions have been working with the people, and especially with the youth and children of the East Side, for more than a decade, and yet juvenile criminality has suddenly become rampant.

If the settlements and other such institutions were all that they claim to be, their decade and more of work on the East Side should have shown better results. Calling the police, or soliciting the cooperation of the District Attorney's Office is not the public service to which these institutions were consecrated; to one mind, at least, it is evidence and confession of failure when they are reduced to this extremity.

If this epidemic of juvenile criminality were due to any inherent moral corruption, it would be unjust to criticize the preventive agencies. But the settlement workers freely admit that this is a new and unexpected phase, quite as startling to them as to the whole community. In fact, they had hoped for better results—especially because they had deliberately chosen an area where, it seemed to them, good results would be more easily obtained than, for instance, in Hell's Kitchen. In this, at least, their judgment was sound.

And, beyond a doubt, they would have had these results if they had not made plans without considering the East Side youth. Here lies the explanation, the genesis of the hideous apparition of juvenile criminality on the East Side. Instead of the wishes of the East Side boy being consulted or reckoned with, the boy-fancies, boy-tastes, and boy-instincts being catered to and directed along the lines of least resistance and greatest good, they have expected him to take advantage of classes for the study of Homer and Shakespeare, to con *Plutarch's Lives* and absorb the philosophy of Aurelius and Epictetus, and to play chess, checkers, fishing-pond, and other lady-like games. That the East Side boy is like any other boy, city or country boy, American boy or Russian boy—in short, a virile, healthy animal, with an exuberance of spirits which finds its natural outlet only in physical expression and boyish pastime—has never crossed their minds. The settlements have conspired with the big city to rob the boy of his inalienable right to play: the city by means of ordinances and prohibitions, the settlements by means of sit-up-straight-and-be-good social rooms, literature clubs, civics clubs, basket weaving, and scroll-iron work.

The consequence is the creation of an unhealthy state of mind, a craving for excitement. This craving has, as recently disclosed, too often found gratification in the frequenting of questionable resorts, in falling in with criminals, and finally in the excitement of "getting away with the goods." The majority of the youthful pickpockets, it has been found, have been swayed not so much by the desire for possession, as by the excitement and the exhibition of skill involved in picking the unwary citizen's pocket, in opening a woman's hanging purse and extracting its contents. The privilege of basking in the presence of an adult "Fagin" and accompanying him to some vile burlesque theater is generally the whole of the young criminal's reward.

It is unnecessary to present proof that the East Side is Jewish, nor does it require any long argument to demonstrate that the Jewish institutions are most likely to be most popular on the East Side, and therefore most successful in influencing the people. But that is not a Jewish institution which suddenly grows ashamed of the name "Hebrew Institute" graven over its portals and covers it over with a sign-board bearing the noncommittal phrase: "Educational Alliance." Nor is that a Jewish institution which stands for something "broader" than Judaism—an invertebrate, anemic, condescending, patronizing sentimentalism that is tolerant even of religion. A Jewish institution is one that stands for Jewish ethics and Jewish ideals, that engraves its Jewishness over its door-posts and nails its Jewishness to the flag-staff, and works in the light that comes from Jewish tradition and Jewish history and Jewish inspiration. Perhaps it is not necessary to have a *mezuzah* on every door in the building, or for every male worker to wear a four-cornered undervest with fringes. But Jewish consciousness must pervade the institution, and Jewish thought dominate it.

It is just this lack of Jewishness that has lost for all of the regenerative work on the East Side the full measure of its usefulness. It would not be going too far to say that what good they have accomplished has been offset by the harm they have wrought. Cleavage of the home tie, depreciation, if not outright repudiation, of parental authority, contempt for the religious opinion of elders, the creation of an unbridgeable chasm between parents and children—all this may with perfect propriety be charged against the non-Jewishness of Jewish institutions on the East Side.

It might be urged too, against the settlements, that they attract, in the main, that element which is already predisposed to goodness, and which would in all likelihood remain good without the aid of a single external influence. In fact, many might have been better; for their goodness, blushing unseen, away from the calcium light of exhibition, would have thrived in a more healthy and less vain, self-conscious manner. The goodness of the settlement graduate is a plume which no one else can possess, and therefore the possessor often considers himself better than the average, who have either not had or rejected the settlement training.

What makes the concrete results indicated here the more deplorable is the fact that these are the unwitting, and certainly the unintentioned, results of work undertaken by men and women who are committed to the noblest human ideals, whose striving has the highest aim, and whose labor in the field of social service represents so much sacrifice.

But the settlements exist, and therefore any discussion of their utility is of less importance than a discussion of a means for giving them their highest utility.

It must be borne in mind that the education of Jews has for

centuries past had a spiritual or, better said, a religious foundation. It is this spirituality, this intense religious motif, that has been the Jew's safeguard against moral degeneration. It was the sway of religion over his daily life that disciplined him so well; that made parental authority so strong; and that dominated him in his relations with men. His code of ethics, his moral conceptions, were not abstruse things; they were concretely expressed in his religion. Perhaps to some it will seem that this is not in keeping with progress; certainly it cannot be pleasing to those who would substitute sentimentalism for religion. But the fact remains that the salvation of the Jew in the past was his religion, and that whenever he has been lacking in religion, he has deteriorated.

Nothing in modern conditions justifies the belief that he has arrived at that point where he can do without his religion.

Rcstorc Jcwishncss to thc Jew in the institutions that are meant for his moral uplifting. Do not outrage the sensibilities of the Jew by erecting Christmas trees in the institutions you wish him to visit, and under whose influence you wish him to come. Suspend all activities on Yom Kippur. Show some respect for the things he holds sacrcd; not mcrcly that distinterested respect which the enlightened have for the sacred things of all people, but a keen personal sympathy and accord. Refrain, also, from compromises which are abhorrent to him—such as celebrating both Christmas and Hanukkah, both Good Friday and Yom Kippur. Let the Jewishness of the institutions be positive. Thus, much of the difficulty that besets social, or preventive, work on the East Side of New York, and on all the East Sides of the United States will disappear. The sympathy and cooperation of the people whose sympathy and cooperation is needed most—that is, the people for whom the work is intended—will be won; greater success will attend the labors of the noble men and women who have given their lives to the regeneration of the masses; and, in time, the need for much preventive work will disappear. For I verily believe that not institutions, but the people themselves, are the best preventive agencies when their highest consciousness, civic and religious, is aroused.

3. Advanced Settlement Work*

BY JACOB BILLIKOPF

I am of the belief that the vast majority of Jewish social workers have come to the inevitable conclusion that, unless a Jewish settlement represents the concepts advanced by Mr. Louis Marshall,[1] it has no *raison d'être*. And at a conference of this character, it would be presumptuous to attempt to present in detail the obvious arguments for the conclusion that the Jewish settlement, if true to its ideals, must concern itself with the problems of Judaizing its clientele.

Then, this question arises: What methods should be utilized to "functionalize Jewish conceptions and to promote Jewish tendencies?" What machinery can be best adapted to the fulfillment of our dual obligation—the Americanization of the Jew, and the Judaization of the immigrant? The reply, and it is only partial, is this: The adoption or furtherance on the part of the settlement of a system of Jewish education which, in the words of Dr. S. Benderly, "should be complementary to and harmonious with the public school system"—a system which should be thoroughly modern and based on sound pedagogic principles.

The recognized institution among our people for the training of their children along Jewish lines is the Talmud Torah. As Mr. Louis H. Levin has so admirably pointed out in an editorial in *Jewish Charities:* "The Talmud Torah is the institution intended to conserve those moral teachings which have appealed to the Jewish heart and mind as the best assurance of an honored and honorable life. It is the scheme devised by Jews for making their children into good citizens—the aim, too, of the settlement." And

* In *Jewish Charities,* vol. V, no. 1 (February, 1915), pp. 161-65. Presented at the Eighth Biennial Conference of Jewish Charities, Memphis, Tenn., May 6-8, 1914.

[1] Louis Marshall, distinguished volunteer leader, New York attorney, and President of the American Jewish Committee.

I may add that no other institution is so intimately related to the lives of our immigrant men and women as the Hebrew school.

Now, it matters little to which particular wing of Judaism you and I may belong or what peculiar construction we may place upon Judaism. There is this certainty on which all of us will agree: that inasmuch as this settlement is an agency for adjustment and interpretation; and inasmuch as the group of individuals in our society mostly in need of adjustment is the immigrant group—any attempt to adjust the immigrant to his American environment must start with the fundamental assumption that the shock of this adjustment should be softened to the greatest extent possible. To that end we must begin by preserving those immigrant institutions that correspond to a fundamental need—moral and spiritual—of the newcomer; those institutions which the immigrant is so eager to keep up, even at great material sacrifice.

As already intimated, it is an undeniable fact that there is no institution which has a more vital hold on the people with whom you and I are called upon to deal than the *cheder* or the Talmud Torah. Practically every Jewish family to be found in our respective neighborhoods will continue to provide instruction in Hebrew for its children. And in his anxiety to have his boy attend a Hebrew school, the average father will sacrifice a great many material things rather than deprive his child of the opportunity to attend such a school. It is true that many objections have been and will continue to be raised against the Talmud Torah system. The close confinement to which weary and fatigued children are subjected day after day in unventilated quarters and in the charge of most antiquated pedagogues, at a time when their minds and their bodies should be relieved of the mental and physical strain encountered in the classrooms during the morning hours, is indeed a serious indictment and cannot be dismissed. But the *cheder* and the Talmud Torah are established institutions, and for a variety of causes appeal infinitely more to the immigrant parents than any of the activities which any settlement has yet perfected for the training of their children. Hence it becomes our duty, as social workers, to help devise ways and means whereby there will be afforded to the Jewish children religious instruction of such a character as will meet the demands of the neighborhood and at the same time conserve the vitality and physical energy of the children.

To illustrate my theory, I would like to present an arrangement, existing in our community, which, with slight modifications to suit the varying needs of the different communities, might be adopted in localities the size of Kansas City.

About two years ago the Board of Directors of our Institute, at my urging, extended to the then newly formed Talmud Torah Association the privilege of maintaining in our main Institute and in the branch building, located in another section of the city, such classes as they wished to establish. This was done in recognition of the fact that the Association, handicapped for lack of resources, would have otherwise been compelled to operate its classes in dingy and unhygienic quarters, with the result that the bodies and minds of the little ones would suffer immeasurably. The Association gladly accepted our invitation. . . .

But perhaps the most significant feature connected with the school, the feature which will interest us as social workers, is the system of playground and recreational activity devised for the children by the Institute. Practically every child belongs to a basketball team, a baseball league or a gymnasium class, and as a result we have in the Institute a steady daily clientele of from two hundred to two hundred and fifty children in the charge of capable paid and volunteer physical instructors. I say a "steady clientele," because the attendance in the Hebrew school is as perfect as in the public schools, notwithstanding the absence of truant officers.

In our building, then, the Talmud Torah Association, with the cooperation of the Institute authorities, has succeeded in working out a course of instruction where the number of hours has been reduced considerably; and through the introduction of games and gymnastic exercises, an interest and enthusiasm have been created in the children such as they would not and could not have otherwise possessed. The dangers of physical deterioration resulting from their attending two schools daily have been minimized considerably by virtue of our recreational system, and in spite of the shortening of the hours of instruction, there has been a decided gain in efficiency in their studies.

To further illustrate the powerful hold which the Hebrew school has on our clientele, permit me to cite this incident. The interval which elapsed between the organization of the Hebrew classes in the Institute and in the branch was two months. For purely local reasons the classes were first started on the South Side, with the promise to the people in the immediate neighborhood of the Institute that as soon as the teaching staff was increased, classes would be organized in the main building. Impatient over the delay, several families, at the end of two or three weeks, moved to the south end of the city, where the branch is located; many more would have moved if the opening of the classes in the Institute had been delayed much longer. Almost every day we received inquiries as to when the school would begin, and complaints to the effect that we showed partiality to the people on the South Side. And since then I have often asked myself the question: Would the introduction or the elimination of any other activity in our settlement have created one-hundredth part the anxiety and commotion occasioned by the establishment of Hebrew classes in our Institute? Which is, in a large measure, the test to be applied to the value of the settlement in a neighborhood.

So much for the purely religious or racial reasons behind the maintenance of Hebrew schools, either as separate institutions or in connection with settlements. There is also this fundamental social justification. For many years social workers have talked about the ever-growing chasm between the immigrant parents and their children. Means have been sought to bridge that chasm and various remedies have been suggested. . . .

Perhaps one of the most distinctive advances made in Jewish settlement work in past years is to be found in the Exposition of the Jews of Many Lands, held at the Jewish Settlement in Cincinnati a little over a year ago. At the Exposition there were presented over 400 charts and diagrams covering the political, social, and economic history of the Jews in twenty-seven different countries. Exhibitions of women's handiwork, displays of articles which have constituted and continue to constitute so important a part in ceremonial Judaism, the arrangement of articles from the Bezalel School of Art, the presentation of a pageant illustrating a variety of aspects of Jewish life—all these attracted widespread attention and brought about in Cincinnati a unification of the various Jewish forces as probably no other past event has done. What were the psychological effects of the Exposition? It afforded to the children remarkable evidence of the riches and the treasures to be found in Jewish ceremonial life. It reproduced in sequence the vital facts in Jewish history, thus connecting the past and the present and investing both with meaning and sanctity. In a word, the Exposition had a tremendous educational value. And to Dr. Bogen belongs credit for the conception of the Exposition idea, which, I trust, he will develop at greater length at this Conference. For an exposition such as was held in Cincinnati is not only of incalculable benefit to the children in that it reveals to them the beauty and significance of Jewish life; it is also of vast importance to a certain class of adults, many of whom, from the moment they land on our shores, are brought in contact with a set of influences so out of tune with their previous environment that their natures undergo rapid and strange modifications, with the result that the shock of freedom throws them into a state of religious anarchy. In the words of Anatole Leroy Beaulieu: "To such the Hebrew chantings have no meaning; the symbolism of the ceremonies is lost; their intellects refuse to accept the teachings in which they were brought up." Does it not become our duty, then, to combat, by means of such educational facilities as are contained in the Exposition, the iconoclastic views which the new environment imposes upon them? . . .

In this paper I have brought out merely two or three features which mark a significant advance in settlement work among Jews.

But whether the one or the other program is adopted by this or that settlement. . . . the most distinctive advance which has been made by settlements in the past few years is this: They have begun to lay more and more stress upon the Jewishness in their work, because they realize more than ever that, unless the Jewish values are emphasized, the need for Jewish settlements must cease.

4. The Public School as the Neighborhood Center*

BY JENNIE F. PURVIN

No one will gainsay that the richest possession of a democratic nation is its public school system. Whatever the demarcations of society, in the public school all children meet on a plane of absolute equality. Here rich and poor, high and low, black and white may mingle in such a manner as to eliminate all class distinction, all lines of poverty or prosperity.

In theory, at least, this is true. In practice, it was the state of affairs until recently. Today, however, the conditions of equality among public-school children are vastly altered, due to the fact that the wealthier class of parents have very largely withdrawn their children from the public schools in favor of privately conducted educational institutions. In fact, the public school of today is about the only public institution of which the poorer classes of society have a monopoly; for by refusing to enter their children in the public schools, wealthy parents have turned over to the less fortunate ranks of the populace this "richest possession" of ours.

Aside from the danger attendant upon the fact that a distinction which formerly did not exist has thus voluntarily been made be-

* In *Jewish Charities,* vol. V, no. 1 (June 1915), pp. 274-76.

tween the upper and lower strata of society, there is a great and important question involved affecting present-day school management—namely, how best to accommodate the schools to those who need them most, and use them most.

This issue is not so new, and it has already been well answered in some communities. Formerly, it was thought quite sufficient to teach children between six and sixteen the rudiments of reading, writing, and arithmetic a given number of days in the week and months in the year. Gradually, as educational ideas broadened, manual training was added for the boys, and sewing and cooking were simply taught to the girls, while a kindergarten was added for the little ones under the regular school age.

The great influx of immigrants was met educationally by opening night schools. This department was of real significance, for it was the first attempt to open the schools at hours other than those for the regular-day sessions. We may imagine that it cost the men who made the original change some considerable effort thus to break away from established precedent. The schools were the closed possession of the regular pupils for so many years that to open them after the supper hour for the instruction of older people was a bold step forward.

Yet this work was educational and entirely under the jurisdiction of the Board of Education. What was probably of even greater import, therefore, was the first step toward the creation of a "social center" in the schools. Here was a move not concerned with the three R's, far from the original purpose of the founders of our school system—a move to provide social recreation for the boys and girls who had passed out of the day school into the factory; a move to bring back into the school building and the school life grown-ups who had supposedly long since passed beyond the influence of the school building.

This was indeed a new recognition of the needs of those classes of society which depended upon the day school for the education of their youth, and upon any form of commercialized entertainment which the public offered for the amusement of their adolescent children. Its significance and value are scarcely to be summed up in a few words. For it was the first open recognition of the great principle which is being slowly evolved by modern society: that a civilization which commercializes the working lives of our youth and gives these lives to society for its material benefit must in turn provide legitimate public entertainment for the hours of leisure and relaxation which come after work time.

The social-center movement is in a measure a public acknowledgement of the fact that the home is no longer the center of attraction for our youth. One wonders why! It is partly because there has ceased to be a sympathetic understanding between parents and children; partly because the young folks who fill our factories by day and our cheap amusement places by night have all too soon become wage-earners, and therefore independent of parental authority; partly because in many families, there are no real "homes" in which the evenings can be spent; partly because the call of the street and its unrest is upon us all, high and low; but principally because commercial enterprise has made amusement so cheap, so alluring, and so profuse.

Except for the "movies," this abundance of commercial recreation serves to accentuate the line of separation between parents and children. The dance hall, the bowling alley, the pool-room, the amusement park, all attract the young folks; supervision and regulation in these places are for the most part absent. Constructive play is unthought of. Initiative in sports is entirely cut off. The "movies," to be sure, entice the whole family away together, but at the expense of nerves and good habits.

It is too late, however, to argue that the proper cure for this unfortunate situation is to encourage the home-staying habit. Before one can start upon any such rash crusade, it is necessary to see that every home is made livable, that every family unit is taught to create its own amusements, and that a better understanding is established between parents and offspring than now prevails among the poorer classes.

And before this can be done it will be necessary to begin with the top ranks of society and ask that better, far more modest and simple examples be set. It will be necessary to forbid the show window which creates the desire for fine clothes, which in turn create a demand for occasions upon which they may be displayed. It will be necessary to stop the quick transportation from all parts of the city to the center, to shut off the street lights and disconnect the telephone!

Surely no one asks or desires that this shall be done. Hence we meet the amusement and recreation problem in a far more earnest manner when we start to find the right kind of place to which the entire family can go together for an evening of clean, wholesome, and intelligent play.

This is where the social center in the public school enters. It is the one "people's clubhouse" which stands ready to solve our problem. Without additional expense, save for modest equipment which all newer school buildings possess, entertainment either purely recreational or entirely educational, or both, can here be established for every member of a family in the manner in which that member desires it. Do the older folks wish a lecture on a sober theme? Do the men wish to discuss politics or literature or whatever? Do the women wish to sew or cook? Do the boys wish to play basketball, to debate or sing, or drill for boy scouts or study or read? Do the girls wish to practice folk-dancing? Do the children care to read or play games? Do the boys and girls together wish to study dramatics? Do the young men care to play billiards? Does the entire group prefer an occasional moving-picture exhibit of the right sort? Is there need to take care of the babies while the mothers are busy elsewhere? All this, and more, too, can be done at one time in the schoolhouse. And here, if anywhere, neighborhood groups can offer competition to the objectionable dance hall by conducting dances in the school hall.

If the boards of education will but provide an official organizer for each school, the neighborhood can be helped to help itself—as has been successfully done in Chicago, Brooklyn, and New York. And this would redeem the amusement situation sufficiently to put it once again on a constructive basis. The passive habit of having our amusements thrust at us is robbing our young folks of the only opportunity left to most of them to show any initiative whatever. Work life is so much a matter of formula and repetition of tasks that if originality and spontaneity are taken from the leisure hour, there is no play left for the imagination.

Hence the great need for this clubhouse of the people, where, with intelligent guidance, young and old may again create their own recreation. What the settlement has been able to do for the few, the school must do for the many. No better use could be made of its classic enclosures. Room for the boy and girl who because of poverty have been forced to leave the day school at the early age of fourteen! Room for the young man and young woman who in the period of adolescence seek a proper outlet for their nervous energies! Room for the tired father and mother who, after a long day's labor, search for modest recreation and diversion! Room for the older men and women who ask for a place in which to spend a quiet hour cheerfully, comfortably, and peacefully. Room for the enthusiastic, energetic people of all ages who demand only lively entertainment of any kind, safe from the seducing power of drink and disorder! And room, too, for the more sober portion of our neighborhoods who would gather in friendly council and debate and make efforts to impress their fellow-citizens with the worth of good citizenship!

V Responsibilities of Wartime Jewish Agencies

BY the outbreak of World War I, not only had the Jewish social work scene become well established, but Jewish community and social-work life had become so complex that the Conference was no longer able to act as both a forum and a planning center for tackling major problems. More and more, the Conference was given over to reporting on current developments. Conference meetings were disrupted by the war, so that much of the record of this period appears only in brief editorials and news items in *Jewish Charities*. The evolution of the Jewish Welfare Board and the American Jewish Joint Distribution Committee are highpoints of the time, but their influence was only sketchily reported in the Conference work.

The problem of providing services to Jewish soldiers was an unprecedented one for the American Jewish community. We find that Jewish groups were eager to be full partners in the general war effort, and while there is no disposition on their part to discourage the use by Jewish soldiers of facilities and services offered by the YMCA and the Red Cross, they have sufficient self-confidence to want to contribute to the war effort as a Jewish community.

Similarly, the American Jewish community was, by 1918, ready to face its obligations to European Jewry within the context of general plans to reconstruct the whole of Europe following the war. American Jewry had succeeded in absorbing refugees from

Europe; it was now confident enough to go to Europe to help Jewish brethren in their own countries.

Local Jewish life was now firmly set upon the road of community development; it was also ready to undertake a national community effort for a sustained period of time. The American Jewish Joint Distribution Committee launched a national program based upon its own observers' analysis of needs abroad, and upon a national campaign for funds. These efforts significantly widened the participation of Jews in American Jewish social work; now all classes were joined in some contribution to a common cause of Jewish as well as national importance. These new givers and their collective energy helped break down many of the "national origin" and religious rivalries which divided Jews locally. The overseas program shared one feature with the Industrial Removal Office of the early 1900's—breadth of scope. It included plans for repatriation, re-establishment of family homes, and industrial as well as individual rehabilitation. In scope and aim and organization, Jewish community life in America can be said to have taken on its modern form by the end of World War I.

1. The Jewish Soldiers (Editorial)*

The Jewish Board for Welfare Work in the United States Army and Navy is undertaking . . . to raise from the Jews of this country $1,000,000 for the activities they have planned. [In view of the fact that] the Jews have responded so nobly to War Relief Charities, Red Cross Funds, and YMCA work there should be little difficulty in securing such a relatively small amount. The character of the men directing the movement—Jacob H. Schiff, head of the money campaign; Jacob Billikopf, chairman of publicity; and Harry Cutler, chairman of the entire board—compels attention to

* *Jewish Charities,* vol. VIII, no. 7 (November, 1917), p. 135.

the campaign in addition to the necessity of the work contemplated. The Board has the entire cooperation of the army and navy officials. . . .

The plan of the Board contemplates specific work in the field and base hospitals. Arrangements will have to be made with Jewish communities near cantonments so that Jewish soldiers on leave can consider them home for the time being. There must be homes where Jewish soldiers can receive hospitality at the hands of their own. In this way there will be precluded a great deal of the discontent and feelings of "aloneness" which arise from being cut off suddenly from all of one's familiar connections. There will be cases where mediation between officers and men will be necessary to remove or interpret slight complaints. Religious services on Friday evenings and on holidays must be provided.

Withal, this plan is based upon the most cordial cooperation with existing [non-Jewish] agencies, so that our Jewish boys will not find themselves set apart from the general camp life. The fact that a small amount of money is being asked for such work is due to the most cordial cooperation with nearby synagogues, Jewish social clubs, and communal buildings. Thus the Jewish soldiers will receive the same opportunities for practicing their own religion as are accorded to others not of our faith.

2. Reconstruction*

BY BORIS D. BOGEN

The problem of reconstruction in Europe is one that calls upon the best efforts of the American people for its solution; the shattered civilian populations, the desolated cities, and the chaotic economic situation demand a gigantic feat of organization, administration, and relief. This work will touch all peoples alike; the war

* *Jewish Charities,* vol. IX, no. 7 (November, 1918) pp. 127-28.

has brought its burden of suffering, famine and misery upon all, with no distinction as to race, religion or nationality; and so the task of reconstruction, to be complete, must also reach all peoples. With the realization of the immensity of this problem and the fine spirit of brotherhood in which it is being approached, the question arises as to whether in the reconstruction program there is room for specific Jewish activities, specific Jewish funds, and specific Jewish organization. Could not the American Jews contribute their share towards the general reconstruction funds, and could not the Jews of the war countries receive their share of benefit from the reconstruction work in common with the other peoples of stricken Europe? If there is no place for the specific Jewish organization in reconstruction, then assuredly such effort should receive little encouragement from the Jews in the United States. If, on the other hand, there not only is room for such specific effort, but there is actual need for it, then it is the solemn duty and privilege of every American Jew to share in the task of retrieving the lives of his people in Europe, as a definite part of the general reconstruction program.

The peculiar position of the Jews in the war countries need not be described here; it is too well-known to need repetition. Socially, the Jews were part of definite entities or communities, outside of which, because of age-old tradition and public usage, it was difficult for them to exist. In small villages, or in the large cities, the Jewish community life, precariously as it may have been balanced, was their [basic form of organization]. With the expulsion of entire communities, the separation of families, and the disintegration of social relationships, the social ties and cohesion of the Jews [have been seriously threatened and in many cases completely] shattered; the restoration of normal existence, amid the national intensities developed through the war, is a definite and delicate problem, vital to the future of European Jewry and peculiar to the Jews alone. Politically, the restrictions and inhibitions that surrounded the Jews before the war may have been intensified or lessened because of the political consciousness aroused through the war. Where the former is the case, it is evident that careful adjustments will have to be made. Where greater tolerance and liberties have developed, the task of adjustment of the fortunate peoples to their new freedom will be a vital one to the future existence of the Jews in those countries. Economically, the Jews have always held a difficult position in European life. Because of political and social conditions, and the historic development of the Jews in the industrial system, trade and the dealings of trade have been their particular portion. And because of this development, and such religious inhibitions as the Sabbath day and other observance, the Jew in trade had established a definite life and routine, industrial habits and economic customs. With the loss of their capital, be it a small margin or a sizable portion, their means of livelihood were destroyed. The shops and stores, the stalls, the trading posts, have been swept away in the maelstrom of the war. Practical industrial rehabilitation in the skilled trades, in farming, and in the productive industries which Europe will now so greatly need will avail the Jews little, for a time at least, until readjustment is made possible; here the peasant and industrial populations of Europe have the advantage. The economic reconstruction of the Jew is a separate problem, involving in the first place the peculiar economic setting of the Jews in European industrial life, and the delicate task of readjustment to their new economic conditions.

In addition to the political, social, and economic aspects of the problem of reconstruction among the Jews, there is the old problem of specific Jewish attitude, case treatment, language differences, and the natural yearning to be dealt with by their own people.

Assuming that there is a specific Jewish problem in relation to reconstruction work in Europe, the question arises as to whether such activity can be carried on without conflicting or interfering with the general program, and without creating the feeling that we Jews are too anxious to "walk by ourselves." In answer to this question it is only necessary to point to the effective manner in which the work of Jewish War Relief was carried on with the approval and cooperation of the United States Government, and the general feeling of appreciation and respect towards it on the part of the country at large. The recognition on the part of the United States Government and the other existing national war work agencies of the place and effectiveness of the Jewish Welfare Board, and of the definite part that it is taking in the entire war work program, is convincing proof that there are occasions when the Jew, working for the Jew, hand in hand with the great unified force of national activity, can most effectively do his share in the broad, humanitarian movements developed to meet the suffering, want, and the urgent human problems that the war has brought upon us.

There is no doubt that all efforts looking towards reconstruction must be made part of a unified, coherent program, fitting into the large general plan, and avoiding duplication, waste, and conflict of interests. It is important therefore that the Reconstruction Program of the Red Cross, of the Government, and of agencies working with it must be carefully studied; the entire plan must be thought through; and when it has been definitely established, the place and nature of the Jewish activities must be so determined as to be a vital and coordinated part of the system.

In the meantime, no efforts must be spared to secure as quickly as possible as much information as is available concerning the needs, problems, and general situation of the Jews in the various European countries. When the time comes to act, there must be at hand a definite foundation of knowledge of existing conditions on which to act.

Sending Jewish social workers into the European lands to study the situation as especially related to the Jews, and to report on what might be done is the one important step before the Jews of America at the present moment. With its skilled representatives in the field, and with constant and earnest effort to share in the big task that America has set for itself, American Jewry will be in a position to best serve the interests of humanity in the task of reconstruction.

3. The Ten-Million-Dollar Campaign*

BY JACOB BILLIKOPF

I have been asked by a few of the delegates to say a word or two about the ten-million-dollar war-relief campaign which we conducted during the past year, and I shall try to point out as briefly as possible some of the essential features in that campaign. . . .

The greatest single factor contributing to the success of the Ten-Million-Dollar Drive was Dr. Frankel's suggestion that a leading Jewish citizen should contribute one-million dollars, provided that an addition ten-million dollars was raised from the country at large. It was Mr. Rosenwald's pledge to give that sum that made the success of the drive possible.

Between April 17, 1917, and June 1, 1917, we contacted about 1,419 communities. I venture to say that there is not a city in America where there is a single Jewish inhabitant in which, at one time or another, we have not made an appeal. . . . A large number of individuals with good ratings were approached and asked to become chairmen of the Jewish War Relief Committee in their own towns.

Between April 15, 1917 and June 1, 1917, we had raised practically six and one-half million dollars throughout the country, more than had been raised during the two previous prosperous years. We raised that amount in spite of the many other campaigns, such as participation in the war, Red Cross, YMCA, Liberty Bond, and a number of others; people contacted us constantly demanding to know whether the money was being transmitted abroad. In a great many towns we succeeded in doubling, tripling and quadrupling the amount raised in the previous two years. Our objective was to raise in each town at least 25 per cent more than we had collected in the previous two years.

* From "Campaign Methods," *Jewish Charities*, vol. IX, no. 11 (March, 1919), section two. Presented to the Annual Meeting of the National Conference of Jewish Charities, Kansas City, Mo., May 12-15, 1918.

On December 3rd we started the campaign in New York City; during the two weeks between the 3rd and the 16th, the sum of $2,000,000 had been pledged. By January 1st, 1918, we had exceeded our ten-million dollar quota by a nice margin, in addition to having raised a million dollars for the Jewish Welfare Board.

When the War Relief Campaign started in New York, the Federation for the Support of Jewish Philanthropies was also planning a campaign. It was feared that the postponement of its campaign might result in a diminution of interest in the Federation cause; that so much money would have to be secured from the people that it would be difficult to collect more; that the captains and lieutenants would be completely exhausted; and that it would be difficult to put over the Federation campaign. Yet, what was actually the case?

The result was this: No sooner was the War Relief Campaign over, than a great many of the same captains and the same lieutenants, only with a much improved and perfected technique, under the direction of Mr. Goldwasser,[1] threw themselves heart and soul into the Federation campaign. About sixty-four to sixty-five thousand new members were added to the Federation, a number much larger than they had ever anticipated getting.

To me the most significant feature of the campaign was not in the fact that we raised ten-million dollars for the War Relief Sufferers—vitally important as that is—but in its spiritual by-product. New reservoirs of generosity opened, and new charitable resources were developed which were unknown up to that time. People never before in the habit of giving and sacrificing to give found it a natural thing to do in this campaign. Another worthwhile result of the campaign was the coming together of all types, classes and kinds of Jews on a common platform—ten million for war relief.

[1] I. Edwin Goldwasser, Director of the New York Federation of Jewish Philanthropies.

VI Toward Intergroup Cooperation and Community Organization

THE conditions of Jewish life in America in 1919 required a fresh approach to community organization, such a solution having been hinted at as early as 1900. At the beginning of the period, emphasis was upon confederation, but mainly for charitable giving, for the consolidation of relief activities. The reasons for cooperation, taken for granted in 1960, were offered as new ideas in 1900—duplication in fund-raising and in appeals; waste of time and money; and well-meaning misdirection in the use of funds.

Efforts to organize affairs more effectively were already then hampered by the rapid specialization which is also a characteristic of the 1960's. However, the early thinking came up against the difficulty of conceiving any form of organization which did not involve administrative control. Thus in 1900 a scheme for joint fund-raising to be controlled by contributors could be advanced but its relationship to welfare programs could not be clearly conceived. By 1916 Waldman recognized that the character and structure of Jewish life had been revolutionized in the preceding decade. Relationships within the Jewish population seemed to have become more complex. A gradualist approach to organizing this newly complex community was outlined, including: partial steps through a national Bureau of Social Research; acceptance of several levels for Jewish association, including the economic, individual, and ideological; and the recognition of Jewish needs apart from charity, which require a total community effort. However, the call for some form of consolidation in community life, without domination by any one group, remained vague and diffused, lacking a means for translating the goal into a working reality.

1. Federation or Consolidation of Jewish Charities*

BY MORRIS LOEB

It has been the boast of our race that we care for the needy and unfortunate from the cradle to the grave. At first, in this country, sporadic cases of distress were relieved privately, or perhaps by congregational effort. But, as the Jewish population increased and many such cases appeared, institutions arose for the shelter of the orphan, the healing of the sick, and the housing of the aged, which are frequently a source of pride, not only to their management but to the whole community which supports them. . . .[1]

Admitting that, with a few exceptions, all such societies that we might enumerate in New York, for instance, are doing necessary or desirable work, we must all recognize some of the evils that a multiplicity of organizations entails. The bad results which I believe arise from too great an individualization of charities are threefold: waste in money, misdirection of energy, and deterioration of the communal spirit. . . .

* From National Conference of Jewish Charities, *Proceedings* (1900), pp. 35-44. Presented at the First National Conference of Jewish Charities, Chicago, Ill., June 11-13, 1900.

[1] Congregational assistance was the rule until the first quarter of the nineteenth century, and independent charitable associations thereafter, while hospitals and orphan asylums began to be organized in the 40's and 50's, and homes for the aged were a post-Civil War development. Individual philanthropy has always been a very minor component of American Jewish social welfare. See Alfred J. Kutzik, "The Social Basis of American-Jewish Philanthropy," unpublished doctoral dissertation, Brandeis University, 1965.

In 1897, at an informal meeting of gentlemen interested in Jewish philanthropy, I read the results of an investigation made by a small committee of enthusiasts on confederation. We had collated the membership lists of the twelve largest Jewish institutions of New York, all those that received at least $10,000 yearly from voluntary contributions: four hospitals, two orphan asylums, one home for the aged, four educational institutions, and the United Hebrew Charities. In these lists appeared 20,704 subscriptions made by 10,282 contributors, who might be said to represent the number of Jews who interested themselves in the truly communal charities. I believe the total amount of the direct contribution did not exceed $350,000, of which two-thirds, say $230,000, were contributed by 209 individuals, leaving the other $120,000 to the credit of 10,000 supporters; of these, over 6,000 gave to but one, and 1,500 to but two institutions apiece. It rather startled us to find that the Jewish community in New York contained less than 3,000 persons who contributed more than the cost of 100 good cigars, or an evening at the opera, to our great benevolent institutions; but these were the facts. . . .

[Concerning the administration of these institutions], the attention given at board meetings to questions of ways and means paralyzes the activity of the management proper; the places on the board for noncanvassing members are so few that but a handful can find time to attend to committee work; and grave questions of internal policy must be decided in a few minutes upon the report of one or two members, who alone have any familiarity with the conditions. But all this is internal and personal. In the mutual rivalry for members, institutions disregard each other's policies and tread upon each other's grounds; there is a constant overlapping of work through lack of systematic cooperation, or because one institution refuses to surrender to another work which the second is better equipped to accomplish. At times, again, necessary but distasteful work is not done because no existing society is willing to take up the burden. Useful societies languish for lack of proper support; useless ones are founded, and if a voice is raised in opposition by some charity worker best qualified to judge of the circumstances, he is accused of jealousy, of spite, of fearing competition. . . .

As a remedy for the evils, material and moral, which I have sought to recall to you, two methods present themselves: (1) consolidation, or (2) federation of the existing Jewish charitable societies in a single city. Both plans have their advocates, and both are being tried more or less thoroughly, here and elsewhere. While I consider complete consolidation preferable to complete individualization, it appears to me that difficulties are introduced that are likely to imperil its success. . . . The chief objection to complete consolidation arises when we consider the probable relation of such an amalgamated society to the general community. It would be inevitable that the directorate would become somewhat autocratic, somewhat opinionated, somewhat self-satisfied. Healthy criticism from outside sources would become more difficult; dissatisfaction could only make itself felt in a falling off of the revenues for the entire system. It would be difficult to persuade a large corporation, proverbially ultraconservative, to take up new lines of work, to venture upon new philanthropic experiments. If an independent organization were formed for such a purpose, it would either be crowded out or, if it succeeded, it would gradually bring back the old state of individualization. Furthermore, if a new but useless or vicious scheme [were brought before the organization,] the consolidated board would be virtually powerless, since it would be compelled to express a single biased opinion if it sought to cause its condemnation; whereas, even now, the consensus of a number of independent boards is sometimes found to be efficacious in suppressing unwise or harmful movements.

To secure freedom of movement in all essentials, coupled with a unity of purpose and concentration of effort whenever needed, and healthful supervision without arbitrary domination, our charities should follow the example of our country; they should adopt a system of federation with sufficient elasticity to meet the wants of the large as well as the small organizations. No organization should be called upon to surrender its charter or its property; in fact, as an inducement for all organizations to join the federation without hesitation, it should be clearly stipulated that any member may withdraw if dissatisfied with the arrangement after giving reasonable notice, without forfeit of any kind. This, I believe, is generally known as the Liverpool plan, since it either originated in that English city or has been most successfully tried there.

As modified to suit the wants of an American Jewish community, this plan might advantageously take the following form. The various cooperating societies, whether incorporated or not, would retain their respective entities, no attempt being made to induce them to surrender their property or their individual subscribers, form of management, etc. They would agree, however, to place the task of the solicitation of funds from the Jewish public into the hands of a general committee, say of fifty or one hundred, chosen perhaps for the larger part from among their own directors. This committee would publish annually a report stating briefly the purposes and methods of the constituent societies, their financial condition, etc., and ending with a list of all the subscribers and the amounts of their respective donations. The committee would solicit, either by circular or through personal appeal, the contribution of an aggregate sum sufficient for the regular annual expenses of all the constituent societies. The subscribers would be asked to make annual, semi-annual, or quarterly payments to a central treasurer, but the subscription blanks would be so worded that the donation might indicate to what extent each particular charity was to benefit; while the subscriber could, if he desired, put a part or the whole of his subscription into the hands of the central committee for appropriate distribution.

This central committee would be a small body of men especially chosen for such a job because of their broad acquaintance with the needs of our institutions, and preferably containing some members not actively interested in any one particular society. It would be called upon to supervise the work of the general committee and to see to the proper distribution of the funds collected through it. The designated contributions would of course be beyond its control; but, assuming that the amount of undesignated contributions would be considerable, the Central Committee would be called upon to apportion them. And herein would lie its most important and delicate function: for the fund should be distributed according to the amount of legitimate deficit appearing in the annual budget of the various societies, after the designated contributions would be distributed. By submitting their accounts to the criticism of this disinterested central committee, the various societies would give their subscribers the best possible guarantee of the economy and efficiency of their management. It often happens that, with the best intentions in the world, one society does too much, another too little. A wise and tactful central committee could do much toward procuring a proper balance in these and other respects. Societies which disregarded the rights of others, showed gross internal mismanagement, or in other respects seemed undesirable, could be dropped by this committee; on the other hand, it might admit new societies with the consent of the general committee. . . .

2. Cooperation Between All Groups in A Community*

BY MORRIS D. WALDMAN

I

In the discussion of this topic we must at the outset assume that there is valid reason for the existence of distinctly Jewish communities wherever a *minyan* (at least ten adult Jews) dwell in one place, because their interests in some respects are distinct from the

* From *Jewish Charities,* vol. VII, no. 5 (Sept. 1916), pp. 92-99. Presented at the Ninth Biennial Meeting of the National Conference of Jewish Charities, Indianapolis, Ind., May 7, 1916.

interests of other people living in the same place. These special interests may be religious, educational, and philanthropic; never political.

In religious matters and in philanthropic affairs, the Jews have followed distinct lines, quite like other religious and racial elements in the population. But in these fields they have not been united; in fact, there have been such sharp divisions as to make the word "community," used as a descriptive term for their organized charities, an inaccurate term if not an actual misnomer.

The reason for these divisions are to be traced ultimately to the fact that the Jews of America, though ethnologically one race, come from many different countries of the globe and naturally possess differences of traditions, customs, theologies, language, culture, and even physique. If we add to these differences in economic condition, perhaps the most vital of all factors, and the differences in the dates of their settlement in this country, we will not wonder at the lack of unity and homogeneity that obtains among them.

Had the influx of Jews into this country from Western and Eastern Europe occurred at the same time, the difficulties in promoting a community of thought and action would have been very much less in spite of the differences obtaining between these two groups. It has been customary for the early settler to regard the later arrival as an inferior. The tendency of the one-year immigrant to regard his fellow-townsman, who has just arrived, as a "greenhorn," an inferior being, has been so common as to prove a subject for humorous treatment by Yiddish writers and playwrights.

The tendency, therefore, on the part of the earlier German Jewish settlers to look askance at the later Russian Jewish immigrants was not to be wondered at, especially since Yiddish, the language which the newcomer spoke, appeared to them to be a badly lacerated tongue. In addition, their uncouth appearance, their ancient ritualism, and their poverty combined to stamp them, in the eyes of the older, more comfortably situated and more polished coreligionists, as of an inferior caste.

Then, too, the two main points of contact between the two elements were such as to provoke friction. The first was intimate industrial contact. In the main the older settlers, already firmly established and prosperous, were largely of the employing class—merchants and manufacturers. The newcomers, who arrived here penniless, were happy to secure employment in their establishments. The antagonism generally obtaining between labor and capital could only serve to intensify the already existing dislike. Where the employee, whether through shrewdness or self-denial and resourcefulness, became a business competitor, the older immigrant became resentful and the notion of caste grew stronger.

The second point of contact was, unfortunately, the charitable organization. As soon as Russian Jewish immigration began, the Jews of this country organized and raised funds to help the newcomers. The spirit which actuated them forms one of the brightest pages in the history of Jewish philanthropy in this country. The help they rendered was both intelligent and generous, testifying to the good-heartedness and liberality of the "German" Jews. But contact with the dependent and poverty-stricken elements of any people is not conducive to respect for them. The erroneous and deplorable though natural impression gained ground even among the best men and women that these applicants for relief were typical of all the immigrants from Eastern Europe. There was quickly established between the two elements the unfortunate relationship of benefactor and beneficiary, which was made still more difficult by unsympathetic treatment on the part of untrained and ill-paid charity clerks and even ignorant volunteer workers on the one hand, and on the other hand extreme sensitiveness and emotionalism on the part of those who sought aid.

Under these circumstances it was but natural, as the newcomers became more firmly established, for them to organize their own mutual-aid societies and even their own charitable organizations. Though they respected the "German" Jew's capacity for organization, they were not in sympathy with the business methods in vogue in their charities. Furthermore, they were not invited in any way to take substantial part in the work of the older philanthropic agencies; when they felt the call for social service, therefore, they organized their own machinery.

The result is that there have developed in every community of any considerable size charitable organizations of varied character, which have frequently duplicated the work of older organizations and have followed policies and methods not approved by these organizations. The aloofness on the part of many well-to-do Russian Jews from the older charitable organizations has moreover tended to give those supporting them the impression that the former are niggardly and lacking in a sense of communal responsibility.

Then again, world currents in Jewish life have moved the newer elements of the people profoundly, whereas the older elements have been quite indifferent and sometimes antagonistic. The Zionist movement, regardless of what our views may be with respect to its final purpose, must be conceded to be a remarkable renaissance of Jewish racial self-respect and dignity. It has largely been viewed with disapproval and distrust and even apprehension by the older settlers, who, basking in the sunshine of American liberty of conscience and action, have feared its effects upon our non-Jewish neighbors and fellow-citizens. Socialism, which had gained many adherents among the newcomers of the wage-earning and professional classes, is another world current which has disturbed the placidity of the bourgeois life-stream of the older inhabitants, who have confused and confounded it with anarchism and regard it as a grave danger to their comfort.

Thus these conservative Jews, who had by their words and deeds striven hard to vindicate their reputation as law-abiding and patriotic Americans, were placed in the position of apologizing to their equally conservative and patriotic non-Jewish fellow-citizens for the disagreeable and to them questionable theories and practices of their co-religionists.

Now that the Eastern European immigrants have become numerically predominant and many of them prosperous, they desire participation in the larger affairs of Jewish life. Some of them have become impatient with the present communal leadership and with what they consider undemocratic methods employed by that leadership. They are motivated by a strong desire to have an equal voice in the selection of the leadership. The European war and the uncertainties of its outcome have afforded them an opportunity of arousing nationwide interest in and sympathy for their plans to establish a Congress, in the face of opposition on the part of those who heretofore have been the spokesmen and leaders of American Jewry. This movement has unhappily sharply accentuated the dissatisfaction arising out of the many differences mentioned above, and has made increasingly difficult, for the time being at any rate, the task of those who have advocated and labored for a united Jewry. The issues have been somewhat confused. There are essentially two issues—one of general policy with regard to the political situation of Jews in foreign countries, the other a question of the organization of the Jewish people of America. If the second issue can be satisfactorily settled, the first will prove less difficult. . . .

That it is desirable for the common good to secure unity of interest and of purpose among these various groups is a premise that we all, I take it, are prepared to establish. In order to do this, we must at the very beginning emphasize as strongly as possible that a union cannot be brought about unless it is predicated upon the basic principle of mutual understanding and mutual respect. Because this principle has not been uniformly recognized but has indeed been frequently violated, these differences have in some respects not only been obliterated but accentuated.

II

In considering this subject, it would be well to take into account the organization problems of local communities, on the one hand, and of the national community on the other.

In a survey of a dozen of the larger communities of the interior recently made, I found many different kinds, ranging from the very loosely coordinated to the closely united community. There was not one completely organized community among them. Where solidarity or cohesiveness was conspicuous, it obtained chiefly with regard to one aspect of Jewish community life—that is, with respect to its philanthropic interests. Indeed, this phase of communal activity apparently has been the be-all and end-all of community planning and articulation. Few even of the most active leaders in these communities have had more than a philanthropic perspective. The concept "federation of charities" has been to them the final word and ultimate idea defining community life. The religious problems, if they have not been of negligible interest, have been considered largely of a private character, circumscribed at best by the walls of the synagogue to which the people happened to belong. The industrial problems have not been considered a legitimate concern of the community except insofar as they have resulted in dependency, when they became a situation with which the charities had to deal. The education of the children and the youth of the community has likewise been ignored as a community problem; like the religious affairs, it has been left to parents, except in those few instances where children are inmates of institutions supported by the community. There are but meager facilities for Jewish education afforded in the social centers supported by the community. Where from time to time the sentiment of the community on other than philanthropic subjects has been expressed, it has been voiced not authoritatively but by an individual or individuals who, by reason of prominence of ability, were called upon or themselves offered to do so. In the smaller communities, this has usually been a satisfactory method. In the larger communities it has not been so satisfactory, and has sometimes proved embarrassing.

In order to develop a rich and comprehensive community life, we must enlarge our vision and look beyond the philanthropic boundaries. We must understand that fortunately, after all, only a very small proportion of our people are in need of charitable aid, but that a larger proportion need aid of a different kind which they can only properly procure by a union of forces *of which they themselves should form an important part.* They must be afforded reasonable industrial opportunities and be protected against industrial exploitation; they must be given educational facilities where they are not provided by the government; they must be protected against all disintegrating forces which surround them and threaten their physical and spiritual well-being by being furnished with wholesome diversion and religious and ethical training, and free scope to conserve and express the culture which they possess as a heritage from the past. They should be encouraged to organize their own activities and to develop them, be they along industrial or social or religious lines, even if the character of such organizations may not be precisely the kind we would create for them. Must they unite into labor organizations for their protection? Then let them; indeed, help them, because the more strongly they are organized the more responsible and responsive they will be to public sentiment. Do they desire to form mutual-aid societies? Let them; indeed, encourage them in every way, for there is no more potent protection against economic disaster and no more effective group discipline than this form of organization. Do they desire to worship God in the same way as their fathers and adhere to their ritual observances and train their children in the same conservative way? Let them, and aid them, even though we may not ourselves observe these forms of worship or educate our children by their curriculum; for there is no surer means to promote good citizenship, respect for law and order and civic responsibility. . . .

[The *kehillah*] has not as yet succeeded in becoming the central authority or the delegated mouthpiece of community sentiment. This it can only become when all the elements and groups join together. It has not yet acquired that position where it can prevent ill-considered deeds and words of irresponsible individuals who presume to speak in the community's name or on behalf of any section of it. But it has attained sufficient prestige to discourage, here and there, injudicious communal activities and to hamper their development. Believing thoroughly in the value of encouraging initiative on the part of all groups for communal work, it has only rarely raised its voice in public protest against irresponsible and unwise movements, preferring to render friendly advice and to direct them into proper and useful channels.

III

Granting then, if we will, the soundness of the principles underlying community cooperation and organization here postulated, we come to a consideration of the national community problem. Here we are also beset with many difficulties. If our local communities were logically and effectively organized on every side, a national union of forces would simply mean a union of local communities. A democratic national federation would be a comparatively simple problem. As I stated in the beginning, there has been much dissatisfaction expressed with the leadership which now obtains in matters affecting our people throughout the country, the way in which this leadership has developed, and some of the methods employed in its exercise. The proposed Jewish Congress is in some measure a protest against it. Though unquestionably this movement for a Congress has not the support of the majority of the important groups, and its leadership is itself not by any means free from just criticism, it indicates that the time has come for the establishment of a unified national organization, analagous to the local community, which must secure its authority to speak from the Jewish people throughout the land. To effect such an organization is no easy task. It is a problem of creative statesmanship which cannot be solved merely by popular clamor and vituperative criticism. The American Jewish Committee was not organized to deal with all Jewish problems arising in this country, but only to prevent the infraction of civic and religious rights of Jews, to secure for them equality of economic, social, and educational opportunity, and to raise and administer relief funds in case of calamities. Of late, however, by virtue of the influence of its membership, it has found itself in a position of responsibility which it had not anticipated, and for which it was not organized. The character of its organization should be changed to meet these newly realized responsibilities. . . . The American Jewish Committee has, up to this time, been the nearest approach to an authoritative body, consisting of men who, by lives of conspicuous devotion to the communal interests of our people, have earned the right to leadership. Nevertheless, the method of their selection has been repugnant even to a great many of the people who are satisfied to follow their leadership. Nor have their methods always been acceptable to the masses. I think it would not be amiss to say that had this Committee been democratically selected, and had it taken more interest in the local problems of interior communities; had it not only invoked their cooperation but cooperated with them; had it not merely uttered fiats but sought their advice; had it not acted under an astonishingly shortsighted policy of administrative economy; had it employed the ablest field staff of propagandists and community workers all over the country, contributing advice and service to interior communities in their local problems, thereby enlisting their good will and placing them under obligations, and coordinating them for national and international purposes, the influence of the American Jewish Committee would have permeated every community. . . .

IV

There is another consideration which must be emphasized because it has been sadly lacking in community effort everywhere. There have been lacking in every community well-defined means of knowing community needs and resources. This has been particularly noticeable in the larger cities, where the population is numerous and the activities varied. The result has been a failure clearly to define programs of community work. Whatever progress has been made has been fortuitous, sporadic, and sometimes unintelligent. Very little systematic study has been carried out of population, of birth rates and death rates; very few other social statistics have been gathered. Our communities are in the position where they do not know themselves.

In New York this situation has been recognized for some time. To remedy it, there has been established the Bureau of Philanthropic Research which, as has been stated, is now in existence and busily engaged in work. . . . After this Bureau has acquired experience and technique, it might well develop into a national bureau not only for philanthropic research but for Jewish research in general, absorbing in the process the present Bureau of Statistics of the American Jewish Committee, so that a knowledge of the life of the Jews from every side may be secured as a basis for action by any particular Jewish community or by the Jews of the country at large.

PART TWO

THE AMERICAN JEWISH COMMUNITY MATURES

Internal Diversity and External Pressures

1920-1929

SURVEY OF THE YEARS 1920–1929

The decade of the twenties provided the environment for a fuller maturing of American Jewish community life. The pressures, emergencies, and new impulses of the previous decade had required community institutions and organizations which were more complex than the philanthropic societies and traditional institutions of the nineteenth century. These new and often *ad hoc* organizations dealt successfully with problems of mass immigration, economic depression, foreign persecution, and war. The Allied victory of World War I brought hope for a new era of peace, stability, and prosperity. Major Jewish communities entered the period with numerous health and welfare institutions which could count on wide volunteer and civic backing, a cadre of employed workers committed to full-time work on behalf of the community, and a highly developed apparatus for financial backing. There was lacking, however, a definite sense of direction: Should emergency agencies and programs be converted into permanent organizations? Why should a sectarian though secular community continue to maintain so many and so large a volume of services, when the pressures of immigration and economic dependency were being sharply reduced? Would it be better to join with other American groups in creating and financing general welfare and social services, or did Jews still require separate facilities? If separate facilities, why, and what were their functions?

The end of the decade found these communities committed to the maintenance of a major network of sectarian social services supported by the widest Jewish community and to serving that community and its internally diverse structure of ideology, opinion, and organization. It became an accepted fact that the "community" was greater than and in fact encompassed a variety of specialized associations and agencies. The mechanism of federation was firmly established as a chosen instrument with which to bridge the many conflicting and competing influences in local and national community life.

Two major developments illuminate the nature of the environment in which welfare and charitable-minded groups worked: (1) the internal diversity and complexity of Jewish life in America; and (2) the enlargement of the role of welfare in the general community, which impelled like-minded groups to replace a sectarian welfare program with a broader one—to embrace or rely upon the general Community Chest or public-welfare legislation. The response of the new Jewish organizations was not fashioned by sectarian loyalty or emotion alone: economic, social, and political changes provided the foundation for the reaction of Jewish leaders, which was sometimes emotional, sometimes sharply rational. Such underlying forces were clearly understood by a few clear-minded leaders, whose addresses to the Conference reflect their astute analyses and proposals. The new conditions can be briefly summarized:

1. *The Drop in Immigration:* Changed conditions in Eastern Europe and the enactment of restrictive immigration legislation in the United States dramatically reduced the pre-war immigration of Jews from the 1,250,000 level between 1900 and 1914. Annual immigration from Europe dropped to between 10,000 and 12,000 in the years 1924 to 1930. Obvious signs of emergency need began to disappear; there was less pressure to receive, absorb, educate, and temporarily care for large numbers of immigrants. The emotional and emergency nature of charity became more sober as it turned to face more far-reaching issues: Must we extend our volunteer efforts to the permanent and continuing obligations of philanthropy? Why? What purposes will be served?

In a more general sense, the American Jewish community was forced to turn in upon itself for future growth and development. The strong flow of new blood and vitality in the form of thousands of new immigrants was diminished. Crises no longer confronted and challenged the creative imagination; or at least the drama and challenge were more remote and not clearly visible. Jobs could be found, but most Jewish families still lived in the slums of large cities, and experienced the problems common to other immigrant groups: low wages, miserable health and housing conditions, job insecurity, or economic exploitation. As Jews, however, their distinctive problem was how to recreate and sustain their own culture. Meanwhile, the new youth was torn between loyalty to European customs and family patterns and the ways of the new world. Community agencies, while accustomed to dealing with such problems, were dissatisfied with the results of their efforts.

2. *Economic Improvement:* As might be expected, the post-war American drive toward "normalcy" had economic as well as psychological roots. The nation was caught up in the dream of a

continuously rising standard of living, even though for the time being the benefits were distributed most unevenly. Despite economic difficulties, some Jewish workers and small businessmen were obviously moving up into the middle class and were thus sharing, more and more rapidly, in the general euphoria of continuous and ever-increasing economic betterment. From their numbers emerged successful small and medium-sized businessmen, industrialists, and professional workers. With their improved economic position, they acquired the means to support new programs, organizations, and agencies in which they had special interests.

The Conference reports on the decline of the need for relief-giving, and the evidence of successful adjustment by the great majority of recent immigrants (measured by economic independence) seemed to prove the effectiveness of the massive charitable, rehabilitative, and welfare efforts of the previous decade. In a sense, it was this very success which helped underpin the case for a permanent structure of social services to meet new problems.

3. *Growth of Community Agencies:* Economic well-being encouraged the development of many new Jewish agencies and associations. The more recent arrivals from Eastern Europe often preferred to organize new social services, homes for the aged, and children's agencies which they would operate and control, in preference to relying upon older family agencies, whose policies were made by other Jewish groups. This tendency was accompanied by an increase in the number of specialized agencies to deal with the needs of children, the convalescent, the aged, the sick, and the tuberculous.

4. *New Scientific Insights:* The new explanations of human behavior put forth by Freudian psychology and psychoanalytic practitioners promised an answer to the social problems which had eluded solution by previously tried methods. Mass approaches through relief charity, education, and resettlement were now supplemented by psychological methods which shifted the area of attack to the individual and his immediate family and environment. These approaches were consonant with the prevailing out-

look of the period; failure was traced to the individual rather than to the political, economic, or social system. Such an approach was also more in keeping with the limited (although growing) financial resources of sectarian, voluntary philanthropy.

These new approaches swept through all the social and health services of the nation, and the Jewish ones could not help but be affected. In this newer, scientific humanism, Jewish leadership saw a new means of accommodating itself to the American scene while at the same time maintaining its Jewish identity.

5. *Forces for Welfare Assimilation:* Even more influential than the new scientific thought was the rapid evolution of philanthropy and social welfare on the general American scene. The major new influence was the success of the Community Chest movement, which had served the nation and localities so well during the war as an instrument for financing and planning needed social services. Although the idea of federation may have originated in, and been tested by, earlier Jewish communities, the success of Community Chests forced a major reassessment of their methods by Jewish Federations. The Chest was a useful social tool which was oriented to national goals, yet adaptable to local differences. Its appeal to Jewish and other sectarian groups was most persuasive. On principle, it was argued that human needs were universal, and their fulfillment was beyond the capacities of any sectarian group; if all specialized groups, including Jewish ones, joined forces, a significant attack could be launched upon human misery without the waste of competition in fund-raising. Such cooperation seemed to promise full acceptance of Jews by the American community, while distributing more equitably the heavy task of raising large sums of money. But many searching and contradictory viewpoints had to be explored before a community policy and approach could be shaped.

By the end of the decade, Jewish communal responses were adapted to meet all of these influences in the form of renewed commitment to separate and sectarian welfare independent of, yet linked loosely with, American welfare at large. Jewish community life was viewed as made of a rich tapestry of many diverse and often competing organizations and agencies. The idea of a unified and tightly knit community, although yearned after by many, was abandoned as new Jewish agencies and associations sprang up and were accommodated by that recent social invention, the Federation.

The sense of an existing, if pluralistic, Jewish community became more apparent and self-conscious. This new form of Jewish identification supplemented the earlier identifications of family, religion, and *Landsmanschaft*. The exigencies of social change, urbanization, and vast migrations further altered the traditional means for establishing and sustaining Jewish identity, especially in the face of an attractive and permissive general American culture. What is surprising is the rapidity with which social-work leadership recognized this shift, and very early sought for a philosophy and a method to replace the older conditions which fostered cultural survival—the ghetto, discrimination, poverty. In this period, the specific content of Jewishness was never defined with any clarity, aside from various religious interpretations; but constant attention was directed to the use of social welfare and charitable agencies as a means for building and enriching that sense of Jewish identity which all but a few Jewish leaders desired.

The decline in emergency pressures resulted in a concomitant fall in volunteer activities by the welfare laity. By the end of the decade, community tasks were more and more assigned to an employed professional community worker, in addition to the teacher and the rabbi. While the loss of wide volunteer activity was decried, laymen still retained effective policy control as members of the boards of directors of these communal organizations. However, the emergence of a professional cadre assured that these men and women would have the richness of experience needed to tackle welfare problems most effectively and the time to reflect on current trends and to propose viable courses of action.[1]

[1] From 1918 to 1924, the Conference was actively involved in efforts to establish a School of Social Work for Jewish personnel, and in 1925, such a graduate school was finally opened in New York City.

The decade closed on a confident note, although many serious problems were still present: differences over national versus local issues; determination of the scope of communal responsibility for Jewish education; and the matter of Jewish identity and how it should be sustained or encouraged. What was new was the community's confidence in its ability to deal with any problem. The social institutions fashioned during the past twenty years had proven remarkably flexible and creative; social-welfare agencies, community centers, and Federations had each grown in strength, although their missions had been altered by the changing years. New organizations were now less often required, as old ones proved suitably adaptable. Above all, the Federation had emerged as the major means for welding together the disparate elements of the American Jewish communities into the minimum of unity essential for community rather than parochial action, while preserving the maximum of variety and diversity in organizational life.

I Problems and Needs at the Opening of the Decade

THE report of the Committee of Nine and the analysis by Morris Waldman, taken together, reveal how well the professional welfare leadership of the early 1920's understood the new period into which Jewish philanthropy and charity was entering. Many of the issues have a strikingly contemporary ring, although couched in the language of the 1920's. The concern over education, anti-Semitism, and Palestinian relief constitutes a bench mark for comparing community methods of 1920 and 1960. As compared with the groping in local community affairs in the 1920's, the latter-day National Community Relations Advisory Council and the United Jewish Appeal represent great progress toward coordination and coherence in handling interests common to all Jews. Yet the early leaders of community thought approached such topics with an enviable breadth of perspective and a concentration upon policy issues which was anything but technical or specialized.

1. Preliminary Report of the the Committee of Nine*

LOUIS M. CAHN, Chairman

The past few years have seen an increasing growth in unrest among the workers in the field of Jewish social service. This spirit

* National Conference of Jewish Social Service, *Proceedings,* (1923), pp.

appeared with greater force at the 1922 Conference in Providence, where your Committee of Nine was appointed.

Though the resolution establishing the Committee of Nine called for a study of the function, scope, and organization of the Conference, it felt it incumbent to take upon itself a much larger task. It feels that the Conference was merely one factor in the many problems facing the field of Jewish social service, and that a thorough study of the Conference would involve a study of all of the ramifications of the field.

We have been able to do no more than prepare an outline of the scope of our study, which we present herewith:

The problems facing Jewish social service in America can be divided into three sections: (A) those involving particularly the smaller communities; (B) those which confront the larger communities; and (C) those which affect the entire field.

(A) In the designation small communities, we include those in which the social-service activities are largely encompassed within one organization, and in which there has taken place no considerable division of function.

1. The standards of administration of casework have as a whole lacked uniformity, system, and scientific basis.

2. In a general way, with certain striking exceptions, inexperienced and unguided personnel have been responsible for a lack of vision and floundering discouragement and deterioration in the service field.

3. Community support has been sporadic, based upon opportunism rather than upon a well-developed, constructive social program. The questions of the development of a community interest, the relation of the workers to the boards, the proper consideration of representation for various community groups—these are all involved in the problem of support.

4. The relation to national Jewish organizations and institutions has not been clearly defined in local communities.

3-7. Presented at the annual meeting of the National Conference of Jewish Social Service, Washington, D.C., May 13-16, 1923.

5. The small community has been an isolated unit. There has not been sufficient contact and interchange of thought and experience between the communities; and there the proper conditions for the development [of such contact and interchange] do not exist, due to a combination of the personnel factors referred to above and the lack of inspiration from within and without.

6. There is an absence of common experience and knowledge as to the extent to which public agencies can and should be utilized. The early policy of parallel public systems of care for the social misfits has not stood up under the pressure of modern conditions, and divisions are being madc in different ways in different communities. Sufficient use of the public agencies has not been made in most communities.

7. The relation to non-Jewish agencies locally, such as the Community Chest and the Council of Social Agencies [has not been properly defined].

8. [We lack a solution to the problems of] immigration and foreign relief.

(B) Except for degree, larger communities face the same problems as those which confront the smaller ones. Division of function results in the presentation of different problems to different people. The Federation movement, as it is developing, should visualize all of these functions as part of a community program.

The danger in larger communities has been a focusing of attention on the part of the individual executives exclusively upon their respective fields, a lack of appreciation of relative values and of the relation of their specific problem to the broad community development. Furthermore, the larger communities should serve as a technical training ground for the smaller centers, and contact between both should be mutually advantageous. The executive in the larger city could then obtain a more comprehensive view of his field, as well as a better understanding of the problems of the smaller community.

Unfortunately, preoccupation with their immediate responsibilities, the absence of standardization in criteria for evaluating their work, and the lack of leisure and consequent lack of perspective, have precluded [the larger communities'] serving as a source of inspiration. Their attitude toward their own work is mechanistic and devoid of a zealous spirit which would give life to the movement, and the character necessary to differentiate itself from non-sectarian social service.

(C) Problems facing the Jewish social-service field as a whole:

1. There is an absence of a *raison d'être,* of a universally accepted philosophy for Jewish social service, such philosophy as exists being individual and deficient in a comprehensive point of view.

2. [There is some controversy as to the relation of Jewish] to non-Jewish national agencies—the National Conference of Social Work, the American Association of Social Workers, the American Association for Organizing Family Social Work, and other such social agencies. There is no need for duplication. We should determine definitely to what extent our common problems require separate handling, and to what extent we can take advantage of and benefit from the advances made in the overall field of social services.

3. Our standing in general social service and allied professions must be determined. There exists a general doubt among non-Jewish social-service workers as regards the need, desirability, and propriety of separate Jewish agencies. Though Jewish organizations in the past have been accepted by other professional workers as being of a high standard, the non-sectarian agencies, as they improve their methods and raise their standards, are scrutinizing the Jewish methods more carefully and are questioning the justifiability of the separation.

4. In the area of personnel, the large turnover in the field is not conducive either to a thorough study of existing problems and conditions or to the perfection of procedures for their amelioration. There are few Jewish agencies in the country which have retained their executives for more than a period of five years. Such

shifting in personnel is detrimental to the best plans for developing a scientific procedure, for social service requires *per se* a long-term program. The problems of recruiting, training, salaries, pensions, status, security, professional attitude—all bear responsibility for existing conditions.

The development of an ethical code is a problem faced by all social-service agencies; it is an especially serious problem for the Jewish group, because of challenges from the non-Jewish agencies, from the communities, and from within the ranks of Jewish social workers. If Jewish social workers are to become community leaders, they must have convictions and the courage to stand behind them.

5. In Jewish social service the problem of lay interests is more than a local one, since Jewish welfare depends for its life upon the interests of the Jewish communities. The relation between board members and professional workers, between formal and informal agencies and the need to professionalize Jewish social service without alienating the laity all constitute a local problem with distinct national implications. There must be a conscious effort to interest and attract the type of layman who in the past has been a force in the development of Jewish social service, and has contributed substantially to its progress.

6. There has been very little control, coordination, or cooperation in the growth of national Jewish agencies and institutions. There exists a confusion of national social service agencies. The relations between the Conference, the Jewish Welfare Board, the National Desertion Bureau, and the Bureau of Jewish Social Research have been ill-defined. The national institutions have developed without due regard for the needs of the individual communities, and have done their work to a considerable degree with little consideration for the economic, social, and health factors in family life.

7. With regard to national problems, immigration, in all its phases, is a problem which requires careful and expert handling.

At the present time, two of the most important phases are being handled nationally and locally by agencies which are not operating on a professional standard. Secondly, anti-Semitism is a problem which needs careful study and scientific handling. The attitudes toward it thus far have been more or less emotional. Social service is endeavoring to develop a methodology for its social control. Should we not concern ourselves with this problem—the development of such methods of control as would be more effective than the procedures which have thus far characterized our efforts?

8. Foreign relief has engaged the attention of American Jewry during the last few years more than any other single problem. Yet Jewish social service, as a whole, has not been seriously concerned with the problem, and emergency international situations have found our personnel unprepared. Nor is there any likelihood of a change in attitude, although the problem is likely to present itself again during the next decade.

Lastly, we have developed no method of standardizing or controlling the growth or organization of Palestinian institutions. They are coming to our communities and deriving their support to an increasing extent from our people.

2. New Issues in Federation*

BY MORRIS D. WALDMAN

I desire to focus your attention upon certain elements in the life of Jewish communities which have a bearing on the Federation movement, and to point out how these forces are tending to modify the scope and content of Federation and to reshape its structure.

* National Conference of Jewish Social Service, *Proceedings* (1925), pp. 210-222. Presented at the annual meeting of the National Conference of Jewish Social Service, Denver, Colorado, June 7-10, 1925.

The content of Jewish social work in this country has been palpably affected by the war in a number of ways. The war has widened our horizons. It has made our interest international. This internationalism was especially evident in the spending of sixty millions of dollars in relief in Eastern Europe. And this internationalism is not a temporary affair. In spite of the liquidation of the Joint Distribution Committee, the needs of Eastern European Jewry have been vehemently brought to our attention. Strenuous efforts have been made to keep this world-wide Jewish interest alive to the tune of as many millions of American dollars annually as can be obtained by distinguished visitors from abroad. And only a few weeks ago the Joint Distribution Committee announced a resumption of European relief work. . . .

The war has had another effect, more subtle perhaps, yet none the less real. The phenomenal commercial opportunities created by the war made large numbers of formerly indigent Eastern European settlers in this country wealthy. The great relief drives gave them an opportunity for communal leadership. These new leaders in giving and serving have been eagerly brought into the local charities. Their influence is having a profound effect upon the content of communal work, and is resulting in a new perspective on communal problems. German Jewish leadership is no longer exclusively in the saddle. . . .

New attitudes toward communal problems resulting from the infusion of Eastern European leadership have accentuated the differences between the old and the new elements. In Boston, after a survey was made of the needs and the resources for Jewish education in 1917, we brought about a united organization for the Jewish schools, and appropriated $30,000 for Jewish education, which represented 15 per cent of the Federation's income; there was considerable suppressed grumbling and dissatisfaction on the part of a number of the older leaders in the community. As time went on, this grumbling diminished. The appropriations for this work grew in proportion to the increase in income of the Federation; this has permitted the development of a comprehensive system of Jewish education, which more recently has blossomed out in the establishment of a college for the training of Hebrew school teachers. In spite of the fact that in this way Jewish education has become firmly established in that city as a community concern—and not merely as the business of a particular group—I should not be surprised if the antagonism toward Jewish education on the part of some of the older element has not yet entirely disappeared. . . .

The problem in Jewish community organization is to find a platform upon which all elements can unite, even if the planks are not uniform in size. We have succeeded in recent years in uniting, to a fairly satisfactory degree, the different classes of the Jewish population on those activities which deal with material relief, except perhaps where spiritual problems are involved.

We have not had much difficulty in uniting our people in local family welfare work; in European relief; in hospitals and orphan asylums. But in those directions where differences of point of view toward the philosophy of Jewish life are involved, much more difficulty is experienced. . . .

So we have here two distinct elements with contrasting traditions as to the Jew's position in the world and his relation to the community at large, yet both part of the same race and religion. Can they be united? This will depend upon a number of factors, among them what the scope of Jewish community life is going to be. . . .

The answer to this I believe is that the scope of Jewish communal activities will be increasingly spiritual or cultural. It will continue to furnish material aid only insofar as religious considerations have a bearing, or in those directions where the state or city and non-sectarian agencies have not yet fully covered the field, especially along lines of social experimentation. And we see distinct manifestations of this tendency in the more recent development of cultural interests [in Jewish communal activity]. More and more emphasis is being laid upon these interests.

The development of Community Chests has complicated the problem of Jewish community organization. For the so-called liberal Jew, who is averse to the distinctly Jewish activities, the Community Fund offers a comfortable escape. However, he who genuinely believes that such affiliation promotes greater cooperation suffers from a confusion of ideas. Cooperation and central fund-raising are not necessarily identical. There is as much cooperative effort between Jewish social-service agencies and non-Jewish agencies, both public and private, in cities where a Community Fund does not exist, or where if it does exist, the Jewish organizations are not affiliated with it. On the other hand, there is no doubt that the Community Fund, by virtue of its control of the finances, ultimately controls the destiny of all its beneficiary institutions. Under such conditions, the growth and development of the Jewish activities affiliated with the Community Chest depend upon the sympathy, understanding, vision, and fund-raising capacity of the Community Chest. . . .

To recapitulate:

1. The more recent developments in Jewish community life in the United States show striking changes over the conditions existing before the war.

2. This has resulted in a broadening and deepening of our communal interests embracing Jewish life abroad, including Palestine, and a recognition of Jewish education as the most vital element in the preservation of the Jewish people.

3. Eastern European settlers have assumed a large share in the leadership of our local social services and are exercising a strong influence in modifying the policies of philanthropic organizations.

4. The general economic improvement since the war affecting all classes, simultaneously with increasing assumption of responsibility for dependents and delinquents on the part of the State, has shifted the center of gravity over to the spiritual and cultural activities.

5. The older settlers are not in sympathy with these activities— to what extent they can be made sympathetic is problematical.

6. The more intensified Jewish character [of the communal-service movement] may drive some of the older settlers away altogether. On the other hand, increasing intermarriage between Eastern Europe and Western Europe, and growing anti-Semitic intolerance will probably strengthen the Jewish sympathies of many Jews who are at present lukewarm.

7. Our dominant non-Jewish environment will act as a weakening and disintegrating force.

8. Though the Community Fund has a tendency to weaken Jewish solidarity, Jewish organizations will feel impelled to join, reflecting the common tendency of all races and creeds to cooperate with one another.

9. The problem before us is twofold: one, to adjust our internal relations in the light of changing community interests; and two, to adjust our Jewish Federation to the Community Fund.

10. This will probably produce a new type of Federation, double-barreled in character, which will reconcile the two conflicting forces [in Jewish social service]—one centripetal and the other centrifugal in nature—and direct them into one channel for the common good.

11 Relation of Jewish Services to the General Social-Work Program

THE early twenties witnessed the solid development of American charity with social work emerging as a profession with standards for varied programs. Compassion for the poor and underprivileged and the mission of church or religious sects were no longer the dominant elements in social welfare. Broad public-welfare measures were taking deep root in the form of mothers' pensions, old-age assistance, and workmen's compensation programs administered by many states. At the same time, new psychological knowledge based upon the works of Freud was introduced, and an academic basis for the education of professional social workers was established.

Such developments stimulated the controversy over the future of the Jewish social agency. Hyman Kaplan saw the issue through bifocal lens: how to use funds released by the drop in immigrant relief—a purely administrative and practical matter; and how to establish a set of Jewish values which would endow the efforts of Jewish social service with greater meaning—a matter of principle. Cutting charitable support and reducing welfare structures was an alternative which was seldom considered. Frances Taussig proposed principles to guide the Jewish relief agency toward a family service agency in which *tzedakah* for the poorest becomes a professional service, communally financed, for all members of the community.

The growing tendency to specialization in social work was recognized by many Conference leaders. Kaplan listed a few of the specialties, almost all of which are still practiced today—psychiatric worker, medical worker, group worker, educator, nutritionist, and nurse. The growing awareness of the usefulness of these fields derived from trends in general health and welfare circles. The work of Mary Richmond, Edith and Grace Abbot and others stimulated more scientific ways of thinking, which in turn encouraged specialized study, training, and practice in more definable segments of welfare problems—child care, mental illness, and others. Other technical considerations supported the growth of many specialized agencies, and freedom to develop new programs provided major assurance that clients' needs would, in the end, be met.[1]

How could this explosion of specializations be controlled? The value of the specialist was accepted, but there also existed the need for a generalist, someone to occupy a position similar to that of the general practitioner in the medical field. The family case worker appeared in 1925, offering the promise of fulfilling this integrating function in charity. The early attempts to impose order often took one of two forms: the use of the family agency or of the general social worker for work with families; or a merger of specialties under a single administrative agency.

1. Visible Effects of the Present Immigration Policy in the Work of Jewish Family Agencies*

BY HYMAN KAPLAN

[1] Jacob Kepecs, speaking at the 1925 Denver Conference, proposed the establishment of small decentralized institutions with fully professionalized and specialized staffs, to care for the most difficult children's problems. This suggestion was not acted upon extensively by Jewish and non-sectarian agencies until after World War II. His advocacy of great variety in agency programs was based upon the conviction that agencies are often preoccupied with their own needs and not those of their clients, a finding arrived at through systematic study by social scientists some twenty years later. See

Immigration Legislation

Up until eight years ago, the motive behind the immigration legislation passed by the Federal Congress had been to prevent the influx from abroad of specified undesirables—foreign convicts, lunatics, idiots, persons afflicted with dangerous diseases, polygamists, prostitutes, and those likely to become public charges—groups which might be classified under the general heading of the mentally, physically, and morally unfit. The exclusion act directed against Orientals was the only exception to what might be termed the [non-]selective principle in immigration regulation.

In 1917, the law was amended by the provision that aliens over sixteen must be able to read English, or some other language or dialect, Hebrew or Yiddish included. This amendment marked the change from the non-selective to the restrictive principle, the object being to limit immigration by making it more difficult to secure entry. The literacy test did not prove adequate for the purpose, however, and in 1921 restrictionists were finally successful in effecting the passage of the Johnson-Dillingham bill. This provided that the number of persons admitted to the United States in any one year should not exceed by three per cent the number of persons of like nationality who were resident in the United States in 1910. The law remained in effect until May 26, 1924, when a still more drastic amendment was passed, reducing the annual quota from each country to two per cent, and using as the base the census of 1890.

Under the three per cent quota—1910 base—the total admissions from Russia, Poland, and Roumania were limited to approximately 68,000 annually; the present law has cut this to less than 10,000. From a practical point of view, therefore, this law is tantamount to an exclusion act.

"The Future Development in Jewish Child Care" in *Proceedings* of the National Conference of Jewish Social Service (1925), pp. 126-38.

* National Conference of Jewish Social Service, *Proceedings* (1925), pp. 108-18. Presented at the annual meeting of the National Conference of Jewish Social Service, Denver, Colorado, June 7-10, 1925.

There has been some general discussion as to the effect of this restriction in immigration on Jewish social service. While the quota law has been in operation but a short time, the average immigration for the seven years preceding its enactment (i.e., from 1914 to 1921) was, due to the war, actually less than for the years subsequent. Jewish immigration decreased from approximately 1,100,000 during the decade 1905-14 to 350,000 for the decade 1915-24.

Has the decline become manifest in the work of the family-care agency?

This question cannot be answered for the country at large without an extensive study of local conditions. For the work of family-welfare agencies has been affected not only by the decrease in immigration, but by such developments as the mothers' pension movement, extension of public outdoor relief, the activity of independent societies, changes in standards of work, and other related factors. Late assignment of this paper permitted only a limited inquiry. One community was considered—Cincinnati—and though the development here is perhaps not representative of the present situation in the large population centers, it does have significance for a number of small communities, and is at least an indication of underlying trends. . . .

Comparative Social Data—Beneficiaries 1914 and Today

Comparison of the group receiving relief at present with that of ten years ago reveals the following significant changes: There is now a much smaller proportion of families with both parents living at home, and the percentage of widows among this group is four times as great. There were few native-born parents then, as now, but the proportion has slightly increased. The average age of parents is appreciably higher. The average length of residence in the United States has markedly increased, only a few having been in this country less than ten years. The proportion of cases known to the organization for a period of ten years and over has more than doubled.

These facts are definite evidence that the native-born and the recent immigrant are practically not contributing to the number of dependents, and that the relief agency is dealing only with a remnant of the old immigration.

Mental and Physical Status

It would be interesting to compare the mental and physical status of dependents today with those under care when Jewish immigration was at its peak. Unfortunately, records of that time are scant, since the importance of medical and mental examinations had not yet been fully recognized. But considering the circumstances—a large influx of destitute families and individuals, and the difficulties of immediate adjustment—we may assume that there were then a large number of beneficiaries mentally and physically normal, merely in need of temporary financial assistance.

What is the situation at present? Tabulation was made of the 70 relief cases now on the [Cincinnati] list, representing 117 parents and 245 children, a total of 362 individuals. Of these, 134 or 30 per cent are suffering from serious mental or physical deficiencies, such as epilepsy, feeble-mindedness, insanity, hyperneurosis, tuberculosis, severe cardiac condition, paralysis, severe diabetes, etc. Minor conditions were not considered, and many children were too young to be definitely diagnosed. The striking fact is that 91 or 78 per cent of the 117 parents are affected. It is evident that the relief problem of this community has [mainly centered around] care for the unfit [or debilitated elements of the population].

Trends in the Volume of the Problem

Quantitatively, the dependency problem has been markedly decreased. Because of changes in methods of compilation common to case-work agencies, it was impossible to compare the statistics of successive annual reports. It was necessary, therefore, to tabulate directly from original records. The number of cases receiving material aid was taken at five-year intervals from 1900 to 1925. Because of the complete centralization of all Jewish relief work during the entire period, the figures thus obtained are an accurate index to the variation in the incidence of the problem.

We find in 1900 . . . . 125 cases
We find in 1905 . . . . 208 cases
We find in 1910 . . . . 245 cases
We find in 1915 . . . . 236 cases
We find in 1920 . . . . 195 cases
We find in 1925 . . . . 111 cases

Note the sharp rise up to 1910 and the corresponding decline, especially marked after 1915, reaching its low point in the past year. The yearly decline from 1920 to 1925 has been consistent and rapid. The number of dependents for the last year is 45 per cent of the number on the list during 1910.

The variation in the taking on of new cases has been parallel [to the changes in case volume]. It was found that in 1900 there were 36 new cases; in 1905, there were 64 new cases; in 1910, there were 82 new cases; in 1915, there were 45 new cases; in 1920, there were 16 new cases; in 1925, there were 10 new cases.

The Transient Problem

There has been a decided change in the transient problem. The non-resident dependent family is, practically speaking, a phenomenon of the past. The number of male transients coming to the attention of the organization [1] is half of what it was ten years ago. An even better index to the trend is the experience of the local Achnosas Orchim, the Shelter House, which is not within the Federation. This institution admits all who apply; yet during the past

[1] Presumably the family-care agency.

few years, the daily census has not averaged more than three, although its capacity of seventeen was once well utilized. The Jewish population is apparently becoming stabilized.

Comparative Expenditures

The average annual expenditure for material relief for families by five-year periods from 1900 to 1925 was as follows:

1900 to 1904	$16,663 annually
1905 to 1909	25,336 annually
1910 to 1914	36,442 annually
1915 to 1919	39,793 annually
1920 to 1924	51,614 annually

Here we observe a continuous and marked upward trend, contrary to what might be expected in view of the sharp decline in relief cases during the last fifteen years. The number of cases receiving material aid during this time was halved, whereas the gross expenditures increased over 40 per cent. The peak of expenditures was reached in 1921, and there has been a gradual shrinkage since. The sum expended on material aid per family in 1910 was $122.00 as against $433.00 in 1925. To some extent this is attributable to rising costs of living, but primarily it is the result of more adequate budgetary standards made possible by the decrease in immigration and diminution of the relief group.

Adequate Budgets

The adjustment of resources to the demands of the relief problem has resulted in the actual application of the principle of adequate budgets to all families under care, a long-sought objective in relief work. Its attainment here has forced to the fore a searching question: Is it socially sound to maintain a dependent group on a plane above the standard of living of a large number of self-sustaining families? The dilemma is one which has not yet been resolved, recent inquiry having revealed a wide divergence of opinion among authorities.

Standards in Case Work

To the small immigration of the past decade may also be attributed, in some measure, the improvement in standards of case work, and the development and extension of facilities necessary for better diagnosis and treatment of clients. When the community was confronted with a large dependency problem, it was difficult to secure appropriations for additional workers, since material relief needs always constitute the first lien upon available funds. With resources for relief being adequate, however, requests for more service met with favorable response. Today the social-service department has an active case load of thirty-five per worker per month, with an exceedingly small turnover, and this—from the quantitative point of view—is an unusual equipment in personnel. Similarly, because it could be done without increasing the total budget of the Federation, there has been developed an unusual cycle of medical and psychiatric facilities, which has been of direct benefit in case work.

Reorganization of Case-Work Plan

The past dozen years has seen a rapid growth of organizations rendering special forms of case-work service. This movement gained impetus from the conviction that the problems of adjusting the difficult boy or girl, of instructing the mother in household management, of following up hospital and clinic patients, to mention only a few examples, is best dealt with by specially trained workers concentrating on particular tasks. It was felt, too, that the general agencies, due to the overwhelming volume of their own problems, could not undertake the intensive care of special groups.

Where social organization has not yet caught up with these problems—as is especially the case in the large population centers—this development has proceeded without arousing comment, for each new agency has found a more or less distinct field of operation. But in the smaller community, such as the one we are considering, the multiplication of activities followed by diminished immigration made necessary a reorganization of the case-work plan. With the narrowing down of the number of families requiring social service, the increase of the average period of care of the dependents and the increasing number of problems presented, the various case-work agencies—both general and special—were more and more frequently finding themselves active in the same homes. It thereupon became necessary to make the general case workers responsible for all problems arising in families under their care, and an effort was made to provide such training as might better equip them for the wider range of their duties.

This problem will inevitably present itself in other communities, if the present immigration laws remain in effect. It would seem that we must go back to the general social worker in order to escape the absurd position of trying to define and differentiate areas of activity of the medical social service worker, the psychiatric social service worker, the visiting teacher, the visiting housekeeper, nutrition worker, neighborhood settlement worker, big sister, big brother, and friendly visitor—in addition to the general case workers and the more technical groups, such as nurses. It has heretofore been assumed that where cooperation between agencies was concerned, conferences to outline concerted programs and to exchange experiences and suggestions would meet the situation. But with the best intentions, cooperation has proved to be almost impossible in practice when half a dozen or more agencies must work together.

The specialist is, of course, essential, but should function in a consulting rather than in an attending capacity; the case worker should correspond to the general medical practitioner.

It may be of interest here to observe that this large requirement has emphasized the need for workers thoroughly equipped by education and training. The new Training School for Jewish Social Work should be a vital factor in meeting this need.

Forecast of Dependency Problem

A forecast was attempted of the extent of the relief problem a few years hence, by making a prognosis in each of the cases now receiving assistance. Definite prospect of institutional care, of assistance from relatives in a few instances, of qualification for mothers' pensions, and above all, of children who are approaching working age, were the guiding considerations. No account was taken of deaths and removals from the city or of increasing facilities for institutionalization. Judging conservatively, on the basis of known factors, it can be said that about 70 per cent of the current cases will be closed within periods ranging from three months to three years; this includes many of the long-term and most expensive cases. As was shown above, the number of new cases and the reopening of old relief cases has been low for several years. The immigration of the past ten years has not contributed at all to the dependent group; and this situation is not likely to alter because of the preference given to immediate family members of United States citizens under the new quota law. It is probable, therefore, that by 1928 the relief problem in this community will again be more than halved. This estimate could be modified in the event of a major industrial depression, although it is significant that the extreme economic disturbance of 1920-21 was without important effect on the local situation. . . .

New Content for Jewish Social Service

What are the implications for Jewish social service? Not so many years ago the giving of material aid in its various forms constituted practically the entire field of social service; the specialized departments and institutions developed through experience with dependents indicated the need for particular types of work. With the diminution of the demand on relief, demands upon the related activities must also decrease. This tendency is definitely visible in the community considered here: in its dispensary, hospital, convalescent home, shelter for children, camp, and community house.

We must look forward to a radical revision of program, to a redirection of released energies, to a new orientation in communal activity. A great social force has been built up by Jewry during the past thirty years, which has expressed itself by a contribution of many millions of dollars annually to local philanthropies, and by active volunteer service of thousands of men and women. This *will* to give of time and money for a common cause has been a vital bond, making for community consciousness and concerted action. We are in a period of transition, and the formulation of programs to conserve basic values must depend upon the initiative and vision of our leaders. In ever larger measure, the social perspective of the American Jew must include the national and world problems of Jewry. Within the narrower field, Jewish social organizations are not in an advantageous position to bring their work to a high degree of perfection, to sponsor the newer ideas, to experiment with the promising, to promote the progressive and preventive. The Conference might well delegate a committee to give this matter thorough study throughout the next year, to stimulate all communities to think clearly and seriously about the whole question and to suggest constructive ideas for redirection, and thus to furnish at the next Conference a basis for discussion which would pool our very best thoughts.

Above all else, the definite and marked decline of poverty in an old Jewish community is inspiring and significant. The exodus of a whole people driven from their homelands to another continent—a migration in numbers and extremities of circumstances without parallel in history—has been accomplished within the space of little more than one generation, and the end of the concomitant problems is already in sight. What eloquent testimony to the native ability, energy and industry of the Jew, and to his ready adaptability under conditions of normal political and economic opportunity! What finer recompense to workers and contributors of the past few decades could there be than the realization that their objectives show promise of attainment! What better refutation to the policy of exclusion could we offer than this record of facile adjustment? The decrease of immigration has been a negative factor, but it has made visible the underlying processes of adaptation and adjustment that have been steadily progressing. These are facts to be emphasized in the hope that there may be some letting down of the barriers in the present immigration policy.

2. Changing Ideals in Jewish Social Work*

BY FRANCES TAUSSIG

Almost a quarter of a century has elapsed since the problems of Jewish social work were first discussed at a National Conference. The half century which preceded had seen the development of the Jewish community in America through the movement from Europe of two distinct groups—the first at its height towards the middle of the nineteenth century, and the second toward the end of the century. . . .

At that time [twenty-five years ago], relief societies were still priding themselves on their low administrative costs, and consequently accomplishing little [in the way of improvement of the condition] of the poor in the land. The idea of the importance of the family in social work was still a theory, and children of widowed mothers, as well as full orphans, were, as a matter of course,

* National Conference of Jewish Social Service, *Proceedings* (1923), pp. 42-49. Presented at the annual meeting of the National Conference of Jewish Social Service, Washington, D.C., May 13-16, 1923.

placed in institutions. Hospitals housed the acutely ill, where possible cured their diseases, and did little out-patient work. Preventive medicine was in its early stages. Juvenile courts were just beginning to be selective in their methods of treatment of juvenile offenders. Institutions for young delinquents flourished. Training for social work had not yet been established on a formal basis and the paid social worker was only too frequently recruited from the failures in the other professions or businesses. The progress which had been made up to that time in social work was due almost entirely to the intelligence, devotion, and insight of an important and not yet forgotten group of laymen, some of whom have continued through the years to point the way to progress. . . .

Some twenty-five years ago, the Federation was first hailed as a panacea for communities which were suffering from overdoses of charity balls and social events. Bazaars, balls, and raffles were no longer considered efficient or dignified methods of raising money to meet community needs. Beginning with the homogeneous group of agencies which formed the early community's philanthropic effort, an experiment in joint financing was tried, and seemed to meet with instantaneous success. The old, expensive methods of raising money were abandoned, and with a decreasing cost of collection, constantly increasing sums were made directly available for use. . . .

Gradually, however, perhaps forced by the constant increase in costs, there began, not so long ago, an epoch of measuring, examining, evaluating. Through the application of these processes, the Federation gradually began to change from an agency whose sole function was the raising of funds to support existing institutions to one which carefully analyzed the community's needs and then organized its resources to meet them. Eventually, the Federation realized that it had the task of not only financing existing organizations, but also of measuring their work in relation to the need—of adding to the equipment of some, of taking the initiative and having the aggressive strength to abolish meaningless, duplicating, or poorly functioning activities, and of creating anew where unmet needs were found.

During this period, as reflected in the more enlightened interest of the community itself, and in the strength of this new leadership, certain important changes are observable in the various fields of Jewish social work. Perhaps the most important of these is the belated discovery of the importance of family services. [Occupied with implementing] their avowed intention of letting no Jew suffer unnecessary want or privation, Jewish relief agencies did not question the strength of the traditional Jewish family life, about which so much has been told and written. For a long time they were content merely to ease with material relief the struggles of Jewish families to maintain their integrity in a new, complicated, and difficult environment. . . .

The next decade completed the transformation of the relief society into an agency for constructive service to families. Investigation became a process of establishing the factors which lay behind the family's failure to adjust itself to its environment; then followed the analysis of these factors with an end to setting up a clear understanding of the situation and the organization of a plan of treatment; then the utilization in the carrying out of this plan of all of the community's resources of service, as well as of adequate material relief if needed. The aim of the process was the rehabilitation of the family through the fullest possible development of each of its members.

Twenty years ago, this Conference studied the possibility of placing motherless children in family homes, and the adherents of institutional care looked forward with dread to the day when the child-care institution, no longer needed, would crumble and decay. A few far-seeing individuals, more progressive than their time, presented a comprehensive program for placing out children in homes. The next twenty years, instead of developing such a program, saw the highest point in the development of institutional care. . . .

In this era of change, we begin to hear less and less of "minimum standards." In the various fields of social work, the *existence* level seems no longer the end to be sought. Educational standards, like many others, have changed, and neither the child in the institution nor the child in the family is restricted to the minimum educational opportunity which is required by law. In most states, the law itself is no longer content with allowing any child of fourteen to work under certain conditions and is beginning to demand of children at work below sixteen certain qualifications of health, maturity, and education; and social work organizations, in helping to carry out the provisions of the law, have again set case-work processes to work to individualize the education of the child. Now, instead of being considered as a potential wage earner who must be productive as soon as possible, the child is looked upon as an individual, who must be assisted with the utmost care and skill to make his entrance into industry [when he is prepared for it]. His educational preparation must be based upon his capacity and his need; and according to these, he may leave the uncompleted grades of the grammar school for vocational training suited to his manual and mental ability, or he may complete high school and go on to college. We have passed beyond the days of being annoyed because the daughters of the poor refuse to do housework, and we ourselves have come to demand for their sons and for their daughters an opportunity in industry for which they are fitted by personality and mental and physical equipment. The contributions of psychiatry and of the new psychology have made possible adjustments which would otherwise have been impossible.

Perhaps the finest evidence of the discarding of the minimum standards as adequate is seen in the changing attitudes toward health. Without the assurance of care for the individual's health, all other assurances—his rights to a home, to the opportunity for development in the family group, to adjustment according to his needs in the environment in which he is to live, and to the educational opportunities which are necessary to that adjustment—are incomplete, according to the modern conception of the responsibility of social work. Family-care societies are beginning to recognize the period of the family's dependency as an excellent time to transform the health liabilities of the individuals in the family into assets.

They are demanding something of the community's medical agencies which those agencies are not yet fully prepared to give—a positive health service—in addition to their work in curing disease. Every family-care society in the country is paying the penalty of its own and the community's failure to recognize and treat disabling diseases in their early stages. Of the 306 individuals in 81 families studied who were chosen at random from among the clients of a family-care society, only two were without physical defects; the greater number of these individuals (204 were children) belonged to that group which private physicians do not see and hospitals and dispensaries cannot admit, because they are apparently well. The early recognition and treatment of physical defects, even though they may be nothing more than neglected teeth, is somebody's job in the community. In some communities, the ultimate economy of early provision of an adequate health service has already been recognized, and the promotion of the health of its members and the curing of their diseases is looked upon as a grave community responsibility.

It is certain that very definite trends have been at work during this quarter century of Jewish social work. Their influence has been felt not only in the above-mentioned fields, but also in the various ways in which the Jewish community has expressed its desire for social effort. Without question, the most important contribution of the period has been the attempt to create in every field a margin of security in the standard which is sought. . . . The minimum is elastic, and its content is becoming more and more inclusive. Slowly there has come to be accepted the possibility of something more than an absolute minimum in the standard which social work seeks to help establish. . . .

Therefore our social work has set itself the task of organizing the community for the more effective preservation of this newer, more adequate basis of life for the individual, the family, and the whole community. Participation in this enterprise is not limited. Orthodox and Reform, radical and Conservative elements serve it in different ways. The Jewish community is no longer neatly, if somewhat unevenly, divided into donors and recipients; in our social work the donors receive and the recipients give of the good which a modern social work program [brings to] the community.

Adequate salaries are now being paid in some fields of social work—usually, however, at the top. The rank and file still struggle with the difficulty of adjusting an enlightened living standard to the limited possibilities of a social-work salary, with too frequent failure. The community is depending upon the social worker more and more for an intelligent, progressive leadership. If this leadership is to be exercised, it must come about through a social-work personnel which, given preliminary requisites for development in a professional field, with the additional qualifications of education and professional training, is free to develop.

Also essential to such a development are conditions of work which will protect the field from all of the dissatisfactions which previously have caused the enormous turnover in the social-work profession. Professional progress cannot be made with a constantly changing staff. The movement of social workers has been motivated not so much by the desire for constant change as by a quest for the proper conditions, for community cooperation and acceptance of standards, and by the hope of finding a democratically organized community job which will give free reign to their qualities of professional leadership.

Since the last meeting of this Conference, a committee has given serious thought to this question of the belated acceptance of personnel standards in Jewish social work. At this meeting the Conference is to be given an opportunity to organize the first important piece of work which it has undertaken since the founding of the National Desertion Bureau. Nothing could be more fitting than to have the Conference itself take the initiative in creating the means of bringing into Jewish social work and keeping in it persons who can carry on the high ideals of the founders of the Conference in the light of modern professional development.

3. Character of Relationships of Jewish Agencies with Public or Non-Sectarian Agencies in the Field of Family Welfare*

BY HARRY L. LURIE

Preface

The relationship of Jewish agencies to non-sectarian and public social agencies is one of the underlying problems which Jewish philanthropy in general, and the National Conference of Jewish Social Service in particular, have been discussing from the very beginnings of organized Jewish philanthropy. In presidential addresses and papers, in the report of the Committee of Nine,[1] and in the Conference discussion regarding the objectives and purposes of the Training School for Jewish Social Work,[2] are to be found earnest attempts to resolve the doubts and perplexities which exist and to enunciate a set of general principles which shall help to guide the policies of Jewish social work in the future. It is this same problem of general principles which confronts us in a discussion of the present topic. The writer is mindful of the fact that any discussion of this problem is merely the opinion of an individual, and it is as a statement of opinion that the present discussion is offered.

At the very outset, it is apparent that Jewish social workers have found it necessary to establish reasons for the continued existence

* From National Conference of Jewish Social Service, *Proceedings* (1927), pp. 20-59; pp. 20-40 of this selection are included here. Presented at the annual meeting of the National Conference of Jewish Social Service, Des Moines, Iowa, May 8-11, 1927.

[1] See above, pp. 168-172.

[2] For an idea of the guiding principles on which the School was founded, and of the "doubts and perplexities" regarding the need for a special training institution under Jewish auspices, see M. J. Karpf, "The Training School for Social Work," National Conference of Jewish Social Service, *Proceedings* (1925), 11-41.

of separate Jewish agencies. It is somehow as though the Jewish social workers [feel they are faced with a challenge of justifying their usefulness]. In 1906, Judge Julian Mack, then president of the National Conference of Jewish Charities, in discussing the reason for separate Jewish Conferences, stated:

A quarter of a millennium ago, when the Jews sought a home in this land, the favor, not the right, was accorded to them, but upon the express condition that they should provide for and take care of their poor, so that they should not be a burden upon the community. Today the Jew no longer need ask the gracious consent of the sovereign power, but may come freely and under the same conditions as all others. Nevertheless, he conceives it to be his duty—no longer to his fellow Americans, but to himself, to his religion, to his fellow Jews—faithfully to carry out this pledge given by his ancestors, the contemporaries of the Puritans and the Cavaliers. This explains the need of our own separate charities, to better and to strengthen which we have created this National Conference.

Surely in the light of modern discussion of this problem, some more logical reason must be found for the continuance of separate Jewish organizations than a harking back to a legendary pledge, or an insistence upon the high moral value which the adherence to such a pledge constitutes. In general, it might be said that the need for re-examination of motives and principles and the self-questioning which this has entailed have not been imposed from without, but have arisen from the ranks of Jewish agencies and Jewish workers themselves. In the past the prevalent attitude of both Jews and non-Jews towards the existence of separate Jewish organizations has been laudatory, commending the fact that the Jews attempt to shoulder responsibility for the problems of their own group; in the minds of most people there seemed to be no reason for raising the question as to whether such policies are in conformity with the highest social ideals. It is only within comparatively recent years that other explanations have been sought both within the Jewish group and by outsiders.

The Development of Jewish Social Agencies

As a result of the conditions which characterized most public-relief systems of the last century, and [in reaction to] the feeling that the persons in need of assistance were less [entitled to comfortable] standards of living than other persons in the community, it was inevitable that an immigrant group coming with radically different habits and attitudes should set up separate agencies and functions.

The Jewish communities could not at first, even if they desired, have undertaken in behalf of the Jewish dependent group to replace the entire network of state and local hospitals and institutions with a complete organization of Jewish agencies. From the very beginning in many communities, the tendency has in fact been for the Jewish agency to act to supplement the services which the general community could offer. Thus we find in several of the communities the practice of using whatever public outdoor relief is available and supplementing such relief by the use of state and local hospitals for physical and mental diseases.

The general [trend in Jewish welfare] included both types of development: the use of available private and public facilities to some extent, and the creation of special Jewish agencies to supplement and to replace existing non-sectarian facilities. There is evidenced in this the double motivation which characterizes the present situation: first, the assumption of Jewish primary responsibility for the care of dependents; and, secondly, the use of non-sectarian and public facilities where necessary. However, there has not been a sharply defined program with regard to the way in which these two elements should properly be combined, and there is considerable variation in this matter between communities at the present time. Gradual changes in the theory of privately organized social work and particularly radical changes in the philosophy of governmental assistance implicit in the state systems of mothers' pensions are the primary reasons why the principles of separate

Jewish relief organizations are again being examined and questioned.

The welfare systems of Jewish communities have never developed a program of complete separation from other community social agencies of a private or public nature. Parallel with the growth of separate Jewish organizations in urban communities, there has been a development of general and specialized nonsectarian organizations rendering some forms of social service to Jewish clients. These special organizations offer services to persons presenting economic, health, and social problems; in most communities we find such agencies being used by Jewish clients, either through direct application or through the intervention of the Jewish family-welfare agency. An example will make this clear.

Each large community has organized a visiting nursing service. With one exception in the cities studied, such service is nonsectarian in nature, and is made use of by Jewish patients and by Jewish agencies in behalf of their clients. One community, however, has integrated visiting nursing service into its own organization, and this service constitutes a part of the community program of the Jewish social agencies. In another instance, that of hospital and custodial care for the insane and feeble-minded, the Jewish family agencies refer their clients to public institutions wherever such help is required. In several of the communities, however, supplementary types of services for such inmates, such as friendly visiting and the offering of recreational and religious services, has been developed under Jewish auspices. Yet there seems to be no insistent demand in this particular field that Jewish institutions take the place of state institutions for such classes of dependents, although private institutions for mental cases do exist. On the other hand, in the field of placing out children, not one of the larger communities has failed to organize a special Jewish bureau or agency to administer the placing out of dependent Jewish children in Jewish homes or institutions. But even here the Jewish children's bureau or agency may avail itself of state institutions for the care of defective and dependent children, of public aid or subsidies, and of the court services of the general community.

Wherever state pensions for mothers and children or for the blind and veteran exist, the prevailing practice for Jewish family agencies is to refer their clients to such public agencies when they are eligible. In such instances the family might continue to receive case-work service from the Jewish agency, or be supervised entirely by the public agency.

In addition to the wide use of the mothers' pension systems, other forms of public outdoor relief are being used with greater frequency as these begin to develop standards of adequacy of service. Boston, Detroit, and Los Angeles are current examples of such tendencies, and it is probable that as standards of public relief in other communities are improved, they will serve Jewish families with the approval of the organized Jewish agency.

It is within comparatively recent times that the state has increased its sense of obligation towards dependents. Previously, responsibility for the social welfare of dependent groups seems to have been concentrated in the care of defectives and persons devoid of normal social status, who were classed as paupers. It is only in the more recent types of compensation legislation and children's codes, and the systems of state pensions to mothers with dependent children, that the public, through its governmental organization, has begun to accept a greater degree of responsibility for caring for dependents and attempting to maintain them and restore them to normal community life. During the last fifteen years, this assumption seems to be undergoing revision, and greater emphasis is being placed upon governmental responsibility. If we accept the state as the super-organization in which every individual participates by right of domain—and this is the current political philosophy—we may agree upon state-wide provisions for the care of dependents and the adjustment of social difficulties for the individual. However, the state at present is far from assuming fully the responsibility for individual and family welfare. There is no logical reason why the existence of state public welfare precludes the development of voluntary means, even though the state is accepted as the primary social organization. The present individualistic philosophy of the state has given it no priority or monopoly over the social welfare features which it is beginning to institute. A mothers' pension is acceptable not because it is public aid, but because it meets with the requirements of social welfare as a means of aiding a dependent mother, whereas a county infirmary for an incurable, defective person may be refused and private sources of caring for that individual substituted, because the infirmary does not measure up to an acceptable minimum of welfare for the dependent. It would, of course, be desirable in all such instances that the Jews, as well as other groups in the community, give attention to the need for improving public systems of aid to an acceptable minimum standard. . . . There seems to be no inherent reason in theory why at some time family and case work fully representative of the aims and aspirations of all of the diversified groups could not be developed in all of our American communities. If visiting nursing service and infant-welfare stations can operate on a city-wide basis, the possibilities for city-wide family-welfare work are not so improbable.

The problems of social organizations, however, are not simple situations that can be solved by recourse to any abstract social or political philosophy, and there are many reasons why coordinated non-sectarian service in the family-welfare field is only a remote possibility in most of the larger communities. In a consideration of the possibilities of amalgamation of Jewish family work with the non-Jewish family agency, the following points would have to be considered:

(a) The reasons for the present existence of a separate Jewish agency.

(b) The possibilities of a general agency meeting the aims and purposes now developed by the special Jewish organization.

(c) The desirability of such amalgamation.

Reasons for the Existence of A Separate Jewish Agency in the Family-Welfare Field

When we come to examine the reasons for separate Jewish family and relief agencies, we find a variety of purposes and explanations. The reasons are to be found both within the Jewish group itself, and in the external influences which affect the situation. Problems of this kind involve a complex of factors upon which social values are established. Change in a given situation depends upon the shifting of these values or the introduction of new factors.

One of the more frequent explanations for the existence of separate Jewish agencies is that the Jews can care for their own group better than other groups or agencies can care for them. This is based upon the assumption that there exists in the Jewish group a sympathetic attitude toward individuals and families requiring service; that this attitude is inherent in a separate Jewish agency, and must, at best, be artificially created in a non-sectarian organization. . . .

Similar to the above reason is the one based upon the variation in standards between Jewish and non-Jewish agencies. Not merely is there a supposition that a friendlier and more sympathetic attitude exists on the part of the Jewish agency towards its clients, but it is felt that in the matter of service the standards of the Jewish organization exceed those of the non-Jewish agency. Whatever the standard of relief of the agency may be,[3] it is no doubt true that the Jewish agency generally throws the client less upon his own responsibility than does the non-Jewish agency. Here again the preferential attitude towards Jews is manifest. For example, Jewish mothers with young children usually have not been accustomed, in the past, to seek work outside of their own homes. In many Jewish agencies they are not expected to do so, even when

[3] The study of relief standards made by Dr. Slawson and the statistics of the Russell Sage Foundation are illuminating on this point. See John Slawson, "Differential Aspects of Jewish and Non-Jewish Relief," *Jewish Social Service Quarterly*, vol. II, no. 2 (December, 1925), 86-104.

they have only a small number of children to care for; and if there are such expectations, special provision in the form of work-rooms are established for them by the Jewish agency. The non-sectarian agency is in general reluctant to set up differing degrees of family responsibility for different racial or national groups. Frequently it is handicapped by lack of funds and must modify its standards accordingly. It is also believed that the Jewish agency, feeling a greater degree of responsibility for its clients, is more concerned with their problems, and on the whole makes greater efforts in their behalf. Whether these differences are true or not cannot be stated without more exhaustive study of this problem, but we do know for certain that Jewish agencies hold them to be true. Not only differences in relief standards, but differences in the size of staff are an indication that a proportionately greater amount of service is being offered the Jewish group than is offered to the community as a whole by the non-Jewish organizations. At the present time, Jewish agencies dealing with a limited portion of the general social problem find it less difficult to raise necessary funds than do the corresponding non-sectarian organizations. . . .

The existence of a preferential attitude and of higher standards in the Jewish agency is, however, not without its drawbacks. As cultural changes take place within the Jewish group, and as the process of assimilation lessens its cohesion and the unity of its cultural patterns, the principle of group responsibility may need revision. Upon what basis shall the feeling of group responsibility for individual members be maintained? In other words, when is a Jewish family entitled to the degree of interest and service available from Jewish agencies? We are increasingly aware of the existence of individuals and families who in their social life are on the periphery of the Jewish group rather than at its center, and whose culture, practice, and affiliations tend to have fewer Jewish contacts than is characteristic of the larger group of Jews. There are Jews who are changing their religious affiliation, who in their general life tend to take on the color of the undifferentiated American group, and who have no organized affiliations with Jewish life.

More specifically, there are the problems of assimilated families. The prevailing practice in American communities has been to consider the family according to the early religious affiliation of the head of the family, but this is not a satisfactory criterion. Shall the division of cases be on the basis of cultural affiliation, widely interpreted to include other than the religious factor? Shall it be the purpose of the Jewish family agency to act as a unifying factor in cultural affiliation, extending its services only to such families as are able to meet specific tests of Jewishness? This is a vexing problem, bound to become more difficult as the trend of cultural differentiation becomes more marked. . . .

In recent years, explanation of the separate Jewish agency has taken the form of a greater degree of understanding in dealing with the Jewish client based upon a knowledge of cultural backgrounds. There is involved in this not only familiarity with Jewish religious customs and dietary laws—these have long been understood to be an important reason for Jewish social work—but there is the further elaboration of this along the lines of group customs, attitudes, and traditions, and the need for the conservation of distinct Jewish culture. The answer to this may be that the non-Jewish agency in its case-work methods is also aware of differences in cultural patterns, that it is sympathetic to religious differences, and realizes the value of the conservation of cultural differences and standards. However an understanding of and a tolerance for culture variations is, in the minds of most Jewish agencies, not sufficient for these purposes. It is supposed that there is needed a more aggressive interest than is to be found merely in toleration; an interest that shall make dynamic use of such culture patterns for the stimulation of individual development. This hypothesis has, in a measure, been taken over by the Jewish Conference, and is one of the mainsprings for the trend of development of the Training School for Jewish Social Work.

When one considers the family agency in its larger aspects, the culture factor becomes a matter of secondary importance. Primarily, the family agency concerns itself with family economics, with problems of employment, health, domestic relations, with matters of community adjustment and of group relationships. While occasionally culture problems are involved in questions of family economics, health, or social adjustment, they do not obtrude themselves with sufficient frequency so as to characterize this factor [as an important individual aspect of] the general run of Jewish social work. These matters are largely determined by the wishes of the family itself. There is in most urban communities an alignment of families with communal matters along religious, educational lines, which is determined by the wishes of the family. A study of family religious observance undertaken by the Chicago Social Service Bureau indicates that dependent families adhere closely to established traditions of religious observances, dietary laws, and the desire for Jewish education. But the case worker rarely becomes an influencing element in such matters in the life of the family. Should these traditions begin to disintegrate in Jewish family life more rapidly than they show any tendency of doing at the present time, it would be extremely problematic to determine how great an influence the Jewish social worker would be in preventing such disintegration through the methods of case work. The forces responsible for such changes are definitely inherent in the group standards and environment, and are under the control of the case-work agency only to a very limited extent. . . .

It would seem inadvisable for a Jewish agency to become a sectarian or proselytizing agency. The purpose of family case work is to restore the family to normal adjustment, and in this it needs to deal with the major social ills which confront the family. It would be unwise to over-emphasize the cultural affiliations of a family in dealing with such problems. Concretely, a family that is suffering from the unemployment of the chief wage earner requires attention primarily from the unemployment angle. . . . It would be of value for the group of Jewish agencies to analyze scientifically the cultural factor in the families with whom they work, and to develop a realistic approach to this factor and its relationship to general social problems.

We might discuss in this connection the tendency for Jewish agencies to attach workers of their organizations to public institutions and agencies. Some of the communities, for example, have workers attached to courts and public social agencies. They make a practice of visiting Jewish persons in institutions, or those who find themselves involved in difficulties with the courts and correctional agencies. When we analyze the purpose of such workers, we find that they largely serve as points of contact with public agencies for the purpose of discovering Jewish persons whom the agency is able to assist; that they can offer case-work service to persons who have not found their way to the doors of the Jewish agency; and can assist the courts or public agency in dealing most effectively with the individual situation. Such assistance usually constitutes supplementary case-work service, and is not based upon the premise that a Jewish social worker can deal better with Jews than can the regular worker of the court or agency. When the public agency or court develops its own social-service departments of acceptable standards, the need for such supplementary services is diminished.

A more basic motivation for separate Jewish agencies than the foregoing lies in the interest of philanthropic contributors and leaders in the problem. Possibly it is the opportunity for self-expression offered by the Jewish communal agencies to their participant professional and lay members which stimulates and sustains their separate existence. This is based partly on the reasons given above, as well as on a desire on the part of Jews to do something for the members of their own group and a desire for leadership in communal affairs. . . . In this respect, the small Jewish relief organizations are significant. That they persist in the face of well-organized and unified Jewish family agencies is an indication that persons able to contribute to charitable efforts seek opportunities for individual self-expression. The centralized Jewish family agency apparently fails to offer this opportunity for volunteer effort to a sufficient number of individuals.

Behind the standards and aims of the work of Jewish agencies, we find the interested contributors of the Jewish community. While many of these persons are motivated by the desire to serve their fellow-Jews and to give social service, they are further spurred by the desire for individual expression through such social activity. The increased participation of Jews in general community efforts would answer such needs to a large extent. However, at the present time, the number of Jews participating in such general enterprises is definitely limited as compared to the number [who are part of] separate Jewish organizations, and it is not likely that there will be any rapid change in this arrangement. Therefore we do not expect to see any difference in the present tendency to create and maintain separate Jewish organizations. While Jewish social work leaders may feel that the efforts of public agencies or non-sectarian organizations may fully meet the need for social service among Jews, private citizens in the community cannot be expected to adjust themselves rapidly to such a point of view. However, as the needs of Jewish families for social service are more and more effectively met by public and non-sectarian agencies, there will be a natural tendency for such persons to divert their interest in Jewish welfare to other than relief and case-work organizations. The variety of Jewish interests offers some scope for such participation; but the compelling motives for charity and personal service to Jews as Jews will not rapidly be dissipated. It would be undesirable for such dissipation to take place until such time as the needs of all persons in the community are adequately met by proper social organizations. If the general improvement in economic conditions which many social workers believe is taking place in the Jewish group and the gradual extension of public interest continues, we may not be far from the time when the problems of relief and personal service will be so reduced that there will be a transference of Jewish interest to other than the relief and case-work fields. This does not preclude the possibility of the further extension of case-work service. There is need for extension of effort into the fields of behavior and delinquency and effective case-work treatment of family maladjustment in groups that do not suffer from economic destitution. An early indication of such developments can be found at the present time in services for the larger community which Jewish agencies are offering along educational and recreational lines. As the case-work method becomes worthy of service for the economically independent group, more and more such persons will tend to avail themselves of such services, and it will be natural for Jewish family agencies to develop in this field. . . .

An examination of our motives for the maintaining of separate Jewish agencies reveals that our arguments contain sound reasons as well as rationalizations that are not so logical. The separation of Jewish social work will continue because we desire it to do so, and because there is back of us a body of community leaders and givers who share our views and our desires. . . .

III What Makes Jewish Social Work "Jewish?"

THE search for an emotional or logical foundation for the pragmatically successful programs of Jewish charitable and philanthropic activities was pursued throughout the twenties with increasing intensity. It took two main forms, which may, to simplify, be called the secular and the ideological approaches. The secular approach was presented most clearly by community organization workers and family-welfare workers; the ideological or religiously oriented approach was most frequently expressed by Jewish educators and community-center leaders. However, spokesmen from all branches of community work were heard actively in both camps. Religious voices, too, were heard on both sides, as the articles by Rabbi Cronbach and others indicate.

The secular view encompassed a wide variety of outlooks which shaded imperceptibly one into the other. At one extreme was the view that the Jewish future lay in a full assimilation with American life and the abandonment of separatist organizations other than the synagogue. Very close to this was the view that Jews must adapt themselves culturally and wholeheartedly to the American tradition, but should maintain some tenuous identity which was never well-defined. At the other extreme was the view that Jewish group survival in America was essential, and to this task all social and welfare agencies and philanthropic enterprises should lend their continuous efforts. Yet the survivalist group also felt that these organizations should rid themselves of narrow or fixed ideologies and in their place should create new values, which would emerge from the work of secular and humanitarian efforts. Close to this approach is the pragmatic view that Jewish identity is found in the bonds of association one Jew feels with others, and finds expression in the groups with which he chooses to associate, and the programs which he chooses to support. Still another approach was that of the immigrant, who stressed the separateness of immigrants *because of* their immigration status—language, habits, and traditions; these differences require separate activities.

In the search for a rationale, it was expected that some common Jewish core or framework would emerge which would unify all Jews.[1] This unity had to be created, since it was no longer possible for it to emerge naturally out of the conditions of life in America. To this end, a communal structure or mechanism had to be established, and all communal institutions had to share in the task.

In the unfolding of these viewpoints, the community center and the synagogue were alternately viewed as competing or as complementary forces. Many contemporary problems and trends were forecast at this time: the community center, with its mission to create and sustain Jewish identity above all else, was formalized as a program in the Janowsky study for the National Jewish Welfare Board many years later;[2] and the idea of a synagogue-center which combined education and social activity is now widely utilized. In those days, Glucksman and others, from different viewpoints, could optimistically visualize center and synagogue as complementary institutions. This view went so far as to urge that one institution alone could never serve the interests of both religion and education, and that separate community institutions were, therefore, essential and mutually enriching. The sharp rivalries of later years represent, by contrast, a decline in community cooperativeness and good-will.

[1] There were, of course, exceptions to this trend towards a unitary view; see the article by John Slawson (p. 214). But the quest for a single ideology proved dominant.

[2] See Oscar Janowsky, *The Jewish Welfare Board Survey* (New York, 1948).

1. What Makes Jewish Social Work "Jewish? Historical Aspects*

BY ABRAHAM CRONBACH

In view of the immense contrast between the civilization of today, on the one hand, with its urbanization and its machine industry and, on the other hand, the rural or small-town civilization of biblical and talmudic times, with its crude and simple handicrafts, we should look for differences rather than resemblances [between these periods] in their respective ways of aiding the unfortunate. Indeed, it is the differences that predominate. Yet, because of those very differences, the occasional similarities which do appear acquire an exceptional significance.

As an example, we may cite the biblical precedent to our chariness about almsgiving. Nowhere in the Bible is almsgiving explicitly commanded. Granting loans to the poor is commanded; our modern free-loan provisions may go back to this. Almsgiving is commanded and even counselled here and there; but it is nowhere in the Bible categorically enjoined.

The Bible meanwhile does abound in what we today would call social legislation—such as the laws that the corners of the fields remain unharvested; and that these as well as sheaves and grapes dropped or forgotten by the harvesters and unclustered grapes or olives be left for the poor; and that, every seventh year when there was no harvesting, the spontaneous growth be placed at the disposal of needy men and beasts. At three-year intervals, tithes were to be shared with the poor, while anyone was free to eat his fill of growing produce at any time, prohibited only from carrying any away in a receptacle. The jubilee laws decreed that every fifty years agricultural land was to be restored to its original owners. The manumission laws liberated and compensated slaves every seven years, and the release laws canceled debts every seven years.

* *Jewish Social Service Quarterly*, vol. VII, no. 1 (Sept. 1930), 3-5. The two articles which follow are part of a symposium.

In later centuries when, under changed conditions, this law made the obtaining of loans difficult for the poor, in the interests of the poor the law was virtually abrogated. Add to these the laws requiring prompt payment of wages; the law against charging interest; the law demanding one day's rest in seven; the law against removing landmarks; the law forbidding creditors to retain pledged garments overnight (for in that day and land, garments were also bedclothes); the law against using as pledges those indispensable culinary implements, millstones; and the law against taking a widow's garment as a pledge. The Bible seems, on the whole, more inclined toward what we call social justice than toward that which we call charity.

In its overwhelming stress on almsgiving and its relative indifference to social change, the Talmud diverges from the Bible. Still we find in the Talmud not a little that accords with attitudes of our own.

The Talmud, for one thing, presents an elaborate system of charity organization. There was the "Kettle," a food supply for daily distribution, and the "Box," a money fund from which weekly allowances were made. The resources of the "Kettle" had to be gathered by three directors, and those of the "Box" by two, while disbursements were made by three men. The "Box" was maintained only for the local poor—not for outsiders. While house-to-house beggars were to receive nothing or only a small sum, transients applying at the proper headquarters would receive a food allowance of not less than one-eighth of a peck per meal and, on the Sabbath, three meals containing beans, fish, vegetables, wine and oil; a bed with a pillow would be provided for the night and clothing supplied if the person were known. At various times and places, the lodge for indigent wayfarers was the synagogue.

The charity administrators had to be men of high caliber and reputation, and had to proceed according to rules carefully devised to preclude anything that might arouse suspicion. And yet, disbursers of charity seem to have been as much subject to the derogations and execrations of their clients as are their modern successors. The doctrine in fact developed that a charity worker ought to rejoice in the curses of the disgruntled, because the more chagrin one endures in this world, the greater will be his reward in the hereafter.

The charity administrators could legally compel people to give a just amount. "According to the camel, the burden" was the proverb. The average subscription was one-tenth of one's income. More was generosity, less was stinginess. The law forbade the giving of more than one-fifth of one's possessions, at least during one's lifetime.

The modern Community Chest did not of course exist in talmudic times, and yet the idea of a Community Chest was not lacking entirely. The following is a passage from one of the writings of that period: "Where Jews and non-Jews dwell in the same city, collections are made from non-Jews as well as from Jews and relief accorded to non-Jews as well as to Jews."

The Talmud also espouses the idea of discrimination in giving. The basis of discrimination may not be identical with our own; yet the principle is there. Witness the rules governing the disbursement of charity:

1. Persons having enough food for two meals were ineligible for the benefits of the "Kettle."

2. Persons having enough food for twenty-four meals were ineligible for the benefits of the "Box."

3. A person possessing 200 *zuzim* (about $5.35) was ineligible for the biblical privilege of gathering what the harvesters had dropped or forgotten in the fields or left unharvested in the corners of the fields. A person with a profitable business worth 50 *zuzim* (about $1.35) was also ineligible for this benefit. Under certain circumstances, the acceptance of help had to be preceded by the sale of certain ornamental belongings, such as silks, jewels, and utensils of gold or silver. An outright miser was to receive nothing, although parsimonious persons might occasionally be granted a loan subject to later collection either from those persons themselves or from their heirs. Poor persons having wealthy relatives

were barred from public charitable assistance, as were persons guilty of extreme deviations from the moral and ritual conventions. Parents were obligated to support their children up to a certain age and children, under certain conditions, to support their parents.

We also encounter in the Talmud the concept of social investigation. The purpose of investigation was to guard against imposture, the Talmud understanding by an imposter a person who pretends to be without means, although in reality he possesses them. Some authorities held that investigation should be made only when food was the benefit asked; others required it only when clothes were desired. Investigation was eliminated in the case of the need deemed the most urgent. One sage was of the opinion that an investigating committee should consist of no more than three persons, lest starvation overtake the sufferer before a larger committee could assemble. All of this is far from the "social diagnosis" of Mary E. Richmond. Still, connection is not utterly lacking.

The importance of vocational training is also recognized in the Talmud. A parent's obligation to teach his son a trade is held to be as great as the obligation to teach him religion. One of the old authorities cautioned: "Whoso fails to teach his son a trade teaches him robbery." Allied to this are the talmudic encomiums on self-support and independence. "Make thy Sabbath like a week day but remain independent." "Whoso needs assistance but, at great sacrifice, foregoes it in order to avoid burdening the community, will live to render assistance unto others." Our modern ideas about self-support and about vocational training need hardly feel strange in this atmosphere.

A near-summary of an important phase of modern social work appears in the talmudic words, "Better than giving is lending, and better than lending is setting up in business"; but the extent to which this adage anticipates modern policy is not as great as some have supposed. The context shows the passage to be merely one of many urging regard for the poor person's feelings. On this point, the Talmud is scrupulous: "Better no giving at all than the giving that shames." "Better to jump into a fiery furnace than to embarrass one's fellow man." The extreme carefulness of the Talmud in shielding charity recipients from humiliation is something that modern social workers will appreciate, whatever the shortcomings of our actual practice.

Much more suggestive of modern views is the ancient homily in which the verse from Psalms, "Blessed is he who considereth the poor," is interpreted to mean not blessed is he who *gives* to the poor, but blessed is he who *helps solve the problems* of the poor. Perhaps ahead of our day is the ancient provision that an owner of real estate, if financially pressed, may secure charitable assistance in order to avoid selling his property at a loss or at an unduly low price. "One man can unburden a beast before it falls, five can not lift it after it falls." The Department of Public Welfare of Detroit little realized that it was following a talmudic precept when, in 1927, it decided that its program of relieving the unemployed should allow for aiding unemployed persons to keep up payments on homes that they had purchased, and should not require them first to sell their homes or their equities in their homes. The problem is one that Jewish social agencies confront recurrently.

In these days when birth control is an issue, it is of interest to know that the talmudic authorities have an occasional good word to say about contraceptives. They counsel their use when the health of the mother or of children already born is at stake. Such protective measures as mothers' pensions, life insurance, and alimony have their talmudic analogue in the *ketubah,* a written document which safeguarded the rights of the wife and specified the settlement or sum of money settled upon every woman at marriage, the principal of which the husband was not permitted to touch because the sum was intended to care for the woman in the event of widowhood or divorce.

In closing, we recall our initial question: "What makes Jewish social work Jewish?" One thing which undoubtedly makes it Jewish is the fact that the group within which it functions is the Jewish group. This group, however varying the rates of its assimilation with other groups, still retains some of its historical peculiarities and uniqueness. The Bible and the Talmud are among the determinants of those peculiarities, and hence among the factors which make Jewish social work Jewish.

While Jewish and non-Jewish social-work techniques differ only slightly, statistics indicate that, for the present at least, Jewish relief allowances are higher than the non-Jewish. In this, the talmudic principle that relief be generous and liberal may possibly be reverberated. So far as the biblical urge for social justice has influenced modern law-making, Christian rather than Jewish mediation seems to have been the more assertive.

Numerous Jews still respond to the appeal of Jewish tradition. These parallels can align tradition on the side of progress. Tradition, often a barrier to innovation, thus may become an aid to innovation and a possible device for persuading various of our people to take certain indispensable steps forward.

2. Communal Aspects*

BY JOHN SLAWSON

. . . One of the chief aspirations in Jewish communal endeavor is to develop a *common, underlying purpose* permeating all of our activities, regardless of the branch of Jewish social service with which one group or another may find itself concerned. While it is difficult to define this purpose because of the variety of interests represented in any welfare scheme, it may perhaps be of help to consider the underlying objective of Jewish communal effort in the United States as being that of raising Jewish life to as high a functioning plane as possible. . . .

This objective of raising our ethnic group to higher planes of thought and action cannot possibly be approached through any

* *Jewish Social Service Quarterly*, vol. VII, no. 1 (Sept. 1930), pp. 11-14.

one channel. A variety of methods must be utilized, and innumerable sources exploited. Social work is one avenue through which certain segments of this goal may be attained, religious activity another, and the cultural program a third. . . .

The rabbi, the social worker, the Jewish educator, and the community center worker have in common this one objective, although different emphases will and should be placed by these communal workers in the program of activities. A multiple approach to the community problem is impossible, however, unless those exercising leadership in the community are cognizant of the unitary nature of this fundamental objective. . . .

The third aspiration may be called the *democratic approach,* as opposed to the self-perpetuating organizational type. In practice of course, the purely democratic set-up becomes almost an impossible objective; but no community can be truly healthy in its social makeup if the administering and policy-forming body is autocratic, self-centered, and self-appointed. The democratic approach calls for proper recognition of all groups in the community that genuinely have a contribution to make as an expression of their own life and work. Concretely, the democratic approach calls for adequate representation of Orthodox, Reform, and Conservative religious groups, the working man as well as the capitalist, the politically conservative as well as the politically radical, on the various boards of the agencies in the community, as well as on the board of the central directing group. . . .

The implication is that the achievements of a community should not be motivated by emulative impulses, but by the needs themselves, met on the basis of objective evaluation and the exercise of social intelligence. For instance, the presently strong drive for the erection of monuments and buildings to perpetuate names and memories which is a detriment to the development and promotion of needed social service functions should be weakened and replaced by a motive for action prompted by a balanced appraisal of the true value and merit of the social service project.

An *integrated approach* is another communal aspiration. Democracy and integration must go hand in hand. Democracy can become the handmaiden of integrated activity, if properly guided. In the family field, where there are, in most communities, in addition to the major family welfare agency a number of smaller relief-giving agencies, integration should be effected through the democratic participation of all interested individuals and groups. In the children's field, where there exists a disparity of points of view as to the desirable types of child care, certainly an integrated child-care program becomes most essential for adequate productivity in that field. The same is true of the health and recreational fields, the latter especially with respect to the relationship between community center and the synagogue center. . . .

Of vital significance is the *Jewish approach* in our communal work. In recent years this factor has been stressed on a number of occasions at conferences and in periodicals. It constitutes the *raison d'être* of all our efforts, because it is a potent element in the underlying purpose of communal action, which we defined above as raising Jewish life to as high a plane as possible. It is the recognition of this Jewish aspect, with Jewish education as the principal mechanism for the injection of Jewish values into Jewish communal life in the United States, that is so necessary if our work is to have a central purpose, compatible with the actual stuff out of which our activities are composed. . . .

The struggle that Hebrew education is experiencing in a number of communities is not due so much to the disfavor in which the teaching of Hebrew is held on the part of a number of influential people in a community, as it is a result of a general indifference to Jewish education as such. No type of Jewish education, whether it includes Hebrew or not, is adequately supported. At best, even the most diluted forms of Jewish education receive only an indifferent and passive approval or support on the part of parents whose children attend these schools. . . .

For a Jewish community to be healthy-minded, another goal must form part of its thinking process, namely, the development of an interest in international Jewish life. Until this is accomplished, the Jewish community does not meet its responsibility, nor is it in harmony with important underlying objectives. Being at one with the sixteen millions of Jews throughout the world is for the Jewish individual a contribution to his ethnic personality. . . .

There is a limitation to the inspiration for communal action that can be derived from the building of orphanages, hospitals, and even community centers. The meaningfulness of Jewish activity in the local American Jewish community depends in a very large measure on the occurrences abroad which serve as a source for fundamental motives of Jewish communal action in the United States. International Jewish interest results in communal dynamics; restriction to local Jewish community matters may, and often does, result in communal stagnation. . . .

It appears that the Federation, as it has been developed, is perhaps the most appropriate agency upon which the responsibility for the approximation of these aspirations can be placed. This is primarily due to the fact that it is of communal and not of congregational composition, and that through the exercise of effective social engineering, it can act as an integrator between social work, cultural, and even religious activities sponsored by the existing organizations. The Federation can be democratic by including representatives of all groups in its considerations of major community problems, and at the same time can act as "a central intelligence" for the entire community. It can approach the community's problems from a multiple point of view, utilizing an all-inclusive approach. This has already been demonstrated by the fact that the Federation is no longer purely a financial instrument, but is rapidly becoming a functional organization. Furthermore, the Federation, in progressive cities, has assumed responsibility for such activities as Jewish education and Jewish recreation, and in at least one community, coordination of the recreational programs of the religious institutions and the community center has been attempted. . . .

If the Jewish Federation is to be looked upon as an expression of Jewish ethnic life in America, and not merely as a palliative instrument, it must concern itself with the accessory as well as with the primary activities of the Jewish community. Not to adhere to this policy is both theoretically and practically unsound: theoretically unsound because Jewish life then becomes split up rather than integrated; and practically unsound because of the energies wasted in repetitious effort which eventually results in an enfeeblement of certain groups of activities. A combined, balanced program makes for one united effort in which all interests, while retaining their identities, derive the maximum amount of benefit.

If the Federation in America cannot adapt itself to this conception, another super-organization concerned with the development of basic Jewish aspects will have to be created, of which the synagogue, Jewish education, the Jewish center, and the Federation itself will be a part. However, it appears that in a number of the more progressive Jewish communities in America, the Federation is meeting the demands placed upon it by the trend of the times and taking upon itself these basic functions.

3. Facing Reality*

ANONYMOUS

An unbiased and clear-cut analysis of "Jewishness" has in the past, and will continue in the future, to reveal that there is nothing inherently unique or different in this phase of group life. To begin with, there is absolutely no agreement on what "Jewishness" is. There are as many conceptions as there are Jews. To attempt a "general common denominator" is as impossible as to try to call by one name six apples, one automobile tire, fifty-seven cubic centimeters of hydrogen, a sense of humor, graft, and a week's vacation in the country.

* *Jewish Social Service Quarterly*, vol. VII, no. 1 (Sept. 1930), p. 15.

From its very beginning, the Jewish way of life has been forced into its "distinctiveness," so-called, by definite economic and social restrictions. As long as these exist, Jewishness will continue as a somewhat recognizable entity. Wherever tolerance, equality of opportunity, and social acceptance have been manifest, the Jew and his "distinctiveness" have disappeared. It has largely been the Jews' own strong separatist inclinations which have built for them the ghetto life and the ghetto spirit against which they have launched their frequent bombardment—futile as long as they insist upon being different and refuse to lose their identity. . . .

One of the great handicaps from which Jewish social work is suffering, which is retarding the raising of proper standards, and which is keeping it on a level inferior to non-Jewish social work, is the Jewish community itself. Ignorance, adherence to vague "tradition," self-glorification, and exhibitionism characterize the behavior of practically all boards of Jewish social agencies. These differences are not conducive either to progress or to satisfactory social service.

In the last analysis, the "separateness" of Jewish social work is merely one of the vestigial remains of a bitter ghetto past, in which one wave of persecution followed another with almost automatic regularity. We are living in a new age, which manifests a more tolerant and a more humane attitude toward intergroup relationships. As we adjust ourselves to the rest of the world, and as we free ourselves from the artificial externals forced upon us by the handicaps of earlier ages, there will be less and less need or reason for a separate and distinctive phase of social work, now called "Jewish." In fact, are we not all striving for that day when social service will be obsolete? The new social order, by its guarantee against economic, social, and industrial injustices, will make social work, no matter what its form or variety, absolutely unnecessary.

4. The Place of Jewish Education in Jewish Social Service*

BY ALEXANDER M. DUSHKIN

As we look back over the programs of the National Conference of Jewish Social Service during the past decade, we are struck by the constantly increasing importance of Jewish education in our discussions. From the time when the problem, and some attempts at its solution, were first presented officially before the Conference some twelve years ago—I believe by Dr. Magnes [1]—to this day, when Jewish education is given place on our program as one of the principal divisions in our work, there has been a constant increase in the time and attention given to a consideration of this field of work. It seems to me that this is of considerable significance, and indicates changing conceptions in Jewish social service. For this growth of interest in Jewish education has not been accidental. Nor has it been due to the enthusiasm of a few devotees. In my opinion, it is indicative of a rather fundamental reformulation of ideals in Jewish social service—a reformulation which has been developing in our midst, gradually but surely, for the past decade; and which I hope this paper may help to bring a little more closely to our attention. I wish at this time to analyze two of the causes which have helped to bring Jewish education within the field of Jewish social service: the first deals with the practice and technique of our work, the second with its purpose and character. . . .

The community-center workers also have realized that their work extends beyond physical and social recreation to the recreation of the spirit, and that no small part of such recreating lies in providing proper conditions for Jewish learning and for Jewish self-

* National Conference of Jewish Social Service, *Proceedings* (1924), pp. 267-79. Presented at the annual meeting of the National Conference of Jewish Social Service, Toronto, Ontario, Canada, June 22-25, 1924.

[1] Judah Magnes, one-time Director of the New York *kehillah* and later President of Hebrew University, Jerusalem.

expression on the part of their young people. They realize, too, in constantly increasing measure, that if their centers are to be real community centers, they must set out conscientiously to provide facilities not only for young people, but for the entire family, as well as the children of the neighborhood; and that for these children they must provide some adequate form of Jewish schooling. . . .

Lastly, those who are shaping the activities of Federations of Jewish Charities have been realizing—and with ever increasing force—that theirs is the responsibility for taking the initiative in developing an adequate community program in Jewish education, including elementary, secondary, and professional Jewish training. . . .

Many thousands of Jewish children receive their instruction in orphan asylums and in community centers. Many thousands of Jewish families are under the influence of family case workers, child case workers, and other district workers. The budgets of the schools, the possibilities for teachers' training, for regulating the status, the salaries, and the tenure of position of Jewish teachers, are in many communities coming to be more and more closely connected with the activities and attitudes of federations of charities. It is impossible, therefore, and unwise, for the Jewish teacher and educator to keep their work aloof and separate from the rest of the community endeavor. . . .

Of late we have been delving into our souls, so to speak, and have been asking ourselves some fundamental questions. One of these has been: "What is the purpose of Jewish social service in this country?" The forces that have led the Jewish social workers to ask themselves this fundamental question are in themselves significant. The lack of enthusiasm, the "emptiness" felt, and reported, by many social workers, may have been one such force. The challenge of our non-Jewish friends in social service, who, as our work keeps growing in proportion to theirs, ask us, bluntly or by implication, why we do not merge our work wholly with theirs and abandon our particular activities and institutions may have been another factor. The need for attracting new workers and for telling them what all this Jewish work is about must certainly have been a contributing cause. Personally, I believe that the challenge of so-called East European Jews, through their educational and religious leaders, in New York and elsewhere, who kept insisting that Jewish social workers must define wherein their work was Jewish, so as to deserve special Jewish interest and support, had not a little to do with raising this fundamental issue.

Whatever the causes, the fact is that many have felt that, in spite of its great difficulty, this question of basic purpose must be raised and grappled with. . . .

I believe that it has dawned on all of us, with more or less force, that the Jews as a group are here to stay—for how many generations we do not know. For, besides the forces for preservation from within, there have appeared the old historic forces from without. How these forces will operate in the future we do not know. But this we do know: that the easy solution of our problem through rapid fusion is not to be expected. Most of our children and our children's children will be Jews, and will be regarded as such . . . and while many individuals will be lost in the general shuffle, as a group we are likely to remain in this country for untold generations. . . .

Our task, therefore, becomes not merely that of social adjustment for the present generation of Jews, but also that of creating the best possible conditions for future generations. And, in viewing future generations, the lines of demarcation between the normal and the abnormal, the adjusted and the maladjusted, the dependent and the independent, become obliterated. The sons of so-called normal families today may become abnormal tomorrow, and the children of the dependent, independent. Our field of work becomes the whole Jewish community, and not some special sections within it. . . .

I believe that many, if not all of us, recognize that the problem of Jewish adjustment in this country is fundamentally not economic, nor political, nor even racial in character, but rather psychological and cultural. To be sure, economic, racial, and even political factors are at work. Jews may be kept out of certain labor unions, excluded from certain public offices, not admitted to certain hotels. Commercial jealousy and racial mannerisms may play their role in creating anti-Semitism. But, in my opinion, these are not of the essence of the Jewish problem. The American Jews are not an economic class, as they were in medieval Europe; nor are they a political party. Nor can we base the Jewish problem merely on race differences, because if this were so, the rate of intermarriage with non-Jews would be much greater than it is—as high, at least, as among other races and peoples in America. When we say that the essence of the problem is religious or national, we mean that it is a matter of psychology and culture—of attitudes.

What are the factors that make for Jewish consciousness beyond the physical fact of birth? They may be stated as follows: family tradition and instruction; the attitudes of our neighbors and friends, both Jewish and non-Jewish; the appeal of fellow Jews, wherever they be, for special sympathy and for cooperation in common purposes; the imposition of Jewish responsibility for each other's acts; the sense of special pride and sympathy engendered by the teachings of Jewish history through its record of achievement and suffering. All of these are psychological and cultural factors, and it is these that create the Jewish problem. To me, the essential factors in this problem seem to be first, the intense wish on the part of the Jewish masses to continue their own family traditions and teachings, and the consequent discouragement of intermarriage, unless intermarriage can be effected without a breakdown of these traditions; second, the attitude of Jewish and non-Jewish neighbors in feeling that "once a Jew, always a Jew," and of imposing Jewish social responsibility for each other, bringing to each Jew the praise or blame for the acts of all others, . . . and third, the challenges and appeals to pride, to sympathy, to relief, to cooperation, made upon each individual Jew by his fellow Jews everywhere in this sufferings and strivings, as well as by the "noblesse oblige" of Jewish history. To help the American Jew adjust himself in his new environment, we must, therefore, help him adjust his *inner* life; and this we can do only if we understand fully the cultural and psychological elements in the Jewish problem. . . .

What Jewish culture is, under what conditions and how it is to be presented—these are the elements of our educational problem. We are very backward in the development of Jewish educational theory and practice, on both the elementary and higher levels. Take the field of elementary Jewish training, for example. Both in extent and in quality, Jewish instruction in America is not a matter of pride, to say the least. You have probably heard statistical data regarding the proportion of Jewish children receiving Jewish instruction. In broad outlines, the situation seems to be as follows: of the 700,000 Jewish children of school age in the United States, one-eighth are being taught in weekday Hebrew schools and Talmud Torahs; one-eighth more are taught in Sunday schools and by private teachers; another one-fourth of our children, who are not now taught, have been given some little instruction in the past or will still receive some instruction before they reach their thirteenth or fourteenth birthdays; and one-half of our children have not, are not, and will not be given any form of Jewish instruction. When we realize, moreover, that the average pupil in Jewish schools attends such a school only for about two years, changing from one school to another during this period some three or four times; and that he is taught after public-school hours by hardly competent teachers, who teach him much that will not function in his life—we get some notion of the immensity and difficulty of the Jewish education problem in America. And yet this problem must be faced and solved, because our children will be Jews; and it behooves us to make them intelligently Jewish, living on the highest possible plane of Jewish life, as taught by our history, by our literature, and by our philosophy of life. And in this grappling together daily with the problems of Jewish education, we shall become clearer as to the content of our Jewish culture and its significance in our American life.

For me, then, the reformulation of the purpose of Jewish social service, of this newer ideal that is to guide us, this common platform—becomes fairly clear. It is to be: "Service to the Jewish people, so as to create the conditions for maintaining its individual and group life on the plane of its finest traditions and aspirations." It is no longer *Jewish social service*, in that it differs from general social service only because it is done by Jews for Jews, but it is *Jewish community service,* service to the communal life and aspirations of the Jews of America. In other words—and this is the crux of my argument—Jewish cases in social service must be dealt with by Jewish workers not so much because we wish to keep these cases away from the State, nor even because their pasts and "backgrounds" have been unique and different, but because their futures, culturally and psychologically, their futures as members of the Jewish community of America, are likely to be different from non-Jewish cases. This is a fundamental reason for our claim that the Jewish social worker can best guide them in their inner adjustment. . . .

5. Tendencies in the Jewish Center Movement*

BY HARRY L. GLUCKSMAN

The term Jewish center, in this paper, does not refer to any particular type of Jewish social or recreational organization. It is employed in its generic sense, and is intended to include every type of organization which attempts to provide leisure-time activities for the entire Jewish community or for a part thereof. Jewish social and recreational organizations are known by a variety of

* National Conference of Jewish Social Service, *Proceedings* (1923), pp. 144-53. Presented at the annual meeting of the National Conference of Jewish Social Service, Washington, D.C., May 13-16, 1923.

names and differ in methods of approach, in the clientele they reach, and also in their motivating philosophies and ideals. . . .

As a movement, the Jewish center is comparatively a new enterprise. To be sure, there have been settlements, alliances, institutes here and there, which were established by the wealthier and well-established portion of the community; but these were invariably philanthropic in spirit and management, and were conceived as a "defensive" measure, to no less a degree than are hospitals, relief organizations, and orphanages. The tendencies of the Jewish center of the present day are toward an affirmative, constructive effort, aiming to serve all elements of the community, not only the underprivileged and the unadjusted; and, as it develops, it must become a democratic enterprise not only in the catholicity of its activities, but in the responsibility for management as well.

The Jewish Community Center—A Definition

People speak as if this type of center—the community center—were already here. That is not so. No Jewish community center, in the true sense, exists in America today. There are approximations of it, for in every community there exist organizations for specific and limited purposes, some of which carry on a part of the work that would fall within the scope of a community center. There is, however, no institution which at present furnishes a common meeting ground for all elements of the community, leading to an interchange of views and to definite community action.

The aim of the community center is to build up an active, articulate Jewish community life as an integral part of the general community. It would furnish a leisure-time meeting place for all people of the community, young and old, carrying on such activities as the community or its groups desire to engage in, self-motivated and self-governed. It would provide a place where the members of the community could create means for their social development and education, for the training and recreation of their children and young people. It would be the Jewish Town Hall, or clearinghouse of ideas for the Jewish community. In short, any activity growing out of the desire and need of the community may be included in [the scope of the center], if it is a part of the general aim of contributing to the welfare and development of the community or of strengthening its Jewish consciousness as a constructive force in American life. . . .

The tendency of the YMHA's and YWHA's is toward the community-center conception. And what is happening in the various communities is happening in varying degrees throughout the country in large and small cities. The development of the center in the larger cities is primarily for service to the neighborhood, which constitutes a community in itself; and in smaller cities, it is for the entire community. In every case noted, with the exception of New York, the effort aims at the establishment of a center with community-wide scope and program; even in New York, only one organization is devoted exclusively to work among young men and boys, and only one to work among girls and young women. It is interesting to note that in almost every instance, the organization was formed not by people desiring to do something for others, but by those desiring to meet their own needs, relying largely upon their own financial resources. . . .

A question that every informed person will at once ask is, Do the various groups mingle freely in these centers? In some few cases there has been a considerable getting together of the several elements—Reform, Orthodox, and Conservative. Sometimes the center is dominated by the Orthodox, and the constituency is drawn almost altogether from this element, although the young people are not necessarily close adherents of Orthodoxy. In the larger centers, the Reform element is dominant in the financial support and the directorates. Yet often only a small part of the constituency comes from this group. Of course, fundamentally, we are confronted here not only with religious differences of opinion, which play a smaller part, but with differences in social status growing out of differences of origin and economic status, which play a greater part. These social differences cannot be overcome solely by the center in individual relationships; they are too deeply rooted. But the center can urge and play a noteworthy part in communal amalgamation, throwing open its doors to the various Jewish organizations, encouraging each to express itself freely, and thus affording a certain independence and a unity to homogenous elements. . . .

Institutes, Alliances, and Settlements

And now what of the institute, alliance, and settlement type of Jewish center? These are comparatively few in number, and in view of the restriction of immigration they are not likely to increase. In the main, they continue as philanthropic enterprises, the participants being regarded as beneficiaries who pay nominal fees for certain activities but not general membership dues. The control of the enterprise is in the hands of those who would serve the poor, the immigrant, and the underprivileged. There are two outstanding exceptions to this general description—the Jewish People's Institute of Chicago, which is developing into a community center, and the Central Jewish Institute of New York, which from the very begininng represented a distinctive philosophy as a Jewish school center.

Among the institutes and alliances, generally, there is a definite Jewish program. Among the settlements, however, which are really a copy of the settlements organized under non-sectarian auspices, there are some, though in Jewish sections, that persist in being non-sectarian and in treating the residents as individuals, without reference to their special backgrounds.

It is an open question for how long a time Jews will continue to support institutions designed to meet the needs of Jews which insist upon an artificial non-sectarianism that is contrary to every modern theory of the social adjustment of immigrant groups. The purely non-sectarian settlement, serving in a neighborhood made up of various races, still has its function to perform in reconciling the different groups, in teaching them mutual respect and confidence, promoting neighborliness and the general welfare of the neighborhood; but a non-sectarian enterprise for Jews and among Jews, it seems to me, means adherence to an idea which must sooner or later give way to the realities.

Synagogue Centers

No discussion of the Jewish center movement is complete without some reference to the synagogue center. Exactly how many of this type there are has not yet been determined, but their number is rapidly increasing. . . .

Three general classifications of the synagogue center may be made: 1. The first attempts to reorganize the synagogue, and to restore its now reduced functions in the light of what it considers the present-day needs of Jewry in America. 2. The second is an effort of the synagogue to serve a certain portion of the Jewish community, who are not necessarily its own members. This type is a synagogue center only insofar as it receives financial support from the synagogue. 3. The third uses the center simply as a practical means of winning or keeping adherents within its particular fold.

It may be pointed out that at least insofar as the first and third classifications are concerned, the synagogue center does not make a community appeal on a broad platform which can elicit the support of the various elements. It is frankly catering to a particular group, and has a specific religious point of view.

Conclusion

The synagogue center appears to be assured of further development and expansion, since so many rabbis and laymen have come to believe in its efficacy for the furtherance of religious life. The YMHA's and YWHA's are gradually merging activities, enlarging their programs, and assuming the functions of a community-wide enterprise. There has been a substantial and steady increase in the number of organizations calling themselves Jewish community centers, and representing a policy and program more nearly conforming to the definition of this type of center. Only the institutes, alliances, and settlements show no appreciable growth in numbers, due primarily to the restriction of free immigration on the one hand, and the changing conditions in Jewish life on the other.

In these manifestations of the Jewish center movement, be it synagogue center, YMHA, YWHA, settlement, or Jewish community center, there are discernible certain differences in program and purpose. Yet there are also very significant elements of similarity that clearly identify all of these organizations with the Jewish center movement. They all aim to aid in the adjustment of Jewish life in America. They seek to achieve this adjustment by various means, but all based on the utilization of the leisure time of the Jewish constituency, through wholesome participation in educational, recreational, and social activities. With the possible exception of the settlement, there is also a desire, common to all of these organizations, to emphasize and make meaningful the Jewish content of the program, thereby supplementing organized Jewish educational efforts and the task of the synagogue. In short, the common goal is to provide an effective instrument for the perpetuation of Jewish life in this country. . . .

IV New Problems in Jewish Communal Life

A SIGNIFICANT elaboration of Jewish charitable and social agencies, both in number and specialization, occurred simultaneously with the emergence of the Community Chest movement, a powerful unifying force for all social welfare overriding sectarian boundaries. Since such developments were on a community rather than a personal or congregational level, it was not known how they would affect the evolution of a widely encompassing Jewish community in America, now cut off from the reinvigorating forces of large-scale immigration. Despite many differences in detail, philanthropic leadership agreed upon three guidelines with which to meet the future: (1) support for skill and quality in all Jewish charitable efforts; (2) cautious exploration of the Community Chest; and (3) full testing out of the concept of Federation as an instrument with which to shape community action and policy.

The new Jewish welfare agencies and organizations were accepted as inevitable, but not without some anxiety about their effect on fund-raising and duplication of effort. Once accepted, advantages were found. The new organizations widened the scope of Jewish participation in community affairs; they made possible a specialization and experimentation which new scientific knowledge justified. These new performers in the arena of Jewish charity had to be accepted as full partners, just as their predecessors had welcomed the newcomer in his early days. Jewish groups with varied cultural, religious, ethnic, and economic backgrounds each supported their own charitable agencies, and their leaders had to find some way to talk and plan and live together if the American Jewish community was not to fall into a chaos of fragmentation.

Moral support for diversification could not suffice, so the idea of Federation, evolved in the previous decades, was tested out and entrusted with new and wider responsibilities. Lowenstein early recognized both the assets and deficits of Federation for the new tasks. The Federation was capable of embracing the most diverse groups, without imposing too rigid a demand for conformity, and it had the apparatus necessary to raise funds and secure citizen support for its decisions. On the deficit side, Lowenstein knew that few Federations had achieved wide participation in 1923; they had difficulty holding their leadership in the face of the attractive Community Chest appeals for cooperation and partnership; and they could not always keep pace with the ever-increasing demands for support.

These evident difficulties were worsened by more subtle ones, which were at the heart of all organizational life and behavior. The leaders of the various community and welfare groups were strong-minded men, although they had as yet developed little social or personal communication or intergroup cooperation in community affairs. Multi-lateral policies could not easily be imposed on or enforced in groups which had freedom to act independently, especially when community spokesmen were drawn from among the early settlement groups and excluded the leaders of the more recent immigrants. Finally, the task of creating a new leadership to broaden Federation roots exposed the Federation to twin risks: the new leadership sometimes became so interested in Federation that they lost influence in their own group; and at other times, they threatened to wrest control away altogether from the older leadership. These more subtle aspects of organizational life in voluntary communities were clearly recognized by both Lowenstein and Kahn, who were the forerunners of a whole school of sociological analysis of organizational life which was to arise twenty years later.[1]

The success of the Community Chest movement posed quite different issues. As Schroeder and Clapp point out, the new social work knew no sectarian boundaries. The urge to fashion an American unity out of the ethnic diversity of the immigrant groups was still very great. Charitable cooperation on a general community rather than a sectarian basis appealed strongly to those who believed in pooled effort as a way to reduce duplication and waste; to those who believed in universal brotherhood as the way to abolish prejudice and discrimination; and to those Jews who sought complete acceptance in the American culture. Some proponents of the Chest saw it as a way to reduce credal differences which underlay discrimination; others saw it as a way to tackle major social ills with more adequate financial backing.

Still other voices, represented here by Hexter and Waldman, were more cautious. They did not close the doors to Chest cooperation, but they expressed the need to retain diversity and variety in charitable work, and to assure that the practical needs of Jews as a group were met and not submerged in any vaguely general approach. Jewish Welfare Funds, very similar in aims to the Community Chest, appeared in the 1920's; but they comprised the full range of overseas, national, and local Jewish interests, whereas the Chests concentrated on local services. The Conference speakers seemed to be urging a wide extension of this approach as a Jewish community policy, despite the practical difficulties early welfare funds encountered in covering so wide a range of charitable interests in one fund-raising organization.

[1] The later work of Talcott Parsons, Robert Merton, George Homans, Alvin Gouldner, and a host of others systematically built up a body of theory which contains most of these early insights.

1. Jewish Communal Organization in America*

SOLOMON LOWENSTEIN, CHAIRMAN

. . . In the opinion of your committee, it can fairly be claimed that the Federations have been successful in improving the financial methods of our communal agencies, in securing a larger measure of support and a more intelligent, just, and efficient distribution of the funds thus realized. It may also be fairly claimed that as a direct result of the Federation movement, there have come about improved standards in the work of the various constituent organizations, amplification of the content of their work, and an expansion of the fields of activity.

It cannot be said so surely, however, that the Federations have shown themselves to be resourceful in meeting new needs, in showing initiative in the establishment of new organizations to solve persistent problems, in enlisting the efforts of existing agencies, or in providing reserve or capital funds for the rehabilitation of antiquated plants or the construction of new institutions. Nor have they been altogether successful in their efforts to secure the hearty cooperation and active participation of all the elements making up the Jewish body politic.

Experience has proved that in practically every instance in which a Federation has been founded upon sound and approved plans, the initial increase in the amount of financial support secured has been great; that with proper organization and intensive effort, this sum can be increased annually both to meet natural losses due to death, business failure, and removals . . . and to provide a gradually increasing amount to meet greater costs of living and maintenance, legitimate expansion of activities, raising

* National Conference of Jewish Social Service, *Proceedings* (1923), pp. 188-99. Presented at the annual meeting of the National Conference of Jewish Social Service, Washington, D.C., May 13-16, 1923. A Report of a Conference Committee.

of standards, etc. In no instance does it appear that as yet the full financial resources of any given community have been realized; though the rate of growth of our communities naturally diminishes from year to year, there does not appear at the present time sufficient evidence to indicate that in any instance the maximum result has been achieved.

It would be presuming too much to claim that the improvement in standards of work of the various affiliated societies is due exclusively to Federation. The development of a class of professional social workers undoubtedly has much to do with the fact that Federations have helped develop social workers. Contact with non-Jewish agencies, offering in many instances examples of superior method and wider vision, has undoubtedly been a drect influence in the development of Jewish work. The increasing interest in social questions and the vast amount of study given them has been shared by Jew and non-Jew alike, and has much to do with the improvement of the technique of our various agencies.

But when all due allowance is made for these and other causes, it is undeniably true that by relieving the executive officers and the boards of control of our societies from a disproportionate and in many instances almost exclusive interest in the necessity for raising funds, there has been set free a reservoir of energy for concentration upon the problems of the work itself; this has brought about the marked improvement of which we are all conscious.

Moreover, the Federation movement has, though it must be admitted in varying degrees, unquestionably brought about a broad community spirit as opposed to a narrow institutional point of view, a recognition of the fact that our various forms of philanthropic effort are but individual expressions of different phases of one central communal problem, rather than independent, self-sufficient activities.

This broadening concept of the meaning of social work has had the effect of attracting large numbers of young men and women of superior education and ability to active participation in these communal enterprises—workers who would have stood aloof from mere absorption in the detailed administration of any single institution, no matter how worthy in itself.

On the other hand, it is alleged by many that this very factor is instrumental in diverting from the management of these essential agencies men and women who might have given themselves freely to their development, thus reducing the number of individuals joining in communal life. On the whole, however, it would not appear that this contention is justified. . . .

The great shortcoming of Federation has been that in many instances it has signally failed to organize the community. This is due to a variety of causes. In the first place, insufficiency of funds has too often restricted the Federation activities to those agencies already existing at the time of its organization and resulted in a great hesitancy in admitting new organizations. This has left outside the Federation list worthy institutions deserving communal support, and compelled them to meet the tremendous competition of a centrally organized body enlisting the financial support of the great majority of large givers in the community. . . .

But the chief cause of failure to create a comprehensive Federation must be sought in the lack of understanding and congeniality between the different national groups within the community itself. Too often the Federation has been merely a Federation of old-line institutions, ignoring completely or partially the new enterprises established by the more recent arrivals. Thus, there has been created unnecessarily a lack of unity which is destructive of any true manifestation of communal life. . . .

A recent study by two of the members of this committee of various Federations throughout the country shows that in the majority of instances, the newer groups in the community are either inadequately or not at all represented in the bodies controlling the Federation. We are witnessing on a much larger scale a renewal of the differences between the original Sephardi settlers and their immediate German successors.[1] But whereas in the earlier period,

[1] While the parallel is sound, this repeats the common error that the American Jews of 1870 were predominately Sephardim. See notes on p. 14.

these differences were of little importance because of the small numbers involved, today the problem is so huge as to require the coordination and understanding cooperation of every group in the community, if a real organization is to be achieved. This difference manifests itself throughout the communal structure. . . .

Morever, there must be a frank recognition of the fact that if all elements of our community are to be represented and to participate in a thoroughgoing fashion in the philanthropic forms of communal expression, with a corresponding share of financial support, they must receive similar recognition in the purely social and recreational forms of organization. If we are to have real communal organization, there can be no place for snobbishness and exclusiveness. In this, as in other respects, all Jews are brethren.

This being granted, there remain, however, real questions as to procedure. It is conceded that the more recent additions to our ranks have not by reason of previous training learned the lessons of systematic organization to the same degree as have those who have been longer in touch with American conditions and methods of administration. Frequently, their institutions are not so organized as to make it advisable for them to enter at once without preliminary experience into the larger life of the Federation. In some instances, their premature inclusion in the Federation has been disastrous to both sides, and has hindered further development along the same lines. . . .

The obverse of the situation indicated above must also be recognized, namely, that as a result of the process of assimilation, there is annually a decrease in our ranks; year by year we find ourselves losing for communal purposes an increasing proportion of those men and women who by reason of heredity, tradition, and longer established residence, should for many years to come furnish the largest proportion of our active communal workers.

If the present diminution of immigration is to continue permanently, it will constitute an ever-increasing weakness in our endeavors to thoroughly organize our Jewish communities. It should also be said that your committee believes that one of the most important functions of the permanent committee which it has recommended for the study of this entire question of organization should be the deliberate and careful consideration of the probable effects of this immigration policy with reference to the field of what now constitutes Jewish social service.

It is manifest that under such conditions many of the needs now so pressing would lose much of their force, and money and energy would be set free for the fuller development of the work of the various institutions, possibly the elimination of a number of them, and the substitution of newer and more needed forms of work.

It is the definite opinion of your committee that the Federation represents but a stage in our communal development, and not the final form. What that form may be, it is impossible at this time to forecast. Papers have been read at an earlier session with reference to two forms of activity which may indicate phases of this newer development—namely, district service and Jewish centers. . . .

The Jewish center offers much hope, if it can be made a democratic expression of all the needs of the community in which it is located and if it endeavors to supply all such wants for family helpfulness, education—both religious and secular—recreation, cooperation with all existing special agencies, etc.; this would no doubt do much to impress upon every member of the community his responsibility and his obligation. It is conceivable that such an organization, working in cooperation with a general community board which will outline policies for the entire city (to be applied locally through such centers) would constitute a form of organization much more immediate and efficient than is at present possible in the highly centralized way in which we endeavor to meet our communal needs. . . .

Questions that must be given very serious consideration before arriving at a conclusion in this matter concern themselves with the amount of financial support to be realized from the Jewish community. In places where the Jewish organizations are invited to join Community Chests, is it possible that the amount to be contributed by Jews will be greater or less than would be the sum realized by an independent Jewish Federation? Furthermore, would the amount contributed by Jews be fairly proportionate to their number and wealth in the community and also to the amount that they should receive for the support of their particular institutions—giving due regard to the obligation of the Jew to contribute to the various non-sectarian activities present in the community? Should the Jewish organization enter such Community Chests as independent units, or only after they have attained such complete local organization as will lead them to believe that they are prepared to enter on equal terms into a joint enterprise. . . ?

2. Our Contemporary Ancestors*

BY DOROTHY C. KAHN

It should be helpful in considering the relationships between Federations and unaffiliated societies to bear in mind that many of the latter mirror the early development of our most modern and highly organized social agencies. . . . To call unaffiliated agencies our contemporary ancestors lays one open at once to all the usual arguments about evolution and contributes [little] . . . to the solution of problems of present-day relationships. . . .

What are the unaffiliated agencies? They might include everything from the unaffiliated relief society to the Jewish Country Club, depending upon our concept of the proper scope of Federation. Practically, however, the term connotes relief societies, loan associations, hospitals, settlements, nurseries, camps, child-care institutions, homes for the aged, Talmud Torahs and Jewish Educational Societies, Young Men's and Young Women's Hebrew Associations, and branches of national and international organizations. . . .

A brief inquiry recently directed to a group of Federation cities, ranging in Jewish population from 10,000 to 280,000, brought

* *Jewish Social Service Quarterly*, vol. 2, no. 3 (March 1926).

forth facts that support a belief in the growing power of non-Federation agencies. In nine of these cities, three of which are members of Community Chests, the non-Federation societies are known to be raising somewhere between five and twenty per cent of the amounts raised by the Federation itself, and none of the Federations supplying this information will vouch for its completeness. . . .

The unaffiliated society (for the purpose of this discussion, the unaffiliated society fostered by the Federation is excluded) is created out of the same factors that contribute to organizations of any kind. They are: (1) community need (real or imagined), (2) personal advocacy of means for meeting this need (this includes the self-seeking type of leadership as well as the most disinterested), and (3) disbelief in or ignorance of the efficacy, adequacy, or flexibility of existing organizations to meet this need. . . .

Federations set out to be all inclusive in their programs of meeting community needs. Such slogans as "give once for all," and extensive publicity showing the all-embracing nature of the activities of the Federation have propagated the idea that all the needs of the community are being met adequately by the Federation. The inaccuracy of this notion is recognized by no group more clearly than the Federation leaders themselves if they are wise, although they have done very little to alter this misleading propaganda. . . .

That the Federation does not provide opportunities for expression for all of the latent leadership of the community is an old complaint, born with the democratic idea and perhaps destined to cause its downfall. In the early days, there were enough parts for all who cared to play; but with the development of more and more centralized organization, including the professionalization of the most appealing and concrete tasks, the actors have become a somewhat unwilling audience, an audience with a more than the usual feeling for drama and a powerful need for self-expression.

There is little doubt that the Federation idea has come closer to the discovery of a common denominator of permanent Jewish interest than any other form of local, national, or even international organization. In its best expression it represents in a fairly permanent membership more varied groups, more diverse interests, and a more heterogeneous collection of people than any other modern institution, not excluding the synagogue itself. It has deliberately gone after and secured members disregarding religious differences, nationality, class interest, in fact even economic status. Anybody *can* and everybody *should* join, and it is no longer a rarity for a constituent organization to number among its clients a contributor to the Federation. Like democratic governments, it has extended the franchise with one hand, and gathered into itself increasing power with the other. But lacking the cohesive force that a political machine lends to popular government, the Federation has opened wide the door to defection or separatism.

One of the most interesting things about unaffiliated societies is that their membership is not as a rule made up exclusively or even largely of non-contributors to the Federation. Their leaders are usually members in good standing in the Federation. The defection, therefore, is within the ranks. If this is true, then these societies represent either unused or unusable leadership material for the Federation and its constituents. . . .

The fact that so many societies of this type have been organized subsequent to Federation, and the fact that so few of them, if any, have been absorbed by the Federation or included in its program of activities, is significant. It is probably true that the Federation has had all it could do in the short period of its history to meet the problem of its own somewhat heterogeneous constituency. Perhaps the unaffiliated society represents a next objective in the Federation program. . . . This condition in itself would not present so serious a problem were it not for the fact that the Federation has left the casework constituents without a philosophy for dealing effectively with these sources of cooperation or interference. . . .

Attempts of a cooperative nature have been along somewhat different lines. Four years ago the family-care agency organized a cooperative council, which acted as a case committee and was made up of representatives of a number of small relief societies.

These societies began years ago with specific purposes, one to relieve consumptives, another to relieve sick persons, a third to give free loans. All of them, of course, have forgotten their original program of work and are simply giving emergency relief from time to time. An attempt in the nature of amalgamation has been made by two of these societies, which meet jointly and distribute equal amounts to the same client as he appeals at their meeting. . . .

Another interesting phase of the situation is the fact that while the Federation agencies have lacked a positive philosophy, the unaffiliated societies themselves, when you strip away technicalities and rationalization, have a very definite and not at all unfriendly attitude toward the Federation agencies. Their members, at least the thoughtful and frank women who are their leaders, will tell you that they recognize differences in philosophy and method between their organization and the Federation agency. They will tell you that in the last analysis they are social groups having as their aim friendly aid, and will point out to you that the fundamental difference between their organization and the Federation agency is that they do not pretend to assume continued responsibility for a program of family rehabilitation. . . . This does not mean that these societies universally carry out in practice the spirit of cooperation thus indicated. Their failure to do so is probably due more largely to the inflexibility and absence of ingenuity on the part of our Federation agencies than to meddlesomeness, ignorance, or selfishness on the part of the unaffiliated society.

There is a further difficulty that cannot be overlooked, and it lies in the varying concepts of Federation. This discussion has assumed, for the most part, that the Federation has set out to organize the Jewish community for social work. Communities have been led to an *a priori* assumption that the Federation means complete provision for community work. Communities have also been led to believe that the Federation represents the community's best attainment in terms of standards of work. There is a third assumption, which introduces an element of inconsistency into the situation, namely, that the Federation is the method for seeking expression of communal needs, the need *to* help as well as the need *for* help. This last is inconsistent only because it is a more dynamic concept than either of the other two. . . .

We cannot permit organization to grip us by the throat. . . . The progress toward democratizing the work of the Federation implicit in the cooperative council idea is only a short step in the direction in which Federations must move, if they are not to give way to some other more inclusive and thus more popular form of communal organization. In a recent attempt at reorganizing an apathetic district committee, it was pointed out by the secretary of a large and powerful lodge that the essential difficulty experienced by Federation agencies in securing effective cooperation from unaffiliated groups in the community was due to their habit of creating figurehead organizations, He emphasized the fact that only a limited amount of interpretation can be expected, if we choose as members of district committees "key people." He called attention to the familiar phenomenon that an individual who represents a group and is selected as that group's representative by some outside organization is very quickly absorbed into the selecting organization, and loses his representative character within the group on whose behalf he was chosen. He insisted that the Federation will never attain the broad popular support which it requires for its continued existence, unless it is willing to take a chance on self-determining and official representation of outside groups in its councils. Individuals, however influential they may be, feel responsible to the group that has chosen them.

Not only must these unaffiliated societies be accorded some form of official recognition in the form of district committees made up on the delegate basis, but the case-work societies will have to be given the same freedom in their relations with unaffiliated agencies that is so readily accorded them in their plan to help families and individuals to the best self-expression of which they are capable. . . .

3. Certain Present Tendencies in the Federation Movement in American Jewish Philanthropy*

BY MAURICE B. HEXTER

About a year ago, at one of the meetings of the Executive Committee of the Conference, Dr. L. K. Frankel suggested that the question of the wisdom of Jewish Federations, as such, in joining Community Chests would gain clarity if a careful scrutiny were made of the history of the federated movement among Jews for the past twenty-five years; this would provide both an inductive as well as a deductive study of those communities in which the Jewish charities as an entity had entered the Community Chests.

With that in view, Mr. Goldsmith [1] and I made an extensive trip through the country. . . .

Relationship Between the Federation and Community Chests

In the Middle West and the Far West, this problem of the relationship between the Jewish Federations and Community Chests had developed much more than it has in the Eastern portion of the country. So far the only large Jewish communities in Community Chests are San Francisco, Detroit, Cleveland, and Cincinnati. Nevertheless, in many other communities the question is being discussed.

. . . There is no clear indication yet of what is the best relationship between the Chests and the Federations. In certain communities, the Federation has gone in as an entity—in other instances,

* National Conference of Jewish Social Service, *Proceedings* (1923), pp. 127-36. Presented at the annual meeting of the National Conference of Jewish Social Service, Washington, D.C., May 13-16, 1923.

[1] Samuel Goldsmith, then Director of the Bureau of Jewish Social Research.

particularly the smaller communities, the individual agencies receive direct subventions. From indications, the best method seems to be that by which the Federation receives a subsidy directly and then reallocates these funds. The only difficulty with this particular plan appears to be that no inherent provision exists for the inclusion of new agencies in the Community Chest where these agencies prefer not to ally themselves with the Federation as it is presently organized. By making a lump appropriation to the Federation, the Community Chest succeeds in enlisting the leading spirits of the Jewish community for campaign purposes. With but two exceptions [San Francisco and Cincinnati], the Jewish communities we visited gave less to the Community Chest than they received for their own organizations. This amount was also generally less than they had raised before the Chest was organized. So large was this [difference in funds given and received] in one of the western communities that the Ku Klux Klan circulated some 5,000 circulars protesting the amount of money taken by the Jewish philanthropies. On the other hand, we have the extraordinary situation in San Francisco where the Jews gave practically one-third of the total income of the Community Chest, and received about thirty per cent of what they gave for their own agencies.

We noticed in most communities that the Jews take a leading part in the campaigns. They often are chairmen of drives or heads of the Distribution Committee; in other words, the Jews do become prominent in the Community Chest activities. Practically universally, we found that the Orthodox element of the Jewish community contributes very little to Community Chests. Efforts to reach them have not been successful. . . .

Certain executives have complained that where Jews are chairmen of the Distribution Committee, in their attempts to be perfectly fair, they lean over backwards when it comes to funds for Jewish agencies. The Cincinnati Jewish community likewise gives more money to the Chest than the Jews receive for their own agencies. Nevertheless, it received much more for its own agencies than ever before. [The same situation holds true] in practically every other community. In Cincinnati, however, the consensus of opinion seems to be that without the aid of the Chest, the Jews could raise as much money as they receive from the Chest.

Wherever we went, we found that the Jews had entered the Chest more or less under compulsion. They felt that they would be damned if they did and damned if they didn't, and they preferred to be damned for doing it. In many instances, too, we found that the Jewish agencies were forced into the Chest by social leaders who hitherto had not been prominent in philanthropic affairs, and who wanted to ride into prominence with the non-Jew by "delivering" the Jewish agencies. In rarer instances, we found that some Orthodox agencies are in the Chest. Somehow or other, they seem to be psychologically removed from this movement.

It is still too early to predict any direct consequences of affiliation with Community Chests. The alliance is still too young. Certain things can, however, be postulated. The first is that more money comes to the Jewish agencies than they received before such merger. Secondly, the Jews partake in an active way in directing campaigns and in budgeting the income. Thirdly, we may be certain that there will be a growing tendency towards centralization of control in the Community Chest movement, just as there has been in the Federation movement. Fourth, I personally have extreme reservations about the ultimate effect of such alliance, particularly when the present generation, reared in an attitude and atmosphere of Jewish philanthropy, will have passed away. The large funds now secured by Community Chests from the Jews, I feel, will become less and less. In one large middle western city where the alliance with the Community Chest is of quite a number of years standing, the ex-president of the Federation stated that he had noticed an abatement of interest in the intimate affairs of the organization.

If one were to ask under what conditions should joinder with a Community Fund be made, we would answer that where the Jewish community organization meets the following three tests, joinder will not be harmful: (a) Where the community has already developed a community spirit and a rather high-type organization of its own, so that the Jewish community is accustomed to large giving. (b) Where the Jewish community can turn over to the Community Fund a strong leadership and personnel for campaign purposes. (c) Where the Jewish community will organically provide much larger sums of money to the Community Chest than it in turn will seek for the support of its own enterprises.

4. What Have Been the Effects in Jewish Social Agencies of Membership in Community Chests and Councils of Social Agencies?*

(a) Psychologically on Jewish Leaders

(b) Practically on Volume of Work of Jewish Social Agencies

BY RAYMOND CLAPP

When this subject was first presented, I questioned what contribution an outsider could make to a problem that had already been so carefully considered by those who thoroughly understand the facts from the inside.

The practical difficulties which stand in the way of proving anything by tabulations of statistics at once ruled out any attempt to use the questionnaire method. The success of the questionnaire method depends upon the ability of the questioner to word his questions so that the person answering has the same understanding of the question; further the person interpreting the answer must understand the meaning of the answer. . . .

* National Conference of Jewish Social Service, *Proceedings* (1927), pp. 138-43. Presented at the annual meeting of the National Conference of Jewish Social Service, Des Moines, Iowa, May 8-11, 1927.

I was asked to evaluate the practical effects of membership in Community Funds and Councils of Social Agencies on the work of Jewish social agencies. From my limited observation and from the reports of others, I feel no hesitancy in stating my belief that the Jewish agencies have received benefit from such membership.

For instance, the Cleveland Jewish child-caring agencies cooperated in a study of child care conducted in 1919 by the Welfare Federation of Cleveland. Following this study, they organized a placing agency, the Welfare Association for Jewish Children, to carry out the recommendations of this study that more emphasis be placed on keeping the child in his or her own home or care in a free or boarding home, and less emphasis on the institution.

The Cleveland Jewish agencies likewise participated in the Hospital and Health Survey. The superintendent of Mount Sinai Hospital reported that the survey resulted in a definite stimulation of increased and improved out-patient and social service, as well as many advances in inpatient care.

The great change in the case-work methods of the old Cleveland Hebrew Relief Association would probably have occurred without a central planning body. But it is significant that the people secured to direct the new program of the Jewish Social Service Bureau were trained in the Cleveland Associated Charities and Red Cross.

The most recent evidence of the benefits to Jewish case work of contact with non-Jewish agencies is the establishment of cooperation between the Jewish Social Service Bureau of Cleveland and the Western Reserve University School of Applied Social Sciences. The plan of training that has been so successful in the Cleveland Associated Charities is thereby made available to the Jewish Social Service Bureau.

It seems clear, therefore, that the Jewish agencies have gained from contact with non-Jewish social work, and that the Council of Social Agencies plan accelerates that gain.

That Jewish agencies are likely to gain financially from membership in a Community Fund, I am unable to prove. That they are likely to lose financially is, in my opinion, also as yet unproven. In Cleveland, for instance, when the clothing industry collapsed, the decreased giving power of the Jewish community was accompanied by a steady increase in Community Fund support of the Jewish Federation.

I have heard it said that in some Community Fund cities the Jews give to the Fund little if at all more than their agencies get from the Fund. If that is the case, it is likely that the Fund would get more money from the Jewish community with the Jewish agencies out than with them in, because many Jewish individuals and firms would give to the general Fund, as well as to the Jewish Federation.

Even if that were found to be the case in Cleveland, I should be sorry to see the Fund go on without the participation of the Jews, because of the greater intangible values that come from participation in the Fund of all groups. . . .

The fundamental question in this whole problem, as I see it, is whether the great cohesive force of the charitable impulse is to be used for the development of a spirit of brotherhood on a city-wide basis, including all races, creeds and conditions of men; or whether it is to be used for the strengthening of group consciousness in Jew, in Catholic, and in Protestant. It cannot be used for both. The Jew may think that he can have his own financial federation and at the same time graciously lend his surplus of interest and support to a general non-Jewish federation, gaining the advantages of both. But I believe that this is a case where he cannot both eat his cake and have it too. . . .

Please do not think that I am attempting to advance the view that the Jew should merge himself in the general population. I believe the Jew has his own contribution as a group to make to society, as have other groups. . . . Harmony is possible in an orchestra of many instruments and in a society of many peoples, when they have learned to work together toward a common purpose.

I am no assimilationist and do not plead their cause. It is because I believe that the Jew has other contributions to make beside charity federation and therefore forces to unite Jewry within itself other than the separate appeal for charity that I plead for the ideal of the Community Fund—a united community, with all races and all creeds working together in harmony to care for those in need, and to lay the foundation for improved health and strength, physical, mental and moral for the coming generations. . . .

Under the Fund plan, the Council of Social Agencies tends to become a vital force attracting and holding the attention of the lay leaders of the social agencies. The task is then important enough to command the best minds and the most influential personalities in the community; this is as true for the Jew as it is for the non-Jew. The Jewish leader in this way has the opportunity to make his contribution in the most effective way to the social planning of the whole city.

Under the Fund plan I have seen both the welfare and the Jewish Federations develop an interest and concern in the fundamental needs of the community. That is, they are using for this purpose the time and thought that formerly went into considering the purely fiscal problems which occupied practically all their attention before the fund-raising task was assumed for both by the Community Fund.

To summarize, I firmly believe that, through participation in the Community Fund and the Council of Social Agencies, Jewish social work improves in effectiveness, and Jewish leadership gains in understanding and in influence in the community. I believe that where the Jew takes an active stand of leadership, rather than a passive willingness to co-operate only after success has been assured, Jewish ideals of community responsibility for the underprivileged may become a pillar of fire. It will help to lead our peoples through the wilderness of misunderstanding and distrust and prejudice to the promised land of brotherly love.

Discussion

BY MORRIS D. WALDMAN [1]

If I essay a critical analysis of the Community Fund in its relation to the Jewish community or take issue with any of the views entertained by Mr. Clapp, please understand clearly that the Jewish people of Detroit have no cause for complaint against the Community Fund. Financially, the Jewish agencies belonging to the Fund are infinitely better off than they were nine years ago, prior to the establishment of the Community Fund, and probably better off than they would be had there been no Community Fund, and had they, therefore, been obliged to fend for themselves. The Community Fund raised in 1920, $2,332,095, appropriating for the Jewish agencies that year $90,727. This year the total raised is $2,978,000, and the aggregate secured by the Jewish agencies affiliated with it is $154,639. In other words, though the Community Fund increased its income by only 27 per cent, its appropriations for the Jewish agencies increased by 70 per cent. Nevertheless, the affiliation of the most important social service agencies with the Fund has complicated, perhaps retarded, at any rate made more difficult, the development of a comprehensive and effective Jewish community organization.

The idea of a Community Fund certainly reflects, in a measure, the existence of a tolerant, cooperative spirit among different elements in the population. Therein obtains a real, though an intangible value. But we shall want to consider carefully whether the Community Fund does really constitute the best approach or, as Clapp seems even to think, the only genuine approach, to the brotherhood of men; or whether it is little more than a gesture of brotherhood, no more or less real than the Kiwanis or Rotary, the Freemasons, or Odd Fellows, the civic organizations or political parties. . . .

There is a natural tendency to exaggerate the value of any enter-

[1] Then Director, Jewish Welfare Federation, Detroit.

prise promoted by ourselves. When Jewish Federations were first conceived, they were hailed by their creators as veritable panaceas for the cure of our social problems. . . .

There has been much confusion of thought with regard to the relation of the Community Chest to cooperative effort. Advocates of Community Chests assume as an axiom that it is the most effective means of cooperation, and even go so far as to imply that without a Community Chest we cannot obtain maximum cooperation. Does experience really prove this to be so? I think not. I have found that in New York, Boston, Philadelphia, Baltimore, and Chicago, where Jewish agencies are not affiliated with the Community Fund or where there are no community funds, there is as cooperative a spirit for the common welfare as in Detroit, Cleveland, and Cincinnati. Cannot people work together for the common good without becoming financial partners? Indeed, financial partnerships frequently result in discord and dissension, especially where the elements are not cohesive. Moreover, I have found that the relation between the Community Funds and the agencies tends to become that of a superior over inferiors—a controlling body over its subordinates. . . . I am sure that to the extent to which cooperative action in social work leads to the brotherhood of men, there is as much brotherhood in New York, Chicago, Philadelphia, Boston, and Baltimore as there is in Detroit, Cincinnati, or Cleveland. Let us not attribute too much value to this fund-raising partnership known as the Community Fund or Community Chest as a promoter of brotherhood. On the contrary, with the Protestant element in control of Community Funds—as is invariably the case, since they are the majority in every city and represent its main wealth and influence—the other elements, the Catholics and Jews, must perforce assume a subordinate, dependent position. It is because this exaggerated interpretation is placed upon the Community Chest as the big, indispensable, and exclusive unifying force in the community that it becomes so embarrassing for a minority group like the Jews or the Catholics to decline to participate in it. Because of the exaggerated function ascribed to the

Community Fund, these minority groups, when they hesitate to join, are exposed to the mistaken charge of clannishness and sectarianism, when in fact they are just as liberal and tolerant and patriotic as the majority group. In short, we must be careful to understand that the Community Fund is not necessarily the only and indispensable unifying force in the social work of a community. In the larger cities, it has proven to be little more than a fund-raising project.

Now when we consider specifically the relation of the Community Fund with the Jewish agencies and the effect of the former upon the latter, we become involved in the intricate and complex study of the philosophy of Jewish life. This is difficult for outsiders to grasp. Very few of us Jews have as yet defined the philosophy of Jewish life in America. We are still floundering. We are still groping in our attempts to adjust our community interests to the general interests. And in our case, the situation is more difficult than that of the Catholics. The Catholics and Protestants, after all, are closer to each other because [of certain similarities in their religious beliefs].

Bonds of this kind will express themselves through common action. The unhappy condition of the East European Jews makes campaigns for funds in this country necessary. To raise these funds, we must have some kind of organization apart from the Community Fund. This is only one illustration among many to indicate that the Jews of America have group interests peculiarly their own—wholly apart from their interests as American citizens. And mark you, these interests, unlike those of the Protestants and Catholics, are not necessarily religious ones. The common interest in the upbuilding of Palestine, by no means an exclusively religious interest, is as vital as any other interest, whether it be synagogue, local charities, or American civic affairs. The Jews, on the whole, feel that Jewish education is indispensable for the transmission of the Jewish heritage, and therefore for the perpetuation of the Jewish people. All these tremendously important goals require that the Jewish community be organized. Obviously the Community Fund cannot embrace these interests; so the Jewish community finds itself in the position where only some of its activities can be included in the community-wide scheme such as the Community Fund. It is obvious that Jewish Federations are necessary in spite of the existence of Community Funds. Community Funds can not promise complete immunity to Jews from charity appeals. . . .

I am constrained to believe that the existence of separate Protestant, Jewish, and Catholic Federations, in spite of Clapp's fears, is not going to retard brotherhood. Because I am thoroughly convinced that if the universal brotherhood will ever come, it will not come in the form of a fraternity of individuals, but as a brotherhood of groups. This is one of the inescapable lessons of the war and its aftermath. The group will-to-live is at least as strong as the individual will-to-live, if not stronger. . . .

5. Jewish Community Chests*

BY SAMUEL C. KOHS

. . . Off-hand, one might take it for granted that any community of Jews has the inherent right to organize a unified fund-raising effort to meet the total Jewish financial obligation for American or foreign philanthropic causes. Yet individuals, local groups, and national agencies have sometimes shown a disposition toward extreme selfishness. They insist that they must be given all that they ask for financially. If not, they will destroy campaign morale and the entire fund-raising machinery. That they thereby secure no funds at all, or deprive fifty or more other agencies of their right to aid, is a matter of no concern to them. They scuttle the ship, and force the other causes to sink with them.

The history of local unified fund-raising for national and foreign

* National Conference of Jewish Social Service, *Proceedings* (1927), pp. 112-19. Presented at the annual meeting of the National Conference of Jewish Social Service, Des Moines, Iowa, May 8-11, 1927.

philanthropic causes will undoubtedly be similar to the history of Federation for local charities. Federation of local Jewish philanthropic endeavors is now generally recognized as a necessity. Yet only a generation ago, this question was vigorously debated, and numerous arguments were presented prophesying the doom of Jewish social service unless this vicious idea of Federation was strenuously combated. But the idea of Federation has triumphed. The trend in the largest centers of Jewish population is itself a sufficient demonstration of this fact. Every one of the fourteen cities having a Jewish population over 20,000 is federated, and every year witnesses new additions among Jewish communities of smaller size.

There has been some preliminary discussion of the advisability of establishing a national Jewish Community Chest. But the idea is not firing any appreciable numbers to organize an effective effort to this end. On the contrary, a new variety of fears and obsessions . . . [seems to surround the issue]. It may be admitted there are dangers inherent in the proposed plan, but dangers are involved in every instrument ever devised by man. . . .

My own feeling in the matter is that we must first lay the foundation for this larger project by successfully creating miniatures of this larger undertaking in the individual Jewish communities throughout the country. Four distinct beginnings already have been made in this direction by the Jewish communities of four cities: Dallas (Tex.), Harrisburg (Pa.), Oakland (Calif.), and San Francisco (Calif.). . . .

I shall limit this presentation to a discussion of some nine reasons for the establishment of local Jewish Community Chests. At another time, a discussion of policies underlying the operation of such Chests, and the problems which such Chests present, might well merit a similar exposition.

Reasons for the Establishment of Local Jewish Community Chests

(1) Every Jewish community of any appreciable size is a favorite stamping ground for every sort of appeal for financial aid.

Throughout any given year, compaign follows campaign for local philanthropies, national institutions, sanitaria, hospitals, orphan asylums, yeshivas and other religious institutions, educational and cultural agencies, soup kitchens, and foreign relief and rehabilitative organizations. All of these are in the field, beside the regular local campaigns to meet the needs of local non-Federation philanthropies. Local groups come into being which sponsor their favorite agencies, and a lively rivalry develops to see which can outdo the other in securing the largest contributions. These frequent campaigns have very decided advantages, but they also develop serious evils. A single yearly campaign to gather the available funds all at one time attempts to avoid these evils.

(2) A multiplicity of separate money-raising efforts inevitably involves an inexcusable waste of energy due to duplication of effort, and waste of funds due to duplication of overhead.

(3) Campaign quotas are assigned to communities by each of twenty or thirty separate money-raising agencies. These quotas are utterly unrelated to monies already contributed to other causes, or monies likely to be called for by other appeals before a given year is over. A most interesting and revealing chapter in the history of American Jewish philanthropy could be written on the subject: "How national quotas are determined and how these are carefully, scientifically, and statistically divided and assigned to the 200 Jewish communities in America". . . .

(4) Among the ten plagues of American Jewry is the *meshuloch*. Well-meaning but misguided, he deserves most sympathetic treatment. I have yet to meet one who is not a problem-personality. He generally comes with credentials and documents stamped with seals, irrefutable character, collecting for some obscure philanthropy in Palestine or in Europe. The average uninitiated American Jew is utterly baffled by the diversity of these causes and the frequency of the visits of these collectors. . . . No one has ever secured accurate figures regarding the fate of the average dollar thus contributed. . . .

(5) Two inevitable consequences of multiple separate drives

and collections are the psychic exhaustion of the givers, and the opportunity for easy escape of all obligations. Repeated appeals for funds and repeated donations of small amounts create a false impression of quantity contribution. . . . A local Jewish Community Chest is perhaps the best instrument for securing the maximum donation to the largest number of Jewish causes requiring financial aid.

(6) In many communities the Jewish leaders have undoubtedly realized at some point that their monies do not always go to major and minor causes proportionately. Often some minor appeal will result in a larger contribution from the community than a major one. This contradiction in results depends on the nature of the leadership, the efficiency of the campaign, the caliber of the visiting propagandist, the spectacular nature of the cause to be supported, and other accidental factors. The development of a local Jewish Chest for national and foreign relief and philanthropic work is motivated by a desire to develop a balanced and sensible communal budget, the aim being to grant greater financial aid to the more urgent and more essential causes, and lesser financial aid to the less urgent and less essential causes. National and foreign philanthropies should welcome more heartily this splendid opportunity for a type of education never before possible on so large a scale.

(7) Community Chests in many cities have made Jewish Federations or the separate local Jewish agencies beneficiaries of the Community Fund. In most cities this joinder has deadened the interest of Jewish leaders in their own local Jewish problems, and has almost entirely annihilated the vital personal interest and responsibility which the entire Jewish community felt toward their own agencies and institutions. This new instrument, the local Jewish National Welfare Fund, or Jewish Charity Chest for non-local causes, is a splendid means for the reawakening of a hibernating Jewish self-consciousness, Jewish morale and conscience. The entire Jewish community thus can again respond to an annual appeal. One or two weeks every year are devoted to an emphasis

upon the problems of Jewry outside the geographic limits of a specific American city. This type of education, this method for keeping alive a Jewish responsiveness to the ills and the aspirations of our people, deserves the support of every clear-thinking individual. . . .

(8) After ten consecutive years of Jewish communal effort, I have yet to see a more effective instrument for uniting and integrating the divided groups in a Jewish community than this Jewish National Welfare Fund. The large number of causes, the varying character of their respective endeavors, and the scattered location of these agencies throughout the world make for an inevitably unanimous responsiveness which throws into shadow the unification of community interest on behalf of the older Federations for local Jewish charity. Here is an antidote to the poisons making for the disintegration of Jewish communities throughout the United States.

In conclusion, may I recommend to the National Conference of Jewish Social Service that in addition to continuing its interest in the establishment of a national Jewish Community Chest, it also sponsor, encourage, and perhaps undertake through the Bureau for Jewish Social Research the establishment of local Jewish Community Chests in those cities which may be interested and may request of us the organization and the development of this desirable method for meeting local obligations to national and foreign relief and philanthropic agencies.

V National Organizations and Their Effect on Community Programs. Toward a Federation of Federations

A NUMBER of national organizations were raising funds for philanthropic causes in the 1920's. Some had developed in earlier decades and survived the war; others were relatively new. Typical examples were the Joint Distribution Committee; HIAS to deal with immigration reception and arrangements; the National Desertion Bureau to supplement local family agency work; the theological seminaries; the Jewish Welfare Board; and various health agencies, among which the tuberculosis sanitaria of Denver were dominant. In addition there were a host of ill-defined groups which raised funds for Palestine. All of them purported to deal with welfare and social problems which were national in scope, or which exceeded the capacities and resources of local communities, such as the problem of tuberculosis (few local communities were considered able at that time to support proper sanitaria).

While such agencies dealt with very real needs, their continued activity also led to critical problems. Many of them were too small to support an effective program. As local community organization matured, conflicts arose between national agency and local leadership about policies, program development, loyalty of local leaders, and above all, over competition in fund-raising and thc allocation of locally raised funds. In some cases, as with the tuberculosis institutions, new scientific thinking, the spread of local hospitals, and the decline in the disease led to a questioning of the need for the extensive national network of hospitals and sanitoria. In 1922, the Conference Executive Committee, through the new Bureau of Social Research, studied the problems of budgeting these national agencies. This led to a proposal, launched at the 1922 Conference, for a conversion of the hitherto emergency Jewish War Relief Committee into a national body to raise funds for varied national, charitable, and educational enterprises, and to organize a procedure for budgeting the allocation of funds to the above agencies.

While there was no immediate perceptible movement to act on this proposal, the issue remained a lively one throughout the decade; five years later, in 1927, a National Appeals Information Service was organized to provide more substantial information about national agency fund-raising needs for use by local contributors and Federations. A number of Federations and several, if not all, national agencies were brought together, at least to seek and exchange information. The organization was in a position to accomplish what individual professional leaders had sought to do through the Conference at the beginning of the decade. A new era of confident cooperation seemed to open in 1930. Local cooperation was reasonably well established through Federations, and this approach seemed well on the way to working on the national scene.

1. Budgeting National Organizations*

LEE K. FRANKEL, CHAIRMAN

The Executive Committee of the 1922 Conference of Jewish Social Workers asked the Bureau of Social Research to make a study of the principal organizations that made national appeals for financial support.

* Presented at the annual meeting of the National Conference of Jewish Social Service, Washington, D.C., May 13-16, 1923. A Committee Report.

The organizations designated to the Conference Committee were: The National Jewish Hospital of Denver; Jewish Consumptives Relief Society of Denver (JCRS); Jewish Consumptives Relief Association of California; Leo N. Levi Memorial Hospital at Hot Springs, Arkansas; Hebrew Sheltering and Immigrant Aid Society, whose principal office is in New York; the National Desertion Bureau; and the National Farm School, located in Bucks County, Pa.

It will be noted, therefore, that such organizations as the Jewish theological seminaries, the Jewish Chautauqua Society, the Jewish Publication Society, the Jewish Welfare Board, and the Bureau of Jewish Social Research, all of which are making, or will make, national appeals for maintenance funds, are not included in the study.

At the Conference meeting in Providence last June, the then assistant director of the Bureau presented a brief statement concerning the study that had been made. The 1923 Conference Committee thereupon asked the Bureau to visit the more important of these organizations and to submit another statement that would not only analyze the general terms of the budgets of the organizations concerned, but would also attempt to make an analysis of the general aspects of the problems which these national organizations were attempting to solve. This summary of the study, which might be read as the report of the Committee on Budgeting National Organizations, presents the findings of the study under two divisions: (1) aspects of the problems of the work done by these organizations, and (2) general aspects of the budgeting of the organizations. The detailed study is available to those who are interested on application at the Bureau.

It might be said in passing that the Director of the Bureau, in the course of his work in the past year, visited personally the two Denver hospitals, the Duarte Hospital near Los Angeles, the HIAS both here and in Europe, the National Farm School, and the National Desertion Bureau. The Hot Springs Hospital was not visited.

It is obvious to social workers that the term "national organization" might be well applied to the two Denver hospitals, the HIAS, the Desertion Bureau, and the Farm School. It is of course understood that at this late date, it is impossible to logically decide that these organizations, or any one of them, should not have come into existence, or that, for instance, sanitaria should no longer function, because local organizations in Philadelphia, New York, Baltimore, or Chicago have had more success in handling the problems of tuberculosis. With such exceptions as we shall note, we must begin with the assumption that these organizations today have a general right to a national appeal.

Summarizing the situation briefly with reference to each of the seven organizations named, we find the following as indicated in the detailed study:

With regard to the Denver hospitals, there are certain general problems that affect their growth or stability. These problems are inherent in the local treatment of the tuberculous. This local treatment, because of varying local support, naturally varies throughout the country. In some communities a decided effort has been made to treat the tuberculous within their own families by moving them to more healthful localities and giving them excellent supervision. Other communities, such as Indianapolis and Louisville, have sent their tuberculous to local sanitaria. Still other communities, such as Chicago, Philadelphia, and New York, have their own local facilities, such as Winfield, Eagleville, and Bedford Hills, to which tuberculous patients are sent for treatment.

New York, with facilities for care of the Jewish tuberculous within their own families under the auspices of the United Hebrew Charities, care of the Jewish tuberculous in a sanitarium, and the after-care work of the Joint Committee, apparently has the most completely organized program of all. A fourth class of communities regularly send their tuberculous people to national or sectional sanitaria. . . .

1. With the exception of the Desertion Bureau and the Farm School, none of these organizations works on a budget.

2. As a detailed study of the finances of these organizations will

indicate, practically all of them with the exception of the two that work on a budget, and the possible exception of the Hot Springs Hospital, have always collected more money than they have spent.

3. All of these organizations, including the Farm School and excluding the Desertion Bureau, renew subscribers and get new subscriptions through solicitors who work on either a salary or commission basis.

4. The total annual collections of these organizations amount to approximately $1,300,000. Excluding the Desertion Bureau, the cost to collect this sum for other organizations amounts to approximately $450,000. The organizations average about 35 per cent of their total for cost of collection. The percentage of cost of collection runs practically nothing for the Desertion Bureau, as opposed to over 40 per cent for the JCRS.

The absence of a budget indicates the fact that most of these organizations work without a definite policy, do not attempt to assess their work in advance, or pledge themselves to definite sums; but, on the contrary, they try to raise as much as can possibly be raised from the communities throughout the country. There is, in fine, no clear-cut financial policy. If large funds are gathered which are far in excess of costs for the year, the tendency on the part of the hospitals would be to put these funds into additional building operations. Without budgeting, an indefinite policy of extension will necessarily continue.

It is not, however, any help to these national organizations to inform them that they err in all these respects, without offering them a definite solution which will give them at least the minimum sum to run the necessary activities which may be mutually agreed upon. For we do realize that the large organizations, with the exceptions that we have already noted, do fulfill a need and do accomplish some necessary work. After experiments with various formulae in the assortment of local communities on behalf of these organizations, the Bureau has arrived at the following conclusions, which may have particular relevance to assessing communities on behalf of the national hospitals.

1. That all communities should pay the patient-day cost, or the client-day cost for all patients or clients from that community treated or helped by the national organization; but that payment should be made for only such clients or patients as register for treatment or care within a year after giving up legal residence in the local community. In this category should also be placed such persons as are directly sent by charitable organizations to the sanitaria or institution concerned. We believe that we can all agree upon this, because if these patients or clients were not cared for by the national organizations, they would be a legitimate burden on the welfare organizations of the community in question. However, if this sort of assessment, with other methods which will be mentioned later, is carried out, sums spent for propaganda, collections, etc., should be discounted in computing the patient-day or client-day cost.

In the *first category* then would be the communities that actually receive service and therefore pay for the service received.

In the *second category* we would place communities that do not necessarily receive service from the national organizations, but should be asked to give a per capita sum, based on the per capita cost of the national organization, because they themselves do not do any work on the problem.

In the *third category* would be communities that now spend more than the per capita of the national organization for handling the specific problem locally. For example, if we assume that the per capita expense of the Jewish Consumptive Relief Society is eight cents—the per capita being based on a Jewish population of three and one-half million—and we take community "X," with a Jewish population of 200,000 and find that this community is already spending more than the per capita cost of a Jewish Consumptive Relief Society and National Jewish Hospital, this community should be exempted from appeals by these organizations, unless these organizations render definite service to people from this community in accordance with category one.

In other words, if city "X" spends $30,000 a year for the care of the Jewish tuberculous locally and is not sending any patients to Denver, in spite of the fact that this community has a very large Jewish population, the two Denver organizations should not have the right to receive funds from it. Exception will have to be made, however, if the national organizations receive insufficient funds from the cities in categories one and two. In this event (and this can be estimated in advance if a budget is used), the sum that is necessary to fill out the budget and is not received from cities in categories one and two should be apportioned among the cities in category three. It is understood that cities in category three that either send patients or clients to the national organizations, or from which clients or patients from the local community come to the national organization, should pay for whatever care these patients or clients receive. Any sums mentioned above refer, of course, only to the custodial or institutional care of patients or clients, and not to the work done through the family-care agencies.

While this method of assessment might undoubtedly prove interesting to the national organizations and possibly lead to discussion and dispute on their part, the question of the raising of the funds still remains.

We must repeat that it is useless to call the attention of the national organizations to their sins of commission or omission with regard to the high cost of collection of funds, unless we give them another specific method for raising funds at a smaller cost.

Possibly you have already seen a statement written by Mr. Billikopf as a result of a conversation he had with the Director of the Bureau. It is undoubtedly true that the most efficient agency that has thus far been developed for the collection of funds from the Jews throughout the United States has been the Jewish War Relief Committee. This Committee has reached practically all the communities that are reached by the national organizations. It has reached these hundreds of communities and many of the thousands of givers of small sums which the national organizations also have reached. It has shown a capacity for raising in a given year a sum upwards of $10,000,000. Such a well organized force has created untold loyalties toward a central organization, has called to itself through its affiliated committees representatives of all classes of Jews—has created a machinery, in fine, that ought, if possible, to continue to exist. At the same time, the personnel of the Jewish War Relief Committee is such that it would have the confidence, on the one hand, of the national organizations, and on the other hand, of the contributors of large sums and the leaders of Jewish communities.

Our suggestion is this: that the Jewish War Relief Committee be asked to continue its work for the purpose of raising the budget not only of the national organizations included in this study, but other national Jewish organizations ministering to the cultural and educational life of American Jewry. Among these latter organizations we have included the Jewish theological seminaries, the Jewish Chautauqua Society, the Jewish Publication Society, the Jewish Welfare Board, the American Jewish Committee, and the Bureau of Jewish Social Research.

A committee organized by the relief committees after the funds are raised might budget and apportion funds to the various organizations. There is no doubt that this would be an inestimable service, in addition to maintaining a well-organized machine for a possible future emergency.

We must bring together all the national organizations, so their budgets can be scrutinized, the value of their work assessed, a limitation placed upon unnecessary expenditures, and above all, funds raised for such work as might be absolutely necessary.

A representative, well-organized committee, in which all of American Jewry and its institutions have confidence, is at hand if it will undertake this task. . . .

2. The Question of Financing Non-Local Jewish Philanthropies*

BY SAMUEL A. GOLDSMITH

You will recall that at the Washington (1923) Conference, I presented a paper (which was the summary of a report made by the Bureau of Jewish Social Research), in which certain basic considerations were projected on the general subject of the budgeting of specific national organizations. These national organizations were: the two Denver Hospitals (The Jewish Consumptive Relief Society and the National Jewish Hospital); The Los Angeles JCRA; The Hot Springs Hospital (known as the Leo N. Levi Memorial Hospital); The Hebrew Immigrant Aid Society; The National Farm School. Mention was also made in this report of the Denver Sheltering Home for Jewish Children and the Ex-Patients' Home in Denver, and the National Desertion Bureau.

The report resulted in a certain degree of cooperation on the part of the representatives of the national organizations present, although—as was to be anticipated—the national organizations could not agree altogether with the report.

Since the Conference, a meeting of the Executive Committee of the Conference with representatives of certain of the national organizations was held. After considerable discussion at this meeting, which was held in December, 1923, in the city of Washington, it was agreed that if the Conference could propose a practical plan to the national organizations by the time of this Toronto meeting, the national organizations would be favorably disposed to consider such a plan. . . .

Unfortunately, it was not possible in the course of the past year to organize a Committee which could adequately deal with the situation and construct a plan with the cooperation of those Jewish

* National Conference of Jewish Social Service, *Proceedings* (1924), pp. 342-52. Presented at the annual meeting of the National Conference of Jewish Social Service, Toronto, Canada, June 22-25, 1924.

citizens whose help is essential in these financial undertakings. In the meantime, the problem persists.

We have had in the Bureau of Jewish Social Research, in the course of the past year, a great number of inquiries concerning the national organizations that we have studied and concerning other organizations, many of them Palestinian, and a number of national organizations not included in the previous "budgeting study." We have discussed the situation with a number of Federation executives. It was their keen interest in keeping the discussion alive and in promoting an endeavor to arrive at some basic conclusions which they might find useful in their local problems that impelled me to call this meeting. I would like to present a few basic facts concerning non-local Jewish philanthropies.

First: Let us view, very briefly, a few basic financial facts. The Federated Jewish Philanthropies, in the year 1923, spent approximately $10,370,000. The national Jewish agencies studied last year, which I have already enumerated, raised approximately $1,700,000. Other national agencies, such as the seminaries, the Jewish Welfare Board, the Bureau of Jewish Social Research, the Jewish Chautauqua Society, the Menorah Society, the National Council of Jewish Women, and the Jewish Publication Society, spent another $500,000 approximately. National agencies of a fairly well-organized character, utilizing their funds for expenditure in the United States, therefore spend approximately one-fifth of the total amount of money that is being spent by Federations themselves.

It is very difficult indeed to estimate the amount of money annually spent by unaffiliated (non-Federation) organizations in different localities. Based on the rather meager information that we have been able to get from twenty-four cities, we should estimate that, including New York, these organizations raised and spent for maintenance purposes something in the neighborhood of $2,000,000. Thus, we have, for purely local charities, approximately $12,250,000 expended; for purely national work in the

United States, including research and educational work, approximately $2,250,000.

The problem of non-local charities, however, does not end with funds spent by the agencies which we have thus far specifically named. It extends more now than ever before into the foreign field. The Joint Distribution Committee's appropriation for 1923 was $9,109,796 for Europe, including Russia and Palestine. There was approximately $12,080,185 spent for foreign constructive or relief work in monies raised in the United States. . . .

In other words, almost as much money was spent in constructive relief work in Europe and Palestine as was spent in the local charities here in 1923. Naturally, of course, it is not necessary to consider the continuance of expenditure of such a large amount of money in Europe, in view of the liquidation of the Joint Distribution Committee.[1] It is necessary, however, to consider the continuation of the expenditure of fairly large amounts of money in Palestine. . . .

If we are to stop giving money to Europe, and if we are apparently to go on giving about $3,000,000 annually to Palestine, non-local Jewish philanthropies are concerned with raising in the United States for their own national organizations and for Palestine and other appeals that may come, a sum that roughly approximates $6-6,500,000 annually. This is a sum almost twice as large as that raised by the New York City Federation, and represents one-half of the total amount raised for the affiliated and unaffiliated societies of all Federations. This is the outstanding financial fact with which we have to deal.

I am not going to discuss the question of the expense of collecting funds. We have discussed that often enough, and I think that, more or less, the national organizations have agreed that if collection of funds could be made much less expensive, they would be

[1] The contemplated liquidation had to be given up in 1925, because of the onset of an economic crisis in Poland and other Eastern European countries.

glad to have them much less expensive. I wish, however, for a moment to turn your attention to some things that are much more basic than the question of expense. There is no doubt that the Jews of the United States, more so than ever before, are going to be confronted with a continuous discussion of immigration affairs. There is no doubt that, more than ever before, the Hebrew Immigrant Aid Society, for example, will be fulfilling a necessary function. But immigration affairs cannot be made the exclusive property of any group in American Jewry, nor can we, as social workers, to whom the problems of the immigrant and to whom the question of his adjustment is so vital, afford to sidestep this problem.

What is involved in the budgeting of the Hebrew Immigrant Aid Society is not a consideration of bookkeeping. . . . If, therefore, through local means or through national means, we can begin to budget or help in the budgeting of the HIAS, we shall begin to think in terms of the immigration problem. This, of course, will not be a new thought to us, but it is necessary to postulate the problem. It will be necessary, in this connection, to coordinate the local activities with Jewish working girls' homes or immigrant homes; to work with immigrant families in relief agencies; to work with mental and medical problems, whether they may be in families recently immigrated or immigrants after the five-year period. There is no reason why work with immigrants should not be work of continuous adjustment until the final adjustment is made, nor why it should be confined to a hearty salute on arrival and temporary shelter for a few days. If we are going to finance the adjustment of Jewish immigration, we must finance it in all its ramifications, and the problem is becoming the property for discussion and for action of all of us who are interested.

We have, for example, nationalized the problem of the Jewish tuberculous. I use the phrase advisedly. But we have not for one moment stopped to consider what the actual problem is: how many beds are available; where they are available; what cooperation remains to be worked out. I endeavored, in a very brief discussion last year, to postulate some of the problems involved and to answer some of the questions raised. But until we are ready to answer these questions; until we are ready to allocate funds; until we know the actual or relative extent of tuberculosis among Jews in the United States, it is absurd to have the present continuous performance of new buildings and new beds without adequate reason for either.

There are a number of agencies working in an effort to interest Jews in agriculture—the Jewish Agricultural Aid Society and the National Farm School represent two such agencies. The question arises whether there is an actual field for effort in this direction. For example, the National Farm School has developed a peculiar type of secondary education. It has the rank of a secondary school, giving, in addition to ordinary education, agricultural training. There is a feeling that this type of training, even if it does not result in many Jewish young men entering active farming or becoming stock-breeders or raisers, is sufficient justification for the maintenance of the school. It is my understanding that there is growing up a closer cooperation between the Farm School and the Agricultural Aid Society than has hitherto existed. Should this cooperation be extended to the Council of Jewish Women in the work they are attempting to do with Jewish women and girls on farms?

In sum, I have here projected three problems: the problem of immigration; the problem of the tuberculous; and the problem of agricultural training, or of work in rural Jewish communities or among rural Jews. None of these has today really centralized discussion, nor can it possibly have, without some basic consideration of the local support that is necessary for the proper maintenance of these activities that will ultimately be found desirable.

I am, therefore, going to propose to you two matters:

1. That there be established through the Bureau of Jewish Social Research, at the request of representatives of the Federations, an Information Service that will deal with the national organizations and organizations making national appeals in the United States on behalf of foreign work.

2. That the local Federations consider the advisability, after a year of study perhaps or immediately if they are ready—of running a separate campaign annually, in the course of which they would raise the amounts assigned to the city for all non-local work—said amounts to be apportioned by the Distribution Committee of the Federation and such other individuals as they may call in, to all non-local charities or philanthropies that the city has been supporting or desires to support. . . .

3. The National Appeals Information Service Moves Forward*

BY WILLIAM J. SHRODER

On December 15, 1929, there was held at Chicago a joint meeting of the National Appeals Information Service and of a number of Jewish agencies that seek its support nationally. Twenty-eight Jewish Federations and Welfare Funds and seven national agencies participated in the conference, all being represented by both trustees and staff executives. Five additional national agencies were present as observers. None of those present had the right to commit the agencies they represented, although advance notices of the matters to be discussed had been given in detail, so that the principals had had every opportunity of impressing their views upon their representatives.

Two formal actions were taken at this conference, whose significance I now propose to discuss.

The first was a joint report of the representatives of The Jewish Consumptive Relief Society, Denver; the National Jewish Hospital, Denver; The National Home for Jewish Children, Denver; the

* *Jewish Social Service Quarterly*, vol. VI, nos. 3-4 (March-June, 1930), pp. 149-52.

HIAS; the Leo N. Levy Memorial Hospital, Hot Springs, Ark.; The Jewish Consumptive Relief Association, Los Angeles; and the Ex-Patients Tubercular Home, Denver. This report was as follows:

> The representatives of the National Agencies at the Convention of the NAIS are in favor of the formation of a Council of National Organizations. They will recommend to their respective boards the inauguration of the experiment in joint fund-raising to be conducted along the lines which they decide.

The second was the adoption of a recommendation by the Federation representatives as follows:

> It is recommended that in fixing the quotas for the various national institutions for the first year, the *status quo* shall be preserved so far as possible, having regard for all possible hazards and contingencies incident to this reorganized effort and the building up of a surplus or safety margin for that purpose; that a joint committee of the NAIS and the national agencies as a group, equally represented, shall, prior to the second year, devise a proper budgetary and accounting procedure based upon the experience of the first year.

These actions followed almost two days of joint and separate discussions by the interests involved, and comprised the first formal expressions of the desire of the national agencies and of the local communities to improve conditions governing the financing and operations of national agencies after almost seven years of continuous effort toward this end.

The successful example of thirty-five years of the Jewish Federation movement, emulated in the Community Chest movement of the past fifteen years to the point where almost four-hundred American cities are enjoying the benefits of coordinated social service and centralized finance, makes it unnecessary to repeat in detail the disadvantages of competitive social service to its recipients, to the active friends of philanthropic agencies, and to the contributors. Suffice it to say that all of the conditions which led to extreme dissatisfaction in the local communities exist as well in the fields of national and international philanthropy. Some of these conditions are characteristic of all of the agencies, all of them of some of the agencies. There is the same waste of service, accompanied by pauperization of individuals. There is the same lack of coordination of programs. There is the same competition for funds at unduly great expense. There are the same repeated demands, resulting in confusion and doubt in the minds of the contributors, and exhaustion of the impulse to service in the voluntary solicitors. There is the same ignoring of budgetary principles, and inability to plan and to operate on other than a hand-to-mouth basis.

In the effort to correct, or at least to improve, these conditions, the National Conference of Jewish Social Service in 1923 appointed a committee to secure the facts for such use as the national agencies might see fit to make of them. The report of this committee was considered by the various interested groups for some years thereafter, but without resulting in a definite program or action. Accordingly, in May 1927, forty-two Jewish Federations, being represented at the National Conference of Jewish Social Service in Des Moines, independently of it, organized the National Appeals Information Service for the purpose of securing and disseminating to its member Federations accurate information with respect to the work, policies, financing, capital, and such other items of interest as might be obtained about Jewish organizations making national appeals throughout the United States.

With the cooperation of the national agencies, this information has been continuously collected and disseminated since that time.

The information thus secured indicated clearly that the individual national institutions could probably secure cooperation both with each other and with the local communities; that it was probable that, with concerted effort on their part, methods of securing contributions could be devised which would to a large extent eliminate competition for funds and a large part of the expense incidental to the competitive method; and that these results could be obtained only through cooperation of the national agencies with each other, and with the larger Jewish communities from which the bulk of their funds are secured.

In the course of reaching these conclusions and their crystallization at the successive annual meetings of the Federation members of the National Appeals Information Service, this organization reached a clearer understanding of its own possibilities and limitations. It does not conceive of itself as necessarily a permanent organization. It does not regard its function as that of the coordinating agency of the national agencies, nor as that of their fund-raising group. It feels that it should continue in existence only so long as it is necessary to supply information assisting in the education of the local communities and of the contributors, and only so long as its help is needed by the national agencies in arriving at solutions of the problems which the operations of these agencies present.

As the foregoing statement would indicate, these problems will center around coordination and fund-raising. It was the opinion of the National Appeals Information Service at its membership meeting in Atlantic City that the easiest approach to coordination was through centralized finance, and that for both of these purposes it was essential for the national agencies to form what, for the lack of a better name, was called a National Council of National Agencies.

Analysis of the present sources of income of national agencies indicates that the contributions come mainly from individuals in the various Jewish communities, but that a substantial portion is secured from organizations which fairly might be said to represent their communities in their philanthropic activities. The Jewish communities might be roughly divided into three groups: first, those that support agencies seeking funds nationally through individual gifts, and that are apparently indifferent to the methods by which the funds are raised (this group is comprised of only a few of the largest Jewish communities); second, those that give through their local Federations or through Jewish Welfare Funds;

and third, those that support national agencies through individual gifts, their philanthropy being entirely unorganized. This latter group, numerically the greatest, is composed of small communities with little possibility of attaining centralized finance.

It had therefore been suggested by the National Appeals Information Service that the National Council of National Agencies might experiment with three different methods in the three types of communities. In the few very large communities, it was suggested that they substitute combined offices for the existing separate offices, and that the solicitations be made for the joint account of the national agencies in the Council. For those communities giving through their own Federations or Welfare Funds, the problem appeared to be more that of educating the communities to an intelligent division of their available contributions than one of changing the method of collecting funds. For the very large number of small unorganized communities, it was suggested that the National Council of National Agencies might substitute single solicitors seeking funds for the combined agencies for the present method of each agency sending its own solicitor. It was recognized that any experiments along these lines would have to be made with the utmost safeguarding of the financial interests of the national agencies involved; it was therefore suggested that an experimental territory be selected in which the present contributions were not very large, so that a failure of the experiment would entail the minimum loss of support.

Closely allied with the problem of method of collection is that of the obligation of each community to the national agencies. No method approaching centralized finance can possibly succeed, unless the contributors are educated to recognizing and meeting their just share of the support of the work so financed. The parallel between individual support of local Federations and community support of national agencies is complete. The problem of the just quota of the various Jewish communities must be solved before a National Council with a national budget can be successful. The National Appeals Information Service has recognized that this problem is one with many involutions, and that any arbitrary criteria of fixing quotas would be unfair and therefore unacceptable to many Jewish communities. The important elements entering into this question are: the size of Jewish population, standards of giving, the budgets of the national organizations involved, the amount now being raised in the respective communities by these national organizations, and the special conditions applying to some communities but not to others. Thus, the reconciliation of two important factors becomes imperative: first, those inherent in the local communities, and second, those incidental to the national organizations' previous development of the individual giving power in the particular community.

All of these questions were considered at the 1929 Atlantic City Conference of the National Appeals Information Service, with the result that committees were appointed to study the elements involved and to report to a future meeting.

The December 15th meeting followed, with the results first herein cited.

What is the significance of these actions? In the first place, they may be regarded as a hesitating first step toward the solution of the two major problems involved in the work of national agencies. This beginning of a national body of national agencies should lead to a more inclusive membership. The existence of such a body will suggest its use for the discussion not only of centralized finance, but also of the general programs of work of these agencies and the better integration of their activities with each other and with the social work of local communities.

In the second place, the agreement of these agencies to cooperate in joint fund-raising experiments should lead to the ultimate solution of the difficult problems involved, and to a direct saving in the cost of raising funds.

In the third place, while the action of the NAIS on quotas was equally hesitating and temporizing, it should lead to the establishment of definite bases for establishing quotas which will assure the adequate support of the national agencies. The very idea of quotas implies the development of sound budgets for national organizations, which in turn carries with it the need for careful planning and orderly development. These are the forward steps, however timidly taken, by the Chicago Conference, and should prove a source of satisfaction to those interested in helping the national agencies and the local communities to cooperate with each other.

PART THREE

ECONOMIC AND POLITICAL CHALLENGES

1930-1945

SURVEY OF THE YEARS 1930–1945

The Jewish social-welfare structure entered this period with justifiable self-confidence. The pre-World War I immigration had been successfully absorbed; whether the extensive social services of previous decades were mainly, or peripherally, responsible for achievements to date could be argued at conferences, but the agencies were widely given credit for the outcome, and the communal foundations for distinctive Jewish service organizations had never been more firmly established. There were only muted warnings of impending triple threats to the world and America—economic catastrophe, anti-Semitism, and war. Nevertheless, from all sides the surge of external events and historical trends were soon to press upon Jewish organizations, as they did upon all others, pointing up the fallacy of any program aimed solely at sectarian isolation and self-sufficiency.

Within four years, by 1933, per capita income dropped by nearly fifty per cent; the number of unemployed rose steeply to between ten and fifteen million; thousands of businesses were wiped out; homes were lost and careers ruined. The shock was world-wide; in the United States, it resulted in more than economic deprivation and physical discomfort, for the depression was a severe shock to the self-confidence of the nation. In the beginning, the reality was hardly accepted, and voluntary organizations tried desperately to cope with the flood of suffering, expecting that the economy would quickly right itself. Jewish agencies, along with others, lived from day to day and improvised emergency measures with such funds as could be raised from private sources.

However, it was soon evident that the crisis was not temporary, and that the instruments of democratic government had to be utilized. Large-scale governmental intervention was essential, in the form of federal funds and emergency-relief organizations, to meet basic human needs for food and shelter. At the start, the Jewish agencies joined with their Protestant, Catholic, and non-sectarian counterparts to administer the funds. But the task was too great, and slowly the voluntary welfare organizations turned to support first emergency and then permanent government agencies in order to help organize relief on a scale commensurate with the large numbers in need due to unemployment, and physical or social handicap. By 1932, it was estimated [1] that all governmental units were spending over $500,000,000 for welfare. Between 1933 and

[1] Fredrick Dewhurst and Associates, *America's Needs and Resources,* Twentieth Century Fund (New York, 1947), pp. 457 ff.

1940, these expenditures averaged nearly two billion dollars annually.

The creation of a comprehensive structure of municipal, state, and federal agencies for both relief and service permanently altered the charitable and social-welfare face of America. Major economic and personal disabilities of old age, orphanage, widowhood, desertion, physical handicap, and unemployment were now aided by minimum governmental programs. All levels of government cooperated through an ingenious grant-in-aid device which funneled federal funds through state and local bodies; these, in turn, fixed local policies within federal standards. In time every county of the nation was assured a skeletal public-welfare agency under minimal civil-service standards. Thousands of citizens began to share in policy-making for these new agencies as members of commissions and advisory boards, while thousands of social workers, including those from the sectarian agencies, moved over to provide the professional and administrative cadres.

These developments were welcomed as the manifest evidence of a new era in social justice and social responsibility, created by the American community and available as a matter of right to all its citizens. The new public programs offered the challenge to create a new world; advancement was rapid; and salary levels often were higher. Nevertheless, some qualms about the future of sectarian philanthropy could not be suppressed. It was likely to become more and more difficult to recruit adequate staff for sectarian agencies. A change of this magnitude also forced a major shift in function upon all voluntary services. If relief could now be provided by a public agency, at a level much more adequate than that usually provided by private charity, and as a matter of law rather than a situation that had to be justified by a confession of personal inadequacy, then a major aspect of private welfare would disappear. The continuation of the private relief function as a part of family rehabilitation would serve relatively few clients. While a few voluntary agencies sought to retain this activity, justifying it through more skilled and individualized service, most private organizations soon turned the energies of their boards and staffs to mapping new functions which could use the apparatus of the voluntary agency.

Family life in a period of depression and threatening war was subject to many disintegrating influences, and the incidence of marital discord, divorce, child delinquency, and parent-child conflict was rising. Mental and emotional illness seemed more widespread than ever. These social and family ills were not limited to the poor or disadvantaged. Many social agencies therefore turned their considerable technical resources to helping individuals and families deal with such problems. In this development, new and stronger alliances were formed with psychiatry and psychology: social-worker training was weighted with knowledge about human behavior; and psychiatrists appeared as important functionaries on the staffs of the agencies.

For the Jewish agencies, the transition was not so direct or single-minded. While the influence of their non-sectarian colleagues pulled them in this direction, their roots in the Jewish community forced them to give equal attention to the problems of immigrant reception, relief, and adjustment. During the thirties, a new, if relatively small, tide of immigration set in again, mainly from Germany and Central Europe, as the Nazi world threatened the existence of European Jewry. By the end of the decade, this became a major function of many Jewish community agencies. Money and organization became vital if any remnant of great Jewish communities was to be rescued. This immigrant relief program differed from the one of 1905 in that the dominant responsibility lay almost entirely with the American Jewish community.

Major action followed these lines, but attention was also directed to long-term trends on the American scene which would continue through depression, war, and prosperity: the steady expansion of the middle-class; the relative decline of unskilled and semi-skilled workers in the labor force; the rise of employment in the service industries; the increasing demand for professional personnel; automation and the threat of technological unemployment; the steady trend toward large economic units in enterprise, which was driving out the small businessman; the employment of married women and mothers; and the steady aging of the American population. Action on any of the social problems resulting from these trends clearly required greater voluntary resources, but the trends also forecast changes in the tasks to which voluntary enterprise could realistically devote itself. These considerations helped shape the new form of Jewish charity.

For a time, at least, the quest for Jewish identity was nearly submerged in the daily task of meeting emergency relief problems for which voluntary welfare was still responsible. The requirements of a beleaguered European Jewry, vast social and economic change in America, and a changing Jewish population, combined to prevent the Jewish social agencies and their supporting communities from following a single course of development. The concentration of historical influences forced the community, the agency, and the professional worker to adopt a many-sided and complex set of programs which were at once adaptable in size and flexible as to policy. For some services, established agencies were converted to new purposes, as in the case of the family, children, and recreation services, which moved into family and marital counselling, treatment of seriously disturbed children, and cultural leisure-time or character-building programs for a middle-class population. For other services, new organizations were created, as in the case of the Jewish vocational agencies and the National Refugee Service. The former took over the job of helping to guide youth, the handicapped, and the newcomer through the changing economy to economic self-sufficiency; the latter organized a major program for refugee resettlement built upon the local work of family agencies.

The communal, charitable forms of Jewish life were thus capable of containing and encompassing the many diverse loyalties of individual Jews and their membership associations. The reserves of financial and volunteer support which were, as a result, mobilized as part of a communal effort served to strengthen the fiber of a diversified Jewish community, and prevented a flying-apart into fragments of unconnected specialized interests in the face of such massive pressures. The great demands made upon Jewish philanthropy to join with public and other sectarian voluntary bodies for essentially non-sectarian tasks were responded to with vigor; but surprisingly, this sharing in general welfare activity was accompanied by an equal strengthening of specifically Jewish programs. While the demand for support from the Jewish community was thus doubled, that community rose to the occasion willingly, and often eagerly, in effect serving two fronts at once.

While local and national organizations were still adjusting to the changes which flowed from the great depression of the 1930's, the tragedy of World War II blanketed the world, and American Jews and their welfare activities were at once caught up in the grave obligations of American citizens, in additions to their obligations as Jews. American Jewry served in the armed forces, on the battlefields, in the war industry. Families were broken up; whole cities of people moved across the nation to military encampments or to new industrial sites; wives and mothers of small children went to work to help maintain the economic machinery of war.

As always, certain consequences of the war especially affected the Jews. Jewish youth, on the move in the army or in industry, sought some tie to their religious-cultural roots; and the movement of anti-Semitism, a backwash from European Fascism and Nazism, increased in strength in the United States. Above all, the rescue of European Jewry lay ahead; the fact of the death of six million Jews had not yet made its impact upon the world. Finally, there was the pervasive uncertainty about the character of postwar readjustment at home and reconstruction abroad: Would the new world offer the same opportunities to enrich the group life of minorities as it had in the twenties? Or would it accelerate the trend toward absorption and adaption in the general culture? Would discrimination increase? While sectarian organizations shared fully in the national war effort, they also thought ahead for the future. For such immediate and long-range planning, the Conference continued to serve as a forum, but more and more the ground plans for action were laid in local community-wide organizations, especially in the Federations and Welfare Funds.

In wartime, the Jewish Welfare Board was used to organize a staff of workers to serve the needs of the armed forces as a part of the United Service Organization, which integrated the efforts of other sectarian and voluntary agencies. The vocational agencies grew as they helped direct and prepare manpower for new military and industrial tasks. The National Refugee Service and HIAS continued to work and hold themselves in readiness for the post-war period, while the Joint Distribution Committee became a major international agency working in dangerous European territories and preparing for a post-war rescue operation. Finally, fund-raising for all voluntary social welfare was affected by the re-emergence of the War Chest as the national and local method for coordinating and conserving both efforts and funds.

Two significant, although in the long run relatively minor events, merit attention. The thirties brought into Jewish philanthropy the political controversies of the time. Plans to meet successive crises depended upon the causal explanations adopted, and such explanations reflected certain biases of current political or philosophical thought. Some interpretations of the functions of philanthropy were based upon the theory of mild adjustments in a free-market economy which required limited control (the New Deal); others explained events in terms of class conflict (the communists and socialists); still others chose the individualistic view of social psychology and personal responsibility. All these views and more were advanced with vigor and heat in an effort to shape the course of agency and community policy. The freedom to experiment meant that all approaches be tested, including the liberal trade-union view of the unionization of agency staffs in major cities.[2]

[2] The social-service employees union, at first independent but later affiliated with the Congress of Industrial Organizations, took firm if not exclusive root primarily in Jewish agencies in a few large cities.

Finally, the long struggle to assure a steady flow of qualified community workers capable of understanding and serving Jewish needs was rewarded by the organization of the Jewish School of Social Work in the late 1920's. It flourished throughout the thirties and attempted to combine in one training center the teaching of the special needs of Jewish communities and the general professional equipment of American social work. Its graduates staffed both Jewish and non-sectarian agencies, although it lacked sufficiently deep roots in local community life to survive the period. Still, it was a significant effort to provide those communities with a steady flow of qualified personnel upon which the conduct of social work in the United States was now fully dependent.

I Economic Crisis: The Rise of Public Relief and Social Security

The great depression of 1929 took the nation completely by surprise, and in the early stages agency staffs assumed that these effects would be minor, although they watched with some anxiety the rising trends in relief applications. Many communities felt, rather than knew, that their own organizations could meet any domestic contingency.

The economic collapse challenged this autarchic outlook, and the doctrine of "we care for our own" was revised. The so-called "Peter Stuyvesant Pledge" was soon seen to be more myth than reality, although it had served as the basic principle of communal policy for many decades. This opened the way for the formation of a new community policy *vis-à-vis* the general community, argued out around the issue of whether needy Jews should depend on public relief rather than upon aid from their co-religionists. Four main approaches were advanced: (1) Active support of public welfare as the wave of the future in solving economic need. Voluntary social work was considered unsuitable for solving deep economic and social problems, but Jewish services could well concentrate on "special problems" of Jews, Jewish culture, and education. (2) A cautious support of the new public intervention, either as a temporary emergency measure, or to finance relief work administered by private agencies. Voluntary organization would remain at the core of this work to safeguard quality, humanitarianism, and scientific method, which could not, presumably, be entrusted to public efforts. (3) Turning Jewish agencies wholly into the path of personal counselling on family adjustment problems. (4) Finally, some counselled that any public welfare was an assault on both American and Jewish concepts of voluntary obligation and would undermine private freedom.

While the debate went on, the rush of events soon fixed the course of action. Large public-relief programs were essential, if urban chaos was to be prevented; these were finally welcomed, even urged, in the form of federal loans to cities, and later as directly administered federal and local relief programs. Boards and staffs of local agencies, and of national agencies, such as the Bureau of Jewish Social Research, joined their counterparts in the Family Welfare Association of America, the Community Chest, and local Family Societies, in urging and administering the new projects. Slowly a shakey confidence was re-established that voluntary agencies would survive, that new social tasks would arise, and that Jewish social agencies would have more than enough work to occupy their staffs and financial resources. Slowly the idea was accepted that underprivileged Jewish families could rely upon public and non-sectarian relief with confidence, and that such relief could be well administered, while voluntary and sectarian groups supported its administration and helped influence its policies through citizen action. Save for certain special areas, such as new immigrant assistance, the voluntary agencies and their Federations were freed to support a strong Jewish life in new ways by strengthening family life, by vocational guidance, and by care of the chronic sick and the aged.

1. What Do We Owe to Peter Stuyvesant?*

BY I. M. RUBINOW

In 1652, Peter Stuyvesant, Governor of New Amsterdam, now

* National Conference of Jewish Social Service, *Proceedings* (1930), pp. 89-104. Presented at the annual meeting of the National Conference of Jewish Social Service, Boston, Mass., June 7-11, 1930.

New York, received a promise from the Jews who came to settle there that they would care for their own poor. Ever since then, the Jews of this country have prided themselves that this sacred promise which the first Jewish settlers in America made has never been broken. . . .

This historic statement imposes certain obligations. In one form or another, it has been repeated a thousand or a thousand thousand times, from the platform, in popular articles, even in serious books.[1] . . .

Is it good history? Have we made a promise? Just what kind of a promise did we make? Have we fulfilled the pledge? And is the promise still binding? Must it control our policies and programs in the future? Here is a somewhat more comprehensive and accurate statement of the situation as it existed two and one-half centuries ago which appears in the book *Justice to the Jew,* by Madison C. Peters. . . :

At this time the Governor was Peter Stuyvesant, a stern, unbending, narrow-minded bigot, whose veins had been inoculated with the virus of Calvinism and to whom all other sects were insufferable, especially the Jews. Therefore . . . he began preparation to have the Jews banished from the community. He petitioned his employers, the Dutch West Indies Company, for permission to drive them beyond the pale of the New Netherlands; but the worthy directors was more tolerant than their representative, to whom they replied, saying that this request was inconsistent with reason and justice. To further show their disapprobation of Stuyvesant's bigotry, they passed an Act permitting the Jews to reside and trade in New Netherlands, stipulating that they—the Jews—would care for their own poor, to which they willingly acquiesced.[2]

[1] See Boris D. Bogen, *Jewish Philanthropy—An Exposition of Principles and Methods of Jewish Social Service in the United States* (New York, 1917), p. 4. This statement, as Dr. Bogen indicates, is a paraphrase of part of the presidential address made by Judge Julian W. Mack, President of the 1906 National Conference of Jewish Charities, in which he raised the question, "Why have we our Jewish charities?"

[2] The substance of the given quotation, though differently worded, appears also in the author's autographed edition (London and New York, F. Tennyson Neely, ca. 1899), p. 22.

May I submit to the gentlemen of the jury that this is quite another story. If this be a promise, evidently it was obtained *under duress,* under threat of expulsion. . . .

As a matter of fact, this whole misconception, supported by a curious mixture of holy tradition, racial pride, and a typical Jewish sense of group guilt, has definitely colored both the theory and practice of our work, and much of the social philosophy of the American Jewish community. . . .

And if we are proud, is the pride justified? Have we, as a matter of fact, always taken care of our poor in this country? If we have made the promise, can we really claim to have kept it? Far be it from me to deny the well-known generosity of Jewish philanthropy in this country, as judged by comparison with other groups. The facts and figures are available. . . . The average family supported by Jewish philanthropic relief agencies receives about twice as much in relief as non-Jewish families from non-sectarian agencies. I believe that in every city where Jewish philanthropic Federations exist side by side with non-sectarian Community Chests, the per capita contribution for the Jewish population is considerably higher than for the general population. In many cities (though there are some sad exceptions) where all-embracing Community Chests exist, it is again a matter of pride with leading Jews that the Jewish contributions to the Community Chest be greater than the amount required by Jewish agencies. It hardly seems necessary to overburden the audience with much statistical evidence to establish the obvious.

And of these things we Jews are proud, perhaps justly so. I say "perhaps" deliberately. Even in this respect there is considerable room for discussion, for it has not yet been established with an equal degree of statistical accuracy that on the whole the Jewish voluntary contribution to public and social needs is in excess of what would be their fair proportion, according to their population and economic resources. . . . Is it necessary to remind the professional worker that the Jews have not built their own insane asylums? Nor have the Jews refused to accept treatment in non-Jewish hospitals, whether public or private. . . . Nor have we worried very much until perhaps very recently that thousands and tens of thousands of our students in colleges, mostly poor, were being maintained partly out of State funds and partly out of philanthropic contributions of non-Jews. And let us come somewhat more closely to the specific problem of relief. Injured Jewish workmen receive large amounts through compensation legislation. Jewish widows are on the lists of most widows' and mothers' pension funds. Presumably, among the 50,000 men and women over seventy years of age who have been put on the roster of the New York Old Age Security scheme, there is no dearth of Jewish names. The plain, unadorned truth, therefore, is that the Jews, as a separate group, have not singly and entirely supported their own poor.

The point of the argument is that the promise itself may have been not only diplomatic, but fair and just in its own day and generation. It was based upon a certain definite social philosophy which, like all other social philosophies, derived its strength from a certain social structure. Two hundred and fifty years ago, and perhaps even fifty years ago, poverty may have been primarily a result of individual factors, or at most group factors. Perhaps the shrewd business people who signed that blank check 250 years ago had good reasons to believe that the amount to be written in need would never become a very heavy burden.[3] But conditions have changed. Very much so! Instead of a quarter of a million Jews scarcely a generation ago, we have four million and a quarter. Instead of being a country of small individual enterprise, we have

[3] The reason the first Jews in New Amsterdam readily agreed to care for their poor was that it was then the norm for Jews to do so. . . . They were primarily poor working people or struggling storekeepers, and not shrewd business people. The most successful of the orginal group of twenty-four, Asser Levy, started as a common laborer, became a butcher, a tavernkeeper and then a trader. Levy was a leader in the struggle against discriminatory conditions for the Jews of New Amsterdam, but not against the agreement to care for their own, which was not considered unusual much less onerous.

become the greatest industrial country in all the world, and in all history. . . .

Why, then, under these conditions, do we have this somewhat naive, antiquated emphasis upon isolation in philanthropic work, in dealing with the problems of economic distress? . . . .

Perhaps it *has* been a good thing, with the emphasis upon the "has." And if it should appear that in this day and generation it has ceased to be a constructive or conserving force, it may be necessary to abandon this rather pretty social myth. . . .

Thus we social workers, and also the successful and charitable contributors, have, until a very short time ago, been living in a sort of fool's paradise. We had begun to feel quite sure that the problem of poverty was rapidly disappearing. Numerous community enterprises were advocated, not only because of their intrinsic necessity, great as that may have been, but in order to find an outlet for the social, the communal, and the philanthropic motive in the heart of the large giver. Were we not, as a matter of fact, definitely promised just five years ago that the volume of dependency has been decreasing rapidly? "It is now half of what it was fifteen years ago," it was said. "Within the next three years, the problem will again be halved". . . . And then came the jolt! . . . .

Time will not permit me to go into a comprehensive discussion of the present economic situation. Within the narrow limits of the problem of Jewish relief, there is enough evidence to prove that only a short time ago, we were sitting on a powder magazine. In almost every Jewish community, exactly as in the non-Jewish communities, the demand for relief has increased by leaps and bounds. Statistics, both Jewish and non-Jewish, have told the story beyond any shadow of doubt. In every Jewish community the available resources for relief have been strained to the utmost. And if this has happened in some communities more than in others, the differences are often due to differences in degree of communal aid rather than existing need. It still remains true, however, that Jewish relief agencies have shown a greater sensitivity, a greater anxiety to meet the situation than many non-sectarian agencies. . . .

But as we sobered up and counted up our losses, and began to estimate our prospects for the future, we had to come to the conclusion that even Jewish philanthropy is subject to the same inexorable law; its resources must become more restricted as the result of the very forces which make for an increasing demand, and the voluntary-group responsibility is bound to be found inadequate in meeting the serious social problem of mass distress.

What shall be the answer of the Jewish social worker to this real and very serious problem? Shall we simply exercise more energetically the old methods of persuasion? Shall we beg and cajole and exhort even more than we have done in the past, in the hope that in this way we might increase the current and philanthropic contributions? That, of course, is the easiest way, theoretically. . . . However, the public has given voice to a resistance that threatens to increase, particularly in view of the ever growing and irritating competition between the numberless appeals. . . . [Nevertheless, this solution remains the most popular answer to the problems presented among those who have closed themselves off to all wider possibilities.]

In the gruesome picture [of economic conditions] which any careful reader of the newspapers would have observed during the last six months—soup kitchens, bread lines, overcrowded lodging houses, flop houses, increased begging, and increased suicide and general mortality rate—the Jews have not played any disproportionate part. The objection to depending upon the method of appeal to the outside community lies in a different direction. It lies in the acquiescence by a professionally trained group to a lack of social [welfare] policy in this country.

It is in this direction that the Jewish community has sinned, and the Jewish professional workers even more so, since they are supposed, if not to lead, at least to point the way. A factor which would retard social progress even in prosperous days becomes especially harmful in days such as these.

In one of the largest Jewish communities, the private relief agency discourages widowed families from claiming the widows' pension, which is theirs by right, by offering them a more generous rate of assistance. In another large Jewish community a few years ago, when the question of a municipal appropriation for relief of the unemployed arose, Jewish leadership remained inactive on the grounds that "we Jews will be able to meet the situation." Not only did this attitude deprive the Jewish dependent of a certain amount of aid that might be made available, but the entire movement to a very large extent remained without Jewish participation, and to that extent was weakened.

Illustrations of this type could be multiplied. Group pride thus may easily become a reactionary force. Consider the wider implications of this attitude. Much of the progressive social and labor legislation in this country dealing with wages, accident compensation, housing reform, public recreation, etc., has been to a very large extent influenced by efforts of American social workers. Hull House, the AICP,[4] the larger schools of social service, the national conferences of social service—these have been the power houses from which came the moving force for the development of broad social programs. How few and far between have been the Jewish social workers active in these movements? How many programs of social reform have been advocated or even discussed at our own National Conference? Insofar as we were dealing with problems of particular interest to the Jewish minority groups, such reticence was wise and commendable; but to the extent to which we have kept the fundamental problems of American economic life within the narrow limits of group philanthropic interests, to that extent we have kept ourselves outside of the progressive current of American life.

Most of us, generous contributors as well as professional workers, have come from the other side. Have we not too readily adopted the prevailing American philosophy that what in Europe constitutes the proper domain of social policy, must in America remain and can be better achieved as an enterprise of private

[4] Association for Improving the Conditions of the Poor, a pioneering social agency in New York.

philanthropy? Have we not, in this effort to accept this philosophy, failed to notice the rising current of progressive legislation? Compensation, mothers' pensions, old-age security, and in the future the possibility of health and unemployment insurance—these movements, except for the interval occasioned by the post-war reaction, have been growing for over twenty years. When they were achieved, we were not above taking advantage of them; but in their achievement we have played almost an insignificant part—surely a very much less significant part than we Jews have played in the development of similar policies throughout Europe. If the cause of such inertia was due to the fact, if it be a fact, that up to now we have been able to meet the problem of poverty in this voluntary way (though there is a good deal of doubt even as to that), even then the result of group pride must be described as a very pernicious one, insofar as our participation in the civic growth of the country is concerned. Is it not possible that we have deliberately kept ourselves in a social and economic ghetto?

If we give due consideration to American economic problems, surely the pragmatic bent of our thinking for which we Jews are so known and of which we may be justly proud, should have convinced us by this time that for all of the publicity given to or purchased by private philanthropy in this country, it is a very [inadequate] method of meeting the problems which it claims to meet. If not for fear of overburdening the audience with statistical figures, comparisons could be made between the total sums available for relief of distress in, for example, "poor" England and "rich" America which would hardly be complimentary to our country. But even limiting ourselves to American conditions, how pitiful, how tragically pitiful, are the figures of private philanthropy and relief as compared with public resources already made available. A year or two ago, our professional journal announced, with a great beating of drums and sounding of trumpets, that Community Chests were collecting the fabulous sum of some $60–$65,000,000 per annum. How much scientific publicity was necessary to obtain this amount? How much flattery was poured out before the generous givers? Yet, at the same time, how many of you remember that for the government relief of only one group of cases—namely, industrial accidents, a comparatively minor cause of poverty and distress in the experience of social agencies—for that group of cases alone, $250,000,000 are paid out each year through the instrumentality of workmen's compensation laws, and the amount is annually rising. Some fifteen years ago, when the mother's pension movement first came up for discussion, the leaders of our profession fought against it on the ground that private philanthropy was amply able to handle the situation and could do it in a more scientific way. And already, some $50,000,000 a year are distributed in mothers' pensions from public funds. . . .

Time will not permit me, nor is it necessary to repeat here at great length, an argument I presented elsewhere: that if it be the purpose and the duty of organized society to eliminate suffering and distress by undertaking the painstaking task of preventing its causes, then "private philanthropy" cannot do it, while public relief and a social policy of compensation and insurance can and does. Today my purpose is a more circumscribed one. I am dealing primarily with the problems confronting the Jewish social worker and Jewish social service. My thesis may perhaps be best summed up in the following statements:

Jewish poverty is not a result of intra-group conditions. It is a part and parcel of the whole economic and social problem of wealth, production, and wealth accumulation of the country as a whole.

The expectation that the problem of Jewish poverty can be met individually and eliminated irrespective of those general economic forces is an expression of excessive group pride uncontrolled by scientific research and thinking.

The sermon of independent group responsibility becomes a definite anti-social force if it destroys Jewish force, Jewish interest, and Jewish participation in national progressive social movements.

I am surely conscious of the danger I am running of a gross misunderstanding of the philosophy underlying these generalizations and of the deductions which follow. Having been a staunch defender of Jewish social service, I have not suddenly committed a *volte-face*. I am not now advocating its abrogation or its immediate merging into the so-called non-sectarian field. Jewish social service has not been an artificial growth forced upon a community by a few energetic social workers. Influenced though it may have been by the development of scientific social work in the country at large, it has grown largely because of at least three reasons:

(1) To perform functions [for the Jewish Community] which otherwise would have been left undone.

(2) To give expression to the need and desire for communal cooperation.

(3) To enable the Jewish minority to make its contribution to the development of cultural, ethical, and even social values and concepts in the community in which we live.

We have made these contributions by introducing and popularizing a higher standard of relief than the community would have been ready to accept without the benefit of our example. We needed a philanthropic effort throughout all these years for the purpose of holding the Jewish community together, when the passion for individual success and the equally strong inclination to internal dissension might have torn the communities asunder. And last but not least, there were many group needs and functions which no one could perform but ourselves, which we have no right to expect that politically organized society will have any concern with, and which we would not want politically organized society to interfere with. . . .

Must our real communal needs, our needs as a national and cultural minority, compete with the widows and orphans, the aged and tubercular, the sick and unemployed? Or, is it not rather time that we draw a very clear line of division between those problems and needs that are distinctly ours, and those which are essentially state-wide and nation-wide in character? Isn't it about time that we clarified our thinking as to what is properly a State responsibility and what is properly a group responsibility? We may then be able to clarify our terminology and to draw a line of demarcation between what is social service for Jews as well as all others, and what may be described as peculiarly "Jewish social service."

Only when these distinctions are clearly marked will we be able to render the service that may be expected of us, both in the Jewish and the national fields. . . .

Having adapted the nomenclature from "charities" to "social service," it behooves the Jewish group in the profession to prove that it really understands the distinction, and that it can adjust its activities accordingly. In that way, I believe, lies the direction of a real constructive contribution of Jewish brains and Jewish conscience to the development of the country.

2. The Cleveland Conference of Federation Executives—A Statement of Principles*

The Bureau of Jewish Social Research, on October 6, 1930, addressed an inquiry to the Jewish Federations concerning the effect of the current economic depression upon Jewish social work as evident in the program of the local Federations. . . .

Replies were received indicating that there are fundamental problems to be considered, and that to cope with them, the cooperative effort of all those concerned in Jewish community organization would be desirable. A group of Federation executives, therefore, joined with the Bureau of Jewish Social Research in issuing a call to a conference at which the problems arising out of the present emergency, as well as practical measures of meeting them, were to be discussed.

* *Jewish Social Service Quarterly*, vol. VII, no. 2 (Dec. 1931), pp. 3-8.

Two meetings of the executives of all of the Jewish Federations were held in Cleveland on January 3 and 4, 1931.

Statement of Principles

Foreword

Jewish Federations and their constituent social agencies are primarily concerned at the present time with the results of adverse economic conditions. There has been an intensification and increase of the problems of distress and maladjustment among the Jewish group. Widely distributed economic dislocation has resulted in increasing the area of dependency. It has also affected to some extent the continued support of established programs of social service, due partly to a shrinkage of surplus income available for philanthropic purposes, and partly to apprehension on the part of those concerned with social-work programs. At the same time, the present conditions increase the difficulty of finding proper support for the added problems created by continued unemployment.

While accurate information concerning the effect of the depression upon the various elements that make up the Jewish population of the United States is not generally available, there can be little doubt of the widespread influence of economic reaction. That portion of the Jewish population that has turned to the existing social-service agencies may be more readily measured. The effect upon the functional social agencies, including the volume of service, the exeprience in financing and the relationship of agencies and types of work to the community program, have been made the subject of an inquiry conducted by the Bureau of Jewish Social Research, and the findings have been summarized in a preliminary report issued by the Bureau in December 1930. The present statement of principles has been formulated as a result of a two-day conference in which representatives of twenty-four communities have participated.

Local Variations

In considering these general principles, the existence of local differences must be taken into account. Communities differ in the nature of their problems, in the extent of the distress created by the emergency, in programs of work, and in financial ability. Some communities may recover later, and others more rapidly. Communities vary considerably in their standards of social work and in the adequacy of the programs which have been established to deal with continuing problems. Similarly, communities have established increased resources for dealing with the present stringency in varying degree. The recommendations made, however, are considered as having general application, modified by the individual conditions which exist locally.

The Extent and Continuance of the Current Depression

The effect of the depression upon Jewish social work has been felt gradually. Increasing unemployment and reduction or stoppage of income for many families have slowly exhausted the self-maintaining resources of ever-widening groups of the population. With the continuance of the depression, there is evident a greatly enlarging area of need which confronts the established social agencies. The financing of social work during the year 1930, based as it was upon the fund-raising capacity of the community for the previous year, has not presented the acute difficulties to the community which may be anticipated as the need is enlarged and the difficulties of raising the required funds are intensified. Although the gradual improvement of economic conditions may be hopefully anticipated, many indications at the present time point to a prolongation of unfavorable economic factors.

Even if improvement in business conditions becomes manifest, social agencies must expect to deal with many new adverse factors. The demoralizing effects of long-sustained joblessness, with its effects of broken health, broken homes, and disintegrated family lives will continue long after the worst phases of the business depression have passed. Many families will regain their former security of independence with difficulty and only after material resources have been exhausted and morale undermined. The new clientele of social agencies developed during the depression will reveal many formerly existing but neglected problems for which continued community care and responsibility will be essential. At the same time, gradually returning prosperity cannot be expected to call forth immediately the increased resources and support which the nature and extent of continuing problems will inevitably require. The quality of community planning which is now being initiated during the emergency and the measures and policies which will be organized in the future to meet emergency needs will determine in large measure the ability of individual communities to come through the present depression with programs safeguarded for future usefulness.

Recommendations Concerning General Guiding Principles

1. In the absence of industrial and governmental provisions for the prevention of unemployment, or for dealing with the destitution created by it, the relief of poverty and distress is an insistent obligation of organized social work. Jewish social work has not and must not hesitate to accept its share of responsibility for the increasing relief measures to deal with the privations which the depression is imposing upon the Jewish group.

2. The new and increased problems of need growing out of the depression should be met by Jewish social work in an adequate manner and with proper standards. At the same time, there is an obligation to protect standards of service previously developed to deal with the continuing problems of the community. The safeguarding of such standards is an important function of social-work organization, particularly because it must be properly equipped to deal with the serious after-effects of the present depression.

3. In addition to the agencies dealing directly with the malad-

justment of families, with dependency of children and the aged, and with problems of impaired health, communities have in the past developed additional agencies as part of a general social program which are concerned with other aspects of the economic, social, or cultural problems. Organized effort to establish community programs concerned with Jewish education, recreation, and culture are considered essential phases of Jewish social work. Some of these services are of recent development and have not as yet established themselves fully. Others are organized nationally and are concerned with widely distributed clients, or with problems of national or international significance to the Jewish group, and have only occasional contacts with local communities. Because of this fact, the Federation as the intermediate agency has a definite responsibility towards national social work. It is important that during the time of distress these elements of the Jewish social-work program in the United States be safeguarded. Similarly, communities have a responsibility for continuing their programs of service to non-residents, as well as to the resident population affected. . . .

The Use of Public and Non-Sectarian Services

1. Many of the problems with which Jewish agencies are concerned have become increasingly the responsibility of tax-supported social agencies as well as the community-wide voluntary organizations. There has been no uniform policy among Jewish agencies for the use of public or community services. Increasingly, however, there is a tendency for Jewish clients, as well as for Jewish social agencies, to accept such services as legitimate means for meeting a part of the social problems of the Jewish group. There is no reason why the trend towards the use of public social work and community-wide services by Jewish clients might not be accelerated during this period of duress.

The use of beds in public hospitals or public subsidies to indigent patients in private hospitals, applications for mothers' pensions and other pension funds, and State or local support for dependent children are some of the measures instituted by the public which might be more fully utilized by Jewish clients, thereby releasing resources in the Jewish agencies for dealing with the added problems of relief for the unemployed.

2. The development of fund-raising machinery with the widest community participation for emergency relief or for emergency work is desirable. Jewish agencies should participate, and where they are not established, may well take the initiative in promoting such general community action. Jewish social agencies can also take the lead in emphasizing the responsibility of the public in the relief of the unemployed through proper measures of work and aid.

3. The acceleration of public development in relief and service should be safeguarded with the development of proper standards of work. Jewish social agencies, in cooperation with other agencies, can contribute to the establishment of proper standards of personnel and case work required to administer adequately family relief and other governmental relief measures and pensions.

3. A Call to the President and Congress of the United States from the National Conference of Jewish Social Service*

Resolution Adopted at the Minneapolis Meeting, June 15, 1931

"WHEREAS, The National Conference of Jewish Social Service, in common with other forward-looking organizations, views the present economic situation as an opportunity for, and obligation on, the social, economic and the political leadership of this country

* *Jewish Social Service Quarterly*, vol. VIII, no. 1 (Sept. 1931), p. 2.

to re-examine and if necessary to modify our social structure, so that human life and happiness, the ultimate goals of social organization, be not destroyed; therefore be it RESOLVED, that the National Conference of Jewish Social Service, in convention assembled, respectfully urges the President of the United States to deal with the present emergency, not only to alleviate present and immediately impending suffering, but to lay the foundation for the effective prevention of similar social and economic catastrophies in the future. Be it further RESOLVED, that the National Conference of Jewish Social Service, representing the entire United States, in all phases of social work, together with other informed individuals and groups, is apprehensive of the consequences of the present industrial depression in terms of its effects on individual and family life, and is fearful that the winter of 1931 and 1932 will be even more severe than have been the winters of the last two years. It therefore respectfully requests the President of the United States to take such steps in the form of federal emergency relief on a large enough scale to alleviate existing and future suffering: the construction of public works to stimulate and revive industry; the formulation of a comprehensive program of social insurance; and the creation of such commissions as will assure social administration of these and other necesary measures. And be it further RESOLVED, that this resolution be transmitted to the President of the United States and to the members of the Congress of the United States.

4. The Present Status of Jewish Social Work: The Need for Critical Examination. A Symposium*

A Symposium

The following article is a general statement prepared by H. L. Lurie, Executive Director of the Bureau of Jewish Social Research, with the cooperation of Dr. Solomon Lowenstein, and Frances Taussig, Chairman of the Continuing Committee of Family Welfare Executives.

The Need for Critical Examination

A period of industrial depression brings to social work not only the distress of the unemployed and increased difficulties in securing funds, but also the need for a critical examination of established programs, functions, and philosophies. The field of Jewish social work offers no exception. . . ; although there are significant differences in degree and emphasis, the problems which concern us are the problems common to all organized social work.

The supposition that there exists an integral relationship between Jewish social work and the other interests and aims of the Jewish group has been offered as the chief justification for our separately organized programs. For this reason, it is important to examine the effect which recent experience has had upon the major objectives of Jewish philanthropy. We may classify the various purposes influencing the status and the developments of social work into two general classes.

The first is primarily concerned with the Jews as a separate population group, whose social and economic problems are important largely because they are involved in the central problem of the survival of cultural integrity and unity. The second outlook is less

* *Jewish Social Service Quarterly*, vol. VII, no. 4 (June 1931), pp. 3-12.

concerned with the maintenance of a homogeneous cultural group, and has limited its interest to the personal welfare of individual Jews in their social and economic settings. From the latter viewpoint, social services are ends in themselves; whereas for the former, they constitute a means toward what is considered a wider and more inclusive program of Jewish welfare. Nowhere in actual community programs, it should be stated, are these purposes clearly differentiated; nor do the actual functions of Jewish social agencies vary markedly between communities that subscribe to one or another of these basic ideologies. Back of the actual programs, however, there is an area of discussion and controversy whose effect becomes evident in the changing forms and adaptations of community programs. The present period of readjustment has particular significance in this respect. . . .

The most striking phenomenon of the past year has been a broader outlook and participation in general community problems in which social work leadership, lay and professional, has been engaged. It is to the credit of this leadership in many communities that they have helped to stimulate the community as a whole to a realistic concern with unemployment problems and relief measures. If, as has been believed, isolation from general programs is a characteristic of sectarian social work, there has been considerable evidence to the contrary in the course of this depression. In fact, many of the leading Jewish social workers were engaged in stimulating the development of community-wide programs for dealing with distress caused by unemployment, long before the acute needs of the Jewish clientele itself made such additional resources imperative. This spontaneous development is a part of a general increasing concern of Jewish social workers with questions of social legislation, especially of social insurance and state-wide relief measures. It is similar to the increasing participation of outstanding Jews in the general interests of their communities, as indicated by their readiness to be identified with political, civic, and philanthropic interests whose objective is the welfare of the entire community and of the nation. . . . Few communities have failed to report [Jewish] participation in general local efforts during the current year.

These general tendencies are having a definite effect upon the programs of Jewish social work itself. The effectiveness of general measures, particularly tax-supported measures, in dealing with dependency is being recognized, and there is less and less reluctance on the part of social agencies to turn over the responsibility for Jewish dependency to the resources of state and municipality. The concern with the standards of such public agencies is no longer a defensive rationalization for reluctance to accept public welfare as such, but a real interest in the adequacy of its performance.

How will the tendency toward greatly enlarged public responsibility for the care of dependents affect the programs of Jewish community organizations? Some of our leaders, who are primarily concerned with Jewish cultural integrity, cherish the hope that the release of energies and resources may be diverted to other problems and other Jewish interests. Others who, in the main, are concerned with individual welfare rather than cultural survival, look favorably upon the development of public relief as offering a more secure and enlarged program for the needs of dependent individuals and families. It may be observed, however, that the assumption of public responsibility for dependents, although accelerated, will nevertheless be gradual. It has taken several decades for the development of mothers-aid relief, and large-scale relief programs for the aged are still in their beginnings. That public relief will be extended, however, in these and other directions is now generally accepted.

Will the activities which organized groups have been gradually undertaking—the cultural and educational activities and concern with the problems of Jews in Europe, Palestine, and elsewhere—succeed local philanthropy as the primary emphasis around which Jewish communal activity will center? The developments of the next decade will determine whether the community organizations called forth by philanthropic interests can be maintained for programs which are not essentially philanthropic in their approach.

To the extent that these newer interests are controversial, and that there exists a diversity of objectives on the part of various divisions in the Jewish group, community organization will need to concern itself more intensively with the reconciliation of divergent philosophies of Jewish adjustment. We cannot assume that the present organization of community interests centering upon problems of dependency and related fields of philanthropy will be held intact during the shift of emphasis to other problems.

So far as can be measured by the experience of the Jewish family-welfare agencies, dependency has increased during the last winter, more markedly in the newer industrial cities and in the larger than in the smaller communities.[1] However, the additional Jewish families receiving relief did not materialize as early or increase as rapidly as the relief loads of public and non-sectarian agencies. The conclusion which might be inferred from this experience—that the Jewish wage-earning group is relatively in a more stable economic position than the rest of the population—is misleading. . . . It is very likely that the Jewish group, which has within it a rather small proportion of immigrants who have been in the country less than fifteen years, has adjusted economically on the same basis as the native population and the older immigrant groups in urban localities. It is believed that a study would be likely to disclose the fact that the effects of the depression upon the Jewish group, insofar as the proportion of families in need of relief is concerned, have been more similar to the effects on the native American white population in urban centers than other nationality groups.

Insofar as can be determined, increased mortality or morbidity have not as yet been indicated; in fact, 1930 mortality rates were considerably below those of 1929. The year 1931 is beginning to show somewhat of an increase over [the figures of] 1930, but it is

[1] Thirty Jewish family-welfare agencies expended $690,750 for relief to families for the first three months of 1931, compared with $513,136 for the same period in 1930 (an increase of 34.6 per cent), and aided 34.8 per cent more families.

as yet too early to determine what the health consequences of the economic depression will be in the registration area. So far as Jewish hospitals are concerned, the effect of the depression is so far visible only in lower returns from payments for service. In the field of child care, although there are significant variations between communities, the total group of thirty-four agencies for which we have information show an actual decrease in intake of approximately 15 per cent for the first three months of 1931, as compared with 1930. Nevertheless, the total number of children under care was approximately 10 per cent greater on March 31, 1931 than on March 31, 1930 for the same agencies. (The number of children in institutions increased by 2.6 per cent; the children in private family homes increased 19.2 per cent in the same period.) An explanation offered for this increase is the greater difficulty experienced in returning children to their own homes. . . .

If the experience of previous depressions may be used as a guide, Jewish social agencies must expect to face the effects of the present depression in succeeding years in a higher incidence of disorganization of families, child dependency, and ill health and occupational disabilities. Following in the wake of the depression there will remain the dislodged wage earners, for whom readjustment is difficult and who are at a disadvantage in finding new opportunities for wage earning. Many will be continuing clients of the family agencies, increasing the volume of relief for a long period after the depression.

There is also a considerable uneasiness, which may be justified, concerning the future economic status of the Jewish group in the United States. What has come to be known as technological unemployment, and concentration of industrial units, including merchandising, may have a continuing adverse effect upon the Jewish group. There is at present a growing concern with the problem of employment discrimination against Jews. This concern may be considered an indication of the more fundamental problem of the occupational and economic distribution of the Jews in the United States. Many of the trades and occupations in which immigrant

Jews and the native-born generation have secured a foothold are beginning to show evidences of oversaturation. In a decreasing labor market, failure to obtain employment emphasizes the incidence of occupational prejudices. The problems, therefore, lead back to the general question of occupation and employment, which confronts not only the Jewish group but the population as a whole. A desirable approach to this problem may best be made through the functions of vocational guidance, which can help to direct and distribute Jewish youth in the occupations offering the greatest promise of security and stability.

Although the uncertainties of the economic future may be dispelled by another period of prosperity, which is being optimistically but cautiously predicted in many quarters, it is unsafe to assume that radical readjustments in economic life will not accompany either the continuing depression or the developing prosperity. Intensified competition, a magnified scale of industrial organization, and further technological changes may be expected. The displacement of small retail units and individual enterprises by chain stores and national consolidations will particularly affect many of the occupations in which Jews are now engaged.[2] The adjustments forced upon individuals and families may not be sufficiently acute to bring many of them to the doors of social agencies, but community life may nevertheless be definitely affected by such changes. . . .

The experience of the Jews in Poland, Russia, and East Europe, where radical alteration in occupations and economic adjustments is taking place, is not altogether remote from our own future. While we may be hopeful that adjustments in this country will be safeguarded by the gradual evolution of a new economic organization from the old, we must be alert to significant problems in this period of adjustment and transition. A clear understanding is es-

[2] The problems of the clerical worker in a changing labor market are equally important. In New York City, the State Employment Bureau reports early in 1931 a ratio of over 900 clerical workers applying for each 100 clerical jobs; but even a year ago before the accelerated increase in unemployment, there were over 400 applicants for 100 clerical jobs.

sential, if we are to guide social-work programs into a position of usefulness for the changing conditions of the future.

The present period for Jewish social work is not a period of discouragement but of readjustment. It is a challenge to marshal energies and abilities, to examine new problems and old philosophies, to formulate new objectives and new programs. Already there are new and hopeful trends, indicated by a more critical attitude toward established assumptions, an enlarged perspective, a greater preoccupation with economic issues, diminishing isolation, and a consequently greater participation in community-wide programs on the part of Jewish social agencies and professional and lay leadership.

5. Wanted—A Return to Basic Values*

BY MAURICE J. KARPF

No one who has observed the situation in which Jewish social work finds itself at present can fail to be impressed by the fact that it is facing a very serious crisis. This crisis is not limited to the financial difficulties which the agencies are facing. It is, in reality, much more fundamental. It goes to the very heart of the future of Jewish social work and Jewish community organization in America. It was in the hope of focusing the attention of some of the leaders of Jewish social work on the dangers of the situation that this article was written.

I

It is natural that at a time like this, when funds are obtained only with great difficulty, if at all, that professional and lay leaders

* *Jewish Social Service Quarterly*, vol. VIII, no 2 (Dec. 1931), pp. 59-63.

of social agencies should cast about for other resources. With a heightened social consciousness on the part of governmental agencies, a constantly developing appreciation on the part of citizens of the principle that the State must bear a large portion of, if not the entire responsibility for, individual and group adjustment in normal as well as abnormal times, and with ever-increasing funds becoming available for out-door and in-door relief purposes from taxation, it is to be expected that Jewish communities will turn to public funds as additional resources in their endeavors to lighten their own burdens.

Nor is there anything inherently wrong or undesirable in Jewish communities seeking their due share of public funds. Hence it is not surprising that the movement to turn over certain types of Jewish problems to public-welfare departments is gaining impetus. It appeals to our sense of belonging to the larger group; it appeals to our sense of justice; it certainly appeals to the giving group in the community, because it lightens their burdens; and it is an outlet for our desire to tell the world that we are as good as our neighbors. The dangers inhere rather in the quality of the work which many public agencies are doing, the conditions under which assistance is granted, the position of the Jew in American life, and the degree of cohesiveness thus far achieved in the Jewish community. . . .

II

What might the consequences be if Jewish communities were to heed some of the ready advice given them and to abandon their dependents to the public-welfare departments? We need not indulge in prophecy to foretell the results. Nor do we have to go back very far into the history of the development of Jewish social work in this country to prognosticate what might happen. We need only recall some of the attitudes, resentments, and vigorous opposition on the part of East European Jews to the organizations they found here which were dominated and controlled by their German-Jewish brethren, and the subsequent mushroom growth of Jewish agencies throughout the country. . . . The East European Jew may not yet give as readily as does his brother of German extraction, and he may be less willing or less able to give because his wealth is more recent and less stable than that of the older settlers, and he may have suffered to a greater extent. He will, nevertheless, make himself heard when he learns that the Jewish community is abandoning the Jewish poor to the public-welfare departments. He will not readily accept such a revision of age-old Jewish tradition. If such practice will not split the Jewish communities and undo what has been accomplished in the last decade in cementing them and in creating united Jewish communities, it will certainly result in the development of small organizations of the type with which all of us are familiar. . . . The derisive attitudes toward the Jewish social worker current during the latter part of the last century and the first part of the present will reappear. The Yiddish press, all-too-eager for controversial issues and none-too-friendly to the Jewish social worker, will not pass up this opportunity to raise a hue and cry that will resound from one end of the country to the other. We shall lose the prestige, recognition, and good will of that portion of the community where our major work lies, unless we exercise the utmost care and recognize the full significance of what we are about.

The above is not a figment of the imagination. It is already happening in some communities. Those to whom the traditions of Jewish life mean something will not willingly acquiesce to a procedure which they consider a violation of every principle of Jewish social living. . . .

III

What about the Jewish client? How will he fare in this situation? It has been a source of pride of Jewish communities and of

Jewish social workers that we do not have a pauper population *per se,* that our agencies have but few second, third, and fourth generations of dependents, that we have no Jukes and Kalikaks. Will this condition continue if we subject our clientele to the conditions prevailing in some of the public-welfare agencies? Are we ready to abandon even our less hopeful clients to agencies counting their case loads per worker in the hundreds, and in some instances almost in the thousands? What will happen to them, and how shall we face and treat them ultimately, when they come back to us thoroughly pauperized and disorganized? Are we willing to abandon our principles regarding the need and efficacy of case work in conjunction with relief? It should be pointed out here that even in those cases where the case work may be done by the Jewish agency with relief coming from the public agency, the situation is not altogether safe. Two dangers lurk there: the Jewish community will become accustomed to accepting public relief and will plan on it, unconscious or unmindful of the cost, and the public agency will demand full authority and responsibility for the handling of the case work where it pays the bills as soon as it can manage to do so with impunity, with its own evaluation of its standards as the basis for its demand.

What about the Jewish community? It need hardly be pointed out that progress in Jewish community organization does not lie in this direction. As already suggested, indiscriminate utilization of public funds under existing conditions may disrupt the Jewish community. No further discussion of this seems necessary at this point. Our older colleagues will remember only too well their trials and tribulations during the early days of this century due to divided communities. . . . As for the younger members of our group, those who neither experienced the above nor are informed of it, one can only hope that the older and more experienced social workers will be able to influence them to proceed more cautiously.

It need hardly be pointed out that the position of the Jew in American life is not yet so stable and secure as to make Jewish community organization unnecessary or superfluous. We need only bear in mind what is happening to other, more stable, and better integrated Jewries in different parts of the world to realize that wisdom dictates caution. Know-Nothingism, Clanism,[2] anti-Semitism are by no means dead in America. And who knows when we shall have a revival of Binghamism [3] in one form or another?

Will the gain be worth the price? Hardly. Eliminate the care of dependents from your community responsibility, and you will find it exceedingly difficult to raise funds for the other needs. Our drives for local, national, and international purposes have been conducted on an emotional basis. Eliminate the emotional appeal which poverty, disease, the widow and the orphan make without long and careful preparation of your giving public, and you eliminate an elemental force in giving. National and international agencies have learned this to their cost. Those who are clamoring for an immediate shift in emphasis to cultural activities have yet to learn this. The very ones who will respond to cries of hunger and appeals for funds for the sick and destitute will find all kinds of reasons and excuses for not giving for purely cultural needs, not the least being a lack of sympathy with a given program. If a shift in emphasis from dependency to cultural work is necessary in fund-raising, the communities must first be prepared for it. With the emotional appeal lacking, with divided communities, with assimilationist tendencies everywhere evident, with divided loyalties between Federation and Community Chest, with examples of lower standards of giving from the non-Jewish contributors to the Chest, and with a false sense of security due to public welfare assistance, Jewish Federations and Jewish communities are bound to go backward. . . .

[2] Refers to various native American movements characterized by group hatred or antagonism, such as the No-Nothing Party, which flourished during the 1850's, and the Ku Klux Klan, which followed the Civil War.

[3] Binghamism refers to the work of Alfred M. Bingham, author and publicist of the 1930's, who espoused dominance by a middle-class technological elite.

6. The Relation of Public and Private Social Work*

BY HARRY GREENSTEIN

There are many problems to be faced in both private and public social work today. In the public field, there are problems arising from the attitudes of different levels of government—federal, state and local—towards each other. There are problems which arise from the operation of WPA (Works Progress Administration); there are problems which come from the complexities of the Social Security Act; there are problems fostered by the scarcity of funds; there are problems arising from inadequacies of personnel and our lack of preparation for so tremendous an undertaking in social-security engineering; there are problems which come from the clash of vested interests; and finally there are problems which we can trace directly to our own impatience and our own unwillingness to explain and interpret our social work needs to that vast group which we all too frequently label the unfriendly community.

All of these problems in the public area have their repercussions in the private fields, and make our task more difficult and more complex. As permanent public-welfare departments emerge from the nucleus of emergency programs, there are many necessary adjustments to be made between public and private social work. Let me particularize in just a few of our functional fields:

Family Welfare

In the family-welfare field the creation of the public-relief agency has brought about certain changes in the scope of the private family organizations. Before the depression and until the establishment of public-relief departments, Jewish communities

* *Jewish Social Service Quarterly,* vol. XIV, no. 3 (March 1938), pp. 320-25. Presented at the Regional Institute, National Conference of Jewish Social Welfare, April 9, 1937.

looked to the family agencies to take care of Jewish needs and distress. This, of course, is no longer entirely true. The assumption of responsibility on the part of the federal government for relief, first through the FERA [1] and now through the WPA, through the development of State and local welfare departments, and through certain categories of social-security legislation, has resulted in the transfer of almost the entire relief burden to public departments. There are, of course, wide gaps in coverage which private agencies are trying to bridge; but as far as the public is concerned, the Jewish family agency is no longer regarded as the only resource in the community to meet Jewish relief needs.

At the present time, private family agencies are attempting to meet certain specific needs. It should be noted, however, that even with respect to the areas in which they are now operating, the work done by them does not fully meet all existing needs. While different family agencies vary slightly in the work they are doing, in general, they are attempting within the limits of their resources to give the following services:

1. Case-work treatments for families that have no need of material relief, but that do need assistance in solving personal problems—such as families in which domestic friction or delinquency is threatening to break up the home, but where there is adequate income.

2. Case-work treatment for a selected number of families receiving relief from public agencies where the needs grow primarily out of personal or family difficulties, rather than general social or economic conditions.

3. Supervision of training in household management.

4. Relief grants to meet individualized or special needs which are not normally allowed by the public agency.

5. Social study of borderline cases where the problem is not clear, and where such study is required to determine the real nature of the problem and the type of treatment to be given.

[1] Federal Emergency Relief Administration, the administrative organization for directing federal relief in the depression.

The public relief agencies should provide the basic material necessities of life on an adequate standard to those families and unattached individuals who are without resources to provide such necessities for themselves, with no distinction between employables and unemployables; they should also provide such case-work service as may be necessary for the effective administration of relief.

Private family agencies are now facing a greater challenge than ever before, and this challenge will have to be met if they are to survive. They will have to give more and more attention to their case-work functions: the rehabilitation of family life and the intensive treatment of behavior problems. This, of course, is easier said than done. It will be a long time before the public agencies will be given the resources to undertake any great amount of work in the field of personalized service. In this area, the family agencies will find their greatest opportunity for constructive work in the years ahead.

Vocational Services

In the field of vocational guidance and placement service, what shall be the relationship and the division of responsibility between the Jewish employment agency and the general community employment and guidance resources in the community?

The establishment of public employment offices raises the question of the extent of Jewish service to be given. Shall Jewish communities set up separate Jewish employment bureaus? If organized, shall they service only clients of Federation agencies, or shall they serve the entire community? Unemployment insurance legislation will result in the development of more adequately staffed public offices throughout the country. There will, however, be large gaps in coverage by public offices. The character of the service is yet to be finally determined. What about the problems of our handicapped people, who must be helped or retrained? Government offices are not well equipped to handle well-rounded programs, not able to cope with problems on an individualized basis. There is a very real need for Jewish vocational guidance and placement services. There will be a larger and larger number of handicapped and borderline cases which will require special vocational guidance and services. Jewish agencies should work closely with public employment offices and should avoid, wherever possible, duplication of services and efforts.

Where there is a well-functioning public employment agency, the Jewish group should cooperate to the fullest possible degree; it should continue on its own basis vocational guidance and special services, and it should look to the public agency to assume as large a burden as possible of the placement of the so-called normally employable Jewish individuals.

The Jewish group should give particular attention to the borderline and problem cases. There should not be too rigid a classification along those lines, but each community should consider its own particular problems in the light of its own set-up.

Where there is no public employment office, the Jewish group should handle the job all the way down the line.

Where the public employment office is politically run, or inefficient, it is our responsibility to join with all groups in the community to bring to bear every possible pressure to correct this situation.

Child-Care Services

It is a generally accepted theory that as the public services for children continue to develop, the private children's agency will have a definite role to maintain, and for an unpredictable period. Public assumption of responsibility for large groups of children, hitherto carried by the private agencies, will, in all likelihood, make for lightened case loads.

We should be able to concentrate our energies more realistically, and therefore more effectively, on strengthening our programs, not only in terms of our own immediate case loads, but also in terms of the needs of childhood and youth throughout the general community. Measures for protection, for correction, for prevention, all offer areas of usefulness for shaping better social opportunities for the younger generation.

We must learn to uphold solid public programs already instituted, and we must learn to fight for their progressive development. We must produce new refinements of skills and techniques. We must make convincing demonstrations of methods and practices that shall ultimately become integrated into the public services. We must keep county, state and federal agencies aware of the individual needs of children in distress, lest in the stupendous undertaking of family-child protection on a national scale these needs are overlooked in the myriads of administrative detail. These are the ideals towards which we must work.

But actually, what can we do? Actually, what are we doing?

It is true that the public agencies cannot attempt to deal with certain types of cases that require much social case-work treatment. The necessarily high case loads, the restrictions of eligibility rulings, to say nothing of the countless administrative problems for which there are no precedents, will make that special service an impossibility for some time to come. This will make it necessary for the private child-caring agency to continue to admit children presenting behavior, health, or other problems demanding expert care, too expert for the public staff, and too expensive for the public purse. Private agencies should also properly care for the short-term cases, especially those that require skilled treatment to maintain family ties which may have been strained by separation because of illness or because of unsatisfactory domestic relationships. This leaves the group of dependent or neglected children whose situations are uncomplicated by need for special services other than long-term protective care as the proper responsibility of the public agencies. When they are willing—as some may already be—to assume this responsibility, will we be prepared to relinquish it? And, if so, on what basis? How many of us wish to give up our relatively uncomplicated problems and keep the more difficult ones? Perhaps we can recognize the problems and obstacles facing the public agencies, but can we be patient, sympathetic, and far-seeing enough to establish a sound, constructive working relationship with them? Can we accept our limitations when they affect our wards? Or, perhaps, more to the point, when they affect our own places in the sun?

Do we really wish to have our case loads lowered so we can devote ourselves to the missions so flatteringly outlined for us by optimistic public and private officials? Can we accept such missions as our chief excuse for existence in an era of growing public service? Can we say we are prepared to perform them?

Up to the present time, our private child-caring agencies have not proved their ability to conduct scientific experiments for the sole purpose of developing general principles and establishing common practices for the benefit of the individual child's needs. There has been little or no interest shown in trying to discover the best means of utilizing all the values inherent in the several types of foster care without regard to agency self-preservation. There has been little or no effort made to explore such related fields as the family societies and the protective agencies represent, in order to plan better coordination of many similar if not identical services, or even for the more simple purpose of becoming better acquainted.

With all our advantages of lay protection and professional equipment, what convictions have we now as to the best practices and techniques? There seems to be no unity in philosophy or method, no disinterested attempts to relate or to correlate our multiple child-caring services. There is little coordination of effort and integration of services between the family and child-care agencies. Can we undertake to blaze trails for the public agencies? Are we sure of the trails that we ourselves have followed before the federal program came into being?

We must face the fact that we cannot develop and foster progressive methods for others if our own programs include practices honored only by time and tradition. If we cannot acknowledge values other than those in our small prescribed areas, for fear of facing our own limitations, and if we persist in the rivalries among our own case-working agencies, then the public agency must appear only as another unwelcome competitor, who will cause us to cry our own wares the louder, and our contribution to general child welfare will be of doubtful value.

Does the responsibility lie entirely with the individual private agency? Have Federations actually provided the children's agencies with adequate resources? Have they actually allowed the flexibility necessary for the laboratory job?

There must be answers to some of these questions. But they must be made the common concern not only of child-care agencies and Federations, but of all our case-working agencies. We must prepare our own group, so obviously interdependent, to marshal its forces for a common goal in the future.

Care of the Aged

The vast expenditure of governmental funds for old-age pensions will undoubtedly affect the character of the population in our homes for the aged in years to come. Those who believed that the effective operation of social-security measures for the aged would spell the doom of private aged homes have been rash prophets. In spite of public assistance to the aged, an ever-increasing number of applications to such homes are reported throughout the country. To ascertain the answer, one must ask what induces the aged individual to seek the security of the institution. While some applicants for admission to aged homes may have always been indigent and dependent, it is safe to assume that the larger proportion have been respectable citizens of the communities. A great many are still healthy, physically and mentally, and are dependent aged only because our industrial and economic system has relegated them to the scrap heap. Public assistance, through old-age pensions, can and will return to the community the type of individual who comes within the scope of this provision. But there is another very large group of aged persons who have not yet reached the age of sixty-five, and who because they cannot be absorbed in the industrial system, are not eligible for old-age pensions. These may be found among the applicants for assistance from private agencies. It is very significant that in several of the largest communities, and no doubt in others as well, the ratio of Jews to the total number of applicants in the community who apply for pensions is markedly out of proportion to the ratio of Jews to the total population.

Undoubtedly, the handicaps caused by lack of citizenship is one of the reasons. This situation will clear up in the course of time, but for the present, it presents a serious problem.

Economic insecurity, loneliness, the need for companionship with others of the same age, maladjustment in the family unit, the need for a more religious atmosphere—all of these are motivating forces which lead the elderly to the doors of our Jewish aged homes.

It is important, however, to point out that the emphasis in our programs for the aged will change, with greater pressure being brought to bear on the admission of the chronically ill aged.

The problems of care for the aged must be related to the problems of the chronic ill. Institutions will have to be modernized, facilities added and competent medical and nursing personnel provided, so that the aged ill can be given the best possible attention.

Greater selectivity should be exercised in the acceptance of applicants to aged homes. Alternative community programs should be made available wherever provision other than institutional care is in the interest of the aged person. For example, it is quite possible that extension of externe service or nursing care in private homes may meet certain situations; foster- or boarding-home care of the aged should be much more carefully explored. Greater coordination of services can and should be developed between the family-welfare agency, the aged institutions, and the hospitals.

The above discussion touches only a few of our many functional activities. I have made no effort to cover them all. Summarizing, I should say a sharp line cannot be drawn between the responsibilities of the public agency and the private agency. Their spheres of obligation are not mutually exclusive. Because of the presence of ever-changing factors, such as changes in general social and economic conditions, the amount of need to be met, the resources available, and the limitations of legislative requirements, no formula can be worked out for a division of work between public and private agencies which will be satisfactory for all times and in all places. Public and private agencies are partners in working for the social welfare of their community, and there should be continuous interplay between them.

However, while we cannot present a specific formula for a division of work, we can state a few principles which may guide us in developing plans to meet special situations.

In connection with the public agency, I would call attention to the following: One of the purposes of government is the promotion of the general welfare. When personal and private resources do not provide the necessities of living, that is, the material necessities—health, education, employment, recreation—it is the responsibility of government to make such provision.

In connection with the private agency, I would call attention to the following:

1. The private agency represents the voluntary assumption of limited responsibility for special areas of social welfare by a comparatively small group of generous citizens.

2. The private agency works in the area of the interest of its supporters; but even there it is unable to assume full responsibility because it is limited by available resources.

3. The private agency should not parallel the public agency in its work; it should serve in its special areas with types of service and qualities of standard not adopted by the public agency which complement the latter's work.

4. The private agency should perform those highly individualized services whose necessity has clearly not yet been accepted as the responsibility of the entire community.

5. The private agency should constantly experiment with the latest standards and methods of service, and the benefits of such pioneering should be passed on to the public agency.

6. If and when public opinion brings about the extension of services on the part of the public agency, the private agency should give up to the public agency work which has come to be accepted as community responsibility; it should go on to new fields of work indicated by new or changed conditions of living.

The future of private social work depends upon the developments in the public-welfare field. Neither the public nor the private agencies can stand alone. It is, therefore, of the utmost importance that both public and private agencies work together as closely as possible to advance the total welfare program in the community.

I should like to suggest that we analyze constantly the content of our daily jobs, and test constantly the methods we are using in the light of results secured. Administration of both public and private social work should be dynamic, flexible, and experimental, if we are to serve effectively the people we are trying to help.

11 Economic Welfare: Jobs, Professions and Discrimination

THE ECONOMIC emergency created by the depression was not dealt with solely by emergency measures. The atmosphere of the 1930's, once the first shock of the depression was absorbed, was positive, constructive and activist—what can we do as a nation to prevent the recurrence of such unnecessary suffering? If our industrial capacity was capable of satisfying most of our material wants, man's imagination must be capable of planning a social and economic structure to serve men's needs in these areas. The Jewish community shared in this constructive approach from its earliest days. In national and local discussions and conferences, the economic shifts of the decade were studied and debated. First, the agencies wished to understand them, and then to assess their effects, if any, upon the Jewish minority. Long-term tendencies were examined: the growing middle-class sector; the changing character of labor; the expansion of professional opportunity to serve a mature, if sometimes stumbling, economy; automation in industry, and its threat to employment and income security; the centralization of economic power, and its threat to the small businessman; and the changing patterns of discrimination against minorities, both Jews and other groups.

The debates on these issues sharply reveal the extent to which in the American economy every attempt to broaden opportunity involved an equivalent risk. Insecurity and change now threatened not only the poor laborer and the uneducated; the professional man, businessman, and the middle-class were also subjected to strange and disquieting pressures—a changing technology, increased market demands, the organization of labor, and new government controls. Out of such concerns grew the Jewish community's recognition that its communal structure must address itself to the requirements of all its members, not only the new immigrant, the handicapped, and the unfortunate.

Recognition of these problems led local service agencies and Federations to consider how they could plan to operate so as to directly improve the conditions of life. The limits of a voluntary association devoted to broad formative programs on economic and social issues were fully recognized; no minority could plan its own economic future single-handedly. Still there existed a few definite points of leverage where a voluntary agency could make a contribution to national policy, e.g., a minority group could join with other groups to shape a democratic governmental economic policy.

In one arena, that of economic opportunity, Jewish groups went further. The Jewish vocational services were extended and enlarged. At this time, economic changes in the area could be controlled only by government activity; but voluntary associations could help guide Jewish youth in the directions best designed to assure them a secure future. Thus, analysis of employment trends, identification of growing and shrinking occupational opportunity, training for new skills, vocational redirection through guidance, were all feasible. At the same time, special groups such as the immigrants and the handicapped could benefit from the same programs. Closely related to this development of a communal program on economic matters was the problem of discrimination, which played a vital part in the shaping of economic welfare activities.

1. The Economic and Industrial Status of American Jewry*

BY I. M. RUBINOW

. . . Modern civilization is subject to change at an ever-increasing rate of speed. It has changed radically during the last half century, changes which I and my contemporaries had the opportunity to observe as eye-witnesses, and which make the preceding thirty years appear almost static. . . .

In this country of economic change, of hope and despair, are four-and-a-half million American Jews. The nation's melting pot . . . has not worked as effectively as was expected; there are large lumps in it, seemingly undigested: two million of us in New York City, and thousands of isolated families or small groups of families in hundreds of small scattered communities. There seems to have taken place no chemical union . . . but a rather crude mixture—yet enough of a mixture to make isolation and identification of the various elements a very laborious, though not an impossible task. This has been a process too often resisted both by the majority and minority elements, particularly in so far as biological, ethical, religious, or cultural melting has been concerned.

The social integration, on the whole, was more acceptable to the minority than to the majority, though even this statement requires some qualifications. It has been frequently charged that we are intentionally living in a ghetto. In examining the problem of Negro adjustment, the late Booker T. Washington created the famous "Five-Finger Theory," insisting that socially the Negro and white must remain separate like two fingers, though economically the

* National Conference of Jewish Social Service, *Proceedings* (1932), pp. 28-38. Presented at the annual meeting of the National Conference of Jewish Social Service, Philadelphia, May 12-17, 1932. Another paper presented at the Conference which outlines major economic trends as they influenced Jewish manpower and Jewish life is "Jews in Commerce and the Professions," by Morris R. Cohen (*Proceedings* [1934], pp. 21-28).

whole American people are like one hand. Jewish psychology has produced the corresponding "Six O'Clock Theory," which argues that the "Jew and Christian must lead a common life until six p. m., the hour when . . . social life begins, for joint social life must mean intermarriage," or, if you will, miscegenation. You might also designate this as the "Soup and Fish Theory" of Jewish life: the preservation of Jewish cultural existence demands that Jew and Christian wear their "soup and fish" and eat in splendid isolation. The theory assumed, therefore, that in economic life no divisions are necessary, and in fact none exist.

How numerous are the exceptions to this as an accurate description of things as they are, we shall have an opportunity to point out presently. Yet there can be doubt that in the economic field, the melting process has been much more complete than elsewhere. The four million Jews, more or less, who have come to this country, mostly during the last fifty years, have made some sort of an economic adjustment; they have penetrated very deeply into American economic life. . . .

We are economically part and parcel of the general American economic scene, whether as employers or employees, buyers or sellers, producers or consumers, practitioners of professions or their clients. The economic position of the American Jew today, and even more so his position tomorrow, is irretrievably interwoven with the economic present and future of the American people. Our problem is their problem. . . .

The probabilities are greatly in favor of a continuation of the present economic depression for some time, followed by a gradual, painful, and only partial recovery; a considerable reduction in the recent standard of living, both in the luxury standard of the upper classes and the comfort standard of the middle classes; a slower rate of the accumulation of wealth, as compared with the decade before the crash, continuation of the process of technological improvement in order to reduce costs and regain profits; a persistence for some time of the army of the technological unemployed, though its makeup may change; a further concentration of wealth because of the reduction of the saving capacity of the masses; a rapid increase in the size of the intellectual proletariat, and possibly the persistence for many years of a serious problem of mass dependency, with a growing participation of government authorities and public resources in its relief.

If that be the rather cheerless but sober and fair statement of the present economic situation and probable economic future of the American people as a whole, a picture which in a general way must apply to or at least affect the Jewish minority group as well, what is likely to be the specific situation of American Jewry? How far, if at all, does the economic outlook of the Jew differ from that of the rest of the population? Can this question be answered?

Obviously, for even an approximate appraisal of the future, some accurate information as to the present is needed as a starting point. . . . We do not have accurate figures on even the size of the Jewish population; on its geographic distribution; its essential data as to birth, death, or marriage; its occupational distribution; its income distribution; its accumulated wealth; its achievements, difficulties and problems. We might have had a good deal of information if we had not ourselves, for some perhaps otherwise valid reasons, objected to the census' recognition of our belonging to a separate group . . . and avoided a thorough study of ourselves by our own group.

We do know that we are substantially an immigrant group in a very modern scene, a very recent immigrant group of only a half-century—1880-1930. . . . There were in 1880 about 250,000 Jews in the United States, and in 1930, 4,250,000—an increase of 1,700 per cent; in 1880 we constituted only .5 per cent of the population, and in 1930, 3.5 per cent, so that even the proportionate increase was sevenfold. Despite the fact that Jewish immigration had almost stopped some ten years ago, the vast majority of us are immigrants or sons of immigrants. We know that while we are not the only important immigrant group of this half century, we have fared materially at least as well as any other, and probably better than most, perhaps better than any. And since there is absolutely no reason to assume that we have been given any special privileges or opportunities, we can at least take pride in the fact that we have taken advantage of such opportunities as existed, and probably worked harder and lived a little more soberly and sanely than the others. . . .

If we were all poor at the time of arrival, many of us are so no longer.[1] There has been a rapid and very effective process of economic differentiation. We have produced our bankers, merchant princes, industrial leaders, and Wall Street bulls. Thirty years ago, the privilege of being a millionaire was reserved for the so-called German Jew, but that monopoly has largely been destroyed since. Probably the majority of us, on the Atlantic seaboard at least, are still members of the wage-working class, and Jewish relief societies and philanthropic institutions do not have to look for clients in vain. Yet the severe test of the last three years has, on the whole, demonstrated that even the Jewish working masses preserved an economic level somewhat higher than that of the rest of the city population. . . .

In other words, the Jewish immigrant mass has been integrated into the American economic system, and has earned a fair measure of the possible awards, not by privilege, but by work, saving habits, probably to some extent by superior business ability—which expressed itself not only in successful trading but also in industrial enterprise—and even by speculative courage.

As to the numbers engaged in the various sectors of industry and commerce, the picture, while not statistically accurate, was fairly well known when the concentration of Jewish labor and enterprise was more clear cut than it is today. So long as the immigrant group constituted a larger proportion of American Jewry than it does today, and so long as immigration from certain countries was primarily and predominantly Jewish—the Jew in economic life was more easily identified than he is today.

[1] While most immigrants were poor and many penniless, a number who fled persecution rather than economic conditions, particularly after the turn of the century, were moderately well-to-do. Most of the early financially successful East European Jews were from this group.

In a study of the economic conditions of Russian Jews made by the speaker nearly thirty years ago (as a contribution to Dr. Bernheimer's symposium on the Russian Jew in the United States) published in 1905,[2] it was quite possible to utilize statistical data on men and women in the clothing industry as a test of the condition of Jewish labor in general. In addition to ready-made clothing, retail trade, dry-goods, and the jewelry business, to some extent the drug, liquor, and theatrical business, real estate, and some professions—namely medicine and school teaching—were listed as the most important Jewish occupations in 1900 or 1905.

A quarter of a century passed, an era of phenomenal industrial development in the United States, of phenomenal enrichment, of which the Jews have had their fair share, perhaps some more than their fair share. . . .

Thus a few years ago a very definite trend could be observed both in Jewish capital and labor which, on the whole, might have been accurately described as a movement "outward and upward." A gradually growing familiarity with American life and American business methods permitted Jewish enterprise to enter new fields; Jewish energy and perseverance made success possible in an atmosphere which was very favorable to success; Jewish ambition and imagination fed on the possibilities of the speculative era. At the same time, the ancient Jewish love of learning and the somewhat more prosaic striving for a professional career (a comparatively recent Jewish tradition which developed in the peculiar conditions of Jewish life in Russia), drove Jewish youth into high schools, colleges, and professional schools. During the years of Jewish mass immigration, this movement into higher occupational levels was partly obscured and more than compensated by the much stronger current of newer immigrants from Eastern Europe; but the respective size of these two streams rapidly changed. The movement of the working class into independent industry, into

[2] Charles S. Bernheimer, ed., *The Russian Jew in the United States: Studies of Social Conditions in New York, Philadelphia, and Chicago, with a Description of Rural Settlements* (New York, John Winston Co., 1905), pp. 101-21 ("Economic and Industrial Conditions, New York").

small and large trade, into the colleges, into professions, government service, and public life—this flow grew in size as the Jewish community gained in experience and wealth, while the current immigration grew thinner and thinner and finally stopped altogether.[3] American Jewry was rapidly becoming middle-class and even upper-class, not only more prosperous but also more polished, more Americanized, and perhaps more cultured. It began to make its cultural contribution to American life at a rapidly increasing rate, truly surprising, considering its short history of some fifty years—a contribution to literature, art, science, music, and the stage. Its economic affluence was reflected in the economic prosperity of its communities: the new synagogues, temples, hospitals, centers, old and young folks homes, clubs (down-town and country), and the swelling budgets of Jewish charities and Federations.

What might the economic development of American Jewry have led to if the economic tendencies of American life between 1922 and 1929 had continued and become permanent, and if no special obstacles to further growth had developed in the path of American Jewry? Some such speculations have been indulged in and some guesses have actually been made.

It would have meant that American Jewry would have continued its population growth at a much slower rate because of the discontinuing of mass immigration, as well as a constantly falling birth rate; that the trend of the Jewish masses from semi-skilled or even skilled trades into the class of employers, of merchants, and other occupations would have continued. As Jewish enterprise became more acclimatized, the narrow limits of specifically Jewish industry and commerce would have broken down, new frontiers would have been penetrated, individual Jewish fortunes would have continued to grow in size and to increase in number (the process of original accumulation would have continued and resulted in an increasing number of small capitalists), and Jewish

[3] Jewish immigration to the United States never stopped, although legislation drastically reduced it after 1923 and the depression in the 1930's reduced it even further. See pp. 178, 179.

poverty would have rapidly decreased and perhaps disappeared altogether. As an inevitable by-product of these changes and a contributing cause to them at the same time, the concentration of Jewish population in the few large centers of the East would have gradually abated since the interior of the country offers a more favorable environment to the financial, industrial, commercial and intellectual capacities of the Jew. . . .

Much of this development has actually taken place—that we know. But how much further may the development proceed in the same direction? Surely, not with the same speed which one might have expected in 1928—because of at least two important forces.

The first of these two forces is a general one: the change in the general trend of economic conditions in the country at large, which has necessarily influenced American Jewry as well. The second force is of a more specific nature—the development of a specific attitude on the part of the people as a whole towards the Jew as a member of a minority group, and his participation in the economic life of the country.

Together with the rest, 120,000,000 Americans, the Jew has suffered from unemployment, from disorganization of industry, from shrinkage of values, perhaps a little less from unemployment and a little more from the shrinkage of speculative values, as a result of his devotion to them during these years. The general economic conditions may have affected the Jews with particular force, because Jewish enterprising capital was more or less concentrated in the luxury trades: jewelry, clothing, furs, amusements—trades which suffered most from the depression.

Just as the first decade of the twentieth century was marked primarily by industrial concentration, the past decade may go down in the economic history of the United States as the period of commercial concentration. The development of the chain store is as characteristic of the 1930's as the great industrial trusts were of the first decade. The chain store, which only ten years ago was somewhat of a curiosity, has now become the standard form of organization of the American retail trade. . . , absorbing a greater and greater part of its total volume. At the same time, the growing use of the automobile has also worked to undermine the small local store, which was so potent an influence in the distribution of the Jewish population away from the large centers to the interior of the country.

This economic process is essentially one that is unrelated to racial or religious group relationships. It is simply the American counterpart of the European process of cooperative trading. It is a natural and on the whole a desirable step towards a more efficient and economical method of retail and consumer distribution. But it also happens to be a force that strikes very painfully at the Jewish middle class, the small commercial class, by tending to reduce the number of independent merchants. The figures of the census of 1930 already bear this out, and the census of 1940 will undoubtedly show it much more.

Thus, recent economic changes have affected and may continue to affect the economic position of the American Jew—not only in a general way . . . but also in a more specific and intensive way, by striking with greater force at those economic activities in which the Jew has been involved. The Jew may thus be only an innocent victim of the triumphant process of economic evolution, perhaps, for all we know, towards a better future.

But there is another social force of quite a different character directed against the Jew, in America as well as in other countries. It is not a new force, but one that has been growing fast during the recent years; it is a force not yet carefully measured, sometimes exaggerated, sometimes intentionally minimized, but nevertheless widely discussed—a force which for all we know may become the predominating factor in shaping the economic destinies of American Jewry. This force is the discrimination against the Jew in the field of employment and economic life in general, the beginning of a movement which in many other countries has been described by the sinister phrase, "an economic boycott against the Jew." Upon the removal of this sinister force, or its further development and growth, the whole economic future of American Jewry obviously depends. . . .

There has been a good deal of journalistic writing and even more of platform and pulpit oratory on the subject, but very little scientific investigation as yet. The writing and speaking consist largely of illustrations of fact and conditions as they have forced themselves from time to time upon public attention. The illustrations are many, but the generous publicity occasionally given to them makes a factual appraisal of the situation very difficult. It is not easy to say how far this tendency already affects and threatens to affect in the future the economic opportunities open to Jews in America.

What is the general situation as it appears, at least from such general observations? Discrimination against the Jew is not limited to the economic field. It is probably stronger in the field of social relationships, such as in the exclusion of Jews from ordinary private social life, from clubs, fraternities, summer hotels, certain high-grade apartment houses, etc. Occasionally this form of exclusion calls forth articulate protests, private or public—it has even led to efforts at special legislation. But on the whole, although American Jewry accepts the situation not very graciously and not very philosophically, it accepts it all the same, and endeavors to adjust its own social and recreational life to existing conditions.

Obviously, economic discrimination strikes at a very much more vital interest. The Jew encounters such discrimination in the field of commercial, industrial, or even professional employment, and as the vast majority of people are forced to earn their living through employment contract, the possibility of discrimination presents a danger for nearly every Jew. Even discounting specific rumors and charges which have been denied, explained, or admitted by individual firms, it is nevertheless fairly well known that in certain important branches of office and clerical work, the door to the Jew is closed. It is understood that very few, if any, Jews can gain a footing inside a bank or insurance company, or a railroad, or a public-service corporation. There are obstacles in many retail commercial establishments, particularly more exclusive ones. There is a growing discrimination against the Jew as a typist, stenographer, or private secretary. The development of the chain-store movement represents a double threat to the Jew, because not only does he lose out as an independent merchant, but he is also unacceptable as an employee, except possibly in distinctly Jewish neighborhoods.

It is a little more difficult to ascertain the exact situation with regard to industrial wage work, skilled or unskilled, though on the whole it is probable that in that field the problem has not yet become quite so acute. Insofar as Jewish labor in large centers has shown a natural tendency to concentrate in certain branches of industry, the decrease of a Jewish proportion in those industries is probably the result of voluntary withdrawal rather than discrimination. When the labor hiring policies are decentralized and depend upon the judgment or whim of the factory foreman, it is difficult to prove any definite policy. However, charges are frequently made and as frequently denied.

In the professional field, the situation is acute, perhaps even more so than in finance or commerce. From the point of view of economic organization, professional work may be divided into two groups: (1) The practice which depends upon an employment contract, e.g., teaching, engineering, chemistry, statistics. (2) Those services in which a system of private independent practice still prevails to a large degree, e.g., medicine, dentistry, law, nursing, etc. It is well known, however, that the employment contract system is gradually, though rather slowly, penetrating this second group as well.

Of course, none of the professions is absolutely closed to the American Jew. In fact, the impression prevails that the professions are overrun with Jews, and this is often cited as justification for the growing policy of discrimination and exclusion. Whether the charge be justified or not, it is widely known that outside of government service (federal, municipal or state)—which constitutes a rapidly expanding field of employment for professional workers either governed by a rigid system of civil service or subject to political influences measured by voting strength—it is in the field of professional employment that inquiries as to the social, religious, racial, and nationality status of the applicant are most searching, and discrimination against the Jewish applicant most frequent. There are opportunities for teaching positions in the public-school systems of the larger cities, though occasional complaints of injustice against the Jew are heard concerning promotions. But the situation in the public schools of smaller towns and rural communities is notoriously bad, as it is in the private schools, with the possible exception of those of the progressive, experimental type. The limitations of a scientific career for Jews in colleges and universities, particularly in the private and denominational colleges, and although more carefully disguised, even in state and municipal universities, raise a grave problem [for the Jew] both from an economic and a cultural point of view; they not only limit opportunities for employment, but also opportunities for a cultural contribution to American life.

The situation is more complex with regard to professions which still preserve the system of private practice. The success of a private practitioner in medicine or law is presumably an individual matter. Whether the social aspects of group discrimination affect the chances of success of a Jewish practitioner would be difficult to say. Naturally, the Jewish physician and Jewish patient may be drawn to each other, but popularity of Jewish practitioners with non-Jewish clientele and vice versa is not at all uncommon. The discriminatory tendencies in this field express themselves in a somewhat indirect but none the less effective way, creating obstacles in the course of preparation for a professional career through the limitation of entrance to professional schools or difficulties in hospitals and clinical appointments. . . .

Assuming that this force of discrimination remains unchecked (and as yet no practical way of checking it has been suggested), and assuming further that it is likely to grow in intensity, what is its influence upon the economic position of the Jew in America likely to be? . . .

What vocations are left open to the Jew? There remain only certain occupational fields in which intolerance to the Jew is weaker or perhaps non-existent.

On the one hand, there is industrial work, factory employment, building construction, perhaps mining or unskilled labor. Not all of these fields are free from the virus of discrimination. Only a very painstaking investigation could ascertain the facts. By tradition, many of these fields have been and remain rather open to the Jew. It is a matter of experience, training, and perhaps of physical stamina. With the disintegration of the lower-middle class, the Jew may more and more be forced in the direction of factory work.

This, in the opinion of many students of the situation, and particularly of some writers for the Yiddish press (which has shown a much more intelligent interest in the problem than most of our so-called Anglo-Jewish press) is a "consummation devoutly to be wished." It revives the glory and dignity of labor. It fits in with the doctrine of the breaking up of the middle class. . . . Yet, it is not as simple a process as the formula would lead us to expect, not as simple perhaps as the industrialization of a declassed Jew in Russia.

To begin with, there is a general economic tendency towards a decrease in the industrial force through technological improvements, while the white-collar occupations of management, accounting, and salesmanship continue to grow. If we look at statistical data on the rapid reduction of the number of wage workers employed in the manufacturing industry, in railroads or mining as compared with the continuous increase in commercial and clerical pursuits, the demand for a return to the wage workers' paradise *en masse* loses a good deal of its certainty.

On the other hand, the growing field of free-lance salesmanship, insurance, installment selling, bond and stock selling—in short, that army of distributing agents which the prevailing system of high-power salesmanship has forced upon a suffering public—can be considered a traditional Jewish occupation, which in the past has contributed little to Jewish reputations.

There remains the higher level of Jewish capital, very restricted except for an accidental or temporary dislocation in the banking business or moving-picture industry. As yet, there seems to be no serious danger or obstacle to the upper Jewish economic strata's continuing to prosper together with non-Jewish capital.

Thus, Jewish energy and initiative may be forced into particular channels of activity not so much by voluntary choice or predisposition as by the action of *vis a tergo,* creating a situation not altogether unlike that which exists in many European countries. A situation such as this obviously creates many serious problems. Large independent or corporate business is a field open only to a small, fortunate minority. Jewish factory labor, particularly in the heavier industries, might become an economic necessity. It is not likely to be a matter of choice. The overwhelming disposition of American Jewry of the present generation to obtain for its children all of the educational advantages available, whether through free municipal colleges or at a terrific sacrifice in other institutions in the face of constantly rising costs, is a tendency that is not likely to be broken down. Observation indicates that there is hardly a Jewish family over the destitution level which does not maintain or expect to maintain at least one child, and if possible, all the children, through college. Not only the upper and middle classes, but even the average and workingman's family have learned to regard a college education as a matter of course, as the legitimate right of a child to rise above his father's station. In every large state university there is an excessive percentage of Jews from the wage-earning neighborhoods of the larger cities. These half-hungry youths often work and starve their way through college. If one out of every twelve youths in the country receives a college education, for the Jew the percentage is at least twice as great—one out of every six. With white-collar employment gradually restricted, with professional schools less and less accessible, American Jewry is likely to develop a growing class of educated workers who will drift unhappily from one temporary occupation to another, most of them maladjusted, perhaps applying their mental abilities to bitter social criticism.

A small minority in the field of big business, an increasing number employed in the hectic field of salesmanship, an unwilling drift to factory work, and a growing intellectual proletariat without permanent occupational status—this, for all we know, may be the future economic position of the Jew, if the present tendencies continue unabated.

Is there anything we can do about it? A Conference paper would seem to be altogether incomplete if the statement of the problem confronting us were not to be followed by a clear-cut remedy.

I must confess, however, that I cannot get very enthusiastic about the plan of organizing special Jewish employment offices, particularly under the auspices of Jewish social-service agencies. The case worker, in his praiseworthy desire to achieve an individual adjustment, may lend all his efforts in that direction; but he often does this without due regard for the more remote but inevitable social consequences. A job at any cost, no matter what the conditions of employment, may be the proper solution for a particular economic and psychiatric situation; but proper relations between economic and social classes cannot be jeopardized in this way. Placement of a few handicapped clients is one thing, and proper organization of the labor market as a whole quite another. The lesson of experience should direct us toward greater consolidation [with general economic trends], and not subdivision of our machinery for bringing job and man together. In the long run, a special Jewish employment office may only facilitate anti-Jewish discrimination and may make for sub-standard conditions of employment for Jewish labor.

This matter of economic discrimination is the very foundation of the whole problem of what the future has in store for the four million Jews in the United States. It is impossible to make any forecasts as to the future, its economic as well as social, cultural and psychological elements, without involving a prediction as to the direction which this attitude may take. The individual's need to pursue a congenial occupation adapted to his capacities, tastes, and choice is an element of primary importance in the process of adjustment to a social group. What is true for the individual must also be true for the group. The existence of an economic boycott—in substance if not in name—or even of a forced direction of Jewish energy and trends into future restricted channels, not only eliminates the opportunities for economic success, but also injures the chances for a satisfying life. . . .

No greater problem confronts American Jewry, and no other problem requires more painstaking study and thought even before any line of action is determined. Unless it is solved satisfactorily, the question of the economic future of the mass of American Jewry is decidedly uncertain. Perhaps it is more uncertain from the point of view of securing human satisfactions than from that of the comparatively simple task of securing in this country of plenty some sort of a living for the Jews during years of prosperity, and a legitimate share of public and private relief during years of need.

2. Planning for Economic Welfare*

BY BENJAMIN M. SELEKMAN

No group of social workers needs to be convinced of the pertinence of socio-economic planning to the problems of contemporary society. For their daily work must reveal to them how the current interest in planning springs fundamentally from two major desires: first, to harness the industrial apparatus of modern civilization so as to serve the community without periodic breakdowns; and second, to make possible the security and rising standard of living implicit in a wealthy economy. If social workers readily see the urgent need for planning, they must, by the same token, be

* National Conference of Jewish Social Welfare, *Proceedings* (1934), pp. 28-33. Presented at the annual meeting of the National Conference of Jewish Social Service, Atlantic City, N.J., May 26-30, 1934.

aware of the obstacles in the way of its immediate realization. Even European dictators, for all their absolute power, do not find it easy to formulate and execute satisfactory blueprints for their respective economies. How much more difficult must it prove for democracies to secure consent from conflicting interests to a national plan, even assuming that the facts, imagination, and skill required are available. And, if it is difficult for a nation, how much more difficult must it be for one small segment like the Jewish group to plan for its economic needs? Yet difficulties in the way of a job that must be done simply make more imperative the earliest and most thoroughgoing consideration of how it can be done. We realize the urgent need of planning for the economic welfare of the Jewish group; we know that perplexities beset any attempt at such planning; we must, therefore, canvass without delay the range of its possibilities and the conditions of its success.

To this end I shall try to discuss three aspects of Jewish economic planning—aspects which I think condition its procedures and its possibilities: First, we must realize that planning for the Jewish community is a process entirely different from planning for the national community. For the Jewish community cannot exercise control over basic economic forces. Indeed, its range of planning must be constantly limited by conditions in the larger community, of which Jews are only a part. Second, we must, however, not let our plans be drawn too largely in terms of such general conditions at any given moment in this era of swift-moving transition. And finally, dependent as Jewish planning may be upon surrounding community developments, we cannot forget that Jews face certain peculiar problems which present a sharp challenge to Jewish communities and their social agencies.

Let us consider just what planning for Jewish economic welfare in America can really mean. It must be at once apparent that in the area of economic activities, the Jewish group can do very little in the way of comprehensive group planning by and for itself. What Jews do or may do in business, in industry, in all of economic enterprise is, and must be, conditioned almost entirely by the dynamics of the American economy as a whole. It must also be apparent, therefore, that planning in American economic life and planning in Jewish-American economic life are two quite distinct things. When nations today face the challenge of planning, they must deal with the growing need to replace the automatic controls and disjointed regulations of a laissez-faire society with the conscious controls of a reasoned and purposive community. But when Jews seek to plan their group economic welfare, they do not face such an issue of fundamental social change, but rather one of adjustment to that change, as it unfolds in the larger community of which they are part. Group planning for them demands a program of *ad hoc* adjustments to a continuously evolving social scene.

This is a significant distinction. For although the long-time trends of social change should bring Jews as all Americans better and more secure lives, such economic planning as America may try in coming years may well operate against their immediate group interests. Our planning for Jewish economic welfare may, therefore, have to concern itself for a time merely with easing the bad effects of a transitional situation. Like all major industrial countries, America has become economically mature. The period of sheer expansion is over. Our vast continental land has been settled from ocean to ocean; our natural riches have been tapped and acquired; our capital equipment has been built; our corporate structure has achieved tremendous size and concentrated power. We now confront the social problems of utilizing our vast productive capacity so as to realize its potentialities of economic well-being for all. We are faced with the problems of socio-economic administration, in contrast to the earlier problems of promotion and development. . . .

This transitional era is pregnant with sharp social conflict. The existence of three rival social philosophies, the tense conflict between fascists, communists, and democrats, indicates the explosive possibilities along the way from an old system to a new one. The old ways of life, the old traditions and old customs of rugged individualism which belong to the period of economic expansion have strong roots, and they are staunchly defended by vested interests employing differential benefits from them. . . . However, while our capital equipment and resources did somehow develop under the aegis of laissez-faire individualism, the efficient administration of that equipment seems to require a large measure of central control and direction. . . .

Let us see, then, how these general considerations apply to the formulation of plans for Jewish economic welfare. The material advance of the Jewish group as a whole under laissez-faire capitalism in America, even without available statistics, can hardly be denied by any who have studied their history here. . . .

But however favorable this economic advance in expanding America may have been, it has obviously left Jews in places particularly hard-pressed by the forces of transition. Like most comparable Americans, our fortunate Jews have prospered by the era's unrestrained promotion of profit-seeking, individual initiative, and private enterprise. But unlike Americans as a whole, the Jewish group does not possess a balanced economic distribution which allows economic gains and losses, strains and tensions, to be spread evenly among their number. Jews are not widely represented on the farms or in manual jobs. The needle trades have employed large numbers, although even here other nationalities have been supplanting them in recent decades. The heavy industries engage few Jews either among employers or workers. Banking, stock brokering, moving pictures and other forms of amusement, real estate, and the distributive trades account for most of our Jewish wealth. The professions, small business, and white-collar occupations yield our large Jewish middle class.

Whether or not the Darrow report is entirely accurate in its accusations of monopolistic tendencies in the NIRA, there has been little doubt among economists that the long-time trends in American life have been making it increasingly hard for the middle classes to which so many Jews belong. Many forces have been squeezing the "little fellow," whether he is in a neighborhood store, a small shop, or an office. White-collar workers also have been displaced from their jobs by technological advances; the adding machine and its fellows, as much as the assembly line, undermine working skills. The professions, especially in the cities, where Jews are concentrated in them, have become steadily more crowded. Discrimination against Jewish students is an economic even more than a racial weapon. . . .

Yet just because planning for Jewish economic welfare must proceed step by step, it must guard against overemphasizing present conditions and trends. Our current days, certainly, are all too dark and stressful. In time, America, like the rest of the industrial world, will have to replace laissez-faire capitalism with planned, collectivist production. But as far as we can see now, no revolution lies around the next corner of American development. The progress of the New Deal in its first year offers little reason to believe that the next decade will witness drastic economic readjustments. Indeed, recovery may well bring a renewed era of prosperity on the familiar models of promotion and speculation, even if within the confines set by the securities and stock exchange acts. . . . Therefore, if any social forecasts can be made in such troubled times as ours, the next decade seems to promise nothing more than an era of progressive reform in America. We shall be fighting for labor organization; mild controls over the issue and trading of securities; progressive, farmer, and labor political parties; social insurance; better wages; shorter hours, and a more even distribution of wealth by means of tax power. Whatever changes may be thus achieved, we will still continue to live in a capitalist society. Many Jews, like other Americans, therefore, will still make their own economic way along familiar economic paths. . . .

By saying that planning is impossible under democracy, we help to make it so. Of all people, the Jews must help win for democracy every chance to show what it can accomplish in creating a new social order. . . . Violence and revolution solve no basic problems of actual social organization. The whole balance of American social forces makes it seem probable that if we do have revolution, it will be, at least in its first stage, revolution on the fascist model.

In any revolution, but especially in a fascist one, European experience has already revealed how handily the Jew can serve as scapegoat for all the conflicting classes. This is an exceedingly important consideration in America, for racial problems here have peculiarly explosive potentialities. The presence of the Negro, the Catholic, the Jew, has already provided outlets for mass discontent and unrest. Time and again organized parties have risen to exploit such antagonisms and prejudices; the depression has produced its Silver Shirts and Friends of Nazi Germany. In self-defense, if for no other reason, it behooves Jews to help secure for democracy every possible aid for achieving peaceful social change.

But simultaneously, we must also make provision for those specific difficulties that the very social process we are helping to advance will create for the Jews. For when an ordered economy is established, rising generations of Jews will find it increasingly difficult to advance themselves freely as their fathers did by means of the urban businesses, trades, and professions in which they concentrated. Logically and theoretically we ought, therefore, to provide for them new places and escapes through a more balanced economic distribution. But I think we must guard in such an effort against any easy assumption about the occupations for which we should retrain our people. True, a comparatively small proportion of Jews are now engaged in industrial or agricultural work. But, at least in America, how much do we want to force them into it? We must realize that these occupations are often as crowded as any of the professions. Moreover, mechanization is progressively displacing many such workers, and restrictive tendencies in some trades are as great as in any non-manual field. Will bricklayers and carpenters, for instance, give Jewish competitors a heartier welcome than Jewish doctors and lawyers now receive? And as for agriculture, which is facing a shrinking market, and the curtailment of one crop after another by the national government, can we say without careful qualification that here is an outlet for Jews who face discrimination in overcrowded businesses and professions? I must confess, too, that I am not entirely sympathetic with the present vogue for decrying Jewish "middle-class and professional leanings." For it seems to me that the idealization of physical work belongs to a past era. Are we not seeking to free all men as far as is possible from the drudgeries of monotonous, repetitive or back-breaking manual labor? Is not the contribution of a doctor or chemist more creative than that of a miner or road builder? Before training too many of our Jewish youth for unwanted manual occupations, we must be sure, then, that they offer the only, or even the most promising, way out in America. . . .

Our recognition of the need for vocational redistribution demands experiment before we can suggest how best to meet it. This constitutes a challenge to Federations, and to Jewish family agencies, in particular. We have often claimed that an outstanding value of private as contrasted with public social work lies just in its flexibility and its willingness to experiment. Since the onset of the depression we have been talking about the dangers of Jewish concentration in middle-class occupations, the lack of opportunity for growing Jewish youth, and the need for experiments in programs of group rehabilitation. But so far no family agency, to my knowledge, has undertaken to discover how we can meet these newly pressing dangers. Everywhere the emphasis has been rather on the preservation of values in the case-work process, and on the therapeutic aspects of case work. Without belittling the importance of case work as a tool, I cannot but be critical of Jewish social work, particularly in the larger communities, for its failure to plan a demonstration program in the all-important task of vocational redirection. Cannot our family agencies in cities like Chicago or New York conduct a laboratory in this primary field for us? What promising new economic occupations can they uncover? For what jobs can they train and retrain surplus workers? Does agriculture offer a promising opportunity for large numbers of Jews? May or may not Jews be expected to continue to make their own way—along the customary economic roads? . . .

As I see it, therefore, planning for Jewish economic welfare in this country during the next decade or so must postulate the continuance of the capitalist system, but operating under mild social controls. We may assume, then, that Jews may continue to enjoy opportunities as economic enterprisers, though on a much more restricted scale, to be sure, than they enjoyed during the latter part of the nineteenth and the first quarter of the twentieth centuries. However, even such a general premise does not help us much. For given the prevailing state of social flux, its broad implications do not facilitate the charting of definite short-term and specific industrial trends. The range of Jewish economic planning is limited just by these uncertain national short-time trends to which we as Jews must make *ad hoc* adjustments. Regardless of exactly what may happen in the immediate future, however, many of the fields into which Jews have crowded have already reached the saturation point; the job of making a living will become, therefore, increasingly difficult. Jewish planning, accordingly, can safely accept as established the need to redirect and redistribute Jewish gainful employment in the American economy. But it cannot assume that promising occupational opportunities are ready at hand, or that even when we search them out, it will be easy to change the habits, mores, and traditions of a people who for centuries have been urban followers of professional and commercial pursuits. We social workers, engaged daily as we are in attempting to influence attitudes, know how difficult and slow a job it is. But no people can fold its hands and wait for the benign or malignant developments of history. We must, therefore, engage in experimentation, and boards of Federations and family agencies should at the earliest possible moment launch experiments in the economic redirection of Jewish unemployed and Jewish youth.

Yet, whatever success such experiments may have, and whatever opportunities individual Jews may yet find in coming decades for winning personal prosperity, the group economic outlook is, I am afraid, not a rosy one. The vast majority of Jews will share with the mass of their fellows all the insecurities inherent in competitive industrialism and social transition. In addition, they will endure specific handicaps just because they are Jews. Our distribution in increasingly crowded economic areas will sharpen the impact of traditional prejudices against us. These prejudices, in turn, exacerbated by the pressures of social conflict, will continuously threaten the Jew with a recurrence of his sadly familiar scapegoat rule.

Before such a prospect, two ways out lie open to us. First, we can and should use whatever energy and influence we possess to help the forward-looking elements in the country wrest from government and the times the maximum social gains for all the people, even while we simultaneously set up defenses for our own people against specific dangers that threaten them. Second, we can and should so strengthen our own cultural and spiritual life—our inner group resources—that it will furnish both the supports against our hardships and the agents for converting them into spurs for the battle for social justice and righteousness that is inherent in the very fiber of our historic traditions.

3. Organization and Administration of Vocational Services under Jewish Auspices

An Outline Statement to the Institute on Social Work Programs of Federations, Philadelphia, January 28-29, 1937.

By a Special Committee of the Vocational Services Section of the Council of Jewish Federations and Welfare Funds [1]

I. Vocational service agencies are necessary because:

A. *Unorganized Job-finding and Preparation Have Become In-*

[1] Irwin Rosen, Chairman; Rabbi J. X. Cohen, Ann Lehman, Doris Maddow, Lucille Naumberg, Dr. Otto Neubeurger, Sarah B. Perlman, Louis H. Sobel, Michael Freund, *ex officio;* Fritz Kaufmann and Dr. Lazare Teper, technical advisors. *Jewish Social Service Quarterly,* vol. XIII, no. 4 (June 1937), pp. 398-401.

creasingly Difficult. Widespread unemployment and the irregularity and impersonality of industry and commerce make it increasingly difficult for the work-seeking population and for those in training for vocations to find or prepare for employment without the aid of organized placement, vocational guidance, and related service agencies.

B. *Many Social-Agency Clients Are of Doubtful Employability.* The difficulty in finding employment is especially severe among the clients of social agencies whose social, physical, mental, and other handicaps raise serious doubts as to their employability; this is true not only in times of crisis and widespread unemployment, but also in times of relative stability in industry and commerce.

C. *Added Employment Difficulties of Racial and Religious Minorities.* Minority religious and racial groups find added obstacles in the path of securing employment, in times of both crisis and stability, because of discriminatory hiring and personnel policies or attitudes in many industries and in certain occupational categories. This tendency is accelerated during periods of widespread unemployment, and creates in the populations affected demoralization and a sense of handicap which has unfavorable repercussions in the community.

D. *Constant Need for Aid in Occupational Adjustment.* Quite apart from current emergency conditions, which exaggerate the needs of the general work-seeking or work-preparing population and the needs of the handicapped and minority groups, there is a constant and fundamental need for occupational adjustment services in any industrial economy subject to rapid technological and social change. In the face of such changes, the resourcefulness of the individual is as limited as is his sense of responsibility for the changes taking place; society must provide the resources which the individual lacks to make a wise choice of occupation, to train for it, enter into it, and succeed in it.

II. Governmental and community-supported vocational service agencies are needed because:

A. *Unemployment Is A Mass Problem.* Only a national (federal-state-local) system of employment exchanges and related services can begin to cope with the mass problem which unemployment represents, or can develop the informational and statistical basis for the scientific management of a training, retraining, labor clearance, insurance, etc., program as required.

B. *Coverage of the Public Agency Program Is Limited.* However, the existing national employment exchange system and the various related governmental agencies and programs, despite a progressive and encouraging expansion since 1933 (as embodied in the new United States Employment Service created by the Wagner-Peyser Act and the unemployment insurance provisions of the Social Security Act) are still admittedly, perhaps due to legislation and budget, of only limited coverage. Thus the local communities, agencies, and minority groups cannot as yet, and probably will not for a long time to come, consider that they are relieved of all employment responsibilities; they must, on the contrary, seek to supplement the work of the government agencies and to stimulate these agencies to expand their programs.

C. *Local Problems Uncared for and Needed Programs Undeveloped.* The Jewish community can supplement the work of the government agencies in two main directions: (a) by providing vocational services for social-agency clients and for the general Jewish population in those localities where discrimination and occupational maldistribution are known to exist, and where the local public vocational service agencies fail to be of special assistance; (b) by actually providing those elements of a comprehensive vocational service program which as yet are only "paper plans" in the government agencies, e.g., vocational guidance, job promotion in the interests of Jewish applicants on register in the public employment office, etc.

D. *Long-term Programs Continue as Responsibility of Community.* It cannot be assumed *a priori* that such supplementary vocational services as the Jewish community organizes will become part of the government agency program, for there are both practical and theoretical difficulties which may preclude such a development.

III. The argument that Jewish vocational service agencies are needed is a purely academic one unless it is added that such agencies must be administered and organized in accordance with certain basic principles . . . .

IV. A national organization to coordinate the activities of the local community agencies by means of central statistical reporting, exchange of job and labor information, standardizing procedures, and promoting and developing community services is necessary for a number of reasons:

A. *The Importance of Regional and National Perspective.* The social and economic forces that condition unemployment and industrial irregularity in the localities are related to national or regional developments; this perspective, which can best be provided by a national organization, must shape any program that calls for occupational redirection of the Jewish work population.

B. *The Essential Nature of Advisory and Liaison Functions.* A national organization could call the local communities' attention to occupational trends and industrial changes which should influence training, guidance, and job promotion programs; this it could do by carrying on central reporting, job and labor information exchange and advisory functions, and by serving as the liaison with national occupational planning and research bodies, such as the National Occupational Conference, the National Youth Administration, the Federal Committee on Apprenticeship Training, etc.

C. *Evaluation Requires A Vantage Point of The Total Population.* The federal control of vast areas of social and economic activity that has developed in recent years constitutes a recognition of the realities in our industrial economy. If the Jewish population is to be integrated in this industrial economy, its needs and objectives will have to be evaluated on a total population basis and interpreted by a national body closely in touch with developments in local communities.

D. *Relating Immediate to Long-Term Objectives.* The organization and administration of new Jewish community vocational service agencies should be influenced by the experience of existing agencies, and should be related to broader objectives as already described. A national agency could best evaluate local experience for the new or projected agencies; it could also interpret the experience and objectives of the governmental agencies.

E. *Providing Important Technical Assistance.* Budget considerations are likely to preclude the development of essential technical aids, such as research, statistics, etc., in the local agencies; a national organization could provide these technical aids for special research projects, statistical analyses, etc.

III Anti-Semitism Renewed: Widening Approaches to Jewish Community Relations

MINORITY groups in all societies have had to be alert to traditional attacks from either a dominant majority seeking conformity to common standards, or from other opposing groups. The restrictions upon minority freedom of action have ranged from subtle social prejudices to legal constraint and physical attack. Early Jewish settlers in the United States, and later the communal organizations which they established, prepared themselves to deal with problems of discrimination and anti-Semitism as best they could. Although such obstacles here were of a less threatening nature than those encountered in Europe by earlier generations, they very definitely did their share in hampering the evolution of a free and democratic society projected under the national constitution. By the decade of the thirties, a number of specialized organizations had been created by various segments of the Jewish population in defense against discriminatory practices: the American Jewish Committee, the Anti-Defamation League of B'nai B'rith, and the American Jewish Congress. Other local associations participated in this work; several communities organized their own community-relations councils to coordinate the work of many interested groups; and new national agencies, such as the Jewish Labor Committee, channeled the energies of more persons to such problems.

The troubled times made new demands upon these specialized agencies and the communities which supported them. In addition to the expression of blatant anti-Semitism in this country, new intergroup anxieties arose as the Jewish community moved more and more toward cooperation with organizations of government and civic associations. This cooperation was often centered around new public-welfare policies, economic reconstruction, and new social legislation—sensitive areas where passions ran high and policy was more often than not a compound of emotion and rational opinion.

There were many interpretations of the causes of discrimination and thus differing bases for framing action, ranging from purely economic explanations (competition over scarce goods leading to envy), to the idea of political class conflict and psychological analysis; the latter attributed discrimination and racial-hostility to emotionally twisted personalities.

Study of the phenomena of prejudice against Jews revealed a complex of causes which pointed the way to broad social programs and actions directed toward improving intergroup relations rather than simple defense measures. At the same time, the demand grew more pressing for some cooperation among these various agencies and groups. It was not only a matter of conserving community energy and funds, but also of using available sources most effectively. Several efforts at coordination among the national agencies were tried, including the organization in 1938 of a General Jewish Council, consisting of the three established national agencies and the newly created Jewish Labor Committee, a precursor of the National Community Relations Advisory Council (1944). At the same time, more local communities began to organize their own councils.

The subject of intergroup relations was affected by the charges of self isolation against some Jewish groups, and counter-charges of discrimination and exclusion by others. Whatever the final explanation, it is clear that Jewish history, education, and experience produced a high proportion of individuals prepared to give time, energy, thought and funds to improve group relations.

1. Problems Facing the Jews Throughout the World and Their Implications for American Jewry*

BY MORRIS D. WALDMAN

. . . Even a superficial inspection of the current Jewish scene reveals that there are no longer distinct problems facing separate communities of Jews, but that, by and large, the Jews the world over are faced with the same social and economic problems. In Poland, for example, it has been estimated that 200,000 Jewish families are in need of relief in one form or another. Unemployment among the Jewish proletariat is enormous; the destruction of the middle class continues, and the opportunities in the professions and the civil service are increasingly restricted. What is true of Poland is equally true of Roumania, Austria, Hungary. In Germany, the ruthless destruction of economic opportunities goes on. In Russia, the Jew as merchant and small trader has been condemned to an economic death. In all these countries, in short, the prevailing economic structure of Jewish life is being persistently undermined.

These conditions are only partly a consequence of anti-Jewish activity. Mainly, they result from the harsh and immutable economic and political forces that in our times have cut freely across national boundaries. Because these factors are international in scope, their effect can be seen upon the American Jews as well as upon the Jews of Eastern and Central Europe. . . .

First, there is the tendency toward State capitalism, or State regulation of economic enterprise. This takes the form in many countries of a nationalization of industries and the creation of State monopolies, a closer regimentation of both capital and labor.

* National Conference of Jewish Social Service, *Proceedings* (1934), pp. 54-56.

Secondly, there is the growing trend toward concentration in industry—the trust or cartel movement—which has the effect of shutting out small industries and business.

Thirdly, there is also the increased striving after national self-sufficiency, as expressed in high tariffs and quotas.

Fourthly, the growth—especially in Eastern Europe—of co-operatives which supersede the old village trader has hurt the economic present and future prospects of many thousands of Jews.

Fifthly, too, there have recently arisen tendencies pointing toward an aggravated feeling of anti-Semitism on the part of consumers, and an increase of "boycott the Jew" movements. There is also an anti-Jewish tendency evident in big business, where interlocking directorates have many times attempted to remove the competition of a Jewish fellow-manufacturer or banker.

In short, and put in its baldest terms, we are witnessing today the suspension in many countries of the principle of free competition, which has been the defining principle of the capitalist system, and under whose aegis the Jew gained his emancipation and patterned his social aptitudes. The Jewish organized labor groups are perhaps best prepared for the new economic developments, but even here, the movement of Jews from labor to commerce renders these unions weaker. Jewish capitalists and merchants are naturally hurt by the decline of foreign trade, the growing anti-Semitism of big business and the consumers, and new centralization [of economic controls]. The Jewish middle class will have to face the problem of declining economic opportunities and perhaps a gradually expanding proletariat. Jewish professional men and students desirous of entering the professions are in the most vulnerable positions.

These permanent worldwide problems facing Jewry today will, and have already begun to, have their effects on Jewish life intrinsically. Religious and cultural assimilation will tend to become less of an issue than it was under emancipatory conditions. Palestine will perhaps assume a new importance as a partial territorial solution. Judaism may be divided by economic and political issues;

or it may conceivably find a new unity, since its fate and future are one for all its members. These questions, perhaps, are imponderables, incapable of solution. Yet they must be faced, and their implications realized by the Jews of America and the world at large.

Added to the prevailing economic factors there is the special problem of anti-Semitism, which, whether officially sponsored or unofficially promoted, aggravates the economic position of the Jew and confronts him with the dilemma of civil and social adjustment as well. . . .

The great danger of this latter-day anti-Semitism is its contagious nature. It appeals to the universal passions of fear, ignorance, and hatred. And, to make it more threatening still, it appeals as an easy strategy or "way out" of the economic and psychological difficulties of our present day. . . .

Because we believe that the ideals for which America stands are so basically antithetical to the tribal system of Hitlerism, our first and immediate problem as Americans as well as Jews is to stem this rising tide in our own land. We must place a high and insurmountable tariff on the importation of these barbaric principles and their dissemination in our country. We must protect our constitution and our institutions from bigotry and race hatred.

The anti-Jewish movement in the United States seems to find its principal support in the active or passive allegiance of thousands of so-called "German-Americans." These people are, I think, generally liberals, since great numbers of them originate in families which left Germany in 1848 as political radicals. However, it is natural that their patriotism is stirred by the new German nationalism, which they believe vindicates all Germans in the eyes of the world. Agitators sent by the German government also have done their work; German *vereins* or clubs in our largest cities have expelled Jews and other dissidents, and have become Nazi "cells"; protests have been silenced by threats against relatives still living in Germany.

Then, too, there still remains latent in the United States the anti-

Jewish feeling exploited not long ago by the Ku Klux Klan and the *Dearborn Independent.*[1] Various demagogues, reviving this spirit and rallying to their standards and their colored shirts, have taken advantage of the situation to incite passion against the Jew.

A great danger is, of course, that out of these apparently unrelated movements a united front may emerge. Such a unity is not an impossibility if inspired by reactionary or Fascist economic groups in opposition to the NRA program. . . .

It is a sad commentary on the progress of man that in this twentieth century the same foul calumnies that were born in the dark Middle Ages and even then condemned by popes and refuted by Christian scholars find currency. To be forced to reply to them in self-defense, to justify our existence and *apologize* for our strength as well as our weakness, for our abilities as well as our defects, is a degrading experience; it threatens to have a demoralizing effect, especially upon those of us who have been born into and have lived in occidental and civilized countries under conditions of emancipation and civil liberty. The danger is that we shall be stampeded into concessions to the anti-Semites, to accept a *numerus clausus* of any kind—in commerce, professional life, civil service, or even in our outlook on life. . . .

If we allow ourselves to become so sensitive to majority prejudices as to condemn any of our fellow Jews for exercising their fundamental, individual, democratic right to belong to any political party they judge best, or, on the basis of equal and not special rights, to achieve the positions and distinctions of which our society deems them worthy—then, indeed, we should be traitors to our ideals as Americans and as Jews. It would mean the acceptance of a political philosophy repugnant to American, English, French, and occidental ideals in other countries, to the principles of Christianity as well as Judaism. We would be bartering our Hebraic ideals accepted by Christendom of justice, humanity, and equality for a mess of pottage.

[1] A notorious anti-Semitic publication sponsored by Henry Ford, who suspended its publication at the end of 1927.

We must not permit the agitation which aggravates the Jewish problem today to throw us back into a ghetto of unhealthy Jew-consciousness and estrangement from our non-Jewish neighbors. Such a compromise would at best be a pyrrhic victory. We may win our lives, but we would be in danger of losing our souls. The Jews must not allow themselves for the sake of immediate security to commit themselves to any policy that would in any way compromise the foundations or negate the meaning of democracy. To do so would be to weaken if not destroy our ultimate security and to betray the ideals of the prophets, the conservation of which is both our high destiny and our *true* justification for existence as a people.

2. The Jew and Social and Economic Conditions in the United States*

Report of a Committee of Practitioners

Our interest in the subject of this paper is not an academic one. As practitioners we are vitally concerned with the welfare of the Jew both as a citizen and as a member of the Jewish group. This interest has been sharpened by events in Germany, and by the emergence of forces in this country similar to those which gained mastery there. Never before in the history of our country has the soil been so fertile for the reception and absorption of an anti-

* *Jewish Social Service Quarterly,* vol. XII, no. 3 (March 1936), pp. 289-307. Presented at the Practitioners' Session of the Lake Placid Convention, National Conference of Jewish Social Service, May, 1935. Committee for the paper: Harry I. Barron, Nathaniel W. Bronstein, Alfred Chalk, Abraham G. Duker, Joseph Kleiman, Mary Pershonok, Elias Picheny, Elizabeth Scharnoff, Irving Schwartz, Lillian Shapiro, Abraham Simon, Sadie Skolnick, Evelyn Spiegel, Frieda R. Unger, George Wolfe, M. D.

Jewish campaign similar to that which has practically destroyed the economic and social foundations of German Jewry. The spread of anti-Semitic activities on an unprecedented scale at the present time is not an accident. It occurs at a time when large sections of the American people are suffering from the effects of six years of a deep-rooted crisis.

In order to achieve a correct understanding of the position of the Jew in America today, we must first acquaint ourselves with the general economic situation of the country, and its effects on the status of minorities in general, and the Jewish group in particular.

The economic crisis which began in 1929 has been the sharpest and the most devastating in the history of the United States. Economic opportunities which seemed to be almost inexhaustable until that year were suddenly reduced to a vanishing point. The New Deal set out to cure the sick condition of American economic life by attempting to eliminate or reduce the cut-throat competition in business, and to increase the purchasing power of the masses. After two years of the New Deal, we can see that this attempt to benefit the forgotten man and the small business has resulted only in bringing benefits to industrial owners. . . .

Accompanying these conditions and the inability of the ownership class to meet the deepening crisis, there developed on the part of those who control the means of production an attack upon civil liberties and rights. For the first time in American history, we witness the simultaneous introduction of a variety of gag bills in the state and federal legislatures directed at curbing the power of organized labor and the working masses. Unparalleled in our history is the introduction of the so-called "ballot bill" in twenty-four state legislatures during the past year, and the passage of these bills in four states.

This bill, sponsored by the American Legion in the various states, generally provides that "no political parties shall be recognized or be given a place on the ballot which advocate the overthrow of the government by force or violence, or which advocate or carry on a program of sedition or treason by radio, speech, or press." This bill proposes not only to set aside such constitutional guarantees as freedom of speech, press, and assembly, but it places a most powerful weapon in the hands of the most dominant political groups to be used for the suppression of their opponents. The experience of the working and generally underprivileged population of Europe has shown that although such bills are directed in the first instance against the most militant workers, they are soon utilized to suppress by violence any attempt by workers to improve their living conditions. In addition to this type of bill there are seditionist, military, anti-alien, loyalty oaths, and criminal syndicalist bills, which are aimed to curtail or abolish free speech, academic freedom, and liberty of the press. The recent expulsions of teachers and students because of their protests against these very bills are an illustration of the extent to which reactionary forces in this country are attempting to crush the rights of liberals and workers alike.

The economic crisis and the attempts to patch up the system which produced it have made the American people more conscious of the tie-up between economic and political forces. The impoverishment of large sections of our population, and the disillusionment with a government that attacks the civil liberties of its people, has given rise to demagogues who try to capitalize upon the desire of the masses for a way out. Father Coughlin and Huey Long are the most popular of these demagogues, who pretend to champion the interests of the workers, dispossessed farmers, declassed businessmen, and unemployed white-collar workers. There is a striking similarity between Coughlin's "social justice" and Long's "share-the-wealth" programs. Supposedly radical and in the interest of the workers and small businessmen, they are reactionary in the extreme, and contain within them the essential features of fascism.

Thus we see how the years of the crisis, including the period of the New Deal, have affected the living standards and civil rights of the American workers and the middle class. The minority groups in our population have suffered further limitations of their right to work, to defend their economic interests, and to give free expression to their political beliefs. . . .

Every bit of available information points to the precarious condition of the small Jewish shopkeeper, tradesman, independent producer, manual worker, and professional. The growth of chain stores, trusts, and monopolies have made more difficult the lot of these groups.

Thus, the American Jew not only suffers from the economic consequences of our chaotic social order; in addition, he is made the target of attacks which threaten his continued existence as a member of society on an equal basis with other Americans. As practitioners, we are vitally concerned with the social and economic conditions which are responsible for this state of affairs. At the same time, we must inquire into the programs advanced by various Jewish groups which deal with the situation.

Let us first examine those agencies whose specified aim is to protect the civil rights of American Jews. The American Jewish Committee, which represents the upper crust of Jewish community leadership, aims "to prevent the infraction of the civil rights of the Jews in any part of the world.". . . The concrete activities of the American Jewish Committee are determined by the social and economic position of its leaders and their conception of the underlying cause of anti-Semitism. . . . By fostering the belief that anti-Semitism can be eliminated by a mere appeal to Americanism, the American Jewish Committee not only is naive, but has no claim to leadership. The leaders of the Committee persist in utilizing this technique, even as did the German Jewish leaders before the ascension of Hitler.

The Anti-Defamation League of B'nai B'rith . . . appeals to American public opinion and enlightens it in the hope that American [democratic] traditions will thus be upheld.

The American Jewish Congress bases its support on the middle class and sections of the working population. . . . The composition of its membership dictates a somewhat more realistic understanding of discrimination and anti-Semitism. But to this day its program has not placed the problem of anti-Semitism in its proper perspective by fighting against the whole onslaught of facism. . . .

This in the main is the point of view and approach of the three important organizations discussed here. A somewhat different attack upon the problem of discrimination and anti-Semitism is represented by the advocacy on the part of some economists and communal workers of programs aiming to bring about an economic redistribution of the Jewish group in America. These programs fall under three heads: (1) a return to trades, (2) a return to agriculture, and (3) the development of specialized economic agencies, such as Jewish communal employment bureaus, to explore the available economic opportunities for Jews. . . .

The various workers' groups discussed here,[1] although differing in their tactics and ultimate aim, realize that only through the enlistment of the broad masses of the population can the rights of workers and minority groups be protected. In this fight, labor has received support from a number of Jewish and non-Jewish organizations which realize the importance of aligning themselves with the groups most affected by the attacks on civil liberties, and the attempts to curtail economic opportunities. Among these organizations are to be found the [Central] Conference of American Rabbis and the Rabbinical Assembly of America. Their pronouncements on social justice specifically indicate that it is the duty of religion "to ally itself with those forces that make for social education and the fostering of a social conscience."

If anything can be said with assurance regarding present social and economic trends in the United States as they affect the Jew, it is that the vital problems of the security and future existence of the Jewish groups cannot be isolated from the immediate problems facing large sections of the general population. The German experience, above all, has taught us that every attempt to limit the civil, political, and economic rights of any section within the general population must have a profound effect on the status of the

[1] Economic planners, labor unions, and socialist and communist groups are identified in the omitted sections.

Jew as a member of a minority group. From this it follows that the interests of the Jew lie with those groups which tend to lose most from discrimination and the limitation of opportunity. . . .

Can there be any question that the Jew must join with all progressive forces to stem the tide of rising reaction? It is not to be supposed that every Jewish group will join this immediate struggle. The interests of some Jews will keep them in the camp of those who propose to limit our rights, but there can be no doubt that the great majority of the Jewish population in the United States can and must align itself with other groups in making secure those rights which are basic for the entire population, and which offer security for the Jew.

We, as practitioners in Jewish social work, call on all social workers to unite on the fundamental questions centering around the preservation of civil liberties, the fight against encroaching reaction, fascism, and anti-Semitism. We call upon you to join with labor in its struggle for adequate social insurance, for child labor legislation, for the thirty-hour week, for freedom of speech and press, for academic freedom, and for all measures which will protect the fundamental rights of the underprivileged workers. No greater responsibility faces us at this critical period. It is not only necessary to accept this basic formulation, but to engage courageously in every day struggles through whatever means possible. . . .

Addendum

This section of the Committee [2] is in full agreement with the underlying thesis of the Committee paper. We concur in the paper's analysis of anti-Semitism as a necessary concomitant of the present economic order. . . .

The solution it offers, however, is not sufficient for Jews who have any interest in Jewish group life, although it may be adequate for all liberal and progressive groups active in the defense of civil

[2] Harry I. Barron, Abraham G. Duker, Joseph Kleiman, Elizabeth Scharnoff, Frieda R. Unger.

liberties. It is not sufficient for a group of Jewish practitioners seeking a radical, thorough-going solution of the Jewish problem. . . .

The conclusion suggested by the Committee paper leaves one with the impression that the united fight against anti-Semitism sets as its goal merely the economic emancipation of the individual Jew. While this is extremely important, such a unilateral emphasis does not consider the essential need for the sustaining of Jewish group life. In cooperating with other groups in the fight against anti-Semitism, the Jewish practitioner must seek specifically Jewish vehicles for that struggle. If we are to make an effective appeal to the Jewish masses, such specific Jewish vehicles are necessary. The Jewish masses can be more easily organized in Jewish groups. Any other attempt at organization will produce a situation of leaders without followers. The establishment of such effective Jewish organizations, moreover, will stem the increasing reaction within the Jewish group. Finally, these mass Jewish organizations must have as their rallying points not merely an appeal for struggle against anti-Semitism and reaction, but also a comprehensive program for reconstructing and revitalizing Jewish group life and activity.

The struggle for survival of the Jews as a group on the modern scene cannot be limited to a program of self-defense against outside hostile groups. To live comfortably and meaningfully as a people, a positive program of Jewish living must be incorporated into the working philosophy of the Jewish practitioner. We feel that no apologies are necessary for our express desire to maintain a distinct Jewish group. The theory of cultural pluralism in this country has been well set forth by outstanding thinkers. Soviet Russia clearly promulgates the principle of national group autonomy. It must be stated that the Jews as a group are not willing to give up their identity and have clung tenaciously to their heritage, as history has shown. As Jewish practitioners in the field of social work, we must, therefore, participate in efforts to preserve the Jewish community. Acting as a positive force in Jewish life, we can help in shaping our community along socially constructive lines.

We propose that our group take advantage of its cultural differentia, instead of carrying them as an added, unwanted, and irritating burden. . . .

A desirable program of action must be formulated. Such a program must necessarily be based on the ideology of a social system which would eliminate the evils of capitalism. Its methods must fundamentally [be determined by] an approach which would ally the Jewish masses with all other working masses and persecuted minorities. It must consider the Jewish problem as one which is international in scope. [The goal of] such a program would [reach beyond] the economic emancipation of individuals within the Jewish group and community. . . .

3. Developments in Jewish Civic and Protective Activity in the United States*

BY HARRY L. LURIE

Our country was settled by European peoples seeking religious liberty and economic opportunity. Our colonial history was a period [characterized by] attempted exploitation by European states. The founding of the United States of America represented the successful effort of a continent to free itself through revolution from [the status of a colonial possession without] full civic equality. Our history, therefore, presented us with the gifts of religious liberty and civic equality, which operated as powerful stimulants in the unfolding of our democracy. Only the vestiges of reactionary traditions imported from our European origins, and elements of our own indigenous conservatism prevented a fuller realization of these ideals in this country. . . . During this development, we were

* *Jewish Social Service Quarterly*, vol. XVI, no. 1 (Sept. 1939), pp. 10-18. Presented at the annual meeting of the National Conference of Jewish Social Welfare, Buffalo, N. Y., June 14-18, 1939.

not completely free from [racial or religious] prejudices, but such attitudes were sporadic and limited and did not materially affect democratic policies. . . . Tremendous advances were made, and for more than a century we progressed along the paths of our democratic ideals. We maintained an open-door policy for immigrants, fought a civil war, and achieved liberty for the Negro slaves.

Jewish defense activities in the United States during the nineteenth century were developed as a logical outgrowth of a generally satisfactory democratic development. Organized efforts were concerned mainly with the problems facing the status of Jews in other countries. This consisted largely of philanthropic work abroad, and securing assistance from our government in resolving some of the anti-Semitic actions of backward nations which on occasion involved the rights of American Jewish citizens traveling abroad. . . .

Toward the end of the nineteenth century, it became evident that the ideals of democracy and equality were losing the widespread appeal they had had in the colonial and the frontier eras. Class and group conflicts were becoming more marked. The older and simpler democracy exemplified by the aims of the Populist Movement of the 1890's met with political defeat. This recession coincided with the point at which we began to question whether our economic structure could continue to absorb the influx of new immigrants. The open-door policy faded, and immigration began to be considered as a threat to the wage and living standards of the resident population. The end of the nineteenth century saw the development of selective immigration through literacy tests and quota restrictions designed to limit its volume. These restrictive measures were accompanied by a resurgence of anti-alien attitudes toward various nationality groups from Eastern and Southern Europe, and involved Jewish immigrants as well. Descendants of former immigrants increasingly began to oppose the admission of new immigrants, on the basis of cultural prejudices as well as economic fears. [The biases of] economic and social stratification were making inroads on the ideals of social equality. . . .

During the last three decades, important economic trends have changed the character of economic rivalry and competition; irritability, fear complexes and antagonism [against certain groups] have begun to develop. This period has created such symptoms as Henry Ford's *Dearborn Independent*, the resurgence of the Ku Klux Klan, and increasingly bitter political rivalries and economic competition between our varied immigrant groups.

During the first three decades of the twentieth century there was a gradual crystallization of anti-Semitism, until at present it seems to have become the residuary legatee of anti-alien and anti-Catholic tendencies which came to the fore in the Ku Klux Klan movement of the twenties and which are now seen to be abating. In fact, recent observers of the fundamentalist Protestant South tell us that proto-fascist and anti-Semitic propaganda is diverting the traditionally Catholic-baiting Protestants of the South into a potential anti-Semitic following.

Up until the last six years, the existence of social prejudice in the United States had only minor political significance. The acute depression and economic dislocations following 1929, accompanied by a reversal of democratic trends in Europe, laid the groundwork for the present phase of anti-Semitic sentiment. The Nazi movement in Germany has made anti-Semitism into a world program, and a component part of the fascist movement in all lands. Threatened with economic disaster and radical social change, former capitalist democracies have either espoused fascist solutions or have become increasingly fascist in temper. Class conflict and social democratic attitudes have been ruthlessly curbed, and anti-Semitism has been [used as an outlet for] a variety of social and economic antagonisms.

Establishment of Protective Agencies

There are four major Jewish agencies now seeking to deal with this situation. All of them were organized in the present century.

The American Jewish Committee, established in 1906, was until recently primarily concerned with the European situation, although anti-Jewish attitudes and the pressure for extreme restriction of immigration in this country were within the scope of its interest. The Anti-Defamation League of the B'nai B'rith, organized in 1913, devoted itself primarily to counteracting social manifestations of anti-Jewish attitudes in this country. The first American Jewish Congress, organized in 1917, had as its objective the participation of American Jewish interests in the settlement of European Jewish problems arising out of the war and involved in the peace negotiations. This original Jewish Congress was adjourned in 1920. The American Jewish Congress which reorganized in 1922 took for its [field of activity] problems [surrounding] the political rights of Jews in this country and overseas. It helped to establish and became a constituent member of the World Jewish Congress; until 1933 it was largely devoted to the problems of Jews overseas and the furtherance of Zionism as a solution for Jewish problems.

With the growing organization of anti-Semitic movements in the United States in this decade, these three organizations began to be more actively concerned with anti-Semitic manifestations here. A fourth agency, the Jewish Labor Committee, was added in 1933, when Jewish labor leaders participated in a program to pit the force of organized labor against the anti-labor movements spreading in the European countries.

Theories and Methods of Jewish Defense Work in the U.S. Prior to 1933

Until very recently, these protective activities seem to have been based mainly upon the belief that we were dealing with sporadic and largely individual sentiments that could be corrected by education and the promotion of good-will. Instances of prejudice and acts of discrimination were viewed and treated as outcroppings of residual attitudes which had been transplanted with the cultural baggage of immigrants who came here from countries of Jewish oppression and entrenched anti-Semitism. The overt instances of discrimination were social in character, and no basic political rights were actually denied or infringed upon. The limited program consisted mainly of meeting individual problems with individual efforts. The work was directed toward dispelling misconceptions by the use of reason and correct information. Persons of goodwill were enlisted in an effort to persuade ignorant, misinformed, or vicious individuals to adopt more reasonable attitudes and actions. With the intensification of anti-Jewish movements, our protective agencies began to intensify their efforts. More and more, we have become conscious of the importance and the extent of the developments which threaten us, even if at the present time there has been no open interference with the civic status of Jews. The agencies engaged in anti-defamation and protective work have little to overcome in the way of resistance or indifference to the problem. As their program of work develops and is understood, assistance and support is being made available to them. Their problems, we recognize, are not essentially philanthropic, but concern us all deeply. Of necessity, their work has become vital to our entire fabric of organized communal effort.

What Can We Do?

The extent of the opportunities for protective work by Jews is, however, circumscribed. We can protest individually and in groups. We can answer malicious charges and slanders. We can attack those who promote anti-Semitism, and point out the vicious character of their motives and their alliances to the supposedly neutral public. We can also hope for a natural antagonism to such fascist and anti-Semitic designs on the part of other groups in our democracy that fear and detest these subversive attacks upon our democratic system. We can try to persuade all persons of good will of the importance of maintaining tolerance and civic equality. We can, in short, contest with the anti-Semitic forces to win over public opinion, hoping that our arguments may be as effective as the organized propaganda of the anti-Semitic groups, and that we may be fortunate in finding the techniques for education and public enlightenment that are positive rather than negative in their effect upon so-called neutral or changeable points of view. All of these and similar actions are being taken by our civic-protective agencies, which are conscious of the extent and severity of the problem, and which will, we may be sure, attempt to carry out the most effective and constructive program that they can create. In our natural eagerness to find solutions for vexing problems, however, we can readily exaggerate the efficacy of our organized activities. Indeed, many of us harbor what seem to me to be fanciful notions of what can be accomplished by educational efforts.

It is a mistake to assume that fascism is an irrational or hysterical phenomenon that can be exorcised merely by statements of reason and enlightenment. The open or, even the secret designs of an organized fascist movement may appear irrational; but therein lies its very danger. For fascism can be made to appear to many unthinking or unprincipled individuals as a solution to unsolved economic and political problems. Poverty, distress, insecurity, hopelessness, and discouragement can so condition the minds of people [as to make them receptive to] fascist ideologies. The ideals of civil liberty and democratic equality bear little weight against the overwhelming political pressures arising from insecurity and frustration. And we must remember that although fascist ideas may spread rapidly among all elements of the population, they are originally supported by, and receive their greatest encouragement from, groups who have a controlling voice in economic and political affairs. We must remember, too, that a functioning fascist program is not necessarily an entirely imported product. We have our own incipient brands of fascism in anti-labor movements, in red-baiting, and in vigilante movements which existed in this country long before we heard the name of Adolf Hitler or the term "fascism."

If we are to deal with the problem of anti-Semitism, therefore, we must deal directly with the forces of reaction which are using it for their own ulterior motives. This is a task for all Americans; but the added threat of anti-Semitism compels us Jews to greater activity than we can expect from other groups. It is obvious that Jews, particularly, cannot afford to ally themselves with the programs of reaction, even if the tie to anti-Semitism is hidden or delayed in these movements. . . .

4. Methods of Dealing With Problems Affecting Jewish and General Relationships*

BY I. M. RUBINOW

There is a Jewish problem in the United States. Until comparatively recently this assertion would have been met with considerable bitterness and resentment by a substantial proportion of Jewish leadership in the United States. It was contrary to the spirit of American institutions, which recognize—so the daily papers have insisted, year in and year out—no distinction between race, nationality, and creed. The last eighteen months have at least had this positive result: they have opened our eyes to the [Jewish] situation, which now is generally admitted and regarded with a great deal of concern and worry. It is admitted not only [by us] but by the country at large. There is an anti-Semitic movement in the United States. That movement represents the substance, or at least the manifestation, of the Jewish problem. We are inclined to blame it entirely upon foreign propaganda. As yet no respectable publication, no respectable party, perhaps no respectable group, would be willing to admit affiliation or even sympathy with the anti-Semitic movement. In public life, in a great many communal activ-

* National Conference of Jewish Social Service, *Proceedings* (1934), pp. 62-66.

ities, and in many important movements, the Jew works side by side with the gentile, and evidences of generous recognition of his contribution to American life are not difficult to obtain. . . . The National Conference of Jews and Christians, backed by the best elements of Christian clergy of all denominations, is endeavoring to perform a noble piece of education for better relationships between various religious groups. Nonetheless, its very existence is evidence that a problem exists, and that its existence has been recognized for years.

Undoubtedly, the new awareness of the problem to a large extent coincides with the Nazi revolution in Germany. There has been, and continues to be, a tremendous amount of vicious anti-Semitic propaganda directly traceable to German influences. Most if not all of the twenty-five such organizations . . . have sprung up since March 1, 1933. Many of them can only thinly disguise their direct contact with their German origins. Nevertheless, it would be naive to describe the entire movement as merely an imported German movement. A smoldering flame has been burning during the last eighteen months. Undoubtedly, the unusual economic and social conditions of the last four or five years have added fuel to the fire. But who can guarantee a rapid improvement in economic conditions, the disappearance of factors of economic and social strife? The gradual development of the problem is at least a warning that its sudden disappearance cannot be anticipated. . . .

Thus defined, the Jewish problem finds its definite place in the domain of sociological theory. It is but a link in the chain of group relations, beginning with tribal wars of primitive society and world conflicts embracing sometimes all of humanity. The study of the problem may begin with a mere explanation. It must end with a program. What can we do to solve the Jewish problem in the United States, or anywhere else, on the assumption that a solution is not only necessary but possible?

Obviously, any effort to outline a complete program, or even more modesty a course of immediate action, must reckon with various steps already taken or suggested.

1. Information. The course of events in Germany during the

last ten years offers a significant warning that the anti-Semitic movement cannot be disregarded. It cannot be laughed out of existence, no matter how preposterous it and its theoretical promises may appear to be. Apparently, there is no inclination on the part of American Jewry to disregard it. The tendency is decidedly in the other direction. Something akin to an anxiety neurosis is developing even in those layers of American Jewry that but recently were quite oblivious to the situation. A sober attitude which neither overlooks nor exaggerates the facts is possible only when the facts are known. On the whole, this immediate task of gathering the facts is being performed energetically and intelligently. The necessary intelligence service has been developed. If the first conclusions of this accumulated information resulted in a shock, it is largely due to previous neglect. Much of what has but recently been discovered has existed for a considerable time. The realization of the plan of economic research which has been under discussion for some years is a necessity.

2. Dissemination of information. *The Jewish Daily Bulletin, Today,* the Anglo-Jewish press and many other Jewish publications, daily, weekly, and monthly, have made the information available to the Jewish as well as the general public. There is some difference of opinion as to the wisdom of throwing the scarlet light of publicity upon the information obtained. With a masochistic tendency, perhaps characteristically Jewish, we love to read of our troubles in Galut, and perhaps grossly exaggerate them. On the other hand, by a process of psychological compensation against this tendency, many of us show a desire to hide the truth. Any effort to place a cloak of secrecy over the facts will invariably lead to an even more alarming exaggeration.

3. Counter-propaganda. The mechanics of the anti-Semitic movement are complicated. Its most common more or less passive instrument may be classified as "defamation" of Jewish character in the past, present, and future. Its more active mechanism is the proposal of legal measures against the Jew—legal expulsion, restriction of legal rights, or extra-legal measures, such as incitement

to isolation, discrimination, social or economic (boycotts.) In extreme cases [anti-Semitic movements have resorted] to direct physical attack (Russian pogroms or German atrocities).

On the American scene where, after all, definite cultural traditions exist, little thought as yet has been given to the possibility of these grosser manifestations of anti-Semitism, even though veiled expression [of such attitudes] may already be observed in the more extreme and cruder anti-Semitic publications. Opinions differ as to whether any real danger of such [anti-Jewish activity] exists. Obviously, any didactic statements as to what the future may bring are worthless.

Defamation is not a new phenomenon. The fact that the Anti-Defamation League of B'nai B'rith was organized more than twenty-five years ago is evidence of this. What can be done to overcome this terrific increase, this veritable flood of preposterously vicious and lying propaganda against the Jew and everything Jewish?

The necessity for counter-propaganda has been recognized. Its organization, however, leaves much to be desired. The Anti-Defamation League has undoubtedly had the most extensive experience, but its resources are limited. On the other hand, a large number of competing or at any rate independent organizations have sprung up, hundreds of committees, and in addition thousands of intrepid individuals ready to undertake the challenge of the slaying of the dragon.

It is assumed that every literary or even every literate Jew, and certainly every Jewish attorney and rabbi, is fit to handle such a job. The long and short of it is that they are not. Effective and honest counter-propaganda requires a knowledge of history, general and Jewish, of comparative religion, of economics, philosophy, statistics, and other sciences and above all an understanding of mass psychology. It should be entrusted only to experts of integrity and recognized standing. . . .

4. Defensive action. An organism that is attacked has a right to defend itself. In fact, it is not even a question of an abstract right;

it is the natural reaction of a healthy organism, individual or social. In social conflicts, . . . the most important factors are strategy and tactics, and sometimes diplomacy.

The danger of physical attacks on the Jews has created the self-defense committees in Tzarist Russia, the Haganahs in modern Palestine. As yet, these dangers have not become very real in our country. There are many [antagonistic] subtle personal and group relationships, however, in which legislative authority is powerless to interfere—unless indeed we were ready to advocate the Russian point of view, which makes not only anti-Semitic action but even an expression of anti-Semitic sentiment a crime against the social order. In such a social setting, the entire problem of group relationships finds itself on an entirely different plane. So long as American traditions of democracy and personal freedom remain, the legal method must be used only in extreme cases and cautiously—despite the fact, or perhaps because of it, that energetic group pressure on our part may often succeed in achieving the desired executive or legislative action. This may give us a temporary sense of victory and power, but it will remain unenforcible and futile, and it will serve as a source of irritation to others, thus making group relations even more difficult.

5. Direct action. Under this somewhat too-general term, certain types of public expression of sentiment and certain efforts involving social and economic pressure may be grouped. Protest meetings, parades, demonstrations, and boycotts are appropriate illustrations. . . .

There can be no question as to the popularity of these methods. In their more articulate form, they are efforts to right a wrong, to punish or at least to condemn the wrong-doer. Unconsciously, they are primarily methods of mass self-expression. In the majority of cases they may be considered as characteristic symptoms of a mass reaction, rather than deliberate remedial measures. Yet occasions may present themselves when such public demonstrations are not only inevitable but necessary and useful, for suppression of mass indignation against the persecutor and of sympathy for the persecuted may present dangers of its own. . . . Yet these are not methods that can be advocated in any wise effort to establish normal and healthy group relations.

6. Education. Group relations are matters of the spirit, whatever the existing material conditions which influence the spirit either of the individual or the group. In the final analysis, the relation of the individual gentile to the individual Jew and of the gentile world to the Jewish group is a question of attitudes, and of influences of the past and the present which shape these attitudes. Insofar as these attitudes are, from the point of view of the Jewish minority, definitely undesirable, they must be corrected. But how?

It does not help much merely to dispose of existing difficulties between the Jewish community or group and the surrounding gentile world by characterizing them as evidences of prejudice, intolerance, and bigotry. Prejudice, intolerance, and bigotry are social phenomena which have existed in all historic eras, and which are not difficult to explain.

It is true that the recrudescence of anti-Semitism (and all other forms of extreme nationalism [which accompany it] for that matter) throughout the world during the last twenty years has apparently justified the deep sense of disillusionment in the efficacy of the educational method. The East European Jew of the past generation, whether in Russia, Poland, or Roumania, no matter how deeply he suffered from the crude anti-Semitism of his time and place, was not without his hope and inspiration. He could and did easily explain this anti-Semitism as a result of the low cultural standards of the community in which he lived. He often went westward to escape religious and racial bigotry, prejudice, and intolerance. Yet here we are with a third of the twentieth century behind us, with general levels of education and culture continuously rising, and anti-Semitism spreading with all its medieval fury. And more than that, modern pseudo-science apparently supports it.

Education has obviously failed us today. What reliance can we put in its ability to save us tomorrow?

Perhaps the answer to this query is that a program of education has never been tried. Mere schooling must not be mistaken for education of the adult mind, if adult education is to be conceived in the words of Dr. Kotinsky—"as an essential component of any effort toward a more desirable social order." . . . Education must remain a component part of any proposed program for meeting a social problem.

There is a great deal of lip service rendered to the necessity for education as a method of solving the Jewish problem in this country, and some efforts in that direction are being made; but the weakness and futility of these efforts, individually and collectively, is pathetic. An occasional pamphlet, sometimes published largely for the purpose of establishing the claim of this or that organization to [carrying out some program], perhaps published under non-Jewish auspices in which the Jewish sources are timidly acknowledged; a few lectures by rabbis and politicians, Jewish and non-Jewish; pathetic grabbing at every kind word said of Jews by prominent non-Jews. These are . . . not methods to change the current thinking and feeling of great numbers of people. In this task of education and re-education, we must admit that the methods of the National Conference of Jews and Christians, sometimes so superciliously spoken of among us, are much more dignified, much more direct, and one may hope more efficient.

It is in contemplating the magnitude and importance of this task that the failure of achieving complete unity of effort among Jewish leadership is most obvious and most distressing. No resources are too great to be used for this vital purpose; no brain trust need be too proud to devote itself to it. We cannot pledge ourselves to apologizing for Jewish cultural traits or explaining them away; we must not teach mere condescending tolerance. We must give to the majority an understanding and appreciation of the cultural values contributed by minority groups, no matter how small. We must boldly disclose the reactionary character of every dictatorial effort at domination by one culture over another.

It is a large task, and it is not to be accomplished in a day. But who can believe that anti-Semitism, with its history of two or three or four thousand years, will be wiped out in a day? And who can believe that the Jewish problem in any country can or will be solved, unless and until such a radical change in group attitudes is accomplished?

7. Self-analysis. In the meantime, life must go on—Jewish life within a gentile environment. It is possible for Jewish life to go on in an atmosphere of misunderstanding, enmity, and even persecution. Shall we assume, in a spirit of fatalism, somewhat tinged by smug self-righteousness, that it was ever so, that the elimination of the evils of prejudice, intolerance, and bigotry is up to the Christian world, and that we can do no more about it than lead a decent life, watch our step—"walk with dignity," as Mr. Arliss-Rothschild [1] has enjoined us, and let it go at that?

Surely I do not intend at this time and before this audience to give support to the advice of the sociologist Faris [2] that we should destroy all differences in custom, habit, or tradition.

The problem of the economic and industrial conditions of American Jewry has already been repeatedly considered in former sessions of this Conference, as well as in other special conferences on the subject. We once expressed a rather smug sentiment of pride, bordering on boastfulness, as we reviewed the amazing economic growth of our recent immigrant group. And then gradually there crept in an undercurrent of grievance as economic discrimination began to threaten the further extension of our opportunities in certain lines of business and professions and perhaps even in labor.

Ours is a serious problem and a serious grievance. It is contrary to the American constitutional guarantees of [individual] equality, irrespective of race and creed. It is contrary to the great American

[1] George Arliss, well-known movie actor who portrayed a member of the Rothschild family in a movie of the same name.

[2] Ellsworth Faris, University of Chicago sociologist and author of *Intelligent Philanthropy*.

tradition that every person is entitled to the greatest measure of personal success which he, through his ability, perseverance, and opportunity, may reach.

But, if we, as members of a group, insist upon retaining our [identity] as a group—and apparently we do—we cannot in the same breath also deny our group responsibilities and insist upon being treated as individuals alone, and [judged on the basis of] our individual merits only.

If we would continue successfully in our climb to the upper ten rungs of the economic ladder, the upper ten per cent of income and occupational distribution, and if we would continue to grow into primarily a middle-class group—manufacturers, shop-keepers, brokers, lawyers, etc.—we will have to pay the price in the kind of attitude which millions of hardworking wage workers and farmers, suffering from unemployment, low prices or high prices, must necessarily hold against this more successful minority. The generalization may be ventured that if American Jewry can furnish evidence of its willingness to do its share of work in factory, mill, farm and perhaps even mine, and not continue to develop as an exclusively middle-class element, as, for instance, German Jewry has done in Germany, it will make the task of reconditioning group attitudes much easier. . . .

IV Organization for Refugee Service

THE nature of the movement of Jews from Europe in the 1930's differed significantly from the immigration of the pre-World War I epoch, and the shift is best seen in the substitution of the later term "refugee" for the earlier "immigrant." The immigrant had sought new opportunity, while the refugee was escaping from tragedy. Estimates of immigration for this period are inexact, for much of it was handled on an individual and family basis, and governmental data excludes reference to religion.[1] The impact of this new influx on local life was in many ways similar to that of the immigration of the early 1900's, but with one major difference: a strong Jewish community fabric was already woven, and at least skeletal administrative and service agencies were in existence to handle the in-flow.

The first urgent need was the raising of large additional sums of money for use at home and abroad; the second was the shaping of an enlarged organization to provide a host of services, from reception to resettlement and readjustment. New organizational structures were necessary and at first reliance was placed on a variety of volunteer bodies in each community, a measure reminiscent of the earlier period.

However, most resettlement work was in fact carried on locally by the augmented staffs of Jewish family-service agencies, under a variety of financial arrangements. It was very soon evident that

[1] See M. Wischnitzer (*op. cit.*, p. 15) for various estimates.

volunteer women's clubs and synagogues lacked the knowledge, organizational skill, persistence, and self-discipline for sustained national action. The result was an augmented welfare operation, built around the staffs and boards of older agencies, but supplemented by new volunteer help from other Jewish citizens and women's organizations.

While most services were organized and supported locally in this manner, a strong national agency was essential to plan, organize, and direct the flow of so large a task. The National Refugee Service (NRS) was established for this purpose. It dealt with the technical aspects of immigrant resettlement, while the bulk of responsibility for movement from Europe to America was vested in other agencies, such as the JDC and the HIAS. The NRS managed the reception of refugees, organized their assignment and distribution to cities beyond the port of entry, attempted to assure that the newcomers were spread throughout the nation, sought to match local employment opportunity with immigrant requirements, and tried to allocate equitably the burden of local responsibility for refugee support. Its staff also advised individual refugees, helped local social agencies develop proper programs, and helped smaller communities organize services which they did not at first believe they could sustain by themselves. Contrary to early hopes, the large city agencies had helped the nearby smaller communities very little, and many of the latter successfully developed their own service programs for refugees. These became the nucleus around which post-World War II family agencies were organized to serve the entire Jewish community with family and counselling services.

In many ways, the national refugee effort was less comprehensive than the immigrant-aid organizations at the opening of the century, which had attempted to implant new Jewish communities in the interior of the country. But the present program rapidly moved large numbers of newcomers to outlying communities and in the course of so doing, it helped spread organized welfare services into many small communities which had hitherto been content to raise funds for national and overseas purposes. Thus, the strength of Jewish community life was extended by formal organization to a wider geographic area. This program further reinforced the various welfare services by recruiting, training, and giving experience to a whole generation of social workers who, after the war, became a major reservoir of manpower for agency staffs.

1. Changes in Jewish Social Work Structure Under the Impact of Refugee Problems*

BY SOLOMON LOWENSTEIN

In considering possible changes in the structure of present-day Jewish social work under the impact of refugee problems, one obviously thinks of the possible parallels with the situation existing at the time of the heavy East European immigration of Jews to this country beginning with the 1880's of the last century. At that time, the Jewish community in America had very elementary forms of organization: a few scattered relief societies, hospitals, orphanages, homes for the aged and Young Men's Hebrew Associations in some of the larger communities; elsewhere there were practically no forms of social organization except possibly in the rabbi's study or in the synagogue.[1] The impact of that large and continuing stream of immigration created the need for a highly diversified scheme of community organization; first came isolated specialized organizations for the care and absorption of the immigrant into the existing Jewish communities, leading ultimately to the creation of

* *Jewish Social Service Quarterly*, vol. XV, no. 3 (March 1939), pp. 313-16.

[1] There were in fact a large number of relief agencies, one or more in all the seventy Jewish communities, which played a major role in helping immigrants. See J. R. Marcus, *Early American Jewry*, vol. II, and H. B. Grinstein, *The Rise of the Jewish Community of New York, 1654-1860*.

[large supervisory and leadership organizations such as] Federations and Welfare Funds. Yet, until the period when immigration was greatly restricted by war conditions and legislation, the immigrant came into a country of abounding industrial opportunity; he adjusted himself, at times with great difficulty but on the whole with great success, and with advantage both to himself and the country at large.

Today the immigrant arrives here under entirely different conditions. He comes into highly organized communities which, with the development of local and national programs, find themselves prior to his arrival struggling with extreme financial difficulties as a result of the increasing complexities and intricacies of these programs; these conditions have been further aggravated by loss of income or greater difficulty in securing it due to a depressed economic condition causing extensive local unemployment, which has persisted in varying degrees for the last decade. Immigration is numerically restricted; employment opportunities are increasingly contracted. The community is already so highly organized that the creation of new agencies for the purpose of caring for the immigrant meets with great obstacles with respect to manpower, financial support, etc. Yet the need is imperative; the appeal is very great; and means must be found for receiving and assimilating this new group into the Jewish body politic.

There is, of course, the offsetting circumstance that there does exist in most communities some central agency or agencies representing both the leadership and the mass of the Jewish public which recognizes the responsibility and obligation to meet this new requirement. This agency or agencies can give the problem the best analysis in each community, as well as the authority necessary to bring about such changes in organization as may be needed, once these have been clearly indicated and understood.

The difficulty in the formation of such agencies is increased by the fact that the conditions of immigrant admission change so abruptly, so repeatedly, and without warning. New emergencies are created by each new and unexpected act of the [European governments]. At first, the new immigrants came slowly and more or less individually. Later, this developed into a mass immigration, within the restrictions of the immigration law, supplemented by persons with temporary visas who came to explore the situation and to endeavor to make arrangements for permanent removal to this country if and when that became possible. Today, because of the horrible events of recent months, the possibilities of admission have been exhausted; quota numbers for visas have been issued by our consuls abroad which will require long periods of waiting.

For reasons utterly beyond the control of the refugees, their economic condition has steadily deteriorated. Increasing taxes, fines, etc., in Germany and territories under its control have made it impossible for the overwhelming majority of these fugitives to bring with them anything in the way of capital, furniture or other material possessions. They arrive here without means, and unless they have relatives or friends capable of rendering them assistance, in many instances they require financial support until such time as they can obtain employment and adjust to their new lives. All this has thrown new and additional burdens of a very complicated nature upon the agencies endeavoring to care for them.

Therefore, the creation of such agencies has been necessarily conducted on a trial-and-error basis. At first there was no organization specifically devoted to these purposes, and the incoming refugees requiring advice, information or assistance naturally drifted to the existing societies in New York City, the chief port of entry. Among such agencies were the family case work agencies, the Council of Jewish Women, employment agencies, synagogues, community centers, etc. None of these was in a position to remedy the entire problem; it soon became apparent that in so large a city as New York, there should be some one central place in which this work might be concentrated, and applicants referred to the particular agency appropriate to their requirements. Moreover, it was equally obvious that this was in no sense purely a New York problem. The mere fact that the bulk of the immigrants landed in New York was relatively immaterial. The problem was one of national scope, challenging the resourcefulness and generosity of the entire country. Of course, a large degree of responsibility rested upon New York, because of its dominant position with respect to population and wealth in relation to the rest of the Jewish community of America. Moreover, recognizing that the problem was international in nature, the League of Nations had created a High Commission to deal with the subject of refugees leaving Germany because of the change in the nature of the political regime in that country. The United States of America was represented on that High Commission, and the High Commissioner was an American citizen.

All these factors resulted in the creation of two bodies: (1) the National Coordinating Committee for the Care of Refugees from Germany, whose duty and function was to bring the entire situation to the attention of the country at large and to endeavor to secure united and cooperative action on the part of all American communities; and (2) a Greater New York Coordinating Committee, including the Jewish Social Service Association of New York City, the United Jewish Aid Societies of Brooklyn (now the Jewish Family Welfare Society of Brooklyn), and the two sections of the Council of Jewish Women located in Manhattan and Brooklyn, respectively. In addition, the National Council of Jewish Women expanded its work for immigrant women; and a new agency was created under the title of the German-Jewish Children's Aid, Inc., to manage the special project involved in the bringing to this country and the placement in family homes of a limited number of children, permitted to enter outside the quota by special arrangement with the United States Immigration Department.

For the remainder of this discussion we will confine our attention to the National Coordinating Committee, since this symposium is not intended to deal with the New York City situation specifically. The National Coordinating Committee, by dint of the pressure of events in Europe spreading from old Germany to Austria, Italy, and Czechoslovakia, has been compelled to conduct its work in a state of constant flux and an increase of responsibility. It has been impossible to plan ahead adequately because each new development affects the already existing structure and adds to its difficulties. It must be prepared for indefinite and continuing changes of this sort; but it is now clear that its work must be organized and supported on such a basis as to give it strength and adequacy and authority throughout the country, through appropriate personnel and complete and whole-hearted financial support. To accomplish this, the National Coordinating Committee has added to its staff and has established separate departments dealing with resettlement, relief, employment, immigration problems, and all the other questions relating to this very highly complicated subject. It has established regional organizations throughout the country corresponding roughly to the regional divisions of other organizations concerned with national and international problems, such as the Joint Distribution Committee, the Council of Jewish Federations and Welfare Funds, the Jewish Welfare Board, etc., in order to minimize duplication and overlap with respect to staff personnel, manpower, and time required for meetings. It has established local or regional committees for resettlement activities, and for the various other related questions.

However, it has also endeavored in every possible way to cooperate with, or to utilize, or to be used by existing local organizations. It has no desire to interfere with or to complicate the already intricate community and regional organizational setup. It has no desire whatsoever to create new agencies, when existing organizations can adequately and properly undertake the work required. Thus, for example, in a well-organized community with a local Federation or Welfare Fund or both, the National Coordinating Committee would prefer that, wherever possible, its work be conducted through such agencies. . . .

The refugee settlement problem is a matter seriously to be considered by each local community, which should so adapt its existing structural organization as to meet the need for absorption of the largest possible number of these immigrants into each new community, or to create if necessary, and only if necessary, new forms of organization to meet the problems arising out of this situation.

2. Local Organization for Refugee Service*

BY SAMUEL A. GOLDSMITH

. . . It is not my purpose, and it would be utterly beyond the scope of this particular paper, to discuss, except incidentally, some of the fundamental problems that confront us in dealing with emigrés in America. It is merely my intention to point out that we cannot seek perfection in this work of rehabilitation and integration of emigrés. Nor, on the other hand, should we continue to flounder in the deep morass of fear and despair because the problem that now confronts us seems so often supremely difficult and hazardous, so far as our own sense of well-being and security may be concerned. . . .

Viewing the Problem from an Organizational Standpoint

The problem at which we are at work is to a very large extent and should remain a problem not only for professional guidance but for professional work as well. It is true that the psychological and other ramifications of the problem have precipitated us into the vague realm of what is called "public relations," into indefinable reaches of controversy and disturbance dominated by the black cloud of anti-Semitism. We should like temporarily to lift the curtain on these phases of the problem and to look at them from the standpoint of organization, with the purpose of bringing about the

* *Jewish Social Service Quarterly,* vol. XVII, no. 1 (Sept. 1940), pp. 119-31. Presented at the annual meeting of the National Conference of Jewish Social Welfare, Pittsburgh, Pa., May 21-26, 1940.

proper integration of badly dislocated people into our American communities.

What are some of the broad characteristics of the problem?

First, as to the distribution of the new immigrants: Of those who were met by dock workers of the National Council of Jewish Women in New York, in 1938 55.7 per cent were destined for New York City, and in 1939 56.6 per cent were so destined. For Chicago, the figures for those two years were 7.4 per cent and 5.7 per cent; Philadelphia, 2.1 per cent and 2.8 per cent. Then follow in rapid succession, Cleveland, Los Angeles, Newark, Detroit, San Francisco, and Baltimore—each one between one and two per cent of the total number; and then of other principal communities, under one per cent and down to less than one-half of one per cent in order: Cincinnati, St. Louis, Pittsburgh, Washington, Boston, Kansas City, and Buffalo.

In 1938, immigrants were destined, in addition to these cities, for 632 other communities, and in 1939 for 402 other communities.

As we know from practical experience, the new immigrants have been spread rather widely over the country, with a comparatively large concentration in New York City. To deal with a widespread problem of immigration which finds its origins in national governmental policies, and whose initial concentration is at the point of debarkation, national agencies and, more important, functioning local agencies, are required.

Local Expenses Surveyed Via Questionnaire

. . . In 1939, thirty-three cities [which were questioned] apparently expended $555,290 for service to emigrés. They expect to spend, in 1940, about $987,070. If their experience proves to be somewhat like the experience of Chicago, their expectations for expenditures in 1940 are lower than what they will actually have spent at the end of the year.

For the usual family and child welfare services, thirty-two of the thirty-three communities normally spend $2,881,992. Roughly then, they will spend approximately one-third more on services to emigrés, principally for family services and services to children, than they spend for these purposes regularly. Of course, the funds spent regularly in many instances are not raised by the Jewish community but by the Community Chests; whereas the funds spent on emigrés are funds raised almost entirely by Jewish organizations, primarily by the Jewish Welfare Funds of the respective cities, or other counterparts of Welfare Funds, known as United Jewish Appeals. In every instance, the cities involved are going to expend more money on emigré services than they spent last year. The percentage of increase runs in certain small communities from practically zero up to approximately 500 per cent.

As for the number of refugees who have come to these thirty-three cities since 1933, the estimates amount to at least 35,750 excluding the cities of Cleveland and Philadelphia, which furnished no estimates. Using the percentage of persons for whom Cleveland and Philadelphia is known to be the city of destination to estimate the numbers going to those cities, there would be approximately another 3,500 to 4,000 people involved. In all probability, however, the numbers for these cities are larger.

Resettlement Work in the Communities

According to the persons responding to the inquiries, 3,623 (in some instances units, and in other instances individuals) came through the National Refugee Service (Los Angeles and Cleveland are omitted from this particular total). Of this 3,623, 1,234 were resettled—that is, were apparently placed in various small communities ancillary to these larger cities for purposes of settlement. In a fair number of these cities, the resettlement program has just been organized; therefore, no fair presentation of its results can be made at this time. Some of the resettlement programs have had rather rocky going; there have been percentages of failure in resettlement ranging from 3 to 100 per cent, though in certain instances the numbers are so small that the percentages are meaningless. In those communities that have had reasonably large experience in resettlement, such as Boston, Chicago, Indianapolis, Philadelphia, and St. Louis, the percentage of failure was noted as "very small" in one instance, and seemed generally to run between 15 and 30 per cent.

Broadly speaking, and again excluding the New York situation . . . we are working in these cities with an expenditure of something under $1,000,000 in behalf of 35,000 to 50,000 people. Of these, approximately 3,000 to 4,000 have come into the communities via the National Refugee Service; and of this latter group, according to the knowledge of the persons in charge of the community programs, possibly 1,200 to 1,500 have come for purposes of settlement in smaller communities.

Finally, this resettlement work is so novel to most communities from the standpoint of sound social organization, that experience with it has not yet demonstrated either its validity or all the problems involved in its execution.

Possibly another $5,000,000 will be spent on an additional 5,000 to 7,500 refugees in the rest of the country—again exclusive of New York City.

How shall we go about using (in these thirty-three cities) the $1,000,000 on behalf of the 35,000 to 40,000 people? . . .

Drawing Agencies Together

In some of these communities, [in the various agencies, and especially the Jewish ones, those desiring to work or actually at work have needed to be drawn together. We know of the activities of] the National Council of Jewish Women and HIAS, which have been at work for many years on problems of immigration; family-service organizations; child-welfare organizations, through special children brought to them by the German Jewish Children's Aid; employment and guidance services that have always dealt with the adjustment of people handicapped by language difficulties, need for industrial retraining, or hundreds of other handicaps; B'nai

B'rith lodges; community centers; and non-sectarian organizations, to whom the American Committee for Christian Refugees or others have brought the problems of the non-Aryan or the Christian refugee.

Profiting from the experience of federated financing through local Federations and local Welfare Funds, these various women's groups and social agencies should have come together into Coordinating Committees or Emigré Service Leagues or groups in order that all agencies, and even all important individuals who can make a contribution to any facet of the problem, might be given an opportunity to render competent service.

With a few exceptions, the work of such Coordinating Committees or central organizations for refugee service has been financed normally by funds raised in answer to refugee appeals or for war relief—in other words, funds of the Jewish Welfare Funds or United Jewish Appeals. . . .

Our communities are probably not concerned with interfering too much with the natural resources of these emigrés, with their spirit of self-help, and with their desire to find their own way so far as they possibly can. It is desirable, of course, that in all communities there exists a local Coordinating Committee or service organization to provide information and service concerning the normal religious, educational, and citizenship affiliations that any intelligent immigrant would like to establish.

Relating the Refugee to Public Life

In this particular field of activity, there is a great deal of opportunity for intelligent volunteer service, provided that in the larger communities where such an arrangement is possible, this service is under the guidance of a really intelligent and competent professional social worker. It is in this area of activity that so many relations are built up with government, with non-sectarian and Christian organizations, and with many Jewish groups. Certainly in the larger communities, when the volume of immigration into the community warrants it, this work should be under the competent leadership of a person skilled not only in case-work training, but also by experience with problems of community organization. In the very large communities, the worker in charge of the Coordinating Committee on service might do this in addition to other things.

Insofar as social services are concerned, how shall we organize? . . . The primary object of the extension of social service to those, of course, who need it (and possibly around 10 per cent at any one time need it) is to give them the advantage of all the rehabilitative aids that now exist in the community. For these things we have the skills at hand in our agencies, as already indicated. But there is something of greater importance; it is well to have firmly fixed in our minds the idea that these people are immigrants and not refugees; that they are in need, and that their needs should be as promptly and as effectively satisfied as the needs of any other Jew in distress or requiring service; and that this should be done under a more calm atmosphere than is possible in an agency confined solely to dealing with problems of people who represent psychologically devastating aspects of the world Jewish situation.

Regularizing Refugee Status Via Established Agencies

Anyone reasonably close to the problems of extending service to emigrés knows what a terrific emotional pull, even on seasoned social workers, there is in the day-by-day contact with the German and Austrian emigré. The suggestion made above is not directed toward minimizing that emotional pull. It is rather concerned with regularizing the status of the emigré or refugee as a potential American citizen, and as a member of the Jewish community to whom services and material assistance are to be granted on the same basis as to any other person in need.

So, from the very beginning, in most cities relief and family service have been extended through the usual family agencies; in comparatively large cities, through the creation of some small departments which are integral parts of the family agency; and elsewhere, through the family agency without the creation of such a department. . . .

Special Characteristics of the Problem

In other words, the usual resources of all organizations, pooled together through a Coordinating Committee, have been at work on this problem in the major cities of the country. It is in these major cities that the bulk of the problem, outside of New York, has been encountered.

There are, of course, certain special characteristics of work with the emigré group which are now coming to the surface.

First, as already indicated in the discussion of the financial expenditures of cities, the problem is not static, but mounting. Naturally, those coming out of Germany, Austria, Czechoslovakia, and, to some extent, Poland, at the present time are much more impoverished than those who left some years ago. Often affiants, with the best intentions in the world, cannot meet the full burden of care of these people. Some who had jobs with relatives or affiants have lost them, as the curve of general industrial employment changed in various localities. People move around. In metropolitan centers, there is an increasing number of persons who are emigrés, who come to these centers and who now require assistance, but whose affiants or relatives are in distant places. Certain professional groups, notably doctors, are concentrating in certain states where citizenship is not yet required for practice. There is a conglomeration of other special situations, all of which demand increasing relief and service measures.

Quite naturally, the solution of the problem of what to do with the unemployed older professional or other emigré worker will follow the pattern of what can be done for people like them in the general community. However, it is important to note that whether a community be large or small, experience indicates that from the standpoint of a logical, reasonable, scientific, and humane policy, the normal agencies should continue their normal program with these people. Only in this way can the process of integration and incorporation in the community be accelerated.

In the City of New York, of course, this policy has not been followed. A special agency—the National Refugee Service—has had a tremendous burden in dealing with the initial impact of problems presented by immigrants when they arrive in this country. In addition, the agency has established employment services, case-work services, and other services for professionals which have been at work on local immigrant problems in New York City. Other organizations in the city, such as HIAS, National Council of Jewish Women, Westchester Committee, and special groups have also been active. There is a natural desire on the part of the National Refugee Service to be relieved of some of the burdens it is carrying; it has been aided by some degree of cooperation on the part of most of the communities.

The Present Resettlement Program

. . . The present resettlement program, frankly, attempts to distribute some problems of relief and also some people who are willing and who can make good adjustments from central headquarters in New York to smaller cities and towns. The fact of the matter is, of course, that the natural process of dispersion of the Jewish population in the United States, and the natural forces within the emigrés and within the country itself, have pulled a very considerable number of emigrés outside of New York without benefit of any special organizational effort. . . .

Requirements for True Resettlement

When we settle these people in smaller communities, removed from the Jewish communities that are well equipped to render social and other services, we cannot expect the normal process of adjustment to go on if the migration from New York is necessarily forced migration, or if true resettlement is based on anything else than the capacity for absorption of the small community in which it is to take place. . . .

Taking the country as a whole, certain quite definite effects of the impact of the work with emigrés can already be seen. The actual financing of this work has added an additional burden for the year 1940 of approximately $5,500,000 throughout the country. True, as already indicated, the Jewish Welfare Funds and United Jewish Appeals are financing this burden at the present time. But the burden is, in most instances, logically and necessarily a local burden. Temporarily, for psychological reasons and because of the relative ease with which this additional money could be raised in connection with a general refugee and overseas relief appeal, we have foisted the burden on the Welfare Funds. We have, naturally, created in the minds of many of our organizations, primarily the organizations dealing with family service and relief, and the organizations dealing with vocational adjustment problems, the idea that people, in the first five years of their residence in this country, can look to the Welfare Funds and to the local organizations for special help, based on their emigré or refugee status.

This is not altogether logical; nor does it carry out, apart from the necessary initial period of adjustment, the fundamental concept of treating these people in some more normal fashion. Only a very few of our family service societies and our Federations have discussed this problem with the Community Chests, from which most of them draw the bulk of their money. Probably very few of our family service societies have discussed intensively with their boards of directors or their staffs the possibility of making this essentially Jewish service and relief problem part of the usual work of the agency. Indeed, the prospect of such a discussion is at times frightening, because it means again, in the larger communities, a review of the case load; a rediscussion of existing relationships with public agencies; possibly additional transfers of cases and the ensuing complications; or, on the positive side, a greatly increased budget to be received from the Federation.

Function of Smaller Communities in Resettlement

. . . The resettlement program should and will, in the main, be developed throughout the country around metropolitan centers, thus furnishing a very interesting opportunity for a further bringing together of the Jewish communities of the country, and particularly of the smaller communities with the larger communities. As the work spreads from the metropolitan centers, it is organized through state and regional groups of representatives from the small towns.

Something very interesting is taking place, and will continue to take place: first, [there is evidence of] a growing interest on the part of metropolitan Jewry in the Jewish communities of their state or region, seen in the establishment of a practical working relationship with these small and scattered Jewish communities; and second, there is a greater possibility of spreading the doctrine of good social work through this collaboration between the large and the small towns.

Particularly in view of recent events in Europe and in view of the imminent period of greatly heightened uncertainty, the work here in America—whether it deals with the integration of emigrés into our American Jewish communities or with any other aspect of the problem—should be carried out with a sound organizational basis; with a view to as good and as rapid an adjustment of the emigré as possible; a full utilization of our local institutions and organizations; and on the basis of advanced planning for a thoughtful extension of the work of local organizations to encompass this problem, both in our larger and in our smaller communities.

Refugee or Emigré?

The very term "refugee" is a pejorative term. The Los Angeles Emigré Service is an infinitely better name for the central organization than the Chicago Committee for Jewish Refugees.

Centering around the term "refugee" there are, however, assets as well as liabilities. The very term, in the popular mind as well as in the technical definition, applies to a person who is temporarily enjoying the hospitality of a land not his own. It gives him no status—certainly no permanent status. It means that he is suffered to be among us rather than that he is among us by right. [The appeal to the uncertain status of such persons] raises some funds; but I question whether as much money could not be raised in the name of the necessary services. [The term has aroused to some extent] Christian sympathy for the lot of these people, and it is unquestionably true that liberal Christian thought is an asset to the Jews in present-day America and the present-day world. But how quickly is the transfer of sympathy made from the refugee Jew to the temporarily debased, suffering average Jew?

We need not be fearful or jittery of the position of all of us in America if we begin, from a quite contrary point of view, to resent the desire of even liberal people to make incursions upon some who are following the normal trend of immigrant life in America, and who have capacities for making great contributions to the further development of America, by singling them out as factors around which to rally some liberal opinion. None of the refugees have come into America, that is none of those who have come in as immigrants, in any other way than under the law. They are not here by sufferance. They are here in accordance with the will of the Congress and of the people of the country as expressed in law. It certainly is our will, since we have organized our own systems of philanthropy, since we have our own religious institutions, our own cultural institutions, our own programs of Jewish education, that these people live among us, as soon as possible, as normal human beings; that we eventually can free them from the cordon of charitable services which began necessarily in Germany, often were applied in Switzerland, Holland, Belgium, Shanghai, Cuba, or elsewhere in the world, and in many instances need to be continued for a time in the United States.

The problem is not large. It has involved, over a period of about six years, about 80,000 to 90,000 people. They are scattered throughout the country. It is true that 50,000 or more are in New York, and it is true that in certain streets of New York, to some extent, German has displaced Yiddish. It is also true that at a time when the resources of our social agencies have been severely taxed to meet great economic disturbances that have come into the general and Jewish community and when, therefore, they have not been able to graduate from their ranks families that normally would have left them, the additional burden of emigré or refugee relief has become serious financially. But in many communities it is being taken in the stride of fund-raising of either the Federation or the Welfare Fund. In many communities, the organization of local resources has been soundly met on the basis of the usual organizations that have dealt with these problems in the usual way.

The Challenge: To Build A Better Commonwealth

True, there have been attacks made on us via the refugee because of his incursion into employment, because sometimes he did not conduct himself well as a professional person; because we demand so much for him; because we have segregated him into a special category of human beings. It strikes me that neither the intelligent emigré nor the intelligent American Jew wants this situation to continue. We, the Jews, have been in a constant process of adjustment and have struggled for the maintenance of human rights, which permit an individual to adjust himself and to live where he finds himself. This means normal living—the creating or the finding of a normal environment for the normal development of these new Americans. We have believed in the development of a full Jewish life, culturally, socially, and . . . the development of the individual as a competent member of society-at-large, and, insofar as possible, a productive economic being. This again means our continuing to struggle not only for human rights in a very broad sense, but in a narrower sense, for economic rights.

Naturally, the emigré, because he has been the victim of a war against Jews, calls from our minds and our hearts the best that is in us; naturally, he presents to us not only the opportunity for charitable service, but truly the opportunity for a demonstration of our will to live and the desire to build a better commonwealth for the people among whom we do live.

This is merely a projection of the development of a normal life in America; while we shall be tested with respect to the absorptive capacities of our organizations and institutions, those capacities are there and will, under the same direction of our professional personnel and the collaboration of our intelligent laity, surmount this present problem too.

Discussion*

BY SAMUEL S. KOHS

Concept of Metropolitan and Regional Areas for Service

One of the by-products that is likely to grow out of the efforts of the Resettlement Division of the National Coordinating Committee and the National Refugee Service is the increasing recognition on the part of the larger cities that they have an important responsibility and a stake in the potentialities and activities for community service in the smaller cities and towns within their area of influence. The efforts to organize refugee resettlement through the Pittsburgh Tri-State Area, to include western Pennsylvania, eastern Ohio, and northern West Virginia, with the city of Pittsburgh as the nuclear city, is a case in point. Similarly, southern California, with Los Angeles as the focal city, carries the responsibility for organizing the metropolitan area towns which number

* See citation on p. 392.

some thirty-five or forty, as well as some of the more remote communities, such as San Diego, Santa Barbara, Bakersfield, and San Bernardino. This new development in community organization makes available for the first time professional service through a well-organized central community which is likely to yield great benefits, not alone in terms of the present needs of emigrés, but also in developing a give-and-take relationship between the larger and smaller communities on other matters of joint communal interests.

In my own personal experience, it has become evident that these smaller communities have many problems which the larger community can help solve and for which the larger unit does have some responsibility—whether the problem is one of building a synagogue or a Jewish center; a problem of transients, or of emigrés; or whether it involves adequate recreational, cultural, and educational facilities for children. The larger central city cannot any longer insist upon its immunity from a concern with these questions.

This new development is likely to revolutionize our Jewish organizational set-up and philosophy. The Los Angeles general population is estimated at 1,500,000; the Jewish population is estimated at approximately 100,000. The metropolitan area, however, has an estimated population of 2,500,000; the Jewish population, outside of the city proper, a possible 15,000; and for the other Jewish communities in southern California, possibly another 10, 000. This would yield a total Jewish population of 100,000 in Los Angeles and 25,000 outside of Los Angeles, in communities of the metropolitan area and in the southern portion of the state. This Jewish population of 25,000 must be integrated in some fashion into the lifestream and activities of the large central city. That responsibility rests upon the shoulders of the professional leadership, which must have the vision, the understanding, and a willingness to develop the necessary measures to tie these scattered groups into a harmoniously working whole.

Putting Local and Regional Work on a Non-Sectarian Basis

Before my dissassociation from the staff of the National Refugee Service, meetings were held with representatives of the Catholic and Protestant refugee organizations to consider the desirability of organizing in some fifteen or twenty communities experimental programs to coordinate and integrate local refugee services. It is to be regretted that this interest and development were not carried forward. It is important to organize centralized local or regional refugee committees which could function jointly for all groups and interests for the purposes of consultation, planning, and such services as are free of sectarian aspects. In the last category would fall such services as aids, advice and guidance on immigration, affidavit work, naturalization, learning English, finding employment, etc. Not infrequently, some local Jewish refugee committee receives a request for service which appears puzzling. . . . Every community should have a central clearance bureau which would provide an index of emigrés in the community requesting service from any one of the community refugee agencies.

It is regrettable that enough has not been done locally to bring about local coordination for refugee service. The instances where that has been achieved are scattered and few.

These are but a few points that one might wish to make to help guide a refugee program toward a more effective and more meaningful achievement of its tasks. Just as the earlier immigrations brought to this country and to its Jewish communities new values, new assets, and new trends, so we are justified in believing that this new immigration will likewise bring us benefits of great social, cultural, and human value.

3. Backgrounds of Some Refugees As Factors in their Orientation*

BY CHARLES H. JORDAN

New immigration—that is, immigration of people who became refugees as a result of Nazi persecution—is now in its eighth year. These immigrants are somewhat different from the earlier immigrants, and at first they caused some confusion in the great community. . . . However, the field of social work has already done a great deal to interpret the refugees to the community, and to create more favorable conditions for their adjustment. Therefore, when we talk as professional social workers about refugees, we do not have to clarify quite as much our own attitudes in relation to them, and can be more objective in discussing some of the problems which exist in their adjustment to a new setting.

The immigrant group as we know it today has changed somewhat as compared with the early arrivals [of the "new" immigration]. Those who first came over were primarily German intellectuals, economically more privileged people, often prominent in one field of endeavor or another. Since the Nuremberg Laws have became more severe throughout Germany, and since the German war machine has conquered other countries, the intellectuals now represent only a small part of the total influx. The larger part is made up of middle-class business and professional workers of various nationalities, many of whom did not belong to the economically privileged classes of Europeans.

Characteristics of Earlier Arrivals

Furthermore, at first we worked with primarily younger people, who were better able to transplant their roots. [By contrast, the

* *Jewish Social Service Quarterly*, vol. XVIII, no. 2 (Dec. 1941), pp. 232-38. This article represents a slight revision of a paper delivered by Mr. Jordan at the New York State Conference on Social Work, October, 1940.

majority of] people now coming to these shores are older people who, after many years of preparation, have succeeded in leaving the countries in which they are no longer wanted.

Many of the early arrivals were outstanding people who had no difficulty in continuing in their own fields in this country, because they had a real contribution to make. But there were others among them who could not follow their chosen work for various reasons, e.g., age, health, and lack of flexibility. Many artists, writers, and scientists presented a real problem because they were unable to make a livelihood in their professions and were forced into other work. The same was true for the later group which came after 1936; in many instances they were forced into new fields of endeavor. But, on the whole, these more recent arrivals have resembled pre-Nazi immigrants, who were small business or industrial people, and therefore could make a quicker adjustment to the traditional American work opportunities for immigrants. . . .

Refugees as Distinguished from Other Immigrants

These refugees are a people who have been persecuted; who have been subjected to a very emphatic reminder for longer or shorter periods of time that they are different—and different in a way which makes them unacceptable. They have been boycotted both economically and socially. They have finally been forced to uproot themselves from places to which they felt they rightfully belonged. Such people, it seems to me, must develop certain traits which distinguish them from people who live and work in freedom and security. . . . The old immigrant knew about the United States only vaguely, and probably mostly from the immigrants from his home community who had preceded him and found the economic security which they sought. They approached the problem of their adjustment purely in terms of getting a job for themselves, and perhaps of obtaining educational opportunities for their children.

The refugee immigrant, however, came to this country at a time when, as a result of the depression, getting jobs was very difficult. And while these people for the most part actually know very little about us, they are laboring under a very definite misconception. Many have heard in Europe that Americans have much lower cultural standards than their own; that Americans are interested only in material things; and that while we are charitable, it is primarily for our own glorification. . . . In general, . . . they do not feel that we have created anything of permanent value in art, music, literature, etc. Unfortunately, the reputation of American creativeness has not reached far beyond the United States, and there is little appreciation abroad for creative efforts in this country.

In many instances, the refugee's conception of our country is derived purely from "typical" American Western movies, so popular abroad, and, of late, from pointedly adverse and derogatory European propaganda. He is led to believe that we are a crude, new people in an uncultivated land of great open spaces. Our West is full of savage Indians; our South abounds with plantation colonels who enslave the Negro; the East teems with gangsters and racketeers. . . .

In many cases, the question of their economic adjustment is complicated by the carry-over of attitudes from the old setting and the old culture into a new setting and a new culture. This ties in with the question of the status which these people have had in such a setting. A lawyer, or a physician, or a butcher, or a cattle dealer may have lived in a small, peaceful European community for twenty years or more where because of his occupation, he was a well-established and respected citizen. . . . The butcher may have been a member of the city council in his community. The satisfaction he derived from his position in the community may have been just as important to him as the advantages he had from his business. When we meet this man today, he is robbed of all the dignity of both a successful businessman and citizen. But this experience is probably the only worthwhile thing he may wish to hold on to.

Are Refugees Overbearing?

We have heard people say that they have been disappointed by refugees to whom they gave jobs—that they were overbearing, over-aggressive, over-assertive. We must remember that the refugee feels he must find some way to tell us that he was once respected and successful. He owes it to his own self-respect to make us see him as he was, even though he may be perfectly willing to accept the reality of his present situation. Thus the emphasis is on the psychological rather than the practical side of the problem, and while the immigrant may be realistic about his change of occupation and willing to take any kind of work, he must still retain his conception of his own importance as a person. This is true not only of small-town people, but also of professional people from the larger cities. . . .

In this connection it is important to remember that the man or woman who is now about forty years of age (and that group represents a large proportion of the refugee group) lived through experiences such as we have not known. They were just beyond puberty at the beginning of World War I, and still adolescents at the outbreak of the socialist revolution. They lived through the terror years of 1919-1924—which saw several beginnings of communist and nationalist upheavals in Germany. They lived through the inflationary period, which robbed many families of their life savings and exposed them to a great deal of insecurity and hardship. They enjoyed only a few years of comparative prosperity and security between 1924 and 1929.

After 1929 they suffered from the same unemployment situation which the United States experienced, and worse, became victims of the Nazi revolution of 1932-33. Many people in business were well-to-do when the Nazi revolution occurred. From this description of their experiences it should become clearer that they must have been a rather strong and resourceful people to withstand all the hazards that are inherent in such a situation over a period of years. Therefore . . . what some call the conceit and high degree of self assurance of these people, and their aggressiveness and persistence in pursuing certain plans which we might call unrealistic [are understandable characteristics in the light of their background]. A similar attitude [can be adopted if we view] refugees purely as people who are threatened in their security, and who therefore quite naturally express their fears in a negative approach to their surroundings. . . .

The "Refugee Experience"

Another factor which creates difficulties for refugees is that preparation for work abroad is careful and intensive and very highly specialized. Even the smallest and most non-technical job requires an apprenticeship of some three years. The apprentices must concentrate on one phase of a particular field, in which presumably they become expert, and it is almost impossible for them to switch to another—even within the same field or profession. Therefore, this experience precludes flexibility in work experience and adds greatly to the difficulty of changing from one field of endeavor to another.

I would like to call attention to one other factor in the orientation of these immigrants to their new setting—the "refugee experience" as such. As I pointed out before, this is the eighth year of Nazi persecution, and many persecuted people left their homes long before they had an opportunity to come to this country. They fled from one European country after another; and while they may have left originally with some money or belongings of their own, they had finally to depend on charitable organizations in the transit countries.

These refugees present a different problem from those who come to us directly from their homes, since the latter have hardly ever been dependent upon outside assistance but have rather been on the side of the giver—either as contributors to organizations, or working actively in them for the benefit of others. But refugees who traveled from Berlin to Vienna to Prague to Paris and on—

always running from the advance of the Nazi armies—have also been wandering from committee office to committee office, and living on hand-outs. This "refugee experience" has greatly affected their attitude toward an adjustment such as we attempt to make possible for them here.

It is [understandable therefore] that these people take on the status of refugees-in-movement and are more or less like transients, who have great difficulties when they finally are faced with the necessity of taking stock of themselves and coming to grips with a situation of permanent adjustment.

Factor of Morale

Another significant factor in refugee adjustment to which attention should be called is the experiences some have had with physical and mental persecution and abuse. . . . We can say that this experience of deliberate humiliation might be limited as far as the total refugee group is concerned. But it symbolizes methods which have been used over a period of years to break down the morale of people, and it is surprising to see how well large numbers of persons so exposed have been able to withstand the pressure.

V Broadening the Jewish Community Base

DESPITE the troublesome dilemmas of the thirties, Jewish community life, especially in its organized form, grew steadily,[1] and neither the spread of governmental welfare services nor the prevailing economic and political insecurity seemed to retard its development. On the contrary, increasingly larger sums were raised for many purposes by a combination of the community efforts of local Federations and Welfare Funds, and the appeals of the national agencies, especially the United Palestine Appeal and the Joint Distribution Committee. The number of sectarian agencies slowly grew and spread to many smaller cities never before believed capable of supporting their own community center, family agency, or home for the aged. New services for the entire Jewish population were added, such as the extended vocational and community relations programs. This was accompanied by an upsurge of Zionist, religious, and other activity, which kept members' attention constantly turned toward critical policy issues.

This manifold activity was viewed with reservation by some, who believed that the diversification of energies proved the absence of a true community of spirit and interest, since it was built upon such a seeming chaos of group and associational rivalry. Others, perhaps the majority, viewed this variety with grati-

[1] For details of the scope of this development, see H. L. Lurie, *A Heritage Affirmed* (Philadelphia, 1961).

fication as bespeaking a vigor in community interest which would lead to a community of cooperation and consent.

Beneath the surface of these new community endeavors and their promising results many old familiar difficulties remained, although expressed in more modern terms: how far should general community programs be used; what should be the essential content and character and purpose of sectarian services; how much central authority should the community exercise over its members and its agencies? All of these questions were re-examined and debated during the annual Conferences, although the Conference no longer took active responsibility for solving problems through its own structure as in earlier years, this now being assumed by the newer agencies specifically designed for such purposes. Many new conditions now surrounded these perennial issues: a strong cadre of professional workers was now developed which was seasoned in the service of the community; agencies had developed their own traditions and a great flexibility and endurance to survive many pressures; and the success of the sectarian agencies made their representatives sought after by general community welfare agencies, the councils of social agencies, and the government programs. Jewish agencies, their boards and staffs, now welcomed two major challenges—building up their own communities, *and* cooperation with general welfare programs—with a reduced sense of conflict or of having to choose one in preference to the other. They evaluated Community Chest affiliation on the basis of whether or not it would help strengthen their communities, and not solely as a desirable means to acceptance by the dominant culture.

The result was an enrichment of community life by the addition of new and stronger voices, and a responsive knitting together of much of this vigor into cooperatively planned community policy and action, at least on major issues. The risk of fragmentation and atomization was past.

For a period, a new central communal structure arose to parallel the Federation—the Jewish Community Council, which strove to contain all elements of community life, no matter how disparate and antagonistic to each other, and to make decisions on all problems. The councils satisfied a desire for "one man, one vote" democracy; but, as an all-inclusive structure they did not wholly reconcile all the divergencies or create the tools of funds and leadership with which to carry policies through to action.

1. Developments in Jewish Community Organization*

BY HARRY L. LURIE

New social forces today are shaping the organized expression of Jewish group interest and concern. Witness first the changing character of the activities appealing for Jewish support, and secondly, the tendencies among individuals and groups to weld their efforts into some semblance of an organized program. Sharply divergent ultimate aims and principles are, to be sure, still acting as a brake on progress. But many activities show an intensity of effort in line with the growing complexity of social problems. In spite of the depression, cities are responding generously to the appeals from overseas, mostly through the form of organized central fund-raising for a number of causes. Problems in the economic and occupational fields are receiving increased attention. In some cities, local councils representative of all groups have been organized or are in the process of formation; together with Federations and Welfare Funds, they are seeking to develop various programs for group action. Elements which were previously wholly indifferent or extremely partisan are becoming more conscious of the possibilities of joint counselling, if not of joint action. The stimulus for improved group organization is fully evident.

* *Jewish Social Service Quarterly*, vol. XV, no. 1 (Sept. 1938), pp. 131-41. Presented at the annual meeting of the National Conference of Jewish Social Welfare, Washington, D. C., May 28-31, 1938.

Few of the important factors that affect our situation grow out of basic changes in the nature or composition of the Jewish group itself. The facts are not accurately known, but variations in age distribution, family composition, birth rate, and other such factors probably constitute minor influences, if any, in our general picture. The fluctuation of the business cycle has affected our economic and social life in about the same manner as it has the population as a whole, particularly the urban population. There has been a general stoppage of immigration, so that the problems of absorbing and adjusting large numbers of newcomers have not loomed large. The present problem of German and Austrian refugees is of a limited volume and specialized functional character.

Politically, the dominant trends in this country have been liberal and democratic, and therefore favorable to the adjustment of minority groups. Increasing length of residence here should in theory contribute to increasing cultural and social adjustment, as we become numerically more of an American rather than an immigrant generation. In addition, the government in the last ten years has assumed responsibility for social welfare so that, in spite of an enormous increase in the number of persons who cannot support themselves, we need not expect any greater intensity of specifically Jewish activity to help maintain decent living standards than we would of voluntary charitable organization in general. . . .

The German and Austrian refugees are a daily living reminder of the malign forces in the contemporary world which, by their assault on democratic culture and civilization, threaten the adjustment and the very survival of the Jewish group. . . . How are organized Jewish activities attempting to adjust themselves to these [threats of anti-Semitism and the spirit of fascism] that are so unfavorable to the welfare of Jews? The democratic basis of American life, with its emphasis upon separation of Church and State, and its liberality in providing for incorporation into American citizenship of a wide variety of national and ethnic strains—these principles have for decades influenced the character of Jewish group activity. In Europe, each state is dominated by a single national or religious group. In this country, Jews constitute one of many ethnic groups desiring to become a part of an integrated American population. The major aspects of American social, political, and economic life, therefore, did not call for intensive Jewish community organization, and were mostly unfavorable to its development. In the main, Jews did not face problems different in character from those facing other groups in a heterogenous population. As in other groups, organization proceeded for the most part on the basis of special cultural or religious interests.

Because of the diversified character of Jewish religious and cultural interests, there was in the past little occasion to organize the community of Jews around a general or comprehensive program of group activities. Congregations of Jews separately developed their own religious institutions. Others associated themselves with social, fraternal, or economic societies on the basis of their particular group interests. The term "Jewish community" has been used to express in a simplified manner the diverse organized interests of those included within the Jewish population. Actually, the term "Jewish community" is an abstraction. Our Jewish population is not organized into any unified or comprehensive form of association. The term "community" is applicable to Jews to about the same extent as it is to immigrants, women, or youth. . . .

Similarly, whatever may have been the form of community organization of Jews in European countries, with their variations of nationality and citizenship status, conditions in the United States have not inspired many Jews to attempt to duplicate European forms of community associaton, or to devise comparable forms in this country. For this reason, there has been no voluntary organization of Jews as a whole. Instead, there have been various associations of individuals around specific and frequently restricted forms of group interest. The natural tendency of such multiple organizations has led to the creation of factions and divided and frequently conflicting Jewish groups.

In some instances, the specific interest of a group or organization has been of so broad a nature that it tended to draw in an increasing proportion of the Jewish population. This has not been true of religious activities because of divisions along lines of national origin, or denominational or congregational lines. Fraternal organizations and social clubs have been even more diverse in character. Cultural activities have also formed a variegated pattern, although increasingly in smaller cities the Jewish center has been extended to larger segments of the Jewish population concerned with cultural and recreational activities. Except for labor unions and a few professional groups, Jews have been organized hardly at all along economic lines.

Jewish philanthropy, because of its broad scope, represents the form of group interest which, in many cities, has attracted the largest adherence of Jews. Membership in agencies and contributions to organized philanthropy have steadily gained acceptance as a social responsibility by the well-to-do and middle-class elements of the population who are able to contribute. Few contributions are received from the lower-income groups, but many of them participate in the agencies as recipients of service. Philanthropy may thus be considered as an instrument of group organization extending to the majority of the Jewish population. The charge is sometimes made that Federations and philanthropic agencies are not democratic. They are not, it is true, under the control of the "Jewish community," but they are under the democratic control of the organization of contributors. The composition and control of philanthropy is changing to the extent that new groups of individuals are constantly reaching an economic level which encourages their interest and participation in philanthropic activities. In addition to local causes, compelling philanthropic appeals of a nonlocal character, such as the post-war campaigns for European relief, have cut across group lines and have enlisted the widest type of participation.

The extension of communal organization from the field of philanthropy to the area of broad group interests has been restricted for more reasons than the fact that the pattern of American life does not stimulate finite group divisions. In fact, all of us have recognized the undesirable character of groups which seek to organize citizens on a religious, racial or nationalist basis for political or economic reasons, or even for self-protection. We know that such movements on the part of others in the nation are an actual or potential threat of anti-Jewish attitudes and programs. It is this general feeling that strongly organized minority national or religious power groups do not fit the American scene, coupled with our own sharp divergencies in group interests, that operate as deterrents to the more inclusive forms of Jewish organization.

We need to recognize in this connection important cleavages among Jews which tend to differentiate us and affect our organization. There have been definite class antagonisms along economic lines in the Jewish population. For many years, organizations of Jewish labor were barred from any collaboration with the Jewish employer class. The passage of years has tended to dull this antagonism, but examples still persist. Jewish labor groups are only now beginning to evidence a cooperative attitude in the least controversial field, that of philanthropy. Even within the domain of social work, there are occasional flare-ups caused by class consciousness and class antagonisms between board and staff. A more important cleavage in community organization is to be found in the lack of agreement on procedures and aims between those who may be classified as Zionists or nationalists, and those whom their opponents label with the supposedly derogatory term of "assimilationists." In this term they include all who do not accept without reservation the concept of the Jewish people as a separate national entity.

Since the difference of opinion in this area relates to some of the most important questions of Jewish organization, the lack of compromise between these ideologies retards the growth of broader forms of community organization. We have a recent example in the sharp differences of opinion expressed at the proposal of the American Jewish Congress for a referendum to determine group opinion on several basic questions, and seeking the election of representatives empowered to speak for the Jewish population. It is obvious that a general acceptance of the proposed referendum would, in effect, constitute the basis for a form of Jewish community organization. The fact that this referendum has been opposed by various groups of Jews organized for philanthropic, fraternal, economic, and defense programs shows the reluctance of these groups to affiliate themselves with a form of association which is being promoted by groups with a definitely nationalist Jewish program. Even within Zionist circles, there are sharp differences of opinion on the methods for achieving Jewish community organization implied in this referendum.

For these reasons, we must consider that the evolution of community organization is still in its earliest stages, and that there are sharply differing theories which are not likely to be speedily reconciled. The social and political background for Jewish organization is not, however, of a static nature, and we must be prepared to face changes in the general social forces, and corresponding changes in the attitudes and opinions of Jews which may lead to different results.

At the present time, all Jews are conscious of themselves as belonging to one classification among the multiple immigrant stocks that constitute the American population. We disagree, however, on our opinion as to whether this separation should be identified and maintained, or counteracted. No Jewish group wishes to jeopardize the status of free citizenship, or to endanger the political and economic rights available under democracy. All groups, in theory, agree on the integrated community basis of democracy, and on the desirability of separation of Church and State; they differ on how that democracy is to be maintained. Therefore, they view proposals for Jewish organization differently, and see varied degrees of group segregation and varied possibilities for cultural differentiation against the general background of American citizenship. Some would like to confine Jewish organization to specialized interests on a defined religious or cultural basis. Others go beyond this minimum and seek to embrace more fully the attributes of a national minority status. The latter group would stretch the theory of cultural pluralism in a democracy to cover organizations concerned with political and economic problems of Jews here and abroad. Although the exponents of the religious-cultural theory similarly concern themselves with political and economic problems as they affect Jews everywhere, they hesitate to incorporate these issues into an all-embracing form of community organization.

Tendencies toward intergroup competition and conflict counteract the equally compelling tendencies toward intergroup cooperation. We may, however, consider the current stage in development as evidencing an increasing stress upon group cooperation. The underlying conflicts have not disappeared, and may from time to time disturb the cooperative relationships. But in general there has been remarkable progress made along cooperative lines. The urge to respond to Jewish problems, to assist in the relief of Jews overseas, to aid in the upbuilding of Palestine, to deal with the problems of group protection and Jewish adjustment, have influenced these developments. The most important indication of this practical cooperation is to be found in the growth of the Jewish Welfare Funds within the last ten years in more than one hundred cities. Acting under the impulse to organize an effective local program, these cities have worked their way into a form of organization which commands a wide degree of Jewish participation.

Welfare Funds, we should repeat, have not reconciled all group differences. There has been no regimentation under pressure of any particular faction or group of leaders. Welfare Funds represent, instead, a practical compromise between the various groups for the purpose of achieving a more effective method of fund-raising for the support of a varied list of activities. The nature of the compromises made differs widely from locality to locality. Permanent and stable funds are possible only in cities able to achieve a substantial degree of compromise or cooperation. There still remains in most cities important differences of opinion concerning the value of particular programs that are being supported, or of the relative values of the list of causes. There are still questions as to the inclusion of certain programs, which are influenced or controlled by adherents of one or another differing theory of Jewish adjustment. Nevertheless, the history and success of central fund-raising, even during years of depression, indicates that some effective form of cooperative relationship can be established between diverse Jewish groups.

We know that not all contributors are satisfied with the central financing type of organization, even though this form of organization is not especially Jewish in character; it corresponds to the general Community Chests, which have been able to achieve cooperation among the philanthropic interests of varied sectarian groups. The existence of diverse points of view makes, however, for intensive preoccupation with particular causes. A few continue to doubt the value of central funds. They believe that cooperation is defined by the extent to which everyone manifests an interest in his particular cause. Some agencies that have the sympathy of large givers are fearful that they may have to share the available funds with other agencies toward which they are lukewarm or antagonistic. In one of the organized regions of the Council of Jewish Federations and Welfare Funds, questions of agency inclusion, budgeting, and relationships are being carefully studied to determine whether definite principles and standards can be introduced into this new form of financing.

Although the cementing factor in Welfare Funds is largely the efficiency of central fund-raising, a more profound type of cooperation is being established in the Community Councils. These are as yet developed in relatively few cities, and are still considered experimental. A committee of the Council of Jewish Federations and Welfare Funds has been studying the local council movement, and a detailed report was presented at the 1938 General Assembly of the Council in Cincinnati. Briefly, local councils, as their name implies, are voluntary associations of selected representatives of all of the important Jewish adult organizations concerned with religious, fraternal, protective, charitable, Zionist, or labor activities. While local councils derive from a large range of group interests, the most important factor of their program lies in their aim to improve Jewish relationships with other groups and to develop relationships among Jewish groups which will be most helpful to these aims. Local councils are overcoming some of the limitations which lack of cooperation among the leaders of national agencies concerned with general Jewish questions has placed on the progress of Jewish group cooperation. Face-to-face contacts and sharing in general local problems have made for a large degree of mutual confidence and cooperation between Jewish groups with diverging programs.

There has been progress in Jewish community organizations during recent years. There has been a heightened response to current Jewish problems. The evidences of increased cooperation between the various Jewish groups are perhaps not conspicuous against the background of deep-rooted differences. We can say frankly that we believe that the cooperative actions . . . can be attributed to the new and increased pressures on the Jewish situation in this country as well as overseas. The most marked results that flow from group cooperation can be seen in the rapid development of central fund-raising for Jewish causes which are primarily national or overseas in scope. This in turn is leading to a greater degree of intergroup cooperation in other phases of our problem.

Developments in community organization can also be seen in the functional services, where there are new developments and increased activity in two directions. Aware of economic and occupational problems stemming from the general unemployment situation, several of the larger Jewish communities are beginning to study and to make available special economic and employment services to the entire local Jewish population. Some attention is also being given, particularly in cities that have organized Community Councils, to various phases of the relationship of Jewish activities to the general American community.

Although these new activities seem to portend a greater degree of group cooperation and the creation of an instrument for bringing together representatives of various group interests, we cannot, with any degree of certainty, assert the permanence or stability of these recent trends. The logic of the situation does not assure us that increased outer pressures and intensified problems will necessarily create a larger unity rather than greater diffusion of Jewish groups. In an emergency, not all of us can agree on a uniform course of action, as we may witness in the growing conflicts in our general economic and political life. It is true that some activities, particularly those directed not toward ourselves but toward Jews overseas, can achieve general acceptance. Conflicts over these philanthropic functions are in a minor key, and threaten to become more acute only when they begin to impinge more directly upon our own adjustment. An evidence of this is the doubt expressed by some concerning programs of aid for Palestine, in the event that these programs may have to be related to the proposed Jewish state.

The only explanation that I can offer for the present tendencies toward cooperation is that the activities involved are generally recognized as palliatives and partial solutions. It is easier to agree upon these activities than upon more drastic programs that are theoretically considered as permanent solutions. . . .

A factor making for group adjustment . . . lies in the uncertain ties surrounding all of the broad programs for Jewish adjustment advanced by different groups. The idea of a Jewish state in Palestine and the intensification of Jewish nationalism in other countries is surrounded by uncertainties no less than the proposals for complete assimilation of Jews as Americans, with or without the retention of our religious or other cultural differences. Not all of the uncertainties are equally acknowledged by all Jewish partisans; but at this stage in human history, the opportunities for self-determination of minority groups are shrinking rather than expanding.

Jewish life and Jewish group organization are conditioned by large political and economic forces. There are tendencies toward dispersion and disintegration of group interest, as well as toward centralization and cooperation. At present, outside pressures are influencing intergroup counselling and cooperation, but no true solidarity or unity has been achieved. There are important doctrines among groups and important special interests that operate as centrifugal forces. Even the present state of cooperation may be dissipated by a change of conditions. A slackening of outside pressures would probably dilute the strength of Jewish group cooperation; more serious crises may tend to bring us closer together. On the other hand, there are few evidences that progress is being made towards the goals that groups acting separately or jointly have set for themselves. We may with increasing tensions experience much impatience with meager results; this may affect the uncertain balance of forces that has been achieved. There is always a tendency for more controversy over unattained goals and purposes than over concrete activities. Then, too, we must not overlook the existence of powerful forces, political, economic, and cultural, that may negate all attempts to try to find a common program for Jewish group activity, certainly in the broader areas, and possibly even in the more limited fields of our interest.

2. The Community Council Idea*

BY ISAAC FRANCK

The Community Council, under a variety of names, and in various forms, is fast taking root in Jewish community life in America. In the present article an attempt will be made to present a clear definition of the Council idea, and to sketch briefly what appear to be some of the forces which brought Community Councils into being; some of the problems with which Councils were to deal; and some of the implications which the Community Council idea may have for the future of central Jewish community organization in America.

* *Jewish Social Service Quarterly*, vol. XX, no. 4 (June 1944), pp. 191-200.

Growth of Community Councils

In 1938, in his book *Jewish Community Organization in the United States,* Maurice J. Karpf observed:

In the last few years the dissatisfaction with the representativeness of Federations and Welfare Funds expressed itself in the demand for a more representative organization. Several communities have been experimenting with a "Community Council," which is made up of representatives of all the organizations interested in communal problems and activities. It is altogether too early to attempt to evaluate this experiment. . . . To a non-partisan observer it seems to represent an interesting effort at democratizing American Jewish community organization.[1]

Much that has happened in the world and in American Jewish life since 1938 has brought to greater maturity the conditions responsible for the appearance of Community Councils. While they cannot yet be said to have emerged from their experimental stage, Community Councils have come into being in increasing numbers, and the need for studying them is being more generally recognized. Thus, in his Summary of the May 1944 joint meeting of Social Workers, Center Workers, and Educators, Nathan E. Cohen stated:

In the intermediate and larger Jewish communities, Community Councils have come into being both because of a demand on the part of the masses for a voice in policy, and the need for an instrument for meeting broad Jewish problems. These councils vary in their origin, composition, and function. . . . Further study of the program, structure, and function of the Council is necessary.[2]

The Council Idea in Essence

The essence of the Community Council idea may perhaps be summarized as follows. There has emerged in Jewish community life a growing awareness of a group of problems whose nature is

[1] Pp. 115-116.

[2] *Proceedings,* Conference of Jewish Social Welfare (May 1944), p. 13.

such that each automatically involves the total Jewish community, and thus has an immediate centrality and community-wide, public character; there is a great diversity of points of view as to how these problems ought to be treated; community unity and discipline are necessary conditions for adequate treatment of these problems; such unity and discipline cannot be achieved without the broadest participation by representatives of all points of view in the discussion and determination of policy; therefore, the broadest possible democratic structure and process are necessary in the central community organization which is to deal with these problems. This brief statement will of course require considerable amplification.

However, it is worth observing at this point that, in the Community Council idea, structure and function are organically related and cannot be separated. It has been customary, in discussions of Community Councils, to present a genetic account of the origin and rise of the Council idea in response to the pressures of elements and groups in the community who have not hitherto been vocal in community affairs. In such discussions, emphasis has usually been placed on the process of economic and social adjustment of East European Jews in America during the past generation, and on the instrumentality of the Community Council in satisfying the desire of these newly adjusted elements for a "voice" in community policy. While an account of this sort is no doubt accurate, it is at the same time incomplete. A comprehensive and analytic presentation of the Council idea must take full cognizance of the recent awakening of American Jews to the existence of a new set of central communal problems. With this awakening also has come the realization that previously existing central agencies were not equipped to handle these problems, because they were not sufficiently representative of all points of view. And it is in the handling of this new set of problems that the "masses," recognizing that they are problems that affect them no less than other groups, have desired a voice.

In effect, the birth of the Community Council idea signalized the maturing of Jewish communities in America. It indicated the beginning of American Jewry's transition from inchoate agglomerations of individuals and groups whose major and often only *central* concern was philanthropy, to fully matured communities with central community recognition of the full gamut of larger group problems, which are inherent in the development of Jewish group life in America. It betokened American Jewry's recognition of the fact that, in addition to *individual* and *family* problems for whose solution the community must organize itself, there are problems of the community *as a Jewish community*, as a *social organism*, which the body as a whole must train itself to meet.

Traditional Central Organization

The central communal problems around which the American Jewish community, with its emphasis on philanthropy, was traditionally organized had their genesis in the need to render certain services to individuals or families, and in more recent years, to contribute to the upbuilding of Palestine, to relief for European Jewry, and help finance the work of national agencies in allied fields. Individuals needed medical care; families needed help in conflict situations between parents and children; young people needed help in finding jobs; old people needed institutional care; children needed foster homes; small businesses needed loans to tide them over difficult periods; young people and adults needed recreation and informal educational facilities; children needed Jewish education. For each of these and similar needs, agencies sprang up in the community; clinics and hospitals, family agencies, vocational agencies, homes for the aged, child-care agencies, free loan societies, community centers, Hebrew and Yiddish school systems. Each of these agencies carried on a program, and each of them needed funds for its work. Funds were also needed for the overseas programs.

Accordingly, central community organizations were called into being by three central needs: (1) central fund-raising for local, national, and overseas programs; (2) allocation of the funds raised; (3) the coordination and planning of the functional programs of local social-service agencies. And it was natural that, in the organization of Federations and Welfare Funds to deal with these central problems, those who gave the biggest share of the money were also those who determined policy. Since they took the lead in raising the funds, they also determined how these funds were to be allocated.

Furthermore, intelligent allocation of funds for local work required evaluation of programs; elimination of duplication; planning and cooperation among functional agencies; and discovery of new social-service needs. Thus, if the home for the aged, the family agency, and the child-care agency all met in the course of their week with medical problems, it was important that some relationship be worked out between these agencies and the clinic or hospital, instead of leaving each of them to solve its medical problems alone. Examples of such coordination can be multiplied many times. There was a logical interrelation between fund-raising and allocations on the one hand, and on the other hand, the coordination of functional programs of the Federation's constituent agencies. While the evolution of Federations to the stage of dealing with this third area was sometimes slow, and a fully-developed program of coordination is of relatively recent vintage in many Federations, it is nevertheless a well-established goal in their work, and is now generally accepted by the community.[3] . . .

Larger Group Problems

As American Jewish communities matured, and as successive waves of immigrants became adjusted to the new scene, it became evident that a number of problems which affect the lives of *all*

[3] "Federations became communal agencies whose function it is not only to provide financial support for their constituent societies, but to plan for the community needs along constructive lines. Today, with a few exceptions, the Federations aim to support, coordinate, and control the needed social service agencies and activities in their respective communities." Karpf, *op. cit.*, p. 103.

Jews, which immediately involve *Klal Israel*, and should be dealt with by an organized, self-conscious, *total* community (insofar as it could be achieved) were either not dealt with at all, or were stabbed at, so to speak, by individuals or separate groups, each on its own. Instead of a unified Jewish community, there were in effect several communities in every city, each almost hermetically sealed, with very little interchange between them.

Among these problems, which we shall call "larger group problems," perhaps most attention has been focused on the community's defending itself against anti-Semitism. It has become self-evident that a case of discrimination against one Jew, an attack on one Jew, is immediately an attack upon the whole Jewish community. It has also become clear that the fight against anti-Semitism cannot be carried on in a sporadic manner, on the basis of emergencies alone. It is a long-range, year-round, day-to-day problem that requires the mobilization of all the resources in the community, and must have behind it the authority and the weight of the whole community. . . . Here discipline and unified action are the *sine qua non* of successful operation; unless the various points of view that prevail in the community are brought to bear on the deliberations, the discipline required cannot be achieved.

The distinguishing feature of the problem of anti-Semitism and of other larger group problems is that they do not involve service to individuals, but rather service, if you will, to the community as a Jewish social organism. They involve the *fate* of the community, its dignity, its social standards, its intellectual and cultural existence, and its relationships, as a community, to the world around it. To a greater or lesser degree, each of these larger group problems partake of this *public, community-wide* character, and are therefore more or less controversial in nature. There is relatively little controversy in the Jewish community as *Jewish* community about the choice between institutional care and foster-home care for children, or about the criteria of eligibility for a free loan. These are technical matters which raise no question about basic philosophies of Jewish group existence. The larger group problems do involve such basic questions, and, affecting as they do the whole Jewish community, they require a solution of differences for unified, authoritative, community action.

Internal Discipline

While the problem of internal Jewish discipline is as old as the Jewish community itself. . . its recognition as a problem in American Jewish life came only with the maturing of the Jewish community. It requires a high degree of community self-consciousness to become aware of the fact that, in some senses, the community transcends the individual, and may require the individual to live up to certain social norms and standards.[4] When individuals or groups violate these norms, the community has a right and an obligation to invoke such biblical dicta as, "thou shalt clean out iniquity from thy midst." In order to maintain social standards, the community has to deal with certain evils which from time to time appear within its social fabric.

[As the community matured, it was agitated more and more by] such problems as occasional unethical practices in Jewish-owned businesses; Jewish-owned stores which stay open seven days a week and disregard the principle of a day of rest; violations or malpractices in the *kashrut* of meat and fowl slaughtering; the annual crop of mushroom synagogues, run for private gain, which are a travesty on organized Jewish religion; Jewish litigation in the public courts, and the consequent exposure of Jewish institutions and traditional ritual to public scorn; and miscellaneous ap-

[4] "American Jewish communities have always exerted controls on individual members. Stringent during the colonial period (see Marcus, *op. cit.*), communal controls were still very strong until the mid-19th century, when the size of the larger Jewish communities and the individualistic American ideology permitted substantial numbers of Jews to avoid assuming what had formerly been accepted as obligations, e.g., membership in a congregation. This trend increased with the even greater size and diversity of 20th century metropolitan communities."

peals for funds which mulct the Jewish public without giving an account of themselves.[5] These evils are not present more frequently in the Jewish community than among non-Jews. But they do exist, and their existence impairs the tone and dignity of Jewish group life and violates the standards of traditional Judaism.

Here again, it is the community as a whole that is involved, and the concept of Jewish group existence. And, since the modern Jewish community is a voluntary association, it is only the consent of the total community that can be instrumental in banishing evils and raising standards. It is precisely because on each of these problems different philosophies of Jewish life produce different opinions that a consensus arrived at as a result of an exchange of opinion is necessary for unified action. Orthodox and non-Orthodox may differ as to whether Saturday or Sunday ought to be the businessman's day of rest, but a thorough discussion participated in by all elements will make it possible to commit the whole community to a reaffirmation of the principle of a day of rest, and to a concerted community effort toward securing the closing of Jewish-owned business places one day a week.

Cultural and Organizational Life

Ethical and social standards in community life are closely related to the problem of the tone of cultural life in the organized community. Jewish life abounds in a multiplicity of individual organizations of various descriptions. Next to the synagogues, it is these many organizations that furnish to their members the only occasions for Jewish group life during the course of an ordinary week. The frequent hollowness and emptiness of the activities of a large number of such organizations stood out in bold relief as the community matured. . . . It is not only the problem of each individual segment of the community to raise its own cultural stand-

[5] For a more comprehensive discussion, see "Internal Jewish Discipline" by Lawrence W. Crohn, *The Reconstructionist* (February 18, 1944), pp. 17-20.

ards; it is the responsibility of the whole communal organism to care for the cultural and intellectual well-being of its parts, since low standards in any of its parts mean the deterioration of the organism as a whole. This requires systematic planning and stimulation of better programming and richer cultural programs in all segments of organized Jewish life, and the coordination of adult cultural activities into as well planned and unified a program as circumstances permit. . . .

Community Voice and Structure

The sum total of these larger group problems has made it evident that the Jewish community needs a central, authoritative voice, and the machinery with which to translate into practice these central, authoritative decisions. Out of this the Community Council idea was born, and here the nexus between its function and structure also becomes evident. If democracy is said to be an essential in Community Council structure, it is not *a priori* democracy in a vacuum. It is democracy which is made necessary by the nature of the central group problems American Jewry has had to face, and by the voluntary character of the American Jewish community. The unity and discipline needed for the treatment of these problems can be maintained only through the broadest base of *organizational* representation. Such representation by its very nature makes possible the presence and participation of all points of view, and the adjudication of differences, and reduces to a minimum the possibility of a numerical majority riding roughshod over minorities. Obviously, such democracy must be real in practice, as well as in principle. The minority point of view must always be heard, and opportunities for influencing the opinion of others, or for arriving at compromises, must always be present. The Community Council structure is such that a minority group, although free to bolt and break discipline, is morally bound not to because of its voluntary affiliation with the council and its full participation in decisions.

These theoretical considerations have a very practical meaning for Community Councils. They mean that, in addition to the broadest organizational affiliation and free discussion and voting by organizational delegates, *all committees,* from the Executive Board down, must have a truly representative character and structure, and include within them all shades of Jewish opinion. Only in this fashion can the growth of community consolidation bear fruit.

Organizational Representation vs. Universal Franchise

The suggestion has often been made that a system of universal franchise in the election of Community Council administrations would be more truly democratic than the system of organizational affiliation and organizational delegates. This wears only a surface appearance of plausibility. It is precisely under a system of universal franchise that the majority rides roughshod over the minority, and minority views are frequently submerged completely. This is workable in a democratic political state, which is not a voluntary association, and from which a minority cannot generally secede, short of staging a revolution.

Secession from the voluntary association of the Community Council is a relatively easy matter. Its stability can therefore be safeguarded only by the mutual respect and understanding which grows out of joint deliberation. This is possible only if *all* views are represented, and can be guaranteed only in a structure of organizational representation. There is a possibility of combining organizational representation with universal franchise. This proposal has not, to the best of the writer's knowledge, been tried, and the mechanism for it would require clearer definition. A tentative suggestion along these lines will appear below.

Relations of Councils with Federations

With the advent of Community Councils, many communities find themselves confronted by the presence of two central agencies.

These communities have often been plagued by the problem of the relationships between these two bodies. The relationships are problematic, both between the lay leadership of the respective agencies, and between their professional leaders. Obviously, much remains to be clarified in these areas. The question is frequently asked: "Who is the community, the Council, or the Federation?" A tentative reply was hazarded by Karpf in 1938:

> It is freely admitted that the Federation is not the Jewish community, and that it would have to be fundamentally reconstructed if it were to become *the* Jewish community. The Community Councils . . . represent one attempt at creating such a representative Jewish community organization. But they have some of the vices of their virtues and may perhaps even threaten the very structure of Federations, unless they are wisely planned and even more wisely conducted.[6]

Whether, in the interval since 1938, any Community Councils have become more truly "the community," it is difficult to say. If they are true to the Council idea as it has been developing, they will have taken substantial steps in that direction.

In the meantime, relations between Councils and Federations can be and should be on the level of mutual respect, and on the basis of recognition of their respective functions in a community, tentative and experimental though the definitions of these functions may be. This should become increasingly possible as Federation leadership admits new elements, and the same faces appear in the counsels of both Federation and Council.

Possibility of One Central Agency

It would perhaps be intellectually dishonest to conclude this discussion without touching on this last problem. As someone phrased it at a recent conference: "Here are two good, important things; isn't it possible to tie them together in one bundle?" Obviously, any answer to this question would have to be largely, if not

[6] *Op. cit.*, p. 150.

wholly, hypothetical. But one may perhaps take the risk of some general observations. It would seem, theoretically at least, that one central community agency, to deal with all problems of a central character, ought to be possible. However, if this were tried, the development would have to be at present in the direction of the Community Council structure rather than that of Federation. While fund-raising allocations and social-service coordination can conceivably continue to be carried on effectively in the present Federation structure, it would appear to the writer that, if the preceding analysis of the Council idea is correct, the larger-group problems cannot adequately be dealt with in any but the representative Council structure, or in some modification of it.

Assuming, however, that such a unified, single, central community agency were tried out, and that the present Council structure would be incorporated in it, it would be a rather serious task to try to chart out its complete structure and method of operation. The following tentative suggestions are made for the purpose of encouraging discussion, and of planting in the minds of some reckless but courageous souls ideas for experimentation.

Functionally, such a central agency might have six departments: (1) Fund-raising (campaign machinery); (2) Allocations (studying budget analyses and requests of national agencies and of local agencies, holding budget hearings, and making final allocations); (3) Coordination of the functional programs of local beneficiary agencies; (4) Civic-protective functions; (5) Program work with constitutent organizations, development of an intelligent public opinion, and of a platform of public opinion; (6) Internal Jewish discipline.

Structurally, each of these departments would have, in addition to its professional staff, an autonomous but thoroughly representative committee, which would in effect be an executive board for that department. These committees would be partly appointed by the executive board of the central agency, and partly elected by the organizational delegates. The executive board and officers would in turn be elected, some by organizational delegates, and others by a popular vote of all adult members of the community. Thus, a combination of organizational representation and of universal franchise would be effected.

Naturally, many important problems are raised by such an arrangement. Is it workable? Is it too cumbersome? How shall membership of an individual be defined? These and similar questions will require much further study and investigation.

3. Jewish Social Services in a Nation at War*

BY LOUIS KRAFT

In his comprehensive survey, designed to provide a broad background for the group discussions at this conference, Mr. Clague [1] has quite correctly pointed up the economic factors that govern the planning of social services in time of war. The economics of warfare, particularly in the case of the United States, which has set out to be the arsenal of the United Nations, is the chief immediate factor in all of life in America today. Stating it in another way, Mr. Clague has analyzed for us many of the broad social problems involved in a total war situation, and it is our task to discover their bearing on the wartime and post-wartime problems of Jewish social work.

The Jewish people of the country, in common with their fellow citizens, share in the experience of being completely involved, as individuals and as groups, in the total war effort. While it is true that, according to the nature of the enterprises in which Jews are

* *Jewish Social Service Quarterly,* vol. XIX, no. 1 (Sept. 1942), pp. 43-50. Presented at the annual meeting of the National Conference of Jewish Social Welfare, Rochester, N. Y., June 4-9, 1942.

[1] Ewan Clague, Commissioner of Labor Statistics and Director, Bureau of Employment Security, Social Security Board.

engaged, they are affected in greater or lesser degree, there is likely to be a general leveling off of differences in local situations if the war continues for a long period. In the discussions that will go on in the institutes,[2] these differentials will doubtless be analyzed and due weight given to them. At the same time, a study of general economic and social trends will reveal the increasingly similar nature of the problems presented by the clientele of the Jewish and non-Jewish agency, with due consideration for differences in degree of these problems. These differences may be accounted for primarily by the fact that Jews are for the most part residents of large metropolitan cities which have not yet felt the full impact of great dislocation of industry and family life.

Jewish Aspects of the War Situation

However, while it is true that we shall not find differences in the essential nature of many of the problems of Jewish and non-Jewish social work in wartime, it is also true that there are areas of Jewish communal interest and specialized Jewish programs affected by the war situation which are not common to the general American scene. These derive from our needs as a Jewish community, and from our responsibilities to Jews in other lands. Since World War I, a vast organization of Jewish service has developed in these areas, involving extensive community organization for fund-raising, for policy making, and for programming. Part of our concern at this Conference is to try to trace the impact of the war situation on the structure and the program that has been developed. And it should be borne in mind that the chief concern of our local Jewish communities in connection with non-local Jewish programs is that of fund-raising through Welfare Funds, the United Jewish Appeal, and other national appeals.

[2] The 1942 Conference program provided for fifteen special institutes, which were to give consideration to the effects of the war upon Jewish social work. For summaries of the discussion at these institutes, see *Jewish Social Service Quarterly*, vol. XIX, no. 1, pp. 80-148.

Participation in War Chests

That this problem of fund-raising is uppermost in the minds of very many is demonstrated by the emphasis in recent discussions on the effect of the growing movement for war chests. Quoting from the report of the recent General Assembly of the Council of Federations and Welfare Funds, which strongly urged increased giving to Welfare Funds:

> Ready acceptance was found for the view that the force of circumstances will determine whether Jewish Welfare Funds must go in or stay out of war chests. Equally accepted was the point that it is necessary not to destroy our essential agencies in fighting to preserve the social organization of communities. Jewish Welfare Funds should be frank in their negotiations with war chests, and insist upon the preservation of the essence of their community organization and their autonomy in fields of community action.

Jews may be counted upon to do their full part in war chests, as they do in all the war effort of the nation. If Welfare Funds do go into war chests, they should seek to preserve the autonomy of the Welfare Fund structure, not only for the sake of freedom to support the causes in which they are interested as a Jewish community, but for the values to America as a whole that are represented in the philosophy and program of the Welfare Fund.

Maintaining National Services

The Jewish Welfare Fund represents a pattern which merits study, along with the experience of USO, as a method for integrating the financing of national programs of private social work.[3]

[3] For a detailed account of the Jewish Welfare Board war-service program and its relation to the USO, see: Louis Kraft, "The Defense Emergency Program of the Jewish Welfare Board," *Jewish Social Service Quarterly*, vol. XVII, no. 4 (June 1941), pp. 339-46; see also Johns Ray, Margaret Creech, Hedlay S. Dimock, and Louis Kraft, "The Experience of the United Service Organizations and Social Work Practice," National Conference of Social Work, *Proceedings* (1944), pp. 193-207.

It supports activities representing an experience in programs of adjustment and reconstruction which will be most useful when America is faced with similar problems in the post-war period. In hundreds of communities in the United States, local groups have learned how to assimilate new immigrants under the leadership of the National Refugee Service. When the war ends, some of the persecuted and homeless people of Europe will find their way to this and other lands, even under the limitations of immigration policies. The experience of the past few years will be of the utmost value in helping the country to absorb these families in a constructive program of economic and social adjustment. That experience needs to be preserved. Similarly, the vast experience of the JDC, the United Palestine Appeal, and their allied services represents a continuing effort and a cumulative growth of knowledge in the conservation of human life, the reconstruction of dislocated economic and social organization, and the building of new lands of settlement. The work of these agencies in the past twenty-five years is rich in example of the possibilities of social and economic reconstruction that conserves the dignity of the individual and enriches society as a whole.

Recently, the President of the United States estimated that twenty million people will have to be aided to find new homes or to be repatriated when the war is over. Undoubtedly, America will have to provide much of the leadership and organization to deal with this gigantic task. It will find value in the continued experience of our overseas service, which will doubtless be available in any plan that is developed. Such services should, therefore, have full freedom now to continue their work.

All that these agencies are able to accomplish during the war will reduce the magnitude of the problem in the period to follow, and if the integrity and effectiveness of their machinery for service is maintained, these agencies will be available to share the responsibility of all Americans in the humantarian tasks that will face us. These programs of the national organizations supported by Welfare Funds are built through national planning, and cannot very well be evaluated by the tests that apply to local programs in the general local community.

Importance of Local Programs

A similar line of reasoning leads us also to urge the need for maintaining the specific Jewish services of a local character that are often included in Welfare Funds. They are primarily in the field of Jewish education and other Jewish communal activity not supported by local Community Chests. They are needed to sustain and to build Jewish spirit and loyalties in Jewish tradition, and to impart Jewish knowledge at a time when similar enterprises throughout Europe have been destroyed. They are a part of Welfare Funds because they have been accepted as a communal responsibility. . . .

The value of such local services to the Jewish community as a whole cannot be evaluated by the same tests that apply to other local organizations in the general community which serve special groups. For similar reasons, the central planning bodies—Jewish Community Councils and the like—represent a need that is exceptional in the pattern of American society, and require freedom to develop their potentialities.

It is particularly important that we, as social workers in the service of the Jewish community, deeply involved as we are in service to the general community as well, should feel the obligation to interpret all aspects of Jewish communal endeavor whenever the issue arises as to the entrance of Welfare Funds into war chests. The pressure to do so will grow. War chests are becoming increasingly popular, because the logic of combined fund-raising becomes stronger as taxes increase and citizen effort for campaigns becomes less available. We need to preserve the full values of our social program of which the system of Welfare Funds, now operating in several hundred communities, is an important part.

There are other areas of the war effort in which we have a special concern as social workers, educators, and communal leaders. No social worker can contemplate the present war situation without thinking ahead to the period of peace and reconstruction. While we have many immediate problems to deal with in our agencies, we know that our work and we ourselves, as professional social workers, will inevitably be affected by the kind of society we have in America after the war, and by the world society which America will be called upon to help develop when peace comes. It is a peculiar characteristic of the present war that military planning and statesmanship comprise one strategy; that while we plan military campaigns, we are also developing the basis for peace terms and the plans for reconstruction of the conquered nations. This we need to do in order to clarify the issues for which the war is being fought, and to sustain the spirit and the hopes of the peoples now suffering under the fascist conquerors. . . .

Social Workers and Post-War Planning

A time will come when the citizens of this country will be called upon to express their views and to make a decision concerning the future program and policy of America in relation to peace and a post-war world. Unless the thinking of this country is clear, and unless adequate and objective information is made available, we are likely to find ourselves unprepared to make a wise decision. As social workers, who are not bound by rigid techniques, we can make a constructive contribution towards clarity of thought by bringing to bear our knowledge of the social sciences and our insights into human behavior as background and perspective for discussions that will inevitably take place, particularly among the citizen groups with which we come in contact. We should not remain aloof from such discussions, or consider them outside of the sphere of activity of technical social work. The mere fact that some eighty-odd organizations, commissions, and committees are already dealing with these problems under various government and national agency auspices indicates the universality of the concern of all professionals with the issues of a post-war society.

As Jewish social workers, as Jewish center workers, and as Jewish educators we have a further obligation to help people in our communities to understand current Jewish issues and problems, especially as they affect the Jewish minorities in European lands and the Jews in Palestine. Many of us have in the past been called upon to advise on the giving of money and on allocations through Welfare Funds, but have had relatively little to do with the beneficiary organizations and movements themselves. The Jewish community needs, and I believe is justified in expecting, communal leadership as well as technical social-work service from its trained professionals. That leadership can come from its trained professionals. That leadership can come from our group if we concern ourselves actively with the broader fields of Jewish policy. The local Jewish communities, far removed from sources of information, are now being asked and will continue to be asked to make decisions, to support one plan or another, and they have a right to look to communal workers for guidance.

I should like to direct attention to another broad field of interest to this group. I refer to the entire area of youth services. You all recall the tragedy of the "lost generation" that followed in the wake of World War I—the generation of disillusioned, skeptical, cynical, and dissatisfied youth. Those young people were prone to blame their unhappy fate upon a callous, materialistic older generation. Perhaps they were correct in their judgment that there was a deterioration of character among the older generation after the war. I cannot escape the feeling, however, that youth itself did little to assume responsibility for creating a better society and a better life for itself. It lacked in large measure qualities of stamina, independence, ambition, and idealism that would have helped to tide over the difficult period of depression. Much of the condition was due to inadequate contact with institutions and organizations that by their nature and programs could have provided these constructive values.

Youth-Serving Agencies

We have these institutions in larger numbers today. They have refined their methods and programs on the basis of a better under standing of children and youth. They are represented in this Conference primarily by the Jewish centers, the Hebrew schools, vocational bureaus, and children's services. To their care is entrusted a large part of the Jewish population of children and young people who will comprise the post-war generation. We need to do what we can to serve this group so that they will not become another "lost generation." This problem is not the responsibility of any particular agency; it is a community problem. This will become more apparent when you discuss in your institutes the psychological effects of the war, dislocations of family life, interruptions of schooling, breakdown of controls that comes with financial independence of young people, breaking up of normal social contacts due to absences of young men in the military service, and similar situations. It is to be hoped that out of consideration of these problems a closer integration may develop among the youth-serving agencies, the Hebrew schools, and child-care and delinquency services as they attempt to meet the need for a wholesome life for the disturbed younger generation.

Closely related to this situation is that of the youth and adult away from home, engaged in war industry. I stated earlier that the Jewish group has not been affected to the same degree as the general population in the shift from the large cities to the boom towns of war industry. But the movement is taking place and will continue to grow. As part of the USO which is concerned with serving workers in the overburdened war-industry communities, the Jewish Welfare Board has had an opportunity to gauge the growth of the problem. Needs for service, primarily in the fields of housing, recreation, and general community assimilation, are growing. The problem is particularly acute in the case of women and girls. It has been found necessary to employ special workers to aid newcomers in war industry communities to make necessary adjustments. We may anticipate an increase in the health, welfare, and recreational services, and in protective services for children, including nurseries and nursery schools.

Family Welfare Problems

Some Jewish family agencies have already discovered a new field of service and a new responsibility in meeting the problem of Jewish families affected by the departure of male members to military service. Frequently the most able member of the family has gone off to war. As army pay is increased, and when allotments and allowances are adopted, more and more men who support and make the decisions for their families will be joining the service. They will leave a host of problems, not all of them financial, behind them. . . . These personal adjustments and difficulties are the natural responsibility of the Jewish social agency.

A New Type of Service

I should like to refer briefly to another area of service which, while it is not the general concern of the traditional field of Jewish social work as such, has a profound effect on the Jewish social worker as a professional worker. I refer to the work on behalf of the man in uniform, popularly known as USO work. This work is generally regarded as that of providing simple social activity and community contacts for the soldier or sailor. It is in fact a more comprehensive task, because it also endeavors to assist in the entire range of the serviceman's personal problems, and deals with many problems of community organization. The JWB for example, now has close to 175 workers in the field, drawn very largely from the ranks of case workers. They serve in communities adjoining camps, and render many services inside the camps. They deal with the total needs of the individual, and have thereby acquired an insight into the motivations involved in the effort to adjust to a new life. These workers also have the rare opportunity to guide the development of community organization services for the men in uniform or workers in war industries in towns which in many cases had no prior organization for communal effort. They are learning fundamental principles of community life and organization as pioneers in these habitations. They are learning also to win acceptance as paid professional workers in communities that never had the experience of working with professionals. . . .

Laying the Basis for Social Gains

While it is somewhat incongruous to think of social values as growing out of a war of such destructive power, we may look forward, nevertheless, to many social gains. . . . Indeed, these gains will not occur by themselves. They will not come about through legislation alone. They will come primarily through social experience. Their validity will be established only by tests of experience. Social workers, because of the services which they are providing for the people during the time of war, are in a crucial position to contribute leadership in developing new services that will provide the basis for the conditioning and acceptance of social gains. That is the challenge that faces us, and that challenge we shall help meet, for this Conference represents a greater strength than it ever had before—a great unity of the professional forces for service to the Jewish and general community, and a broad understanding of our role in this time of great need of our country and our people.

4. The Impact of War Upon Jewish Social Service*

BY PHILIP BERNSTEIN

The theme of this Conference has been the impact of the war upon Jewish social work—a war not confined to military activity, but a total war which affects all of us directly, and in which all of us are engaged—a war which has been termed the greatest of all wars and the greatest of all world revolutions. . . .

In general, the Conference examined: (1) the effect of the war upon America, economically, politically, and sociologically, and with respect to social work activity; (2) the effect of the war on Jewry and specifically upon Jewish social service . . .; (3) what is being done about post-war planning with regard to Jewish problems; and (4) the implications of all this for us as social workers and as Jews.

Effect Upon America

The effect of the war upon America was brilliantly sketched by Ewan Clague[1]. . . . He predicted a national income of 125 billions of dollars next year, about one-half of it represented by war production, and the other half by civilian production. Not only is this the greatest national income in our history, with the war production figures alone greater than our entire national income in 1932, but it is being built up with tremendous speed. . . .

This means that with 17,000,000 people in war production and 4,000,000 in the armed forces, a total of 21,000,000 out of our normal working force of 55,000,000 will have been taken from

* *Jewish Social Service Quarterly,* vol. XIX, no. 1 (Sept. 1942), pp. 153-166. Presented at the annual meeting of the National Conference of Jewish Social Welfare, Rochester, N.Y., June 4-9, 1942.

[1] See "Security in Wartime and After," *Jewish Social Service Quarterly,* vol. XIX, no. 1, pp. 26-42.

civilian production—and with the great expansion of industry, that force of 55,000,000 will have to be increased. This can be done only by drawing from the ranks of the unemployed, and from persons who heretofore have not been in the labor market at all. Already the figures has risen to 58,000,000 and may go up to 65,000,000—in other words, one out of every two people in the United States may soon be working in war or civilian production, or may be serving in the armed forces.

Obviously, this is going to mean a great change for America, and a great adjustment in our own thinking and planning, which for ten years has been geared to mass unemployment and economic depression.

But the picture is complicated further by the paradox that although we have a labor scarcity, we are confronted at the same time with a labor surplus. For the scarcity is not uniform; it exists only in certain skilled fields, while other persons, forced out of civilian occupations because of material priorities and other causes, do not have those skills, and can find little or no outlet for their experience. And so we find not only a labor shortage and labor surplus side by side, but high wages for those urgently needed, and low wages for those with surplus skills.

Another problem is created by racial and religious discrimination which still bars the doors of some companies to persons of certain background who do have the skills our war industries badly need. In this respect, it should be clear that the problem of discrimination no longer is confined to the realm of ideals and ethics. Neither is it just a Jewish or a Negro problem. In an immediate and real sense, it is now an American problem, and the breaking down of these barriers has become a practical necessity in the nation's war effort.

The transfer to war production has had the effect, too, of shifting large numbers of people from one part of the country to another, uprooting and breaking up families. The sociological effects and the problems of adjustment to a new family situation, to a new community life, to housing shortages and other elements are obvious.

Insecurity

In addition to the economic forces, a second major effect of the war upon America has been the insecurity it has caused. We are living in a world in flux, with widespread, deep, and fundamental uncertainty as to what the future holds. We do not know from one day to the next what is going to happen to us during this war—if young men, whether or not we are going to be drafted for active service; if older men, whether or not we will be shifted from our present occupation to some other; if women, what will happen to our husbands, whether or not we shall be able to get various supplies, and how we are going to make ends meet financially. And we approach these problems as a population already unsettled by a long depression, which cut more deeply into the lives of our people than any other in our history.

Nor do we know what will follow after the war. The men in the armed forces are asking themselves whether there will be jobs to come back to, whether their companies will still be in existence, and whether they can start again to build up their professions. . . .

Social Services

Major effects of the war upon our social services can already be seen. There has been a decline in such functions as unemployment benefits, public assistance, in the relief rolls, and in such agencies as the NYA, the CCC, and the WPA,[2] which in fact now face the possibility of being eliminated altogether.

On the other hand, there is taking place an expansion of services such as vocational training of men and women for war industries.

[2] Emergency federal relief agencies: National Youth Administration, Civilian Conservation Corps, and Works Progress Administration.

The increasing employment of women is bringing about important changes in industry itself, involving hours, conditions of work, safety measures, etc., and the awareness of an increased need for facilities for day care of the children of working mothers.

Other important effects include the forced removal of civilians from their home areas, such as on the West Coast, and the scarcity of physicians and dentists in some areas of war service. State and local services will also be affected—particularly when we realize that states derive an average of 60 per cent of their revenue from automobiles, which will be drastically reduced on account of tire shortages and gasoline rationing.

In the field of private service, too, we are facing important changes. The wealthy and middle classes, which have supplied the bulk of support for private social work, are likely to be severely affected by the program of war financing, and the foundation may thus be pulled out from under the structure of private agencies. On the other hand, the majority of wage earners are in a much better position than they were before the war with a total annual wage bill estimated at seventy-five billions of dollars. Increased taxes are not taking the entire increase, and community funds will have to concentrate more on these new sources in order to carry on.

Effect on Jewish Life

With this picture of the effect of the war upon America and upon social work before us, what are the effects upon Jewish life? . . . Dr. Baron [3] approached the question from the perspective of what happened to American Jewry after the last war. He pointed out that the Jews of America came to maturity, attaining a stature of equality with the other large Jewish communities in the world, developed an incipient leadership, and for the first time became a

[3] Dr. Salo W. Baron, Professor of Jewish History, Literature, and Institutions on the Miller Foundation, Columbia University. See "The Effect of the War on Jewish Community Life," *Jewish Social Service Quarterly*, vol. XIX, no. 1 (Sept. 1942), pp. 10-22.

world force. Up to that time Jewish affairs had been dominated by the Jews of Europe.

The last war brought the creation of the Joint Distribution Committee—which Dr. Baron termed one of the greatest communal achievements of American Jewry—and saw the formation of the Provisional Committee for Zionist Affairs, another evidence of the emergence of American Jewry from a provincial group to a world power in Jewish life. The last war and post-war period saw the creation of the Jewish Welfare Board, the New York and other Jewish Federations, the formation of Jewish Welfare Funds and Jewish Community Councils, the establishment of some schools of higher Jewish learning, and the expansion of others. . . .

In the present conflict, the transfer of population to centers of war industry is bringing about an internal migration of Jews along with others. With a majority of Jews living "within 200 miles of Times Square," this dispersal away from the Atlantic seaboard may require many new adjustments and may achieve automatically what previous organized efforts at a wider population distribution were unable to accomplish.

In the cultural and ideological realm, there has been some indication of a recent "return to religion," particularly among the men in the armed forces, reversing the previous post-World War I trend which Dr. Baron reported. Whether this will continue, it is too early to predict. Dr. Baron pointed out, too, that the whole cultural and ideological atmosphere is different in this war than it was in the last: the messianic fervor of that war seems to be missing, and has been replaced by a more matter-of-fact concern with practical strategy and mechanics.

Community Relations

Within that general setting, the specific effects of the war upon Jewish life and social work were brought out in their day-to-day aspects by the various institutes of the Conference. The institute on Jewish community relations revealed that contrary to the expectation and belief of many persons, the war has provided an opportunity for increased anti-Semitic propaganda, advantage having been taken of tensions which are inevitable in a period of stress. In many cities false rumors have been spread that the Jews are responsible for the war, that Jews avoid army service, that they have the "softest" jobs in the army, and the like. To combat this vicious propaganda, our national civic-protective agencies and local communities are trying to call attention in many ways to the large number of Jewish men in the army, and to the awards and citations many have received for outstanding valor and service. Similarly, we may expect a post-war fascist and anti-Semitic drive, blaming various evils and problems upon the Jews, and the time to prepare for it and prevent it is now.

At the same time, however, the war has provided an opportunity for better interfaith understanding and unity, through the mingling of all groups in the armed forces, through cooperation in such activities as the USO and civilian defense, and through the acceptance of minorities in some companies and industries previously closed to them. It was felt by the persons participating in the institute that conscious planning should be carried out to preserve these gains after the war, possibly by continuing agencies such as the USO with post-war functions, and by giving further attention to the problem of employment discrimination.

The institute considered the question of Jewish participation in foreign-relief drives, such as Russian War Relief and British War Relief, and came to the conclusion that it is not advisable to form separate Jewish sections for these campaigns and organizations—rather, it is preferable to participate in them as do all other Americans.

An investigation was also made of the propaganda drive to stir up anti-Semitism among Negroes, and it was suggested that Jews should develop positive programs to prevent and overcome such anti-Semitism, and to build up greater intergroup cooperation.

Community Organization

The institute on community organization examined the effect of the war on the various functional fields of Jewish social work, on Jewish education, and on other community services and needs. From its discussions have come a set of requirements for community organization in the field of voluntary social work—standards which, in fact, all Jewish social agencies must have in order to succeed: (1) a necessary program; (2) strong lay leadership; (3) serving an unduplicated need; (4) high quality of performance; (5) acceptance by the community; and (6) a proper relationship to the non-Jewish as well as the Jewish community.

The war was seen as a potential threat to voluntary agencies in that it caused competition for the interest of lay leaders, a possible reduction in contributions, and restrictions in the programs of agencies. On the other hand, the war has created new needs and opportunities by making welfare programs part of the war effort, has boosted morale, and has provided an opportunity for constructive interpretation. Agencies will have to become more flexible, taking the lead in calling the community's attention to the needs outlined above and in making sure that they are met.

Another development in Jewish community organization resulting from the war was pointed out by Louis Kraft. This has been the introduction of 200 Jewish Welfare Board workers, many of them giving service to communities which have never before known professional social workers. The result is an experience in generic social work which should be carefully weighed, and a group of new community workers who will be available after the war.

Fund-Raising

The questions of fund-raising . . . were given detailed attention by the institute which concentrated on that specific problem. . . . Attention was called to the Chicago Assembly of the Council of

Jewish Federations and Welfare Funds, at which it was urged that Jewish Welfare Funds preserve the autonomy of their structure in any war-chest relationship, not only in order to maintain their own values, but their contribution to democracy in general. They have established a pattern of operation which serves as an example to national agencies, both in financing and in the integration of their programs. We must be careful, likewise, to protect and strengthen Jewish cultural and educational programs, which to date have not come within the scope of Community Funds, to provide for the development of community planning bodies such as Jewish Community Councils, and to assure the preservation of our overseas agencies, whose experience will be sorely needed in meeting the tremendous post-war problems that will arise.

Economic Adjustment

In the field of economic adjustment, the institutes revealed that the war has brought about a change in the content and emphasis of service work rather than in its techniques, to meet the changing needs of the individual and the community. Specific trends include: (1) increased attention to short-term vocational counselling, rather than career planning; (2) a continued, demonstrated need for both individual and group vocational counselling because of war problems; (3) increased attention to "borderline" groups, including the handicapped, very old, very young, and others; (4) increased need of special job solicitation for dislocated workers, refugees, and "residual" groups; (5) an aggravated problem of refugee counselling and placement.

It was revealed, further, that the United States Employment Service has been taking more complete control of the labor and job market, concentrating on recruitment for war industries, and that Jewish agencies should supplement its work through aid in recruiting and by supplying the intensive placement and guidance service which the federal agency cannot give. More definite and formalized working relationships must be developed by private agencies with one another and with the federal agency, and steps are now under way in that direction.

A very important development has been the activity of the federal government in combatting discrimination in industry, following the executive orders of the President and his establishment of the Committee on Fair Employment Practice. Jewish agencies obviously must do their part in cooperating with the government in this effort . . . to help meet an immediate and pressing American problem. . . . Unfortunately, there has been evidence that some of our communities and agencies have not realized the urgent need for full cooperation, particularly with other minority groups. It should be abundantly clear that this is not an isolated problem of our own, nor is it a problem which we ourselves can solve. . . .

Family and Child Care

The impact of the war on other functional fields was examined by institutes dealing with family and child welfare, refugees, and the aged. The family agencies in general are experiencing a decline in requests for service and relief, offset in part at least by higher per capita relief costs due to the higher cost of living. There is a feeling that in order to help meet the new stresses of the war, the agencies should offer their services to a wider clientele, including a non-dependent group, possibly on a fee basis to some. In war industry cities there is a serious housing shortage accompanied by the serious problems which inadequate housing may cause: increased delinquency and crime, and more women in factories resulting in harmful effects on family life and greater need of day care for children and closer supervision of adolescents.

Smaller agencies in primary war industry cities apparently are feeling the full impact of the war more directly than the large agencies in other communities. War services offered by family agencies in general include aid to draft boards in investigations, participation in first-aid programs, sale of War Bonds and other civilian services, assistance to clients in handling questionnaires and in understanding their problems, and help in adjusting families of men in the service. Thus far there has been no widespread shortage of professional personnel, although some of the agencies are experiencing difficulties. . . . In general, war pressures are pointing to the need for a re-evaluation of case-work skills and techniques, as well as some of our case-work philosophy, in order to meet more effectively new problems and developments under existing circumstances.

Some of the same effects have been noted by the child-care agencies, particularly with reference to broken families, day care, and delinquency; however, it was recognized that there are as yet insufficient facts to support any conclusion of a general increase in delinquency throughout the country. The dangers created by young people leaving school to enter industry, the pressure to relax child-labor standards, and the permanent hazards involved in having young people cut short their educational training to enter war industry only to face later on the question of continuing in industry or going back to their original choice of occupation—all these require serious consideration and close attention. . . .

Refugees

Turning to the effects of the war upon refugee problems, at least four items should be mentioned here.

1. There has been a pressing need for accurate information about the citizen status of the immigrants, particularly because many refugees are technically classed as "enemy aliens," and thus are subject to special government regulations—although there is no doubt that they are among the most ardent champions of the cause of peace. The National Refugee Service is attempting to meet this need by issuing frequent bulletins to inform aliens and those working with them of new developments as fast as they occur.

2. The problem of refugee employment has been aggravated by the refusal of some companies to employ aliens, despite the fact

that government regulations stipulate the exclusion of non-citizens only in work done under secret contracts, and prohibit employment discrimination in other fields.

3. Aliens are accepted for military service, and physicians eligible to practice in the United States may enlist as privates, obtain their citizenship and then apply for comissions, it was reported.

4. With regard to requests for information from government agencies on specific aliens, it is important to know exactly what information is desired, and then to cooperate with skill, intelligence, and maximum care, so that the information is accurate and can be fully substantiated.

Care of the Aged

Finally, looking at the effects of the war upon the functional fields, the institutes concerned with the care of the aged pointed to the fundamental fact that an increasing proportion of our population is in the aged group, and that basic planning for this group, nationally and locally, has become a necessity. Public and private agencies must cooperate not only in caring for those who are dependent, but also in meeting the medical, housing, and recreational needs of this entire age group. In this task it is important to understand individual needs, and to focus attention on the strengths rather than the limitations of the aged, who have much to offer in this war effort. Important consideration must be given to the formation of community-wide councils for the aged and chronic sick as instruments for central planning where such councils do not already exist.

Institutions for the aged are experiencing a shortage of personnel, which they are trying to overcome through increased use of volunteers. Drawn from board members, auxiliaries, and affiliated groups, volunteers have filled some of the gaps, particularly as nurse's aids and clerical workers; but maintenance work remains a problem, only partly met by the greater use of the aged residents for some tasks.

Anticipating a shrinkage in private agency income, administrators of the homes for aged have been studying their budgets. They felt that expansion is unavoidable because of higher costs and increased demands. It was their conclusion that they should not cut standards or intake, but rather should look for increased income from public tax sources, and from relatives of residents, in addition to exercising the fullest economy through such measures as cooperative purchasing. . . .

Post-War Planning

If the United Nations wins the war, America will be the key to the destiny of this century. If we retreat once more to an isolationism that will bring high tariffs and narrow economic and political nationalism, the inevitable result will be another war. With practically every other major country devastated by war, we will be the one great producing nation left. Therefore, we must gear our peacetime economy to the gigantic task of world reconstruction, exporting all the goods we can possibly produce and spare, under the most liberal arrangements. This will not be an act of great humanitarianism alone; it will equally be an act of enlightened selfishness. For history certainly should have taught us that democracy and liberty are directly related to rising production and high standards of living, and cannot continue without them.

We must expect, however, that as soon as the war is over the cry will be heard that we have all we can do to meet our American problems, that we must concentrate on the tasks at home, and that much of what happens overseas is none of our business—theories which should be recognized as completely outworn by this time, but which unfortunately have not been and will not be forgotten. We must make sure that we do not "save" ourselves into another depression and another war, and that we spend whatever is necessary to rebuild lives and communities, as readily as we are spending vast sums to destroy them. And the planning and leadership for this must come now. It has been the tragic failure of social work, and indeed of all community planning, to arrive too late, with too little. This time we cannot and must not repeat that mistake.

The task that will confront us overseas will be tremendous. The relief needs will be far greater than after the last war, and the countries will lack the resources which they had then for their own reconstruction, when they were able to more than match the help which came from outside. As Clarence Pickett [4] told us, such sums will be completely beyond private resources, and enormous public funds will be required. And, as he also emphasized, this reconstruction must be planned by the United Nations and not just by the United States and England; it must be carried out so that it is more than an immediate service, but becomes a medium for permanent gains in sound social organization, in a healthy relationship between peoples, and a lasting contribution to the peace of the world.

Post-War Planning for Jews

As for the Jews, I have already mentioned the growing general concern with practicalitics, in contrast to the messianic fervor which characterized Jewish leadership after the last war. Dr. Baron has pointed out the danger of a Jewish isolationism which would attempt to solve the problems of American Jews without reference to world Jewry, despite the fact that all such attempts have failed in the past, and are certain to fail again. At this time, there are no other Jews in the world who can save our people, if we in America fail.

He noted, however, an improvement during the past two years in the perspective and approach of American Jewry to the post-war problems, demonstrated by the various agencies which are giving special study to the problem. Thus far, however, only beginnings have been made. With the possibility that there may be a prolonged armistice of five or ten years before the peace treaties,

[4] Executive Secretary, American Friends Service Committee. See "Post-War Relief and Reconstruction," *Jewish Social Service Quarterly*, vol. XIX, no. 1 (Sept. 1942), pp. 51-55.

he suggested that Jewish peace studies concentrate on a two-fold program of (1) immediate action to follow the war, and (2) long-range proposals for the permanent peace.

This whole question was given detailed analysis by Abraham Duker [5] in his comprehensive and penetrating paper. You will recall that he listed five different national Jewish organizations at work studying war and post-war problems as a basis for proposals to be made at the peace conferences. The studies thus far have been historical in part, looking at the effects of Nazi persecution in Europe, and the problems of reconstruction that have been created. But the discussions to date have not been as intensive as those during the last war, hampered in part by the vagueness of the peace aims of the United Nations.

Relief and Reconstruction

Two major attitudes characterize the approach of Jews to the post-war era: (1) that there are no special Jewish aspects of the problem, and that our problems are part and parcel of the total needs. . . , and (2) the view that there are specific Jewish aspects in the situation which require special attention.

Among the latter there are some who hold that there is no future for the Jews in Eastern and Central Europe, where they will be faced with total impoverishment and a deep-rooted anti-Semitism which will not disappear with the end of the war. The solution, according to this group, is wholesale evacuation.

At the other extreme are the "optimists," including some socialists and laborites, who say that Jews have no right to emigrate, that they are equal partners with other groups that make up the nations of Europe, and should remain to help work out a democratic and socialist reconstruction.

[5] American Jewish educator and historian, associated with the Graduate School for Jewish Social Work and later Director of the School for Jewish Studies, Chicago. See "Political and Cultural Aspects of Post-War Problems," *Jewish Social Service Quarterly,* vol. XIX, no. 1 (Sept. 1942), pp. 56-66.

The majority opinion, in Mr. Duker's judgment, lies between these two extreme views; it believes that while large numbers will have to emigrate from Europe, many others will have to remain, and that we must recognize both these factors in our post-war planning. Although Zionists emphasize the necessity of emigration, and non-Zionists the reconstruction within Europe, there is widespread recognition even among the latter that Palestine can play a major role in the post-war salvation of Jewry; the difference is one of degree.

At least two points of agreement are emerging from the planning to date: (1) there must be equality of rights for Jews everywhere; and (2) there must be an international Bill of Rights guaranteeing that status, with international machinery to enforce it. Among the Zionists there is the further requirement that Palestine must definitely become a Jewish commonwealth.

. . . Mr. Duker pointed not only to the psychological-cultural problem of Jews in Nazi-dominated countries who will be unable to remain in the poisoned atmosphere that has been created, even though legally permitted to do so, but also to the situation of Jews in Russia who cannot bring themselves to adjust to the abolition of the Jewish religion there. For such Jews, he said, there must be an international agreement permitting emigration from these lands, as well as immigration into others more desirable to them. Thus, the United Nations must assure not only racial and national equality and security, but also the sanctity of the human personality under religious freedom and due process of law. In such a world the validity of cultural pluralism will be accepted as a fundamental tenet of democracy. . . .

Our Fundamental Goal

I should like to take a final moment to look at what all this implies for us as social workers and as Jews. This war is being fought for fundamental human values—values that are the common basis of social work, of democracy, and of Judaism. Our way of life, as well as our survival as a people is at stake in this conflict. As social workers we face, in the words of Kenneth Pray,[6] the basic necessity of adjusting society and the individual so that we achieve security and stability on the one hand, and freedom for individual creative venture on the other. No society and no government has been able to attain that balance as yet. It is the goal of democracy. It is our goal as social workers.

And as Jews we must bring to that task the leadership, the resources, the experience, and the great moral message which has been our heritage, and which the world needs now and will need more than ever in the days to come.

And if I may be permitted one personal word in closing, it seems clear from all this that we are living in a great moment of history—a moment that will determine the course of human events for this century and perhaps for many more to come. I believe that we shall know within our own lifetime how well we have met its challenge.

[6] Dean, School of Social Work, University of Pennsylvania.

PART FOUR

YEARS OF CONSOLIDATION

1946-1958

SURVEY OF THE YEARS 1946–1958

The years following the close of World War II were years of growth and consolidation of the national life, overlaid by the anxieties and uncertainties of rapid social change and international tensions. But fears of a major post-war economic collapse were nowhere realized, although short-term recessions in economic activity did occur. Instead, a growing population met growing employment of unprecedented dimensions, a growth sometimes obscured by the persistence of a hard core of unemployment which especially affected youth, the aged, and minority groups. Income was more widely distributed upwards, although those at the lowest end of the economic scale benefited least, and the gap between the poorest and the wealthiest grew.

International tensions caused by the cold war between the United States and the Union of Soviet Socialist Republics led to a high level of military and defense expenditure and rapid technological change. Military weapons development led to the study of nuclear energy, and to the exploration of space. At home, the tensions led to an outburst of intolerance for many forms of independent thought, culminating in the Senate investigations of the Committee on Un-American Activities led by Joseph McCarthy. Abroad, the United States embarked upon a massive program of foreign aid, first to help Western European nations rebuild their economies, and then to help new or underdeveloped nations build more sound economic foundations.

Jewish immigration continued at a steady pace, but was overshadowed by the more extensive movement to Israel. The establishment and support of the new State of Israel was a signal event for Jewish philanthropy. Its effect upon social services in America was slight, but it significantly affected Jewish community organizations, which greatly increased their fund-raising to help support both the new State and the growing demands of a stable American community.

Social problems at home persisted in the form of an incidence of mental illness, outbreaks of juvenile deliquency, and continued discrimination against racial and ethnic groups, especially Negroes. At the same time many health problems were progressively brought under control, although there remained certain long-term illnesses for which there was no successful treatment. The flux of population from the East to the West and Southwest, and from core city to suburban fringes, resulted in a fluid population, with a consequent loss of local rootedness and an intensified search for meaning and significance in daily life.

The decade also witnessed a remarkable rise in governmental, and especially federal responsibility for health and welfare services; social problems were perceived to be national in scope and thus to require national involvement in their solution. New alignments between government and voluntary social work were in the making.

Jewish social services demonstrated the solidity of the foundations upon which they had been built over the preceding fifty years. American Jewish communities emerged from the war era as the largest, wealthiest, and most secure Jewish population in the world with world-wide responsibilities for the rebuilding of European Jewish communities and the re-creation of the State of Israel, as well as the maintenance of a large network of domestic welfare services. Jewish communities continued to examine their purposes and directions, but with fewer doubts as to the validity of their existence or their rationale. Jewish communal organization was secure, encompassing the diverse interests of Jewish life in Federations, Welfare Funds, and religious associations. Jewish agencies accepted the permanence of their being and their value. Re-examination was now concentrated upon a selection of directions for the future, upon improvement of standards, and maintaining flexibility in the face of continuous change. By and large, Jewish welfare services now were viewed as instruments to serve the entire Jewish community; social problems affected all groups and were not confined to those who were poor or dispossessed.

Community services continued to evolve, but along different lines. The family and child-welfare services became more and more professionalized, concentrating upon the treatment of psychological and inter-personal stresses, as did their counterparts under other auspices. More and more the language and theories of psychiatry became the cornerstone of personal service programs. Recreation and community centers concerned themselves more than ever with the character of Jewish communal life; their broadened programs were matched by a corresponding broadening of interest on the part of synagogues, many of which organized congregational leisure-time services in lieu of community-wide activities. Jewish education grew steadily, and began to deal with the problems of an all-day school system in some cities, and the improvement of teaching standards in all communities. Community relations councils grew in number, and, along with the national agencies such as the American Jewish Committee, American Jewish Congress, and Anti-Defamation League, dealt with broad civic issues such as race relations, and international issues such as the growth of the State of Israel.

Philanthropic giving in Jewish communities grew apace, reaching an unprecedented level—over a billion dollars was raised in this decade by means of central fund-raising campaigns. Despite this high degree of cooperation, however, the needs of Israel, as it sought to establish itself on a firm basis, seriously strained community capacity to support the growth of local communal services. As a result, service agencies turned to new sources of support such as government subsidies and the collection of fees for services.

Throughout the course of these changes, nearly all Jewish-supported services were accepted as contributing, in one way or another, to the health, vigor and viability of Jewish life in America, a Jewish life which combined sectarian distinctiveness with integration in the mainstream of American life.

I The Jewish Health and Welfare Services—Purposes and Goals

THE welfare developments of this period are in a direct line of descent from the activities designed to elevate the social condition made at the beginning of the century. Re-reading the first Conference Agenda and the first Presidential Address in 1900, we find the expression of the same interest in community cooperation, refugee resettlement, family well-being, child welfare, and economic security; but by the 1950's the institutions created for these purposes are seen as permanent in nature, and as indispensable for communal welfare.[1] The early impulses which led one human being (or one Jew) to help another in distress through acts of personal kindness have given way to a conviction that professional and often esoteric skills are required to cope effectively with widespread social problems. These skills are seen as mainly clinical in nature, based upon medical, psychological, and psychiatric models of treatment. There remains only a faint echo of the global aims to alter society by purely philanthropic and humanitarian methods which were so often proclaimed in earlier periods.

The family service agencies had completed a decade of work of resettling many thousands of refugees; but this dramatic social task was often perceived as a temporary obstruction to the central task of the agencies, that of expanding and improving professional skill for personal counselling of individuals and families to help them confront their realities, one by one. Child welfare services are no

[1] See Appendix, p. 622.

longer sustained by the appeal to nurture and care for the orphan or the abandoned child, but are seen as complex psychiatric and social therapy institutions to treat the most persistent and serious emotional disorders of youth. The vocational services acknowledge that the existence of discrimination in employment can be attributed to certain root causes, but their tasks are limited, by and large, to acquiring and practicing those technical skills necessary to advise and retain the individual handicapped or disadvantaged citizen for the contemporary labor market, or to match his skills to a specific job. In such fields, the Jewish services have become solidly rooted in the mainsoil of general American social service.

Jewish services for the aged and Jewish hospitals were forced into a pioneering role by the demands of chronic illness, giving leadership to new forms of social organization. Jewish homes for the aged introduced medical, psychiatric, and skilled nursing care into their programs, converting hitherto custodial institutions into medical and quasi-medical institutions. Jewish hospitals began to develop into comprehensive community health centers as various social agencies claimed a common identity between social and health institutions. The Jewish communities' stress upon a living link between community supported institutions provided the framework for extended hospital services to homes for the aged, to family and children's agencies, and for the development of new forms of medical care, such as the provision of hospital-level service for the long-term sick and the aged in their own homes. The professional staffs of these agencies were soon in demand by governmental and by other service groups to further the spread of these ideas in social-medical relationships.

For both the health and welfare services, the increasing complexity of methods of treatment has produced two complementary movements, clearly discernible in all of the documents included in this section: (1) an increase of professionalization of manpower in all services, with stress upon the clinical and therapeutic disciplines; and (2) a demand that the now specialized agencies synchronize their various functions in some coherent fashion so that the risk of overlooking the needs of the individual or the family in a maze of administrative detail will be reduced. Since services and skills were expected to alter almost continuously, the development of resources for a parallel form of continuous planning for coordinated activity was seen as inevitable.

1. Current Purposes and Goals of Jewish Family Agencies*

BY MARCEL KOVARSKY

The family agency is at one and the same time the oldest and the newest member of the congregation of Jewish communal services —the oldest, because in most communities it represents the first organized attempt, outside of the synagogue, to implement the biblical injunction of caring for the stranger within our gates; [1] the newest, because during the past two decades it has been continually reviewing its purpose and goals, and in that sense has several times been reborn. A more accurate description, perhaps, would be to say that it has shed its outer skin and emerged as a new kind of animal; so new and different at times as to be almost unrecognizable by its parent, the Jewish community. . . .

The current review [2] of Jewish family agency scope and pro-

* *Jewish Social Service Quarterly,* vol. XXX, no. 3 (Spring 1954), pp. 282-88. Presented at the National Conference of Jewish Communal Service, Atlantic City, N.J., May 27, 1953.

[1] This biblical injunction refers to non-Jews; but the author's contention is correct, since the Jewish benevolent societies, the direct ancestors of the Jewish family agencies, were the first non-synagogal Jewish welfare organizations in the U.S.

[2] See Theodore R. Isenstadt, "The Role of the Family Agency in the Jewish Community," *Jewish Social Service Quarterly,* vol. XXXI, no. 2 (Dec. 1954), pp. 208-12, and Comments by Milton Goldman, pp. 213-15; also Martha K. Selig, "The Role of the Family Service Agency," pp. 216-23. The points made by Isenstadt are that "the very heart of Jewish Family Service today in 1954 is the counselling (or case work) service,

gram was initiated two and one-half years ago, and has been carried on, as were the earlier ones, under the auspices of the Council of Jewish Federations and Welfare Funds. It differs from others, however, in having involved a much wider representation of family agencies, as well as of persons from the Federation field. This review was motivated by the fact that most Jewish family agencies had for a period of four or five years prior to 1950 been devoting a major share of their time, effort, and interest to the adjustment of newly arrived immigrants. While the understanding and skill which these agencies had developed out of their previous experience contributed immeasurably to the effectiveness and economy of time with which they were able to help the newcomers, the priority of attention which this group demanded had its inevitable effect on the "normal" program of the agency. At the end of 1950, when it became apparent that large-scale immigration was on the decline, and the end of the New American program was in sight, many agencies became concerned that (as had happened once before with the development of public-assistance programs) a major portion of their clientele, and hence an important reason for their existence, would disappear. This constituted a particular problem for some of the newer agencies that had not had an opportunity to build much of a local base before they were engulfed by the pressure of refugee service. . . .

It is important to note, and not just in passing, that the general family service field is also in the process of taking inventory. The Family Service Association of America has for several years had at work a Committee on Method and Scope, and publication of its report is eagerly awaited.[3] There are many problems—as, for ex-

---

which devotes itself primarily to aiding families, individual members of the family, and unattached individuals in attempting to resolve and modify problems arising out of strained or distorted interpersonal relationships"; also that "both Federation and Family Agency used to view program development on a joint and shared basis, and . . . Federations are obligated to understand the needs, aspirations, and special problems of operating agencies."

[3] Family Service Association of America. *Scope and Methods of the Family Service Agency* (New York, 1953).

ample, the difficulty of interpreting an almost intangible helping process to the community—which Jewish agencies share in common with the general field. At the same time, there are important differences: the Jewish agency must be much more responsive to the sentiment of its constituency, and its normal development has been sidetracked for five or six years by the impact of the refugee program. . . .

In considering the objectives and functions of a Jewish family agency, two fundamental questions present themselves: What can family service contribute to community well-being? What are the special and unique contributions which a Jewish family agency can make?

In its early days, the family agency was necessarily a general practitioner. The need for specialized agencies had not yet been established, so that the early family-service bureaus had business loan and consultation departments, offered vocational services to adults and scholarships for children, and in some cases operated dispensaries and visiting nurse services under their auspices. They were also very much concerned (this was perhaps more true of some of the non-sectarian agencies) with improving the conditions of community living through social reform; they worked for better housing, tenement laws, and the minimum wage. Gradually, the more specified activities—even those dealing with social legislation and reform—were split off, and became independent agencies with their own boards. Regardless of what anyone may think of the merits of this development, we must recognize that it merely parallels what has been happening in other professions and services. Medicine provides a striking parallel, and to an extent so do engineering and the physical sciences.

Unquestionably, there are both values and losses in this general trend. The gain is in the more intimate knowledge and higher degree of skill which specialization makes possible; the principal loss lies in the increasing difficulty of seeing the person, or family, as a living operating whole. This observation holds true for medicine as well as for case work. The question before us is not whether we ought to return to the general practice of social work. Realistically, we do not have that choice; we could not turn back the clock even if we wished to. The question, rather, is how to preserve as much as possible the values of general practice, while at the same time utilizing to the full the advantages of specialization. A full-blown solution to this problem does not yet exist; but I would like to suggest that it may lie in a direction analogous to group practice in medicine.

The characteristic which differentiates family service from other case-work services is that is always family-centered. The Jewish agency has a special orientation because of its interest in the family as a unit in the total Jewish community. Its primary objective is the prevention of family breakdown, the strengthening of family ties, and the maintenance of healthy and satisfying family living. In the course of this work it helps individuals, but always against the background of the family constellation, and with the underlying purpose of strengthening the family fabric.

Family service is unique in that it keeps in focus the family as a whole and its members in their family interrelationships. Other services with specific interest in individual family members, such as a vocational service or a mental hygiene clinic, may benefit the family as a whole incidental to the primary service they provide. However, since the family is the primary source of mental health, family agencies contribute directly to the general mental health of the community.

In its analysis of the areas in which Jewish family agencies currently operate, the Committee on Purpose and Function has defined three principal categories. These are: (1) problems of family and personal interrelationships; (2) concrete services administered through case-work; and (3) information and referral service. Under the first category are included marital problems, problems of parent-child relationships, and adjustment of individuals. The concrete services which a Jewish family agency may offer will vary according to the availability of public and other resources to support social and economic requirements for family well-being.

Such concrete services may include interim financial assistance, homemaker service, boarding care for the aged, or even making available psychiatric treatment. All of these services are administered by a caseworker, and have as their aim the strengthening of family life. The Committee also felt that information services which help families make full use of all community resources are a valid part of family service, when such a program is administered through case-work methods and with case-work objectives.

There appears to be substantial difference of opinion regarding the priority of counselling vis-à-vis concrete services. At one point in the Committee's discussion, there appeared to be agreement that counselling should be regarded as the common core of family-agency service, with concrete services varying from community to community and occupying a peripheral position. Those who espoused this view did not point out that a preponderance of time and staff must be devoted to counselling before an agency may properly consider itself as rendering a family service, but merely stressed counselling as the hallmark of any family service, no matter how large or small. In the most recent draft of its report, the Committee further suggested that while counselling service is an essential characteristic of a Jewish family agency, concrete services, although necessary for healthy family living, need not be administered under Jewish auspices. While this point of view has been borne out by [individual studies], there is an important body of opinion which believes that, on the contrary, certain concrete services are more acceptable to the Jewish community when administered under Jewish auspices, while counselling service may be more readily acceptable from non-sectarian sources. The relatively free use by Jewish families of child guidance and other mental hygiene clinics, which are generally under public or other non-sectarian auspices, as against the more limited use by Jews of the services of non-sectarian family agencies, is urged in support of this viewpoint. However, this argument is inconclusive, because in the few instances in which child-guidance service is available under Jewish auspices, very full use of it has been made by the

Jewish community. It is an area in which much more exploration needs to be done before we can be certain of any conclusions.

It may be interesting in this connection to examine the services which non-sectarian family agencies are called upon to give. In its analysis of service statistics for fifty representative agencies (mainly non-sectarian), the Family Service Association of America found that relatively little change has occurred over the past three years in the distribution of problems for which case-work service was given. Family relations led the list, constituting a factor in half of all the cases served by the fifty agencies. Economic problems ranked second as a focus of case-work service; they were reported in slightly more than one-third of the cases. Third place was occupied by problems of personality adjustment, which occurred in slightly more than one-fourth of the caseload. Other important problem areas were: planning substitute care of children (fifteen of the fifty agencies also offered child placement service), physical illness, employment, housing, and mental illness—in that order. It may be of further interest that of the cases with difficulties in the area of family relations, about two-thirds had marital problems, and nearly half had problems of parent-child relations. In the area of personality adjustment, case-work service was usually given to adults, although help for personality difficulties in adolescents was not unusual.

Although it is not possible to classify these "problem areas" as either counselling or concrete services with any degree of certainty, it is apparent that general family agencies are rendering a substantial amount of service in both fields.

This brings us to the crucial question of the validity of sectarian Jewish service, specifically Jewish family agencies. It is unquestionably true that while in the early days most clients of Jewish agencies were immigrants, who required specifically Jewish services because of their special language, cultural, and religious needs, today the problems brought to the Jewish family agency are for the most part of the same general nature as those coming to the non-sectarian private family service. Nevertheless, there is ample evidence, both from the Springfield study [4] and from the comments which agency and Federation executives have made on the Committee's report, that this circumstance alone does not justify the discontinuance of Jewish family agencies. As one person put it, "A sectarian service, by its very existence, is an instrument of Jewish survival, regardless of its specific content."

I think it is in this area that the Springfield experience has most to teach us. Those of you who have read the study will recall that, new Americans aside, there were almost as many Jewish families utilizing a combination of non-sectarian services as used the Jewish agency. Furthermore, these nonsectarian services were of good professional quality, and those Jews who used them apparently felt comfortable in doing so. Nevertheless, when a representative sampling of Jewish community opinion was taken on the question of whether a separate Jewish agency should be maintained, the predominant majority believed that it should, while at the same time insisting that its service should be of superior quality and skill. The principal reasons adduced for this preference were community pride, easier identification for the community and for some clients with a Jewish agency, the belief that in the long run the maintenance of high professional standards can more safely be entrusted to Jewish auspices, the possibility of recurrent crises (such as the refugee problem) which are specifically Jewish, and the aforementioned survival value. It is interesting that in Springfield the opinion was expressed that families requiring financial or medical services could probably make use of non-sectarian sources quite adequately, but where personal problems are involved, a Jewish agency is invaluable. Regardless of the divergence of opinion on this last point, I think we may safely assume that family service under sectarian auspices is here to stay, at least in the foreseeable future.

This brings us to the final point of where the responsibility for the planning of family services within the community properly lies.

[4] See "A Jewish Community Looks at Case-Work Services—Survey Report of the Jewish Social Service Bureau of Springfield, Mass.," by Robert Morris, Council of Jewish Federations and Welfare Funds, 1952.

I have heard this argued pro and con on many occasions, with Federation executives pointing out that the central communal agency is in the best position to assess community needs, and agency representatives maintaining that only the group which renders a professional service can possibly determine what and how much it is able to do. Out of my own experience—and the discussions in the Committee on Purpose and Function in which I have participated have certainly played a part in shaping this—I have developed a firm conviction that neither agency nor Federation alone can do this job, and that we need to promote opportunities for agency and Federation people, both lay and professional, to sit around the table on a year-round basis (not just at budget distribution time), so that there may be developed out of the specific experience of each a common understanding of what services the community needs, what it is willing to pay for, and what services agencies are currently equipped to offer. Out of such joint effort can flow the community of understanding and purpose which will insure the most appropriate and effective level of service by the Jewish family agency, both now and in the future.

2. Changes in Child Care and Their Implications*

BY MARTHA K. SELIG

During this period there has been a sharp reduction in the number of children in placement, reflecting both fewer applications and the refinement of professional skills. Due to methods of carefully screened intake, there were fewer children admitted, and intensive under-care service reduced the length of time they remained in

* *Journal of Jewish Communal Service,* vol. XXXIII, no. 1 (Fall 1956), pp. 73-86. Presented at the Annual Meeting of the National Conference of Jewish Communal Service, St. Louis, Mo., May 28, 1956.

placement. The number of orphans and semi-orphans has declined, and parents have become increasingly involved in the life of the child in placement. Disturbed children represent an increasing percentage of the children in placement. Our diagnostic and treatment skills, together with the addition of ancillary services of all kinds, particularly psychiatry, have made it possible to deal with highly disturbed children who in the past we could not have helped, but only have referred them to mental institutions or reformatories. Services have been opened to a broader segment of the community. While the number of children in placement has declined, applications for child guidance, day care, family counselling and homemaker service have increased. Expenditures have risen sharply due partly to the general rise in price levels, but far more to the shift from less expensive to more costly types of care and enrichment of all services.[1]

Neither professional workers nor communities have remained indifferent to these changes, and there have been many modifications in concept, methodology, and in the types of service facilities. Communities have responded in a number of ways: one was to consolidate child-placement agencies, with a perhaps too-rapid abandonment of group-care facilities. Another was to merge family and children's agencies. Some communities transferred part of the child-placement program to non-sectarian auspices, and others sought increased public subsidy to meet mounting costs. Many increased their emphasis on mental health, and opened their social-welfare resources to the wider community. . . .

Of particular significance is the increasing awareness of the

[1] The factual data gathered in the New York Federation study (*To Serve the Children Best. A Community Program for Jewish Child Care*, by Martha K. Selig, 1956) confirmed the above trends: The number of Jewish children in placement declined from over 4,000 to 1,677, or a two-thirds reduction, while the Jewish child population in New York City under 21 dropped by only 11 per cent; at least 85 per cent of the children showed some personality abnormality; 12 per cent were half-orphans and two per cent were full orphans; 93 per cent of the families had some form of physical or mental illness; the vast majority of the families were in the lower economic bracket; adoption services expanded to include older and exceptional children; expenditures doubled, and per capita cost increased six-fold.

value of preventive services, and the expansion of such services as child guidance, parent-child counselling, homemaker services, group-day care, and, more recently, foster family day care, to prevent family disintegration, the most frequent cause of placement. This has stemmed from the recognition that the aim of child care must be directed toward the preservation of the family, wherever this is possible; that, at best, placement should be regarded as a temporary phase in the life of the child. . . .

While each community may have specific problems, I believe that there are three generic questions which have applicability to all, large and small, and which require our concern. These are: (1) services to the disturbed child in terms of nature and variety of facilities, administrative auspices, and relationship to psychiatry; (2) the need for a broadened view of child care and its relationship to family service; and (3) the increased cost of care and the obligations it imposes. . . .

Varied Services for the Disturbed Child

. . . With the development of broad social-welfare programs designed to keep families intact, and with the increase in family-service and child-guidance facilities, many "normal" children who would formerly have been placed can now remain at home. The population in placement has become, by and large, a residual and selected group, representing the more disturbed children and families in the community.

In the past, there was a tendency—and perhaps there still remains a strong residue of this—to think of services to the more disturbed child, particularly the acting out and aggressive child, in terms of placement away from home and in institutional facilities only. With more acute differential diagnostic appraisal, pointing to a broad continuum in the category of disturbed children, there developed an ever-increasing awareness of the need to provide a wide variety of services for this group, geared to their special needs, both in placement facilities and at home. Many children who formerly had been placed are now treated successfully in family-service and child-guidance agencies; the value of day-treatment centers, which provide an all-day school and treatment milieu without complete separation, is being tested; the effectiveness of foster homes for a number of these children has already been validated. Small "residential-treatment centers" are serving some of these children.

We must, however, continue to scrutinize our disturbed children carefully, so that we do not view them indiscriminately and feel that we have done our duty by them simply by providing more psychiatric care. For, many of these children, because of the nature of their emotional problems, require special services different from and more extensive than those generally associated with the traditional child-care agencies.

A community plan for services to the more disturbed child, then, must include both provision for "home care" and "foster care." The disturbed child who can remain at home could be helped through child-guidance clinics, family counselling facilities, and day-treatment centers. When placement is indicated, we might think of at least four broad categories: (1) special foster homes, including the group foster home; (2) the educationally oriented group-care facilities, with a therapeutic milieu for delinquent and/ or aggressive disturbed children who do not require a closed environment; (3) the psychiatrically oriented small-group facilities, utilizing education and case work and ancillary services for the more highly disturbed in the group; and (4) the hospital ward for those requiring a closed environment.[2]

The adoption of this concept of variegated services for the disturbed child by the smaller communities, which cannot establish expensive facilities, will permit more disturbed children to be cared for *within the local community*. For, all too frequently, with the

[2] The New York Federation study projected three additional services for the "less disturbed" children requiring placement—regular foster home, a facility for the less disturbed child who cannot live in a foster home, a group facility for the somewhat retarded child. These services are described in detail in the full report.

belief that the disturbed child can benefit only from the most highly specialized services, now known as the "residential treatment centers," many communities have discounted their own resources. This has resulted in the abrogation of community obligations to this group; the responsibility for such children is turned over to public agencies, or they are referred to "regional" specialized organizations.

Use of Regional Placement Facilities

In this connection, it would be desirable to reconsider the present use of regional placement facilities for these children.

The placement of a child in a facility hundreds and sometimes thousands of miles away from home does not enable adequate or integrated work with the family. Since this is a vital part of child care, such separation should be undertaken only as a last resort. Obviously, there will be some children in the smaller communities for whom a special service may be required and is not locally available. If regional agencies are necessary, it would seem desirable to establish several of them throughout the country, each serving communities within a reasonable commuting distance. Thus, the special service would be more readily available, and reasonable contact could be mantained with the family.

I would see even these regional facilities utilized only for those children for whom alternative possibilities within their own communities have been considered and excluded.

Size of Units

We must also at this time give consideration to the question of whether the disturbed child can be served most effectively in large settings of 150-200 children. This question requires serious exploration to determine whether "treatment" can go on beneficially en masse. We have come to accept the concept that function and structure should be interrelated. Is it not, therefore, desirable that along with a change in function from an institution serving the "orphan child" to one serving the "highly disturbed child," the structure of the institution should also be modified to insure the most effective operation? I believe we will find that smaller units will be more effective in serving the disturbed group. In these units children can more easily be seen as individuals, and the effects of regimentation in the larger institution can be avoided. Furthermore, smaller units assure, to a greater degree, flexible use of program and resources to meet the changing needs of children under care.[3]

The "Residential Treatment Center"

Child-care workers will also want to be more discriminating in the use of the term "residential treatment center," which is appearing more and more in the literature of the field. On the one hand, the term applies to institutions serving very large groups of children with a wide variety of personality problems; and on the other, to small units serving twenty to twenty-five seriously disturbed children at the other end of the curve whose needs are predominantly psychiatrically oriented. The differences between these services are significant and warrant a separate nomenclature, so that the services are not confused. . . .

If, for the moment, the term "residential treatment center" is restricted to the highly specialized, psychiatrically oriented small units, I would then like to urge a word of caution with respect to the too-rapid duplication of such units. There appears to be no agreement at the moment as to just what a residential treatment center is. The existing ones are new, and have had insufficient experience to warrant any conclusive findings. We do not yet know, for instance, the best size for such units; the extent to which mingling of different types of disturbed children is feasible; the full

[3] In the New York Federation study we recommended that the cottage-plan units now serving these children give serious consideration to "reorganizing and relocating these facilities to bring us closer to our goal of smaller units located within the mainstream of community activity." Jacob Kepecs made similar proposals in 1925. See citation, p. 178.

potentialities of special foster homes for these children; or the value of an enriched program in some of the existing facilities in solving problems for at least a part of this group. We are only now beginning to experiment with the day-treatment center for the disturbed group. Despite all of these uncertainties, many communities are planning to establish "residential treatment centers" as a panacea for their problem.

Coordination among services now available for the highly disturbed child has been insufficient to provide differential criteria for intake, program, and structure. Further experimentation and cooperative evaluation should be undertaken, before large capital investments are made for services which may be swiftly superseded. The field urgently needs a continuing and intimate exchange of experience between the different types of services for this group, in order to find guideposts for further developments.

Need for Coordination of Services

The diverse nature of children's difficulties makes it desirable to seek a structure that would facilitate the selection of the most appropriate service for the individual child, and the flexible utilization of the various facilities as they may be required. . . . As child-care services are becoming increasingly diversified or differentiated so as to correlate more closely with a highly developed diagnostic differentiation of children's needs, it becomes all the more important to strive for a central intake facility.

Awareness by each agency of the facilities of the other does not necessarily guarantee the most effective utilization of these facilities. One of our executives made a very interesting observation along these lines. She said, "I am not so certain that we are free of prejudice in favor of our own agency, and whether this prejudice does not blind us to the consideration of perhaps a different placement facility. I wonder whether we do not interpret the term 'intake' as 'eligibility for *our* services.' This applies to that group of children who qualify for care from the agency to which the application is being made, but could be more appropriately served in another agency."

Implied in all of this is the necessity for every community to evaluate critically existing facilities and programs, to experiment with modifications of existing services, and to create new approaches. And above all, to coordinate all services for the disturbed child in order to serve his needs best.

In the concern for the highly disturbed child and the lure of the "treatment" centers, I hope we shall avoid the pitfall of creating in this field, as we have done in the past in other fields, a hierarchy of values which will result in insufficient attention to our obligation to provide basic case-work services which are the *sine qua non* of a good child-care agency.

Roles for Psychiatry and Case Work

The increasing number of highly disturbed children has brought in its train two additional problems which require clarification: the use of psychiatrists in a child-care agency, and the auspices of psychiatrically oriented services.

The experience of child-care agencies has demonstrated that a substantial portion of children and their families can utilize successfully the services which case work can offer. In some of these instances, the agencies sought help in the form of consultation with the psychiatrist, with the objective of gaining from him the clarification necessary in carrying out the case-work goal.[4] Case work however, remained the primary service, and psychiatry an auxiliary service, with no direct psychiatric treatment of the client involved.

The sharpening of our diagnostic skills, however, has helped to

[4] Agencies use the consultant psychiatrist in a number of ways. If time permitted, one could raise many questions regarding the direction of this trend, particularly when the psychiatrist is asked for a diagnosis without seeing the client, or where the consultant psychiatrist directs the case-work plan, or what often becomes a psychiatric plan carried out by the case worker.

identify a group of children whose difficulties are of such a nature as to require direct psychiatric treatment to supplement the casework milieu. Agencies have been assuming this responsibility in an effort to provide a total service to the client. Treatment is arranged through panel, staff, or private psychiatrists. Psychiatry is described as "closely related" or an "integral part" of the child-care agency, although there is, as yet, no clarification as to whether this responsibility is financial, supervisory, and/or administrative.

An examination of this trend raises serious question as to whether direct psychiatric treatment, which is distinct from case work, should be the function of a child-care agency. When an agency assumes responsibility for providing psychiatric care under its own aegis, to that extent it is operating as a "psychiatric clinic," and assuming what is regarded as a medical responsibilty. A monograph entitled *The Relationship of the Consultant Psychiatrist to the Family Agency* clearly describes the differences between social work and psychiatry, and the obligation to keep these processes distinct. It states:

> The fact that a family-service agency has a consultant psychiatrist on its staff does not justify any expectation on the part of the community that the agency will accept added *medical responsibility*.[5]

This applies equally to child-care agencies.

It would therefore appear to me desirable that a psychiatric service of any nature be affiliated with a medical setting having appropriate psychiatric facilities. Association of a psychiatric program with a hospital is particularly important because of the manner in which psychiatry has developed, and the growing importance of the medical and chemotherapeutic aspects of the profession. An adequate psychiatric service of any nature should have at its disposal a total range of services, from intensive individual psychotherapy to medical intervention, to be drawn upon as

[5] Prepared by the Committee on Psychiatry and Social Work of the Group for the Advancement of Psychiatry, 1956. Italics in quotation are mine.

needed. Identification of psychiatric services with medical facilities provides this opportunity in a properly structured setting, where members of the staff can be alert to the new trends in the discipline.

In the past, case-work agencies may have been compelled to offer direct psychiatric treatment because of lack of such facilities in the community. There were few out-patient departments in psychiatric hospitals, and those that were operating were not prepared for a joint relationship. Unfortunately, the medical profession and hospital management have, until recently, neglected this important responsibility. When such agency relationships were sought with hospitals. . . , experiences were disappointing because the psychiatric ties were artificial and not indigenous to the hospital function. Indeed, many of the case-work agencies may not have been ready for an association with hospitals. However, as many of the hospitals are making rapid strides in developing psychiatric programs and in demonstrating broad, socially oriented attitudes, and as case work has developed its own inner security. . . , it may now be the appropriate time to move toward a closer relationship between the case-work agency requiring psychiatric service and the hospital.

While this relationship is being explored, and so long as direct psychiatric treatment remains within the orbit of the case-work agency, it would seem to me that the agency would wish to be as scrupulous with respect to its supervison and control as it is in its case-work service. It should, therefore, not be content with just "handing over a case to a psychiatrist," regardless of his qualifications; but it should wish to establish a structure which would identify the psychiatric program as apart from the case-work program, with provision for proper orientation and adequate supervision at its own level of competency.

To differentiate these services and provide the necessary supervision, it may be necessary to establish an agency psychiatric department, which, while remaining related for the time being to the case-work agency, would be supervised and directed by a psychiatrist and identified with a psychiatric hospital or university medical school. Thus, each discipline would operate in an appropriate milieu while adequate communication would insure [cooperative treatment] in the best interests of the client.

Auspices of Psychiatric Services

There is an additional aspect of this problem—namely, the auspices of those child-care services that are primarily psychiatrically oriented.

By studying the success or failure of programs for children under care, case workers are beginning to recognize that, for a segment of children in placement, the case-work milieu may no longer be adequate. Special psychiatrically oriented units have developed—residential treatment centers—especially for the highly disturbed child. Due to past associations, some of these psychiatrically oriented units have evolved from case-work agencies, and have remained under case-work auspices as one of several facilities—as indeed have child-guidance clinics—without basically changing their identification. I believe that this only helps to confuse the picture, since the auspices, direction, and supervision of the service should clearly reflect the nature of its program.

For, when the clientele of the case-work agency—whether it is a placement or an extra-mural service—changes in character to the degree that the basic service required is a psychiatric one as opposed to a case work one, and psychiatry becomes the primary and case work the ancillary service, then we are dealing with a *psychiatric agency*. We would expect the total administration, direction, and supervision of the agency to change in relation to the new function and responsibility, and organic ties to be sought within the appropriate discipline—in this instance, psychiatry.

If the service of a psychiatric agency were administered and supervised by psychiatric leadership, two values would obtain: It is reasonable to assume that internal operations would run more smoothly, and, on a communal basis, that a clearer demarcation would obtain between case-work agencies under case-work leadership and psychiatric services under psychiatric leadership. Through lack of proper identification of agency services, the case-work function frequently becomes synonymous with the psychiatric function. Case work runs the risk of losing its distinguishing characteristics, and it is this that we should try to avoid.

While acknowledging the necessity for a total psychiatric agency unit under the direction of psychiatrists, many agency executives are fearful that supervision and direction by a psychiatrist of a psychiatric program of a child-care agency as part of a hospital setting would result in "psychiatric and hospital domination" of the entire agency. May I suggest that this is an unnecessary fear; a clear differentiation of the functions of the two disciplines can only enhance both, and we should be eager to make available to our clients the best possible services. . . . Only when hospitals assume their full responsibility for child as well as adult psychiatric problems will the case-work profession be assured of the most effective utilization of all techniques available, and will case work be freed for the further development of its own services and skills. . . .

Child Care and Family Service

I should like now to deal briefly with the need for a broadened view of child care, and the implications for relationships between the child-care and the family-service agencies.

While we accept the fact that child placement may be a positive step, and often a very necessary one in the eventual rehabilitation of children and families, we have also come to recognize that separation should occur only as a last resort, and when we are certain that the problems cannot be dealt with without this drastic step. Such a judgment involves a thorough understanding of the family and its potentialities. Child-care workers must, therefore, inevitably become involved with families, and family-service workers involved with children.

The whole problem of placement has become more complicated, not alone because of the nature of the families and children coming under care, but also because our new knowledge and skills have increased the responsibilities of agencies for the social and psychological rehabilitation of children and their families.

The more we examine the children and families who come to the placement agencies, the more we recognize that child care can no longer be considered in isolation, but must be viewed as a "family-care" problem. The entire concept of child care should be emancipated from the narrow view of placement [and institutional care] with which it has so long been associated, and should give more serious attention to preventive services—homemaker, child guidance, parent-child counselling services, etc.—designed to prevent family disintegration. As this comes about, the boundary lines between the responsibilities of a child-care and a family-service agency will grow more and more indistinguishable. Even now it is becoming difficult to distinguish between child-parent counselling and marital counselling where there are children involved, and between such counselling and child guidance, except in the orthodox use of the term as a "clinic service."

The separation of functions which necessitates referral to another agency [for specific problems] adds to an already complicated problem in the client, and sets up artificial distinctions which have no counterpart in the life of the client. With the recognition that a total service is necessary to achieve greater comfort for the client, as well as the goal of family rehabilitation, some of the placement agencies are even now thinking of setting up as part of their structure such adjunct services as counselling prior to placement, "child-centered homemaker services," and after-care counselling. I would seriously question this development, since the proliferation of duplicate services would inevitably lead to fragmentation of the total community services rather than to their integration. . . .

While professional cooperation and communication can be attained by good will, and while any single structure in and of itself does not necessarily insure good service, the combination of both may alleviate a great many of the above difficulties, make it possible to render a more effective child and family service, and prevent further fragmentation of services. It is with this point of view in mind that the child-care agencies should move toward closer integration and, if possible, eventual merger with the family-service agencies.

The Increased Cost of Care

Let us now deal with the third major consideration, the increased cost of child care.

Child-care agencies throughout the country have experienced a sharp rise in per capita cost, largely because of the nature of the services and the more comprehensive programs. Expenditures for service to children designed to build wholesome relationships may in the end be an economic investment for the community; the emotional advantages, of course, can never be calculated in monetary terms. But we must be sure that we are spending this money wisely.

There are many facets to this problem, but I would like to restrict my comments briefly to three: (1) the obligation to examine basic processes and procedures including flexible use of available facilities to assure maximum efficiency and productivity; (2) the most effective use of professional time and skill; and (3) the effect of other sources of income.

We need to review critically such administrative procedures as scheduling interviews, length of interviews, recording, time spent in conferences and seminars, etc., to achieve more economical methods of operation.

We also should review critically the criteria for using supplementary resources, such as psychological examinations and psychiatric consultation, which may be desirable in certain instances but not necessarily effective for others, so that these do not become routine and costly procedures. Greater flexibility in the selection of placement facilities will reserve the more expensive types of service only for those for whom there is clearly no alternative solution. The need for more foster homes for an increasing number of children who are now referred to more costly institutional care may require modifications in the traditional home-finding procedures, more flexible criteria for selecting foster mothers, and a modified method of payment to provide reimbursement for service, in addition to expenses. There is further implied the need to experiment constantly with new ways of serving the children; for such endeavors may be less costly, and may open up new vistas of professional service as well.

The critical personnel shortage which often impedes the implementation of programs has affected all the agencies throughout the country. While additional personnel is being recruited, perhaps this is a good opportunity to evaluate the function and responsibility of the highly skilled professional worker, so as to reserve for him those aspects of a total job which require professional skill and training, and delegate some of the other responsibilities to case aides and even volunteers. This has been accomplished in the medical field by means of medical aides, attendants, and practical nurses, who assume many of the burdens formerly carried by the registered nurse; the latter are now free to administer the highly skilled aspects of patient care. Similarly, in the teaching profession today experiments are going forward in the use of teacher aides to alleviate the critical teacher shortage. The increased utilization of such persons for subsidiary jobs which now drain the skilled workers' time would make it possible for the trained worker to assume responsibility for case work with more children, and thus reduce the per unit cost.

The problem is more complicated, of course, in the case-work field, where so much depends on the case-work skills required in the person-to-person relationship. But implementation of this suggestion would carry with it the concomitant advantage of recruiting additional personnel to the field, and of activating the interest of lay people in the operation of the case-work agencies. A positive approach to this immediate crisis could result in a constructive solution to an otherwise critical situation.

In the light of increasing financial burdens, it is quite natural that agencies are giving a good deal of thought to income from other than philanthropic sources. One possibility, of course, is the extension of child-care services to fee-paying clientele in the wider community. Here, too, there are many aspects which require careful consideration. If child-care agencies are to take into account income from fees in budget-making, does this not imply a decision concerning percentage of free, partial-paying and full-paying service rendered? If no quotas are set, and a "first come first served" policy is established, then the income becomes a very unreliable one.

The changed character of our social services, plus the introduction of the fee, has made for a new step forward in the evolution of the philanthropic idea; but again we must consider the implications. If the trend is to extend service to the upper economic group at the expense of the poor, it is no longer philanthropy. If the trend is to develop a communal service, then one cannot select primarily from the paying group. Service could be extended to this group if added facilities were available which did not reduce the level of operations to the non-paying group, in which instance a "profit" might possibly ensue. . . . This is important and should not be underestimated; child-care agencies should know the direction in which they are moving, lest in their desire to increase income they neglect their philanthropic responsibility.

Public contributions are representing an increasing percentage of the total cost of care. I venture to say that this should be encouraged and the partnership between public and private agencies maintained and enhanced, for only with increased public subsidy can the philanthropic organizations hope to continue to maintain the extent and level of service required to meet the needs of the children and their families. This, however, need not influence the nature of the service to children, which, I believe, should continue under sectarian auspices, since this reflects the expressed wish of the Jewish community.

It is incumbent upon Jewish agencies, particularly the placement agencies acting in *loco parentis,* to provide the essential cultural and religious identifications. This is consonant with [the basic principles of] a democratic society, which emphasize the validity of a cultural pluralism.

Our Basic Responsibilities

These, then, are some areas of concern with which we would wish to deal as we continue to develop child-care services.

The experiences of the past and the guides to the future lead us to anticipate several strong probabilities.

1. As extra-mural services expand, as a healthy economic climate continues, and as benefits of the welfare state extend even further, the census in placement agencies will continue to decline.[6]

2. In the remaining agency population there will be a higher proportion of children with serious emotional disturbances.

3. This population will require more of the specialized placement services, and less of the traditional forms of both care and foster-home facilities.

4. There will be a greater demand for a number of different services to meet a wide variety of needs.

5. The cost of service will remain substantially the same, despite a decrease in the number of child patients, largely because of the intensification of the services.

A courageous, yet cautious, approach must influence our decision to eliminate, retain, or expand services. Projections are at best estimates based on obtainable facts and figures, and while they are invaluable in pointing a direction, they are subject to too many intangibles and unforeseen contingencies to warrant translating them rigidly. This is all the more important in social planning, where human beings play a vital and unpredictable role. Only time can tell what further effects diagnostic techniques, new methods of working with clients, or development of chemotherapy for mental illness will have upon the needs for our total child-care services.

[6] In New York City we estimated a decline of about a third in the next decade.

An altered picture in any of these areas might substantially influence the need. Above all, we should be influenced by the conviction that while we would wish to be guided by experience, future plans should not be circumscribed inflexibly by past patterns.

A pattern of services developed for any community should derive from an understanding of the child and his family. If in the light of our newer understanding of people in trouble, the way to serve them best implies changes of a sometimes sweeping nature, it is nonetheless our responsibility to adapt our tools and services to the needs of families, rather than expect families to adapt to our traditional tools and services.

It has become rather trite to say that the development of child care is at the crossroads; yet we are in a position which offers us a most creative opportunity. Case workers have made rapid strides toward attaining maturity and toward finding a place in the community in relation to the other professions. An obligation of a mature profession is constantly to examine and re-examine the nature and quality of services rendered, rather than to be concerned with status and chances of survival. The crucial questions are: What are the services our clients need at the moment? How can we bring all our capacities to bear upon the development of these services?

Either we ally ourselves with vested interests with the purpose of preserving our old though outmoded face at any cost, or we take the leadership in determining what is obsolete in social-work policy, what services are required, and what is the best structure within which to offer these services. This is our challenge.

3. Trends in the Care of the Aged*

BY MORRIS ZELDITCH

Care of the aged has been recognized for a generation as one of the most pressing areas of need for community support. It is one which receives very substantial financial support, both public and private, and in both the general community and the Jewish. Yet it is only in the last five to ten years that we have come to a full appreciation of the rapidity of change in the needs of the aging population, and the necessity for parallel changes in service programs to maintain pace with those needs.

The basis for change can be seen in two sets of statistics: one concerns demographic figures, and the other a calculation of length of life of the aged part of our population. The American population is changing rapidly; it is increasing at the rate of between 1.5 and 2 per cent per year. The birth rate continues to be high, and the future outlook, as a whole, is for a much larger population than was originally anticipated.

The small numbers of aged in the population in the early 1900's, combined with the relatively short life expectancy of the population at that time, made it unnecessary to do much planning in our communities for the care of the aged. We were content to establish institutions where those who were fortunate enough to survive to old age could retire to a refined atmosphere in a Jewish home for the aged to live out their remaining years in peace.

Today, the population over age 65 contains 8.5 per cent of the total population or 14,200,000, and the prediction is that by about 1975 it will probably stabilize at between 9 and 10 per cent of our population. Present estimates are that on this basis, we should have an aged population of about 21 million in 1975, out of a total population of about 220 million. Translated into the Jewish population, this would mean that we have currently about 456,000

* *Journal of Jewish Communal Service,* vol. XXXIV, no. 1 (Fall, 1957), pp. 126-140. Presented at the Annual Meeting of the National Conference of Jewish Communal Service, Atlantic City, N.J., May 27, 1957.

Jewish people above the age of 65. I have not seen any projections on the Jewish population in the United States in 1975; but it certainly will substantially exceed the present figures, since we Jews are sharing in the high birth rate of today's general population, and the percentage of Jewish aged, it is fair to assume, will probably be the same as for the rest of the population. I think it would be safe, under these circumstances, to assume that there will be at least 750,000 Jews in the United States over the age of 65 by 1975, or better than half as many as we now have.

More important is the change that has taken place in life expectancy rates. The Metropolitan Life Insurance Company published a table in one of its recent statistical bulletins stating that the expectation of life at the time of birth in the year 1955 is seventy years for all persons in the United States. This is primarily due to the fact that infant mortality has been so greatly reduced that the large number of children who died in infancy now survive and live on to old age. Nevertheless, this statistic reflects a gain in 1955 of 23.7 years of life for everybody in the population over what he would have had in 1909; and a gain of thirty-six years over the life expectancy range in 1890. Putting this another way, the Metropolitan statistical bulletin reports that in 1955 any person reaching age sixty-five has a life expectancy of fourteen additional years on the average; 12.5 years for males and 15.1 years for females.

If we could play this as a straight numbers game, there would be no occasion for a paper such as this. We could simply increase the number of beds in institutions for the care of the aged in proportion to the increased number of older people in the population. . . .

But there are two other important forces pressing in upon the aged community. These change the nature of social planning for the care of the aged from a simple arithmetical expansion of facilities to a far more complicated problem. We are first confronted by the change in the physical and mental condition of the aging population. So many of our aged have now reached their seventies, eighties, and nineties that the number among them who are seriously handicapped by physical or mental deterioration or enfeeblement due to age is very much greater than it used to be. Statistics on the extent of these conditions are unknown. But the increasing frequency with which they occur has brought about modifications in the needs of the aged, and hence in the forms of community service for them.

Another force which affects community planning for the aged is the quality and range of care which we are now prepared to give. The development of a high degree of professionalization in the social services and the ability of the communities to raise vastly greater sums of money, both privately and publicly, than was possible in the past, has reflected both the desire and the capacity of the community to provide more and better services to our aged than ever before. In short, we have and we will continue to have more old people, and a substantial proportion of them will need community help for their health and social problems. The community is both more alert to these and better able to provide services to meet them.

Today's trends in the care of the Jewish aged reflect these conditions. Instead of concentrating all the community effort in institutional care, programs for helping older persons to remain in their own homes have begun to develop. The expansion of non-institutional services is a marked part of the trend. The major form of service is still the institution, but this is showing the most dramatic changes in program to meet these changing needs. The most obvious program change is the transformation of the home into a nursing institution. From one-half to two-thirds of all beds in Jewish homes for the aged are now occupied by chronically ill patients. Moreover, between twenty and twenty-five per cent of all residents in the Jewish homes are considered senile, and constitute, therefore, a problem in mental health which we are only just beginning to tackle. And the average age of population in the homes is above seventy-eight years. In the light of this data, let us look at the nature of the institutional programs for the aged as they are today, and glance at the trend toward new programs which the institutions are beginning to initiate.

Institutional care by the Jewish community in the United States is more than a century old. It began in 1855 with the establishment of the first home in St. Louis. Today we have eighty-five homes, with bed capacities ranging all the way from six to over 1,000. In all the communities where they exist, they are a most important part of the program of care of the aged. They used to constitute the entire community program, and in a few communities they still do.

Originally, the home was a large boarding house to which old Jewish people could retire. Today that is no longer true. The increasing number of chronically ill, feeble, and senile aged persons, and the inadequacy of hospitals and public facilities to care for them, has compelled our homes to become a combination of nursing home, mental hospital, group residence, and social agency. Of the eighty-five homes in the Jewish community today, not more than half a dozen limit admissions to ambulatory old persons. Nearly all admit the chronically sick and senile as well. Some also handle terminal cases. Changing needs have compelled the home for the aged to become the community's nursing home. Moreover, it has begun to include day care for non-residents, and home care for aged in their own homes. . . .

It is the medical-care program, together with its component parts of physical therapy and psychiatric care, that is developing into a complex affair. What are the elements of a good medical program? In any home, large or small, there must be continuity of medical contact between residents and physicians. Therefore, there must be a medical director. In the larger institutions there must, of course, be physicians in residence or available at all times and on the premises for a substantial part of each day. In smaller institutions it is not necessary to have a physician in residence; but it is essential that a doctor visit regularly for examinations and sick calls and that he is available at all times for emergencies.

The older system of volunteer doctors who rotate their services free of charge to the institution is gradually giving way to the practice of paying one or more physicians for part- or full-time service; [this medical arrangement] is supplemented by a panel of specialists which contributes its services as needed. [Allocating] the [medical supervision] to one physician assures regularity of examinations, the maintenance of adequate records, and the centralization of responsibility for the health of all the residents in the institutions.

It is also of the greatest importance that the medical program of an institution for the aged be tied closely to a good general hospital; at the very least, the medical director should be a member of the hospital staff. It is far better if the home's medical program operates as an extension of the hospital's scientific and teaching program. Aside from the obvious advantages of the home's use of the hospital for surgery and complex medical service for its residents, the entire level of medical care in the home, its possibilities for preventive work, better treatment, and research, are directly related to the closeness of its ties with the full scientific apparatus and personnel of a hospital. Only the very largest homes can afford to "build in" this quality of care without such a connection by themselves operating as hospitals.

Of equal importance to the doctor, and many think probably of greater importance to the patients, is the nursing care provided. The exact number of nurses required by this for the operation of a home for the aged is not a known or fixed quantity in proportion to the number of residents. The kind and the number of nurses will depend on the quality of care to be provided and the amount of nursing which the condition of the residents requires. Unless the institution operates on a hospital level, the bulk of the care is provided by practical nurses and nurses' aides, with registered nurses usually in charge of the total nursing program, and attending to medication and treatment as prescribed by the doctor. . . .

Physical therapy is another important activity. Practically all homes, except the very smallest or most backward, now set aside space for physical therapy equipment. Their use reflects a constructive point of view regarding the health and the physical condition of the residents in the home. And the use of a trained physical therapist, or sometimes even a nurse, under the direction of the doctor, is an indication that the institution regards the conditions of its residents as capable of improvement, and does not consider enfeeblement or illness as a state for which nothing can be done. The presence of a physical-therapy program is related to other parts of the treatment program, and gives hope to the residents.

An important activity now generally used in all but the smallest of homes is occupational therapy. For this, too, space needs to be provided for equipment and materials and occupational therapists. This program may or may not be prescribed by the doctor, but it is open to all residents in the home including those confined to bed care. . . .

Some of the larger homes are installing special sheltered work shops for both their residents and for older people from the neighborhood who wish to keep themselves usefully occupied. A sheltered workshop is an essential part of the occupational therapy program, and has added value in that residents are paid for their work. Certainly, the more useful the work done by the residents, the greater the sense of productivity and of sharing in a useful activity for the home and for the community. . . .

A most important program for a modern home is in its use of social case work. A good rule of thumb to guide the home in determining how to utilize social work is to assume that all homes require case-work help. The case worker may assist the admissions committee in the investigation of the social and financial condition of applicants for admission, and his presence in the institution is invaluable to help the residents with their personal problems and relationships, to maintain contact with the family, to maintain relationships with other social agencies serving the residents, and to help the psychiatrists or physicians to carry out their programs wherever personal contact is needed which cannot be provided by the nurse or attendants. The smaller homes may utilize the services of a case worker from the Jewish Family Agency, at least for social investigation of applications; the larger homes provide their own social-service departments, both for admission purposes and for intramural services.

All the programs I have enumerated so far are necessary for the successful operation of today's home for the aged. In the larger and more progressive home, all are present. In smaller homes, some and parts of many are to be found. The extent to which a fully rounded program is provided varies first with the attitude of the board of the home, and secondly with the availability of skilled personnel.

Changing needs have resulted in three new kinds of programs. None of these is in very wide use as yet, but each may be seen in a few homes. The first is the organization of programs designed to treat and care for senility. Because senility has been accepted as part of the responsibility of nearly all Jewish homes, mental health in the home has become a major problem. Hence, a psychiatric program in the home for the aged has now become a necessity. This is not always easy to establish, largely because of the shortage of good psychiatrists; but where possible it is an invaluable element in the successful operation of the home. The psychiatrist can help not only in the screening of admissions of patients of doubtful mental health; he can also provide psychotherapy for selected residents; and he can, with the help of the social worker and psychiatric nurse, orient and train the staff to deal with senile and mentally affected residents. In short, the more our homes care for senile and disturbed older persons, the more essential it becomes to have a psychiatric program as part of the medical program.

Secondly, home care, for at least those on the active waiting list for the home, is now beginning to come into practice. It is invaluable in helping to maintain a feeling of security in older people, who fear that they need the institution, but can and would prefer to remain at home as long as possible. For this form of service the social-service department must marshall all kinds of help—doctor, nurse, homemaker, social worker, occupational therapist, physical therapist, and volunteer assistant. These services may be provided by the home or by other agencies; but the net effect is to maintain the person in his own home, while providing the feeling of security that, if needed, the institution is available to him. The effects of a home aged care program have been to expand the capacity for care of the institution, . . . to maintain the family in its own home.

Finally, there is the day-care program. A number of homes have begun to allow residents to come in during the day, take full part in the daytime activities of the home, and go home or to a room in the neighborhood at night. An even more dramatic variation of this concept is the use of the home as a recreation and community center for large numbers of older people from the entire area served by the institution. A recreational and cultural program of broad scope under these conditions is extremely beneficial: it makes the home a place of service not only for those who are within its walls, but for a substantial number of older people who can come in by day, use its facilities, and associate with one another there.

This review of the elements of program necessary in the modern home for the aged is neither complete nor all-inclusive. Other forms of service in homes will also develop. Needs are becoming more complex, and the galaxy of services provided by the institution must increase accordingly. There is little choice. If the services are not provided by the homes for those for whom it is necessary, then the community will find them elsewhere or create them.

The trend in homes is to expand in two directions: development of a high quality of medical and social programs within the institution, and provision of services outside the institution to older persons living in the community.

An interesting semi-institutional development can now be seen in three or four Jewish communities in the acceptance of responsibility for the housing of semi-independent aged. Currently, this takes the form of what is known as apartment projects, or residence clubs, in which lonely older members of the community can live in groups, yet are free to come and go as if they were living in a hotel. All the present residence projects of this type are attached to Jewish homes for the aged. The Home for Aged and Infirm Hebrews in New York City is the best known of these. Most recently, the Philadelphia Home has completed plans for housing about 240 Jewish aged in a hotel-like building on the Home's grounds, with a community recreation center built in, and other facilities for serving a large aged population. In effect, what this does is provide a room and board arrangement under the protective wing of the home. Usually, the buildings are near enough to the institution to permit the residents of the units to participate in the life of the institution. . . . If or when they become ill or feeble, they feel assured of admission into the home, and the protective care it will provide for them. This security seems to be of tremendous importance. It is analogous to the sense of security which the patients under home care feel. At the same time, it permits the community to serve a larger share of its aged population, and to help delay or prevent altogether the necessity for admission into the nursing home, which is the institution. . . .

It has rarely been found necessary for the Jewish community to set up new agencies to serve all these needs of the aged. The established health and welfare agencies of the community have been able to change their programs and assume their share of the services. Thus, in addition to the program directions noted in homes for the aged, we find that other agencies have been adapting their programs to meet the needs of the aged. This is especially true for the Jewish community center, the family agency, the vocational service agency, and the Federation itself. Let us examine the trends in the functions of each of these in turn.

Recreation for the aged is now widely accepted as a need for which communal services are necessary. . . .

The Golden Age Club is the most common device for organizing old people into groups for recreation, and it is most successful. These clubs are developing interesting sidelines other than recreation: visiting of the sick, friendly visiting to the helpless, and the seeking out of opportunities for other forms of service besides recreation. . . .

This picture of recreational programs for the aged is designed solely for old people. But older people can and do take an active part with adults of all ages in the whole range of adult activities in Jewish community centers. They may not be active in the gym or the swimming pool; but in many centers they are to be found mingling with adults of all ages in the arts and crafts groups and in social events, etc. Such activities provide recreation and companionship. Other needs which old people indicate while in these groups include opportunities for productive work, desire for assistance with individual and family problems, assistance with housing, provision for long-term illness, financial difficulty, and personal problems only indirectly related to the normal programs of a recreation center. The opportunity of the center to refer people to appropriate agencies for their problems, or to bring to the center persons from other agencies to assist the aged with such problems, is evident.

One of the most pressing needs of older people is opportunity for productive work. There is a good deal of talk about extending the age of retirement, of campaigns for the employment of older workers, and of altering pension systems so as to make it possible for older persons to engage in productive work without financial penalties, keeping in mind the fact that most of the unemployed older workers are widows with grossly inadequate incomes. Such measures are part of the responsibility of the total community. They are hardly within the range of what the Jewish community can undertake. However, there are some things which can be done by the Jewish community. One is the trend lately observed in the Jewish vocational service agencies to undertake special programs for the aged. These take three forms: placement service for older workers; vocational guidance to older individuals; and the establishment of sheltered workshops for the employment and training of older workers.

Placement service for older workers has been part of the program of Jewish vocational service agencies in a number of cities. The New York Federation Employment and Guidance Service has had a special department for the placement of the aged for several years, and reports considerable success in maintaining sustained contact with selected employers to hire older workers for jobs within their capacities. The Cleveland Jewish vocational service reports that it recently established a system in which groups of potential employers meet directly with older potential workers with a view to employment. Other Jewish vocational service agencies are finding that as long as our economy remains in a healthy state, the opportunities for placement of older workers often need only the conscientious efforts of a trained vocational worker to find the employer willing to depart from the conventional and employ older persons, and to match the skill and capacity of the worker to the job. . . .

Sheltered workshops are a rapidly growing communal service. The Jewish community already supports a number of them. Formerly these shops limited their service to handicapped persons who could be trained to work in industry, refusing to accommodate older workers unless they could be so prepared. If the condition of the worker was such that he was unable to hold a job, the sheltered workshop did not keep him and he was therefore thrown back into the community, with no opportunity for productive work. The trend is now for the Jewish vocational services to re-examine this premise; some careful thought is being given to the extension of the sheltered workshop idea to include terminal workers—that is, workers who cannot be placed in business, but who will be retained under the protected conditions of the shop for an indefinite period. Some of the larger homes for the aged have established such sheltered workshops on their premises as a sort of extension of the occupational therapy of the home. But it is to be noted that most of the sheltered workshops in homes open their doors to older people in the community as well. The terminal workshop for the older worker is a desirable and useful service, which can be established at relatively little cost, and it should be encouraged.

The auspices can be lodged almost anywhere; in a community center (as in Cincinnati); in a Jewish vocational service; in a family agency; in an independent setting.

When we think about the development of non-institutional services for the aged, we think first of the family agency. It is used in many ways for serving the aged: case work with individual and family problems; family foster home care; intake for homes for the aged, especially in smaller homes; referral and information service; homemaker service, etc. Although the family agency has been quite slow in its development as a major non-institutional service to old people, an examination of the case loads of the Jewish family agencies today shows them to be very heavily involved in aged programs.

In a study made by the Council of Jewish Federations and Welfare Funds in 1954, it was found that an average of twenty-three per cent of the active case loads of all Jewish family agencies consisted of persons over sixty-five years of age. We have no 1957 data on this point, but it is our impression that the size of this load in the family agencies is growing, especially in the larger communities. For instance, the Jewish Community Services of Long Island (New York) estimates that forty per cent of its present case load consists of clients above the age of sixty-five. When we take into account the fact that the case load of aged persons tends to be cumulative, and consider the larger numbers expected in the future, it becomes apparent that the role of the family agency in the services offered to the aged will be increasingly important. . . .

A number of special programs for the aged are developing which call for some redirection of older forms of service. Thus the use of homemakers to provide temporary services to families in emergency periods is developing into a major resource to keep the families of aged persons going and to keep families intact in their own homes. . . .

Among the newer programs which have been developed especially for the aged is family foster care and boarding care. While not entirely a new program, not more than a dozen or so Jewish family agencies are engaged in any extensive effort to place aged clients in substitute family homes. It is an expensive operation, as the costs of foster care are sometimes equal to the costs of institutionalization for an aged client. . . .

The job of coordinating the agencies' services, so as to avoid duplication of activities and make posible efficient inter-relationships between agencies, is obviously one which only the Federation can undertake. In the past this function has been served by a commission or council of agencies in the aged field. Cleveland employs a social planning professional staff for its commission on the aged, and the Chicago Federation assigns a substantial proportion of the time of one of its social planners to the coordination and planning functions of its council on care of the aged.

Only through a central commission, operating under the auspices of the Federation, can successful communal planning be done. The very close connection between planning for the chronically sick and planning for the aged, for instance, requires the recognition of the complexities in both areas of service, entails an inevitable overlap of activities. Thus, if a Federation operates a council on chronic illness, it may also operate a council on care of the aged. Yet there is a very large common interest between the two fields, and great care should be taken to efficiently integrate their work for the benefit of the programs of hospitals, institutions, and agencies. It is also clear that a forward-looking council on the aged can explore as yet unfilled needs and gaps in service, and encourage the development of research in the programs and the application of improved methods of care.

There is one other job which the Federation can profitably undertake, although at this writing not too many of them are doing so. This is in the field of social action. Without going into detail on this subject, I should like to indicate that some Federations are becoming interested in joining with other agencies in the community to try to effect better economic and social conditions for the aged. Such efforts are being directed at improvements in the housing supply for the aged, increasing the amounts of grants to the aged through assistance or pensions, exerting pressure for better and more widespread work opportunities, etc. . . .

4. The Function of a Jewish Vocational Agency*

BY SIDNEY LEWINE

. . . . The earlier Jewish vocational agencies were set up largely for the purpose of assisting Jewish people to find jobs at a time when jobs were difficult to find, especially for the disadvantaged Jewish job-seeker. The generally accepted present-day function of the Jewish Vocational Service (JVS) involves the provision of vocational counselling as well as job placement services with the goal of the vocational adjustment of Jewish persons of all levels of the community. Critics of the agencies have claimed that such services should be rendered by the public agencies.[1]

The conclusion seems obvious that the functional development of the Jewish vocational agency has been in keeping with the general movement in Jewish social agencies to provide broader services, and to make such services available to all levels of the Jewish community. Possibly because of its more recent origin among the family of Jewish agencies, the vocational agency has been quicker to offer a wider range of services to a broad clientele. . . . The criticisms of the Jewish vocational agency are of the same general nature as criticisms of the other Jewish social services.

* *Jewish Social Service Quarterly,* vol. XXIV, no. 1 (Sept. 1947), pp. 119-26. Presented at the Annual Meeting of the National Conference of Jewish Social Welfare, Baltimore, Md., May 30-June 4, 1947.

[1] For more recent developments in the area of Jewish vocational service, see Roland Baxt, "Jewish Vocational Service," *American Jewish Year Book,* vol. 55 (1954), pp. 103-09; "Community Services Keep Pace with Times: Changing Needs Have Resulted in Broader Range of Services by Vocational Agencies," *The Jewish Community,* vol. XII, no. 1 (April 1947), pp. 12, 16-17.

Because of its youth and its vigor in offering wider services to a wider clientele, it is not unlikely that the vocational agency will play a crucial role in the dispute over the validity of the broader functional approach. A more detailed description of its clientele and its services may therefore well be in order.

An examination of the clientele of most of the Jewish vocational agencies, and especially those which have been more recently organized, will show that these agencies are truly Jewish "community agencies"; they serve both a wide range of the Jewish community and a large numerical portion of it. These vocational agencies have become Jewish community agencies not as a result of the empire-building tendencies of a group of young, ambitious executives, or of the fortuitous development of agency programs, but by virtue of the expressed wish of the Jewish community, translated into services by careful planning consonant with the best principles of proper community organization.

A broad clientele and a wide breadth of service were goals explicit in the very original statement of function of the Jewish Vocational Service of Cleveland. The statement of agency function contained in its articles of incorporation dated October 27, 1939 reads as follows: "To unify and intensify the efforts of the Cleveland Jewish community in the fields of vocational guidance, vocational training, and vocational placement, to the end that the members of said community may find more employment and more suitable and stable employment." In the seven and one-half years since the Cleveland JVS began operation, it has rendered individual vocational services (aside from additional persons "reached" through its group programs) to more than 17,000 different persons. In a community of 85,000 or 90,000 Jewish people, an agency serving this number in a period of seven and one-half years is truly a Jewish community agency! In addition, spot studies of agency clientele have shown a reasonable sample of each Jewish neighborhood represented, indicating roughly a clientele drawn from all socio-economic levels.

Not at all Jewish vocational agencies have been able to serve so large or representative a cross-section of a local Jewish community. Philadelphia, for example, with a Jewish community three times the size of Cleveland, supports a Jewish vocational agency no larger than the Cleveland agency. A recent study of vocational agency budgets compared with local Jewish population size showed an even greater variation in relative sizes among the agencies.

The general approach in most cities has been to interpret the agency broadly within the community, and at least to attempt to serve in some way almost all members of the Jewish community who come to the vocational agency for service. The evidence shows that agency services are well understood by the Jewish community, that large numbers of Jewish persons feel they need vocational services, and that the local Jewish vocational agency is a resource to be used in securing such services. The response of the Jewish community has in fact led to a constant selective intake problem in some vocational agencies, and at times in all such agencies. The nature and severity of this problem of "whom to serve" has naturally varied with the relative size of the agency and with other factors. Among all agencies, however, the most successful solution to the selective intake problem has been found in selection for service based on two criteria: urgency of need and treatability. When the agency has asked itself, "How badly does this applicant need our service?", and, "How well can he make use of our service?", there have been no insurmountable problems regarding whom to serve. Further, this approach has enabled some agencies to define rather clearly the applicant population which was not being served, and to secure the staff expansion needed to meet requests from the relatively less urgent group.

Difficulties have been encountered, and naturally so, in vocational agencies which have attempted to serve large numbers of clients without the requisite staff. Problems have also arisen in instances in which the agency has requested additional funds or help without clearly demonstrating the needs of the applicant group not receiving service. These occurrences are indeed unfortunate. They have sometimes led not only to unjustified curtailment of agency programs, but also to further questioning of the basic function of the agency and its role in the community social-service program.

An interesting sidelight in the acceptability of Jewish vocational services has been the application for services by non-Jews. In many agencies, the decision has been made by the lay boards to render such service as could be offered without serious curtailment of service to Jewish applicants. In some cases, strong expression has been made in favor of the public relations value to the Jewish community of the services rendered by the Jewish vocational agency to non-Jews. With only one minor exception, however, the agencies have not deviated from their basic function of serving Jewish people, and the numbers of non-Jews served have generally been fewer than five per cent of the total agency intake.

In the further definition of the Jewish clientele of the vocational agency may be found the total rationale for Jewish vocational services. In brief, the Jewish vocational agencies serve a clientele of Jewish job applicants who have special job problems because of employment discrimination, and Jewish clients who have special problems in the choice of a career because of employment discrimination and discriminatory practices of our educational and training institutions. The *primary* job of the Jewish vocational agency is *not* to combat discrimination directly, *not* to reduce discrimination by the direct reallocation of Jews to occupations in which there is little representation of Jewish workers, and, more obviously, *not* to improve the lot of Jewish job applicants by changing the general economic situation. The vocational agency may attain some of these goals indirectly. Its primary, direct task is to assist the individual Jewish client in securing a satisfactory job, or to assist the individual Jewish client in developing a satisfactory career plan.

In the application of the intake criteria of need and treatabilty, the young adult population has comprised the major portion of the vocational agency clientele. The young person faced with immediate decisions regarding career choice and the problem of finding a job is generally the client group felt by agencies to need vocational service urgently, and to be in a position to make immediate constructive use of the service.

Among persons in this general age group, probably the most urgent need for vocational services was presented by some of the veterans who applied in such vast numbers one and two years ago. Although veterans as such did not as a general rule receive service priority, their urgent problems often required immediate help. For example, veterans applying to the Cleveland JVS during 1946 almost completely cut out the in-school youth from our active client files. Yet this came about entirely on the basis of a case-by-case determination of need and treatability. Veterans and non-veterans went into the same file of those awaiting service. . . .

This experience underscores the fact that the Cleveland JVS, along with other vocational agencies, has not considered its clientele in terms of groups or categories, but in terms of individuals, each with his own set of needs. Service has been rendered to clients on basis of individual need, and not because of membership in any particular client group. Two possible exceptions to this policy should be cited: the client referred by another Jewish social agency, and the refugee. Most vocational agencies, having had some origins in case-work agencies, have given from the beginning precedence to clients referred by other agencies, and in no instance has this practice been modified. Priority of service to the refugee has likewise been a traditional and unchanging practice among the vocational agencies. It is important to note, however, that although these two client groups have enjoyed priorities in vocational service, the principle of individualized selective intake has not been badly violated. Most individuals in both groups have presented extremely urgent problems calling for immediate service. . . .

Such has been the character of the clientele of the Jewish vocational agencies. The nature of that clientele, and the problems met in defining the client group, should be marked by representatives of all functional fields who are interested in the broadening of the community served by social agencies.

The definition of *services* rendered by the vocational agencies has not engendered as many problems as the definition of the proper clientele. The primary services rendered by virtually all agencies are vocational counselling and job placement, in the generally accepted meaning of those terms.

Job placement service, because of its direct dependence upon the local economic scene, has varied tremendously in quantity and quality over the past ten years. With mass unemployment, broad job placement efforts were made in the employer group, and a major portion of time was allocated to the promotion of job openings. However, the job applicant group was large, leading at times to "streamlined" registration of job applicants. The war years reversed all those trends. The employer became the applicant solicitor, applicant loads were small, and frequently consisted of difficult-to-place persons, requiring a great deal of intensive work with each individual.

It is hoped that the more individualized type of placement service will continue to be rendered in the future, . . . and there is indication that this will actually occur in the increased professionalization of the worker operating in this area. . . .

In defining the job placement function, the vocational agencies have generally agreed that their job is to attempt to place any and all Jewish applicants who apply to the agency. Special efforts are made to place those who are difficult to place, on the basis of the conviction that such applicants need the agency service more than those who can be placed easily. In line with this thinking, there has been a healthy emphasis more recently on qualitative aspects of measuring the placement services, rather than an emphasis on large numbers of placements. The difficult-to-place clients are often transferred from a placement department to a counselling division, where more intensive service is possible. In some agencies, an intermediate type of service staffed by workers who are "special placement counsellors" has been developed to meet the more difficult placement problems.

One of the important aspects of the placement function which needs clearer definition is the role of the employer. Basically, the employer is secondary, or even incidental, in the placement service. Although the agency has the responsibility of maintaining professional and ethical standards in its relationships with employers, and will for its own effectiveness concern itself with good employer relations, it should be understood that the agency function is that of serving the job applicant, first and last. There have been one or two statements made by vocational agencies regarding services to employers which violate this very elementary principle.

While rendering job placement services to a wide range of Jewish applicants, most vocational agencies have taken pains to define their placement service as an added service available to Jewish people, rather than as the sole placement service in the community to be used by Jewish job-seekers. Most have taken concrete steps to encourage their Jewish clientele to apply as well at the local public employment office. This is in keeping with the generally accepted philosophy that the public agencies have the basic responsibility of providing vocational services, and that our voluntary vocational agencies have a supplementary, a complementary, and an additive role.

In further recognition of the primacy of the public employment service, many Jewish vocational agencies have been active in promoting improvement of the services available through the public agency, through participation in community advisory groups, and through promoting of pertinent legislation.

In providing vocational counselling services to young people, the vocational agencies have likewise reiterated the primary responsibility of the public agency—in this case the schools—to carry on this function. Through the development of specific demonstration programs, the encouragement of referrals through the schools, and follow-up work with the schools in carrying out students' vocational plans, the vocational agencies have attemped to educate the schools to a full awareness of this responsibility, and to assist them in developing their techniques to meet this responsibility.

The Jewish vocational agencies have been fighting on a broader and more important front for the promotion of more adequate vocational counselling services. Before the war the vocational agencies had developed counselling techniques which emphasized an individualized, non-authoritative approach; these techniques were closer to a case-work approach than the vocational guidance procedures then in vogue at schools and so-called vocational guidance clinics. With the end of the war, and the surge of demand from veterans for vocational reorientation, the worst aspects of the older technique were practiced. At many "guidance centers" sponsored by the Veterans Administration and universities, vocational guidance meant wholesale testing of clients and hurried vocational prescriptions written by ill-trained counsellors, who did not even attempt to identify the veteran's real vocational problem or its many complex motivations. The Jewish vocational agencies have been active both in professional circles and in community groups in combatting this injurious type of service, and in promoting a more sensitive, more complete, more professional approach.

There is also evidence that within the agencies themselves, advances have been made along these lines. Progress has been made in integrating psychological services more closely with counselling procedures, so that fewer psychologists are running their own separate offices within the agencies. Closer operating relationships and better mutual understanding between vocational and family agencies are evident. Finally, and most significantly, increased attention has been given to the training of vocational counsellors, with proper emphasis on field work and on more rounded academic training.

In addition to the primary services of vocational counselling and job placement, some of the vocational agencies have operated such related programs as "group guidance," vocational training, scholarship assistance, and small-business consultation.

The group vocational programs have had as their basic purpose the stimulation of thought among groups of young Jewish people regarding choice of occupations, and the dissemination of such valid occupational information as would assist the members of groups in making wise vocational choices. The primary skill of the "group-guidance" worker has been considered his knowledge of a wide range of occupations, although attempts have been made to assign workers to this field who have some group-work skills. Evaluation of such a program is difficult, and too often the number of referrals from such a program is difficult, and too often the number of referrals from such a program to the vocational agency for further service has been used as a criterion of success. Where this criterion has not been misapplied, and where the worker assigned to this service has been properly selected and oriented, the group vocational programs are thought to have positive intrinsic value.

Vocational training programs operated by the vocational agencies have been few in number. The agencies have rightfully turned to public and private training resources for all client training needs. To meet special client demands which could not as well be met otherwise, some agencies have set up training programs in such skills as sewing and jewelry work. Such programs have usually been necessitated by the special needs of a refugee group.

More recently, a few vocational agencies have assumed a larger responsibility of service in the area of scholarship loans to Jewish persons to assist them in training for their chosen occupations. This step was taken only after intensive community study, and was accompanied by an amalgamation of scholarship resources making for improved service to the total community. The vocational agency has assumed the task of evaluating the applicant's vocational plan, while a lay group has the final responsibility of passing on the application for funds.

One further extension of agency activity is found in the assumption of small business or self-employment advisory service. The offering of this type of service came as a natural outgrowth of the interest of some Jewish job applicants in opportunities for self-employment. Finding commercial resources for help in this area inadequate in many ways, some vocational agencies have developed small groups of businessmen who have offered to provide consultation where necessary. Agencies do not directly offer advice regarding plans for self-employment.

This overall, over-simplified review of the functions of the Jewish vocational agencies clearly indicates some progress in defining their clientele, services and skills. Some errors both in service and in interpretation of service have been made. But generally, the response of local communities has been positive. . . . Where disagreements have arisen because of local errors in service, or errors in interpretation of service to the local community, it is hoped that such errors will be recognized [as temporary and minimal]. It is also not too much to hope that local leaders of the Jewish community, both lay and professional, will lend our relatively young, relatively small vocational agencies the type of constructive assistance which leads to growth and maturation, rather than discipline and rejection when they err.

Finally, we record the hope that our work shall not be bound too much by either family-agency-mindedness or by the more traditional philanthropy-for-the-needy type of thinking, and that our Jewish vocational agencies will be permitted to act out their destined role of serving the total Jewish community.

5. Local Community Planning Towards an Integrated Health Program*

BY ROBERT MORRIS

. . . Four factors in the general health field which call for general community attention may be touched on briefly. First, there is the matter of desperate shortages of professional personnel. Since a

* *Jewish Social Service Quarterly*, vol. XXVI, no. 1 (Sept. 1949), pp. 169-75. Presented at the Annual Meeting of the National Conference of Jewish Social Welfare, Baltimore, Md., May 30-June 4, 1947.

community's health depends upon a skilled and trained health personnel, it naturally has an interest in such shortages. The situation varies from community to community and is different in rural and urban areas, but in general, there is an overall shortage of doctors with adequate specialized training to keep them abreast of modern developments in medical science. Although personnel tends to be concentrated in urban areas, even in cities there is a serious shortage of trained and registered nurses to staff hospitals and to meet private patient needs. Shortages of hospital beds are a little more difficult to assess. There is no adequate and established standard of bed ratio to population; but in many communities doctors must wait for long periods of time before they can admit patients for elective treatment, and treatment facilities for the chronically ill as well for patients with mental diseases are very inadequate.

A second area of general community interest is the continuous and steady growth of public understanding and public information on problems of health. While there is much yet to be desired, there is no doubt that the public is more health-conscious, continues to seek out doctors for preventive services, and is more ready to make use of hospital and clinical facilities than ever before. Much of the fear of hospitals and clinics and doctors is being slowly overcome. This growing public understanding has been furthered immeasurably by the rapid extension of hospital-insurance plans, which have brought hospital services within the reach of moderate-income groups in the community, and have enabled them to experience at first hand the use of good health facilities.

This extended public knowledge has, of course, placed a heavy strain upon medical institutions, since the demand for their services has grown so rapidly. This third factor contributes to the pressure for such expanded hospital construction.

A fourth area already touched upon has to do with the sometimes slow but very steady progress of science in the conquest of disease. This development has made the practice of medicine incredibly complex, and continues to demand the perfection of the most flexible and elaborate mechanisms for the treatment of disease. Research has continued to broaden. However, the understanding of what is needed to maintain and expand this steady conquest of science has not grown as rapidly in the minds and hearts of the community. There is still a wide gap between the general belief in using health services, and the understanding and support necessary to the growth of such facilities. . . .

Jewish health as well as welfare services are a very small part of the complex battery of services which the Jewish community uses in any city. Jewish philanthropy develops and supports institutions and agencies which cannot by any stretch of the imagination be expected to meet all of the needs of all of the Jewish residents. Despite this sharp limitation, Jewish hospitals and health agencies play a very important part in the extension of community-wide facilities. It is still true in this country that despite the rapid growth of public services, many needs of citizens still are met by programs supported by sectarian and voluntary philanthropy. As long as this is true to any extent, the responsibility of those who support voluntary sectarian philanthropy must be examined. . . .

The percentages of operating income received from the central financial bodies are varied and at first glance do not seem very important. Of all hospitals studied, there was an average of about twelve per cent total operating income received from Community Chests or Jewish Federations. Eight hospitals received twenty per cent or more of their total income from these sources, while thirteen received less than five per cent. Generally, hospitals in larger communities receive a larger proportion of their income from a central source, while hospitals in smaller communities tend to be more dependent upon patient income and other non-central sources of income. . . .[1]

However, the basis for Federation interest in hospital affairs is not limited to financial matters. In many communities, Federations, Welfare Funds, and Community Councils, as well as Community Chests and Councils of Social Agencies, are increasingly

[1] For more detailed statistics, see the *Yearbook of Jewish Communal Service,* published by the Council of Jewish Federations, 1946.

exercising a social planning role in relation to local services. During a period when hospitals confined themselves to the limited function of providing beds for sick people, there was more basis for considering hospitals as completely separate from other community affairs. However, the discussion today has already touched upon the expanding and changing role of the general hospital in the community. There is widespread consideration, and in a few places actual development, of hospital services in new areas. To mention only a few: providing top-notch research and medical care for the chronically ill, who no longer have to be housed in a general hospital; improved psychiatric treatment facilities in general hospitals; the bringing of psychiatric services into the total program of medical care of the general hospital; providing adequate home-care medical services in the homes of people who have serious disabling and chronic illnesses, rather than keeping them for prolonged care in expensive hospital beds; the extension of diagnostic and case-finding services, to assist general practitioners in the community to diagnose conditions of disease earlier in their early stages; services which call for more flexible use of hospital out-patient clinics and laboratories; and the provision of adequate medical care in homes for the aged and children's institutions. These, and a host of other developments of recent years, have brought the hospital into the closest association with other community agencies, family agencies, homes for the aged, nursing homes, and so on. As soon as one institution begins to rub elbows with several others in this way, many problems of planning, cooperation, and coordination arise. In very few instances does effective cooperation between such diverse organizations come about naturally or easily. In many communities, Federations are assuming an active role of responsibility in helping functional services of this kind come together and work together more effectively. The problems with which central organizations can help functional agencies in such a cooperative venture are, I hope, obvious. . . .

The second significant development in the field of medicine is the steady growth of the medical center idea. The medical center idea has many forms. In general, it reflects the need for some types of effective coordination of health institutions in a given community. This type of coordination or cooperation, if it is to be developed into an effective medical center, must be anchored in the most skillful and effective medical service that any community has to offer. In other words, it must be not only cooperative but scientific as well. In the Jewish field, there are no communities which have as yet put into operation a fully developed and comprehensive medical center. However, movement is proceeding steadily in that direction in all of the larger communities. The development of the medical center has followed two or three broadly defined paths. The first, which has received the greatest amount of attention to date, has been the development of a medical center through the expansion of the activity of a general hospital. This is possible only where the hospital has a predominant position of prestige and is known for a high level of service in a given community. In this situation various less developed institutions, such as chronic hospitals or nursing homes, have become directly affiliated or have merged with the general hospital and become specialized departments within that hospital.

A second line of development is in the partial merger of several independent medical institutions into one corporate entity. In this instance the new corporate entity, through a board and an executive staff, carries on certain centralized responsibilities which are delegated to it by the constituent members of the center. These responsibilities may concern personnel, bookkeeping, finance, housekeeping, and so on. The constituent institutions retain some independent identity through their own boards and professional staffs, which, on internal professional matters, are responsible only to themselves rather than to the center administration. The New England Medical Center in Boston is an example of such a plan.

A variation of this type of center is the assumption by one hospital of responsibility for medical service in affiliated agencies, leaving them full autonomy in all other matters. This is the direction of center development in St. Louis, and perhaps Boston.

A third line of development, which has been proposed only recently in communities such as Milwaukee and Boston, calls for the development of community health planning boards or committees which are a part of the central Federation. Such a planning body is composed of representatives of the various agencies which are concerned with health matters, as well as representatives of the Federation. On behalf of the entire community, this planning body then works out patterns of coordination and cooperation, sets working standards, and so on. The authority of the committee is usually advisory, and does not directly affect the autonomy of individual agencies. However, since it does provide a community-wide sounding board, it can play an important role in the furthering of community understanding and support. In particular programs it can assist agencies to cooperatively work out their differences, and can be considered an instrument for achieving more complete medical-center organization over an extended period of time. . . .

The sequence and planning of events [in any medical-center program] places a very real challenge before all communities—how to plan in a world of constant change. This challenge is not the concern of the hospital boards alone. In such a world, planning does not end with the erection of a handsome building. It continues daily, throughout the year, and involves the support of many scientific disciplines, the cooperation of many interests, and the understanding of all of us.

II Communal and Educational Developments

WHEN we turn away from the more narrowly defined welfare services to the area of Jewish community activities, we find many of the same trends and developments, but the issues take on a more controversial hue. The controversy is not, as in the past, between Jewish institutions and their external environment in a struggle for place and survival. Rather, it is a competition between several types of Jewish institutions, and involving multiple conceptions of the means to insure group continuity. Since American Jewish communities had, by this period, determined to maintain their cohesiveness, they faced the choice between religious, cultural, and educational tools to achieve this end. No "all or nothing" choice is implied in these alternatives, but the situation was such as to encourage rivalry among the relevant institutions—synagogue, school, and leisure-time cultural agency—as each sought to define its role and relative position in communal affairs.[1]

To cite an example, the debate outlined by Solender between community centers and synagogues over the place of the so-called synagogue-center in Jewish communal life can be viewed either as a conflict between religious and socio-cultural approaches to the subject, or as an attempt by one set of social institutions (e.g., the rapidly growing Conservative synagogues) to secure a larger share

[1] Although the context is quite different, the debates in this period bear some resemblance to the arguments about social adjustment on the East Side of New York, which were so provocative when Jewish settlement houses were established. See Part One, pp. 114-133.

of philanthropic funds in its competition with an earlier established institution, the community center. In some respects, the differences between the community and the congregational school can be viewed in the same light, the focus of the conflict here being the methods of scientific pedagogy employed by the communal schools versus the more traditional teaching methods of the synagogue.

These issues emerged obliquely in the Conference *Proceedings,* for the predominately religious spokesmen were not part of the Conference constituency. But the issues were heard nonetheless. Solender and Ruffman give comprehensive analyses, although they defend their own institutions strongly and selectively. Solender persuasively presents the case for the community center as an independent social and educational institution, while the argument for the rival synagogue-center was advanced in the periodicals of Conservative Judaism, [2] and in the budget and building plans of many synagogue congregations throughout the country. The synagogue-center proponents held that the central institution for Jewish continuity is the synagogue or the religious congregation, and that the diversity of Jewish life can be given adequate expression through the individual congregation. Such groups, it was felt, also constitute ethnic, national, and cultural units which have played a large part in Jewish history, and therefore should perpetuate their group values. It is taken for granted that these institutions will avail themselves of the best modern methods for education and for group organization, provided that such techniques serve to further congregational goals, and are not merely professional operations divorced from Jewish values. Modern pedagogy for religious education and modern methods for shaping the character of youth should be utilized, but each synagogue should have its own building for communal activities, its own school, and its own teaching staff and materials. To such advocates it was unreasonable to assume that all Jewish youths could share the same educational and cultural facili-

[2] See *Conservative Judaism,* vol. XVI, nos. 2 and 3 (Winter-Spring, 1962), "A Symposium on Relationships between the Synagogue and the Center"; and vol. XVII, nos. 1 and 2 (Fall-Winter, 1962), Jacob Neusner, "The Synagogue and the Center—The Symposium in Retrospect."

ties, manned by a neutral professional staff serving all equally alike. In such circumstances professional skills are not seen as primary, though they are accepted as useful.

The situation in Jewish education appears more flexible and less polemical, as the emergence of dominant congregational schools and of religiously supported all-day schools was absorbed within the framework of general educational theory. Educational analysis suggests that the trend toward advancement and experimentation, so well delineated by Ruffman, was probably due not so much to the rise of new ideological forces as to a simple problem in logistics. As Jewish populations were dispersed widely into suburban communities, their members had to recreate institutional forms to sustain their Jewishness. For such a purpose the earlier community religious school did not expand rapidly enough, and it seemed only natural to Jews, who of course built a synagogue when they moved, that they should attach to this new synagogue other functions not yet provided for them.

Similarly, the barrier between religious education and general community support was hurdled, perhaps slowly, but without major controversy. The consolidation of American Jewish life can be seen nowhere more vividly than in the recognition by Federations that they could finance religious education, in both communal and congregational settings, and should do so on a clearly rising scale of allocations. By this time, the one seriously divisive issue, that of governmental support of parochial education, engaged only extremist groups. Most spokesmen found a more suitable alternative in Jewish communal support. Federations were willing to increase their local service allocations, in contrast to the United Community Funds, whose local allocations continued to keep pace with price-level changes, but not with increased service requirements.

Perhaps the most widespread confrontation was between vertically organized national Jewish organizations (not only religious bodies, but welfare organizations as well such as the United Jewish Appeal, the national civil rights agencies, etc.), which supported their local units, and the horizontally organized local community enterprises such as the community center, community religious school, and Federation, which, in turn, encouraged cooperative efforts for commonly shared ends. This situation is dealt with at length by Pekarsky, who saw that planning on a national scale, to be effective, had to accord greater recognition to the problems and abilities of the local community agencies, and their role in shaping national affairs and policy.

Whatever lens is selected for viewing these subjects, however, it is clear that in the overall context, an affluent America was now tolerant and accepting of religious (if not of political or color) minorities. Moreover, the infusion into American Jewish life of new vigor from Orthodox and Conservative religious proponents coincided with the renewed Jewish self-awareness engendered by the creation and support of the new State of Israel. Both of these phenomena served to re-emphasize the significant role of the synagogue in group life. The earlier congregational isolation of the synagogue from modern concepts of pedagogy, group appeal, and character formation of youth began to disappear, and many synagogal groups sought to develop these skills for the furtherance of their own institutions.

The period ends on an olympian note of cultural exchange. Just as, in the first years of the century, Jewish institutions drew upon contributions from the cultural past of their organizers and blended them with borrowings from their American surroundings, so in the 1950's, Jewish Federations were recasting their functions in the light of the cultural needs of their constituents, and also guiding themselves by the experiences of the United Community Funds and Councils in an effort to resolve the dilemmas of national-local agency relationships, now seen as issues of contemporary American life, and not as sectarian issues at all.

1. Current National Trends Affecting Jewish Communities*

BY GEORGE W. RABINOFF

This paper will attempt to present a number of national trends which are influencing the entire American [Jewish] community. Political-economic-international developments [which have occurred] within the post-war decade are producing profound changes. Equally significant are the changes taking place in the social climate and the sociological setting within which the social services function; the organization of the community for social welfare is being modified accordingly in its philosophies and structure, its financing, and in its position in the community. It is interesting to speculate on how much the professionalization of community organization has been the product of these forces, and the extent to which professional leadership has influenced the course of action. . . .

In the United States, newly acquired and uncertain leadership in the political and economic field and dependence on the well-being of the world for the continuance of our high standard of living means that we must maintain what our government calls a "position of strength." Hopefully, other countries will share in the benefits, likewise work to achieve their maximum social and economic independence. This "new normality" requires a defense and military establishment such as we have never known before in peacetime; production for civil and military use must rise to ever higher levels with improved techniques, administrative effciency, better organization, and close interrelationship between labor and management. The resultant problems—the armaments race, the hazards of corporate and governmental concentrations and controls, the effects of the increased tempo on individual and family

* *Jewish Social Service Quarterly*, vol. XXX, no. 1 (Sept. 1953), pp. 19-25. Paper presented at the National Conference of Jewish Communal Service, Atlantic City, N.J., May 26, 1953.

personality and relationships—can only be resolved by forces beyond the ken of social welfare. . . .

[A related item is the population problem.] New immigration legislation has reversed our traditional attitude towards accepting the "outcasts" of the world so aptly expressed in the Emma Lazarus poem on the Statue of Liberty. According to the 1950 census, the shift from rural to urban centers continues, although 40 per cent of our people live in cities of 2,500 or less. Overall growth continues; we, too, have had an increased birth rate for the past dozen years. Is this a temporary bulge, incidental to the wars and the depression aftermath, or a reversal of a long-time trend? Is our "average size" family going to exceed 4.2, where it has hovered for several census periods? The population move is from the big cities to their suburbs; the big cities are losing, the metropolitan areas are gaining, and at an accelerated rate.

Incidental to the defense effort and the extension of industrial plants, a new crop of cities is springing up in open country areas and around small and previously self-contained villages. Under federal defense legislation, 231 places have been designated "critical housing areas" (as of January 1, 1953); the in-migration has been so great as to compel special provision for housing.

The average family in these new suburbs and new towns is younger and has more small children. The proportions of skilled and professional persons are higher, incomes above average. Mobility of population aside, these places are demonstrating that the people need welfare services, be they rich or poor. Personal and marital guidance, day-care centers, recreational, educational, and religious facilities are in great demand. These are rare opportunities for testing, experimenting, providing services to "normal" communities—new housing, new roads, new schools, new sewers and other utilities. We have had no such opportunity for integrating social welfare into town planning since federal legislation sent surveyors into the woods of the Northwest Territory (Ohio, Illinois, Indiana, Michigan, and Wisconsin), to lay out the new townships and allocate lots for schools, churches, and town halls.

Within the Jewish group we have no statistics on the move to the new towns, but the numbers are probably small. However, we know that clusters of suburban high-ratio Jewish population centers have grown up around practically all of the large cities and many of the small ones. Here is virgin territory for Jewish community organization. What kinds of Jewish services are these towns wanting and providing? Are they asking the old-line agencies for guidance, following time-worn patterns, or are they venturing into more indigenous cooperative and multi-service agencies? Are their relationships to their general communities of the same character as in the older places, or are they taking new forms?

What are the current trends in the social field that affect the services of the Jewish communities? We note the shifts in age distribution among the general population, the continuing rise in the ratio of older people, and the drop in the birth rate during the thirties, evident today in the smaller proportion of young people. The birth rate rose again in the forties, bringing overcrowded elementary and high schools and an unpredictable future. Second is the health situation, which shows a continuing decline in death rates. Medical science is making important advances, and the principles of public health and preventive medicine are being more widely understood and practiced; researches in the degenerative diseases are bringing results comparable to the earliest victories over infant mortality and the infectious diseases. More people are living longer; work and retirement habits and attitudes are being accommodated, avocational interests being cultivated. Third is the favorable economic situation as income strives to keep pace with higher living costs and taxes. Equilibrium is being sought in the higher ranges of the production-consumption spiral. Fuller employment and higher standards of living round out this series, with some question of prospects if the lines should turn downward. Data on these phenomena, as they affect Jews, are non-existent or spotty.

This brings us to the Federal Social Security system, which has been the largest single factor conditioning the Jewish social services as well as the general welfare programs. The federal-state-city coverage of the basic need categories of dependent children, the blind, old age, and since 1950, the permanently and totally disabled, now reaching some two and one-half million beneficiaries, has largely eliminated relief as a function of private social agencies. These measures are supplemented, unevenly in manner and quality, by local authorities, through general assistance for persons ineligible for the social-security categories. Old Age and Survivors Insurance, completely federal in administration and based on the contributory principle, is now covering 80 per cent of the nation's paid civilian jobs; over four and one-half million individuals were drawing monthly benefits under its provisions as of June 30, 1952. As OASI is extended, and more persons are protected when they reach retirement age, old age assistance, aid to dependent children, and the other security categories are declining. This raises new questions about categorical relief, since it limits the unprotected group largely to persons with particular and individual problems requiring technical attention beyond the capacity of untrained or semi-trained persons carrying large case loads.

Public outdoor relief, as it was known before the security system took over, has become an integral part of our body politic; it is no longer challenged in principle. Operating standards and methods have improved in adminstration, in personnel, in in-service and other training programs, and even in community understanding. No longer is it taken for granted that there must be great disparity between the public and the voluntary agencies. We may still reach the level where social security against life's hazards is accepted as normal. . . .

These past several years have witnessed mounting attacks on public assistance, based reputedly on humanitarian, political, or economic considerations. The attackers insist that local administration, without federal subsidy or controls, would result in smaller assistance rolls and reduced relief expenditures. Exposing the assistance lists would also cut relief loads, say these advocates. Furthermore, they assert that relief is demoralizing, encourages illegitimacy and recklessness. To cap their argument, they look with alarm at rising taxes, which they assert are inhibiting commerce and industry; the economy cannot afford to carry so large a proportion of the population on a non-productive basis. The evidence thus far available from the states which have opened their public assistance records does not bear out the first contentions; nor can we ignore the extent to which welfare expenditures (some $16 billions annually, taking into account all social security, veteran's aid, railroad retirement, and the ongoing welfare and related services) make a decent life possible, directly for the persons lacking other sources of support, and indirectly for the rest of us, through the added strength such protection gives to our total economy. On the other hand, it is basic to the concept of any governmental service that it requires periodic examination, and this may be the time to do it. It is going to be done in any case, and it behooves its friends to assure competent and adequate evaluation.

No statistics are, or could be, available as to the participation of Jews in the social securities. Be it in proportion to population, or less, as is more likely, the Jewish community has a heavy stake in these equities.

Another recent trend affecting the security of Jewish individuals is the expansion of welfare and retirement funds under cooperative, corporate, or union stimulus and controls. With some measure of governmental regulation, they are reaching increasingly larger numbers of the population. They are a standard feature of our American "way of life," adding another buffer against unpredictable hazards. Also included in this category are the cooperative health insurances—Blue Cross, Blue Shield and others. Although they are still expanding, these programs still reach only a minority of the population, according to the recent report of the President's Commission on Health.

The trends in the technical phases of social work can hardly be detailed within our theme. We can note that technical proficiency rates increasingly high; standards are being tested and questioned but accepted; and methods are ever more refined in group work, case work, and the other techniques. Specialized training for social work is coming of age, both in the technical and in the professional sense. The trade and mechanical "know-how" phases are being balanced by emphasis on wisdom and statesmanship. The keen inquiries and suggestions made in the Hollis-Taylor [1] study of social-work education in the United States (1951) contributed handsomely to this goal, which is being advanced by the new Council on Social Work Education. Are the Jewish agencies, who are well in the fore of this technical procession, any clearer as to their basic Jewish function? Is continuing existence of the Jewish agency still being rationalized because there exist other sectarian agencies, and because some Jewish clients prefer to be served by a Jewish agency? We know that there has been a breakdown of the old rule under which Jewish agencies accepted only Jewish clients, except in the hospitals, and Jewish clients went only to Jewish agencies. Technical progress, among other forces, seems to have shuffled case loads, staff, boards, finances, and other agency elements to the point that Jewish agencies are largely indistinguishable from others.

Community organization has seen many major developments. The Jewish Federation, Jewish Welfare Fund, and Jewish Community Council, were all forms that evolved to meet specific phases of Jewish relationships to American life—i.e., the local services, the special Jewish and overseas needs, and the Jewish community relations, internal and external respectively. All three phases have been influenced profoundly in structure and operation by the trends cited in these pages, as Jews have integrated into normal community groupings, as overseas pressures have stabilized, and as intergroup relations have been found to affect all groups as well as Jews. The more assured status of Jews has undoubtedly brought them to a greater measure of community participation. Jews and Jewish communities have benefited from the favorable economic climate, improved standards of living and of health, and

[1] One of several studies of social work education issued as a report by the Council of Social Work Education, and published as Ernest V. Hollis and Alice L. Taylor, *Social Work Education in the United States* (New York, Columbia University Press, 1951).

show greater interest in the affairs of the world. They have shared in the evolution of the social securities and in the concern for their present evaluation.

Recent trends in the Community Chest field are of more immediate interest. Most Chests started in the post-World War I period as contributors' protective associations, but they have pretty well come out of that stage. The National War Fund and the rapid burgeoning of huge national health agencies have precipitated democratizing processes, and an increasing sense of community obligation. The standard Chest today is a true community servant, governed by an increasingly representative board of citizens as trustees of community needs and interests. With its affiliate, the Welfare Planning Council, the Chest is concerned with public and voluntary health and welfare programs, and conceives of them as supplementary and complementary, rather than competitive. It recognizes organized labor as a major policy-making partner, a channel for wide community support in program and money. The trend of Chest support is up, after a pre-war decline; the concentration of income in corporations and in employee groups has brought these two sources of support to the point where they are providing practically 70 per cent of all Chest income. . . .

Few would hold that the Chest-Councils and their national body, Community Chests and Councils of America, even when joined by the National Social Welfare Assembly and its 68 affiliated national organizations, are adequate to serve the huge galaxy of voluntary welfare effort. Welfare planning has the limitations of other phases of the democratic process, dealing as it does with the inequalities and the variables of human relations. However, rooted in the people, responsive to their needs and to their expression thereof, it seems to be basically sound.

The American Jewish community, indigenous to American life, made up of individuals and agencies constantly exposed to all of these national trends, is undoubtedly accommodating its practices and philosophies to them. It is certain that these trends are sufficiently all-pervading to require careful cultivation of channels of communication between the Jewish community agencies and the general community groups. Jewish communal services have affected general community developments, and have been affected by them. That tendency must be encouraged, despite intensified professionalization on both sides. Community isolation is a hazard; it must be guarded against, as part of the process of strengthening and further professionalizing the Jewish community and its agencies. It is of concern to keep the issue before the Conference, and to give leadership in this process.

2. The Place of the Jewish Community Center in Jewish Life*

BY SANFORD SOLENDER

We have entered a fruitful and challenging era for Jewry, climaxing a century both of tragedy and of tremendous progress. Out of the cross-currents of change have come the potentialities for a period of creativity and fulfillment unparalleled in our American experience. But realization of these possibilities requires identifying our assets, fully utilizing them, and carefully correlating all our efforts. Against this background we shall consider the place of the Jewish community center in America today, and its relationships with other Jewish organizations.

From our earliest beginnings on these shores, we American Jews have been adapting our Jewish heritage to life in a democracy. . . . We have accommodated our ideas and institutions to the voluntarism and freedom of America. We have created many social instruments to facilitate this process and to meet our [unique] requirements. We have replaced the legacy of [communal] so-

* *Journal of Jewish Communal Service,* vol. XXXIV, no. 1 (Fall, 1957), pp. 36-54. Presented at the Annual Meeting of the National Conference of Jewish Communal Service, Atlantic City, May 1957.

cial organization inherited from a self-contained and relatively isolated European ghetto life by the adaption of old institutions and the development of new ones to satisfy our modern needs. . . .

The Distinctive Role of the Jewish Community Center

1. The center and the Jewish person. The Jewish community center is an institution indigenous to our American Jewish experience and one which is peculiarly well-suited to meet many basic modern Jewish needs. Dr. Salo W. Baron refers to it as ". . . a major American contribution to Jewish life in the emancipation era."[1]

The center can be understood first in terms of its capacity to affect in a positive manner the development of the personality of the Jew through Jewish group experience with skilled leadership. Serving persons of all ages in varied, natural, and voluntary groupings, and basing its programs upon individual interests and needs, the center can have an important influence upon the healthy growth of the Jewish people. It can help individuals to better relate to one another, to groups, and to the community. The educational impact of experience in center activities can mature youthful participants, and can further healthy personal adjustment.

A wide range of personal needs can be satisfied in center programs, whether they pertain to physical well-being, rewarding association with others, the broadening of cultural horizons, or the intensification of civic participation. Through its service to individuals in Jewish groups, the center can foster identification of the Jew with his group, greater knowledge of his Jewish heritage, and involvement in many aspects of Jewish group and communal life. Jewish persons who have only an inchoate feeling of Jewish identification, but no formal relationship with synagogues or other Jewish groups—the so-called unaffiliated Jews—can find in the center an entree to Jewish participation which may lead to a wide variety of

[1] Salo W. Baron, "The American Experience," p. 477 in *Great Ages and Ideas of the Jewish People,* ed. by Leo W. Schwarz (New York, 1956).

Jewish interests. The breadth of experience open to individuals in center programs, bearing simultaneously on universal and Jewish needs, can contribute to the unity of the personality of the Jew. By providing enduring values for individuals through the significant use of their leisure time, through recreation, and informal group association, the Jewish community center can enrich their lives immeasurably.

2. The center and the Jewish group. The Jewish community center is well suited to the satisfaction of the group-life needs of the Jewish people, in particular the need for positive and active Jewish identification. In our "group-oriented" society, persons achieve identity by association with many types of large and small groups. Jews join Jewish groups to reinforce their connection with the Jewish people, whether merely through Jewish friendships, or more formally through affiliation with the Jewish community. The center is able to help a cross-section of Jewish groups to increase the value of their programs and to fortify their relationship to Jewish life.

The center has the potential resources for fostering Jewish cultural advancement in America. By its influence on Jewish organizational programs, the center can increase awareness of [and participation in] Jewish cultural expression in the arts. . . . By broadening and educating the audience for Jewish cultural endeavor in America, and through workshops and other cultural activities, the center may ultimately stimulate greater musical, dramatic, and other artistic activity in a characteristically American Jewish idiom.

The center can be an important force for advancing sound Jewish communal growth in America. Because of the representativeness of its constituency, the center is a microcosm of the Jewish community. Individuals and groups in the center thus are associated with a Jewish community in miniature, a valid setting in which to nurture sound communal identification and unity. Participation in the center's recreational, cultural, and community activities by members of various congregations and organizations can broaden the scope of Jewish associations, and can foster Jewish unity based upon respect for Jewish differences. The center program can increase understanding of Jewish problems, encourage participation in Jewish affairs, discover and train Jewish leadership, and teach enlightened Jewish citizenship.

The center can further the identification of Jews with the total community, founded on Jewish self-acceptance and self-respect. It can demonstrate the harmony of Jewish and democratic values as it stimulates its members to participate in broad civic affairs, and advances relationships between Jew and non-Jew through intergroup activities. As part of the recreational resources of the general community and as a participant in the Community Chest and Council of Social Agencies, the center represents Jewry in the family of community leisure-time activity.

Distinguishing Characteristics of the Center

The uniqueness of the center [2] lies in the fact that it does these things within a framework which: (1) Recognizes the vital place of leisure in our life and of the importance of programs which enable people to benefit from the satisfactions and values inherent in certain leisure-time pursuits.

(2) The center accepts the fact that the personal interaction which results from group association is significant. . . .

(3) The center is committed to the conviction that the service of professionally trained social-group workers is essential, if the above values are to be gained from group association. Trained social workers with insight into human behavior, group dynamics, and community life, who possess professional skill in work with individuals, groups, and communities, are best equipped to help persons satisfy basic Jewish needs through group experience. A

[2] For a more complete development of the distinctive character of the Center see the writer's "The Unique Function of the Jewish Community Center," National Jewish Welfare Board (New York City, 1955).

corner-stone of the center's distinctiveness is its utilization of the knowledge and skill of social work for the discharge of its functions.

(4) Inasmuch as the center is sponsored by the whole community, it is obligated to make its services available to all members of that community. This enables the center to work with Jewish groups in a manner different from that of any other body concerned with Jewish group experience. The center can function as the expert group-work resource for the Jewish community, dedicated to aiding all types of Jewish organizations to enrich the Jewish group association afforded their members. For this reason, the center is usually regarded as the "chosen instrument" of the official Jewish community for group-work service: the agency is assigned responsibility by and on behalf of the organized community for providing service in this area.

(5) The center provides specialized facilities designed exclusively for group-work programs, administered so as to enhance such service, and always available for these programs.

(6) The center has a high degree of mobility and adaptability, and a capacity to move and change with its members and to shape its services to new needs and locations. It is concerned with constant appraisal of community changes, and social planning with broad participation by other social agencies and organizations.

(7) The center has an informed lay leadership, for whom the accomplishment of center goals is of primary interest. . . .

(8) The Jewish community center is identified with a national movement of centers dedicated to similar goals on behalf of Jewish life and operating through a national body, the National Jewish Welfare Board.

Importance of Service to the Group Life of the Jew

The importance of the need of Jews for Jewish identification and association, and of their leisure time and group life as an opportunity to satisfy this need, is attested to by the interest of other Jewish institutions in this area. This is an appropriate concern for many of these groups. On the other hand, duplication and serious overlapping causes needless waste and is detrimental to community life. The needs of the Jewish community are met best by specialized community services, which have well-defined and generally accepted functions. There should be close interrelationship between all agencies, but the association should be based upon the employment of each by the other as discreet, competent, and responsible organizations with a mutuality of concerns. Representative community planning must be employed to determine needs, the competency required to meet them, and the institutions best able to satisfy these requirements. Individuai and group needs are served best by this approach, and resources are used to best advantage. Each service is more effective by virtue of its relative freedom from competitive concerns, its broad acceptance, and the advantages resulting from cooperative endeavor.

Jewish Community Center and the Synagogue

We turn now to the relationships of centers to other organizations interested in this field. We will first consider the synagogue, since its concern with the leisure-time [of its congregation] sometimes impinges upon the area of activity of the Jewish community center. The position of the synagogue *vis-à-vis* the Jewish community center can be better understood if we can clarify the respective functions of the synagogue and the Jewish community center in American Jewish life. This paper does not presume to attempt a [comprehensive or definitive] statement on the functions of the synagogue. Such a definition falls within the province of our religious leadership, though it is doubtful that there can be any single interpretation.

It is likely that there is unanimity that the synagogue has a fundamental role with respect to the religious and Jewish educaional needs of its members. But the aspiration of some synagogues to a major center role requires closer examination. . . . Among religious leaders, and particularly those in the rabbinate, there are several conceptions of the role of the synagogue with respect to leisure time and recreational services for its members. The first ascribes to the synagogue functions which are primarily religious and educational. It holds that it is appropriate for the synagogue to sponsor related supplementary group activities, such as brotherhoods, women's auxiliaries, and congregational youth groups, which strengthen congregational adherence and increase participation in religious activities. According to a second viewpoint, the synagogue should embrace the *totality* of Jewish activity, including center work. It is from this view that the "Synagogue-Center" concept flows. In the first approach, it may be assumed that primary responsibility for leisure-time and group-work service under Jewish auspices belongs to the Jewish community center, and that there is no conflict between the synagogue and the center. In fact, there are rich opportunities for cooperation between the two. The second alternative poses the greater threat of conflict and therefore requires examination.

Basis for Establishing Synagogue-Centers

A review of the factors which motivate congregations to establish synagogue-centers can throw light on this problem. For some leaders who have spoken recently on this matter, especially among the rabbinate, the synagogue-center aspiration is based upon a philosophical conviction about the nature of Jewish life and the place of the synagogue in it. This defines Jewish life now—and increasingly so in the future—as essentially religious in character. It minimizes such concepts as "peoplehood," "Judaism as a civilization," or other definitions which view Jewishness as a blending of religion, culture, group identification, and ethnic factors. Those inspired by this concept believe that the synagogue should be the center of all that is Jewish. This viewpoint has far-reaching implications, not only for the replacement of the Jewish community center by the synagogue, but eventually for the substitution of synagogue activities for many other programs and services now conducted by communal agencies.

The school of thought which holds that Jewish life in America in the future will be exclusively religious in character emphasizes its belief that this is the norm of Christian society—which will shape the milieu of the Jew.[3] There are many who take exception to this viewpoint. However, it is of interest to note that even if we hold this hypothesis as correct, the American pattern strongly indicates a trend towards secular organizations committed to the enrichment of the life of the religious groups which function outside the church. The experience of the YM and YWCA's reflects this very fact. Thus, even within an exclusively religious context, the function of the Jewish community center is distinct from that of the synagogue.

In general, however, one cannot help but be impressed with the highly speculative character of the predictions being made regarding the future of Jewish life. We strongly suspect that a pragmatic approach provides the soundest guidance for institutional planning —an approach which appraises Jewish needs, and employs the most up-to-date knowledge in meeting them.

The remarkable growth of Jewish interest and affiliation in recent years is a gratifying phenomenon. It has manifested itself in the membership and programs of congregations, community centers, and other forms of Jewish activity. It is apparent that overall it is a search for Jewish identity—for ways to give meaning to Jewishness, and to enrich the Jewish dimension of life. This opens new vistas of opportunity for service by all of these institutions, each of which brings something distinctive to the task. The [group-oriented] nature of this need points to the unique capacity of the Jewish community center to contribute to meeting it.

In reality, practical rather than philosophical considerations seem to be the stimuli for organizing synagogue-centers. Much synagogue affiliation today is motivated by a wish for Jewish identi-

[3] Will Herberg, "The Triple Melting Pot," *Commentary* (August 1955), and "America's New Religiousness," *Commentary* (September 1955).

fication and contact, rather than for [an exclusively] religious experience. Herbert J. Gans speaks of the fact that "the people who flock to the synagogues go there not so much to practice the traditional Judaic religion, as to feel and express their Jewishness —both for themselves and their children."[4] This causes many congregations to place great emphasis on their center plans, a tacit acknowledgment that this, rather than the religious appeal, is a prime attraction to membership. Competitive congregations can quickly gain an advantage by utilizing this appeal, and synagogues often virtually are forced, although reluctantly, into the center area. Marshall Sklare points out that "the successful congregation must have active affiliated organizations to serve as an inducement for synagogue affiliation."[5]

Provision for the children and young people in the family also is a primary reason for synagogue affiliation. But religious activities touch only a small fraction of the children and youth. The formal school reaches most of the children, but [Jewish education is pursued by] only an insignificant proportion of youth above bar mitzvah or confirmation age. In the search for programs that may engender response from the young, synagogues try (though for the most part fruitlessly) to stress the center and social activity aspects of their work. Such an interest in forming a center often arises less from a belief in the inherent merit of this program than from an anxious search for something to fill the gap created by the lack of response to the religious and educational programs.

Fund-raising considerations also play an important role in the formation of synagogue-centers. Because social factors are primary motivations for synagogue affiliation, successful fund-raising for buildings used for social purposes necessitates promoting the construction of facilties which will satisfy this interest. Nathan Glazer, writing of post-war synagogue construction, pointed out that in these buildings "the schools and community center facilities

[4] Herbert J. Gans, "American Jewry—Present and Future," Part 1, *Commentary* (May, 1956).

[5] Marshall Sklare, *Conservative Judaism* (Glencoe, Illinois, 1955).

often loom larger than the house of worship itself." [6] Many synagogues call themselves "Jewish Centers" because this name is more attuned to people's interests than such appellations as "temple" or "synagogue."

Except for the limited number of situations in which the synagogue-center is based upon philosophical conviction, it is a product of expediency rather than of principle. One often suspects that there is little understanding on the part of sponsors of what is involved in creating a synagogue-center, or any serious consideration of the implications of erecting such structures. The center aspect appears to be an incidental factor which is deemed necessary for the success of the primary goal of the congregation—to build a large and impressive synagogue building.

In a number of new, developing suburbs, Jewish residents, moved by a genuine concern for the various Jewish services they require, attempted to establish a single institution which could encompass the functions of the synagogue, school, welfare fund, and center. However, as the suburb has grown, and its institutions have multiplied and diversified, it has become clear that these efforts—while deserving understanding and respect—cannot provide a satisfactory answer to the community's needs.

The Functioning of the Synagogue-Center

These conclusions seem to be confirmed by the experience of most congregations which have planned synagogue-centers, raised substantial sums for them, and built large buildings in which center facilities are featured. Irrespective of their motives, the center commitment of most has been only nominal. They have not developed and sustained significant center services. Their center-type programs are limited in number, generally inferior in quality, and serve relatively small numbers, mainly members of the congregation. Professionally trained social-group workers are lacking al-

[6] Nathan Glazer, "The Jewish Revival in America," *Commentary* (December, 1955).

most completely, and group leadership is inadequate. Center facilities are restricted in their availability, and often are little used. Genuine interest in center work usually is absent on the part of most of the synagogue's leadership, whose prime concern is with the congregation's religious and educational activities. The center program has a low priority in interest and support as compared with other congregational activities. While scientifically determined conclusions are impossible, an overview of synagogue-centers in the country raises a serious question as to whether the "synagogue-center movement" in American Jewish life has proved to be no more than the theoretical promise or unrealized ambition of its sponsors. . . .

Jewish Community Center and Synagogue-Center Compared

The difference in performance of the group work and leisure-time services of Jewish community centers and of the synagogue centers in America is not accidental. The vastly greater success of center programs operated under *communal* auspices as opposed to those sponsored by *synagogue-centers* can be understood by a comparison of the characteristics of each. Such a comparison will reveal the essential dissimilarities between them and the appropriateness and suitability of the Jewish community center as the setting for organized Jewish group work and recreational and leisure-time services.

Sponsorship and Purposes

Turning first to the sponsorship of center work, the Jewish community center's community outlook and responsibility embrace the total community. By contrast, the synagogue's sponsorship is particularistic and limited, directed at those who share its denominational commitment. It represents a circumscribed segment of the community, is responsible only to its own membership, and often is institutionally rather than communally oriented.

To examine the purposes of each as regards center work, the community center is a social agency concerned with the development of the individual and the community, which views Jewish group experience as essential to the achievement of this end. The constructive use of this experience is the main interest and function of the center. Recognizing the close relationship between the spiritual, cultural, and social growth of the individual, the center is actuated by a concern for the development of the whole person. It fosters community values, integration of the many dividing tendencies within Jewry, understanding between Jewish groups, unity within Jewish life, and relationships with the general community. The synagogue, on the other hand, considers religious and educational programs as its primary concern, and group experience as secondary to these purposes. Work with groups is not regarded as having intrinsic value, but more as a means for maintaining synagogue adherence. Congregational group activities tend to focus on religious content, attitudes, and knowledge, and to be "subject-matter centered," rather than "individual-personality focused" or "relationship-centered." Whereas the community center views Jewish life in broad and inclusive terms, the purposes and program of the synagogue are oriented to the needs of its particular congregation.

Methods and Program

. . . The Jewish community center emphasizes intensive social-group-work practice. Knowledge and values are transmitted, and personality development is furthered by group experiences. Concentration is upon voluntary group associations, with concern for the principles of group composition and homogeneity. The community center utilizes a permissive approach. Members have opportunity to question and challenge and to experiment with ideas and solutions to problems: to grow in their understanding through experience under able leadership. The community center emphasizes the *process* as well as the *content* of program planning and development.

In the congregational center, the method of work with groups generally is more formal, tending even to the didactic. There is less encouragement to challenge and question, especially in discussions of religious doctrines and practices. Emphasis is upon transmission of concepts and practices, and the method of doing so is often doctrinnaire. In the congregational center there is little concern for the nature of groupings, and the stress is on large groups. . . .

The congregational center program is based far less on membership interests, needs, and background, inasmuch as program content is often predetermined by the philosophy and doctrine of the congregation. Moreover, in the synagogue, program activities are more narrow and limited in scope, and center-type programs generally are focused upon youth rather than upon the whole age range. Programs usually are fragmentary and episodic, lacking careful planning and unity. Heavy emphasis is placed upon mass programming, rather than on a wide range of group experiences. Abraham Fleischman, commenting in 1951 on a study of synagogue-center programs, referred to "the lack of special interest groups, such as those organized for dramatics, arts and crafts, etc." [7] On this same subject, Sklare writes: "Most Conservative synagogues have been satisfied to leave elaborate leisure time programming to the Jewish community center. . . . It [the synagogue] carries on only as much of a center program as is necessitated by the desire of its own adherents, the need to attract new members, the competition of other congregations, and the strength of the center movement in the community." [8]

[7] Abraham A. Fleischman, "The Challenge of Youth Activities to the Synagogue Center," *Reconstructionist* (November 16, 1951).

[8] Marshall Sklare, *Conservative Judaism*, pp. 138-39.

Constituency

With respect to constituency, there are pronounced differences between the Jewish community center and the synagogue-center. In the former, membership is inclusive and covers a broad cross-section of the community. The nondoctrinal, generic Jewish outlook of the center makes it a hospitable base for participation of Jews with varied backgrounds and viewpoints, and persons with both religious and secular outlooks may find a common meeting ground in the community center. . . . Its constituency is drawn heavily from families with congregational affiliations, and the whole range of synagogues is represented amply in its membership. Families who are not synagogue-affiliated are also actively involved in center programs. Some synagogue leaders have appraised the constituency of the center inaccurately, as the following quotation indicates: "No longer do they [Jewish community centers] constitute the social, recreational, and cultural center of the entire Jewish community. They will tend to attract and serve mainly the 'unaffiliated' young people of those loosely organized synagogues which concentrate on the religious needs of the grandfather rather than those of the grandson. . . . In such [large] communities, they [Jewish community centers] are needed as the social and recreational center of people affiliated with program-less synagogues." [9] An analysis of the comprehensive nature of center membership reveals that this [description is inaccurate].

In a congregational center, the constituency is limited mainly, if not entirely, to the congregation's own membership. There is a tendency for synagogue-center participation to be narrow in scope, in contrast to the inclusiveness of the center. Marshall Sklare comments that "congregationalism is *incompatible* with the center concept, for . . . the local religious group tends to form a *social unit*. As a result, while the institution does not become an exclusive organization, the strain towards homogeneity in respect to

[9] Max Arzt, "The Center in Contemporary Jewish Life," *Judaism*, (Fall, 1954), p. 485.

class and status is strong."[10] The breadth of involvement in the community center, which contrasts so sharply with the restricted participation in the congregational center, enables the former to provide a totally different Jewish experience. It should be noted, also, that participation in group activities by non-Jewish friends can come about more easily and naturally in the community center, whereas the congregational setting is far from a congenial one in this respect. Vigorous rejection of such participation is not uncommon in the congregational center. Moreover, in large metropolitan areas, where service in a definable neighborhood is involved, the community center can focus its services upon the neighborhood as a social unit—an approach not feasible for the congregation.

Personnel

Comparison between the two organizations reveals the difference between them in professional personnel used in center work. Social work is the primary professional discipline to which the Jewish community center is committed. Professional competence for the community-center worker is rooted in specialized preparation for social-group-work practice, within the context of the goals of the Jewish community center. Other disciplines such as education (health education, adult education, nursery education, etc.) have an important function in the community center, and operate within the social-group-work context. . . .

In the congregation, on the other hand, the primary professional disciplines [utilized in center work] are those of the rabbinate and the teacher. Group activities are usually directed and led by them, or by less trained or completely untrained workers, but certainly not by personnel with social-work interest or capacity. [Outside] personnel assigned to this work is usually employed on a part-time basis, and for only part of the year. The organizational structure and practice needed to underpin social-work services are absent in the congregational center, and competent supervision of staff usu-

[10] Sklare, *op. cit.*, p. 138.

ally is lacking. The congregation naturally is identified with the general religious community, rather than with a social-work community. A center operated under congregational auspices has little opportunity to provide the impact and stimulation which result from participation in [dynamic group experience].

It is important to note that the mere addition of a trained social worker to a synagogue-center staff does not alter this situation. In view of the synagogue's different approach to the purposes, concepts, and functions of the program, a trained social worker would find himself on a lonely island in a congregational setting. . . .

Lay Leadership, Financing, and Structure

The contrast [in orientation of center work] between the two organizations also is evident in the lay leadership which each provides. The primary concern of the leaders of the Jewish community center or agency is the center program, and for them it is not a lesser or secondary interest in an organization with other purposes. They acquire specialized knowledge about center work and the capacity for creative leadership in this area because this is the dominant focus of the agency. Special efforts are made to recruit and train board members for enlightened community center leadership through board member institutes, manuals, and similar approaches. The center's leadership is drawn from all sections of Jewish communal life, and the structure of its leadership is democratic.

In the congregation, the primary commitments of the lay leadership are to the religious and school programs. In the community center, the board is concerned entirely with the center program, and gives its prime attention to this, whereas the top board of the congregation has minimum interest in or time for the center function, which is relegated to sub-committees. Frequently, the new, young, and less influential leaders are assigned to the center committees. In this connection, Abraham Fleischman remarks that the adult youth activities committees in the synagogue-centers he studied "met very infrequently and had little prestige in the institution. Little opportunity was given to them to report at meetings of the Board of Directors, and the laymen who were interested lacked sufficient guidance and stimulation." [11] Under these circumstances, the center program is unlikely to gain the recognition, understanding, and support which it warrants and can only hope to achieve where it is the primary focus of lay interest.

The differences between these organizations are reflected in their fiscal structure as well. Community-wide participation in the community center, and maintenance of sound standards of work require a budget combining community subsidy and self-support, with a fee structure which assures the availability of the center to all. The communal auspices of the community center enable it to receive Community Chest and Jewish Welfare Fund grants, which are essential to such a financial arrangement. . . .

The congregational center must be totally self-supporting, since it is not eligible for Community Chest or Jewish Welfare Fund allocations. Thus, its fees tend to be too great for certain economic and social groups. Moreover, because other functions have a higher priority upon congregational funds, the center service in a synagogue-center receives only those monies available after the needs of the religious and educational programs have been satisfied. With rare exceptions, funds assigned to center work are insufficient to even begin to maintain a center program of high quality. Irving Brodsky made the following statement in a recent article on this subject: "In a new building costing over $300,000, in a heavily populated Jewish neighborhood, the youth program budget to serve 300 young people was about $1,500 a year. (It is unfortunately typical of many synagogue-centers, with elaborate structures and large budgets, that an infinitesimal proportion of their budget is expended for recreational youth services)." [12] This confirms Abraham Fleischman's earlier findings which pointed out

[11] Abraham A. Fleischman, *op. cit.*

[12] Irving Brodsky, "Experimenting in Cooperation Between Synagogue and Center," *The Reconstructionist,* vol. XXII, no. 20.

"the very meager percentage . . . of the budget used for this program as about three per cent of the total."[13] It is economically unfeasible for a synagogue to support a center program operated according to sound standards. . . .

Facilities

Finally, the comparison of the facilities of the two types of center programs reveals their further differences. Jewish community center buildings are planned exclusively for center purposes. The size of given areas, their relationship to one another, types of space planned, and the facilities and equipment of community center buildings are tailored for center work. The center program always has priority in the use of the facilities of the community center building, and there is a permissive attitude about the use of the facilities which is conducive to the atmosphere of freedom so essential to successful group work, especially with youth.

The facilities of the congregational center are primarily designed to accommodate religious and educational activities, and planning for center use follows these considerations. Use of synagogue buildings for center programs generally requires adapting space designed mainly for other uses to the requirements of the group-work program. Severe limitations on the suitability of synagogue-center buildings for center purposes are common. Likewise, the constant use of synagogue-center buildings for school purposes sharply curtails their usefulness for center purposes. The understandable priority which is given to the use of assembly halls and other congregational space for weddings, bar mitzvahs, and other synagogue activities reduces their availability for center purposes, and prevents their sustained and planned employment for center service. In addition, restrictions generally are imposed on the freedom of groups using synagogue facilities, especially youth, in order to protect the facilities for more formal use. This is quite the opposite of the relaxed and permissive atmosphere which prevails in the

[13] Abraham A. Fleischman, *op. cit.*

community center. We may also note that centers within congregational facilities often require participants to observe practices related to the congregation's religious commitments, as for example, the wearing of yarmulkas at Orthodox synagogue center activities. . . .

Implications of this Study in Contrasts

No doubt there are objections to some aspects of this characterization of center-type services under congregational auspices, and there are exceptions which can be pointed to. Such variations from the norm are likely to be the result of special center interests or backgrounds on the part of certain leaders or other exceptional circumstances. Varying approaches to center service due to differences in stage of development, leadership, and other factors may be found in *both* the synagogue-center and the community center. Generalizations are ever ready targets for critics. Yet, if we make no attempts to compare these institutions as regards their provision of center service, clarity cannot be achieved—the clarity which is an essential prerequisite for mutual respect and healthy cooperation. The general description offered here is deemed to be a reasonably accurate one. . . .

This contrast between the two organizations suggests the following general conclusions: First, programs concerned with the enrichment of Jewish group life as conceived and carried out by the Jewish community center are essential ingredients in a well-conceived program of Jewish communal service in America. Second, such programs can be soundly achieved *only* under Jewish communal auspices, and by independent agencies specifically charged with carrying out this function. Third, center-type programs in congregations serve a valuable function within the scope of the congregation's activities but constitute a different service than that of the Jewish community center. Fourth, the primary service in this area cannot be provided under the auspices of congregations, which must be seen as fundamental institutions in Jewish life with a basically different function than that of the community center. . . .

It is significant that the progress of Jewish community-center work has paralleled congregational expansion in America. It is evident that communities have found that each institution fulfills a distinct and discreet function, that both are needed, and that they are thoroughly compatible. It is noteworthy that the predominant leadership of community centers has been drawn from those who are congregational leaders as well. For them, there is complete harmony between the two institutions, each of which complements rather than conflicts with the work of the other.

Community Center as Community Resource: Cooperation with Synagogues

One of the distinguishing characteristics of the modern Jewish community center is its commitment to strengthening every facet of Jewish group life. Because of the center's assumption that individuals and communities grow through significant Jewish group experience, the center is interested not only in providing valuable Jewish group associations under its own roof, but in making its skills in enriching Jewish group life available to other Jewish organizations and groups as well. There is a growing pattern of such cooperation between Jewish community centers and many Jewish organizations and groups.

Patterns of Community Center-Synagogue Cooperation

This cooperative trend is true especially with regard to synagogues. As the Jewish community-center movement has grown in its resources, its technical proficiency, and its communal orientation, cooperative movements between centers and synagogues have evolved in many communities. This collaboration has proved most effective when each institution respects the other as performing distinctive functions in American Jewish life, and when each desire to benefit from the special skills and resources of the other. Among the forms which these relationships have taken are the following:

1. Provision of direct leadership or supervision by community center to the synagogue in the group activities conducted by the latter. Here the center provides specialized group-work service in activities sponsored by the synagogue. The use of center aid for a youth group, an older adult program, a young married group, a sisterhood, or extra-curricular activities of a synagogue school are examples of such cooperation.

2. Jointly sponsored programs in which the community center supplements its main program by operating the equivalent of a branch in congregational facilities. Such a project is jointly sponsored by both the Jewish community center and the synagogue, with the center providing leadership, supervision, and direction and the synagogue supplying the facilities. A guiding lay committee is drawn from both organizations and responsible to each.

3. The community center may conduct its own extension program, utilizing synagogue facilities. Here the community center secures the use of synagogue facilities (on a rental or other basis) in which to house an extension service under its own auspices and direction. This plan, as well as jointly sponsored programs, are means employed to extend community-center programs into unserved areas where existing congregations have facilities which can be used for this purpose.

4. The community center may provide advisory help on congregational group activities to synagogues in the form of counsel to synagogue staff or lay committees.

5. Centers often offer coordinating and central services which . . . are utilized simultaneously by synagogues and other organizations. These include club leader recruitment and training, community-wide youth councils and inter-organizational youth activi-

ties, and community-wide cultural councils and program events, such as those related to Jewish book and music festivals. . . .

Experience in Center-Synagogue Relationships

A recent survey of Jewish community center-synagogue relationships revealed much progress in such cooperation. Close to three-quarters of the 102 community centers reporting have either formal or informal synagogue representation on their boards. Over a third of the centers conduct activities in synagogues, and half of the centers provide program consultation or other services to congregations. Over forty per cent of the centers reported use of their facilities by synagogues, and a quarter indicated that they receive active assistance from the synagogues in the conducting of community-center programs. Over a third of the centers stated they conducted joint activities with congregations.

This advance in cooperation between the two is encouraging. Community centers have learned from this experience that such work can be a constructive supplement to their own basic programs. However, it is clear that such cooperative projects with synagogues cannot replace the primary work of the center, which can only be carried out effectively in communal facilities and under the circumstances we have described. Viewed as an adjunct to and a secondary resource for community-center work, this approach is clearly valuable for both organizations. It can help the synagogue to enhance its religious and educational work, and can enable the center to increase its effectiveness in enriching Jewish group life.

A review of the experience of Jewish community centers and synagogues reveals the problems which have arisen between them. Conflicts have occurred especially in two situations. The first is in communities with a well-developed Jewish community-center program, where synagogues have accelerated their group activities with the object of replacing center services under communal auspices with synagogue-conducted programs. The other area of conflict is in new suburbs which lack Jewish community-center services, and where synagogues developed first. Tensions sometimes arise when an interest emerges in establishing a community-center program in such communities. This interest eventually is linked with the planning of the Jewish community center (or centers) in the metropolitan area. . . .

Lack of mutual understanding and respect by the leaders of one institution for the functions of the other, and misconceptions about their respective roles, often are contributing factors to tension. For example, the erroneous tendency of some congregations to look upon the community center as a secular-oriented agency makes for misunderstanding, as does the failure of community-centers to recognize that many group activities have a place in the congregation. Efforts of one organization to perform activities which are clearly the province of the other are another source of conflict. The trend away from center sponsorship of worship services or formal Jewish education has alleviated some of these tensions. As the aspirations of some synagogues to absorb community-center functions lessen, another source of friction will be eliminated. . . . Difficulties also may grow out of conflict situations such as the breakdown of a cooperative plan or of negotiations to achieve such a plan, coincidence and conflict in building-fund campaigns, or competition in given activities. . . .

Prospects for Center-Synagogue Relationships

We view the future relationship of the Jewish community center and synagogue with much optimism. Each succeeding year brings greater clarity about the functions of the community center. As communities conduct studies and replan and expand their center work, there is new awareness of the value of the Jewish community center. We have passed through a period of great change and witnessed a dramatic migration to the suburbs. There are perceptible signs of stabilization, which should bring about clarification of institutional patterns. As the realization spreads that healthy communities need both effective synagogues and Jewish community centers, tensions between these institutions should be replaced by mutual acceptance and sound cooperation. . . .

Center Relationships With Other Bodies

In considering the relationships between Jewish community centers and other community bodies, we have dealt extensively with the synagogue. Because of its community orientation, the center is associated with many other organizations interested in the group aspects of Jewish life. These relationships are of two types: First, association with communal agencies whose primary roles are in other functional areas, but with whom the community center has mutual concerns. . . . The center has natural opportunities for association with the Jewish school regarding activity approaches in its curriculum, extra-curricular programs, and summer camping under Jewish educational auspices. Centers cooperate with homes for children or aged persons with respect to recreational programs for residents. Centers collaborate with family-service and child-care agencies regarding referrals and the group aspects of casework services. Relationships between centers and vocational agencies are common, both for referral purposes and for the conduct of group-guidance programs. Where Jewish communal camps for children are operated under auspices other than the center (the incidence of such situations is decreasing as camps are being integrated into community-wide center organizations), many relationships exist with the center. These involve intake, camp program and operation, and follow-up service after the camping season. Centers have a basis for mutual concern with Jewish hospitals in such fields as recreational therapy and the provision of pre-school care for the children of nurses. Centers and Jewish Welfare Funds and Federations have relationships affecting Jewish communal planning, fund-raising, and matters of broad Jewish community interest, as well as leadership development and the conducting of youth divisions of Welfare Funds.

The second category of center relationships with other community groups covers those with Jewish organizations and groups providing leisure-time and recreational services within the particular organizational or ideological framework of the sponsoring group.

The contributions which the center can make to these community groups are of an advisory nature, and often involve direct responsibility by the center for service within the framework of the other organization. . . . The first type of cooperation involves counsel to lay and professional leaders of organizations by the center, to advance the quality of the group association or recreation conducted under their auspices. An example of center advisory help is the advice given to local Zionist Youth Commissions in leadership training or program planning. The center can likewise benefit from the counsel it receives from cooperating organizations. Family agencies can assist the centers in planning family-life education programs, or Jewish education agencies can serve as resources in the planning of Jewish cultural center programs.

The second type of cooperation refers to the obligations assumed by the center for providing direct service in its area of competence within another agency setting. Examples may be found in center supervision and/or direct professional service with respect to recreational services in homes for the aged, or the provision of service to residents of homes within the center's older adult program. Similarly, such cooperation is evidenced where centers house and provide leadership and supervision to B'nai B'rith Youth Organization groups, or where centers give staff service to the youth divisions of Jewish Welfare Fund campaigns. Other agencies can provide direct service to centers, such as is the case with vocational agencies which conduct group-guidance programs in centers, or Jewish education agencies which operate formal adult Jewish classes in centers.

The Jewish community center's commitment to serve all aspects of Jewish group association, in the interest of enriching every avenue of Jewish living, imposes a compelling mandate upon it to intensify its cooperative relationships with other groups. There is steady progress in such collaboration; it is receiving ever-wider acceptance, reflecting the forces within the whole community, within Jewish life, and within the social-work field which impel us toward greater unity, collaboration, and integration. Emphasis and support must be given to these relationships to insure the richest exchange of the competencies of all community resources. . . .

3. Trends and Recent Developments in the Field of Jewish Education*

BY LOUIS L. RUFFMAN

In any review of program in the field of Jewish education, first consideration might be given to the status of pupil enrollment in Jewish schools. For the limited scope of this report, only a few salient facts indicating significant developments will be singled out.[1] The data shows a steadily continuing upward trend in the number of pupils enrolled in our schools. In the spring of 1951, there were 302,454 pupils attending Jewish schools, an increase of 13.4 per cent over 1950. This compares with an increase in 1950 over the previous year of 4.2 per cent and in 1949 of 6.9 per cent. It has been roughly estimated that the total Jewish child popula-

* *Jewish Social Service Quarterly,* vol. XXIX, no. 1 (Fall 1952), pp. 29-37. Presented at the Annual Meeting of the National Conference of Jewish Communal Service, Atlantic City, N.J., May 27, 1957.

1 For additional statistical information, see Oscar I. Janowsky, *The JWB Survey* (New York, 1948), and *Jewish Education Register and Directory,* 1951, published by the American Association for Jewish Education. For more recent data, see the annual reviews of development in the field of Jewish education in *American Jewish Year Book,* 1952 to 1958; A. M. Dushkin and U. Z. Engleman, *Jewish Education in the United States* (New York, AAJE, 1959); Oscar I. Janowsky, "Jewish Education, Achievements, Problems and Needs," *The American Jew: A Reappraisal* (Philadelphia, 1954), pp. 123-174.

tion of school age is about 650,000. It follows therefore that about 43 per cent of this Jewish child population is enrolled in organized Jewish schools. This represents a considerable increase over the estimate of between 25 and 30 per cent which had been generally accepted a decade and more ago.

The statistical evidence that we have indicates that the structural pattern of American Jewish education has become fairly well crystallized, with the congregational week-day Hebrew school and Sunday schools constituting the predominant types. About 75 per cent of the week-day Hebrew schools are presently under congregational auspices. It is interesting to note that the trend in the congregational week-day schools is more and more towards the pattern of three-day week sessions, although the schools operating on four- and five-day sessions still represent the majority. Whereas in 1964 these schools represented 62.7 per cent of the total as against 29.6 per cent for the three-day week schools, in 1950 the four- and five-day week schools constituted 55.3 per cent of the total and the three-day week, 34.7 per cent.

The most revealing and striking development in terms of structural pattern has been the growth of the all-day school. In 1935, there were only three communities conducting seventeen such schools with a total enrollment of 4,600; in 1945, fifteen communities operated seventy-eight all-day schools with an enrollment of 9900; in 1950, fifty communities conducted 130 such schools, with an estimated enrollment of 21,500. This increase seems to be continuing. The enrollment in the all-day schools constitutes eight per cent of the total enrollment in Jewish schools, and over 16 per cent of that in week-day schools (in New York City, where a large percentage of the all-day schools is concentrated, this proportion is considerably higher). While largely under Orthodox sponsorship, the all-day school has aroused considerable interest among other groups. A number have been established by Yiddish groups and some by Conservative congregations.

The growth of the congregational school as the dominant type, and the rise of the all-day school as a significant and substantial factor in Jewish education have been accompanied by a steady decline in the community-sponsored Talmud Torah, which formerly occupied the central role in the structure of supplementary week-day Jewish education. While the limited scope of this review does not permit a comprehensive analysis of the basic causes responsible for this change, it is important to bear in mind that the growth of the congregational school as the predominant type is closely linked with the steady and continuing shift of Jewish population from thickly settled and closely concentrated metropolitan areas to the suburbs. There is a growing tendency in these newer areas for larger numbers of Jews to affiliate themselves with the synagogue, and to center their Jewish interests more and more around the congregation.

The growth of the all-day school has aroused a good deal of controversy in the American Jewish community, and it might be well to dwell briefly on a number of points which have caused misgiving and require some clarification.

The position taken by some that the all-day school is a Jewish parochial school, which represents a threat to American public-school education, is hardly justified at the present time. Actually it is a private school conducted and supported by a local membership group to provide a form of Jewish and general education which meets the particular needs of this group more adequately than the prevailing system of public school and supplementary Hebrew school education. It performs the same function on the American educational scene as the many other private schools whose position has long been recognized. While the all-day school has grown at a very rapid pace and may continue to do so for some time, it is hard to imagine that it will displace the supplementary afternoon Jewish school, which meets outside public-school hours, as the dominant type in American Jewish education. The costliness of the all-day school, and the deep-rooted commitment of the overwhelming majority of American Jews to the American public-school system will set definite limits on the continued expansion of the all-day school. It seems reasonably certain that the Jewish educational needs of the preponderant majority of Jewish children in this country will continue to be filled by a supplementary system of Jewish education.

The all-day school must compete successfully with the public school in terms of physical facilities, effective teaching, administration, adequate concern for children's needs and interests, sound financing, etc., if it is to maintain its present position and survive on the American scene. It follows that those who sponsor all-day schools have a responsibility for maintaining acceptable standards governing all aspects of their school program and practice; these must at least equal, if not exceed, the minimum standards prevalent in the better public-school systems in this country, particularly those in the communities in which the all-day schools are functioning. The threat to the continued growth of the all-day school, or even the maintenance of its present position, does not lie in the elements who oppose it on principle as a threat to the public school system of education; it comes, rather, from proponents who take the position expressed by one zealous adherent that "the poorest and worst yeshiva is better than the best Talmud Torah." The expansion of the all-day school has reached a point where its sponsors must give increasing attention to consolidating the quantitative gains already made, and concentrate their efforts largely on improving the quality and effectiveness of program, teaching, and administration. The financial base of most of the existing yeshivas needs to be greatly strengthened and physical facilities substantially improved, if the all-day schools are to hold their present position.

In a number of instances, questions have been raised about the responsibility of the community to contribute to the maintenance of all-day schools. While the Jewish community has a right to require that those groups which undertake the organization of all-day schools must also assume the basic responsibility for providing adequate financial support required to maintain acceptable standards, the community itself, functioning through the central Jewish educational agency, certainly has an obligation to help the all-day school through subsidies and other services to the same extent that it helps other types of schools to reach and maintain such standards.

The adherents of the all-day school who would have Jews press for federal aid to parochial schools are misguided; in the final analysis they are doing a disservice to the future growth of this type of school. So long as private and parochial schools do not benefit directly from federal and other governmental aid, they cannot constitute a real threat to the principle of public-school education in America. Should the sponsors of all-day schools press for and advocate federal aid, they will tend to justify the argument that they do constitute such a threat; they will consequently alienate the sympathies of the majority of Jews, who are committed to the public-school system, but who feel that the all-day school, as a private school, has a legitimate place on the American Jewish scene.

Intensification of Jewish Education

The relatively rapid growth of the all-day school is the most dramatic of a number of recent indications of a clearly defined trend towards the intensification of the program of Jewish education which has emerged during the past decade. This is in sharp contrast to the trend which prevailed up to a decade ago, when a general watering-down of school programs and lowering of a standards accompanied the emergence of the congregational school as the dominant structural type.

The last decade has witnessed an organized and sustained effort among those sponsoring the congregational school to intensify its educational program, improve overall standards, and raise the level of achievement. The Conservative congregational schools are now in the process of limiting one-day-a-week attendance to a restricted age group, thus eliminating the Sunday school as a competing unit with the week-day Hebrew school; raising the number of hours per week of instruction to a minimum of six; providing more adequate budgets and more qualified staff, and, in general, trying to follow a carefully planned program designed to raise standards governing all aspects of school administration, program, and practice to a level considerably higher than that which has prevailed in these schools until recently.[2] Many of these congregational schools have now set up definite requirements of eligibility for the bar-mitzvah ceremony. This has served as an effective instrument for the retention of pupils over a longer period, and the intensification of instruction.

Among the Reform religious schools, which have been and still remain predominantly one-day-a-week or Sunday schools, there is in evidence a marked trend toward the organization of week-day Hebrew instruction, extending from one to three days a week.

Another outstanding evidence of the intensification of Jewish education is the recent development of the foundation school, an all-day school on the level of early childhood education, covering nursery, kindergarten, and primary grades only. The pioneer school of this type has been the Beth Hayeled of New York, which is now [1952] celebrating its thirteenth anniversary. It has experimented extensively in developing a workable bicultural program, which provides a complete fusion and integration of both the Jewish and American elements of the program, and in creating a suitable environment for the harmonious blending of American and Jewish influences in the life of a very young child. The orientation in programming and method is progressive, focusing primary attention on the personality development of the child. The aim is to establish an adequate foundation for follow-up with an intensive Jewish education in an afternoon week-day Hebrew school, and continuation of general studies in a public school beginning with

[2] See "Statement of Objectives and Standards," United Synagogue Commission on Jewish Education.

the third or fourth grade. The teachers who function in this type of school are expected to handle both the Jewish and general elements of the program, and thus effect complete integration. A good deal of attention has been given to the problem of involving the parents as much as possible, and bridging the gap that so often exists between the school and the home. The nursery and kindergarten levels of the foundation school have been instituted in many communities and in a large number of schools of all types during the past ten years; but the total pattern developed by the Beth Hayeled, which includes the first three primary grades, has not been followed as extensively. An organized effort within the Conservative synagogue group to establish such foundation schools among their affiliated congregations has recently been started, with the organization of a special department for the foundation school by the National Commission on Jewish Education of the United Synagogue. The National Education Committee of Mizrachi recently established a special training program to prepare teachers for this type of school. For those who earnestly desire a more intensive form of Jewish education than can be expected in the typical congregational school, and yet want their children to attend the public school, the foundation school offers a very promising alternative to the all-day school, which covers all the grades.

A major factor in the trend towards a more intensive Jewish education has been the steady increase in the number of Jewish educational summer camps organized throughout the country. These camps have been established by central Jewish educational agencies and various communal groups and institutions. In a number of them all communication is in Hebrew; in others, provision is made for formal classroom study at stated periods; a third group provides extensive Jewish cultural experiences without formal instruction. What is common to all is the pattern of complete Jewish life which they are in a position to provide during the two summer months because, unlike the Jewish school, they have available all the time and energy of the children, and can create a total Jewish environment which will appeal to the innate interests of the child.

Community Responsibility for Jewish Education

During the past seven years, a total of twenty-two central agencies for Jewish education were established in communities where they did not exist before. This represents over 50 per cent of the total number of such agencies currently functioning. Whereas in 1936, twenty-nine communities reported contributions to Jewish education from Federation and Welfare Funds amounting to $523, 749, in 1950, sixty communities reported such contributions, amounting to $2,400,000. During the past few years, between eight and nine per cent of allotments of Federations and Welfare Funds for local needs has been allocated for Jewish education. Prior to 1945, the percentage ranged from five to seven. A study of the budgets of twenty-one central agencies of Jewish education for each of the three years from 1946 to 1949 shows an increase of 52.8 per cent in their total budgets during this period. While in 1946 the Federations and Welfare funds contributed 66.5 per cent of the aggregate budgets of these agencies, this proportion rose to 77.2 per cent in 1948.

This is indeed convincing indication of the increasing recognition on the part of our community leaders of the principle of total community responsibility for Jewish education, which maintains that all Jews must collectively assume the obligation for the Jewish education of all children in the community. Moreover, these agencies have become more inclusive in nature, and have assumed a broad range of functions, covering every aspect of Jewish education as it operates in the community, and servicing all groups regardless of ideological differences. A pattern of community organization and function has developed which is based upon the principle that, while there is a unity of community responsibility for the improvement and expansion of Jewish education, . . . there is room within this unity for a wide diversity of approach in the form and content of the Jewish education advocated by the various groups. This development represents a long step in the direction of minimizing the potentially disparate elements in Jewish education, and enabling it to function as a great unifying force in the community.

The development of this sense of community responsibility for Jewish education was greatly stimulated by the success of the first national conference for Jewish education held in the winter of 1951, under the joint sponsorship of the American Association for Jewish Education and other national communal organizations. One of the positive outcomes of this conference was the decision to conduct a national survey of Jewish education. This survey has already begun and is in its early stages. . . .[3]

As the field of Jewish education has become increasingly recognized as an integral part of Jewish communal service, it has been establishing closer contact with other functional fields on a local and national level. The most advanced development in this connection has been the closer working relationship that has been established between the fields of Jewish education and Jewish center work, with the organization of the Joint Committee of the American Association for Jewish Education and the National Jewish Welfare Board, in which both the National Council for Jewish Education and the National Association of Jewish Center Workers are participating. A statement of common objectives and areas of cooperation in the fields of Jewish education and Jewish center work, issued by this Joint Committee, has defined a broad area of common interest between the two groups, and recognized the need for a maximum degree of coordination and cooperation.[4] It is now formulating very specific recommendations for the actual implementation of a program of cooperation on the part of the

[3] Since this essay was written, the study has been completed and published by the American Association for Jewish Education in 1959 as *Report of the Commission for the Study of Jewish Education in the United States,* vol. I, by Alexander M. Dushkin and Uriah Z. Engleman.

[4] Since published: *Recommendations on Jewish Education for Youth,* Joint Committee, National Jewish Welfare Board and the American Association for Jewish Education, January 1951; *Report of Committee on Planning and Coordination of New School and Center Buildings,* January 1951; and *Recommendations on Day and Country Camps,* January 1951.

school and center on a local level and is trying to develop a joint training program which will provide needed training in group work for the Jewish educator, and the necessary background in Jewish content for the center worker. During the past year, a joint two-day institute covering experiences in different communities in implementing such a program of cooperation was successfully conducted.

Personnel

A number of distinct advances have been made in the professional status of workers in the field of Jewish education which mark the beginnings of stabilization. The rise in school enrollment and in the number of community agencies for Jewish education has opened up new positions on the teaching, supervisory, and executive levels which did not exist a decade ago. The opportunities for growth and professional advancement have been greatly enhanced as a result. Many congregational schools which did not engage professional principals a decade ago require such personnel today. The scope of the job of principal in a considerable number of these institutions has been expanded to cover other areas beyond the elementary Hebrew school. There has been an increasing demand for teachers in specialized fields such as the nursery, kindergarten, and the various fields of arts education. Many communities now have local boards of license, and conduct a system of licensing teachers on the basis of definite qualifications designed to maintain acceptable professional standards. A National Board of License has been functioning for some years for the purpose of establishing such standards and coordinating the work of the various local boards. During the past few years a number of communities have adopted community-wide Codes of Practice governing the relationship between teachers and schools, including salary scales which come close to those provided by the public-schools systems in those communities. This development is by no means general. By and large the salaries actually paid by Jewish schools are below those prevailing in the field of general education, particularly in the larger communities, which employ the vast majority of Jewish teachers. What is significant in this development, however, is the fact that it represents a growing recognition on the part of Jewish community leaders of their responsibility for protecting and advancing the professional status of the worker in Jewish education on a community basis. These are very substantial achievements indeed, and indicate the very great progress that has been made in recent years in establishing a solid professional base for the field of Jewish education.

Yet the profession is still faced with an acute shortage of personnel, both in terms of quantity and quality. A recent survey has estimated that the combined output of graduates from all the existing Hebrew Teachers Training Schools is sufficient to meet no more than 20 to 25 per cent of the annual need for new Hebrew teachers. The causes for this shortage are fairly obvious and need no elaboration here. A qualified teacher in a Jewish school must have a basic general and Jewish education on a college level, and be thoroughly grounded in pedagogy and child psychology. Moreover, to be successful under the difficulties inherent in a voluntary and supplementary system of education, he must be imbued with an uncommon sense of dedication to his calling. This is a rare combination difficult to find in adequate numbers, even under the most favorable circumstances. The actual situation shows, however, that Jewish education has to compete for personnel on unfavorable terms with other areas of Jewish communal service. The professional codes and salary scales referred to above, which represent a great step forward, are still inadequate to cover the field, and are often difficult to enforce even where they have been adopted. One of the very serious problems faced by the profession is the insecurity caused by the narrowing hours of instruction provided by an increasing number of schools. A recent study [5] re-

[5] "The Status of the Teacher in Jewish Schools," by Dr. Emanuel M. Edelstein—paper delivered at the Conference of National Councils for Jewish Education, June 4, 1952.

vealed that in the larger communities employing a minimum of twenty full-time teachers, only 11 per cent worked on a schedule of twenty or more hours a week, the average schedule approximating thirteen hours per week. In the smaller communities employing fewer than twenty teachers, only 6.5 per cent taught more than twenty hours per week, and the average schedule was close to fourteen hours per week. Under the circumstances, the job of the teacher in many communities is not a full-time one, unless it is supplemented by other duties. This study also showed that in New York City the average length of stay of teachers in the profession of Jewish education was between eight and nine years as against an average length of stay of 24.5 years in the public-school system.

It is obvious that the improvement already noted in the economic and social status of teachers in Jewish schools must be extended to the point where the field of Jewish education will not only be in a position to retain the present limited personnel, but will also attract new, adequately trained men and women in sufficient numbers to meet its expanding needs.

While the existing teachers training schools can by themselves do little to meet the numerical shortage, they must assume a measure of responsibility for shortcomings in the quality of teaching—at least to the extent that the training programs they provide fall short of desirable standards. A recent comprehensive survey found that there is a great disparity in the requirements for admission and graduation among our training schools; they do not offer well-balanced curricula which provide adequately for the pedagogic elements essential to sound professional training; and insufficient attention is given by them to a carefully planned program of student observation and practice teaching. To this may be added the need for training in related disciplines, such as group work and adult education, which will make possible the provision of full-time positions in schools which provide only a limited schedule of classroom teaching.

The American Association for Jewish Education, which sponsored this survey, has taken steps to establish adequate machinery for coordinating program planning among the various Teachers Training Schools, and establishing the proper base for cooperative action among them. Should this effort succeed, it will go a long way towards bringing about the necessary improvements in training qualified teachers.

Curriculum

The point of view in curriculum construction that seems to have received the widest acceptance in the field of general education assumes that the school curriculum must be focused around the child, on the one hand, and around the society into which it seeks to induct the child, on the other. In the field of Jewish education, whatever reconstruction of the Jewish school curriculum and redefinition of its aims and emphasis which has taken place in recent years has been in the direction of meeting more fully the needs of the Jewish child living in the American environment, and reflecting the changes that have occurred in Jewish life, both in America and outside of it. The more recent curricula provide much more adequately for active pupil participation in living Jewish experiences related to all areas of the curriculum. More and more the school has been forced to assume what had formerly been the major function of the home in educating the child and creating for him a living Jewish environment in which he can express himself Jewishly through a variety of media. Particularly evident has been the more widespread introduction of the various forms of arts education, in providing some measure of activity program for the child in the Jewish school. In terms of the content of the curriculum, its scope has been substantially broadened to reflect more closely the changing pattern of American Jewish life and its needs. Thus, definite provision is now made for organized study of the American Jewish community, its history, institutions and relationship with the other Jewish communities the world over; the rise of Israel, and its relationship to America; and contemporary Jewish life. The study and observance of the Sabbath and festivals has become an essential element of the curriculum, and a good deal of progress has been made in making the study of this aspect a live and meaningful experience. New teaching materials designed to make the content of instruction more vivid and meaningful to children—(filmstrips, various types of dramatizations, children's magazines, and similar aids that form the components of the growing field of audio-visual materials)—are now being produced in significant quantities. While the curriculum of the Jewish school is still largely centered around the training in skills of Jewish observance and the imparting of knowledge, these elements do not occupy the exclusive role that they formerly played in the curriculum of the Jewish school.

These developments have not been manifested evenly among all elements concerned with Jewish education on the elementary level. Because of the pluralistic nature of the American Jewish community, there inevitably remains a great deal of variation in curriculum conception and practice prevailing in the various types of schools functioning in our community. However, a very significant effort has been made in recent years towards the development of a common core of content and values, which all but the most extreme groups could accept as a working basis for their respective curriculum programs. This does not entail the development of a uniform curriculum for all groups, which is manifestly out of the question. It rather seeks to single out those elements in Jewish life and tradition which could be considered indispensable to the program of any school concerned with the survival of Judaism and its way of life. It was felt that each group could then incorporate these elements into its own curriculum program, to the extent and with the particular emphasis which best reflected its own particular ideological outlook on Jewish life. This offers many interesting possibilities for further development, and represents a substantial step in the direction of building a common curriculum for the Jewish child growing up in the American Jewish environment. It is interesting to note that this development in the direction of common elements in curriculum planning was in a measure induced by the recent tendency on the part of the community to assume over-all responsibility for the Jewish education of all children in the community and involving all groups.

A dynamic program of curriculum development is inextricably bound up with an organized and sustained program of research and experimentation. In the general field, the initiative in maintaining adequate research and experimentation has been centered largely in the teachers training schools and education departments of universities. In the field of Jewish education, the existing teachers training schools have apparently been insufficiently concerned with the aspect of experimentation, and as a result the field of Jewish education can show little development in this area. The recent establishment of such graduate departments in Dropsie College, Yeshiva University, and the Jewish Theological Seminary, among others, is a very significant development indeed, and should in the course of time stimulate effective research and experimentation in the field of Jewish education.

The central problem remains that of developing a common curriculum program applicable to all Jewish children (except possibly those associated with extremist groups on either end), which will have relevance for them in their present American Jewish environment, and yet be adequately rooted in the past and its traditions to insure continuity. The vagueness which characterizes the daily expressions of Jewish life among large elements of the Jewish population in America militates against such a development even more than the pluralistic nature of American Jewish life. Perhaps such a curriculum program, assuming that it is desirable, will only be possible when this vagueness will have been transformed into a truly indigenous American Jewish life, which the child will experience as a matter of course in his home and in the general community, as well as in the school, and which will supply the social setting in which such a curriculum can be rooted.

4. New Developments in Jewish Community Organization*

BY HERMAN M. PEKARSKY

Charles Merriam, in his provocative essays on "Public and Private Government," points up the basic principle underlying our whole discussion of the Jewish community. He states, "Democracy is the formula for social gains and cannot abandon these gains without abolishing itself. Democracy means social gains in practical application. . . . In a democracy organization is not an end but a means, not a vested right of the few but the tool of the many." These ideas are fundamental considerations in any discussion of the Jewish community. The community exists for a purpose. It was created originally, and has continuously been fashioned through the years, in an effort to meet certain group responsibilities and needs. It has undergone constant change. It has evolved from the very limited functions vested in it in earlier days into a comprehensive organization concerning itself more and more with the total life and activities of the Jewish people at home and abroad. These changes did not always follow consciously charted directions. Force of circumstance, as well as external and internal pressures, have exerted their influence and left their stamp on its character and physiognomy. Throughout its planned and unplanned life, there has always been noticeable the attempt to develop the kind of an organization which would thrive in democratic soil, which would be in keeping with the American community, and which would be so constituted as to effectively and efficiently discharge the total complex of the community's responsibilities.

Community organization is an evolutionary process, with gradual changes and modifications based on experience and developing problems and needs. There are many trends which we have been

* *Jewish Social Service Quarterly*, vol. XXIV, no. 1 (Sept. 1947), pp. 6-15. Presented at the Annual Meeting of the National Conference of Jewish Social Welfare, Cleveland, Ohio, 1949.

observing for years, and which gradually, year by year, have taken on more form and substance, so that today, we look at them with greater understanding as to their meaning and influence on Jewish community life.

In the area of Jewish community organization concerned with the structure and form of the central community mechanism, a number of very interesting and encouraging developments are taking place. Communities are becoming more aware of the importance of a strong, effective, and responsive central community instrument. The experiments which are being tried in a number of communities are evidence of this greater concern and interest. No one can say that we have found the perfect form of central community organization, which fully reflects the wishes and the desires of the people, or which can adequately meet all the needs of the community. But some of the experiments, more than others, point toward the development of a representative type of Jewish communal organization which is in keeping with the concept of democratic living. Many of the fears about democratizing and broadening the central Jewish community organization are being dissipated by the actual experience resulting from the day-to-day operations of the newer forms of community organization. I do not fear that the larger masses who are now in a leadership position will be less reasonable, less objective, or less concerned with sound community development than the more selective leadership prevalent in the past. Many able, responsible people are ready to take their places in the self-government of the community.

If we accept the fact that the community exists for the people, then the people should have the opportunity to express their ideas and to reflect their desires and wishes through a central organization, which will be responsive to the needs of the total community, which will recognize present-day realities, and be ready to assume its responsibilities not only in the traditional sphere of what we call "social services," but also in the much larger developing sphere of Jewish communal life that is concerned with the pressing problems of the large majority of the people.

We cannot overlook the influence of impinging world-wide forces on the development of the Jewish community. We cannot debate the validity of overseas and Palestinian needs, and the responsibility which has fallen upon the American Jewish community which demands a concentration of its efforts, its time, and its funds on this gigantic task. The eventual solution of this problem is in the hands of the governments of the world. . . . Until a solution is found it will remain the common task of the American Jewish community to continue palliative measures, to keep alive those who remain in Europe, and to strengthen the hand of the Yishuv in Palestine.

While this development has for the present pushed into the background local needs and projects, the excitement caused by multi-million dollar campaigns in local communities has made more Jews conscious of their communal responsibilities. We have involved them in fund-raising activities, and are testing their leadership abilities. In every community, recruits in communal work have been obtained through the expanded fund-raising programs of the last few years. In the years to come, many of those whose first association with community activities has been on the fund-raising level will be the leaders of our local communities, and will grow in their understanding not only of overseas needs, but of local problems and objectives as well.

As to how much of this leadership can be conserved once the appeal for overseas funds is reduced—that is a question which cannot be answered at the moment. But this very question also offers a challenge to all of us—to our ingenuity and resourcefulness in developing a good working relationship with these individuals [who are new to communal leadership], and in the promotion of an educational and interpretive program about our community which will help to maintain the interest of this new leadership on a continuing year-in and year-out basis, and make these men and women loyal and persistent advocates and supporters of the local community.

Related to the overseas problem is the question of local needs.

Generally, the experience has been that with the disappearance of the drama and patriotic appeal of the War Chest, the Community Chest movement has slowed down to a prewar pace, with resultant limited funds for the needs of local agencies. In those communities which receive funds from the Chest, the problem is becoming more acute, and the gap between the needs of Jewish agencies and potential support from Community Chest funds is widening every year. We are at a stage where the Jewish community has broadened its interests and has seen the necessity for providing services, not only of a philanthropic nature, but also those which service the entire community, rich and poor alike.

Our programs have been expanding, and the funds available from Community Chests have been insufficient to meet these programs. The budget allocations of sixty-six Chests increased 55.2 per cent in 1964 compared to a base period of 1935-1939. Using the same base, we find that by December, 1946, the consumers' price index rose 53.3 per cent, approximately the same rise as reflected in Chest allocations to agencies. The increased cost of commodities, services, and wages during the same period have more than offset the dollar increase in allocations, so that very little opportunity has been afforded for expansion of programs or the addition of new services. Consequently, the call to our own Welfare Funds for supplementary support of our local-service programs has been growing from year to year, and in some instances the point is being reached where aid from Welfare Funds is almost equal in dollars and cents to the funds provided by the Community Chest, the agency which historically was supposed to provide full-deficit financing for those local services traditionally included in the Chest. Other communities, to date, have staved off supplementation of Chest agency aid, but the pressure is increasing because of the need for agency expansion and new services. Sooner or later, they will have to succumb to the pressure and need for supplementation, unless the picture changes radically and the Chest finds itself able to, once again, assume its full responsibility.

Within the Jewish community, a number of problems are

beckoning for attention. We have increasingly accepted responsibility for Jewish education. But unfortunately, the acceptance of responsibility has not been extended to the formulation of guiding principles for determining the nature and extent of our responsibilities. While we recognize the diversity of various Jewish educational endeavors, we are still faced with the problem of developing criteria for determining which Jewish educational programs should be accepted as the common concern and responsibility of the entire community, and what should be the scope and character of such activities.

Recent developments in the field of Jewish education make it necessary for Jewish communities to address themselves more directly than ever before to this question. We assumed and rationalized for ourselves the principle that the responsibility of the central community for Jewish education was only binding for certain types of schools, primarily communal Talmud Torahs, and to a limited extent even in these schools. We developed Jewish education associations, and emphasized standards of personnel, curriculum, and facilities, but in a sense dodged the question as to how far the Jewish community must go, or should go, in the direction of actually providing full-deficit financing for our educational institutions. The growth of Jewish parochial schools in the last ten years has resulted in an intensification of the urgency of this issue, and is forcing the community into a position where it may have to choose between opposing ideologies [with respect to community responsibility for financing Jewish education], or accept all of them. We must approach the entire problem in a more direct and courageous fashion.

As a community, we must begin giving greater attention to the entire field of Jewish scholarship, research, and cultural development. To date, the Jewish community has given very little consideration to these aspects of American Jewish life. The greatness of the European Jewish community rested, in large measure, on its eminence in Jewish scholarship and its rich Jewish culture. Without these European Jewish contributions, our American Jewish life would be much poorer. Unfortunately, the main sources of European Jewish scholarship have been destroyed and exterminated. It now devolves upon the American Jewish community to maintain the steady stream of the centuries-old Jewish learning. This is not a matter to be treated within the context of philanthropic services. It is a necessity which the growing Jewish community must accept as one of the main sources of its nourishment and well-being. I cannot improve on Elliot Cohen's words on this subject. In a recent issue of *Commentary* he states,

> The Jewish community still tends to classify culture as a seductive but forbidden luxury—like that second mink coat. . . . The bottleneck lies in an obsolete kind of community thinking. We live by a kind of charter that permits us worship and charity and social adjustment and self-protection, and while the intellectually hungry knock at the door, we sit searching the fine print of the charter: In the matter of culture, *is* one permitted or is one *not* permitted?

Elliot Cohen's comments are a challenge to all of us. As a mature community, we must give adequate recognition to scholarship and research, not only in the fields of group relations and anti-Semitism, but in the whole realm of Jewish life and thought. It is one of the essentials of purposeful and rich Jewish living and experience which goes beyond our social service endeavors and our fight for the protection of our civil, political, and religious rights. . . .

We must also develop a more direct interest in the life of the community as manifested in its various organizations of a fraternal, benevolent, or social nature. The paucity of their programs and the poverty of their content are matters which should deeply concern the organized Jewish community. These organizations are the social life-blood of the large mass of people. We cannot continue to prate about educating our community, about having it realize its responsibilities and potentialities unless we reach into the very heart of Jewish life as represented by these organizations. Unimportant as these organizations may seem to some in relation to the total Jewish community, they have residual strengths which could be helpful in developing a much better community. An effort must be made to integrate them into the larger community, to provide them with the kind of service which would enrich their programs, widen their horizons, and enable them to develop an interest in local community agencies and needs.

Our local services are being subjected to more vigorous and frequent challenge. We may expect this to continue as these agencies expand and their financial needs multiply. We should have the courage and the determination to review their programs critically, to liquidate agencies if their usefulness is doubtful or obsolete, to merge where merger is indicated, and to develop new services and new programs when called for. We should not wait to be pushed into a situation, but should take the initiative in testing the validity of services and of their needs within the community.

The pattern of the past is not necessarily the guiding light for the future. Over the years, many of our agencies have changed. Some have disappeared, and new ones have developed. This change in communal service, however, has been a relatively slow process. We are now living in the atomic age, and in a community where the forces from within and from without create constant conflict, disorganization, and change. We must make adjustments at a much more rapid rate. We cannot afford the luxury of following the path of least resistance, and of hoping that five years from now we may reach the goal that should be our objective for today. Perhaps we need a change in our philosophy of the function and the role of the central agency. Perhaps it is time that the central agency assumed more than the responsibility for advising, guiding, planning and budgeting. It may be necessary for it to become the determining force in the community in dictating policy, as opposed to its present role of merely prescribing the medicine and letting the patient decide whether or not to take it. It may have been desirable in the past for the central agency to act in the role of advisor, giving a gentle push here and a pat on the back there, but leaving it to each agency to determine its own destiny and to decide its own direction and usefulness. But is this desirable now?

I know that there are many who will disagree with this view, but perhaps in the community of tomorrow, it will no longer be a question of choice. This very responsibility may be forced upon us by circumstances beyond our control. Certainly, if the central community organization becomes more representative in its composition and more responsive to the needs of its people, it will have to play a much more dominant role in shaping policy and program for community service, and in its relations with its member agencies. If central planning is to have real meaning and validity, it must assume more than the function of providing blueprints and hoping for their implementation. It must have the power and the force not only to plan but to implement, not only to suggest but to order.

There are also rumblings in another direction. The validity of certain social services as distinctive Jewish institutions is being questioned. Dr. Samuel Kohs challenges the Jewish family agency as it is now constituted. He says:

> As far as the Jewish family agency is concerned, its structure and function today are much more the result of Christian and of so-called "non-sectarian" pressures than of Jewish tradition, of the needs of Jewish community life and the demands of the organized Jewish community. . . . The Jewish family agency is becoming more and more of a stranger in the association of Jewish communal organizations with a vanishing interest in the problems of Jewish life. . . . If this change in the Jewish family agency is necessary and desirable, then it should be no longer a *Jewish* community responsibility.

The same thought is echoed in the recent JWB survey:

> Jewish group-work agencies, however denominated, must be Jewish, or they have no reason for existence. . . . A non-sectarian Jewish settlement or educational alliance is a contradiction in terms. Either it is dedicated to a Jewish purpose, or it is a neighborhood institution concerned with the all-embracing aspects of American

life. . . . Non-sectarian agencies should be under non-sectarian direction. They should not be sponsored and financed exclusively or predominantly by the Jewish group.[1]

It is reasonable to expect that this kind of a yardstick will be applied more frequently as more funds out of purely Jewish sources are provided for such services. The further democratization of the community may also lead to more vigorous challenge of our current position on this subject.

We recognize the contribution of national organizations to the fields of social work and to the local community. They played an important role in the past, and are continuing today to expand and extend our social welfare horizons. In a sense, they have been circuit riders, carrying on missionary work, winning over new converts, helping communities to organize their own programs, and demonstrating the values of sound social-work development. It is as a result of this greater development of the local community that the problems of national-local relationships are in the forefront today. It is not only in the Jewish community that this problem in relationships is at the top of the agenda. The entire May, 1947 issue of *Community,* the publication of Community Chests and Councils, is devoted to an analysis and discussion of the problem of national-local agency relationships in the general community. And as Ralph Blanchard points out in his introduction to this special issue of *Community,*

We in the field of health and welfare are not the only ones who face this problem. Business has it. Labor, too, wrestles with it. So does the Church. Government is constantly struggling to reconcile federal, state and local interests and needs. In fact it represents one of the basic problems of our age, since, it appears, differing only in detail, as the most difficult issue facing the United Nations.

The local community is no longer the community of the early decades of the century, or even the community of pre-war days. Without a doubt, the local community is finding itself and, regard-

[1] Oscar Janowsky, *The JWB Survey* (New York, 1948), pp. 276-77.

less of the type of central community organization which it has, is developing greater competence, better understanding and more alert leadership able to wrestle with the problems of concern to Jews at home and all over the world.

The local community will not forever continue to acquiesce in having its responsibilities discharged and its decisons made by proxy by national agencies. The national agencies, sooner or later, will realize what the local communities have already realized —that the strength of the community and its institutions lies in the grass-root development and interest in the local community; that planning on a national or overseas scale cannot be satisfactorily superimposed from above on local communities without regard to their views, problems, abilities, capacities, and interests.

Central planning and coordinated fund-raising in local communities are among the major forces which have contributed to the success of our overseas efforts in the last two years. Without the organization and sound experience developed by local communities in the last twenty years, this could not have been achieved. Greater recognition of this fact on a national level will add to our total community strength.

The time will come when national and overseas planning will reflect the interests of the local communities in greater measure than ever before, and will evolve much more specifically out of the deliberations and thinking of the local communities. I do not say this critically. I say it with the sincere conviction that when that day comes, the foundations of national agencies will be strengthened, their causes will marshal greater support, and their interests will not be the interests of national versus local, but those of the total American Jewish community.

Anarchy which exists today in the planning of national services, and in the fund-raising appeals resulting from this, cannot continue to be tolerated in the years ahead. The day is bound to come when "national advisory budgeting" will become a necessity in American Jewish life if we are to continue to plan intelligently and adequately for our needs—local, national, and overseas. When we settle down to a more normal fund-raising level, the scarcity of the dollar and the greater competition for this dollar by local, national, and overseas agencies will inevitably result in some national plan which will try to look courageously and intelligently at all appeals and services—put them in their proper relationship, and provide the funds in keeping with their valid needs.

Fortunately, there are signs of greater cognizance of the role of the local community in helping to determine national affairs and shaping national policy, as demonstrated by the following developments.

The communities, through their central organization—the Council of Jewish Federations and Welfare Funds—and the major overseas agencies recognize the importance of obtaining full and complete information concerning the needs which must be met overseas and the effectiveness of plans and programs being developed to meet them. An Institute on Overseas Studies is therefore being organized, under the auspices of the Council of Jewish Federations and Welfare Funds, on a continuous basis, to gather information from all sources concerning Jewish needs and Jewish plans and programs in Europe and Palestine and other areas of potential settlement.

This project will aim to develop a comprehensive and coordinated body of information, which would be helpful both to agencies that are responsible for planning and carrying out functional programs, and to an informed community leadership responsible for raising funds. The Institute will concern itself with four aspects of the problem: (1) The general economic and political position and prospects of the overseas Jewish population; (2) activities undertaken by Jewish and non-sectarian voluntary agencies and by governmental and inter-governmental agencies in aid of Jewish populations; (3) adequacy and effectiveness of Jewish agency operations in various fields of work; and (4) Jewish agency planning for the future development or modification of their work, and the basis for such planning.

The Institute on Overseas Studies will not recommend agency

budgets, but will develop factual information bearing on budgetary needs and campaign goals. In addition to presenting full, factual data both on underlying needs and on agency programs, the study may include, and I personally hope it will include, evaluations of an agency's work in relation to overlapping of services, quality of service provided, and administrative efficiency. This development is a hopeful start in sound national-local cooperative planning.

The recent reorganization of the United Jewish Appeal, providing for the inclusion of one-third representation from local communities on the Administrative and Executive Committees, is another step toward better national-local relationships. Perhaps it would be better to term it a half-step, since this reorganization is hedged by protective devices, as examplified by the provision that the representatives selected by the communities must be acceptable to the UJA. This, in essence, means that the UJA reserves the veto power in the selection of local representatives. Furthermore, the area in which the local representatives may exercise their rights is thoroughly circumscribed and limited. The distribution of funds among UJA beneficiaries, and the decision on the continuance or dissolution of the UJA at any time, are still entirely in the hands of the Joint Distribution Committee and United Palestine Appeal. But even with all these restrictions and limitations, it is a step toward greater recognition of the local community.

The development of the national finance council device as utilized by the National Jewish Welfare Board, the American Fund for Palestinian Institutions, and more recently by the Joint Defense Appeal, is also evidence of increased recognition of the local community. While the individuals serving on these finance councils do not officially represent their communities, it nevertheless is a recognition of local community leadership. Although the finance council device is primarily aimed at promoting the budget needs of a particular agency in the local community, it gives local leaders a chance for joint thinking and discussion, and for reflecting local community opinions.

Let me also point out that the general community has been

developing some special devices for planning, coordination and budget review of national services. The National Social Welfare Assembly was organized in 1946 as the successor to the National Social Work Council, to provide central machinery through which national planning and coordination of health and welfare agencies could be carried forward on a broad base. The National Budget Committee was formed in 1946 to continue a task which was started in 1942 in conjunction with the National War Fund. Its function is to provide central review of the budgets of national health and welfare agencies, particularly those appealing for support through Community Chests. The basic purpose of the National Budget Committee "is to provide an orderly procedure through which national agency program plans and requests may be channeled to local communities." Its powers go beyond those vested in the budget service of the Council of Jewish Federations and Welfare Funds, since the National Budget Committee issues reports to the Chests, which indicate the specific amounts for which national agencies are warranted in appealing, and outline the methods by which the appeals are to be made. Naturally, the responsibility for determining which national agencies should be included in local Chests and the amount of inclusion rests with the local Chests.

Another development in the general field of fund-raising for health and welfare services is the proposed establishment of a National Quota Committee, under Community Chests and Councils auspices, to restudy the question of quota plans for national agencies. The objective of the Quota Committee would be to suggest to national agencies and to local communities a plan for establishing local quotas on an equitable basis, adjustable to the varying conditions affecting different types of appeals.

There is one more development in the general community which should be of real interest to Jewish communities. During the last year, some states and a substantial number of communities have established appeals review boards (1) to act as a central agency to clear all proposals for community-wide fund-raising campaigns; (2) to evaluate the necessity and justification of each such appeal; (3) to coordinate the time and method of all appeals; (4) to encourage public support of approved fund-raising campaigns. The review boards, however, assume no responsibility for raising funds for the agencies or services which they approve. As can be seen, our problems and plans are part of the warp and woof of the general community philanthropic and fund-raising fabric.

The national Jewish service and coordinating agencies have a more specific relationship and responsibility to the local community and its programs. Some of these national agencies were created to stimulate and promote the development of certain services in the local community. Others have grown out of the needs of local community programs to coordinate their efforts, channel information, exchange experience, and provide specialized guidance in carrying out these programs. Such national agencies have an obligation to the local communities to re-evaluate their own programs and philosophies in the light of changing needs, and to crystallize their functions in relation to the local communities, as has been done in recent months by the National Council of Jewish Women and the National Jewish Welfare Board.

Let a journalist speak on this point. Dr. S. Margoshes in *The Day*, issue of May 21, 1947, states:

> To my mind the year-long survey of Jewish Center and Jewish Welfare Board work . . . marks an epoch-making departure in American Jewish life . . . for two reasons: first, because it sets an example which other organizations will be obliged to follow, if they wish to maintain their position in the Jewish community; and second, because Dr. Janowsky's recommendations, when followed, are sure to usher in a new period of enlightenment and creativity in Jewish communal life in America.

As to the survey method, Dr. Margoshes states,

> I cannot see how some of our top-ranking and highly expensive organizations can further avoid using it to prove their work to the

Jewish community in general and their contributors in particular. I could easily list ten national Jewish organizations which, among them, spend half of the Jewish communal budget in the United States, and which could much improve their standing with the community as a whole by a strict accounting not so much of the sums spent, as of the value received.

The JWB report raises some questions about the relationship of a national service agency to the local community and its institutions. Some of the answers will be provided within the next year by the local Jewish centers and central community organizations in their discussions of the report recommendations. Even though some of the recommendations may be challenged by local communities, out of the discussions there will grow a sounder understanding of the role of the Jewish center and of the relationship of the JWB to the local centers and communities.

Sidney Hook makes some very interesting and pertinent comments on national-local relations in his survey report of the National Council of Jewish Women. He states that:

> We must first distinguish between the position Council must take on a national level, and the position of the various sections. This distinction is necessary in view of the diverse character of the sections, and the statement from some of them that because of the homogeneous social composition of their particular communities they have no acute unmet needs. . . .

He further observes that the national office of the Council is not called "to invade sections with blueprints about section needs or with breathless news about the very latest developments in the field of social work. . . . As distinct from the national office, sections may very well focus their activity on a social welfare project depending upon the local situation. This decision must be largely left to the sections themselves." Here, very definitely, is a recognition of the growth of the local community, its ability to cope with its own problems, and the fact that programs conceived nationally cannot be superimposed without specific relation to the needs and resources of the local communities.

There are signs of growth and development in the Jewish community. There is greater alertness and more conscious direction in community affairs and accomplishments. To build the Jewish community which will be adequate and strong enough in the days ahead will require from all of us—lay and professional leadership—determined pursuit of those objectives which are so vital in our organized Jewish community life.

PART FIVE

RETROSPECT AND PROSPECT

1899-1958

Man has consistently sought to understand his history by review and assessment of the past; and to anticipate developments by projecting past and present trends into the future. The 1950's were years of both growth and uncertainty, and the completion of fifty years of Jewish philanthropic history provided a natural opportunity for stocktaking. The papers of this period, of which Waldman's is typical, reflect a backward look through the eyes of men and women who had lived through the strenuous past and a look ahead on the basis of a lifetime of experience.

The retrospect reveals how far and rapidly American and Jewish life have moved. Shifts in political and economic relationships among the nations give perspective to the narrower world of social welfare. The development of an American welfare state in no way diminished the need for, and vigor of, voluntary and sectarian social agencies. The American Jewish community evolved through an intense exchange with American society at large, both contributing to it and drawing from it. The hardly credible rapid expansion of Jewish philanthropy is a measure of the tempo with which new immigrants found a place for themselves in a new world. Even the savagery of World War II and the threat of Fascism appeared as an opportunity to strengthen a world-wide humanitarianism and to reinforce confidence in man's capacity to cope with the uncertain future.

The prospect revealed no diminution in great issues and challenges. Technical changes in program-content and policy were forecast, but even more striking are the bold anticipations of a great change in the character of American Jewish philanthropy and charity: the spread of some welfare programs to serve all members regardless of class or economic position; the great development of cultural, religious and educational programs carried on by community organizations to enrich community life; and the progressive sharing of certain protective or social welfare tasks with government, labor and industry.

Predicting the future is more hazardous than synthesizing the past, but Hexter's detailed look into the next generation of social welfare has been confirmed in many respects by developments during the ten succeeding years. By 1965, a checklist was available with which to test the accuracy of these predictions. A few are summarized here:

(1) Governmental programs have continued to expand; personal insecurity has been minimized by increasing social insurance for the disabled, the unemployed and the aged sick. Personal social-work services were introduced and expanded for public-relief agencies through federal legislation in 1962. In the middle 1960's the federal government launched extensive public programs against poverty (at least one fourth of the American people were still

living below the poverty line), for better care for the mentally retarded, and for local community care of the mentally ill.

(2) While unions have remained powerful, their membership has not expanded along with the rest of the population, but their welfare influence has grown as the reserve of union-management welfare funds reached over thirty billions of dollars.

(3) Suburbs have continued to enlarge metropolitan areas but it was not clear at first that this has been an expression of an increase in population as much as of an increase in urbanization. New social agencies to serve these areas have not been produced at any great rate; the social problems at first appeared to be regional in scope; and neither sufficient funds nor trained manpower were available to generate enough services fast enough for both inner and outer city.

(4) In the area of the aged, Jewish and general concern and agency programming expanded as predicted with more Jewish philanthropic support, more institutional and medical care for the sick aged, and more comprehensive care for the elderly living in their own homes. Only the unions failed to enlarge their own services, preferring to support expansion of Federal programs in housing and medical care for all citizens.

(5) Family agencies have continued to become more professionalized, with significant increases in attention to a fee-paying clientele and a modest development of more tangible service for the aged. Contrary to prediction, and except for New York City, family agencies have not moved closer to hospitals or to the synagogue, and psychiatric policy has not been consolidated in the general hospital. The massive Federal support for community mental-health centers was unpredicted and its effects are not yet discernible.

(6) In almost every respect, the predictions for services for children have been borne out. Community care has increased, and institutional care has become even more specialized and costly, continuing to treat the very disturbed child. However, mergers

between family and child-care agencies have proceeded slowly.

(7) Community centers have not seriously affected the growth of religious institutions, but have become more building centered, serving a middle-class suburban population. While more professionalized, they have equally relied more and more upon volunteers. While government support was not forthcoming, the national stress upon overcoming poverty in the city center led to support for centers which still remained in underprivileged districts.

(8) Hospital predictions have proven accurate in the main, as improved public medical centers intensified competition for staff. Ambulatory and home care, branching out from the hospital, expanded and became more adequate and hospitals continued the trend to comprehensive medical centers without regard for the physical limits of the hospital.

(9) Jewish education experienced a renewed interest in professional quality, built around the requirements of congregational schools. Jewish training for social work continued to receive attention at Yeshiva and Brandeis Universities, although basic professional training continued to be provided by general professional schools.

(10) Jewish Federations continued to serve as the centers for community welfare growth expanding their social planning staffs, and incorporating the best of social science research methods.

With these positive predictions confirmed, it is possible to disern certain divergencies in the agendas for American and for Jewish social welfare. In the middle 1960's America was tackling the problems of persistent poverty; racial, not religious, discrimination; enlightened community care for the mentally ill and retarded, which subsequently revolutionized the mental-hospital system; and a further shift from public relief to social insurance as the main protection against social hazards. Jewish social welfare seemed to have as its main goals: professional service for a primarily middle-class, suburban population; further growth of religous freedom; and cultural enlightenment.

1. A Backward Look*

BY MORRIS D. WALDMAN

. . . Picturing to myself the bodily resurrection of one of the founders of the Conference, I imagine what his impressions would be if he were to review world events during the past half century, the circumstances of Jewish life in Europe and elsewhere, and particularly the development of organized Jewish life in the United States.

The astonishingly rapid transition from a horse and wagon civilization to an atomic age would be bewildering to him. Life was relatively placid in the decades at the turn of the century. The country was prosperous, people were friendly, and American ideals of democracy held the promise of early fulfillment. There were few racial tensions, at least among the white population. Immigration was at its height, and the immigrants who represented many different races and nationalities were all welcomed and eagerly invited to become the bone and flesh of the body of American citizenry. The brotherhood of man seemed right around the corner. . . .

The early founder of the Conference would be speechless at the tremendous advance in the sciences, pure and applied, and the countless new mechanical devices for physical comfort, increased speed, and rapid communication. In his day the wireless telegraph, the cinema, the radio, the airship, the submarine, and refrigeration were still in their experimental and embryonic stages. Jet propulsion and atomic energy were the still vague dreams of imaginative and adventurous scientists.

If our founder had an interest in world affairs, he would be thunderstruck by the current startling economic and world revo-

* From presentation on the occasion of the Fiftieth Anniversary Celebration of the National Conference of Jewish Social Welfare, *Jewish Social Service Quarterly,* vol. XXVI, no. 1 (Sept. 1949), pp. 23-28. Presented at the Annual Meeting of the National Conference of Jewish Social Welfare, Cleveland, Ohio, June 4, 1949.

lution. . . . He would be astonished to find that great Britain has been relegated to a secondary role in the commercial, financial, and political spheres, the British Commonwealth having become little more than a tenuous association of completely independent countries, and no longer the chief supplier of manufactured goods; that the American dollar has replaced the pound sterling as the stable currency basis and criterion of foreign exchange; that the United States has become the almoner of a mutilated and impoverished Europe; and that most of the European countries have been obliged by a succession of grave crises to follow the stern policies of a state-controlled economy, with Communist countries appearing on the greater part of the continent and Communism making alarming inroads in an awakening Far East, in the Pacific Islands, and other hitherto backward countries.

The founder would be extremely happy to see the progress which has been made in humanitarian enterprises, and in the areas of child labor, public health, recreation, higher education, social insurance, and other welfare measures undertaken by increasingly socialized governments. However, having belonged to a generation that believed that the best government was the kind that governed least, the founder might be somewhat disturbed by the paternalistic trend reflected in these public activities, and more recently in Franklin Roosevelt's New Deal and Harry Truman's Fair Deal. These were the objectives the pioneers in professional social work were only just beginning to agitate for in the halls and committee rooms of our state legislatures.

Our founder would be tremendously impressed with the achievements of organized labor, the diminution of the political power of the moneyed classes, and the growing political power of the trade unions. He would be agreeably surprised at the statesmanship of the Jewish labor leaders, who have contributed signally to worker prosperity and peaceful employer-employee relations in the garment industries. He would be filled with admiration for the social and educational institutions which labor has established and developed over the years.

He would be amazed, also, at the drastic changes that have taken place during the past half century in the trustees in the institutions of the Jewish community, leaders of German origin having given way almost completely to East European leaders and their sons and daughters.

Recalling the pronouncement at the convention of the Central Conference of American Rabbis, viz: "America is our Zion and Washington our Jerusalem," and having viewed the Zionist movement with distaste and derision as the hare-brained scheme of fanatics, he would be astonished to find that the State of Israel is now a reality, and is receiving the enthusiastic moral and financial support of world Jewry. Despite his sentiments when he was alive, he could not help but swell with pride over the courage, self-restraint, and political wisdom displayed by the Jews in Palestine, which have evoked the respect of the world and have raised the prestige of all Jews everywhere. But he would be amused to learn that on this very evening, the Hebrew Union College, in his day the fountainhead of anti-Zionism, is conferring honorary degrees on Dr. Ralph Bunche and Aubrey Eban for their services on behalf of the State of Israel.

The founder would feel uneasy over the shift of emphasis from the internal problems of Jewish life to the relations of the Jewish community with the general community, a shift unhappily produced by a revival of racial hostility that he had firmly believed was relegated to the limbo of the past. In the days when the Conference was first established, animosity toward Jews rarely assumed a more serious complexion than an occasional offensive word by a street urchin, or exclusion from clubs and private homes in what was known as "society."

The Conference was founded before social work became professionalized. Philanthropy was exclusively in the hands of volunteers and ladies bountiful. Case workers were called "investigators." They were referred to as "paid" workers, not "social" workers. Later they were called "visitors." Now, even that term is obsolete; they are called "counsellors." These changes in nomenclature are a significant reflection of the changes that have taken place in the objectives and techniques of social work. An article such as the one which appeared in the latest number of the *Jewish Social Service Quarterly* under the title, "The Generics of the Supervisory Process," which even I, in touch with case work only twenty years ago, plowed through with some difficulty, would be Greek to the founder.

The founder might recall the ominous report issued by the United Hebrew Charities of New York in 1901 about the menace presented by the mass immigration of Jews from East and Southeast Europe. Pointing to the immigration statistics, that report stated that chronic poverty, appalling in its immensity, was developing in the Jewish community of New York, and that the horrible congestion in which so many of our co-religionists lived, the squalor and filth, the absence of even the most basic necessities, the vice and crime, the irreligiousness, lack of self-restraint, and indifference to social conventions were daily growing more pronounced and more offensive.

This was a terrifying picture and a gloomy prospect. Happily, it proved to be a passing phenomenon. Ten years later, having succeeded Lee K. Frankel as managing director of that organization, I happened to compare the current statistics on immigration and dependency with those of the preceding decade. I discovered, to my surprise, that in spite of the continuing heavy immigration, the number of applicants for relief at the "Charities" kept on diminishing. In 1901, the number under our care was 11,447. In 1910, it was 9,283. Yet during these ten years the Jewish population had virtually doubled. Had the number of applicants continued to increase in proportion to the number of new immigrants, it would have risen to 20,000.

When I presented these figures before this Conference shortly thereafter, they were received with incredulity. Indeed, I suspected that some of my colleagues questioned my intellectual integrity, and probably recalled Mark Twain's famous analogy between the positive, comparative, and superlative degrees and "lies, damned lies, and statistics." The founder would be pleased with my discovery that the Jewish immigrant was not a pauper; on the contrary, he was self-respecting and self-reliant, and rapidly adjusted to his new and strange environment. He was a hard-working and thrifty person, prudent and resourceful in creating mutual benefit societies of various types to which he could repair in case of emergencies due to unemployment or illness.

The founder would be surprised indeed to find that few, if any, of the families under the care of the Family Welfare Service are receiving material help from that agency; that it is concerned today only with rendering constructive advice and treatment; and that those in need of material aid are provided for by the City Welfare Department. He would undoubtedly be disturbed over the fact that the city is engaged in outdoor relief work. In his day, the only outdoor relief was the "blind dole," a trifling sum given by the city to a small number of blind dependent people. Public outdoor relief was frowned upon by the private agencies; indeed, it was regarded as anathema. Though public relief is more consistent with principles of democracy than private charity, he would regard the change with considerable apprehension; he would remember the flagrant political corruption which prevailed in his day when the notorious Tammany boss, Richard Croker, confessed to newspaper reporters that he was in politics for his own pocket, and his younger colleague, Congressman Tim Campbell, gave voice to the famous utterance, "What's the Constitution between friends?"

The founder would be astounded, yet pleased, to witness the generous outpouring by the Jews of America of hundreds of millions of dollars for the relief of Jews abroad. In his day, American Jewry had not yet become a benefactor of European Jewry. In a sense, we were the beneficiaries of European generosity, in the form of substantial grants from the Jewish Colonization Association to American Jewish organizations dealing with the settlement of immigrants on farms and in industrial centers throughout the country. America's role as a benefactor began in 1904, when through the hastily and temporarily created National Committee for the Relief of Sufferers by Russian Massacres, on which I happened to serve as secretary, there was collected from American Jews a million and a quarter dollars, a large sum in those days, for the relief of the surviving victims of the pogroms in Gomel, Kishinev, and other towns in Tzarist Russia.

He would be impressed, too, by the achievements in Jewish education, and its present emphasis upon the positive elements in Jewish life, the comprehensively developed school systems—as contrasted with the unorganized, unrelated *chedarim* and Talmud Torahs of his day—by schools and colleges of today directed by scholarly and able educators, staffed by well-trained pedagogues, and supported by the community as a whole, instead of only by individual synagogues and other private groups.

The founder would be gratified to see the growing cohesion in the American Jewish community, the merging through marriage [and social intercourse] of the various peoples from a score of countries, and the solidarity of interests reflected in "Federation," "Welfare Fund," and "Community Council," which have helped to bridge the chasm of ideological and cultural differences that prevailed in his time. In brief, he would find that American Jewry has attained maturity, national consolidation in spite of organizational rivalries, an organized generosity and a sense of collective responsibility for both domestic and foreign needs—a striking contrast to the schismatic, chaotic condition of unrelated communities and institutions of his day.

The high level of social work attained during this fifty-year period is a challenge to the low level of ethics now common in international relations. Treaties between nations have been cynically regarded as valueless scraps of paper by even the most advanced countries. Before the adoption of the Kellogg-Briand Pact which outlawed war, armed conflict between nations was sanctioned by the conscience of the world. Despite that pact, war is still endorsed by international legal codes. War even receives ecclesiastical blessing in every country. In recent years, in Germany, Italy, and Japan and their satellite countries, national ethics have degenerated into arrogant contempt for human life and human dignity. What a paradox! On the one hand, we have witnessed sadistic torture and deliberate butchery of many millions of innocent men, women, and children; and on the other hand, we have practiced tender solicitude for the weak and lowly in our highly developed social services. . . .

What is perhaps as tragic as the recent relapse into primitive savagery has been the callous reaction of Christendom to these horrors. Except for occasional denunciations by some good-will groups, few men and women were so deeply shocked and moved as to permit the pleasant routine of their lives to be affected. Christian churches, whose spiritual cornerstone is the doctrine of the sanctity of the human person, rarely alluded to the unspeakable atrocities of the war. What condemnation they did utter was virtually confined to complaints over Nazi interference with their ritual worship and the curricula of their schools. Many shepherds of Christ seemed unaffected by the odious crimes for which the surviving leaders were later hanged by judicial process.

Happily, Nazi and Fascist power has been destroyed and humanitarianism has survived. "Not by power, not by violence but by My spirit, saith the Lord." That the human spirit still lives is due less to ecclesiasticism than to the social conscience that motivates welfare endeavors. As that conscience grows more sensitive to the sufferings and frustrations of human beings, social work will develop even more elaborate techniques—so that fifty years hence, the charming and able young author of "The Generics of the Supervisory Process" will have as much trouble reading an article in the *Quarterly* of 1999 by some young case worker of that day as my hypothetically resurrected founder would have had understanding the technical language of her recent essay.

The higher the levels reached in welfare work, the less likely that the world will witness another recession to barbarism. In a real sense we social workers, by virtue of the very labors in which we are engaged, are among the peacemakers. This Conference symbolizes that fact.

2. The Next Twenty-Five Years in Jewish Communal Service*

BY MAURICE B. HEXTER

. . . I assume for the purposes of this paper that we shall not have an all-out third world war and/or a repetition of the crisis of 1929-33 in the economic life of this country. Both of these contingencies would play havoc with all that we have worked for, and with all of the fields in which we work.

My next assumption and indeed, prediction, is that the Welfare State is here to stay and to expand. I say this regardless of whichever of the two major political parties is in power. . . . I think it important, however, to utter a word of caution that the existence of this Welfare State does not necessarily carry the key to heaven for all of the communal agencies represented at this Conference. Indeed, some of the agencies in this Conference may well be threatened by wider State subventions to certain aspects of private philanthropy, although obviously the State will not enter for many years into all of the areas of operation of the average Federation. If some of these agencies get more and more financial support from the State, the ties that bind them to central financing will become weaker. . . . The Welfare State will eventually enter into areas far afield of those which it now supports. It would be impossible to postulate the continuance of a permanent public relief policy based only on the determination of eligibility. The time is not far off when the Welfare State will no longer ask why a person

* *Jewish Social Service Quarterly,* vol. XXXII, no. 1 (Fall, 1955), pp. 30-48. Presented at the Annual Meeting of the National Conference of Jewish Communal Service, Atlantic City, N.J., May 23, 1955.

is eligible, and will make every effort to prevent [the causes which make relief a social necessity].

My next prediction is that the unionization of labor is bound to grow, deepen and become stronger. . . . More and more, the demands of labor at the bargaining table will deal with what we now euphemistically call "the fringe benefits". . . . In 1929 less than one per cent of wages and salaries went to welfare benefits. In 1954, the percentage was almost 6.5—a fantastic increase in ratio. In 1929, there were very few, if any, contributions to private pensions and welfare funds of unions. There were also no contributions to an unemployment insurance scheme, and it was not until 1937 that the contributions to Old Age Survivors Insurance Funds were secured by unions. The aggregate contributions of welfare benefits in 1954 totalled over $10.5 billion. . . .

The next development which is bound to grow, and must form a basis for our communal planning, is the rapid suburbanization of our population, and its concomitant of increased leisure. This has a tremendous impact upon all of our agencies, and especially upon the intramural services. Is the development to be a proliferation of agencies, or the expansion of our existing agencies? . . . We have found it easier in New York City to develop new agencies in the suburbs than to persuade our existing agencies to render branch services. The dynamics . . . can be well understood. Most of the agencies are so overwhelmed with demands for services in the areas in which they are located that they find it easier to be unreceptive to needs from new areas. The problem at the center—Federation, if you will—is somewhat different. . . . In order to expand the base of giving, new agencies must be created in the new suburbs which are springing up all around our metropolitan areas. We will follow to the suburbs the families who move there. . . .

The next postulate is that we shall in the future develop closer ties with Israel, and that there will be a greater interchange of experience and knowledge in our field than has prevailed up to this point. . . .

My final postulate is that we will witness a strengthening of the synagogue, since its growth is closely related to the trend toward suburbanization. In general, the Hitler epoch has brought about a realization that we do not need the gas chambers to say our *Shema,* but that it is wise and helpful to bear it in mind even in good days and in free climes. In our metropolitan area [New York] the growth of new synagogues and the rebuilding of old ones has been fantastic in the extreme, and, at all levels, surprising. While one could have hoped for a less chaotic development, and financially a stabler basis, this expansion has important consequences for our field. . . . While there will still be separation between the synagogue and social service, the influence of the synagogues will be more manifest in the years ahead than it has been in the immediate past. . . .

I turn next to some of the functional fields. . . . Even in the large cities, we shall witness less and less separation between the [specialized] fields. When after so many years separate fields have been tilled so intensely, the borderlands between them usually are extremely fertile; this, I believe, will be one of the great developments in the years ahead. That applies to the relationship between all of the fields; I shall have something more to say about certain individual areas further on. However, at this point, let me cite a few of the examples already in progress on our own stage. There is a very close relationship between our psychiatric hospital and one of our family agencies, in which the family agency places discharged patients and patients on the waiting list in boarding homes; reciprocally, the psychiatric service of the family agency is provided by a panel of physicians jointly appointed and supervised by the psychiatric hospital.

Our sheltered workshop works closely with our psychiatric hospital. Our community centers and case-work agencies have an intimately related program, and we now have on our drafting boards a plan for supplying recreational service to one of our institutions in which patients are bed-bound by one of our community centers. The eradication of party lines will continue and proceed apace.

Services for the Aged

. . . We shall see deepening programs for the care of the aged; and because of the terrific financial impact of the self-interest and perhaps the voting strength of the aged, we are bound to see more and more governmental assistance to local programs in this area. A substantial beginning has already been made, and the pattern of these local programs is more than dimly outlined. We shall witness (perhaps in some way coordinated with industry and trade-union programs) the enrollment of people in old-age programming even before they will have reached the retirement age. . . . I do not think it possible to provide institutional care for the aged, because of the avalanche of numbers; nor do I foresee that as a desirable goal. We shall continue to find alternate ways of meeting this need. We shall have to increasingly make use of the recreational resources of the community, its nursing and home-care resources, and an extensive medical supervision program directed by our hospitals. . . . Our institutions for the aged will become almost completely populated by house-bound residents. These house-bound residents will include increasingly the large proportion of residents suffering from the mental ailments of the aged. We shall cease sending such unfortunate people into state institutions or into, what frequently is worse—nursing homes. These services for the aged will not be confined to those who are public charges, but will include individuals who can pay and pay well, just as hospitals have for many years included patients who can afford even the high rates of the private pavilions. . . . The trend away from the care of aged relatives by the individual family will continue. . . . New homes for the aged will be erected in as close proximity to general hospitals as is feasible. We will not build them far away from [city centers] and kin. I predict the goal of practically complete coverage of care for the aged under sectarian auspices, with a larger proportion of the cost coming from government and trade unions. . . .

I foresee the unions stepping into this field with much vigor. . . .

And since the unions have entered into housing developments, the time is not far distant when they will invoke the aid of voluntary agencies in setting up and supervising their own program for their own union membership. . . . What I have said with respect to trade-union-supported housing projects applies with equal and probably greater vigor to public housing developments. . . .

The Family Agencies

. . . I believe that we shall no longer spill so much blood and waste so much time on problems of methodology (i.e., Rankian versus Freudian psychology; counselling versus case work) which really are meaningless, and falsely assume that there is but one road to salvation. . . . We are going to recapture more and more of the warmth [and personal approach] which we had a generation ago in family work, some of which we have lost in this search for more and more scientific and objective treatment processes. For a while it appeared that a hierarchical order was springing up between counselling and case work. This distinction will continue to fade, however, for if there is any difference between the two (which I doubt), it is a grave mistake to assign an inferior position to one or the other. . . . The family agency still remains the agency to which the community instinctively turns, not only for a solution of the "interpersonal problems of living" but also for a variety of concrete services; some of these services the family agency perhaps cannot give, but it can certainly take people by the hand and show them where they may be found. . . . The Jewish family agency still remains the same good friend of people who are in trouble and whom they are in business to help; as Frederick Almy said some seventy-five years ago, "what people needed was not alms but a friend." I see great developments ahead in the social-service field for the upper economic classes. . . . The recent establishment of the Arthur Lehman Counselling Center in New York City points the way to counselling and family guidance for those who can afford to pay well for such help. When this service in our family agencies shall have been expanded to those who can pay at least cost and possibly more, family case work will then have reached a competence equal to the other professions. . . . I believe that in this field we shall see a gradual elimination of the separation from medical services. There are already signs that medical social-service programs in hospitals are coming closer to the family agency, and I believe that reciprocally, family agencies are bound to come closer to the hospital. On our own drawing board, in response to an invitation from a donor, are the blueprints of a project for setting up in an appropriate hospital the full range of services found in a well-equipped family-service agency.

The family agencies will . . . make a desirable alignment with the synagogues which have a progressive rabbinate. . . . The courses which we ourselves have helped to establish in pastoral psychiatry will sooner or later have a profound influence in this direction. The rabbi, like the doctor, frequently has a unique contact and relationship with people who need help, and who do not know where to find it. We shall close that gap between us and the rabbinate as soon as we have lost our false sense of insecurity. . . .

I am fully convinced that psychiatric service for the clientele of our agencies will be supplied, in the long run, by hospital-appointed and hospital-supervised psychiatrists. I do not believe that in this field we are going to be any more content with separate clinics and out-patient departments than we have been in the field of physical medicine. If the last two generations of hospital development and innovations in the field of public health have shown anything, it has been that the independent clinic is undesirable and less effective, however specialized and adequately staffed it is, because it tends to fractionalize the problem in question. This is all the more true in the field of psychiatry, where a number of important advances have already been made and others are being explored in the test-tube stage, such as chemo-therapeutic treatment of psychiatric disturbances. This transfer probably will take place when our social agencies feel less insecure and less committed to any one ideological psychiatric school. Here, too, there is no one road to salvation.

The Children's Field

The children's field, like the other functional fields, has undergone major, indeed radical changes in the past decade. It would be superfluous here to reconstruct the social, economic, and professional factors that have influenced this development. It is enough that the children coming to the attention of the social-welfare agencies today are different both in their number and the nature of their disturbances. These differences have markedly influenced the nature of services available, and the cost of these services.

We have seen a drastic reduction in the number of children in placement throughout the country. . . . In 1940, prior to the merger of several of the child-care agencies in New York City, there were almost 4,000 children under care. Today, this agency has a clientele of about 1,000. In the past decade, we have seen the closing of large congregate institutions, and the increased use of foster homes and small-group living units for all types of children.

The number of children who do not require special services is, in my judgment, apt to continue to decline. The rise in the birth rate a number of years ago will be reflected in the agencies ten years from now, and we should take stock now to determine whether the institutional resources for our children's needs are ample. I have a vague uneasiness that perhaps in some communities the move from group care to foster care may have gone too far and too fast. The success of closure rests upon the availability of an adequate supply of suitable foster homes to meet various and specialized emerging needs.

The day of the large institution is over, because of the lack of elasticity inherent in such institutions. The so-called "normal child," save in exceptional cases, will not be sent to a large institution; where a family is unable to accept foster-home placement, there will be small apartment projects, or small homes, in place of large institutions.

This last decade has witnessed an increasing trend in specialized and differential services for particular types of children. In the area of foster care for children, I predict an even greater development in the specialized services as specialized needs are shown. . . . The time is not far off, especially for children requiring special services and heavy dosages of psychotherapy and psychiatric social work, and indeed for children with other handicaps, when we shall turn to foster homes, because of the flexibility this form of service permits and the lower cost of operation. . . .

The term "disturbed children," in varying degree, is appearing more and more frequently in the literature, and the "Residential Treatment Center" has become the most recent "therapeutic milieu." Though the number of children under care has decreased, the cost of care has spiralled, due to smaller case loads and an increased use of ancillary services. Heretofore, the child-care agencies in most communities assumed responsibility for almost complete coverage of children requiring placement away from home. With the increased cost of service, there is now some question as to whether private philanthropic resources can be asked to finance this total program—especially in the case of the highly disturbed or exceptional child—without substantial cushioning from public resources. . . .

Any predictions regarding the number and nature of the children requiring foster care must necessarily consider the impact of the expansion of the adoption program in more recent years, seeing how fewer social and professional taboos of the past have continued to limit the horizons of this program. Permanent homes are being found for the children, and in addition to the incalculable emotional advantages of such an arrangement for their children, it is financially advantageous for the community.

Consideration must also be given to the development of extra-mural services geared to keeping the family intact—child guidance, family counselling, homemaker service, and day-care facilities.

. . . The further development of the mental-hygiene movement and the concentration upon preventive programs will shift the balance from intra-mural to extra-mural services. As this gradually penetrates our current operations, the volume and cost of these extra-mural services, particularly child guidance and family counselling, will reach a critical point—if indeed it has not already been reached—where public support of these services will be commensurate with the support of intra-mural services, which is now a well-established fact. A small beginning has been made through contracts with the city for special services, but I visualize a pattern which will call for more and more public recognition of this service. . . .

Historically, children's agencies have developed separately from family agencies, since the needs each served in the past were in most instances distinct and separate: the children's services were concerned by and large with orphans, while the family agencies dealt with relief administration. I believe that to retain this separation today in the light of current theory and practice is not a wise procedure, in view of the fact that both agencies now, and even more so in the future, will be concerned with the entire family. Child-care agencies work closely with parents. It is becoming more and more difficult to differentiate between the cases carried by child-guidance agencies and those treated by family-service agencies. The child population of families under the care of our family agencies is frequently larger than the population serviced directly by the children's agencies, and we shall exploit more and more the preventive possibilities that inhere in such a condition. . . .

The Jewish Component

I would be less than candid if I did not say a few words about the so-called "Jewish components," the *casus belli* of many a great battle in this forum. I am personally unregenerate, and still adhere to the basic belief that there is something different or, in my judgment, there should be something different, in our processes from those of the general approach to social problems which I believe is generally now practiced, or at any rate proclaimed. I do not believe that basically these proclamations are lived up to. I happen to believe, also, that only Jewish eyes can understand the distress in the Jewish eyes which face him or her. I am quite aware of the fact that I am talking of feelings rather than demonstrable data. . . . Lack of identification with the client, however justifiable on psychoanalytical grounds, dares not include a severance from [or ignorance of] the ethnic past and suffering of the person who seeks our help; I predict that any attempt at cutting off identification [in agency work] will fail and lead to the establishment of agencies which possess such Jewish components.

Community Centers

The last two decades have shown that the concept of settlement houses, especially as applied to the Jewish community, is on the way out, and that the community center has displaced it; . . . community centers will increasingly be placed in the better income neighborhoods and . . . the degree of self-support enjoyed by them will be augmented. . . . "Adult education" will grow, and in our Jewish centers there will be increasing emphasis upon the Jewish elements. The community center is still for many the secular equivalent of the synagogue. It is secular, however, only in the sense that it does not insist that its membership adhere to a single ideological viewpoint. It is open to all sections of the Jewish community, and while it accepts non-Jews, its focus is certainly not sectarian or even inter-sectarian. As its professionals become more self-conscious as Jewish communal workers, I believe from all of my talks with many of them, and without taking any personal position on the justice of what I say here, that they will even begin to challenge the recent growth of religious institutions, and the assertion that the synagogue is the primary institution in Jewish life. I believe that in that effort they will fail, but I think they are heading towards such a confrontation. I remember that at the Conference in 1914 in Memphis, Tennessee, a paper was given by one of the outstanding community-center leaders of the day, in which he challenged the place of the synagogue in Jewish life. One of the giant philanthropists of the day, Mr. Cyrus Sulzberger, reminded the speaker that when the Temple was destroyed, they started a new Academy at Yavneh—not a community center. . . . After the attempt to challenge the primacy of the synagogue will have subsided, the community centers may claim their movement as a fourth force, different from Orthodox, Conservative, and Reform Judaism, and appealing to a substantial, although in my judgment declining, proportion of the American Jewish community that is either not identified with the synagogue or temple (as in large cities) and yet wants to be identified with Jews and Jewish community life; or that, if synagogue affiliated (as in the middle or smaller cities), believes that the synagogue should be restricted to religious and educational functions.

The community centers will, in my judgment, provide an increasing proportion and quantity of recreational facilities over long weekends, holidays, and during the summer, when school houses are closed. The trend towards large buildings for community centers, I think, is in for a revival. The growth of what appears to be permanent suburbs makes such centers desirable and almost inescapable.

All centers now insist on professionally trained leadership with thorough training in both the Jewish background and in the skills and knowledge required for programming. I predict a reversion to the volunteer worker, because there probably are not and will not be enough professionally trained people to go around; also because the volunteer has something to give which the professional worker does not have in sufficient degree. And, if the volunteer cannot be recruited for center work, the outlook for the further development of the community center is grim indeed. . . .

I do not see rosy prospects ahead for public support of a substantial share of center activities, because they are sectarian; I believe that the trend is toward the sectarian development of community-center activities. It is likely that here and there government support can be captured for specific programs in which the government may for the moment be especially interested, as, for example, a delinquency prevention program. More and more, . . . the nonsectarian agencies will find refuge in the school house or in public housing; and the sectarian agency will be more adequately housed, and not confined as in the past to poor neighborhoods, but distributed in the better neighborhoods as well. . . .

Hospitals

At the present time, there are some sixty-six general and special hospitals under Jewish auspices, some fifty clinics, and quite a number of institutions for the care of the convalescent and chronically ill. Every Jewish community with a population of at least 30,000 has at least one hospital; and some ten communities which have less than 30,000 Jews have Jewish hospitals. This development took place for the most part *after* the heavy Jewish immigration of our times, even allowing for a time lag. Note, too, that this development [has occurred despite] the fact that . . . the Veterans Administration hospitals necessarily siphon off, and will continue to siphon off, an ever-increasing segment of our adult patients—not to speak of raids upon nurses, doctors and other technical personnel. . . . These hospitals have been established at a time when it has become increasingly difficult to staff our medical institutions, and to find good department directors. . . . At the same time, there is increasing emphasis upon the need for more and better teaching, not only from the standpoint of the staff development, but also because of the pressing need for adequately trained interns without whom no good medical program can long endure. . . . [Moreover, the acceleration of programs] for better trained medical personnel comes at a time when fewer and fewer patients are available to serve as teaching material. More and more the resident patient in the hospital is found in the private and semi-private resources. . . , and even in the wards, the patient more often than not enjoys his stay due to the help of third-party agencies. This situation will diminish, in my opinion, with the passing years as voluntary schemes for hospital insurance proliferate, and as unions provide this care for their members. . . . Unions are planning to purchase hospital accommodations from the voluntary agencies in the not-too-distant future, and. . . . there are already signs that some of the unions would like to transfer their clinics to appropriate hospitals under suitable priority arrangements. This will come about because it is right and good, but it will not faciltate the production of teaching material without some further labor. The time is not far distant when most, if not all, private and semi-private cases will be used as teaching resources. . . . The situation is further aggravated by the rapid externalization of hospital services through the development of their out-patient departments and their home-care and educational programs. The future will witness a further development of these services under which OPD's [1] are expanded into [hospital supervised] housing developments. . . . Nor do I foresee . . . that the increasing acceptance of Jewish physicians in other [sectarian and non-sectarian] hospitals will present less difficulty in the future than it has in the past. Jewish physicians will continue to turn to Jewish institutions for their training and for staff appointments.

In the larger cities, particularly, I foresee a very grim picture for the small Jewish hospitals because they cannot develop into good educational centers. The bulk of the medical care for the community will be provided by governmental authorities, either directly or through heavy subventions, and the major goals of the voluntary hospitals, and especially Jewish voluntary hospitals, will lie in the exceptional training that they offer to able Jewish physicians at the intern level, the resident level, and the staff level. Training of

[1] Out-Patient Departments, usually of general hospitals.

professional men and women is a task which voluntary agencies not operating in mass production can perform more uniquely and efficiently; and I predict that in at least our large cities, our Jewish hospitals will be forced to become large medical centers offering a full range of special services and treatment, . . . that there will occur an efflorescence of the full-time system, and that our professional men will again become prophets and seers. . . . Central financing agencies will be bound to increase their grants to hospitals rather than diminish them, even and perhaps especially in those cities in which there is substantial state aid for medical programs. I predict, too, that some of the smaller hospitals, even in some of the smaller cities, will wish to fall within the orbit of a large Jewish medical center in a nearby city or in the same city, in order to provide better training, to attract better interns, and in due course, better residents. In those cities in which there are several smaller Jewish hospitals, there most likely will take place either merger or alliance, so that at least some measure of the full-time system can be instituted and better training facilities obtained.

I predict, too, the development of a fine professional Jewish medical school, which will in due course attract the best students. I underline the words "in due course." In the medical boat the Jews have more than rowed their own freight, and I believe will continue to do so. Positive contributions in this area will come with increasing frequency after this program is established.

I would like to add a word about the national hospitals, for which I do not see a rosy picture, at least in the field of tuberculosis. The climatic element in that therapy has long ceased to be important; as a matter of fact, the disease itself will probably be conquered within the next decade. Trudeau has closed, and one of the other national hospitals already has changed its emphasis to cancer research. I doubt whether, in the long run, we can justify a national cancer hospital, unless it be primarily geared to patients from the very small rural communities. Nor do I see good future prospects for other specialized hospitals, such as those for children suffering from asthma or heart disease. This does not mean that they will disappear. . . .

Jewish Education

Here in Atlantic City, I believe in 1916, some of the outstanding Jewish educators of the day predicted that the synagogue school would disappear, and be replaced by the communal school. Perhaps that should teach me a lesson of caution in predictions, because they were completely wrong. The synagogue school has prospered and thrived at the expense of the communal school. I feel that this trend will continue and that the basis of (at least primary) Jewish education will be in the synagogue, and not in the communal school. The future of Jewish secondary education is not so easily foreseen, and may require central support. I do not see a productive stretch ahead for the all-day school, because I believe it is basically in disharmony with the basic concept of Jewish adjustment in America. I say this despite the fact that some very fine people are associated with that movement. I do not think that our soil is a fertile one for its development.

I see too in the not-too-distant future a revival of a definite school for Jewish social work. I believe the development at the Yeshiva College points the way; I will risk a guess that a good school will be built and developed there within the next decade. We must re-emphasize our life as Jews; we cannot rely upon the chance decisions of community leaders, especially in the upper echelons. Perhaps, too, we may see a development of the department of Human Relations at the Hebrew Union College. Perhaps it is utopian to believe that the forces of these two institutions, plus the Seminary, will combine to project a good school of Jewish social work. At any rate, that development is definitely in my picture, because I am certain the school created in the twenties by this Conference did not close because of the "dynamics" of the situation.

Vocational Guidance and Employment Service

. . . Despite the passage of anti-discrimination bills, and despite the fact that discrimination is waning, I predict that there will be, certainly for many years, a real field for specialized employment service for our people. But I am bound to add that the great future for these agencies is in the specialized field of vocational guidance for our youth—vocational guidance not alone for the poor, and not alone for the children of our agencies, but for the wider community as well.

Federation and Welfare Funds

I am sure that it is generally accepted that the Jewish Welfare Funds will continue to grow, and that the Jewish Federations will not be displaced by Community Chests. More and more, as I read the times, Jewish philanthropic institutions are looking for a greater part of their support from Jewish sources, rather than from the Community Chest. I don't know why it should be so unpalatable to say and to hear that, somehow or other, Jews give more to Jewish causes than to general causes. The difference is not due completely to better organized campaigns; it's in our blood.

I foresee that unavoidably, there will be more planning, rather than less, by the central communal agencies. We may need another 1929 to bring this about; I hope not. At any rate, I definitely believe communal planning is on the march, and that we are just seeing the beginnings of it, dynamic as those beginnings have been over the past generation. In the *smaller* cities, I believe that the role of the community councils will increase.

I see a continuing important role for the Council of Jewish Federations and Welfare Funds; with the passage of time, it will pay more attention to our local scene than it has in the past decade and a half in which, understandably, a good deal of attention was paid to overseas needs geared to campaign goals. Its platform will not be used to proclaim the primacy of overseas needs.

My picture of the future includes an improved status for the B'nai B'rith and the Council of Jewish Women. We have not yet learned to use these organizations on a national scale. They have a unique function in the smaller communities; likewise, a definite function in promoting to the public certain broad concepts such as Big Brother and Big Sister movements, help for the aged, etc., in even the larger communities. . . .

I would say, too, in this, my final appearance at this Conference, that I see a brilliant future for Jewish social work when it shall have freed itself from fear, competition, and semantics. The maturity of the American Jewish community requires a developing professional social work force which is dignified, self-respecting, well-trained, and ethically motivated.

This is the end of my story. Any person can paint his own picture of the future, and he can really live with it. This is the one I like to live with. I don't ask you to like it. I only ask you to believe that it comes out of the experiential wisdom of some forty-four years in the service of the Jewish community as a paid official. Thank you for having invited me to be here.

APPENDIX

Selected Documents on the Origin, Purposes, and Evolution of the Conference of Jewish Charities

PROGRAM OF THE FIRST MEETING OF THE NATIONAL CONFERENCE OF JEWISH CHARITIES IN THE UNITED STATES, CHICAGO, JUNE 11-13, 1900.*

PROGRAM

Monday, June 11, 1900

Registration of Delegates
Address of the President
Report of Committee on Finance
Appointment of Committees
Report of Committee on Transportation
Discussion
"Federation vs. Consolidation of Jewish Charities in a City"
Prof. Morris Loeb, New York City
Report of Committee on Desertions
Discussion
"Relations of Bad Housing and Poverty"
Dr. M. Reitzenstein, New York City

Tuesday, June 12, 1900

"Causes of Poverty and the Remedial Effects of Organized Charity"
Morris Goldstein, Cincinnati, Ohio
"Tuberculosis as Affecting Jewish Charities"
Dr. Lee K. Frankel, New York City
Report of Committee on Friendly Visiting
Mrs. Charles Haas, Chairman
"Friendly Visiting" Miss Minnie F. Low, Chicago
"The Ethics of Friendly Visiting" Dr. E. G. Hirsch, Chicago
"The Friendly Visitor" Miss Hannah Marks, Cincinnati, Ohio
"Friendly Visitor, a Factor in Preventive Charity"
Dr. Lee K. Frankel, New York City

* National Conference of Jewish Charities in the United States, *Proceedings* (1900), pp. 9-10.

"Cooperation Between Public and Private Charities"
Dr. C. R. Henderson, Chicago, Ill.
"The Place of the Individual in Modern Philanthropy"
Dr. Emil G. Hirsch, Chicago, Ill.

Wednesday, June 13, 1900

"The Problems of Jewish Charities in the Smaller Cities"
Rev. Dr. E. Calisch, Richmond, Va.
"Progress in Jewish Charity" Mrs. S. Pisko, Denver, Colorado
Report of Committee on Uniform Records and Statistics
Discussion
Election of Officers
Reports of Committee on Resolutions, etc.

THE RAISON D'ETRE OF THE CONFERENCE *

BY MAX SENIOR

That the necessity for a Conference of this nature had been felt for some years was recalled last year at the preliminary meeting in Cincinnati, which led to the formation of this organization. It seems, as perhaps some of those present may remember, that an attempt was made to form a similar union some years ago at St. Louis. It failed, for lack of that feeling of unity and common interest.

Since that time, the necessity for an organization of this character has become ever more pressing, for two reasons. It need hardly be stated that, on account of the immigration during the last fifteen years, the demands for charitable organizations have grown to great proportions, and call for the expenditure of sums which some years ago would have seemed fabulous. Every possible form of distress had to be provided for: poverty, sickness, and incompetence; and an alien population had to be put into accord with American life and American ideals as quickly as possible. For these purposes, the loose benevolent but spasmodic organizations of the past were not equipped. But the Jews of America have recognized their duty. Strong permanent organizations have been established in all the large cities to disburse the large sums subscribed; cooperation in all branches of charitable work has been the order of the day; and the work of rehabilitation has gone steadily on with ever-gratifying success. But the problems involved in the carrying out of this work are so vast, so complicated, that they are still far from solution. It is with a view to aid in the solving of these many questions that we are assembled for deliberation and suggestion.

Never in the history of the world has the condition of the poor been the subject of so much concern as it is today; and never has the best thought and the best efforts of so many able men and women been devoted to the uplifting of the lowly and unfortunate. The admirable work of such bodies as the National Conference of Charities and the

* From "Presidential Address," National Conference of Jewish Charities," *Proceedings* (1900), pp. 12-14.

New York Charity Organization Society has not failed to leave its impress upon us. Through the length and breadth of the land the conviction has spread that better methods of administering charity must be recognized, and every effort made not to break down character. The introduction of this idea into Jewish charity work has called for almost a revolution of methods. Open-handed but indiscriminate alms-giving, and a cordial but unthinking welcome to the stranger within your gates have ceased to be the be-all and end-all of charity. It has come to be recognized that personal service is the cornerstone of true charity, and that a new system and new methods must be built around and upon it.

It was the recognition of these facts that induced the United Jewish Charities of Cincinnati to call the preliminary meeting last year; it led to so prompt and cordial an endorsement of the constitution of this Conference that we now have enrolled in its membership thirty-six cities, representing twenty-five states, and embracing almost without exception the principal cities of the country. It is for mutual aid in carrying out ideas here expressed that we are assembled today.

CONSTITUTION OF THE NATIONAL CONFERENCE OF JEWISH CHARITIES IN THE UNITED STATES *

ARTICLE I.—NAME. This association shall be known as the National Conference of Jewish Charities in the United States.

ARTICLE II.—OBJECTS. The objects of this association are to discuss the problems of charities and to promote reforms in their administration: to provide uniformity of action and cooperation in all matters pertaining to the relief and betterment of the Jewish poor in the United States, without, however, interfering in any manner with the local work of any constituent society.

ARTICLE III.—MEMBERSHIP AND DUES.

Sec. 1. Any regularly organized Jewish relief society of the United States may become a member of the association on application made to the secretary and on payment of membership dues.

Sec. 2. The annual membership dues for each society shall be one-tenth of one per cent of the amount expended by it for its corporate purposes during the preceding year, not less, however, than $5.00, nor more than $50.00. Such dues shall be payable February 1st of each year.

Sec. 3. Each constituent society shall be entitled to one delegate but may appoint as many as it sees fit to attend the biennial meeting. All such delegates shall be entitled to participate in said meeting, but each society shall have but one vote.

Sec. 4. Each constituent society shall certify to the Secretary on or before January 1st of each year the amount of its expenditures for its corporate purposes during the preceding fiscal year. . . .

ARTICLE VI.—MEETINGS.

Sec. 1. This Conference shall meet biennially at such place and time as the Executive Committee shall designate.

Sec. 2. Delegates representing fifteen constituent societies shall constitute a quorum at such biennial meetings.

* National Conference of Jewish Charities, *Proceedings* (1900), p. 3-4.

EXCERPTS FROM CONSTITUTION AND BY-LAWS OF THE NATIONAL CONFERENCE OF JEWISH COMMUNAL SERVICE

Adopted 1951 *Corrected 1953.*

CONSTITUTION

Article I–NAME

This association shall be known as the National Conference of Jewish Communal Service.

Article II–PURPOSE

Section 1

The purpose of this Conference is to serve as a forum for the discussion of programs of Jewish communal service on a professional level, and of the application of general professional techniques to service in Jewish communities.

Section 2

The Conference is not primarily an action body. It may, however, take an official position on matters within the general scope of Section 1, when there is broad unanimity of opinion among the membership as determined in accordance with Article LX, Sections 4, 5, and 6, of the By-Laws. . . .

Article VI–ASSOCIATE GROUPS

Section 1

The National Association of Jewish Center Workers and the National Council for Jewish Education shall be Associate Groups of the Conference.

Section 2

The Associate Groups conduct activities in accordance with

their respective purposes. In recognition, however, of common interests in the total field of Jewish communal services and in the forum purposes of the Conference, the Associate Groups shall participate in the Annual Meeting of the Conference, shall assist in maintaining and extending the membership of the Conference, and shall otherwise have such privileges, duties, and responsibilities as may be prescribed in the Constitution and the By-Laws. . . .

CONFERENCE PUBLICATIONS: *1900-1958*

PROCEEDINGS OF THE BIENNIAL AND ANNUAL MEETINGS:

National Conference of Jewish Charities in the United States, 1900-18.
Published biennially: as separate volumes, 1900-12;
in *Jewish Charities,* 1914-18.
(National Conference of Jewish Social Service, 1919-22.
None published.)
National Conference of Jewish Social Service, 1923-36.
Published annually: as separate volumes, 1923-30;
in *Jewish Social Service Quarterly,* 1931-36.
National Conference of Jewish Social Welfare, 1937-51.
Published annually in the September and subsequent issues of the *Jewish Social Service Quarterly.*
National Conference of Jewish Communal Service, 1951-present.
Published annually in the September and subsequent issues of the *Journal of Jewish Communal Service.*

SPECIAL PUBLICATIONS

Recent Trends in Services for Children. (Papers presented at the 1957 annual meeting of the National Conference of Jewish Communal Serivce.) New York, *Journal of Jewish Communal Service,* 1958.

Meeting the Needs of the Aged. (Papers presented at the 1957 annual meeting of the National Conference of Jewish Communal Service.) New York, *Journal of Jewish Communal Service,* 1958.

PERIODICALS

Jewish Charity, 1904-06.
Monthly. Established October, 1903, by the United Hebrew Charities, New York. In March, 1904, it was designated as "the official organ of the National Conference of Jewish Charities." Merged in March, 1906 with *Charities and Commons* (later the *Survey*).

Jewish Charities, 1910-21
Monthly. Established August, 1910, and designated *Bulletin of the National Conference of Jewish Charities.* In June, 1919, the title was changed to *Jewish Social Service.* Ceased publication, May, 1921.

Jewish Social Service Quarterly, 1923-56.
Established by the National Conference of Jewish Social Service, February, 1924. In June 1924, it was given the sub-title: A Record of Communal Trends and Developments, which was changed in September, 1946, to A Journal of Professional Trends and Developments. In September, 1953, further addition was made to the sub-title, Incorporating the "Jewish Center Worker" of the National Association of Jewish Center Workers. In March, 1956, the title was changed to: *Journal of Jewish Communal Service*—A Quarterly of Professional Trends and Developments.

MISCELLANEOUS PUBLICATIONS

Information Pamphlets. Published by the Field Bureau of the National Conference of Jewish Charities.
Vol. I, No. 1: *The National Conference of Jewish Charities,* 1917.
Vol. I, No. 2: *Transportation Rules,* 1917.
Vol. I, No. 3: *Transportation Decisions,* 1919.

Transportation Rules and Digest of Decisions of Transportation Committee. 1929.

Constitution and By-Laws of the National Conference of Jewish Social Service. Adopted 1919. Amended 1929 and 1930, 1936, 1936, 1940. (Mimeographed.)

Report from Self-Study Commission as adopted by the Executive Committee, April 1, 1951, for action by the Annual Business Meeting on May 22, 1951, in Atlantic City. (Proposed Constitution and By-Laws.)

National Conference of Jewish Communal Service Constitution—By-Laws—Procedures. Corrected as of July 31, 1953. (Mimeographed.)

Report of Committee on Palestinian Charities. 1912. (English and Yiddish.)

Hollander, Jacob H., *The Unification of Jewish Communal Activities,* 1908. (Reported from Proceedings of the Fifth Biennial Session of the National Conference of Jewish Charities, Richmond, Va., 1908.)

———, *Forces and Tendencies of Jewish Charities,* 1910. (Reported from Proceedings of the Sixth Biennial Session of the National Conference of Jewish Charities, St. Louis, 1910.)

YEARS AND MEETING PLACES OF BIENNIAL AND ANNUAL CONFERENCES, 1900-1958

YEAR	MEETING PLACE
1900	Chicago
1902	Detroit
1904	New York
1906	Philadelphia
1908	Richmond, Va.
1910	St. Louis
1912	Cleveland
1914	Indianapolis
1916	Memphis
1918	Kansas City
1919	Atlantic City
1920	New Orleans
1921	Milwaukee
1922	Providence
1923	Washington, D.C.
1924	Toronto, Canada
1925	Denver
1926	Cleveland
1927	Des Moines
1928	Cincinnati
1929	Atlantic City
1930	Boston

YEAR	MEETING PLACE
1931	Minneapolis
1932	Philadelphia
1933	Detroit
1934	Atlantic City
1935	Lake Placid
1936	Atlantic City
1937	Indianapolis
1938	Washington, D.C.
1939	Buffalo
1940	Pittsburgh
1941	Atlantic City
1942	Rochester
*1943	*No Regular Meeting
1944	Cleveland
*1945	*No Regular Meeting
1946	Atlantic City
1947	Baltimore
1948	Atlantic City
1949	Cleveland
1950	Atlantic City
1951	Atlantic City
1952	Chicago
1953	Atlantic City
1954	Philadelphia
1955	Atlantic City
1956	St. Louis
1957	Atlantic City
1958	Chicago

PAST PRESIDENTS

1900 Max Senior
1902)
1904) Max Herzberg
1906 Julian Mack
1908 Nathan Bijur
1910 Jacob H. Hollender
1912 Lee K. Frankel
1914 Minnie F. Low
1916 Aaron Cohen
1918 Fred M. Butzel
1919 Felix M. Warburg
1920 Louis H. Levin
1921 Solomon Lowenstein
1922 Frances Taussig
1923 Maurice B. Hexter
1924 Ludwig B. Bernstein
1925 Louis M. Cahn
1926 William J. Shroder
1927 Morris D. Waldman
1928 Samuel A. Goldsmith
1929 Boris D. Bogen
1930 Philip L. Seman
1931 Maurice J. Karpf
1932 I. M. Rubinow
1933 Jacob Billikopf
1934 Ben M. Selekman
1935)
1936) Harry L. Glucksman
1937 Harry Greenstein
1938 Joseph J. Schwartz
1939 John Slawson
1940 Maurice Taylor
1941 Israel S. Chipkin
1942 Kurt Peiser
1943 Louis Kraft
1944 Isidore Sobeloff
1945 Harry L. Lurie
1946 Harold Silver
1947 Louis H. Sobel
1948 Samuel Levine
1949 George W. Rabinoff
1950 Charles Zunser
1951 Martin M. Cohn
1952 Marcel Kovarsky
1953 Philip Bernstein
1954 Judah Pilch
1955 Roland Baxt
1956 Edward M. Kahn
1957 Miriam R. Ephraim
1958 Walter A. Lurie
1959 Herbert H. Aptekar
1960 Judah J. Shapiro
1961 Donald B. Hurwitz
1962 Philip Soskis
1963 Jacob T. Zukerman
1964 Bertram H. Gold
1965 Maurice Bernstein
1966 William Avrunin

PAST SECRETARIES

1899-	Boris D. Bogen
1900-1904	Hannah Marks
1904-1908	Solomon Lowenstein
1908-1916	Louis H. Levin
1916-1919	Boris D. Bogen
1919-1928	Samuel A. Goldsmith
1928-	Hyman Kaplan
1929-1933	George W. Rabinoff
1933-1936	Michael Freund
1936-1939	Moses W. Beckelman
1939-1945	Marcel Kovarsky
1945-1949	Herbert H. Aptekar
1950-	Joseph Antman
1951-	Eli E. Cohen
1952-	Preston David (*Executive Secretary*)
1953-1954	Meyer E. Fichman
1955-	Frieda Romalis
1956-	Benjamin R. Sprafkin
1957-1958	Joseph L. Taylor
1959-	William Pinsker
1960-1961	Morris Grumer
1962-	Bertram H. Gold
1963-1964	William Avrunin
1965-	Sidney Z. Vincent
1966-	Martha K. Selig

BIOGRAPHICAL NOTES

BENJAMIN, EUGENE S.: U. S. communal worker, born Kansas (1862-1941). President, Benjamin and Co., 1905-13; later President, Baron de Hirsch Fund, 1910-1922; President, Woodbine Land and Improvement Co.; Vice President, Jewish Agricultural Society.

BERNSTEIN, LUDWIG B.: social worker, born Latvia (1870-1944); came to U.S. 1892. Superintendant, Hebrew Sheltering Guardian Orphan Asylum, 1903-18; credited with originating private foster-home placement of dependent children (1906), and cottage plan for institutional care of children (1909); Executive Director, Bureau of Jewish Social Research, 1919-1920; Executive Director, Federation of Jewish Philanthropies, Pittsburgh, 1921-44; Lecturer in Sociology at the University of Pittsburgh, and in Child Care at the Graduate School for Jewish Social Work; President, National Conference of Jewish Charities, 1924.

BERNSTEIN, PHILIP: U.S. social worker, born Ohio, 1911. Assistant Director, Cleveland Jewish Welfare Federation, 1934-43; Survey Director, National Commission on Training for Jewish Social Work, 1941-44; Vice President, National Public Relations Council of Health and Welfare Services since 1961; President, National Conference of Jewish Communal Service, 1953-54; Executive Director, Council of Jewish Federations and Welfare Funds since 1955.

BILLIKOPF, JACOB: social-work executive, born Vilna (1883-1950); came to U.S. 1897. Superintendant, Jewish Charities, Milwaukee, 1905-07; Superintendant, United Jewish Charities, Kansas City, 1907-19; later organizer and member of Kansas City Board of Public Welfare; President, Missouri State Conference of Charities, 1911-12; Executive Director, Federation of Jewish Charities, Phila.,

1919-35; President, Conference of Jewish Social Service, 1933-34.

BLAUSTEIN, DAVID: Russian-born educator and social worker (1866-1912); came to U.S. 1886. Rabbi of Congregation Sons of Israel and David, Providence, 1892-1898; Director, Educational Alliance of New York; Instructor in Semitics, Brown University, 1897-98; Director, Chicago Hebrew Alliance, 1908-10.

BOGEN, BORIS D.: Russian-born social worker (1869-1929); came to U.S. 1888. Superintendant, Baron de Hirsch Agricultural School, Woodbine, N.J., 1900-04; Director, United Jewish Charities, Cincinnati, 1904-10; Director General, Joint Distribution Committee, 1917-24; Superintendant, Federation of Jewish Welfare Organizations, 1924-25; International Secretary, Independent Order of B'nai B'rith, 1928-29; President, National Conference of Jewish Communal Service, 1929.

BRESSLER, DAVID M.: German-born attorney (1879-1942); came to U.S. 1884. General Manager, Industrial Removal Office, 1900-17; President, National Conference of Jewish Social Workers, 1914; later organizer of the 1915 War Relief Campaign; Secretary, Joint Distribution Committee, 1915-24; Chairman, Emergency Committee for Jewish Refugees, 1924; National Co-Chairman, Allied Jewish Campaign of JDC and Jewish Agency for Palestine, 1930; member, New York State Planning Board, 1934.

CAHN, LOUIS M.: U.S. (Ohio) born communal worker (1874-?). Secretary and Director, Maxwell Street Settlement, Ohio; President, National Conference of Jewish Social Service, 1925-26; Executive Director, Chicago Jewish Charities, to 1930.

CLAPP, RAYMOND: Community Chest and Council Executive, Cleveland, Ohio.

CRONBACH, ABRAHAM: American-born rabbi, Indiana, 1882. Rabbi, Temple Beth El, South Bend, Indiana, 1906-15; Assistant Rabbi, Free Synagogue, N.Y., 1915-17; Rabbi, Temple Israel, Akron, Ohio, 1917-19; Chaplain, Chicago Federation of Synagogues, 1919-22; Vice President, National Council for Prevention of War, 1947; Honorary Vice President, American Council for Judaism, 1950. Professor of Social Studies, Hebrew Union College, 1922-50; Emeritus, 1950-.

DUSHKIN, ALEXANDER M.: Educator, born Poland 1890; came to U.S. 1903. Secretary, American Jewish Relief Commission to Eastern Europe, 1916; Secretary, Board of Education, Zionist Commission, 1919-21; Inspector, Jewish schools, Government of Palestine, 1920-21; Director, Board of Jewish Education, Chicago, 1922-34;

founder and instructor, College of Jewish Studies, 1922-34; Associate Director, New York Bureau of Jewish Education, 1922-35; President, National Council for Jewish Education, U.S., 1931-32; Professor Emeritus, Hebrew University, Jerusalem, since 1959; Professor of Educational Administration and Director, Undergraduate Studies and School of Education, 1935-59; Special Professor of Jewish Education in the Diaspora, Institute for Contemporary Jewry, since 1962.

EPHRAIM, MIRIAM R.: U.S. social welfare executive. Director of Extension Activities, Central Jewish Institute, N.Y., 1924-35; Director of Activities, YM and WHA, Pittsburgh, Pa., 1935-45; President, National Assoc. of Jewish Center Workers, 1937-38; President, National Conference of Jewish Communal Service, 1957-58; Director, National Program Services, National Jewish Welfare Board, 1945-65; Associate Editor, *The Reconstructionist;* member: National Youth Reference Board, Hadassah; Board of Directors, Teachers Institute Alumni Assoc., Jewish Theological Seminary; National Council for Jewish Education; National Assoc. of Jewish Center Workers; National Conference of Jewish Communal Service; National Assoc. of Social Workers.

FRANCK, ISAAC: Organization executive, born Russia 1909. In U.S. since 1923. Director, Jewish Community Center, Manchester, N.H., 1937-39; Director, Jewish Council of Detroit, 1941-46; Executive Director, Brooklyn Jewish Council, 1946-47; Director, Jewish Community Council of Greater Washington since 1949; Consultant, U.S. State Department, International Information Administration, 1951-54; member, faculty of American University, since 1956.

FRANKEL, LEE K.: Philadelphia-born insurance executive and civic worker (1867-1931). Manager, United Hebrew Charities, N.Y., 1899-1909; Director, Jewish Chautauqua Society, 1897-1899; Instructor in Chemistry, University of Pennsylvania, 1888-1893; President, National Conference of Jewish Charities, 1912-13; President, American Public Health Assoc., 1919; Second Vice President, Metropolitan Life Insurance Co., 1924-31; Vice President, Training School for Jewish Social Work, 1925-31; Editor, *Jewish Charities.*

FREUND, MICHAEL: Social welfare executive, born in Poland (1883-1962). Came to U.S. in 1904. Reconstruction Department, JDC, 1920-23; credited with revival of the Jewish Credit Cooperatives of Poland; director, Industrial Workshop, Jewish Family Service Agency, Chicago; Secretary, National Conference of Jewish Social

Service, 1933-36; Director of Social Research, Federation of Social Agencies of Pittsburgh and Allegheny County, 1946-47; Associate Professor in Social Research, University of Pittsburgh School of Social Work.

FROMENSON, ABRAHAM H.: Publicist, born Chicago (1873-1934). Originator and Editor, English Department, *Jewish Daily News-Jewish Gazette,* N.Y., 1899-1907. Later Managing Editor, *Jewish Tribune,* N.Y.; Publicity Director, Joint Distribution Committee Campaign; Publicity Director, Commission for General Zionist Affairs, 1917-21; Former Chairman, Education Committee and member Executive Council, Federation of American Zionists.

GOLDSMITH, SAMUEL A.: U.S. social worker, born N.Y., 1892. Executive Director, Bureau of Jewish Social Research 1920-30; President, National Conference of Jewish Social Service, 1928-29; Executive Director, Jewish Federations and Welfare Funds, Chicago, 1930-66; President, Illinois Welfare Assoc., 1948-49; Chairman, Mayor's Committee on Relief Problems, Chicago, 1936.

GOLDSTEIN, MORRIS: Philadelphia-born rabbi, 1904. Rabbi, Temple Beth El, Niagara Falls, N.Y., 1927-29; Rabbi, Liberal Jewish Congregation, Liverpool, Eng., 1929-32; Rabbi, Congregation Sherith Israel, San Francisco, since 1932. President, Jewish National Fund, S.F. Council, 1934-44; President, Board of Rabbis of Northern California, 1937-39, 1946-48; President, Association of Jewish Organizations, S.F., 1948-49; lecturer on Old Testament, Pacific School of Religion, Berkeley, since 1948; President, Western Association of Reform Rabbis, 1954-55.

GREENSTEIN, HARRY: U.S. social worker born Baltimore 1895. Executive Director, Association of Jewish Charities and Welfare Funds, Baltimore, 1928-65; President, State Relief Administration of Maryland, 1933-36; President, National Conference of Jewish Communal Service, 1937-38; President, American Association of Social Workers, 1939-40; President, Baltimore Council of Social Agencies, 1935-39; Director, Welfare in the Middle East, UNRRA, 1944-45.

GLUCKSMAN, HARRY L.: American social worker, born New York (1889-1944). Founder, Jewish Community Center movement in the U.S.; Assistant Executive Director, 92nd St. YMHA, N.Y., 1913-15; Executive Director, YHMA of New Orleans, 1915-17; Executive Director, Jewish Welfare Board, 1919-1936; President, National Conference of Jewish Social Service, 1935-36.

HEXTER, MAURICE B.: American-born organization executive and social worker, Cincinnati, 1891. Executive Director, Milwaukee Federation of Jewish Charities, 1915-17; Executive Director, Federated Jewish Charities, Boston, 1919-20; President, National Conference of Jewish Charities, 1923-24; Director, Palestine Emergency Fund, 1929-38; President, Agro-Joint, since 1942; Executive Vice President, Federation of Jewish Philanthropies of N.Y. since 1941.

JORDAN, CHARLES H.: U.S. organization executive, born Philadelphia, 1908. Director of Central Intake and Reception, National Refugee Service until 1941. Director General, Overseas Operations, Joint Distribution Committee since 1955; Director, Caribbean area, 1941-43, Far Eastern activities, 1945-48, Emigration Department, Paris, 1948-51; Chairman, Board of Governors, International Council of Jewish Social and Welfare Services since 1961; President, European branch, National Association of Social Workers of America, since 1961.

JOSEPH, SAMUEL: Russian-born educator (1881-1959). Associate Professor of Sociology at the City College of New York, 1936-52; Assistant Professor, 1929-36; Chairman, N.Y. Federation for Food Administration, and N.Y. Director, American Relief Committee during World War I; Chairman, Committee on Puerto Rican Communal Services of the Welfare Council, N.Y., 1934-35.

KAHN, DOROTHY C.: U.S. social worker, U.N. official, born Seattle (1893-1955). Executive Director, Jewish Welfare Society, Philadelphia, 1929-32; Director, Department of Economic Adjustment and Family Service, National Refugee Service Inc., 1941-43; Technical Director, Office of War Information, 1944; President, American Association of Social Workers, 1934-36; Executive Director, Welfare Council of N.Y., 1946-50; Chief, Social Services Section, United Nations, 1951-55; Advisor on Social Services to Government of Israel, 1953.

KAPLAN, HYMAN: American social worker, born New York (1893-1958). Assistant Executive Director, Bureau of Social Research, 1920-21; Secretary, National Conference of Jewish Social Work, 1928-29; Executive Director, Jewish Welfare Federation, San Francisco, 1929-58; Former Executive Director, Jewish Family Service Agency, San Francisco.

KARPF, MAURICE J.: Social-welfare executive and psychologist, born Austria (1891-1964). Director, Jewish Social Service Bureau of Chicago, 1919-25; Director and President, Faculty, Graduate School of Jewish Social Work, N.Y.; President, International Conference of Jewish Social Work, 1930-48; President, National Conference of Jewish Social Service, 1931-32; President, American Association of Schools of Social Work, 1932-35; Executive Director, Federation of Jewish Welfare Organizations, Los Angeles 1942-47; President, American Association of Marriage Counsellors, 1951-53.

KOHS, SAMUEL CALMIN: U.S. social worker, born N.Y. 1890. Executive Director, Jewish Welfare Fund, Oakland, Calif., 1924-26; Executive Director, Federation of Jewish Charities, Brooklyn, 1928-33; Chairman, Department of Social Technology, Graduate School of Social Work, N.Y., 1929-38; Director, Resettlement Division, HIAS, 1938-40; Director, Refugee Service Commission, Los Angeles, 1940-41; Director, Administrative Field Service, Western States Section, Jewish Welfare Board, 1941-56; Director, Bureau of War Records, N.Y., 1942-47.

KOVARSKY, MARCEL: Assistant Director, Jewish Board of Guardians, N.Y.; Executive Director, Jewish Family Service, Pittsburgh, 1949-59; Secretary, National Conference of Jewish Communal Service, 1939-45; Executive Director, Jewish Child Welfare Association, St. Louis, 1944-49; President, 1952-53; Director of Business and Finance, Family Service Association of America, 1959-.

KRAFT, LOUIS: Communal worker, born Russia, 1891. National Executive Director, National Council, Jewish Welfare Board, YHMA's, 1938-47; General Secretary since 1947; National Executive Director, World Federation, 1947; Consultant, Joint Distribution Committee, 1953-61; Honorary President, National Association of Jewish Center Workers since 1947.

LEWINE, SIDNEY: Director, Jewish Vocational Service, Cleveland; Executive Director, Mt. Sinai Hospital, Cleveland.

LOEB, MORRIS: U.S. chemist and philanthropist, born Cincinnati (1867-1912). Professor of Chemistry, New York University, 1891-1910; Director, Chemical Laboratory, New York University, 1895-1906. Director, Jewish Agricultural and Industrial Aid Society, 1900-14; Founder, Industrial Removal Office (1901), and Jewish Agricultural Experiment Station, N.J.; President, Hebrew Technical Institute; Trustee, Jewish Theological Seminary of America, 1904-12; Founder, American Jewish Committee and Educational Alliance.

LOWENSTEIN, SOLOMON: U.S. rabbi and social-service executive, born Philadelphia (1877-1942). Superintendant, Hebrew Orphan Asylum, N.Y., 1905-20; Deputy Commissioner, American Red Cross in Palestine, 1918-19; Executive Vice President and Director, Fedration for Support of Jewish Philanthropies, N.Y., 1920-35, 1935-

42; President, National Conference of Jewish Social Service, 1921-22; Chairman, German Jewish Children's Aid, 1934; President, National Conference of Jewish Social Work, 1938; Trustee, American Jewish Committee and Joint Distribution Committee; Vice President, American Friends of Hebrew University.

LURIE, HARRY L.: Social worker, born Latvia, 1892; came to U.S., 1898. Research Director, Associated Charities of Detroit, 1915-20; Faculty member, University of Michigan, 1922-24; Superintendant, Jewish Social Service Bureau, Chicago, 1925-30; Director, Bureau of Jewish Social Research, N.Y., 1930-35; Executive Director, Council of Jewish Federations and Welfare Funds, 1935-57; Editor, *Encyclopedia of Social Work,* since 1962.

MACK, JULIAN W.: U.S. judge and Zionist leader, born California (1866-1943). Director of Jewish Charities, Chicago, 1892-1911; Professor of Law, University of Chicago, 1902-11; appointed Judge, U.S. Circuit Court, 1913; Chairman, Commission of Jewish Delegations to the Versailles Peace Conference; President, National Organization of YM and YWHA's, 1917; President, American Jewish Congress, 1917; President, Zionist Organization of America, 1918-21; Chairman, Board of Trustees, Jewish Institute of Religion; Board of Governors, Hebrew University, Jerusalem; Honorary President, World Jewish Congress.

MORRIS, ROBERT: U.S. professional social worker and educator, born Ohio, 1910; Editor-in-Chief, *Journal of Social Work,* 1962-66; Fellow, Gerontological Society of America and President Elect, 1966-67, and American Public Health Association; Editorial Board, *Encyclopedia of Social Work;* former Chairman, Social Work Advisory Council, Veterans Administration, Washington, D.C.; Professor of Social Planning, Florence Heller Graduate School, Brandeis University; Fulbright Lecturer, Italy, 1965-66; member: Research Grants Advisory Panels, National Institute of Mental Health, Welfare Administration, Department of Health, Education and Welfare, Washington, D.C.

PEKARSKY, HERMAN M.: Polish-born organization executive (1907-1963); came to U.S. in 1927. Acting Director, Detroit Jewish Welfare Fund, 1943-44; Managing Director, Council of Social Agencies of Metropolitan Detroit, 1944-45; Executive Director, Jewish Community Council, Essex County, N.J., 1945-63; President, New Jersey Welfare Council, 1954.

PURVIN, JENNIE FRANKLIN: U.S. business executive, born Chicago 1873. Executive, Mandel Brothers Department Store, 1934-?; Board of Directors, Scholarship Association for Jewish Children, since 1915: President, Chicago Women's Aid, 1911-15; Organizer and first Secretary, Jewish Welfare Board, Chicago section, National Council of Jewish Women, 1920-22; Board of Directors, Board of Jewish Education, 1931-35.

RABINOFF, GEORGE W.: U. S. social worker, born New York, 1893. Superintendant, United Jewish Charities, Hartford, Conn., 1914-18; Director, Case Work, United Jewish Social Agencies, Cincinnati, 1920-21; Executive Director, Jewish Federation, Indianapolis, 1921-28; Associate Director, Bureau of Jewish Federations and Welfare Funds, 1932-?; President, National Conference of Jewish Communal Service, 1949-50.

RUBINOW, I.M.: Russian-born economist, statistician and social worker (1875-1936). Director, Bureau of Social Statistics in Department of Public Charities, N.Y., 1917; Director, Jewish Welfare Society of Philadelphia, 1923-28 & 1932; Executive Director, Zionist Organization of America, 1928-29; Vice President, National Conference of Jewish Social Service, 1927-32; Secretary, Independent Order of B'nai B'rith, 1929.

RUFFMAN, LOUIS L.: Polish-born educator, born 1904; in U.S. since 1907. Principal, Congregational Hebrew Schools, N.Y., 1927-40; Assistant Director, Jewish Educational Commission, N.Y. since 1950; President, National Council for Jewish Education, 1952-54; Editor, *Jewish Education,* 1957-61; Visiting Lecturer, Dropsie College, 1957-62.

SABSOVICH, HIRSCH LEIB: Russian-born chemist and agricultural expert (1860-1915). Active in many early welfare organizations; Superintendant of the Baron de Hirsch Agricultural and Industrial School, 1894-1915; Mayor of Woodbine, N.J., 1903-1915; General Agent of the U.S. Baron de Hirsch Fund, 1905-15.

SELEKMAN, BENJAMIN M.: U.S. educator, arbitrator, born Pennsylvania (1893-1962). Research Associate, Russell Sage Foundation, 1916-27; Executive Director, American Office, Hebrew University, 1928-1929; Executive Director, Association of Jewish Philanthropies, Boston, 1929-45; President, National Conference of Social Work, 1934-35; President, Mass. Conference of Social Work, 1937; Kirstein Professor of Labor Relations, Harvard University Graduate School of Business Administration, 1945-1962.

SELIG, MARTHA K.: Clinical Psychologist, C.C.N.Y. School of Education, 1934-37; Case Worker and Supervisor, Pleasantville Cottage School, N.Y., 1938-40; Intake Service, Jewish Child Care Association, 1940-42, and Foster Home Bureau, 1942-43; Executive

Director, Jewish Community Services of Long Island, 1943-45; Consultant, Family and Children Services, Federation of Jewish Philanthropies, 1946-; Secretary, Communal Planning Committee, Federation of Jewish Philanthropies, 1962-; Second Vice President, National Conference of Jewish Communal Service, 1966.

SENIOR, MAX: U.S. businessman and philanthropist, born Cincinnati (1862-1939). Pioneer in U.S. in movment for the federation of Jewish Social Agencies; Founder, United Jewish Charities of Cincinnati, 1896, and President, 1899; President, National Conference of Jewish Charities, 1900-02; Director, Cleveland Jewish Orphan Asylum; Director, National Jewish Hospital for Consumptives, Denver; Representative to Holland, Joint Distribution Committee, during World War I.

SHRODER, WILLIAM J.: U.S. attorney and civic leader, born Cincinnati (1876-1962). Chairman, Cincinnati Board of Education, 1926-34; Chairman, National Appeals Information Service, 1928-32; Later President, Council of Jewish Federations and Welfare Funds, 1932-?; Chairman, Jewish Welfare Fund, Cincinnati, 1936-37; Chairman, Executive Budget Committee, Cincinnati Community Chest for 30 years; Vice Chairman, Joint Distribution Committee, 1939-52; Lecturer, University of Cincinnati; Founder and first President, Council of Jewish Federations and Welfare Funds; Founder and first President, Cincinnati Jewish Community Council.

SILVER, HAROLD: Russian-born social worker, 1900; came to U.S., 1913. Bureau of Jewish Social Research, 1926; Associate Editor, *Jewish Social Service Quarterly,* 1927-30; Superintendant, Case Work, United Jewish Social Agencies, Cincinnati, 1930-33; Director, Jewish Social Service Bureau, Detroit, since 1933; Director, Michigan Jewish Family and Children's Service, Detroit, since 1933. President, National Conference of Jewish Communal Service, 1945-46.

SLAWSON, JOHN: Russian-born social-welfare executive and psychologist, 1896; came to U.S. in 1904. Assistant Director, Jewish Welfare Federation, Detroit, 1924-28; Executive Director, Jewish Welfare Federation, Detroit, 1928-32; Director, Jewish Board of Guardians, N.Y., 1932-43; President, National Conference of Jewish Social Service, 1939-40; Executive Vice President, American Jewish Committee, 1943; member, U.S. National Commission for Unesco, 1952-55; Executive Committee, 1954-57; Special Advisor, President's Committee on Juvenile Delinquency and Youth Crime, 1962.

SOLENDER, SANFORD: U.S. social worker, born New York 1914. Executive Director, Council Educational Alliance, Cleveland,

1942-48; Director, Jewish Center Division, National Jewish Welfare Board, 1948-60, and Executive Vice President since 1960; President, National Association of Jewish Center Workers, 1948-50; Vice President, National Conference of Jewish Communal Service, 1950; President, Board of Education, Mt. Vernon, 1957-58; Chairman, Temporary Inter-Association Council of Social Work Professional Organizations in the U.S., 1953-55; President, National Conference on Social Welfare, 1962-63; Chairman, National Association of Social Workers, 1956; Chairman, Liaison Committee, Government Advisory Council of Public Welfare since 1957.

TAUSSIG, FRANCES: U.S. social worker, born Illinois 1883. Executive Director, Jewish Aid Society, Chicago, 1912-19; Executive Director, Jewish Family Service, N.Y., 1919-49; President, National Conference of Jewish Social Service, 1922-23; President, American Association of Social Workers, 1932-34; Director, Jewish Social Service Association, New York.

WALDMAN, MORRIS D.: U.S. rabbi born Hungary (1879-1963); came to U.S. 1883. Director, Galveston Movement, 1906-08; Executive Director, United Hebrew Charities, N.Y., 1908-17; Founder, National Desertion Bureau, 1910; President, N.Y. State Conference of Charities and Correction, 1812; Co-founder, Committee for Care of Jewish TB, 1915; Founder, Bureau of Philanthropic Research, 1915; Executive Director, Federation of Jewish Charities, Boston, 1917-19; and Detroit, 1924-28; President, National Conference of Jewish Charities, 1927-28; Secretary, American Jewish Committee, 1928-42; Executive Vice President, 1943.

ZELDITCH, MORRIS: U.S. organization executive, born Baltimore 1899. Director, Community Studies, Council of Jewish Federations and Welfare Funds, since 1962; Director of Social Planning, 1945-62; Superintendant of Public Assistance, Washington, D.C., 1941-43; Director of War Activities, Family Service Association of America, 1943-45; Secretary of the Board, National Council on Aging, since 1959; Chairman, Social Welfare Section, Gerontological Society since 1962.

ZUNSER, CHARLES: Attorney and social worker, born Russia 1881; came to U.S. 1890. Counsel and later Secretary and Chief Counsel, National Desertions Bureau, 1911-48; Director, Committee on War Orphans, 1920; Chairman, Committee on Domestic Relations Courts, Welfare Council of N.Y., 1931-34; Chairman, Committee on since 1948; President, National Conference of Jewish Communal Service, 1950-51; Member, Executive Committee, YIVO, since 1955.